'This is a hugely impressive work on a hugely important subject: how should an economy's performance be measured? For decades we have relied, with no justification, on GDP and related measures. However, recent advances in theoretical reasoning have shown that the metric that should instead be used is the economy's wealth, that is, the social value of its capital assets (including natural capital). The author is among the first to prepare a full-blown account not only of the theory, but also of attempts to estimate the wealth of nations.'

SIR PARTHA DASGUPTA, University of Cambridge, UK

'We argue over GDP and (de)growth because we've lost a deeper historical understanding of wealth – one that saw more than income. McLaughlin returns to that tradition, not out of nostalgia, but to restore a wisdom we can no longer afford to ignore.'

PAUL SHARP, University of Southern Denmark

'Imaginative, well-written, and timely.'

KEVIN O'ROURKE, Sciences Po, France

'Are people better off now than in the past – and if so, will economic progress continue? It depends on the wealth of the nation, properly defined to include its people and natural resources as well as infrastructure and machines: do we now have what we need to be productive, and can it be sustained? This book suggests not, but suggests that measuring wealth instead of GDP could change this.'

DAME DIANE COYLE, University of Cambridge, UK

'Adam Smith may not have lost much sleep 250 years ago worrying about fossil fuels and global warming – nor did he need to. But as we learn from this fluent, timely, and highly original work, Smith's framework for analysing the limits to sustainable economic growth has a very modern ring to it. In linking his insights to the concerns of environmental economists in 2026 and building on them, Eoin McLaughlin's *The Inclusive Wealth of Nations* contributes to both the history of economics and the economics "of what lies ahead".'

CORMAC Ó GRÁDA, University College Dublin, Ireland

'The kind of book I have long wanted to be able to put into students' hands: intellectually ambitious, historically grounded, and immediately useful for teaching. It returns to Adam Smith in the only way that matters pedagogically – not as a set of slogans about pin factories and invisible hands, but as a moral philosopher concerned with the wealth of nations in the fullest sense. This is a book that will sharpen classroom discussion, travel across different teaching contexts, and reward rereading – precisely the qualities that make it an outstanding teaching text.'

CHRIS COLVIN, Queen's University Belfast, UK

'Debates about progress now oscillate between optimism and alarm. Eoin McLaughlin takes a longer view, returning to Adam Smith's broader vision of political economy, one that bound markets to morals and prosperity to its natural foundations. The result is a timely and carefully argued book. At a moment when societies cannot afford to give up on growth, yet can no longer ignore its costs, McLaughlin shows how a fuller account of wealth can reconcile human flourishing with environmental limits.'

JOHAN FOURIE, Stellenbosch University, South Africa

'Professor McLaughlin rose to fame for revealing trends in the wealth of nations over the past 200 years. Now, in this timely work he offers the key insights into how our nations can maintain their wealth for the next 200 years.'

MATTHEW AGARWALA, University of Sussex, UK

The Inclusive Wealth of Nations

ALSO AVAILABLE FROM BLOOMSBURY

Macroeconomics, William Mitchell, L. Randall Wray and Martin Watts
Recharting the History of Economic Thought, Kevin Deane and Elisa Van Waeyenberge
Economics of Development, A.P. Thirlwall and Penélope Pacheco-López

The Inclusive Wealth of Nations

Prosperity, Sustainability, and the Future of Economic Progress

EOIN MCLAUGHLIN

BLOOMSBURY ACADEMIC
LONDON • NEW YORK • OXFORD • NEW DELHI • SYDNEY

BLOOMSBURY ACADEMIC
Bloomsbury Publishing Plc, 50 Bedford Square, London, WC1B 3DP, UK
Bloomsbury Publishing Inc, 1359 Broadway, New York, NY 10018, USA
Bloomsbury Publishing Ireland, 29 Earlsfort Terrace, Dublin 2, D02 AY28, Ireland

First published in Great Britain 2026

Cover design: Grace Ridge
Cover image © Dilok via Adobe Stock

A catalogue record for this book is available from the British Library.

ISBN: HB: 978-1-3505-4415-4
PB: 978-1-3505-4414-7
ePDF: 978-1-3505-4416-1
eBook: 978-1-3505-4417-8

Typeset by Deanta Global Publishing Services, Chennai, India
Printed and bound in Great Britain

For product safety related questions contact productsafety@bloomsbury.com.

To find out more about our authors and books visit www.bloomsbury.com and sign up for our newsletters.

To my family: I made it, meh! (I said meh!)

CONTENTS

FIGURES

TABLES

PREFACE

Adam Smith's *An Inquiry into the Nature and Causes of the Wealth of Nations* is the landmark text in economics and one of the most influential books written in the past 250 years. While the book is seen as kick starting an intellectual revolution, the evolution of economic thinking and writing since the time of Smith has lost many of his messages and the nuances inherent in his thinking. Smith was first and foremost a moral philosopher and *The Wealth of Nations* was part of his broader intellectual project. This was demonstrated clearly in the preface of the sixth (and final) edition of his *Theory of Moral Sentiments*, where an elderly Smith reflected on how he had set out to write on the principles of law and government, the 'different revolutions' that society had undergone in terms of justice, and 'what concerns police, revenue and arms, and whatever else is the object of the law'. Smith said he had 'partially executed his promise' in *The Wealth of Nations* and had hoped to continue it, but his advanced age prohibited further work.

Taking an introductory economics (Econ 101) textbook off my shelf, Adam Smith is only given a passing reference. There is a small text box introducing *The Wealth of Nations*, it quotes an iconic passage about how self-interest drives market behaviour, and it emphasizes the importance of the (rather than 'an') 'invisible hand'. This is a very superficial summary of a very complex book (rather, a book of books) that Smith continually revised over his lifetime. Ironically, the 'invisible hand' that is so often attributed to Smith was only mentioned once in *The Wealth of Nations*, although so much has been built around this powerful image. What is seldom mentioned is that 'an invisible hand' first graced the pages of *The Theory of Moral Sentiments*, yet modern economics has largely distanced itself from this text and its original context. Smith was writing at a time when mercantilist thinking was on the ascent in Britain. This worldview was zero-sum, viewing the world in binary (winner and loser) terms. It was this mercantilist thinking that placed constraints on the development of the US Colonies and ultimately led to the drive for independence: restraint of trade became equated with constraints of liberty.

My introduction to Adam Smith came via the study of history, which is not surprising given how Smith has effectively been sidelined by modern economics. I first read *The Wealth of Nations* when I was studying the economic history of Ireland. Adam Smith and his intellectual successors played a key role in the analysis of problems pertaining to Ireland in the 1700s and early 1800s. In the 1700s, Ireland bore the brunt of the various mercantilist restrictions that Smith rails against in *The Wealth of Nations*. The Woollen Acts, for example, were laws enacted by the English parliament that restricted the development of woollen industries in Ireland. Smith cited these as an example of the injustices of mercantilism. Later discussions focused more heavily on overpopulation as emphasized by Malthus but when analysing the problems of poverty, contemporaries in Ireland had first turned to Smith to understand why Ireland was poor: it had a scarcity of capital.

I initially sought out Smith to see what he said about banking in the Dutch Republic (the Bank of Amsterdam in particular), because eighteenth-century Irish thinkers (the so-called Irish School of Economic Development) had looked to Dutch examples. The beauty of *The Wealth of Nations* is that it was not just a treatise on economics, but it was a broad summary of Smith's philosophical approach to thinking about economic affairs, surveyed across a range of countries; it is both theoretical and empirical. Smith had both read and travelled widely. He had been an academic and quit to become a travelling tutor. In later life he became a bureaucrat, taking up a position as customs master in Edinburgh, ironically earning a salary from collecting the taxes on trade that he had argued against. Reading Smith first-hand (something I would highly recommend), I came away with a greater appreciation of the masterpiece and also an understanding that context in analysing the formation of ideas was an important part of the history, something that seems to have been lost by mainstream economics.

With the 250th anniversary of the publication of *The Wealth of Nations* approaching, my colleague Robbie Mochrie planted the seed in my mind to write a book to commemorate the event. I have done so, but not how you might expect. This is not a book about Adam Smith and the development of his thought in Enlightenment Edinburgh. This book is not a defence of free trade or the benefits of free market capitalism- I leave that case for others to make. What I want to show is how the ideas of Adam Smith are still relevant for society today and in the future by illustrating how his ideas align with the current views of economists about sustainable development; to be more specific, how economists have inadvertently and, in most cases, unwittingly rediscovered Adam Smith.

The genesis of my idea comes from Book II of *The Wealth of Nations*, a passage that I have quoted on numerous occasions but perhaps one that is not as well known to the wider public:

> To maintain and augment the stock which may be reserved for immediate consumption, is the sole end and purpose both of the fixed and circulating capitals. It is this stock which feeds, clothes, and lodges the people. Their riches or poverty depend upon the abundant or sparing supplies

> which those two capitals can afford to the stock reserved for immediate consumption.

The 'stock' that Smith was referring to was not capitalism, the concept that is so frequently and erroneously attributed to him. He was, in fact, thinking about the wealth of society. My book addresses this idea and how it relates to wider questions of immense importance regarding how we think of our planet and how we approach the idea of what legacy we leave behind for the future of humanity.

Many people associate Adam Smith with self-interest and greed, but this omits the importance of his other classic, *The Theory of Moral Sentiments*, which is a book on moral philosophy that, above all, devises a way to judge our ethical behaviour through the lens of the 'impartial spectator'. Applying this core idea from Smith, what if the impartial spectator is a descendant of ours looking back. How would they judge our actions? Did we maintain and augment the capital stock (what I refer to in these pages as Inclusive Wealth) for them, or did we deprive them of the opportunities that we had?

There were many starting points for this book. The first was a longstanding research project, originally funded by The Leverhulme Trust from 2011 to 2013, which I have been pursuing for almost 15 years. Initially, I began working on quantitative estimates of historical sustainable development indicators for the UK and the US. The focus was on the change in (Inclusive) wealth, broadly defined to include conventional measures of capital (e.g., investment in buildings, machinery, infrastructure), but also natural capital (e.g., coal, forests, pollution), and human capital. The idea behind the project was not simply to estimate the changes in wealth, but to test a theory that said these were predictors of future well-being. The project was a professional and personal success. I was based in the School of History, Classics, and Archaeology at the University of Edinburgh, where I worked closely with my mentor and friend David Greasley. I learned the trade of an economic historian from this master craftsman and I also co-authored several papers on genuine savings (with David Greasley, Nick Hanley, and Les Oxley) that were published in environmental economics journals – some of the material within this book is based on articles published in *Journal of Environmental Economics and Management*, *Oxford Review of Economic Policy*, *Environmental and Resource Economics*, *Journal of Economic Surveys*, and *Environment and Development Economics*. To cut a long story short, the change in Inclusive Wealth is a good predictor of future well-being over the long run, but only if we include a measure of technological progress.

It was during my time at Edinburgh that I had the fortune of hearing a talk from the Club of Rome on the 2012 update to the *Limits to Growth*. The talk piqued my interest in the origins of the ideas of sustainable development and the importance of the *Limits to Growth* and the evolution of the ideas of sustainable development became another motivation for this book. It inspired me to delve deeper into the history of the ideas and become more of an environmental (economic) historian. This was the future, or so I thought.

If life were simple, this book would be one purely examining environmental economics and what lessons Adam Smith could offer to the world today. It would be about how Smith's optimistic approach (rather than the pessimistic approach associated with those who came in his footsteps) can help manage environmental problems. But this is not what this book is about – or rather, it is not *all* about that. There is a reason for this. I had the luxury of test driving some of my more innovative ideas in a classroom full of hardened environmentalists and they did not take kindly to my impertinent economic imperialism. So, like Smith's work, this book also began life as a series of lectures. Over a decade ago, I taught in the Department of Geography and Sustainable Development at the University of St Andrews, where I was primarily tasked with teaching classes on environmental economics and I found myself explaining the origins of sustainable development to many students. I particularly remember one of my first classes. It was an eye opener. The class soundly rejected the idea of the economic approach to sustainability. Every point and assumption was (rightly) queried and questioned. Economic growth was in this group seen as bad, it had led to all sorts of social and environmental evils (even though I had presented a theory on sustainable development that emphasized inter-generational well-being and equity). Economists were the villains of the piece, there was no redemption for them.

Part of this was an erosion of trust; following the 2007-8 financial crisis it became *de rigeur* to criticize economists and this blame throwing continues to ebb and flow. Most famously, the Queen, when visiting the London School of Economics in November 2008, asked why no one had seen the crisis coming. Economists have also not fared well in the Covid and post-Covid era. The inflation shock post-Covid was deemed by the most respected economists as being transitory. It was not. If economists had missed crises that were under their noses, then how could they be trusted to advise on an existential crisis that would evolve many years in the future?

As a postgraduate student during the global financial crisis I was certainly questioning some core assumptions. I heard confident statements from economists and politicians that the problems associated with the economy had been solved; the Nobel laureate Robert Lucas assuredly stated that economics had solved the original problems of macroeconomics, and the UK Chancellor Gordon Brown believed that there would be no more boom and bust. The experience during the global financial crisis led many to question the central premises of economics as taught and practised. I do not think more of the same economics is what is needed here. One of the things lacking in mainstream economics is an understanding and appreciation of history, both the history of ideas but also the history of the economy.

As a teacher, I wanted to understand the origin of the view among environmentalists that the thinking of economists is inherently wrong. As a researcher, I wanted to go beyond the superficial article (this article was published in whatever year and it said x, y, and z). I wanted to know where the ideas that underpinned my research originated and why they emerged when they did. This led to discussions with colleagues and chats with friends. One of the latter led me to a book that had not been on my radar: Paul Sabin's book *The Bet* (an excellent read). Sabin used the infamous bet between Julian Simon and Paul Ehrlich in the late 1970s as a metaphor for the division between environmental advocates and sceptics. Overly confident prognostications on both sides are bad for society and the environment. The other book that has been hugely influential on my journey was Heinz Arndt's *Economic Development* on the history of the idea of development.

The book that I have written is the result of my journey down a rabbit hole of the history of ideas. It is a history of ideas but also a history of the economy; it mixes both the history of thought and economic history with issues pertaining to environmental economics. It is the result of a career working in history, geography, and economics departments and an amalgam of different views and concepts. I have written this book to be accessible and so I have purposefully omitted mathematical notation throughout, but for those keen to see a more thorough mathematical exposition, please see my review published in the *Journal of Economic Surveys* and a recent overview published in *Ecological Economics*.

Before I began writing the book, I was advised to keep referencing to a minimum for the sake of readability. I must apologize, I failed in that task. At times I have even committed the cardinal sin of allowing a dialogue to emerge between the footnotes and the text. Unlike Adam Smith, this book is replete with references, not for ornament but in the hope of advancing the issues discussed and encouraging others to do the same.

Eoin McLaughlin, Panmure House, Edinburgh December 2025

ACKNOWLEDGEMENTS

I have accumulated enormous debts of gratitude over the years, for everything from simple reading suggestions to more deep and meaningful conversations.

First, I must show my appreciation to two enormous influences who sadly passed away recently: David Greasley and Kirk Hamilton. Being honest with myself, David would either be writing this book with me, or he would have told me I was wasting my time. Sadly, David is no longer here to set me straight, but I would be remiss if I did not thank him for all of his mentorship and support over the years. Kirk was an invaluable supporter of the work of estimating long-run Genuine Savings (what I call the change in Inclusive Wealth). He was generous with his time and wisdom, and without his assistance, I do not think the work on historical UK Genuine Savings would have advanced as quickly as it did. At St Andrews, we honoured Kirk by naming one of the rooms the 'Kirk Hamilton Room', and I hope this book continues to honour his memory.

I owe huge thanks to Nick Hanley, whom I have worked with on sustainable development metrics since the 2010s (with the support of the Leverhulme Trust) and who is still a great source of knowledge. Nick is widely recognized as one of the leading figures in environmental economics in the UK but perhaps what many do not appreciate is Nick's keen interest in history. Nick has been a mine of information and a constant source of encouragement for which I am very grateful. I would also like to thank Les Oxley (the second half of the iconic Greasley & Oxley partnership in economic history), whom I have had countless discussions with over the years and who introduced me to the beauty of New Zealand. Special thanks also go to two long-standing friends, Matthias Blum and Cristián Ducoing, without whom much of this work would not be possible. Matthias was intrigued by the ideas behind the economics of sustainable development and helped spread the word. Matthias also introduced me to Cristián, and together we wrote an early version of a 'Global Genuine Savings', which is featured on *Our World in Data*. Cristián enthusiasm sustained (pun intended) my interest in the topic of sustainable development, and here I must thank the Riksbankens Jubileumsfond for funding our further research on global genuine savings. Last, but not least, thanks to Matthias Beck, who introduced me to the wild and wonderful world of existential risk.

I am deeply grateful to the many friends and colleagues who read various drafts (some rougher than others), offered invaluable feedback and encouragement, or who gave me useful reading suggestions (or – in one case – donated a mountain of books to me). My sincere thanks go to Tobias Börger, Antje Brown, Graham Brownlow, David Cobham, David Crichton, Martin Chick, Dan Clayton, Chris Colvin, Enda Delaney, Adam Dixon, Louis Dupuy, Nathan Foley-Fisher, Seán Kenny, Jan Kunnas, Jason Lennard, Richard McMahon, Darren McCauley, Brendan Mee, Robbie Mochrie, Cormac Ó Gráda, Rowena Pecchenino, Graeme Roy, Mark Schaffer, Paul Sharp, Alex Trew, Sally Tuckett, Paul Warde, and Niall Whelehan. Special thanks to John Turner, Diane Coyle, Romesh Vaitilingam, Ashley Lait, and all of the team at the *Economics Observatory* for giving me the opportunity to develop some early ideas and helping me appreciate how fun it can be to communicate economic concepts. Similarly, I wish to thank Steve Vass and all of the team at *The Conversation* for giving me the opportunity to present my research to the wider public. I am also grateful to Matthew Agarwala, Frans de Vries, and Mirko Moro, who helped organize a session on Adam Smith and the environment as part of the Adam Smith Tercentenary celebrations at the University of Glasgow. The event helped me consolidate my thoughts and spurred ideas for further research. Lastly, thanks to Arnab Bhattacharjee and Adrian Pabst for the opportunity to speak about the project at the National Institute of Economic and Social Research.

I wrote this book in the 2024–25 academic year when I had the privilege of being a fellow at Panmure House, Adam Smith's former residence. I wish to thank Adam Dixon and all of the staff at Panmure for their hospitality and support.

I owe particular thanks to my wife, Adrienne, for her patience with my late-night and early-morning writing sessions (and for keeping the home fires burning while I lived like Adam Smith). I can not thank you enough for enduring my often chaotic attempts to explain half-formed ideas (likened more than once to Charlie Day's 'Pepe Silvia' pinboard), and for critically reading several iterations of the book. My dear, I hope the final draft does you proud.

CHAPTER ONE

The Inclusive Wealth of Nations

Adam Smith's *An Inquiry into the Nature and Causes of the Wealth of Nations* – published on 9 March 1776 – was an inspirational treatise that set the foundation for modern economic theory and policy. The *Wealth of Nations* is considered a classic in academic and financial circuits, but as the economist William Barber (1925–2016) wryly surmised, it 'has suffered the fate accorded to most classics: it is more talked about than read.'[1] With the 250th anniversary of the publication of the *Wealth of Nations* looming, it is a timely moment to return to this famous work and consider what the *Wealth of Nations* now means in the twenty-first century.

Anniversaries are an ideal time to reflect on where ideas started, how they have developed, and where the field is going. Personally, the 2023 tercentenary of Adam Smith's birth, marked by events in Glasgow, Edinburgh, and his hometown of Kirkcaldy, drew me back to my well-worn copy of the *Wealth of Nations* that I had read as a student. It made me reflect on Smith in relation to my own work on economic sustainability.[2] Smith took a holistic view of the economy and sought to understand what exactly contributed to the wealth of nations. Arguably, it is this broad broad-based approach to understanding the economy that was lost to Smith's descendants. While many honour Smith as an intellectual ancestor, they have not paid careful attention to the arguments of the *Wealth of Nations* in its entirety, or appreciated that the *Wealth of Nations* was part of a larger intellectual project embedded within moral philosophy.

There have been many debates, discourses, and discussions about Smith over the centuries mainly with a particularly keen focus on free trade. One of his core messages, that of the importance of capital for economic development, has tended to be sidelined. Many representations of his legacy have highlighted growth in income, but not necessarily growth in *wealth*. The modern preoccupation with income owes much to the revolutionary work of John Maynard Keynes (1883–1946) and his followers. The reason for this shift of focus from wealth to income is largely because of short-term fluctuations in the economy that became particularly pronounced in the 1920s and 30s (see figure 7.4). Economists therefore came to rely on Gross Domestic Product (GDP) as the central measure of national income, an indicator that reflects how extensively resources are being used within the economy. But GDP is, at its core, primarily a short-term indicator. As Keynes infamously remarked, 'in the long run, we are all dead.' While that may hold true for some of us, we hope it will not be the case for our children, grandchildren, and future generations.

The difference between income and wealth is still not widely recognized today. Income is a flow that is measured over a discrete period of time (e.g., quarterly or yearly), while wealth is an accumulated stock; for example, the annual salary (income) of a worker may be high, but their net worth (wealth) may not be due to various other factors, including student or personal loans, spending habits, and so on. The same principle applies to companies; they may report high revenue, but their balance sheet might not be as healthy. The analogy extends to nations as well, they could have a high national income (GDP), but their national wealth might not be in rude health. Having GDP growth when we run down our environment (our natural capital) is like heating a house by ripping up the floorboards: it undermines the foundations of our wealth.

Unlike some modern economists, Smith thought about economic progress as the transformation of the different forms of wealth. He saw how we take natural capital (both finite and renewable), make produced capital (machines), and ultimately human capital, which is the basis of economic growth. It is the maintenance of the capital stock that generates future income. Smith was clear on this: 'it is this stock which feeds, cloaths, and lodges the people. Their riches or poverty depend upon the abundant or sparing supplies which those two capitals can afford to the stock reserved for immediate consumption.' Returning to the centrality of wealth in the *Wealth of Nations* brings us into debates about the impact of economic growth on the environment. Simply put, income can be a drawdown on an increasing stock of wealth that leaves real wealth unimpaired, or increasing income can involve running down wealth. This is the crux of the *Wealth of Nations* and essentially how sustainability has come to be understood (or rediscovered) by economists today.

Over the past 50 years, there have been continuing debates surrounding the environmental impact of economic growth and its long-run sustainability.[3] This has led to efforts to change how we think about economic growth and how it should be measured. A consensus approach is to move away from thinking about growth of national income (GDP) and instead focus attention on managing national wealth.[4] Inclusive Wealth is a measure of national wealth that includes all assets (produced, natural, and human) from which people obtain well-being or welfare.[5] A key facet of this is how our stock of wealth changes over time and that changes in Inclusive Wealth (per person), whether positive or negative, can tell us if our economic growth has led to sustainable (or unsustainable) development.[6]

Paying homage to Adam Smith, the 2006 report *Where is the Wealth of Nations?* was a landmark publication from the World Bank that attempted to shift the focus away from measuring a nation's income towards measuring its wealth. This was also the central message of the 2021 UK government report, *The Dasgupta Review of the Economics of Biodiversity*, arguing that, 'in order to judge whether the path of economic development we choose to follow is sustainable, nations need to adopt a system of economic accounts that records an inclusive measure of their wealth.'[7] Partha Dasgupta reiterated this point in his 2025 book, *On Natural Capital*, where he argued that Inclusive Wealth should be regarded as, 'the index we should use for assessing economic progress,' adding that, 'movements over time of inclusive wealth should guide our reading of the way the human economy is treating the biosphere.'[8] Similarly, in her 2025 book *The Measure of Progress*, Diane Coyle argues that current approaches to measuring innovation and economic progress are outdated, and she makes the case for shifting focus from GDP to broader measures of wealth (including human, natural, and intangible capital).[9] These examples from the past 20 years indicate a slow but steady return to Smith's holistic view of the economy. More, however, can be done to incorporate these historic lessons, which is the aim of this book. The story, though, does not begin in 2006, but with the work of Adam Smith and how our understanding of economics as a philosophy and a science has co-evolved with the economy over time.

This book aims to contextualize the modern Inclusive Wealth approach by outlining the history of how economists have thought about the wealth of nations, and how it is effectively a return to the original principles of Adam Smith. It also aims to show how the Inclusive Wealth approach emerged through a history of critiques of economic growth in the 1970s, in particular environmental critiques but also criticisms of those in developing countries that felt their needs were not being addressed. This led to the uneasy (and contradictory) compromise between environmental sustainability and economic development.

The goal of this book is to show that revisiting and moving beyond the original (some unresolved) critiques of economic growth in the 1970s can provide a blueprint for a sustainable future. The book will also critically evaluate the theory and application of Inclusive Wealth. It will show that while there is a theoretical consensus in how we should measure the Inclusive Wealth of nations, the application of theory has led to some inconsistencies. The book will assess the usefulness of the Inclusive Wealth approach by applying the concepts to a case study of Britain's economic history, and by assessing whether the theory can offer us any new, or useful, information about Britain's past that may help us navigate future challenges. Finally, the book will contrast the ideas of Inclusive Wealth with alternative paradigms *en vogue* today, namely 'degrowth' and 'doughnut economics.'

Anniversaries

Reflecting on the importance of Adam Smith's work has been helped by other momentous anniversaries. The year 2026 also marks the 70th anniversary of the publication of arguably one of the most monumental studies of economic growth since the days of Smith: Robert Solow's (1924–2023) classic 1956 study, 'Contribution to the Theory of Economic Growth'. The central message was to move away from seeing capital as the source of economic growth towards recognizing technological progress as the ultimate driver of growth. Solow's model of economic growth is still central in mainstream economics; it features in widely used undergraduate textbooks on macroeconomics and the article itself has over 47,000 citations in academic journals (per Google Scholar). It is still a key part of any intermediate macroeconomics class, while sadly Adam Smith is not. Solow's work is the foundation on which later theories of economic growth, including Solow's own work on sustainable development, were built. On the 50th anniversary of the publication, Solow's work received renewed attention in special issues of two economics journals, *Oxford Review of Economic Policy* and *History of Political Economy*, notably with retrospectives from Solow himself (who was still active until the ripe old age of 99).

Solow, a Nobel laureate in economics, was a giant of twentieth-century economics, but he has often been vilified by critics of economic growth. Such criticism seems to have missed the point of his research, as Solow explained in an interview recorded in 2023, just months before his passing:

> First of all, the fact that I've spent much of my life studying the way growth occurs in modern industrial capitalist economies does not mean I'm an enthusiast for it. I could have spent my life studying the bacteria that caused tuberculosis. That doesn't mean I'm in favor of them . . . I do not think that growth itself is or should be a particular objective for a modern economy.[10]

Another anniversary that is directly relevant to my study is the 50th anniversary of the publication of what could be considered an antithesis of Solow's model: the Club of Rome's *Limits to Growth* (*LTG*). Published in 1972, *LTG* warned that the world was teetering on the brink of collapse and that there would be an 'overshoot and collapse'. *LTG* was controversial as it implied that humanity had to change track or face the abyss. Unsurprisingly, it received almost instant backlash from both academics and politicians. Economists, including Robert Solow, were among the most prominent. One of the best known responses was the book *Models of Doom* published in 1973.[11]

Yet, *LTG* is still influential and widely utilized with over 35,000 citations to date,[12] not too far off Solow's total. Writing in 2011, Ugo Bardi, a professor of physical chemistry, speculated why there was such a backlash and resistance to the message from *LTG*. Bardi assured his readers that the model was correct and continues to be right as the various updates have shown, implying that there is some conspiracy against the message of *LTG*. Bardi highlighted the existence of a conspiracy of industry against Rachel Carson's work on pesticides, the lobbying of big tobacco against research showing the health effects of smoking, and also the Climategate scandal when climate researchers' emails were leaked in the 2000s. This is pure speculation as Bardi notes, 'we have no document available that proves that, in some smoke filled room, representatives of extractive industry gathered to decide what measures to take against the authors of LTG'.[13] Bardi's faith in *LTG* is not shared by the environmental scientist Vaclav Smil, a prominent critic of economic growth. In his 2019 book *Growth*, Smil dismissed *LTG* because he understood the programming language that was used to build the model and when he, 'deconstructed the model line by line (not a very difficult task, as their model of the world fit into fewer than 150 lines) and [he] quickly realized the number of indefensible simplifications and misleading assumptions.'[14]

As the Club of Rome marked the 50th anniversary of the publication of the *Limits to Growth* in 2023, it hosted a webinar with Dennis Meadows, lead author of *LTG*, Johan Rockström, an earth system scientist and lead author of the Planetary Boundaries reports, and Jayati Ghosh, a development economist and a commissioner associated with the Club of Rome's Earth4all. After Meadows presented on *LTG*, Rockström lauded the prescience of Dennis Meadows and the *LTG* project:

> Dennis Meadows, you are absolutely one of my top heroes in the world and you've influenced me and so many of my peers in the world. I would say you're the father behind system dynamics modelling, what has become modern earth system modelling and you're so humble when you always emphasize that you were not doing any predictions but you were sitting there with your team in the early 1970s . . . So it has really guided science and our understanding of human relations with your system for this whole time . . . We still follow a pathway to disaster.[15]

Therefore, we have two models of economic growth in the twentieth century and beyond: one uber optimistic model of continuous growth driven by technological progress, and another that was utterly pessimistic regarding the collapse, and possible extinction, of human civilization. There is a continued disconnect between these visions, which I will explore throughout this book.

Existential Risk

Since written records began there has always been fascination and concern with things outside of our control. An early written example is the Book of Revelation (6:1–8), which aimed to offer succour in times of Christian persecution through an apocalyptic lens. As scientific knowledge has advanced, we have become more aware of possible threats to the existence of life on our planet. There have been five known mass extinction events on this planet in the last 3.5 billion years, and it is argued that we are currently living through a sixth.[16] There have also been additional extinction events identified that are believed to be associated with near-Earth objects (NEOs) (i.e., asteroids, comets, meteors, etc).[17] Humanity has not been exposed to such extinction events, but recent evidence suggests that our ancestors may have survived such an event 117,000 years ago.[18] As humanity has progressed, it has become the first species that is able to remake our world, but also has the capacity to destroy it too.[19]

Recent global concerns, such as the climate crisis, Covid-19 pandemic, Artificial Intelligence (AI), and the recent re-emergence of the risk of nuclear war, have created a heightened awareness of global catastrophic risk (although perhaps not the expression itself) among the public and the mainstream media.[20] Yet, such global catastrophic risks (GCRs) have traditionally been overlooked in national risk assessments.[21] There is also another underutilized field of risk research, Planetary Boundaries (PBs), that shares many similarities with the GCR approaches to monitoring and evaluating existential risks to humanity, but the two approaches have tended to be siloed.

Planetary Boundaries are parameters beyond which there is a level of risk that can undermine the long-term survival of humanity. They act as markers of 'safe operating spaces' for humanity that can be quantified, and it is posited by Rockström and colleagues that once these are crossed, consequences for human survival can be irreversible.[22] GCRs also assess risks to humanity that have potential for enormous harm at a global scale, but the focus of GCR research differs from that of PB in that it contemplates a broader array of global risks to the survival of humanity, such as AI, biothreats and pandemics, and climate change.[23]

The philosopher Nick Bostrom and the astrophysicist Milan Ćirković summarized GCRs using a three-fold categorization:[24] risks from nature, unintended consequences of human activity, and hostile acts.[25] Vaclav Smil offers a different approach for classifying GCRs and divides risks into three types: known catastrophic risks, plausible risks, and entirely speculative risks. Known risks are events that have occurred in the past (NEOs, volcanic mega eruptions, and pandemics) and therefore can be assigned a non-zero probability that they will occur again at some point in the future. Plausible risks, by contrast, have not yet occurred (examples include a nuclear war or a 'pandemic caused by an unknown pathogen') but are nonetheless conceivable. Recent events like the Covid-19 pandemic demonstrate that such risks can no longer be dismissed. Finally, speculative risks are those lacking historical precedent (e.g., Artificial Intelligence [AI]) or clear scientific foundation (e.g., a new omnivorous bacteria capable of reducing the biosphere to dust). Writing in 2012, Smil pointed to speculation that AI might surpass human intelligence as implausible. At the start of the 2010s, he was sceptical, remarking that 'we have been promised superintelligent, omnipotent robots for several generations. There are no such machines today.'[26] In light of recent advances, however, this particular risk is increasingly viewed as plausible, if not yet fully realized.

While the PB and GCR ideas themselves are distinct, there is an element of overlap between the two conceptualizations of existential risk.[27] The linkage between PBs and GCRs can be traced back to the work of the sociologist Ulrich Beck (1944–2015), who focused on risks that are the by-products of modernization/industrialization, such as climate change and nuclear waste.[28] In work with my colleague Matthias Beck, we argue that a holistic approach is more appropriate to ensure focus is not directed on one type of risk only, thus missing crucial overlaps and interactions between PBs and GCRs. While there needs to be clear definitions of both of the concepts, PB and GCR demarcation should be carefully assessed because the siloing of thought hampers the conceptual understanding of key global risk constellations beyond the confines of particular lenses of risk. The approach we take is represented in Figure 1.1, which presents PBs and GCRs as overlapping risks with the arrow indicating interactions between the two.

This argument for a holistic approach to existential risk is supported by the fact that there is no absolute demarcation line between PBs and GCRs. Bostrom and Ćirković offer some guidance on what would, and would not, constitute a GCR by defining damage, global in scale, in terms of deaths and economic damage. For deaths, the range for a catastrophe is between 10 thousand and 10 million (or more) fatalities, and for economic damages it is $10 billion and $10 trillion (or more) worth of economic loss, 'even if some region of the world escaped unscathed'.[29] This is similar in many respects to the definition of harm from crossing a PB threshold as outlined in Rockström and co-authors, namely, 'widespread severe existential or irreversible negative impacts on countries, communities and individuals from Earth system change, such as loss of lives, livelihoods or incomes; displacement; loss of food, water or nutritional security; and chronic disease, injury or malnutrition'.[30]

The Covid-19 pandemic offers a recent example supporting this argument. Researchers and international bodies have speculated about links between coronaviruses and human encroachment into wild habitats, or the degradation of ecosystems, leading to calls for greater protection of biodiversity. There have also been suggestions that the virus was man-made.[31] These concerns have been framed within both the PB and GCR

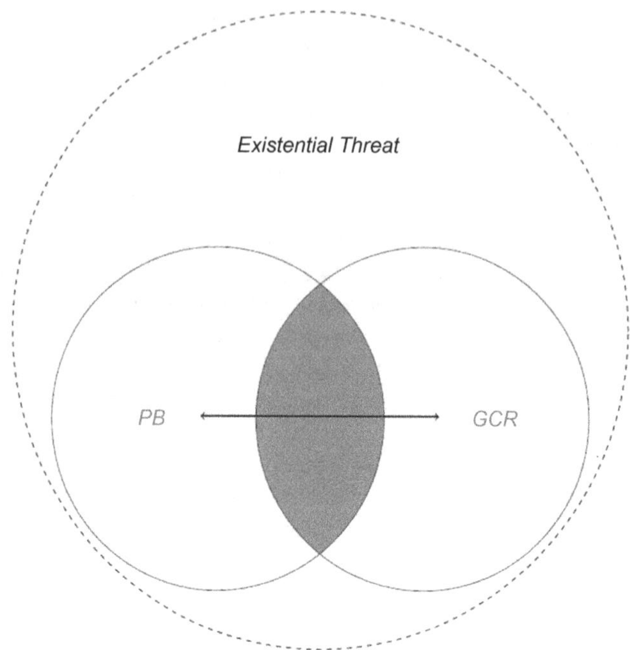

FIGURE 1.1 *Speculative reorganizing conceptualizations of existential threats. Source: McLaughlin and Beck (2025), 'Managing and Mitigating Future Public Health Risks'.*

paradigms.[32] Global excess deaths for Covid-19 were estimated at 18.2 million from 1 January 2020 to 31 December 2021, and arguably this figure could have been higher if it were not for the various mitigation efforts implemented globally.[33] The economic costs associated with Covid-19 were staggering; the estimated costs for the US alone amount to $16 trillion in 2020.[34] Under the definitions of both GCR and PB, it is clear that Covid-19 constitutes a GCR as pandemics are part of this framework, but it also falls within the PB framework as biodiversity pressures are a key PB. Yet, one could still question whether Covid-19 falls under either a PB or a GCR framework, or both. This distinction matters for how we plan for future such PB-GCR type events.

How would Adam Smith have thought about the myriad existential risks that we face today? Smith was famously an optimist and embraced the miraculous improvements of his own lifetime, but he was also aware of risks. In Book I of *The Wealth of Nations*, Smith discussed risk (albeit at a general level) and highlighted how 'chance of loss is frequently undervalued', giving the example of how few fire and maritime insurance policies were taken out. Similarly, the work of philosophers of catastrophic risk, such as Toby Ord, argues that we are underestimating existential risk.[35] A similar argument about underestimating risk is also made by the economist Martin Weitzman (1942–2019) when analysing the likelihood of catastrophic climate risk.[36] So if we are underestimating these risks we need to incorporate ways to more adequately assess risk, and I argue that revisiting the work of Adam Smith can help us achieve this.

Justice (For All Generations)

After identifying a risk typology, what should we do to address this? This is clearly an ethical (normative) question that relates to justice, especially in regard to the future generations of humanity. One of the most influential texts on justice in modern times has been the work of the philosopher John Rawls (1921–2002) in his *Theory of Justice*.[37] Among many things, Rawls set out an idea of intergenerational justice and a 'just savings principle', whereby each generation contributes towards future generations and that each subsequent generation receives a bequest from their predecessors. In the revised version of the *Theory of Justice*, the section on just savings was edited as Rawls was 'trying to make it clearer', but the essence of his explanation of intergenerational justice remains the same:

> Each generation must not only preserve the gains of culture and civilization, and maintain intact those just institutions that have been established, but it must also put aside in each period of time a suitable amount of real capital accumulation. This saving may take various forms from net investment in machinery and other means of production to investment in learning and education.[38]

There are no guidelines for how this intergenerational accumulation and distribution of real wealth should be allocated, but Rawls does provide some ethical constraints. Rawls contrasts a utilitarian view with his own view of contracts. In the utilitarian view, future generations may have higher well-being if capital accumulation and technological improvements lead to improved conditions in the future (and an ability to support a larger population). Therefore, higher savings in the poorer generations could disadvantage them.[39] Rawls then compares the utilitarian approach to the contract approach, or the 'veil of ignorance', where people do not know what generation they belong to. In that context, it is better to develop a consistent savings rule as every generation, apart from the first, would gain if a 'reasonable rate of saving is maintained.'[40]

The Rawlsian approach to intergenerational justice influenced how economists have approached the issue since the 1970s.[41] Both the Nobel laureate Ken Arrow (1921–2017) and Robert Solow – two key figures in how economists have thought about the idea of sustainability – were explicitly drawing on a Rawlsian approach in early studies analysing the intergenerational allocation of resources. Arrow focused primarily on produced capital as conventionally defined, whereas Solow expanded the definition of capital to also include finite natural resources. Solow also operationalized the Rawlsian approach as maintaining constant consumption per capita across generations. The application of the Rawlsian ethical approach adds greatest nuance when the role of non-renewable natural resources is considered, as this creates a challenge when trying to balance constant consumption per capita in perpetuity when resources are finite. Ultimately, in the case of non-renewable natural resources, technological progress is the saviour, because, as Solow notes, 'unlimited technological progress may be unlikely, but it is not, like unlimited population growth on a finite planet, absurd'. This proves to be key to Solow's application of Rawlsian intergenerational justice, but one of the problems is that it is maintained by the assumption of perfect substitution between produced and natural capital (i.e., that produced capital can act as a substitute for non-renewable natural resources). Following Solow, the economist John Hartwick showed how intergenerational equity could be achieved by a savings/investment rule, 'invest[ing] all net returns from exhaustible resources in reproducible capital'.[42] This is what Solow later referred to as the 'Hartwick Rule'.[43]

The Rawlsian interpretation of justice is very similar to one of the most influential descriptions of sustainable development, the 1987 Brundtland Commission, which stated that, 'sustainable development is development that meets the needs of the present without compromising the ability of future generations to meet their own needs.' Within the Brundtland definition, there were two key concepts: the first was 'needs', where the emphasis was on, 'the essential needs of the world's poor, to which overriding priority should be given', and second was environmental limits to present and future needs that were, 'imposed by the state of technology and social organization'.[44] While Rawls is not cited in the report, the Brundtland definition of sustainable development in terms of intergenerational justice has a clear Rawlsian fingerprint.[45]

In setting out his theory of justice, Rawls sought to distinguish his views from the utilitarian tradition that had come before him; Rawls grouped Adam Smith (and David Hume (1711–1776)) in with utilitarians such as Jeremy Bentham (1748–1832) and John Stuart Mill (1806–1873). While Smith places weight on utility, this was not the primary basis for action and, in this sense, Smith is closer in thinking to earlier classical thinkers. As the economic historian Deirdre McCloskey argues, Smith was a virtue ethicist.[46] Smith's work on moral theory is often analyzed in isolation from his canonical text on political economy, but when read together the two inform the other and help to reconcile Smithian and Rawlsian approaches to justice.[47]

Underpinning the *Wealth of Nations* was a justice framework, with justice seen as one of the essential roles of the state in Book V.[48] However, what Smith meant by 'justice' is most clearly outlined in his other masterpiece, *The Theory of Moral Sentiments*. Justice is central to Smithian thought as it is 'the main pillar that upholds the whole edifice [of society]. If it is removed . . . [society] must in a moment crumble to atoms'.[49] One of the most famous quotations from the *Wealth of Nations* relates to 'natural liberty', but what is equally important is the adherence to the 'laws of justice':

> All systems, either of preference or of restraint, therefore, being thus completely taken away, the obvious and simple system of natural liberty establishes itself of its own accord. Every man, as long as he does not violate the laws of justice, is left perfectly free to pursue his own interest his own way, and to bring both his industry and capital into competition with those of any other man, or order of men.[50]

Because society does not reward good behaviour, Smith saw justice as a negative virtue: it only punishes infractions on liberty. Positive virtues can be fulfilled without a requirement to take action.[51] While Smith was an advocate for liberty, this was not to come at the expense of wider society, noting that, 'though his own happiness may be of more importance to him than that of all the world besides, to every other person it is of no more consequence than that of any other man.'[52]

Smith outlined a framework for judging one's actions based on the perception of an 'impartial spectator', and that to 'disturb the happiness' of others because it stands in the way of our own would be intolerable to the impartial spectator.[53] Smith had a clear hierarchical structure to justice, with the greater the crime the worse the punishment. Murder 'is the most atrocious of crimes', followed by theft and breach of property, which were considered greater crimes than breach of contract. It is through the application of justice:

> that man, who can subsist only in society, was fitted by nature to that situation for which he was made. All the members of human society stand in need of each others assistance, and are likewise exposed to mutual injuries. Where the necessary assistance is reciprocally afforded from love, from gratitude, from friendship and esteem, the society flourishes and is happy. All the different members of it are bound together by the agreeable bands of love and affection, and are, as it were, drawn to one common centre of mutual good offices.[54]

Justice was of great importance to society, and injustice could potentially destabilize and even 'destroy' it.[55] For Smith, justice was not only a matter of individual perspective but also concerned the broader social implications of an action. Negligence, stemming from an absence of care regarding all possible outcomes of an individual's action, was a key concern:

> A person [who] happens to occasion some damage to another, he is often by the law obliged to compensate it . . . [As] nothing, we think, can be more just than that one man should not suffer by the carelessness of another; and that the damage occasioned by blamable negligence should be made up by the person who was guilty of it.[56]

This is reminiscent of what we think of today as a negative externality, a public cost arising from a private gain. While Adam Smith's views of justice have been criticized as being too thin (as they do not consider broader welfare), others see Smith's views as having wider applicability.[57]

The Nobel laureate Amartya Sen, who sees his own work in the tradition of Smith and other Enlightenment thinkers, indicates that Smith was aware that there are 'several different meanings' of justice.[58] Sen, in his 2009 book *The Idea of Justice*, draws on traditions of Indian jurisprudence to make a distinction between *niti* and *nyaya*: *niti* is the 'organisational propriety and behavioural correctness' of justice, while *nyaya* refers to 'realised justice'. Sen used the motto of the Holy Roman Emperor Ferdinand I (1503–1564) as an extreme example to illustrate the distinction: 'Fiat justitia, et pereat mundus [let justice be done, and let the world perish]'. There is clear *niti* but the consequences in terms of applied justice are catastrophic. In terms of the applicability of *niti* and *nyaya*, Sen sees Rawlsian justice as a form of *niti*, while Smith and other Enlightenment thinkers are more in the *nyaya* approach.

In discussions of sustainability, Sen defers to Solow, particularly praising his work on intergenerational equity. Sen believed that Solow had applied the Brundtland Commission's concept of sustainable development to economics. This is not entirely correct; Solow's work predated the Brundtland Commission and was directly influenced by Rawls's idea of 'just saving'. Regardless of this intellectual lineage, Sen broadened the Rawls-Solow-Brundtland framework, proposing that sustainable development should be understood as preserving (and if possible expanding) the capabilities and freedoms of the current generation 'without compromising the *capability* of future generations' (emphasis added).[59] This brings us back to the idea of 'just saving': it is through the maintenance of capital (broadly defined) that we can preserve the capabilities of future generations.

The economist Eric Neumayer argues that sustainable development is a concept that is like 'universal peace' or 'freedom', something that is hard for politicians, activists, and academics to argue against.[60] Yet, understanding what exactly the concept means has been somewhat elusive. Until the 2010s, the Brundtland definition of sustainability was the most widely cited interpretation of the concept. Today, sustainable development is more widely recognized through the United Nations' adoption of the Sustainable

Development Goals (SDGs) in 2015, as part of its 2030 Agenda. The SDG framework comprises 17 goals and numerous sub-targets, ranging from ending poverty (SDG 1) and achieving gender equality (SDG 5), to taking climate action (SDG 13) and strengthening global partnership to achieve the goals (SDG 17). The goals are highly visible on university campuses worldwide, with many institutions signing up through initiatives such as the UN Principles for Responsible Management Education (PRME).

While the goals are undeniably ambitious, they do not always align coherently with the Brundtland Commission's original definition of sustainable development. As Partha Dasgupta has argued, certain goals are in fact in direct tension. For instance, the pursuit of economic growth (SDG 8) can conflict with the conservation of life on land (SDG 15) and the conservation of life below water (SDG 14), raising the risk of promoting unsustainable rather than sustainable development. Moreover, the academic literature distinguishes between two competing visions of sustainability: one that emphasizes the substitutability of different forms of capital, and another that insists there is no substitute for natural capital. These tensions are explored further here in Chapters 6 and 9, but the main argument is that these differences are more theoretical than real, and that in practice there is a fundamental alignment in scope.[61]

The break between Brundtland and SDGs came via a series of UN conferences: the 1992 UN Conference on Environment and Development (the Rio Earth Summit) and the 2012 UN Conference on Sustainable Development (Rio + 20). The 1992 Rio Declaration placed humans at the centre of sustainable development (principle 1) and affirmed states' sovereign rights to develop their natural resources (principle 2), thereby prioritizing development over intergenerational equity. However, principle 3 emphasized intergenerational equity, stating that the right to development must, 'equitably meet development and environmental needs of present and future generations'. This narrowed the Brundtland definition by excluding the phrase, 'without compromising the ability of future generations'. Following the 1992 Rio Earth Summit, a UN Commission on Sustainable Development was formed to develop sustainable development indicators in line with Article 40 of Agenda 21.[62] The Commission recommended a smorgasbord of more than 100 indicators across environmental, economic, and social dimensions, but placed little emphasis on intergenerational equity.[63] By Rio + 20, the intergenerational aspect of sustainable development, while acknowledged, was much further down the list of resolutions (paragraphs 39 and 86 of the *Future We Want*), and emphasis shifted towards poverty eradication and the elaboration of SDGs.

Although it has been argued that sustainable development, 'is institutionalised by the UN in the 1987 Brundtland Report', the distinction between sustainability, economic development, and sustainable development has since become blurred.[64] In doing so, the UN arguably diluted the conceptual clarity of sustainable development. In what follows, I have purposely chosen to adhere to the original Rawlsian-Brundtland definition, which places intergenerational equity at its core. In using this approach, we can utilize the Smithian 'impartial spectator' concept as a way to assess the 'just saving' and the path of sustainable development.

A Survivalist's Rationale for Measuring the Inclusive Wealth of Nations

If we can agree on a risk typology, and the reason for taking action, the question becomes how these risks can be effectively mitigated and managed. Many GCRs are considered 'natural risks' and require geological and astrological monitoring. Other GCRs, those driven unintentionally and intentionally by human actions, should also be monitored. The GCRs from intentional human actions refer to nuclear or biological warfare, while the unintentional actions can be consequences of economic activity. Effectively, this breaks risks into a dichotomy of those that arise outside of human activities (exogenous) and those that are generated by human activities (endogenous). This brings us to the question: how should we measure the economy to provide a better indicator of the impact of economic activity on the environment (e.g., explicitly on PBs but also on GCRs)?

In terms of the wider applicability of a Smithian conceptualization of justice, we return to the question of existential risk and recent work stressing 'safe and just' planetary boundaries.[65] These are attempts to place the planetary boundaries framework, and its critics in the global south, within a wider social and environmental justice framework. In these applications justice is seen through a Rawlsian lens, although it could be expanded to incorporate Smithian principles.[66] It is these Smith-Rawls-Sen views of justice that underpin the approach that I take in this book.[67]

The conventional way to measure the economy is by calculating a nation's Gross Domestic Product (GDP), which is a measure of an economy's income, and the change in GDP is used to measure economic growth.[68] GDP as a measure is a flow and it tells us what economic activity was over a certain period of time, but this does not tell us what is happening to underlying stocks (the accumulated value of stocks at a point in time) that went into generating the flow. Therefore, instead of measuring the economy in terms of gross income, we should also measure the Inclusive Wealth of an economy.[69] This in turn relates to wider calls for how we measure the economy, such as those raised in a 2023 editorial in the journal *Nature*, echoing an earlier plea to measure wealth rather than income to fully appreciate the effect of economic activity on the environment.[70]

A proposal for improved risk management would centre on adopting a more careful and considered approach to maintaining the integrity of natural capital, broadly defined. Figure 1.2 highlights a recent empirical application of so-called

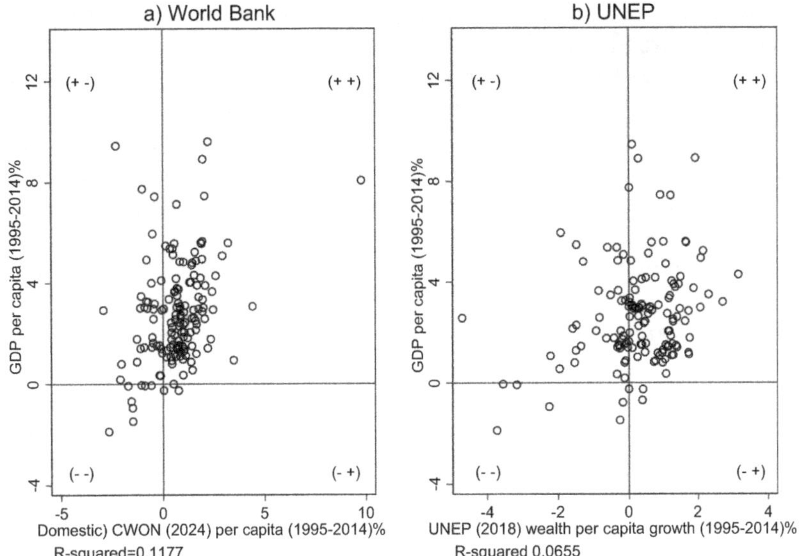

FIGURE 1.2 *GDP per capita growth and Inclusive Wealth per capita growth (1995–2014). Note: There are empirical divergences between the World Bank and UNEP approaches to measuring Inclusive Wealth, these are discussed in Chapter 6. Source: World Bank data from Changing Wealth of Nations, 2024. UNEP data from Inclusive Wealth report, 2018.*

'wealth accounting' by the World Bank and another by the United Nations Environmental Programme (UNEP).[71] Figure 1.2 shows that the growth in Inclusive Wealth per capita differs significantly from the growth in GDP per capita.[72] According to World Bank estimates, 10 countries showed negative GDP per capita growth compared to 41 countries that experienced a decline in Inclusive Wealth per capita. While UNEP data showed that 7 countries had negative growth in GDP per capita, compared to 45 countries that experienced negative growth in their Inclusive Wealth per capita (see discussion in Chapter 6 on the difference between World Bank and UNEP approaches). Inclusive Wealth is a more appropriate measure for monitoring what is happening to our natural capital in the long term, while GDP should still be used for monitoring short-term fluctuations.[73] This would help provide an indicator that can monitor risks which are internal, or 'endogenous', to our economic system.

It has been argued that, when it comes to preventing catastrophic disasters, a simple cost-benefit analysis of individual events is an imperfect tool; instead, greater emphasis should be placed on prevention itself.[74] The *Dasgupta Review on the Economics of Biodiversity* uses the Inclusive Wealth framework in the context of PBs only. Therefore, instead of a narrow definition of existential risk, I argue for a more holistic definition where both GCRs and PBs are included and also possible interactions between the two concepts are identified.[75]

The global economy is vulnerable to GCR and PBs but the risks that are driven by economic activity are underestimated because the most widely used metrics for measuring economic activity tell us little of what is happening to the underlying natural capital.[76] Inclusive Wealth is therefore an approach that I advocate for risk management by placing greater emphasis on the management of all forms of capital, particularly natural capital, both nationally and globally. While Inclusive Wealth is typically not discussed in the PB or GCR research,[77] the conceptual link between Inclusive Wealth and the GCR-PB framework comes from their focus on human well-being, which is central to all concepts.[78] The Inclusive Wealth perspective highlights the importance of all forms of capital, particularly our natural capital, where natural capital is usually defined as all 'gifts of nature'.[79] This is illustrated in Figure 1.3, which places human well-being at the centre and the link between the different frameworks.[80]

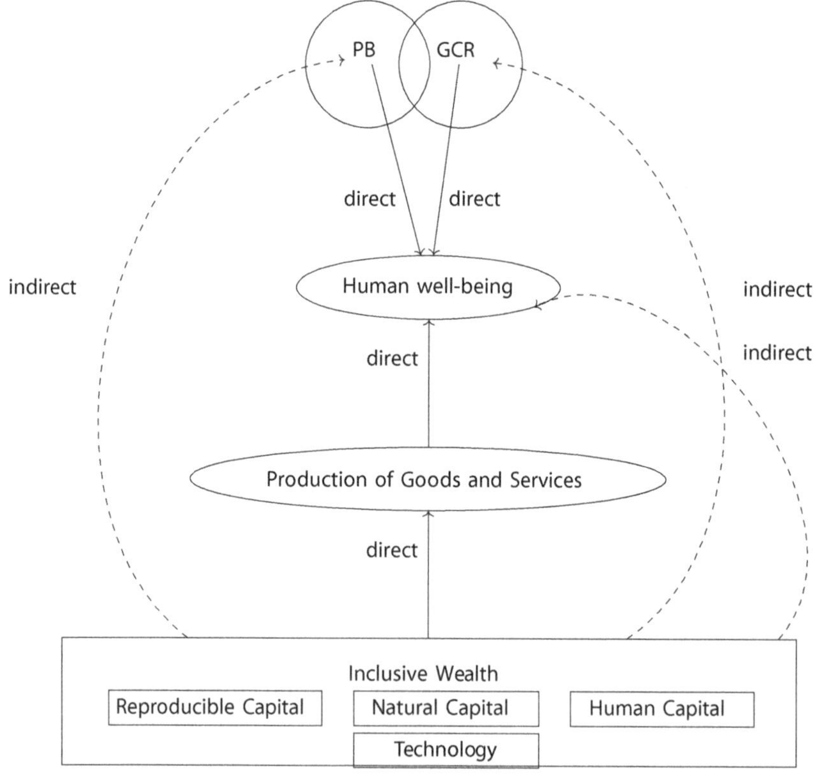

FIGURE 1.3 *Conceptualization of link between Planetary Boundaries, Global Catastrophic Risk, and Inclusive Wealth. Source: See Figure 1.1.*

Sustainable Smith?

There is a (mistaken) impression that economists do not engage with the subject of climate change and the environment more broadly. Most people with an eye to sustainability will have heard the phrase (widely attributed to Kenneth Boulding [1910–1993], a former president of the American Economic Association), 'anyone who believes in indefinite growth in anything physical, on a physically finite planet is either mad – or an economist'. This quip is based on a caricature of economists as being only interested in economic growth.

Not only is the taunt widely quoted, but it has also been used by influential members of the global intelligentsia, including as a punchline by David Attenborough in his 2011 Royal Society of Arts (RSA) president's lecture and by Vaclav Smil in a 2019 op-ed in the *Financial Times* (and in his 2019 book *Growth*). The sentiment was echoed by prominent environmentalists. In 2019, speaking at the United Nations Climate Action Summit, Greta Thunberg remarked: 'We are in the beginning of a mass extinction, and all you can talk about is money and fairy tales of eternal economic growth.'

Economics as a discipline is often used as a strawman in debates over sustainability. For example, historians Fredrik Albritton Jonsson and Carl Wennerlind's study of the conceptualization of scarcity over time sees neoclassical economics as a wrong turn, where economists had assumed people had insatiable desires and that faith in technology was a solution to problems of environmental scarcity. For Jonsson and Wennerlind, the problem is that, whether it is for a full specialist degree or only a brief introduction, neoclassical economics is what is taught across Western universities.[81] Others have argued that neoclassical economics and neoliberalism (inspired by neoclassical economics) were responsible for 'form[ing] one of the principal driving forces of environmental destruction and social injustice'.[82] There is a belief that the assumptions of neoclassical economics have led to undesirable social outcomes and that by replacing the dominant approach with one that takes the environment (or rather ecology) into consideration, it can cure a whole host of social ailments.[83]

A recent contribution to this trope is Genevieve Guenther's 2024 book, *The Language of Climate Politics*, where some of the main villains are 'the ivy-league economists celebrated by both the Nobel Prize committee and fossil-fuel front groups' because they underestimated the cost of future climate and were overly optimistic about future economic growth. Guenther, an English Renaissance scholar turned climate activist, argues that economists have focused solely on growth and that continued economic growth, in the face of climate change, 'is a myth'. The reason that Guenther sees it as a myth is because she sees that there are two 'dogmas': 'first, that technology can always substitute for nature, and second, that wealthy societies have nearly limitless capacity to adapt to global heating'. She believes that these assumptions, 'sustain the myth of economic growth as a form of salvation from climate change'. The main villain for Guenther is Robert Solow, both for his 1956 article and for the additional crime of being a PhD advisor to the Nobel laureate William Nordhaus. Despite the accusations against Solow, it is somewhat ironic that Guenther lauded another of Solow's graduate students, Martin Weitzman.[84]

The criticism of economics as an academic discipline has a long lineage, although with somewhat greater deference in the past. In their 1970 book *Population, Resources, and Environment*, the environmentalists Paul Ehrlich and Anne Ehrlich saw that 'economics and politics can usually be viewed as two sides of the same coin' because political decisions could be justified using economic rationale. For the Ehrlichs, it was not so much neoclassical ideas *per se* but economics in general, and they saw equal problems with both capitalist and socialist economic systems as they generated ideas of growth,[85] a view echoed by modern-day degrowth scholars. In fact, the Ehrlichs actually heaped praise on the seventh edition of Nobel laureate Paul Samuelson's (1915–2009) *Economics*, published in 1967, as 'excellent' and 'one of the great texts of all time' (a view widely held by economists too, I must add). However, they decried the text for the absence of discussion of environmental problems. They ended on a positive note that perhaps future generations of economists could change and incorporate more of the criticisms laid out by environmentalists. It must be acknowledged that this criticism was somewhat disingenuous, as the first edition of Samuelson's *Economics*, published in 1948, did contain discussion of externalities. Samuelson referred to 'external diseconomies' or 'external economies' and thought that 'certain lines of activity deserve to be contracted and others to be expanded'. This suggests that perhaps the Erhlichs had not fully appreciated how economists understood environmental problems.[86]

In any case, the Ehrlichs did not have to wait long for their satisfaction. The eight edition of Samuelson's textbook, published the same year as the Ehrlich's book, went a long way towards alleviating their concerns, with a new chapter devoted to the 'economic problems of race, cities, and the polluted environment'. Samuelson noted that:

> the climate of the world changes as a result of what the Industrial Revolution has done to the concentration of carbon dioxide in the air. Some scientists believe that the irreversible accumulation of lead in the air we breathe will soon become a problem everywhere in the world. Strontium 90 and radioactive trace elements have been the consequence of atomic testing; and the threat of the ultimate-doomsday cobalt bomb which will end all human life forever is more than an old-wives' bogey tale. Even noise pollutes the urban environment.[87]

Comparing the first and ninth editions of Samuelson's textbooks, the economist W. Robert Brazelton illustrated how the ideas and definition of economics evolved. Later editions of Samuelson's textbook included greater coverage of various social and environmental issues, such as the affluence of the West and the desirability of 'zero population growth'.[88] The most recent edition of Samuelson's textbook included William Nordhaus, one of the most eminent climate economists, as a co-author. Other introductory economic textbooks now include sections on externalities relating to pollution, so in a sense, the 1970s environmentalist concerns were addressed, at least somewhat.

While it may be a stretch to attribute a host of social and environmental problems to an academic discipline, there appear to be two separate issues. The first is that there is a conflation of the functioning of commercial economic systems with economic thought. Another issue relates to how economics as a discipline has evolved. While many economists today would see Adam Smith as their progenitor, it is unlikely that he would recognize modern economics as descended from him. Smith was a moral philosopher who wrote about economics from a holistic perspective, taking account of the historical, social, and political context of economic activity,[89] whereas the modern economics profession evolved with a narrow perspective on a single aspect of Smith's work.

Book outline

In what follows, I will attempt to contextualize both Smith's work and the evolution of economic thinking, and I will conclude with some ideas to move modern economic thought forward, incorporating a more rounded Smithian framework.

In Chapter 2, I adopt an *ad fontem* approach, returning to the original text of *The Wealth of Nations* to offer a concise summary and to draw lessons for Inclusive Wealth. In Chapter 3, I look at how the understanding of economic growth has changed over time. The most important theme that emerges is how capital has gone from the core of thinking, to the periphery, and now returned to the centre. Technological change is now seen as the biggest driver of growth; this is consistent with the views of Adam Smith. In Chapter 4, I outline the evolution of key ideas about development and environment and how these two fused into the concept of sustainable development. I show that Adam Smith's optimism is inherent in the approaches to development, but it is the pessimism of Smith's followers that has permeated the modern environmental movement.

In Chapters 5 and 6, I look at the history of the measurement of the economy. In Chapter 5, I show how the evolution of thinking about measurement culminated in how we measure the economy today and why it is that we think in terms of income and not the wealth of nations. This is based on thinking from the economist John Maynard Keynes, and it is centred around short-term fluctuations. This approach to measurement has worked to date because there are agreed definitions and there is a consistent approach to measurement, but it overlooks key aspects such as environmental degradation. In chapter 6, I demonstrate how the idea of Inclusive Wealth has evolved. There is a general consensus going back at least to the 1970s that the way we measure the economy is not a good indicator of the well-being of society, but devising an alternative has been stifled by the lack of agreed-upon definitions and consistent applications. In Chapters 7 and 8, I use the economic history of the UK as a case study for the application of conventional theories of economic growth and ones based on Inclusive Wealth. I argue that taking a more holistic view of Britain's economic history can shed new light on the country's contemporary productivity slowdown. In the final chapter, I explore alternatives to Inclusive Wealth, namely 'doughnut economics' and 'degrowth', and argue that neither of these is satisfactory primarily because they have taken a narrow approach to the concept of existential risk. Overall, my argument is that we need a more holistic understanding of economics and balancing the short-run and the long-run. While I agree with Keynes that we will not live to see the long run, I hope that our descendants will. I am writing this book in the hope for a sustainable future for our children and all that follow.

Part I

History of the Theory of Economic Growth

CHAPTER TWO

Wealth of Nations

A Synopsis

O wad some Pow'r the giftie gie us To see oursels as others see us! It wad frae monie a blunder free us, An' foolish notion: What airs in dress an' gait wad lea'e us, And ev'n devotion!

ROBERT BURNS "TO A LOUSE"[1]

Adam Smith (1723–1790) is widely considered to be the founder of modern economics. He was born over 300 years ago in Kirkaldy, a small coastal town in the east of Scotland. Smith entered the University of Glasgow at the tender age of 14, where he studied moral philosophy under the tutelage of the Irish-born philosopher Francis Hutcheson (1694–1746), the father of the Scottish Enlightenment. Smith then won a scholarship to study at the University of Oxford, where, although he was disappointed by the quality of teaching, he found recourse in the literary treasures held there. Smith returned to Scotland, delivering lectures in Edinburgh before being appointed to a professorship, first of logic and then of moral philosophy, at the University of Glasgow in 1751 (replacing Hutcheson). It was at Glasgow that he wrote his famous treatise, *The Theory of Moral Sentiments*, first published in 1759. He resigned his professorship in 1763 to take on the tutorage of the young Duke of Buccleuch, and in his new role he toured Europe and met with the leading French philosophers of his day.[2]

It was in France that Smith began drafting his most famous work, *An Inquiry into the Nature and Causes of the Wealth of Nations*, although the bulk of the book was written when he returned to Kirkaldy in 1766. On his return from France, Smith was elected a member of the Royal Society where he expanded his circle of influence. The *Wealth of Nations* was finally published on 8 March 1776, which fortuitously was the same year that the American colonies declared independence (4 July 1776). Smith had correctly predicted the future greatness of the colonies, cementing his place in the rare pantheon of successful prognosticators.

The Wealth of Nations is comprised of 5 books: book I outlines the theory of the division of labour and the source of wealth of a nation; book II relates to the accumulation of capital; book III focuses on differences in economic growth across countries; book IV discusses different approaches to political economy and is the battleground between the ascendent mercantilist view and Smith's liberal approach; and book V relates to the role of the state.

The Wealth of Nations was an evolving project. The genesis of the work can be found in Smith's lecture notes from his time at Glasgow that were posthumously published by a former student. In 'On Jurisprudence', where Smith laid out the four great objects of law: 'justice, police, revenue, and arms'. Perhaps surprisingly, the wealth of nations was considered under the heading of 'police', given that the word carries a much different connotation today. But 'police' was a term borrowed from the French *police*, which in turn derives from the Greek *politeia*, itself rooted in *polis*, which signified the policy or organization of government. Smith outlined that, 'the objects of police are the cheapness of commodities, public security and cleanliness . . . under this head we will consider the opulence of the state'.[3] It is in these lecture notes that the division of labour was introduced, although the concept borrowed heavily from Hutcheson.[4]

In all, there were five editions of *The Wealth of Nations* published in Smith's lifetime. The first edition sold out within six months, while the second edition, published in 1778, only had minor differences. Smith noted that in the third edition, published in 1784, he had 'made several additions' including new books and chapters that made a considerable difference to the previous editions.[5] Effectively, this was the final version; there were minor edits to the fourth and fifth editions, published in 1786 and 1789 respectively, but there were no substantive changes.

Within his lifetime, Smith witnessed revolutionary changes in the British (especially the Scottish) economy. Some of his famous contemporaries were intellectuals, such as David Hume (1711–1776), Adam Ferguson (1723–1816), Joseph Black (1728–1799), John Sinclair (1754–1835), and James Hutton (1726–1797), as well as famous inventors, such as James Watt (1736–1819). He was an eyewitness to the Industrial Revolution, and he documented what were the foundations of the wealth of a nation. It is often said that Smith makes no mention of the Industrial Revolution that was occurring around him, but this is not quite a true reflection. For example, Smith referred to a remarkable 95 per cent decrease in the prices of watches as well as price decreases in other metal wares in Sheffield and Birmingham. Watches were the high-tech sector of their day and were relatively neglected in conventional accounts of the Industrial Revolution. Inspired by Smith's observation, economic historians Morgan Kelly and Cormac Ó Gráda have shown that there was a substantial fall in the price of watches, indicating a rapid rise in productivity at 2 per cent per annum, which was higher than in other sectors of the economy.[6]

The cultural milieu was clearly an important factor in the development of Smith's thinking. He was an active participant in the Scottish Enlightenment and engaged socially with the main figures of the day. The Scottish Enlightenment is something difficult to characterize as it encompassed a large swathe of time. The first phase is associated with 'the age of Francis Hutcheson', whose main influence was on those whom he educated at Glasgow University. Hutcheson, however, was not active in the clubs and societies that formed in Glasgow, and Edinburgh was 'terra incognita'. The second phase of the Enlightenment was associated with the influence of the Edinburgh-based David Hume and his historical approach to philosophy. Smith was close with Hume, twelve years his senior, who was a pivotal influence on Smith's thinking. It has been said that the relationship between Smith and Hume was both critic and disciple.

The 'High Enlightenment' phase was associated with Adam Ferguson, William Robertson (1721–1793) and Adam Smith. It is here that Smith played a key role both as an academic, having lectured in both Edinburgh and Glasgow, but later as a public figure and in his role in the Oyster Club in Edinburgh. Smith also entertained other key figures of the Enlightenment; James Hutton and Francis Black were close friends. It was rumoured that he later inspired the great bard Robert Burns (1759–1796) as attested by Burns' poem 'To a Louse', which references *The Theory of Moral Sentiments* and the role of the impartial spectator. It was in the later stages of the Enlightenment that Edinburgh became known as a 'hotbed of genius' and 'Scotland became one of the most important centres of intellectual culture in the western world'. The University of Edinburgh became renowned for its medical school, which was one of the best in the world by the early 1800s.[7]

Several wars and subsequent political unrest occurred during Smith's lifetime that undoubtedly influenced his thinking. When he first returned to Scotland after his studies at Oxford, the country was in the throes of the final Jacobite rising of 1745; the city of Edinburgh had recently fallen to the Bonnie Prince and his army. Soon after, the Seven Years' War (1756–1763) changed the shape of Europe and the nature of the British Empire. Finally, there were what he called the 'present disturbances' in the US colonies: the US War of Independence (1775–1783). Smith actually delayed publication of *The Wealth of Nations* as he moved to London to be closer to news about the American Colonies. Smith's world was also one of competition between warring European nations, where trade was restricted by monopolies, and where parliaments placed restraints on international trade.

Adam Smith was born after the Union of the Parliaments of England and Scotland in 1707. Before the Union, Scotland had been a relatively poor and peripheral European economy, driven close to bankruptcy by the failure of the Darien scheme, its ill-fated attempt to emulate colonial ventures in the

New World. The Union was slow to deliver material benefits, but it created a common market that encouraged trade across the island and laid the groundwork for greater industrial development north of the border. By the early 1760s Scotland was beginning to see clear advantages of the Union, and prosperity continued to grow until the outbreak of the American War of Independence in 1775, with 'practically all classes of Scottish society' becoming part of a noticeably 'richer society'. [8] In Smith's lifetime Britain underwent dramatic economic change. Its population grew by about a quarter, with Scotland seeing the fastest growth in its towns and cities.[9] One of the most striking changes was the marked increase in British national debt during the Seven Years' War: national debt soared from £95 million to £148 million. Such pressures on public finances undoubtedly shaped Smith's thinking.[10]

It is Smith who is seen as the founder of the discipline of economics and who is widely admired. This is evident in the writings of some of the most esteemed economists. John Maynard Keynes, who is generally considered one of the greatest economists, held Adam Smith in highest regard: 'Economists must leave to Adam Smith alone the glory of the Quarto, must pluck the day, fling pamphlets into the wind, write always *sub specie temporis*, and achieve immortality by accident, if at all.'[11] In his defence of the study of the history of economic thought, Kenneth Boulding was similarly effusive: 'Adam Smith may well be considered not merely the founder of economics as a scientific phylum, but even of social science in general.'[12] Smith is still revered today, for example Amartya Sen refers to Smith as 'finest political economist of all time'.[13]

Division of Labour

The opening gambit of *The Wealth of Nations* lays out a then revolutionary idea (and probably still a revolutionary idea for certain politicians) that the wealth of nations is not the hoarding of bullion but that the 'annual labour of every nation is the fund which originally supplies it with all the necessaries and conveniences of life which it annually consumes'.[14] As Smith tells us in the introduction to *The Wealth of Nations*, Books I to IV are about the 'revenue of the great body of people' across 'nations and ages', while Book V relates to the wealth of the 'sovereign' or the 'commonwealth'. Within this classification, it is perhaps better to think of Books I and II as the development of the theory of *The Wealth of Nations* and Books III to V as applications of the theory. Book I sets out some foundational ideas in economics, namely supply and demand for labour and commodities and markets determining the prices. While some of the nomenclature might not be what many people are familiar with today, the concepts still lie at the core of modern economics.

The starting point is the division of labour. This is the specialization of tasks that enables society to become more productive. The famous example that Smith used to illustrate the division of labour was from a 'very trifling manufacture': pin manufacturing. This was reportedly derived from a mixture of personal observation, but also from Denis Diderot's (1713–1784) *Encyclopédie*, although whether either of them actually witnessed the process of pin making is debatable. The argument that Smith made was that there were several tasks involved in making a pin: drawing out the wire, straightening the wire, cutting the wire, pointing the wire, grinding it to receive the head of the pin, then making the head of a pin, whitening the pin, and then placing a pin in paper. If one person performed all of the tasks, they would only be able to produce a handful of pins in a day. But if the tasks were broken up in a supply chain (or an assembly line), then the output could be increased 4000-fold. Not included in the classic example of the division of labour is the mining and smelting required to make the base metal. So, the productivity is even greater than the original exposition indicates.

Smith gave other examples, such as the 18 tasks involved in making a jacket. This clearly has a lot of resonance with the way global supply chains work today. A modern example could be the smartphones almost everyone in the world carries. The phone is not made as one unit but involves tasks divided up among supply chains. Take only one component: semiconductors. They are designed in the United States, manufactured in Taiwan using machine tools from the Netherlands, and made from quartz mined in North Carolina. Consider that when looking at all of the other components; the camera, antenna, microphone, speakers, battery, display screen, and so on, all have similarly complex supply chains. All of these components are then brought together and assembled in factories in China or Vietnam. There is specialization in each layer of the supply chain, and this division of labour enables smartphones to be mass produced. If one manufacturer had to make each component plus assemble the final product, it would take longer and be a much more expensive process and the price for the final product would be significantly higher.

Smith noted three benefits from the division of labour. The first is that workers can increase their experience and expertise on a particular task. This is effectively a learning-by-doing argument: the more time spent at one task, the better we are at it. This then leads to improvements in productivity. To this we add the second benefit: the time saved that otherwise would have been spent moving between tasks. Rather than having to change our focus on a task that may be completely unrelated to the previous one, we can spend time repeating the same process, enforcing the learning-by-doing method. The last benefit is that focusing on one task creates understanding, and incentives, to innovate and invent, 'a great number of machines which facilitate and abridge labour, and enable one man to do the work of many'.

The question then remains what conditions lead to specialization as, 'it is not originally the effect of any human wisdom, which foresees and intends that general opulence to which it gives occasion'. Smith's answer: it arises from human inclination to exchange, that is to trade. Specialization requires a market because for people to specialize in one particular occupation requires someone else to specialize in another, and for some trade to happen between the different occupations. This is best illustrated using the iconic passage:

> It is not from the benevolence of the butcher, the brewer, or the baker that we expect our dinner, but from their regard to their own interest. We address ourselves, not to their humanity, but to their self-love, and never talk to them of our own necessities, but of their advantages.[15]

The degree of specialization then grows hand-in-hand with the size of the market. In Smith's time (before the advent of railways), rural communities, particularly in the Scottish Highlands, were often isolated. As a consequence, there was less specialization in these areas compared to towns and cities. Smith saw water carriage (transport) as being a greater facilitator of trade and thus of urban settlement. This observation has modern resonance, as urbanization rates are now higher than in Smith's time, and the global urban population has surpassed the rural population.

The next question is how trade takes place. It is awkward to try and barter (the examples are butcher, baker and brewer), say, beer for bread or bread for meat, well, how much beer for a loaf of bread or how much bread for a pound of mutton (or for a haggis)? This is where money enters the equation; it is a medium of exchange that enables trade and thus facilitates the division of labour. The end result is that everyone is living by exchange, or rather everyone is effectively a 'merchant', and the society 'grows to what is properly a commercial society'. A commercial society therefore needs prices to facilitate trade, and prices are distributed between the key inputs into production: wages for labour, profit for capital, and rent for landlords. Smith, however, was keen to illustrate that there is a clear distinction between money prices and the real value of a commodity.

Smith contrasted an opulent that is one (that is, growing) society with, a stagnant society and one that is going backwards. The feature that distinguishes each society is what is happening to real wages. He continually refers to England as an example of an opulent society and China as an example of a stagnant one. Smith obviously preferred growth, 'the cheerful and the hearty', to stagnation ('dull') or decline ('in melancholy'):

> The demand for those who live by wages, therefore, necessarily increases with the increase of the revenue and stock of every country, and cannot possibly increase without it. The increase of revenue and stock is the

> increase of national wealth. The demand for those who live by wages, therefore, naturally increases with the increase of national wealth, and cannot possibly increase without it.[16]

An increase in real wages then would lead to an increase in the number of inhabitants, which Smith considered 'the most decisive mark of the prosperity of any country'. If population increased without a complementary increase in capital, then real wages would instead fall. Smith uses China to illustrate this point, noting that it has 'acquired that full complement of riches which the nature of its laws and institutions permit it to acquire'.[17]

A key point made in Book I is the distinction between the 'value of use' and the 'value of exchange'. To explain the distinction between use and exchange, Smith drew on the Water-Diamond paradox. Water is essential to life and is widely used, but it is ubiquitous and therefore has a low value when it comes to exchange. Diamonds, however, are not essential and are not widely found; they are scarce (well, that was until synthetic diamonds could be manufactured), and so they had a low use value but would have a high value of exchange.

Accumulation (and Division) of Capital

Capital is central to the Smithian conceptualization of the economy. Although Book I of *The Wealth of Nations* opens with the division of labour, Smith is clear that there can be no specialization without capital to facilitate it: 'capital must be accumulated beforehand'. Smith argues that capital accumulation leads to increased output but also that this increased output leads to greater specialization. So it ultimately leads to further growth. The key point then is that:

> To maintain and augment the stock which may be reserved for immediate consumption, is the sole end and purpose both of the fixed and circulating capitals. It is this stock which feeds, clothes, and lodges the people. Their riches or poverty depend upon the abundant or sparing supplies which those two capitals can afford to the stock reserved for immediate consumption.[18]

But what exactly does Smith mean by capital? Smith sees that there are three types of capital: durable consumption goods (i.e. furniture), fixed capital, and circulating capital. Fixed capital is divided into four categories: 'machines and instruments of trade, which facilitate and abridge labour'; 'profitable buildings which are means of procuring a revenue', these include warehouses, work-houses and various farm buildings; improvements in land;

and 'the acquired and useful abilities of all the inhabitants and members of the society'.

Today, we would consider all of these as forms of capital; while circulating capital is more like working capital in modern accounting and it is fixed capital that enables future production. Although the latter two components of Smith's fixed capital may be considered natural capital and human capital, respectively. Smith included them both as part of fixed capital because they could be 'regarded in the same light as those useful machines'. Improving land is effectively equivalent to increasing the amount of land, and increasing human capital can mean the ability to invent new machines. A charitable reading of Smith in this light could therefore be seen as anticipating what later became known as 'endogenous growth', that the means to generate economic growth is derived from the power of human capital.

Circulating capital was defined as consisting of four elements: money, stock for sale, raw materials, and inventory. The circulating capital is then used within a year and either goes towards the consumption of durable goods or is added to the stock of fixed capital. This leads to another key point in Smithian capital theory: it is not simply a case of accumulation, but the capital needs to be 'continually supported' and maintained. Capital depreciates (through wear and tear) and can become obsolete, hence the need to think in terms of net, not gross, capital formation.

Effectively, Smith saw circulating capital as investment and it is ultimately derived from the 'produce of land, of mines, and of fisheries'; i.e., natural capital in today's parlance. The process of economic growth therefore transforms natural capital into fixed capital. But not only does natural capital transform into physical capital, when fixed capital is applied to natural capital it increases the produce of natural capital and it 'is in equal proportion to the extent and proper application of the capitals employed in them'.

Smith saw capital as augmenting labour and saw the increase in the annual produce of land and labour as being driven by an increase in productive labour; or 'the productive powers of those labourers', and that this productive increase could only be achieved by an increase in the capital stock. Smith saw limits to this, noting that 'the capital of all the individuals of a nation has its limits, in the same manner as that of a single individual, and is capable of executing only certain purposes'. Although it must be noted that Smith made a distinction between productive and unproductive labour, unproductive labour being services, a distinction which is not recognized today. However, the idea of the capital intensity of industry increasing labour productivity still holds true.

Capital accumulation was ultimately driven by profits, first at an individual level but then scaled up to the level of a nation:

> The capital of all the individuals of a nation is increased in the same manner as that of a single individual by their continually accumulating

> and adding to it whatever they save out of their revenue. It is likely to increase the fastest, therefore, when it is employed in the way that affords the greatest revenue to all the inhabitants of the country, as they will thus be enabled to make the greatest savings. But the revenue of all the inhabitants of the country is necessarily in proportion to the value of the annual produce of their land and labour.[19]

The allocation and application of capital across the economy was determined by the 'private profit' of the owner of capital. This meant that the owners would invest in sectors where they perceived the highest return and the wider aggregate implications ('the different quantities of productive labour which it may put into motion') of such investment decision are never considered ('never entered into his thoughts').

Security and property rights are essential conditions for the accumulation of capital. Without which there is a high risk of expropriation by the state (or by marauders). Smith saw capital accumulation in England as being in spite of government exaction and was driven by efforts of individuals to 'better their own condition' with liberty to do so and being 'protected by law'. This Smith saw as maintaining 'the progress of England towards opulence and improvement'.[20] Smith also warned against 'prodigals and projectors' who would 'waste and destroy' the capital of a country through crowding out investment from more productive uses. In this sense, the original promoter of market economy warned against excessive risk and misallocation of capital to bubbles of various kinds.[21] Smith was emphatic that, 'capitals are increased by parsimony, and diminished by prodigality and misconduct.'[22]

In analysing the growth of capital, Smith was keen to emphasize a long-term view over decades ('at periods somewhat distant from one another') rather than a short-term perspective; i.e. fluctuations over years would make growth appear gradual, but over a long period of time the full extent of growth (or lack thereof) could be seen.

The 'Progress of Opulence'

The themes of Books I and II are expanded in Books III and IV. In Book III, Smith takes a historical overview of economic growth, or what he calls 'progress of opulence', across different countries. One of the key themes that emerges is the interaction between rural and urban and the gains from exchange between both. This relates back to the key themes from Book I, the bigger the city, the 'more extensive that market' and the greater the benefits of trade both within the city but also with its rural hinterland. The benefits to the agricultural community are higher prices for their produce while the urban community benefits through food and exchange for their wares.

Smith outlined three benefits of growing cities for the countryside, the first is to create a market for the produce of the land which encourages 'further improvement' in agriculture. Second is that merchants acquire land in the country and can bring this into cultivation, and the last point is that expanding cities can bring greater liberty and security to the countryside which has 'lived almost a continual state of war with their neighbours'. But for a city to grow, the agricultural community must first be able to generate a surplus, i.e. produce beyond its subsistence. Here, by highlighting the benefits of trade, Smith is using urban and rural trade as a metaphor for international trade and attacking the mercantilist position of 'balance of trade', that trade is a zero-sum gain. Again a charitable reading of Smith here could be that he is anticipating what later become known as Marshallian externalities, or agglomeration effects of cities, due to knowledge spillovers and common pools of resources within cities.

One of the key themes to which Smith repeatedly returns is the role of institutions, particularly pernicious ones that place restraint on trade, in multiple forms, not only through tariff barriers. A lot of attention is placed on laws that prevent access to land (e.g., feudalism). Smith highlights the divergent growth patterns of the American colonies and European countries.[23] In the latter, there is industry and commerce, but land had been restricted for generations, while in the former, it was an open frontier. For Smith, the reason why the price of land was so high in Europe was because of monopoly prices and this was the result of the 'laws of progeniture and perpetuities of different kinds, prevent the division of great estates, and thereby hinder the multiplication of small proprietors'.[24] While some authors have interpreted this as Smith implying agricultural land was the source of wealth, it seems more likely that Smith is implying that institutions can create market distortions. Smith saw the natural order as being the division of labour following an agricultural surplus and he sees legislative interference in this process as a distortion:

> Had human institutions, therefore, never disturbed the natural course of things, the progressive wealth and increase of the towns would, in every political society, be consequential, and in proportion to the improvement and cultivation of the territory or country.[25]

Smith also reflected on the impact of wars and revolutions on wealth. These events can lead to a flight of merchants and dissipate the 'sources of wealth that arise from commerce only', but the capital stock is more durable and thus can lay the foundations of recovery.

Capitalism *avant la lettre*?

Adam Smith is seen as a founding figure of capitalism, yet the word capitalism does not appear in the pages of *The Wealth of Nations*. As Smith is at pains to make the distinction between wealth as capital and wealth being synonymous with money 'as a popular notion'. As was outlined in Book II, the wealth of a country is its capital, not the stock of money, and 'it is not for its own sake that men desire money, but for the sake of what they can purchase with it'.[26] Book IV focuses on the systems of political economy which Smith classified as either 'commercial' or 'agricultural'. The commercial approach is what we know today as mercantilism, which is associated with the belief that trade is a zero-sum gain (balance of trade) and a focus on accumulating bullion, and the agricultural approach is what is associated with the French physiocrat school, which places agriculture as the source of wealth. By emphasizing these two distinct approaches to political economy, Smith aimed to place his work as an alternative to both. Concluding Book IV, he wrote:

> All systems either of preference or of restraint, therefore, being thus completely taken away, the obvious and simple system of natural liberty establishes itself of its own accord. Every man, as long as he does not violate the laws of justice, is left perfectly free to pursue his own interest his own way, and to bring both his industry and capital into competition with those of any other man, or order of men.[27]

As Smith had placed emphasis on internal trade, or rather exchange, this placed his views at odds with the mercantilist approach which emphasized international trade. Smith accused the mercantilist tradition therefore of ignoring 'the most important of all' sources of wealth, internal trade between cities and the countryside. While Smith is seen as one of the main critics of the mercantilist system, it was David Hume who offered a more devastating theoretical critique of the mercantilist system with the quantity theory of money. The mercantilist system would ultimately be self-defeating, because the attempts to attract gold would lead to a rise in the price level which would ultimately lead to an increase in imports and an outflow of gold and a return to the original price level.[28]

Smith opposed market distortions, particularly import restrictions, which he believed led to the creation of domestic monopolies. These monopolies, while beneficial to some interest groups, did not benefit the nation as a whole. But the biggest issue that Smith had was that government intervention could distort markets and create incentives. It was uncertain whether the 'artificial direction is likely to be more advantageous to the society than that into which it would have gone of its own accord'. Without government interference, Smith saw capital being allocated according to where the owners of capital best saw fit (i.e., 'an invisible hand'):

> As every individual, therefore, endeavours as much as he can both to employ his capital in the support of domestic industry, and so to direct that industry that its produce may be of the greatest value; every individual necessarily labours to render the annual revenue of the society as great as he can. He generally, indeed, neither intends to promote the public interest, nor knows how much he is promoting it. By preferring the support of domestic to that of foreign industry, he intends only his own security; and by directing that industry in such a manner as its produce may be of the greatest value, he intends only his own gain, and he is in this, as in many other cases, led by an invisible hand to promote an end which was no part of his intention. Nor is it always the worse for the society that it was no part of it. By pursuing his own interest he frequently promotes that of the society more effectually than when he really intends to promote it. I have never known much good done by those who affected to trade for the public good. It is an affectation, indeed, not very common among merchants, and very few words need be employed in dissuading them from it.[29]

Smith makes the case for the benefits of trade, noting that, 'if a foreign country can supply us with a commodity cheaper than we ourselves can make it, better buy it of them with some part of the produce of our own industry employed in a way in which we have some advantage'.[30] Smith acknowledged the benefits of free trade but argued that mercantilist restrictions distorted trade and increased inefficiencies.

Smith gave extensive discussion to the 1703 Methuen Treaty, a treaty which gave favourable reductions in tariffs for Portuguese wine in exchange for preferential access to the Portuguese market for British woollen textiles. The Methuen Treaty was negotiated at a point of unequal power relations between the British and Portuguese governments during the War of Spanish Succession (1701–1714), where Portugal accepted the terms in return for defence protection. Smith criticised mercantilist logic behind such agreements, noting that some commercial treaties were regarded as advantageous not because they promoted mutual benefit but because they were thought to yield a favourable balance of trade and an annual inflow of gold and silver:

> some treaties of commerce, however, have been supposed advantageous, upon principles very different from these; and a commercial country has sometimes granted a monopoly of this kind, against itself, to certain goods of a foreign nation, because it expected that in the whole commerce between them, it would annually sell more than it would buy, and that a balance in gold and silver would be annually returned to it. It is upon

> this principle that the treaty of commerce between England and Portugal, concluded in 1703 by Mr Methuen, has been so much commended.[31]

Smith also included a translation of the three articles of the Methuen Treaty in the text of *The Wealth of Nations*. It is therefore somewhat surprising that a mercantilist treaty became the canonical illustration of comparative advantage in David Ricardo's (1772–1823) work. The example used by Ricardo was Portuguese wine traded for English textiles; Portugal could produce wine at a lower cost than England, while England could produce cloth at a lower cost than Portugal, thus providing a basis for trade. However, he did not acknowledge that the historical pattern of costs and trade he invoked had been strongly influenced by the 1703 Methuen Treaty. [32]

Furthermore, Smith highlights the myopic nature of the mercantilist worldview as tariffs lead to retaliation in kind and ultimately make consumers worse off and lead to the oppression of industry in both countries. As Smith noted, 'there may be good policy in retaliations of this kind when there is a probability that they will procure the repeal of the high duties or prohibitions complained of'. However, if the retaliation does not lead to a removal of the barrier, then it is only taxing ourselves. Smith saw tariffs as 'a real tax upon the whole country, not in favour of that particular class of workmen who were injured by our neighbours prohibition, but of some other class'. But then, how should the tariffs be removed? Here Smith argued for a gradual withdrawal of protection because of the livelihoods built up under the protectionist regime.

Smith ultimately saw mercantilism as 'beggaring all their neighbours' and believed that commerce between nations, as between individuals, should be treated as friendship and union and not hostility.[33] Smith saw mercantilism as interest groups imposing restrictions that were against the interests of the bulk of society. He did not see the advantage of imposing tariffs on neighbouring countries because 'the wealth of a neighbouring nation, however, though dangerous in war and politicks, is certainly advantageous in trade'.

Smith was also hostile to market distortions in the form of export bounties as he did not believe they should be used for sectors that can be carried on profitably without them, as they distort the market. Smith argued that export bounties were effectively a double taxation because they require a tax to pay the subsidy and they also impose a higher price in the domestic market. Foreshadowing future views of famines, Smith did not see famines as being natural disasters but rather man-made catastrophes resulting from market distortions, arguing that free trade was 'the only effective preventative of the miseries of a famine, so it is the best palliative of the inconveniences of a dearth'.[34]

One of the most interesting chapters in Book IV is on colonies. Smith looks to the history of colonization back to antiquity and also the colonization of the Americas. He draws a distinction between the motivations of the

Greeks and Romans, whom Smith attributed their expansion to population pressures, in a manner later echoed by Malthusian arguments, and the colonization of the Americas, which he saw as driven not by demographic strain but by the lure of mineral wealth. Smith believed that a colony in an area with sparse population which replicated the institutions and laws of their own country would see 'advances more rapidly to wealth and greatness than any other human society'. And that 'there are no colonies of which the progress has been more rapid than that of the English in North America'. Smith highlighted the importance of freedom to manage affairs and better treatment compared with other colonies. The French and Spanish colonies were used as a counterpoint, as a reason why the US colonies thrived but they did not have control over their external trade due to the mercantilist system. This view has been echoed in the work of Nobel laureates Daron Acemoglu, Simon Johnson and James Robinson, who stressed the importance of institutions in settler economies.[35]

The Role of the State: *Dirigisme or Laissez Faire*?

While Smith is normally presented as a pioneering advocate of free markets, this caricature seems to forget the last book of *The Wealth of Nations* which relates to the role of the state in a market economy. Also, there is no reference to the concept of *laissez-faire*. As Smith clearly outlines:

> Commerce and manufactures can seldom flourish long in any state which does not enjoy a regular administration of justice, in which the people do not feel themselves secure in the possession of their property, in which the faith of contracts is not supported by law, and in which the authority of the state is not supposed to be regularly employed in enforcing the payment of debts from all those who are able to pay. Commerce and manufactures, in short, can seldom flourish in any state, in which there is not a certain degree of confidence in the justice of government.[36]

Smith outlined three roles of the state: national defence, justice, and the provision of public goods and institutions. Effectively, these are the roles that are not performed by the free market.[37] These roles, Smith argues, are for the 'general benefit of the whole society'.

Smith sees the state as a provider of defence as an outcome of the division of labour. In hunter-gather and shepherd societies, everyone was a warrior but as agriculture developed, so too did the need for professional soldiers. As warfare became more sophisticated, this increased the need for a professional soldiering class funded by society. Thereby compulsory military training for all members of society in peacetime contradicts the division of labour. The wealth generated by the division of labour 'provokes the invasion of their neighbours'. Without provision for defence by the state, a wealthy nation is 'incapable of defending itself'.[38]

The options for the state are either to provide some continuous training to all citizens or to create a professional army. Smith reflected then on the nature of military training required pre- and post-introduction of firearms; prior to the introduction of firearms, soldiers needed greater experience in the use of arms and needed strength and endurance as well as experience on the battlefield. After the introduction of firearms, while skill was necessary, less experience was required. But greater discipline was needed in an army with firearms, and Smith believed it was harder to get this level of discipline in a militia than in a standing army. Here, an obvious issue arises over fears of liberty, as 'men of republican principles have been jealous of a standing army as dangerous to liberty'.[39] Smith gave examples from antiquity, but also the relatively recent historical experience in Britain; Cromwell was only 120 years prior to the writing of *The Wealth of Nations*. Although the fear of an army was ultimately about who the army was answerable to and here he made the case that liberty was best supported by a strong army in order to prevent anarchy; clearly, the experience of the Jacobite uprising left a lasting impression. Smith concluded, therefore, that:

> The first duty of the sovereign, therefore, that of defending the society from the violence and injustice of other independent societies, grows gradually more and more expensive as the society advances in civilization. The military force of the society, which originally cost the sovereign no expense either in time of peace or in time of war, must, in the progress of improvement, first be maintained by him in time of war, and afterwards even in time of peace.[40]

Defence increases in cost as a society experiences economic growth and Smith saw this cost also increasing with technology. Noting the great reversal of fortune, in earlier epochs opulent societies found it difficult to defend themselves against the 'poor and barbarous' while in the modern era it was 'the poor and barbarous [who] find it difficult to defend themselves against the opulent and civilised. The invention of firearms, an invention which at first sight appears to be so pernicious, is certainly favourable both to the permanency and to the extension of civilization.'[41] Ultimately, defence was seen as important because it provided security for ongoing investment, capital accumulation, and the division of labour.

The second role of the state was to protect 'every member of the society from the injustice or oppression of every other member of it'.[42] This Smith saw as essential to the functioning of the market-based system. Successful people acquired property through their hard work or over generations of hard work but 'for one rich man, there must be at least five hundred poor' and this inequality would prompt envy. The role of the state was therefore to protect private property which meant that it was an institution for 'those who have some property against those who have none at all'. Here is where cross-reference to Smith's other *magnum opus* is needed. Smith had intended to write another work on jurisprudence after *The Wealth of Nations*. In the final paragraph (and in the second advertisement) of the final edition of *The Theory of Moral Sentiments*, which he revised before his death, Smith highlighted the link between the two books:

> I shall in another discourse endeavour to give an account of the general principles of law and government, and of the different revolution they have undergone in the different ages and periods of society, not only in what concerns justice, but in what concerns police, revenue, and arms, and whatever else is the object of law.[43]

This was a continuation of a passage from the first edition of *The Theory of Moral Sentiments*.[44] In the advertisement (preface) to the final edition of *The Theory of Moral Sentiments*, Smith wrote that he had 'partly executed this promise' in *The Wealth of Nations* but the other facets on jurisprudence he would not be able to address owing to 'very advanced age'. Regardless, it is clear that Smith saw justice as a core aspect of *The Theory of Moral Sentiments*, as was outlined in Chapter 1. Thus, it was liberty of contract backed by a system of justice that enabled capital accumulation to take place and the state provided the necessary security of investment.

The final role of the state was facilitating public institutions and public works that were of the 'highest degree advantageous to a great society' but which were too expensive for individuals to provide by themselves. The two examples, apart from national defence and the administration of justice, were institutions to facilitate commerce and public education. In terms of institutions to facilitate commerce, this relates to infrastructure such as roads, bridges, canals and harbours, as well as treaties and ambassadorial staff, to facilitate trade. Infrastructure, Smith argued, could be financed through the use of tolls and this need not be an additional burden on society.

For education, Smith makes the case for public provision of primary education. He supports 'the education of the common people', especially to 'read, write, and account'. Because the parents of the 'common people' could not afford the expense and 'scarce afford to maintain them even in infancy'. Smith advocated for parish schools, similar to what was in existence in Scotland which taught the three R's (reading, writing and arithmetic). But he also wanted a more practical syllabus with less focus on teaching Latin and more emphasis on 'geometry and mechaniks' because of its applicability to common trades. Smith also alludes to the positive externalities of education, or rather the negative externalities associated with the 'gross ignorance and stupidity, which, in a civilized society, seem so frequently to benumb the understandings of all the inferior ranks of people'. Smith was also in favour of public education in science and philosophy as well as public provision for the arts to provide 'gaiety of publick diversions'. Smith also alluded to the benefits, or rather the positive externalities, for the other role of the state, justice, in having a more orderly populace; thus education expenditure could offset the cost of the administration of justice.

To finance the roles of the state, Smith outlines the various revenues of state monopolies but also how tax should be levied. For taxes, these should be paid on the revenue of individuals from three sources he outlined in Book I: rent, profit, and wages. Smith's principles of taxation are still key to how taxation is interpreted today: equality, certainty, convenience, and cost-effective system of collection.[45] That taxes should be in proportionate to the means of an individual, there should be no arbitrariness in the levy of the tax, the timing of the tax should be convenient to the payer, and the apparatus of tax collecting should not become wasteful of the taxes it raises. The final chapter of Book V looks at sovereign debt. Here Smith sees public debt as an outcome of wars because there is only revenue in the treasury for carrying out peacetime administration. Smith argues that sovereign borrowing can be facilitated by the development of commercial society. Which brings us back to the main question: what leads to the development of a commercial society?

Conclusion

The Wealth of Nations is a lengthy and complex work, covering an expansive range of subjects. Its richness allows readers to draw a variety of interpretations and insights, depending on their interests and perspectives. *The Wealth of Nations* is the sum of all books: it is a body of knowledge; it is both theory and empirical observation. It is not simply free markets, nor is it a homage to capitalism. It is an optimistic account of economic development and economic growth that was rooted in the Scottish Enlightenment. The importance of free trade is that it can facilitate the division of labour. Capital accumulation is a necessary prerequisite for the division of labour to function. The alternative systems (mercantilism and physiocracy) for the allocation of scarce resources were inadequate. And lastly, that the state could either hinder or facilitate economic growth.

Kenneth Boulding saw two different approaches to the incorporation of the history of thought in economics. One which saw the classics as scripture and where they must be pored over to extract their true meaning. The other, an antihistorical view, took the extreme that economics is an evolutionary science and that going back to past masters was learning the mistakes of the past. Boulding took a halfway point between both views, that the history of thought was a complement to the study of economics. The classics can help shed light on current questions by revisiting them afresh. Boulding held the *Wealth of Nations* in particular reverence because it was the origin of the species:

> Works like *The Wealth of Nations*, therefore, are inevitably part of an extended present, which shows no signs of coming to an end, in the sense that one can still go back to Adam Smith even after many rereadings and find insights which one has never noticed before and which may have a marked impact on one's own thought. Any writer who is capable of affecting the thought of people who are living and thinking after he is dead may be said to be seminal in this sense and also part of the extended present.

Boulding's approach was to 'study them [the classics] from the point of view of what they have to say to us today, rather than from the point of view of what their place is in the historical record'.

In terms of thinking along the lines of Inclusive Wealth, *The Wealth of Nations* offers several lessons. There should be greater emphasis on long-term thinking and moving away from short-termism. Today, when governments release reports and these receive media coverage, they focus on the latest growth figures. These are short-term focused, from quarter-to-quarter and year-to-year, without taking a long-term perspective. Liberty is an important part of the wealth of nations, but liberty should not come at the expense of the wider body politic. Justice is core to Smithian thinking and without justice the edifice of the wealth of nations will collapse. Institutions are important aspects of this and are key to capital accumulation.

Amartya Sen describes Adam Smith's view of development as 'market-inclusive' because Smith recognized a role for the state, particularly in providing education.[46] This aligns with Sen's own perspective, in which development involves building human capabilities to enable participation in a growing economy. Using Sen's definition of sustainable development from Chapter 1, we can expand on Smith's emphasis on promoting human capabilities by incorporating natural capital within an Inclusive Wealth framework. This approach supports Sen's idea of enhancing capabilities not just within a single generation, but across generations.

The different systems of political economy that Smith highlights still have relevance today. The 'commercial' system can be seen in the neo-mercantilist views as espoused by the United States and China. While the views of the physiocrats could be seen in the ecological school which places the environment above all else.

CHAPTER THREE

Where Is the Wealth of Nations? A Short History of the Theory of Economic Growth

Introduction

As *The Wealth of Nations* was essentially a theory of economic growth, this chapter focuses on the intellectual history of economic growth from Adam Smith until present times. The economist John Kenneth Galbraith (1908–2006) argued that 'there is value in knowing what was once believed or thought worthy of belief.'[1] The interwar period until the late 1960s was the 'golden age' for the study of the history of economic thought. During this period, economists used the history of economic thought to analyse contemporary economic problems (i.e., what would Smith think of x).[2] By the 1970s, the history of economic thought had developed into its own separate, and marginalized, discipline within economics, and arguably, economics is poorer as a result. Mainstream economics became anti-historical, a view that Kenneth Boulding argued was, 'common in the US . . . so that one can become a full-fledged, chartered Ph,D. economist without ever reading anything that was published more than ten years ago'. Boulding's critique was that anti-historicism had led to a creation of mindless technicians:

> who know how to use computers, run massive correlations and regressions, but who do not really know which side of anybody's bread is buttered, who are incredibly ignorant of the details of economic institutions, who have no sense at all of the blood, sweat, and tears that have gone into the making of economics and very little sense of any reality which lies beyond their data.[3]

The classic text that analyses the question of economic growth, or rather how economic growth as a policy objective fell in and out of favour, is Heinz Arndt's (1915–2002) 1978 book *The Rise and Fall of Economic Growth*.[4] The book prematurely declared an end to the interest in economic growth as a policy objective and as a matter of intellectual curiosity because there was renewed interest in the economics of growth from the 1980s onwards. I have taken a slightly alternative tack to Arndt and attempted to chronicle perspectives on the theory of economic growth using various surveys of the history of thought written at distinct points in the twentieth century. The first was written by French economists Charles Gide (1847–1932) and Charles Rist (1874–1955) and published in 1909, later translated into English in 1915.[5] A review of Gide and Rist, in the *Economic Journal* in 1909, declared that it was, 'destined to be placed, and to remain among the most welcome and valued possessions of every serious student of economics in France or elsewhere who can boast of the ownership and use of an adequate library'.[6] The second was a best-selling survey written by William J. Barber, *A History of Economic Thought*, published in 1967, which was one of the most successful books of this period.[7] Barber's book was based on teaching experiences where he did not want to bog students down in the 'big books' of the past, but to give them a flavour of the 'analytical properties' and distinguishing between their 'master models'.[8] The more recent surveys are Roger Backhouse's acclaimed 2002 (revised in 2023) book *The Ordinary Business of Life,* which surveyed the development of thought from ancient Greece to modern times, and Robbie Mochrie's 2024 book *How to Think Like an Economist,* which also took a much broader view of the development of economic thought.[9]

This chapter will survey how economists have thought about the sources of wealth of countries and about economic growth. It will start with Adam Smith, the classical optimist, and then move on to classical pessimists (Malthus and Ricardo, followed by Marx, and finally Mill) who thought that population growth was ultimately the constraint on economic growth. After introducing these important concepts, the chapter will show how views have changed over time, especially in the post-1945 era. One of the major changes in economics was the shift from literary-based to mathematical-based analysis over the course of the twentieth century. Refocusing the emphasis, though it brought greater clarity to economic analysis, created a barrier to non-economists.

One of the biggest changes that occurred over the twentieth century was the shift in the Anglosphere from British to American dominance of economic doctrine. In a review of *Ricardian Rent Theory in Early American Economics*, a study of early American economists, published in the *American Economic Review* in 1922, it was lamented that there were very few US economists featured in the Gide and Rist survey of economic thought.[10] There continued to be few US economists discussed in Barber, while the more recent historians of economics, such as Backhouse and

Mochrie, emphasize the rise of US economic thought and how the United States became an exporter of economic ideas after the Second World War.[11] Today, US-based academics are the leaders in the study of economics and it is very rare to find a Nobel prize-winning economist who is not based in the United States.[12] This US dominance of economics is a relatively recent phenomenon and in the nineteenth century it was 'heavily influenced by doctrines formulated abroad'.[13] Arguably one of the biggest influences US academia has had is its contribution to the revival of the subject of economic growth, which effectively had been dormant since the time of the classical economists in the early nineteenth century.

The common thread of this chapter is the role of capital in economic growth theory. The core theme is that Adam Smith's explanation of growth, being driven by capital accumulation and increasing returns to labour, lasted until the rise of an alternative pessimistic view which emphasized diminishing returns and population pressures. In the twentieth century, the focus shifted to one based purely on capital accumulation followed by a revolution in thought that emphasized technological progress. The most recent iteration has emphasized the importance of explaining the sources of technological progress, which has once again placed capital at the centre and returned to the ideas reminiscent of the old master, Smith.

The main theme is the connection between the classicists and their 'concern with the progress of economic growth' and their interest in the big questions: what drove growth over prolonged time periods and how was the distribution related to future prospects.[14] Barber argued that, 'the relevance of these issues has not diminished since they wrote; in fact, in much of the modern world, the questions to which they addressed themselves are the dominant economic issues. The classical approach, though susceptible to considerable updating and refinements, still has much to offer to mid-twentieth century readers.'[15] In fact, these issues are still of interest to audiences in the twenty-first century, where the desirability of economic growth is still debated and so too is the distribution of the gains of this growth (i.e., inequality) for future well-being. I do not wish to take a retrogressive narrative that we need to reclaim old ideas for the present, but rather I wish to emphasize that we should be aware of the various debates and their associated pitfalls.

A key facet overlooked in the various theories is what exactly capital is and how it is measured. This is an unresolved controversy. In what is considered the last word on the capital controversy, the economist Christopher Bliss wrote that 'when economists reach agreement on the theory of capital, they will shortly reach agreement on everything else. Happily, for those who enjoy a diversity of views and beliefs, there is very little danger of this outcome.'[16] Given the importance of capital to the theory of Inclusive Wealth, such issues from capital controversy are magnified and understanding the issues at stake becomes important if they are to be reconciled and if any value is to be had from applying the concepts.

Ideas in Context

Alongside various theoretical drivers is of course what is happening in the economy contemporaneous to the writers and how this directly, or indirectly, influenced thinking. Most of the protagonists in these debates in the Anglosphere were based in Britain or the United States: first Scotland in the latter part of the 1700s, then England in the early 1800s, then, as the balance of economic power shifted in the twentieth century, US-based writers became more dominant.

The Nobel laureate John Hicks (1904–1989) advocated for the use of a history of economic thought but reminded his fellow economists that:

> The history of economics, so understood, cannot be discovered by poring over old textbooks, even old "classics." That is no more than a part of what has to be done. The books must be read against their background, the events which prompted the analysis, and what happened to the analysis when it went out into the world. All that is part of the tradition which we have inherited, and from which, if we are to do our job, we cannot escape.[17]

Context is key as it provides stimulus to thought. Seeing Edinburgh overrun by a Jacobite army in 1745 clearly left an indelible impression on Adam Smith and the rest of the Enlightenment thinkers who sought to understand why it had happened and how to avoid the repetition of such an event. For Smith, it was a post-war project but also the contemplation of what would happen if the American colonists were to declare independence. War time dislocation also affected both Malthus and Ricardo and this facet of their work is often overlooked. In the twentieth century, war time dislocation affected the inter war economic recovery and Keynesian policy prescriptions for the post-First World War fall-out were the proximate influence on Roy Harrod. Similarly, growing up in the Great Depression was a profound experience for Robert Solow. But many of Solow's generation were also affected by their war time service and a host of early and mid-twentieth-century development practitioners had either direct or indirect exposure to the Second World War. For Solow and other Western economists the post-Second World War recovery and Cold War world were salient factors. New growth theory emerged towards the end of the Cold War and the (re-)emergence of globalization and it was ebullient about future growth prospects.

Another important context is how well the economy is perceived to be at the time of writing. Conventionally, or at least going by modern mainstream macroeconomic textbooks, whenever we teach introductory macroeconomics, the tendency is to tend to start with three indicators of the economy: GDP, inflation, and unemployment. There is a logic to this as these have become the standard public barometer of how the economy is performing. Of the three, inflation is something that can be tracked easily and at a relatively high frequency, although challenges arise when we think of new, or likewise obsolete, goods and services, as well as changes in preferences. Unemployment is also relatively straightforward to track in modern times, although with some caveats in terms of definitions that can sometimes give conflicting signals. GDP is something that takes longer to measure; estimates are released but they are subsequently revised as more data comes in (see Chapter 5). I have highlighted trends in these figures for the United Kingdom and the United States, as the key contributors discussed in the chapter are authors from these countries.

I have illustrated the prevailing rate of inflation in Figure 3.1 as a way to contextualize the theories that are discussed in this chapter. Inflation is something that impacts people in their daily lives and intellectuals are not immune to such pressures. This point is alluded to by the economic historian Walt Rostow (1916–2003), who argued that the pessimistic debates tend to occur during Kondratieff upswings (long-run trends lasting over 50–60 years).[18] Adam Smith had the fortune of publishing the *Wealth of Nations* during a relatively turbulent-free period, vis-à-vis inflation, although the book was published just months before the American colonies declared their independence. Malthus was writing in the midst of the French Revolutionary Wars, after an infamous financial panic and run on the reserves of the Bank

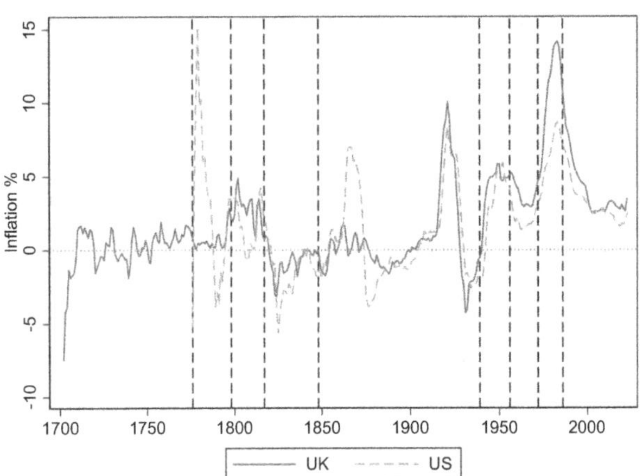

FIGURE 3.1 *Inflation trends in the United Kingdom and the United States, 1700–2023. Note: Inflation represented as a 10-year moving average. Dashed vertical lines indicate years of publication of key texts (1776, 1798, 1817, 1848, 1939, 1956, 1972, 1986). Source: Gregory Clark, 'What Were the British Earnings and Prices Then? (New Series)'. MeasuringWorth, 2025; Lawrence H. Officer and Samuel H. Williamson, 'The Annual Consumer Price Index for the United States, 1774-Present.' MeasuringWorth, 2025.*

of England in 1797 that forced it to suspend payment of notes on demand. Riccardo published his work in the years immediately after the end of the Napoleonic Wars when the economy was still experiencing dislocation. Mill published his *Principles* during the hungry 1840s while Marx and Engels' *Communist Manifesto* was similarly published against the backdrop of the 1848 revolutions in Europe. After that point there was a gap in an explicit focus on economic growth until post-Second World War.

When it comes to Solow's 1956 paper on economic growth, there is a marked difference between experiences of inflation between the United Kingdom and the United States. The UK was experiencing what were known as 'stop-go' balance of payment crises and dollar shortages, and it was also the year of the Suez crisis with pressure put on the British pound (see Chapter 7). The US economy was in much better shape in comparison, which perhaps explains Solow's exuberance. The apathy towards the theory of economic growth from economists and the publication of *Limits to Growth* (discussed in more detail in Chapter 4) coincided with an upswing in inflation, which is in part explained by the pressures of the Vietnam War, Keynesian demand-management, and the collapse of the Bretton-Woods system of fixed exchange rates. Although Rostow saw *Limits to Growth* as coinciding with a fifth Kondratieff curve upswing.[19]

A key motivator in the twentieth-century growth models was the experience of the Great Depression (1929–1941).[20] This was the period that had the highest annual rates of unemployment in the twentieth century in the United States and the United Kingdom, shown in Figure 3.2. The macroeconomic instability of the interwar period was a key influence on the development of the thought of John Maynard Keynes, the towering figure economics in the first half of the twentieth century, who questioned the prevailing orthodoxy as being more focused on long-run adjustment while ignoring short-run dynamics. Keynes sparked an 'intellectual revolution' with the publication of his *General Theory of Employment, Interest, and Money* in 1936 and effectively created the field of macroeconomics.[21] While Keynes had not explicitly addressed the long-run, his supporters, of which there were many, attempted to apply his insights to the long-run and to the question of economic growth. The early growth theorists had also been influenced by the Great Depression. Roy Harrod (1900–1978), who, although not part of the 'Keynesian circus' at Cambridge, was a close friend of Keynes (his 'Oxford representative') and had sent a letter to the US President Franklin Delano Roosevelt (1882–1945) advocating public works.[22]

Another important facet underpinning the understanding of economic growth is how economists perceived the trajectory of the economy. Measured using trends in GDP per capita growth, Figure 3.3 highlights how the interwar period stands out as a period of exceptional volatility. This would have influenced how twentieth-century theorists approached the idea of economic growth. Whereas for earlier thinkers, although they would not

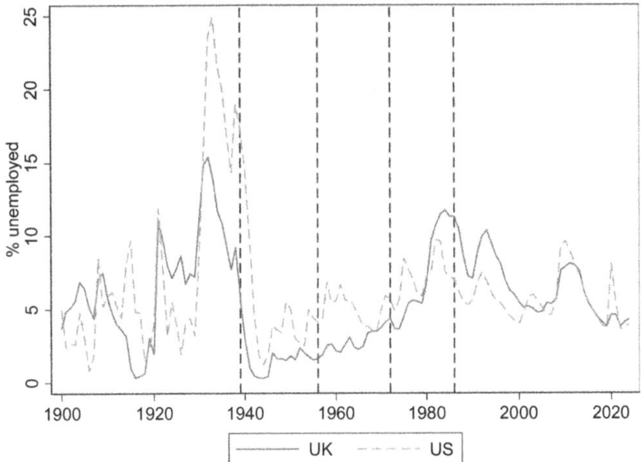

FIGURE 3.2 *Unemployment rates in the United Kingdom and the United States, 1900–2023. Note: The dashed vertical lines indicate years of key publication (1939, 1956, 1972, 1986). Sources: Bank of England (2024). A millennium of macroeconomic data for the UK: The Bank of England's collection of historical macroeconomic and financial statistics, v. 3.1; S. Lebergott (1957). Annual estimates of unemployment in the United States, 1900–1954. NBER; Federal Reserve Economic Data (FRED).*

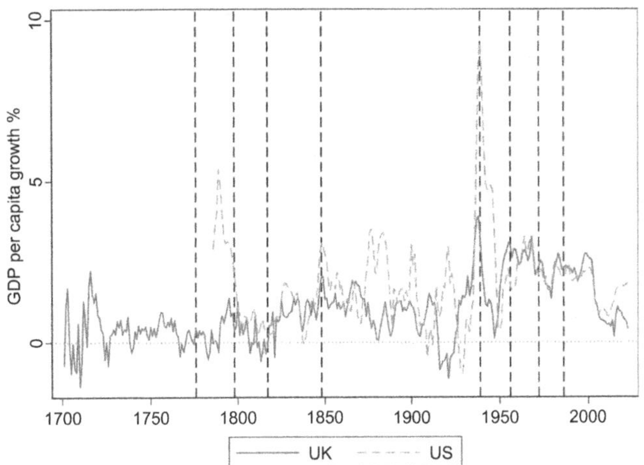

FIGURE 3.3 *Trend GDP per capita growth in the United Kingdom and the United States, 1700–2023 Note: The dashed vertical lines indicate years of key publication (1776, 1798, 1817, 1939, 1956, 1972, 1986). Source: Ryland Thomas and Samuel H. Williamson, 'What Was the U.K. GDP Then?' The Consistent Series, MeasuringWorth, 2025; Louis Johnston and Samuel H. Williamson, 'What Was the U.S. GDP Then?' MeasuringWorth, 2025.*

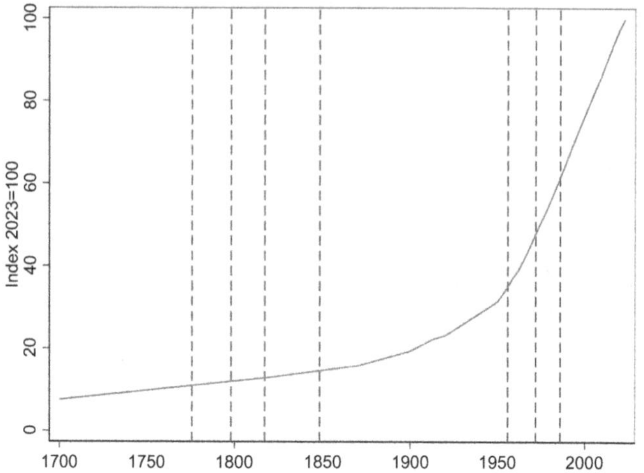

FIGURE 3.4 *Global population index, 1700–2023. Note: Vertical lines represent the year of publication of key publications (1776, 1798, 1817, 1848, 1956, 1972 and 1986). Sources: A. Maddison (2009). Historical Statistics of the World Economy: 1-2008 AD; and World Development Indicators.*

have had anything equivalent to GDP growth figures (see Chapter 5), they were aware of a palpable need for growth and thus were preoccupied with increasing economic growth. Later thinkers had the luxury of being the beneficiaries of previous bouts of sustained economic growth.

Population trends are also a key factor underpinning many of these debates. Global population has increased tenfold since the time of Adam Smith, from around 0.8 billion at the time of the publication of *The Wealth of Nations* to 8 billion today (Figure 3.4).[23] The rapid population growth clearly alarmed some more than others, but it is a key contextual variable that explains the preoccupations of intellectuals, particularly in the mid-twentieth century (see discussion in Chapter 4).

Context then is an important consideration when assessing the prevailing views of economists and understanding the optimism or pessimism of subsequent work.

An Inquiry into the *Wealth of Nations*

The Wealth of Nations is first and foremost an outline of the treatise on the drivers of economic growth and, as Roger Backhouse highlights, 'Smith was concerned with the process of economic growth,' much more than any of his predecessors.[24]

Perhaps one of the biggest shifts over the twentieth century has been the re-appreciation of Adam Smith. Gide and Rist, writing in the early twentieth century, were highly complimentary of Adam Smith and saw him as 'the true founder' of economics, but by mid-century Smith's contribution was questioned by Barber who noted that, 'while it is true that his great work – published in 1776 – launched the classical tradition of economic thought, a larger claim for his innovating role would not be justified.'[25] By the beginning of the twenty-first century, Smith's position was restored and Smith is seen by Mochrie as 'the common ancestor of all the ways of thinking about the economy which exist today' and that *The Wealth of Nations* was a 'founding document of modern economics'.[26]

While Barber was critical that there was little original content in *The Wealth of Nations*, [27] the main achievement of Smith was in synthesizing a wide range of perspectives into a coherent body of thought for the first time.[28] Although a modern reader could take a hypercritical perspective on Smith, a more 'sympathetic' (as Smith would argue in *The Theory of Moral Sentiments*) reading shows key themes that are enduring.

In fact, one of the biggest changes in the twentieth century has been the re-appreciation of Adam Smith the moral philosopher. Barber dismissed *The Theory of Moral Sentiments* as having had 'little distinction as a contribution to philosophy',[29] whereas Backhouse and Mochrie see the arguments that were developed in *The Theory of Moral Sentiments* as being pivotal in Smith's understanding of capital formation. The dismissal of *The Theory of Moral Sentiments* by Barber is not surprising as many economists have seen the two as unrelated works. Indeed, criticism of Smith tends to also overlook *The Theory of Moral Sentiments*. For example, at the bicentennial of *The Wealth of Nations*, it had been argued that Smith had a 'pernicious legacy', but here it is clear that this criticism was based on a narrow reading of Smith from *The Wealth of Nations* and not what is elaborated in *The Theory of Moral Sentiments*.[30] There is a clear connection, as was illustrated by the use of both *The Theory of Moral Sentiments* and *The Wealth of Nations* in the work of Rawls and Sen.

The Theory of Moral Sentiments is where Smith first invoked the concept of 'an invisible hand' as the mechanism that 'advance[s] the interest of the society'.[31] Smith saw this as a way that society had ordered itself through the actions of the poor to emulate the rich:

> It is this deception [that the poor can emulate the rich in achieving convenience] which rouses and keeps in continual motion the industry of mankind. It is this which first prompted them to cultivate the ground, to build houses, to found cities and commonwealths, and to invent and improve all the sciences and arts, which ennoble and embellish human life; which have entirely changed the whole face of the globe, have turned the rude forests of nature into agreeable and fertile plains, and made the trackless and barren ocean a new fund of subsistence,

> and the great high road of communication to the different nations of the earth. The earth by these labours of mankind has been obliged to redouble her natural fertility, and to maintain a greater multitude of inhabitants.[32]

In sum, it was 'an invisible hand', according to Smith, that drove economic growth and overcame limits.[33]

The Wealth of Nations is not without faults; for example, Gide and Rist highlighted the 'useless controversy' over productive and unproductive labour where Smith viewed services as unproductive. While this is no longer a view held in economics, it persisted through Marxian thought and was embodied in Marxian views of how to measure the economy. While Smith emphasized capital, Gide and Rist saw this as a 'threadbare controversy' because by the early twentieth century economists had viewed aggregate output as a function of land, labour *and* capital, and thought that, 'the amount of produce raised must depend upon the amount of each of these factors employed, and not upon the amount of any one of them.'[34] Adam Smith did not comment on the forces that were driving the Industrial Revolution and he was certainly not 'the prophet of industrialism'.[35] What Smith describes are the conditions in the period immediately before major advances in modern industrialization, where growth was driven by the division of labour and gains from trade.[36]

While Smith is almost universally optimistic, he does admit to some limits to progress. He notes that the entire population is 'equally maintained by the annual produce of the land and labour of the country. This produce, how great soever, can never be infinite, but must have certain limits.'[37] Smith's work has been interpreted, not so much as being rooted in ideas of infinite growth, but rather that under the right conditions, growth can perpetuate itself. Smith did not advocate for a steady state, a point where growth would cease. As he noted:

> It deserves to be remarked, perhaps, that it is in the progressive state, while the society is advancing to the further acquisition, rather than when it has acquired its full complement of riches, that the condition of the labouring poor, of the great body of the people, seems to be the happiest and the most comfortable. It is hard in the stationary, and miserable in the declining state. The progressive state is, in reality, the cheerful and the hearty state to all the different orders of the society. The stationary is dull; the declining melancholy.[38]

Smith was also optimistic about England's future prospects, which he attributed to the role of institutions that had 'maintained the progress of England towards opulence and improvement in almost all former times, and which, it is to be hoped, will do so in all future times'.[39] He was critical of the abilities of governments to act frugally, but emphasized that the law nonetheless protected citizens. The institutions that Smith referred to were primarily legal protections that 'allowed liberty to exert itself'. While the term *institutions* can be thought of quite broadly today, at its heart is property rights and protection from expropriation. Smith also recognized the role of political institutions, particularly in the English colonies, which he described as being 'more favourable to the improvement of the cultivation of land'. The importance of institutions has been taken up in more recent times by economists such as Mancur Olson (1932–1998), Nobel laureate Douglass C. North (1920–2015), and the Nobel laureates Daron Acemoglu and James A. Robinson.[40] In this perspective, the main benefit of institutions was in reducing uncertainty in economic decision-making and thus enabling investment decisions whose returns might take years to materialize.[41] Institutions help facilitate the accumulation of capital that is required for the division of labour. Thus, Smithian growth was driven by capital accumulation and the continual expansion of the capital stock: achieving growth required savings (investment) to form a relatively high share of net income, a condition enabled by supportive institutions.[42]

Smithian growth was rehabilitated in the early twentieth century in the work of Allyn Young (1876–1929), who interpreted Smithian division of labour as implying increasing returns: as an input used in production is increased there is a more than proportionate increase in output (see Figure 3.5 for an example).[43] In doing this, Young was effectively thinking in terms of positive spillovers, or what we think of today as agglomeration effects, associated with increased specialization in an area that was highlighted by Alfred Marshall (1842–1924).[44] The economist Morgan Kelly showed how Smithian growth, which requires increasing returns, is subject to threshold effects: if the extent of the market is too low there will be limited growth, but if a market increases in size there can be rapid acceleration in growth.[45] In the hands of the economist Haim Barkai (1925–2006), the Smithian model loses its explicit increasing returns property but it still does not display diminishing returns akin to later Malthusian and Ricardian approaches. Nevertheless, even this model shows a 'Smithian variant of the stationary state', which is somewhat at odds with the central message of *The Wealth of Nations* that capital accumulation could 'ensure eternal progress'. Capital was central as both a 'social product' and a '*sin qua non* of technological progress', as capital embodies technological change.[46] This means that the capital produced in any given period embodies the technology of that era, so newer capital incorporates more up-to-date technology than older vintages.

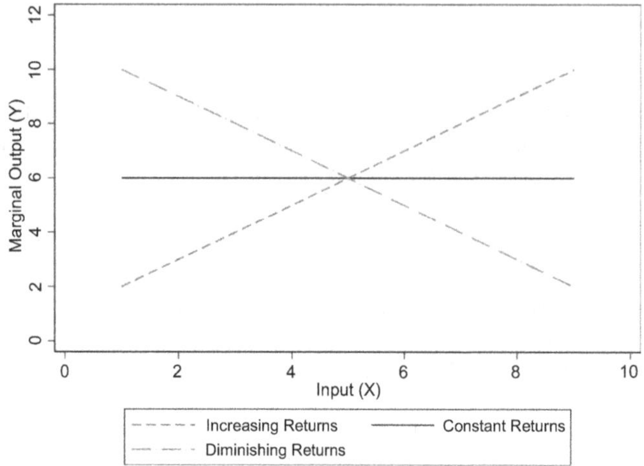

FIGURE 3.5 *Illustration of the concept of increasing, constant and diminishing returns.*

An Inquiry into the Poverty of Nations

Economics earned itself the derogatory title of 'dismal science',[47] not because of the work of Adam Smith, but from those who immediately followed in his footsteps. While Smith was universally optimistic, his immediate successors were anything but. Gide and Rist remarked that Smith's successors 'had no faith in what we call progress';[48] here it should be noted that the concept of economic growth used to be understood as 'progress'. Despite this pessimism, Keynes placed Thomas Robert Malthus's (1766–1834) work in the same tradition as Smith, as it 'had great influence on the progress of thought';[49] and Ricardo was held in equally high regard. While Malthus is perhaps more widely remembered today outside of economics, Ricardo has had arguably as strong an influence on economists as Smith himself. Both Malthus and Ricardo were close correspondents and thought highly of each other; Ricardo applied Malthusian logic in his own work.

Malthus was (temporarily) a practicing clergyman and earned the title Reverend before pursuing an academic career. Malthus became the world's first professional economist as he held a post as professor of history and political economy at the East India College in Hertfordshire, and through his work he also became the 'best-abused man of the age'.[50] The *Essay on the Principle of Population, as it affects the Future Improvement of Society* was published anonymously in 1798 (lest it disturb people that a clergyman thought in this manner). There were six editions of the *Essay* with the final edition published in 1826. Drawing inspiration from Adam Smith, Malthus opened with a question that is still very much relevant today: whether man would experience infinite economic growth 'or be condemned to a perpetual oscillation between happiness and misery, and after every effort remain still at an immeasurable distance from the wished-for goal'.[51] But, Malthus took Adam Smith's conclusions to the extreme, and, as Barber put it, Malthus distorted Smith's vision into the 'Poverty of Nations'.

Malthus is best remembered for his *Essay*, which surmised that 'the power of population is indefinitely greater than the power in the earth to produce subsistence for man.' Malthus argued that population, if unchecked, grows geometrically while subsistence grows arithmetically. Humanity is dependent on subsistence; if population growth exceeds the level of subsistence, then 'a strong and constantly operating check on population' exists to bring the two back into balance. The intuition of a Malthusian approach is best illustrated by plotting two curves to represent the geometrically increasing population and the arithmetically increasing 'means of subsistence'; for an example, see Figure 3.6.

In this world, there can be no sustainable population growth unless there is a way to increase the means of subsistence; increases in subsistence, that is, an increase from the initial level, could be achieved through improvements, in seed quality to generate higher crop yields, more extensive use of fertilizer or the use of better farming equipment. But if the means of subsistence did increase, that is, if there was an increase in income, then population would also grow. The crux of the problem is that if population grows faster than the means of subsistence, then checks bring the population back into balance. Malthus referred to 'positive checks' (e.g., famine, war and pestilence) and 'preventative checks' (e.g., celibacy and birth control) that perform this role.

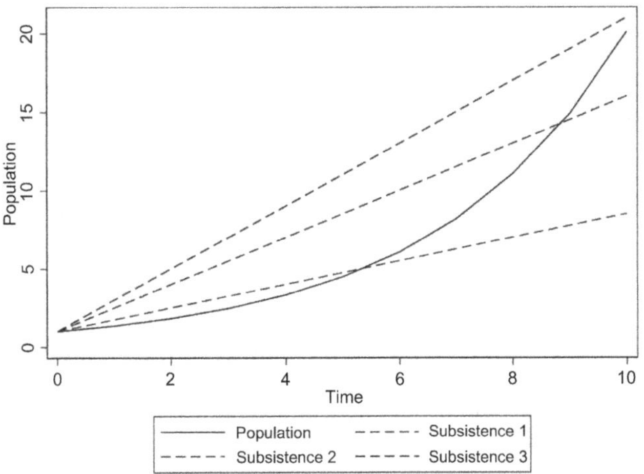

FIGURE 3.6 *Malthusian equilibrium.*

While Malthus had been steadfast in his warnings about overpopulation, in his final work he nuanced his own findings:

> From high real wages, or the power of commanding a large portion of the necessaries of life, two very different results may follow; one, that of a rapid increase of population, in which case the high wages are chiefly spent in the maintenance of large and frequent families; and the other, that of a decided improvement in the modes of subsistence, and the conveniences and comforts enjoyed, without a proportionate acceleration in the rate of increase.[52]

There was thus freedom for humanity to choose how to use its wealth; overpopulation (with checks) was not predestined. Although Malthus was more circumspect, this caution in his work seems to have been lost on subsequent generations.

Malthus is, of course, also famous for the law of diminishing returns, although there were three others (David Ricardo, Edward West (1782–1828) and Robert Torrens (1780–1864)) who arrived at the same conclusion independently.[53] In his *Principles of Economics*, Malthus lays out the concept of 'the diminishing productiveness of labour on the last land taken into cultivation'.[54] By this he means that as we increase the number of workers, each additional worker generates a smaller amount of output (see a visual illustration of this concept in Figure 3.5). Diminishing returns only applied to agriculture and not to industry, but it was a direct challenge to *The Wealth of Nations* where Smith had implicitly assumed increasing returns. Ultimately it is this process of diminishing returns that slows growth and leads to a steady state because population growth reduces wages to subsistence and 'the increase of produce occasioned by the labour of the additional number of persons will have so lowered its value, and reduced profits, as to determine the capitalist to employ less labour'; this in turn leads to a collapse in 'effectual' demand.[55] Furthermore, Malthus highlighted the variation in soil quality and how marginal land was used as population grew. It is clear that Malthus saw clear constraints in this world: 'living as we do in a limited world, and in countries and districts still more limited'.[56] Malthus also broke ranks with Smith when it came to free trade as he was in favour of the Corn Laws (tariffs on grain imports into the UK) and tariffs on agricultural imports. Here his rationale was consistent with his theories on population: Malthus did not trust the reliability of trade in the event of war and the Corn Laws would give greater incentive to increase domestic production of food.

Another important avenue for surplus population in a Malthusian world, of course, was migration, with large-scale migration to the United States and other colonies. Malthus was heavily influenced by developments in the new world.[57] In fact, his population figures were based on records from the American colonies that showed a doubling of population in twenty-five years. This rapid population growth Malthus saw as 'the consequence of these favourable circumstances united, was a rapidity of increase probably without parallel in history'.[58] The 'favourable circumstances' were liberty, equality, institutions that encouraged the use and division of property, absence of tithes, and very productive agricultural land. Malthus also took the opposite view to Smith on the causes of emigration, and he saw colonies as a result of population pressure because 'a great emigration necessarily implies unhappiness of some kind or other in the country that is deserted'. Emigration became an issue in the twentieth century when neo-Malthusians began worrying about the 'closed system', as previously open land was now unavailable for settlement.[59] Neo-Malthusians saw population density as a key influence of emigration in the nineteenth century, a view echoed in recent research on the drivers of migration in that period. [60]

Within the British Isles, Ireland has long lived under a Malthusian shadow.[61] The Great Irish Famine (1846–52) was seen by many as divine providence and a realization of Malthusian principles, referred to as 'the great Malthusian panacea' by Marx. One of the most infamous anecdotes relates to the Oxford-based economist Nassau William Senior (1790–1864) who is reported to have said that 'the famine in Ireland would not kill more than a million people, and that would scarcely be enough to do much good'.[62] Yet, recent evidence does not support the Malthusian view that overpopulation was the main cause of the Irish Famine and that other factors, such as the distribution of wealth, were important.[63] Malthus was also more nuanced in his assessment of positive checks which he implied meant a generational lowering of living standards and that the 'sons of labourers are very apt to be stunted in their growth, and are a long while arriving at maturity'. The Irish were renowned for being taller than their British counterparts, a difference attributed to their monotonous yet nutritious diet of milk and potatoes.[64] Recent evidence finds conflicting evidence of stunting during the Irish famine where the places most affected by the famine actually saw an increase in peoples' heights and places relatively unaffected showed signs of stunting.[65]

With the benefit of hindsight, it is clear that, just as it could be argued that Smith had missed the industrial revolution that occurred around him, Malthus had overlooked the importance of technological progress and trade in alleviating population pressures. The first British census in 1801 had shown a population of 10.5 million and this increased by 34 per cent by the 1821 census that was held before the publication of the final edition of the *Essay* in 1826. By the 1831 census, the British population had increased by 54 per cent since 1801.[66] It was the Industrial Revolution that had prevented one of the Malthusian checks from occurring in Britain.[67]

David Ricardo, Malthus's great friend and peer, was another pivotal influence on the direction of economic thought. Ricardo was a successful London stockbroker who became interested in political economy after reading *The Wealth of Nations* in 1799. He published his main work, *The*

Principles of Political Economy and Taxation, in 1817. His views were conditioned by his economic context; Ricardo witnessed rapidly rising grain prices during the Napoleonic Wars and saw that landlords were the main beneficiaries of this inflation in foodstuffs. In his lifetime Ricardo was also a Member of Parliament, purchasing a seat in Portarlington, Ireland, from 1818 until his death. When in Parliament, he lobbied for the removal of the Corn Laws, and he later became a landlord and received the rents he had earlier complained about so bitterly.

Ricardo's main focus was the distribution of income between landlord rents, capitalist profits, and labourers' wages; of the three, Ricardo saw labour as, 'by far the most important class in society'.[68] For Ricardo rent was a constraint on economic activity, noting that it, 'is a creation of value, but not a creation of wealth; it adds nothing to the resources of a country, it does not enable it to maintain fleets and armies; for the country would have a greater disposable fund if its land were of a better quality, and it could employ the same capital without generating a rent'.[69] The issue of rent was further exacerbated by the limited availability, and the variation in the quality, of land. If land was unlimited and uniform, there would be no rent. But because of population growth, marginal land is brought into cultivation, and rent is paid on it. Ricardo stressed the limited availability of land and how that interacts with the dynamics associated with Malthusian population growth. The higher population growth, the more rent is paid for the scarce resource.[70]

In fact, Gide and Rist saw Ricardo as much more pessimistic than Malthus because after rent has taken its share of income, capitalists and labour must fight over the residual. As capital's share gets eroded, there is a disincentive to invest and there is no longer an accumulation of capital. But if capital growth slows, so too will wage growth, as Ricardo saw the two as intertwined. In this situation society reaches a steady state because both capital and wage growth are stationary. Ricardo highlighted two ways to alleviate the pressures from the stationary state. The first was through the use of technology and the other was through international trade; the former was a labour-saving technology, and the latter reduced the cost of labour by reducing the price of grain.[71]

Karl Marx (1818–83) was last in the line of classic pessimists. Marx became highly influential in the twentieth century, and it was recently argued that this legacy is more due to the political upheaval in Russia than to the ideas of Marx himself.[72] This assessment seems too harsh; Gide and Rist dedicated a chapter to an analysis of his views showing that he was widely read among economists in Europe. They further remarked that Marx was 'frequently quoted but seldom read', and that, 'no work has exercised a great influence upon nineteenth century thought, probably, no work, with the exception of the Bible and the Pandects, has given rise to such a host of commentators and apologists'.[73]

In earlier writing, Marx and Friedrich Engels (1820–95) were in awe of the great strides that capitalism had achieved in:

> creat[ing] more massive and more colossal productive forces than have all preceding generations together. Subjection of Nature's forces to man, machinery, application of chemistry to industry and agriculture, steam-navigation, railways, electric telegraphs, clearing of whole continents for cultivation, canalisation of rivers, whole populations conjured out of the ground – what earlier century had even a presentiment that such productive forces slumbered in the lap of social labour?[74]

In Marx's epic *Das Kapital*, volume 1 published in 1867 and volumes 2 and 3 published posthumously, the focus was more on predicting the collapse of the capitalist system through its own internal contradictions than on economic growth *per se*.

Marx shared similarities with the other classicists and is sometimes viewed as the last of the classicists as he uses a similar framework and addresses the questions of distribution of income and growth, although he uses his own interpretation. Similar to earlier classicists, he saw capitalist surplus (profits) as the source of capital accumulation, and that population growth responded to wages (Malthusian influence), thus creating a tendency for profits to fall. For Marx, the key issue is the power associated with ownership of the means of production, or rather the 'monopoly of the means of production', because the worker must 'produce the means of subsistence for the owners of the means of production'.[75] Unlike other classicists, Marx saw a dichotomy between capitalists (with landlords subsumed within a general classification of capitalists) and labour. Seeing the distribution of income like this, it effectively becomes a tension within the process of capital accumulation:

> Accumulation for accumulation's sake, production for production's sake: by this formula classical economy expressed the historical mission of the bourgeoisie, and did not for a single instant deceive itself over the birth-throes of wealth.[76]

Somewhat confusingly, Marx defines capital as constant and variable, whereby constant capital is the 'value of the means of production', and variable capital is 'the sum total of wages'.[77] In some senses this is similar to the division of capital into produced and human, although not exactly expressed in these terms. But effectively this implies a substitution of capital for labour, which, taken to the extreme would mean complete capital substitution. This would effectively imply a collapse in demand from labour for the goods that capital produced.

While Marx was critical of the classical tradition, some of his greatest critiques were reserved for Malthus, deeming that his 'work in its first form is nothing more than a schoolboyish, superficial plagiary of De Foe, Sir James Steuart, Townsend, Franklin, Wallace, &c., and does not contain a single sentence thought out by himself.'[78] Referring specifically to Malthusian population dynamics, Marx saw these as a result of capitalist modes of production with historically idiosyncratic rules that were valid within a specific time period and that 'an abstract law of population exists for plants and animals only, and only in so far as man has not interfered with them'.[79] Marx attacked Malthus in order to place greater responsibility on capitalists for the plight of the working class; otherwise, the burden of blame falls on the workers themselves.

It is of course more customary to go from Malthus and Ricardo to John Stuart Mill as the close of the classical period of political economy. The thirty-year period between Ricardo and Mill was not a void, but Gide and Rist, somewhat unduly and harshly characterized it as being, 'occupied by economists of the second rank, who apply themselves, not to the discovery of new principles, but to the development and coordination of those already formulated'.[80] There was a sense that the science was already complete.[81] By the time Mills' *Principles of Economics* was first published in 1848, most of the issues that Ricardo had advocated for had come to pass: the Corn Laws were repealed and banking was reformed. There was a belief that the science was settled, and Mill was seen as just a refined version of Malthusian/Ricardian theory. Mill is therefore seen as a bridge from the classicists to the neoclassicists. Confusingly, Mill is seen as a 'Neo-Malthusian' by Gide and Rist because of his obsession with population growth;[82] similarly, Hicks sees him as a neo-classicist.[83] His views on the stationary state were similar to Ricardo in many respects but Mill was a more eloquent writer and he was able to express the 'stationary state with its melancholy vistas . . . in such eloquent terms that we are almost reconciled to the prospect'.[84] The rationale for a steady state is one of the most powerful there is:

> Nor is there much satisfaction in contemplating the world with nothing left to the spontaneous activity of nature; with every rood of land brought into cultivation, which is capable of growing food for human beings; every flowery waste or natural pasture ploughed up, all quadrupeds or birds which are not domesticated for man's use exterminated as his rivals for food, every hedgerow or superfluous tree rooted out, and scarcely a place left where a wild shrub or flower could grow without being eradicated as a weed in the name of improved agriculture. If the earth must lose that great portion of its pleasantness which it owes to things that the unlimited increase of wealth and population would extirpate from it, for the mere purpose of enabling it to support a larger, but not a better or a happier population, I sincerely hope, for the sake of posterity, that they will be content to be stationary, long before necessity compels them to it. It is scarcely necessary to remark that a stationary condition of capital and population implies no stationary state of human improvement. There

> would be as much scope as ever for all kinds of mental culture, and moral and social progress; as much room for improving the Art of Living, and much more likelihood of its being improved, when minds ceased to be engrossed by the art of getting on. Even the industrial arts might be as earnestly and as successfully cultivated, with this sole difference, that instead of serving no purpose but the increase of wealth, industrial improvements would produce their legitimate effect, that of abridging labour.[85]

In sum, the classical economists saw limits to growth driven by diminishing returns and culminating in a steady state. The views of the classical school were later criticized by Joseph Schumpeter (1883–1950) as being infected with the 'Ricardian Vice', that is 'the habit of establishing simple relations between aggregates that then acquire a spurious halo of causal importance, whereas all the really important (and, unfortunately, complicated) things are being bundled away in or behind these aggregates'. For Schumpeter the issue was that there were oversimplifying assumptions made for theoretical tractability, but policy lessons were being drawn from such oversimplifications.[86]

Optimism Rebounds

After Mill, growth theory was in abeyance for eighty years, and it appeared that growth theory had found its own steady state. John Hicks argues that the disinterest in growth theory arose partly because of the influence of Mill, whose *Principles* was the best-selling work on economics up until the 1890s.[87] Alfred Marshall, another giant of neoclassical economics, held views similar to Mill when it came to the steady state but thought that it had not been reached yet. Marshall saw 'economic progress' as being driven by international trade and regional specialization, particularly the increasing returns of industry and the external economies associated with industrial co-location.[88] As the issue of growth was seemingly solved, the focus of the neoclassicals was then on stability and market allocation of goods and services.

The interlude of growth theory was punctuated by the First World War, post-war dislocation, and the Great Depression. The focus of economists during the interwar period was on macroeconomic stability and short-term business cycles,[89] the immediate economic environment and attempts to address the deteriorating global economy (see Figures 3.1, 3.2 and 3.3 above). Key here is the publication in 1936 of John Maynard Keynes, *The General Theory of Employment, Interest and Money.* This was a revolutionary change in how economists thought about short-term fluctuations in the aggregate economy. In his earlier work Keynes had seen short-term stabilization as a key role of economists. As noted in chapter 1, he famously quipped that 'in the long-run we are all dead'. For Keynes, by assuming away short-run fluctuations, 'economists set themselves too easy, too useless a task if in tempestuous seasons they can only tell us that when the storm is long past the ocean is flat again'.[90] Keynes had intended for his *General Theory* to be the solution to the interwar economic malaise. He saw short-run equilibrium, 'given situation of technique, resources and costs', whereby employment was dependent on income. In turn, income, or rather aggregate supply, was determined by the propensity to consume and the volume of investment and this was 'the essence of the General Theory of Employment'. Investment was seen as central to aggregate demand, and Keynes maintained that 'employment can only increase *pari passu* with an increase in investment'. Keynes defined investment in net terms as:

> the net additions to all kinds of capital equipment, after allowing for those changes in the value of the old capital equipment which are taken into account in reckoning net income. Investment, thus defined, includes, therefore, the increment of capital equipment, whether it consists of fixed capital, working capital or liquid capital; and the significant differences of definition (apart from the distinction between investment and net investment) are due to the exclusion from investment of one or more of these categories.[91]

Keynes concluded his discussion on the importance of investment highlighting how it had been underappreciated, 'capital is not a self-subsistent entity existing apart from consumption. On the contrary, every weakening in the propensity to consume regarded as a permanent habit must weaken the demand for capital as well as the demand for consumption'.[92] Keynes also highlighted a distinction between his definition of investment and depreciation to that adopted by the Austrian School in their definition of capital formation and capital consumption but noted that he had 'been unable to discover a reference to any passage where the meaning of these terms is clearly explained'. While these points may appear moot, they would take on tremendous importance in empirical analysis. It is also important to highlight that Keynes was also seen as having been infected by the 'Ricardian Vice', 'namely, the habit of piling a heavy load of practical conclusions upon a tenuous groundwork, which was unequal to it yet seemed in its simplicity not only attractive but also convincing'. For Schumpeter, and others, this was due to his focus on the short-run and the extrapolation of short-run dynamics to the long-run.[93]

The rediscovery of economic growth followed the publication of *The General Theory* and came in two phases. The first phase were Keynesian-inspired approaches that extended the short-run analysis (multipliers and financial accelerators) into the long run. The second phase was neoclassical-inspired approaches that focused on aggregate production functions that specified the relationship between outputs (national income) and inputs (factors of production), and the substitutability of inputs (between capital and labour). The latter were a direct critique of the former and the argument centred around the application of tools for short-run analysis to the long-run (the so-called 'Ricardian vice'). There were some similarities in the approaches as both the Keynesian and Neoclassical approaches centred on capital-output ratios. Although, the Keynesian-inspired approach primarily focused on demand side instability, whereas the neoclassical focus was supply-side only.[94]

In *The General Theory*, Keynes was explicit that he would not concern himself 'except in occasional digressions . . . with the slow effects of secular progress'.[95] Keynes suffered a heart attack in 1937 and was convalescing for two years, so he was unable to continue his intellectual revolution, this task was left to his supporters. If one were to speculate how Keynes would approach economic growth, clues are in *The General Theory*, as he believed that expectations were 'embodied in the to-day's capital equipment'. Therefore, capital, embodying technological progress, would be central to any Keynesian approach.

The Keynesian-inspired growth models were derived independently by Roy Harrod and Evsey Domar (1914–97), and are collectively known as the Harrod-Domar model.[96] The Harrod growth model aimed to extend Keynesian business cycle analysis into the long-term using a dynamic framework, while the Domar model was focused on the relationship between capital accumulation and employment.[97] Both became textbook models of economic growth.

The Harrod-Domar approach sees capital-output ratios as being central to economic growth. Harrod's model focuses on three growth rates: the actual, the warranted, and the natural growth rate. In essence, Harrod's work is an extension of short-run trade cycle theory into a medium- to long-run setting, as he regards 'dynamic analysis as a necessary propaedeutic to trade-cycle study'.[98] The warranted growth rate is a 'moving equilibrium' growth rate, and the focus of his original essay was to illustrate how the 'moving equilibrium' is 'unstable' as it can be self-aggravating (either leading to inflation or unemployment). This was because the parameters that influenced it were determined outside the theory (i.e., they were exogenous). At the heart of the problem is that there is nothing in the theory to make the growth rates converge towards each other, hence the term 'Harrod's knife-edge' as it creates a 'secular instability problem'.[99] Domar arrived at similar conclusions, albeit from a different starting point. Domar's observation is that Keynesian thought treats investment as an 'instrument for generating income' but does not consider that investment can also increase productive capacity. The key assumption of the Harrod-Domar approach was constant returns to capital, so that an increase in investment would have a proportional increase in output (e.g., see Figure 3.5).[100]

An important contextual factor explaining the popularity of the Harrod-Domar model was the rapid development of the USSR which had come about through state planning (see Chapter 4). In an era where development meant target growth rates and state planning, the attraction of the Harrod-Domar model to contemporary development planning lay in its ease of application in formulating target growth rates. Using Harrod's example, 'if 10 per cent of income were saved and the capital coefficient [incremental capital-output ratio] per annum (C) were equal to 4, the warranted growth rate would be 2½ per cent per annum'.[101] In his essay on the history of the *World Development Report*, the economist Shahid Yusuf illustrates the centrality of the Harrod-Domar framework as a policy guideline for economic growth, and it placed capital at the centre of economic development.[102] The Harrod-Domar model continued to be used in developing countries long after it lost sway in academic circles to the alternative neoclassical models. Although it must be acknowledged that Domar never intended for the model to be used to target growth rates, it was anticipated to be a way to monitor short-term fluctuations. Domar and his generation had expected another Great Depression after the end of the Second World War and were looking for ways to avoid this.[103]

The view that investment was required for sustained economic growth was further popularized by Walt Rostow in his 1960 book *Stages of Economic Growth*.[104] Rostow also sought to counter the influence of Marx and with the not-so-subtle subtitle: '*a non-communist manifesto*'. Rostow's distain for Marxian thought was evident in earlier work, and he felt that 'Marx's framework for relating economic, social, and political factors has found its way much more deeply into Western academic thought than most practitioners were aware'. Ironically, he felt that Marxist analysis was 'oversimplified', criticism that was later levelled at Rostow himself.[105] Rostow outlined the conditions for economic growth using aeronautical metaphors; 'take-off', which was essentially an increase in net investment from 5 to 10 per cent of net income leading to a sustained increase in income per capita.[106] The theoretical underpinnings for Rostow's approach was an article he had published in the *Economic Journal* the same year as Solow's more famous article, discussed below, and his 1952 book *The Process of Economic Growth*.[107] In *Stages*, Rostow's argument was a descriptive economic history that centred on the 'scale and productivity of investment in relation to population growth' and the rapid increase in investment, and he documented such associations for a number of countries and dated their 'take-offs'. Many of Rostow's 'take-offs' were not matched with the real experience; his predicted 'take-offs' were too late, and there was no 'smooth and stable cruising' found after the actual 'take-off'.[108]

The neoclassical growth models of Robert Solow and Trever Swan (1918–89) appeared almost simultaneously in 1956. Both emerged as a direct response to the Harrod-Domar model, with Solow using the assumptions at the heart of the Harrod-Domar model as explicit motivation and Swan also clearly comparing the neoclassical approach with Harrod's model.[109] Solow critiqued the application of short-run tools to a long-run problem ('the land of the margin'). One of the key criticisms of Solow was the constant capital-output ratio and a lack of factor substitutability (that is substitution of capital for labour and vice versa) in the Harrod-Domar model. A key distinction in the approach taken by Solow and Swan was the explicit use of an aggregate production function (the idea being a specified relationship between output and the inputs (capital and labour) used in production). The explicit production function was a significant difference compared to Harrod-Domar, and the function chosen was an off-the-shelf approach based on the work of the mathematician Charles Cobb (1875–1949) and the economist Paul Douglas (1892–1976).

Cobb and Douglas studied the relationship between output, capital, labour, and 'technique' in American manufacturing. Part of the issue for Cobb and Douglas was how to account for the variation in labour (overtime or in the short-term (i.e., underemployment)) while not making similar allowances for capital (intensity of use), but also that a 'third factor of natural resources' was excluded. This meant an assumption of a relationship between inputs (factors of production) to generate an output (income).[110] Given the centrality of this approach to modern economics, it is curious how its origins are unclear. In the original study, Cobb and Douglas refer to 'J. B. Clark, Wicksteed et al.'. Some claim it originates in the work of the Swedish economist Knut Wicksell (1851–1926), but a later retrospective by Douglas claimed it could be found simultaneously in the work of John Bates Clark (1847–1938) and Philip Wicksteed (1844–1927).[111] The key assumption of Cobb and Douglas was that the production function itself (that is the combination of factors) displayed constant returns but that there were diminishing returns to individual factors. This meant that output rose (or fell) in proportion to the increase (or decrease) of the inputs used in the production function but if one factor input increased, and if the other was kept constant (i.e., did not change), then there would be diminishing returns to the increasing input. The implications of this approach were that the combination of inputs led to a proportional increase in output (e.g., see the visualization of the concepts in Figure 3.5).

The use of the Cobb-Douglas production function by Solow and Swan led to the finding of no 'knife-edge' as the system adjusts to the growth in labour, through a price mechanism via relative factor prices (that is wages and interest). Another avenue for convergence between the warranted and natural growth rate of Harrod lies in the diminishing returns to capital. This second assumption deals with the implication of the Harrod-Domar model, that 'growth by raising an investment quota seems somehow too easy an approach'.[112]

The main implications of the neoclassical growth model were that long-run growth was effectively independent of capital accumulation, as increasing investment can temporarily increase growth and shift an economy to a new steady state but not lead to a sustained increase in the long-run growth rate. Secondly, exogenous technological change is seen as the driver of long-run economic growth. In a companion paper, Solow applied his theory to US data from 1909 to 1949. The application fitted an aggregate production function using US data on non-farm private GNP, capital (corrected for idleness), and labour (in man hours) from 1909 to 1949. The key finding was that shifts in the production function drove growth over the time period (accounting for 87.5 per cent of the increase in gross output). This residual, now known as Total Factor Productivity (TFP), has also been described by Moses Abramovitz as 'a measure of our ignorance about the causes of economic growth'.[113]

The other result of the Solow-Swan model was that, in the long run, countries would converge because lower-income countries, having lower capital-to-labour ratios, would experience higher levels of growth per capita. This occurs because poorer countries have a higher marginal product of capital which, given the assumption of diminishing returns to capital, encourages capital accumulation in parts of the world with lower levels of capital.

Apart from the headline results, what is of note in the application of the theory is the relatively broad definition of capital ('one that will really drive a purist mad'), 'for present purposes, "capital" includes land, mineral deposits, etc.'.[114] Solow noted that, 'ideally, what one would like to measure is the annual flow of capital services. Instead one must be content with a less utopian estimate of the stock of capital goods in existence'. Solow noted in the qualifications to the work some of the 'cobwebs . . . [that] have been brushed aside', the most notable of which are in the consideration of capital. Equating savings as investment overlooks some of the short-run Keynesian critiques, and the assumptions of 'perfect foresight into the future' were problematic, and the 'absence of risk, a fixed propensity to save, and no monetary complications' in the investment function.[115]

The Solow-Swan growth model has been central to the theory of economic growth for over half a century. Two outstanding issues are still debated. The first, as the economist Harold Hagemann shows, is that the problem of combining short-, medium- and long-run macroeconomics has not been resolved.[116] One aspect of this is that the neoclassical approach ignores the demand side of the economy, while Keynesian approaches ignore the supply side.[117] Also, the neoclassical model did not address the two dimensions of the instability in the Harrod-Domar model: the divergence between the warranted growth and the natural rate, as well as the 'short-run instability problems that arise when the investors base their decisions on expectations of a higher or lower rate of growth than the warranted rate'.[118] Solow later summarized the contribution of neoclassical growth theory to 'relate growth to asset pricing under tranquil conditions'.[119]

Solow himself was later critical of aggregate production functions as they were a 'dubious tool' given the issues associated with measurement. One such issue was how capital, as had been defined in the original 1956 article, was treated as a homogenous group without giving attention to the age composition of the stock. Noting that 'casual observation that many if not most innovations need to be embodied in new kinds of durable equipment before they can be made effective'. Solow addressed the issue of technology and capital in a subsequent work where he discussed embodying technology within new capital. The solution was to redefine the production function into subcomponents that attributed output to different vintages (ages) of capital. This approach reshaped the importance of capital and reduced the significance of the residual, which was now equal to capital. Other important issues related to the utilization of capital and greater attention to capital utilization might also reduce the weight of technological progress.[120]

New(er) Growth Theory

Growth theory was effectively dormant again from the 1960s to the early 1980s and re-awakened with the emergence of 'new' growth theory, alternatively known as 'endogenous growth theory'. After surveying the research on economic growth from 1939 to the early 1960s, the economists Frank Hahn (1925–2013) and Robin Matthews (1927–2010) felt that 'diminishing returns may have been reached' in the study of economic growth because greater understanding would require new ideas being brought to bear on the concept of growth.[121] Heinz Arndt's *The Rise and Fall of Economic Growth*, published in 1978, explains some of the lack of interest in economic growth because it was no longer seen as the primary objective of economic policy and thus of less interest to economists.[122] Surprisingly, Backhouse's more recent survey of the history of economic thought has less to say about developments in economic growth theory. This is partly explained by a predominant focus on short-run macroeconomic instability especially in the interwar years but again in the 1970s with the monetarist revolution against prevailing ideas of Keynesianism which had, up to this point, dominated discourse. Growth theory was also revitalized as part of these intellectual revolutions.

The renewed interest in economic growth came from the increasing availability of estimates of national income that showed how countries had performed over the previous thirty years (see Chapter 5). The results appeared to be at odds with predictions from standard neoclassical models, as there was limited evidence of convergence.[123] The increasing availability of data, also long-run historical data, enabled cross-country comparisons of growth performance to test which approach fitted the data.[124] Furthermore, cross-country data highlighted the positive spillovers associated with equipment investment and economic growth which were at odds with conventional theory.[125] This led to observations about the variation in experiences of economic growth across countries in the post-Second World War era and led to a focus on factors which could explain the sources of growth, namely technology.

In a series of articles in the 1980s, the Nobel laureate Paul Romer attempted to explain technological progress which had been considered equivalent to manna-from-heaven in the Solow-Swan model. Romer focused on the increasing return properties of new ideas and used human capital (that is the skills, education and experience embodied in labour) and knowledge as a way to explain technological change, with the result that 'per capita output can grow without bound'.[126] Another key contribution was that of the Nobel laureate Robert Lucas (1937–2023), Romer's PhD advisor at the University of Chicago, who emphasized the importance of human capital as a way to explain economic growth.[127] In the model devised by Lucas, human capital had both an internal effect and external effect which enabled increasing returns and economic growth. Other studies, such as the economist Sergio Rebelo's 'AK' model (so called because it is effectively a model of capital (K) without any diminishing returns), placed emphasis on broad capital which included both human and physical capital.[128]

The Nobel laureates Philippe Aghion and Peter Howitt used the framework of Schumpeter's creative destruction, that is, innovation renders old processes (and old capital) obsolete, as a way to model economic growth; in so doing, they brought Austrian economics into the mainstream. Later work by Aghion and Howitt focused on the embodiment of technology in capital. This approach implied that the latest technology is embodied in the newest capital, giving greater importance to investment for economic growth. The complementarity between capital and technology then runs counter to the original Solow-Swan model which effectively assumes disembodied technology (i.e., technology as independent from the capital stock). Other innovative aspects of the endogenous growth research are applications focusing on how short-run macroeconomic instability can impact future growth.[129]

The generalized AK model of endogenous growth assumes a broad capital stock, 'implicitly defined as being proportional to the sum of all different types of capital', with increasing returns to scale. In the original Romer setting, it is produced and human capital, but it can be extended to all types of capital. The model was a rediscovery of an older contribution from the economist Marvin Frankel (1924–2021) that, as Aghion and Howitt commented, 'seems to have gone unnoticed by the profession'.[130] In Frankel's study he contrasted the Solow model with the Harrod-Domar model by translating the Harrod-Domar model into a similar production function (leading to the so-called 'AK' model).[131] The modern focus considers capital to be much broader than originally envisaged by Harrod and Domar. Romer had effectively revitalized the AK approach which in turn meant a rehabilitation of the Harrod-Domar model.[132] The Harrod-Domar model is now seen by Aghion and Howitt as an 'early precursor of the AK model'.[133] Or some have more forcefully argued that the AK model *is* the Harrod-Domar growth equation. So twentieth-century growth theory came full circle.

How new was the 'new' theory of economic growth? There had been criticism of assuming that the residual equated solely to technological progress because, as Charles Kennedy (1923–97) and Anthony Thirlwall (1941–2023) demonstrated, it could also reflect other factors such as the substitution of capital for labour, economies of scale, learning by doing, educational improvements, resource shifts, organizational improvements, or measurement errors.[134] Many of the underlying arguments amount, in some respects, to a rediscovery of the work of the Keynesian economist Nicholas Kaldor (1908–86).[135] In a series of articles in the 1950s and 1960s, Kaldor offered a Keynesian-based alternative to the neoclassical growth models. A particular emphasis of the Kaldor's approach was to focus on technology embodied in capital. There were also precedents in Kenneth Arrow's study on learning by doing from 1962, and Hirofumi Uzawa's (1928–2014) 1965 study that embodied technical change in labour (i.e., human capital).[136] The argument that there were no diminishing returns to investment in broad capital was also made in 1944 by the economist Frank Knight (1885–1974).[137]

Hints of endogenous growth can also be found in Rostow's earlier and 'more scholarly' work, which was a subtler study of the dynamics of economic growth.[138] *Stages* had overshadowed Rostow's previous book, *The Process of Economic Growth*, which was an attempt to bridge the gap between history and economics to develop a theory of economic growth. Rostow's application of economic theory to history was later praised by Douglass C. North who saw Rostow as a precursor to the development of 'new' economic history as he had pioneered the application of economic theory to the study of history.[139] Rostow, who was a colleague of Solow's at MIT, had originally been sceptical of applying Keynesian short-run analysis to long-run problems. He critically discussed various aspects such as changes in production function as well as defining capital to include 'land and other natural resources, as well as scientific, technical, and organizational knowledge'. Rostow also saw the development of 'fundamental science' and the importance of investment in science for the 'flow of potential innovations coming forward', where he saw science as being the 'pool and flow of knowledge'.[140] Other factors that Rostow emphasized were related to the impact on capital-output ratios; these included the duration of time of an investment, and the length of time an investment generated a service, as well as externalities of investment.[141]

Capital Theory and Capital Controversy

Capital accumulation is a central concept in economics, but precise definitions of capital have proved elusive and caused much debate,[142] with multiple definitions still co-existing within different schools of thought.[143] In 1935, the economist Ludwig Von Mises (1881–1973) wrote that 'the view of scholars on the definition of capital are more divergent than their views on any other part of economics.'[144] Three decades later, Hahn and Matthews commented that, 'as far as pure theory is concerned the "measurement of capital" is no problem at all because we never have to face it if we do not choose to'. [145] This is true; in theory, measurement is not an issue and never has to be addressed but once any attempt is made to *apply* the theory then there is a requirement to actually measure capital. This is when problems surface.[146]

This chapter gave a brief account of growth theory where capital went from the centre to the periphery and then returned to central importance. But there was no clarification of what exactly was meant by capital. That was intentional given the lack of a consistent definition of capital in the classical period. Effectively, two perspectives on capital had a seminal influence on capital theory, those of Irving Fisher (1867–1947) and John Hicks.[147]

In 1896 Irving Fisher made the case for a coherent definition of capital after documenting the many inconsistent ways the term had been used.[148] Fisher clarified the definition of capital by thinking in terms of stocks and flows and adding a time dimension. Another important observation was the challenge of valuing capital, and Fisher highlighted how physical capital can be increased without a corresponding increase in value; the example he gave was of the doubling of the number of ploughs, which reduces the price of ploughs and thus the value of capital is constant.

Fisher defined wealth as the 'material objects owned by human beings' and he emphasized the link between wealth and property rights, where ownership limited the use of the future services generated from wealth. Fisher's definition also saw wealth as being related to the 'welfare of the community in general' and the goal of wealth accumulation was the 'final satisfactions in the human mind' (i.e., utility).[149] Fisher noted that there were two definitions of capital: 'wealth in its more general sense' and 'wealth in its more restricted sense'. In terms of the 'general' wealth, Fisher distinguishes between land (immovable real estate), commodities (movable) and human beings (both free and enslaved) (see Figure 3.7); 'restricted' wealth excludes human beings as they were considered 'a very peculiar form of wealth'.

Fisher noted a distinction between measuring units of wealth in their physical quantities and measuring them in terms of their value (price times quantity). In an example, Fisher was keen to stress the physical units, price and value 'represented different modes of measuring wealth' but that a common denominator (the valuation in monetary units) made it possible

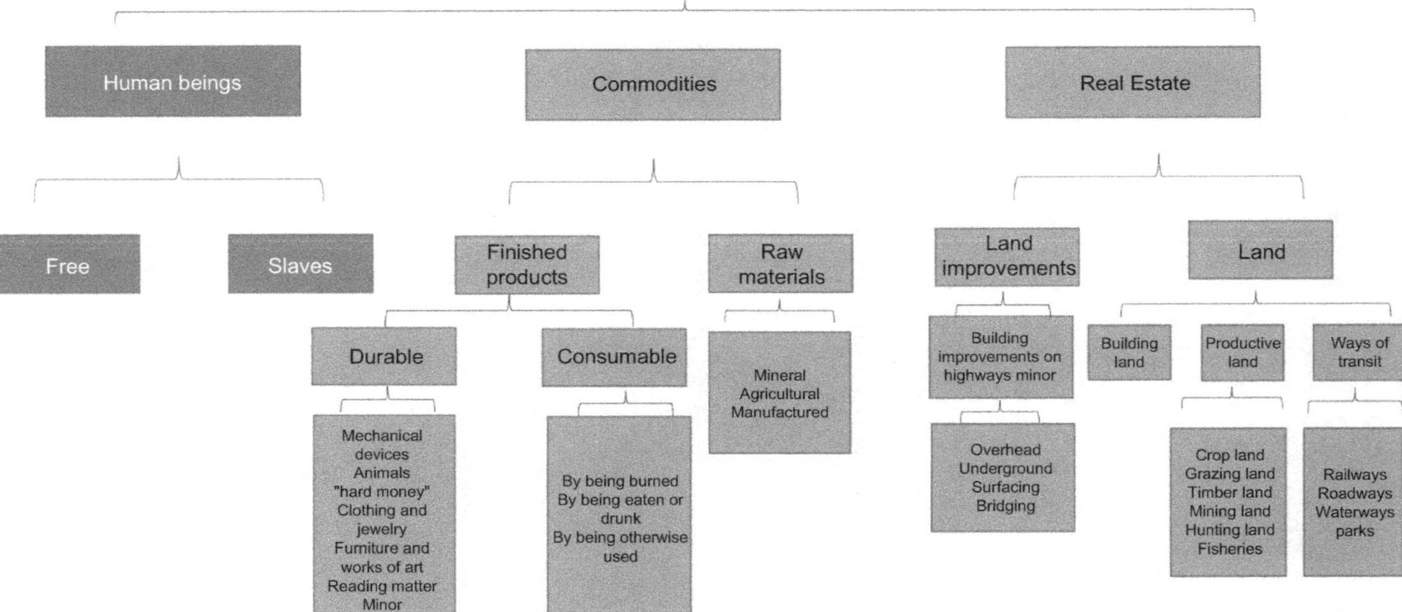

FIGURE 3.7 *Fisherian Wealth. Source: Fisher (1906), The Nature of Capital and Income.*

to aggregate wealth. He added that 'it would be a great mistake to suppose that it gives what may be called the "true measure of wealth"' and that 'measurement, is practically, a very inaccurate affair'. For Fisher it was most important to differentiate between capital and income. Capital (as represented by wealth) is a stock at a given period of time and income is a flow, as well as a service of wealth, through a period of time. Fisher also distinguished between capital-instruments, with each measured in its own unit of measurement, and capital-value which is measured in a common unit.[150] While Fisher's attempts to define capital were contested, ultimately his approach won out.[151]

The concepts were revisited again in the interwar period owing to the general upheaval associated with Keynes' *General Theory* as it contained numerous definitional contributions that generated further debate and revision. While many contributed to the definitional revisions, the most notable contributions were from John Hicks in his 1939 book *Value and Capital* through his critical assessment of the definitions of income, savings and depreciation.[152] Hicks outlined the ambiguity that income can be clearly defined in static analysis (or at the steady state) when income is then equal to one person's receipts, however, when applied to dynamic settings, it becomes more troublesome to define.

Hicks thought of capital through its relationship with income, or rather the 'capitalized money value of the individual's prospective receipts'. Uncertainty or irregularity in the payment of receipts creates the need to differentiate between what is income and what is to be dedicated to maintaining capital constant. According to Hicks, the purpose of an income calculation is to 'give people an indication of the amount which they can consume without impoverishing themselves'.[153] If a person were to make any saving, then they would intend to improve their circumstances and if their consumption exceeded their income then they intended to be in a worse position in future.

Hicks gave three different definitions of income and how they related to capital. In the first definition, income was the maximum amount of consumption that kept 'the capital value of prospective receipts' intact. The second definition of income was the maximum amount an individual can consume in a week and still expect to be able to consume the same amount in subsequent weeks. The first and second definitions are effectively equivalent as long as there is no change in the rate of interest. If there was a change in the interest rate, Hicks's third definition of income was: the maximum amount of consumption in a week consistent with the expectation of being 'able to spend the same amount in real terms in each ensuing week'.

These concepts were then aggregated and scaled up to 'social income', where differences in social preferences and expectations meant that the aggregate figure was an 'aggregate of possibly inconsistent expectations'. Hicks also maintained that there were three definitions of savings and investment that corresponded to his three definitions of income, making a distinction between *ex ante* and *ex post* saving. *Ex ante* total saving represented, '[the] planned increment in the value of physical capital' and *ex post* total savings are, 'the increment in the value of physical capital; which is what seems to be meant by investment'. The *ex ante* and *ex post* distinctions matter more for empirical measurement because what is measured is the *ex post* realization and not the *ex ante* expectations.

While these seemed satisfactory definitions of income and capital, the underlying issues of how to measure capital and whether it can be aggregated continued to be of concern. This bubbled up during the mid-twentieth-century debates surrounding the theory of economic growth. The various theoretical complications (what Solow dismissed as 'cobwebs') resurfaced during the so-called 'Cambridge-Capital Controversy'. This was a longstanding theoretical argument relating to the difficulties of measuring capital due to its heterogenous nature. One major issue was the presence of 'Wicksell effects', which refer to how changes in the prices and real returns affect the valuation of capital.[154] Other key concepts included 'reswitching' and 'capital-reversing', these were situations where the relationship between capital and labour inputs change in non-intuitive ways as interest rates shift, challenging the neoclassical assumption of a smooth, predictable substitution between capital and labour. The protagonists in the debate were based in Cambridge, United Kingdom (many of whom were Keynesians), and those in Cambridge, Massachusetts, United States (primarily neoclassical economists).[155]

The first part of the controversy had to do with productive combinations and the idea that not all combinations of factors are equivalent (e.g., Cobb-Douglas). The economist Joan Robinson's (1903–83) critique of the aggregate production function is a good example here:

> the production function has been a powerful instrument of miseducation. The student of economic theory is taught to write O = f (L, C) where L is a quantity of labour, C a quantity of capital and O a rate of output of commodities. He is instructed to assume all workers alike, and to measure L in man-hours of labour; he is told something about the index-number problem involved in choosing a unit of output; and then he is hurried on to the next question, in the hope that he will forget to ask in what units C is measured. Before ever he does ask, he has become a professor, and so sloppy habits of thought are handed on from one generation to the next.

The theoretical and empirical difficulties of measuring capital are central to Robinson's critique.[156] She argued that capital was inherently heterogeneous: its variation in age, quality, and type meant it could not be reduced to a common unit.[157] For example, capital goods such as roads and bridges differ fundamentally from machinery in both form and function. Consider a bus company: its fleet may include vehicles built at different times, at different costs, and varying in their fuel consumption. Some of the older vehicles might be diesel-powered internal combustion engines while the newer vehicles are fully electric. This diversity complicates efforts to measure the firm's total capital stock in a coherent way;[158] and this complication is scaled up in an aggregate production function.

In the neoclassical model discussed above, the key parameters of the Solow model relates output of 'only one commodity' which is either saved or consumed, the accumulated savings form the capital stock again simply defined as 'an accumulation of the composite commodity' with the relationship between output and inputs defined via a production function. Swan's treatment is similar but there was no specification of what constituted capital. Although Swan referred more explicitly to Robinson's critiques, effectively dismissing them as he viewed Robinson as being 'mistaken in her view'.[159]

These theoretical reservations about capital were effectively dismissed in the neoclassical approach. In his review of the intellectual history of capital theory, Solow explained that, 'the status of capital theory is unsettled' and he highlighted the debates 'between Bohm-Bawerk and J. B. Clark in the 1890's, between Hayek and Knight, going over much the same ground, in the 1920's and 1930's, and between Mrs. Joan Robinson and almost everyone else outside of Cambridge, England in the present'.[160] At the core were the issues raised by Fisher (how should capital be measured) and Solow believed this was an important issue but he argued that the disputes were due to mistaken questions rather than due to any deep theoretical importance. Solow noted that, 'this is a matter of some significance, because when a theoretical question remains debatable after 80 years there is a presumption that the question is badly posed - or very deep indeed'. Solow came down on the side that the question was badly posed and not that the issue had any deep theoretical significance.[161] While for Robinson these were issues of fundamental importance.

A symposium on production functions and economic growth published by the *Review of Economic Studies* in 1962 brought together many of the key figures in the capital controversy but no consensus was reached. This was evident in the reflections of the opposing sides to the symposium (Robinson and Kaldor on the Cambridge, UK side; Solow and Samuelson on the Cambridge, MA side). It was also evident from Solow's opening gambit that 'I have long since abandoned the illusion that participants in this debate actually communicate with each other'.[162] What was most interesting about the symposium was that it contained two novel contributions and they would later be seen as precursors to endogenous growth theory.[163] Samuelson later acknowledged the reality of reswitching and that 'the fact of possible reswitching teaches us to suspect the simplest neoclassical parables'.[164]

Reviewing the 'Cambridge-Capital Controversy', the economist Richard Chase (1932–2018) highlighted how the main questions (e.g., was there sufficient substitutability within the system) was effectively an empirical question, but that, 'the reswitching anomaly, along with its theoretical developments and implications, have been placed in abeyance'.[165] While the economist Geoffrey Harcourt (1931–2021) saw the controversy reflecting methodological differences of those that had started their working lives before the Second World War and those who entered a changed environment, the former were hostile to the neoclassical methodologies while the latter embraced it.[166]

The 'Cambridge-Capital Controversy' faded without resolution or consensus; there were no decisive knock-out blows, the questions were unresolved and the controversy petered out only because the main protagonists on the Cambridge UK side were already veterans and they passed away.[167] Therefore revising and resolving the controversy is essential for any theory of Inclusive Wealth to be meaningfully operationalized.[168] Furthermore, as highlighted by the economists Avi Cohen and Geoffrey Harcourt, part of the problem was that, 'ideology and methodology, two subjects most economists would rather avoid, were pervasive undercurrents fuelling the controversies'.[169] Reflecting on the Cambridge Controversy, Solow stated that he was 'trapped' because it was primarily ideological in origin.[170]

Yet it is generally viewed, well at least among proponents of endogenous growth, that it was the Cambridge UK side that were right. When introducing his views on endogenous growth theory, Robert Lucas (at the University of Cambridge) noted that the Cambridge UK had won the capital debate and that, for him:

> the development of the theory of human capital has very much altered the way I think about physical capital. We can, after all, no more directly measure a society's holdings of physical capital than we can its human capital. The fiction of 'counting machines' is helpful in certain abstract contexts but not at all operational or useful in actual economies – even primitive ones. [171]

In an address to the American Economic Association, John Hicks reflected on the Cambridge-Capital Controversy noting that, 'we need to know the history of our concepts in order to know what it is that we are handling'. Hicks made the distinction between capital as a volume as it is measured ('materialists') and the value of capital ('fundist'). From Hicks's perspective the Cambridge Controversy arose from these different perspectives on what constitutes capital: materialism versus fundism.[172]

The issues in capital controversy flare up periodically and lead to some recurring debates about the nature of capital. This matters primarily in the context of this chapter because growth theory is framed around capital (either its importance or unimportance) and whether these controversies matter or not. Ultimately all capital controversy revolves around the tension between physical and value conceptions of capital.[173] These issues are still pertinent, especially as we broaden our definition of capital in later chapters. While mainstream economics appears to have disregarded the capital controversy as insignificant, they have been embraced by heterodox economists of all varieties. Harcourt and Cohen predicted that the unresolved nature of the controversy would result in a future flare-up.[174]

Summary

John Kenneth Galbraith referred to accepted ideas that form a consensus as 'conventional wisdom'.[175] Ideas of economic growth became conventional wisdom until the 'march of events' led to challenges to the prevailing consensus. The main changes were wars that shook the established wisdom and the dislocations following wars that led to different ways of interpreting the world.

The shift in economic methodology also explains some of the changes. This was particularly evident in the Cambridge-Capital Controversy, as it reflects how economists in the United States had eclipsed the British/Cambridge approach to economics. The traditional Marshallian approach, that was dominant in Cambridge, UK, had been anti-mathematical and Harrod himself admitted in a letter to the Nobel laureate Jan Tinbergen (1903–94) that, 'I fear that my mathematics are rather rudimentary and that any singlehanded attempt to give a rigid mathematical formulation to my theory would not be successful.' The shift in economics had resulted in more economists reading the American academic journals such as *Econometrica* and *Review of Economic Studies* that were more heavily maths-based than the then more philosophically orientated *Economic Journal*.[176] More recent studies of economic growth reference Kaldor's stylized facts of growth but do not give much credence to his models of growth as these were deemed to be mathematically intractable.[177]

Growth theory is alive and well and recent developments have spurred greater focus on explaining the drivers of technological progress. Since the 1980s, there has been a vibrant field of research that led to the establishment of the *Journal of Economic Growth* in 1996 and an increasing array of studies focusing on various aspects of economic growth.[178] These include theories that attempt to bridge classical and modern theories of growth in a unified framework.[179] With the increasing availability of data and the fall in cost of computing power, there was an explosion of empirical studies looking to test the various growth theories in the 1990s and early 2000s. Despite the prevalence of endogenous growth theory, the traditional neoclassical model continued to rule the roost as TFP growth continues to explain a lot of cross-country variation.[180]

Reflecting on the future of the field of economic growth in light of his own research, Solow highlighted three interrelated aspects of growth: one is the shift to service-based economies and how well traditional growth models reflected these developments, second was the more explicit inclusion of the environment in economic growth models, the last was how the rapid development of India and China might impact on the other two developments. Many of the recent growth models have addressed the structural changes in the economy but there is less of an explicit focus on the latter points.[181]

Macroeconomists have also been reflecting on the state of their discipline, though much of this reflection has focused on the apparent convergence of views around short-run adjustments. Writing in 2008 (just before the global financial crisis), Olivier Blanchard, a former Solow student and MIT professor, famously declared that 'the state of macro is good'. He pointed to productive work being done on both short-run dynamics and long-run growth. Blanchard acknowledged a major omission: the medium term, the crucial phase that links these two ends of the macroeconomic spectrum. In a more recent reflection, Blanchard noted that although macroeconomists have converged in terms of methodology, the medium term remains under-theorized and largely neglected.[182]

Capital theory returned to mainstream attention in the early twenty-first century via the work of the economist Thomas Piketty, particularly in *Capital in the Twenty-First Century*. Piketty defines capital as 'all forms of real property (including residential real estate) as well as financial and professional capital (plants, infrastructure, machinery, patents and so on) used by firms and government agencies' and explicitly excludes human capital in this definition.[183] In some respects, this is returning to the restrictive Fisherian concept of capital (e.g., Figure 3.7). At the same time it also re-opens long-dormant questions about capital and its measurement.[184] Piketty briefly addresses what he called the 'Two Cambridges Debate', but he frames the disagreement primarily as an empirical one, noting 'that participants on both sides lacked the historical data needed to clarify the terms of the debate'. In doing so, he downplays the deeper theoretical divisions that remain unresolved. Without engaging with the core issues of the original controversy, the significant omission remains.

It is only fitting that the last word should go to Robert Solow. On the fiftieth anniversary of the publication of the original neoclassical growth model, Solow reflected modestly on the origins of the papers and expressed the hope that future historians of economic thought would find other contributions equally worthy of attention. He reminded them that:

> there is a piece of background wisdom that historians of economic thought must all know in their bones, but that they may tend to forget in the momentum of later discussion. When I did the research and wrote those papers more than fifty years ago, I had no inkling that they would be important or influential papers.[185]

Part II

History of the Global Economy

CHAPTER FOUR

Conflicting Futures

Development and Environment in the Twentieth Century

With over 100 million deaths, the world wars of the twentieth century were the most destructive events in the history of humanity.[1] The Second World War ended with Japan's surrender after it experienced the devastating power of the newly developed nuclear capabilities of the United States of America. The end of the Second World War marked the beginning of a new epoch in international relations, ushering in a Cold War between the United States and the USSR, accelerating decolonization, and revealing the destructive capabilities of modern technology.

In the aftermath of the Second World War there was an increase in the number of independent countries in the world.[2] Former colonies won their independence and sought their place in the world. Economic growth and development were desired policy objectives that were associated with modernization, industrialization, and national security. In terms of international relations, the multi-polar world of the European powers that had dominated the nineteenth century was swept away in the aftermath of the two world wars; a bipolar world emerged with the United States representing free market capitalism and the USSR offering an ideological alternative based on (Marxist-Leninist inspired) communism. The emergence of the Soviet Union as a global power also gave countries a template for rapid development through the use of extensive planning. Given the development of nuclear energy and other scientific advances, there was a techno-optimism around the prospects of future economic development.

The atomic age also signalled 'man's mastery over nature'. Between 1945 and 1963, over 500 above-ground nuclear tests were conducted leaving a distinctive radioactive layer in sediments.[3] The consequences of these atmospheric nuclear explosions stimulated thoughts on environmental issues and ushered in an environmental revolution in the second half of the twentieth century.[4] Building on an earlier tradition that was primarily concerned with overpopulation, an environmental movement emerged with greater awareness of the environmental consequences of economic progress. This led to greater criticism of economic growth as a policy objective and culminated in the 1972 *Limits to Growth* report.

The thirty years following the Second World War are crucial years both in terms of the emergence of economic development as an idea and environmentalism as an intellectual and social movement. Covering the period of the first Cold War until the breakdown of détente in 1970s, this chapter outlines the conflicting interests of development and environmentalism. Development was a concern of the newly independent states in the Global South, while environmentalism emerged in the Global North where the region was aghast at the possibility of further global economic growth. The chapter ends by focusing on arguably the most important report of the modern era: *The Limits to Growth*. The report was shocking in its depiction of a pending disaster awaiting the prevailing economic system.

Ultimately, there were two visions of economics at play. The first was the classical optimistic views of Smith that saw the wealth of nations being driven by free markets, division of labour, and capital accumulation. This was seen in the application of the ideas of Smith to the problems of development, such as in the early work of Arthur Lewis.[5] Environmentalists took the counter stance, embracing the pessimistic views of Malthus that saw population pressures as an excessive strain on the environment. The Marxist underpinnings of the USSR make for a possible third vision, although the Marxism of the USSR was more in line with the views of Smith (albeit with no role for free markets) than with Malthus given Marx's hatred of classical Malthusianism (as discussed in Chapter 3).

The realm of international development and environmentalism was seen as two sides of the same coin. In 1970, *Time Magazine* evoked the Cold War 'domino theory' to the case of the environment because 'man has violated these [natural] laws and endangered nature as well as himself'. The view was that reduced mortality through advances in medicine had distorted the natural order and, 'started a surge of human overpopulation that threatens to overwhelm the earth's resources'.[6] Although early visions of development soured, *The Limits to Growth*, and environmentalism more broadly, implied an end to the development agenda based on economic growth. Attempts to reconcile the two led to an uneasy compromise following the 1972 UN conference on the Human Environment held in Stockholm, Sweden. The fusion of the conflicting interests of development and environment persists in the form of the concept of 'sustainable development', and this underpins the approach of Inclusive Wealth discussed in Chapter 6.

The chapter gives an overview of the emergence of the idea of development and the rise of environmental awareness. It emphasizes the role of the Cold

War both as a driver of development and a factor that delayed the emergence of environmentalism. *The Limits to Growth* became a focal point for the tension between the goals of development and environmental sustainability. While environmentalists embraced the warnings of *The Limits to Growth*, proponents of economic growth and development were quick to dispute its assumptions and conclusions.

Decolonization and the Meaning of Development

From the end of the eighteenth century, European economies demanded increasing amounts of raw materials to fuel their industrialization and economic development. This was met by importing raw materials from the rest of the world, parts of which were later colonized by European powers such as Britain, France, and the Netherlands. Trade became dominated by flows of manufactured goods from Europe in exchange for primary commodities and raw materials from the Americas, Africa, and Asia, not to mention the trade in slaves from Africa.[7] The 'Age of Empires' was at its height at the 1884–85 Berlin Conference when European powers carved up the African Continent for their own interests. This led to the creation of extractive political institutions in Africa, the most heinous case of atrocities were found in the Belgian colony of Congo.[8]

Following the First World War, several empires were dismantled. Some former imperial territories, such as those of the Austro-Hungarian Empire, were granted independence; others, like the colonies of Germany and the Ottoman Empire (Turkey), were transferred to the victorious powers.[9] Under Article 22 of the Covenant of the League of Nations, 'there should be applied the principle that the well-being and development of such peoples form a sacred trust of civilization and that securities for the performance of this trust should be embodied in this Covenant'.[10] At the heyday of the British Empire, King George V declared in his 1920 speech that, 'it will be the high task of all my Governments to superintend and assist the development of these countries according to their varying degrees of advancement for the benefit of the inhabitants and the general welfare of mankind'.[11] This was known as the 'dual mandate' of British colonies to 'develop' colonies and to promote the welfare of their subjects.[12] Although it would later be interpreted as a colonial scramble for oil-rich territories in which Britain secured a disproportionate share, but it was portrayed differently at the time.[13]

Economic development as a distinct concept, one that combines both growth and welfare, emerged in the immediate post-Second World War era. Prior to this there was a different lexicon to describe what would later be known as development. Classical economists referred to 'material progress' and even up to the eve of the Second World War economists thought in terms of 'economic progress'. There were two exceptions: Marxists and economic historians. Development implied historical processes and stages in Marxist thought. To economic historians, particularly those studying overseas colonies, development represented something that was the purposeful action of government to convert natural resources into production, such as in Canada or Australia.[14]

The meaning of development changed over the course of the Second World War and in its immediate aftermath. This is illustrated by the development economist Paul Rosenstein-Rodan (1902–85) who, in 1944, wrote that:

> If we want to ensure a stable and prosperous peace, we have to provide for some international action to improve the living conditions of those peoples who missed the industrialization 'bus' in the nineteenth century. Since the 'economic forces,' the automatic mechanism of supply and demand, the movement of population and of capital between the different parts of the world failed to achieve over a hundred years what was expected of them, there is no doubt that they must be regarded as having had their chance and that many people have lost patience waiting for a solution by this means.[15]

The shift in the meaning of development was not coincidental. After the Second World War, African, Asian, and Latin American countries aspired to develop quickly. This push was driven by an awareness of the relative economic position compared to their former colonizers. This disparity was made visible through the publication of national income league tables from the 1950s onwards (see Chapter 5 for discussion). More importantly, the aspirations for development were closely tied to concerns about national survival and to the ambition of fully realizing the benefits of independence.[16]

The post-Second World War period saw the creation of major intergovernmental organizations. The United Nations (UN) became a successor to the failed League of Nations of the interwar period. The 1945 Charter of the UN made explicit reference to development as a way to ensure peaceful relations between countries and aimed to encourage 'higher standards of living, full employment, and conditions of economic and social progress and development'.[17] The UN created a variety of subsidiary agencies that were directly involved in development, such as the World Health Organization (WHO) founded in 1948; Food and Agriculture Organization (FAO) founded in 1945; UN Conference on Trade and Development (UNCTAD) founded in 1964; the UN Development Programme (UNDP) founded in 1965; and the UN Environment Programme (UNEP) founded in 1972. Due to its independent status, the UN was widely recognized as a leader in addressing various development challenges. However, the one area where it was notably absent was in relation to the sensitive issue of population growth as it 'was not treated, or accepted, as a major policy issue', despite concern from early environmentalists.[18] In the immediate aftermath of the Second World War, UN commentary on the global economy highlighted the importance of economic development. For example, in the 1945–47 UN *World Economic Situation* report, the Chinese diplomat Peng Chun Chang (1892–1957) stressed that without developing under-industrialized regions, global 'economic tranquillity' was impossible.[19]

Economic development was synonymous with economic growth in the immediate post-war period. For example, when pioneering development economist Arthur Lewis published the first comprehensive book on economic development in 1955, it carried the title *The Theory of Economic Growth*. Contemporary development theory emphasized the prevailing wisdom and was based on the Harrod-Domar growth models (see discussion in Chapter 3).[20] In this context, development theory emphasized capital accumulation and high savings rates. For instance, the 1951 UN report *Measures for Economic Development of Under-Developed Countries* advocated for increases in capital accumulation and that annual investment rates of 20 per cent of national income 'might raise national income by about 2 ½ per cent per annum' (although this would need to be higher to accommodate rapid population growth.)[21] This led to many highly capital-intensive, but symbolic, projects such as dams and other forms of infrastructure. As high savings rates were required, many countries did not have the capital available domestically and were required to import capital (what would be thought of as Foreign Direct Investment [FDI]) or receive developmental aid.

The 1960s were a UN 'Decade of Development' with a target of 5 per cent growth of national income per capita. There was rapid economic growth, and some countries experienced higher growth rates than developed countries had experienced in the nineteenth century. Although, in the first UN Development Decade, the meaning of development was reinterpreted; 'development is not just economic growth, it is growth plus change'.[22] The 1970s was a second UN Decade of Development with a target of 6 per cent growth of income per capita, but a problem emerged where high growth rates did not eliminate poverty and resulted in higher inequality. This led to disappointment with economic growth as a proxy for economic development, and equating development with growth was seen as misconceived. Resulting in the emergence of alternatives such as 'basic needs' from the 1970s.[23] 'Basic needs' was concerned with 'providing human beings, but particularly the poor and deprived, with the opportunities for a full life'.[24]

Other influences on the change in emphasis in development thinking were the failure of attempts to implement import substitution industrialization; these were capital-intensive attempts to industrialize by restricting the import of capital goods. This was predominantly practised in Latin America but also in remote parts of Western Europe (Ireland). By contrast, countries in Asia operated under export-orientated models of development and saw much faster economic growth. Japan was the poster child for rapid growth in the immediate post-war period followed by other so-called Asian 'tigers' (Hong Kong, Singapore, South Korea, and Taiwan). The shift to export orientation was slowed by the gradual removal of trade barriers erected during the interwar period. Various rounds of the General Agreement on Trade and Tariffs (GATT; now the World Trade Organization) were a response to the need for freer trade and the view that 'aid can be no substitute for trade'.[25]

The shift in thinking towards a more inclusive definition of development came from disillusionment with economic growth delivering meaningful change.[26] The shift in perspective came in the 1960s when there was greater emphasis on human capital as opposed to physical capital accumulation.[27] In making the case for a wider definition of development, the UN-based development economist Hans Singer (1910–2006)[28] reflected that the formative period of development was 'the great days of the Harrod-Domar formula', but regrettably 'the Harrod-Domar formula turned out to be so unstable as to be useless as instruments of economic planning'.[29] Singer was alluding to the importance of 'residual factors' in economic growth, those that became associated with the neoclassical growth model (see Chapter 3). The shift towards human capital meant greater effort to improve education and training in developing countries.

The distinction between economic growth and economic development led to calls for alternative ways to measure development. One of the first was the 'Physical Quality of Life Index' (PQLI) developed by the economic historian Morris David Morris (1921–2011) for the Overseas Development Council, a US-based think-tank focusing on developing countries. The work was later sponsored by US Agency for International Development (USAID). PQLI was a simple index of infant mortality, literacy, and life expectancy at age 1, with the index intended to show basic human needs of the population. Challenges implementing the PQLI related to data availability, and an initial attempt to apply the PQLI at a subnational level in India ran into data difficulties. Others were critical of the focus on physical indicators as a measure of well-being as this missed other aspects of development, such as justice and political freedom.[30]

Another alternative measure of development came through the Human Development Index (HDI), which was instigated by the UNDP-based economist Mahbub ul Haq (1934–98). The HDI approach was based on the capabilities approach of the development economist Amartya Sen, and as a result both ul Haq and Sen are often attributed with the creation of the HDI.[31] Human development as captured by the HDI aimed to shift the focus of development economics from national income accounting to people-centred policies.[32] The UNDP HDI has been published since the 1990s and tracks different aspects of development; it is comprised of GDP, education, and life expectancy. The HDI was intended to be used 'as a more genuine measure of socioeconomic progress', given that '[h]uman progress may be lacking in some societies despite rapid GNP growth'.[33] Different aspects of development, such as inequality and political freedom, have been

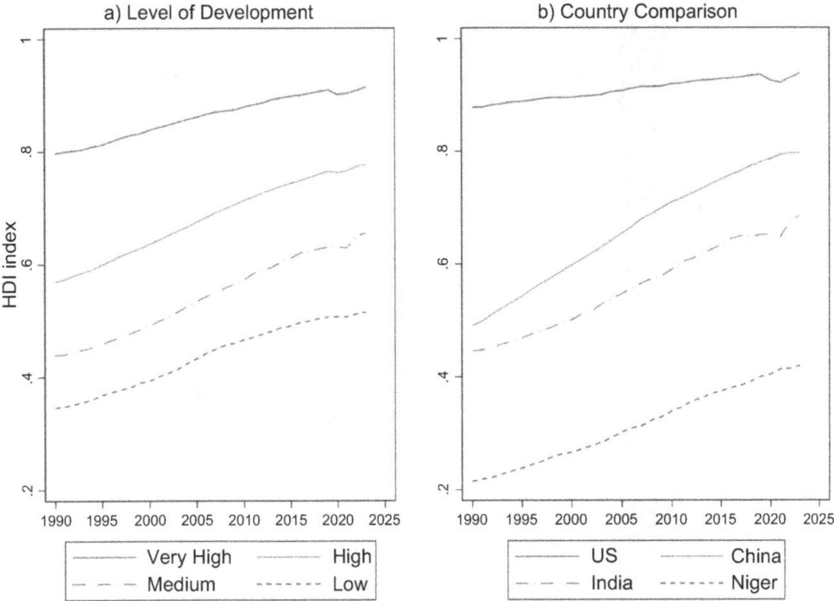

FIGURE 4.1 *Human Development Index, 1990–2023. Source: UN Development Programme. Human Development Reports.*

incorporated to augment the HDI but environmental considerations have yet been fully incorporated in this measure of development.[34]

Figure 4.1 shows trends in HDI across different levels of development, as well as trends for China, India, Niger, and the United States. China's rapid improvement in HDI indicates that the recent Chinese economic growth miracle was accompanied by significant human development. During this period, China graduated from the category of 'medium human development' to 'high human development'. In contrast, India's progress has been modest, remaining within the 'medium human development' range. The figure also shows that while Niger's HDI rose from 0.215 in 1990 to 0.419 in 2023, it still ranks among the world's lowest in terms of HDI.

Neo-Malthusian Concerns about Development

The twentieth century saw a population explosion. Global population rose by approximately 61 per cent between 1900 and 1950 and increased by 140 per cent in the second half of the twentieth century (see Table 4.1).[35] Some parts of the world saw a slowdown in population growth due to the demographic transition (particularly evident in Europe), where mortality rates were falling followed by a decline in birth rates. Other parts of the globe

TABLE 4.1 Population and population growth in the twentieth century.

	1900	1950	1970	2000	1900–50	1950–70	1970–2000
	Population (billions)				Population growth rates (%)		
Western Europe	0.23	0.31	0.35	0.39	*0.54*	*0.73*	*0.36*
Eastern Europe	0.12	0.18	0.24	0.29	*0.74*	*1.51*	*0.58*
USA	0.08	0.15	0.21	0.28	*1.39*	*1.50*	*1.07*
Latin America	0.06	0.17	0.29	0.52	*1.90*	*2.76*	*2.03*
China	0.40	0.55	0.82	1.26	*0.63*	*2.04*	*1.46*
India	0.28	0.36	0.54	1.00	*0.47*	*2.07*	*2.08*
Asia	0.87	1.39	2.09	3.61	*0.93*	*2.09*	*1.83*
Africa	0.11	0.23	0.37	0.81	*1.47*	*2.39*	*2.69*
World	*1.56*	*2.53*	*3.69*	*6.08*	*0.97*	*1.91*	*1.68*

Source: See Figure 3.4.

continued to see high population growth despite the fall in mortality rates which led to concerns about the implications of unconstrained population growth.

Many have seen global population emerging as a problem during the Cold War era, but the historian Alison Bashford shows that concerns about overpopulation emerged in the wake of the First World War.[36] The economist (and civil servant) James Bonar (1852–1941) noted in a 1926 reprint of Malthus's *Essay* by the Royal Economic Society, 'the interest in Malthus has rather increased than diminished since 1895'.[37] The increased demand is reflected by the views of some who saw the First World War as an example of a Malthusian positive check; for example, the economist Edwin Cannan (1861–1935), when reviewing Warren Thompson's (1887–1913) *Population: A Study in Malthusianism* observed that, 'the increase of population in Europe is having one of Malthus' "positive checks" administered with very great sharpness'.[38] In *The Economic Consequences of the Peace*, John Maynard Keynes saw population pressure as one the main causes of the First World War and commented that 'the great events of history are often due to secular changes in the growth of population and other fundamental economic causes, which, escaping by their gradual character the notice of contemporary observers, are attributed to the follies of statesmen or the fanaticism of atheists'.[39] The view that population pressures were a cause of war was espoused by the economist Harold Cox (1859–1936) in his 1922 book *The Problem of Population* and the population biologist Raymond Pearl (1879–1940) in his 1925 book *Biology of Population Growth*.[40] Similarly, there were prominent commentators, such as the ecologist William Vogt (1902–68), that saw overpopulation as the cause of the Second World War.[41] This view was echoed by the conservationist Henry Fairfield Osborn (1887–1969) who saw the world wars as an outcome of an underlying conflict with nature; the world wars were a visible conflict 'spawned' by an invisible war with nature and that the war with nature 'contains potentialities of ultimate disaster greater even than would follow the misuse of atomic power'.[42]

If Adam Smith is the common ancestor of economics, then Malthus is perhaps the last common ancestor of economics and other sciences. The influence of Malthus is most visible in demography and ecology. The fusion of political economy with biology came via Charles Darwin's (1809–82) *Origin of Species*:

> It is the doctrine of Malthus applied with manifold force to the whole animal and vegetable kingdoms; for in this case there can be no artificial increase of food, and no prudential restraint for marriage. Although some species may be now increasing, more or less rapidly, in numbers, all cannot do so, for the world would not hold them. There is no exception to the rule that every organic being naturally increases at so high a rate,

> that, if not destroyed, the earth would soon be covered by the progeny of a single pair.[43]

In his autobiography Darwin acknowledged the influence of Malthus on his work, stating that he read Malthus 'for amusement' in 1838 'and being well prepared to appreciate the struggle for existence which everywhere goes on from long-continued observation of the habits of animals and plants, it at once struck me that under these circumstances favourable variations would tend to be preserved, and unfavourable ones to be destroyed'. After reading Malthus, Darwin was inspired to begin writing his theory, but he did not begin for a number of years, as he was 'anxious to avoid prejudice'. Thus, it was Malthus that inspired Darwin's subsequent work on the theory of evolution.[44]

As Alison Bashford documents, Malthus was held in high regard among leading figures in demography and ecology, such as Raymond Pearl and William Vogt.[45] This brings a clear lineage from classical political economy to ecology. The environmental historian Donald Worster argues that Malthus 'introduced a new ecological dimension to Adam Smith's study of human economics, and at the same time offered a gloomy reappraisal of the economy of nature'.[46] The term 'ecology' (oecologie) was coined in 1866 by Ernest Haeckel (1834–1919), a staunch adherent of Darwinian, and by proxy Malthusian, principles. He labelled the new science 'the economy of nature [Naturhaushalt]'.[47]

The connection between ecology and economics was most explicit in the ecology book *The Science of Life* written by the science fiction author Herbert G. Wells (1866–1946) in collaboration with Julian Huxley (1887–1975) and Wells's son, George P. Wells (1901–85). The connection between Malthus, Darwin and ecology was explicit.[48] Ecology was referred to as 'biological economics'; they opined that economics should be subsumed into ecology as it was, 'human ecology, it is the narrow and special study of the ecology of the very extraordinary community in which we live'.[49]

This Malthusian-Darwinian influence percolated through into the modern environmental movement. The ecologist William Vogt, whose scientific career began as an amateur ornithologist, parroted the ideas of Malthus in his book *Road to Survival* with his predictions of famine in London and that, 'hand in hand with famine will walk the shade of that clear-sighted English clergyman, Thomas Robert Malthus'.[50] Henry Fairfield Osborn's view was that Malthus was 'not so far wrong' and while highlighting Malthus' lack of foresight on the role of technology, Osborn extrapolated this to mean that Malthus had overlooked the devastating impact of the internal combustion engine. Unlike other commentators who viewed Malthus as missing the beneficial impacts of technology, Osborn instead saw that technology was hastening humanity's doom as it 'has so incredibly accelerated the capacity to exploit the earth's resources of forests and croplands. This invention has brought its innumerable benefits and wreaked its irreparable damage.'[51]

Eugenics, a once respected science, was a movement that arose in the wake of Darwin's *Origin of Species*, and it was the result of the Malthusian-Darwinian fusion. At its core, eugenics was an attempt to affect reproduction through heredity.[52] Eugenics was originally developed by Darwin's cousin Francis Galton (1822–1911) who saw eugenics as an alternative to 'natural selection' through selective reproductive of traits among the human population. Galton gave his interpretation of eugenics as he saw it in 1908:

> I conceive it to fall well within his province to replace Natural Selection by other processes that are more merciful and not less effective. This is precisely the aim of Eugenics. Its first object is to check the birth-rate of the Unfit, instead of allowing them to come into being, though doomed in large numbers to perish prematurely. The second object is the improvement of the race by furthering the productivity of the Fit by early marriages and healthful rearing of their children. Natural Selection rests upon excessive production and wholesale destruction; Eugenics on bringing no more individuals into the world than can be properly cared for, and those only of the best stock.[53]

This view was shared by the eminent statistician Karl Pearson (1857–1936), who argued that a relative decline in intelligence in the British population was caused by relative shifts in fertility. He maintained that 'the only remedy, if one be possible at all, is to alter the relative fertility of the good and the bad stocks in the community'. For Pearson, intelligence could be 'aided and trained' but it could not be 'created' through education or training; instead he insisted that 'you must breed it' and envisioned a role for 'statecraft'.[54]

Another prominent eugenicist was the biologist Garrett Hardin (1915–2003) who was chair of the American Eugenics Society from 1971 to 1974 (and he had been an active member of the society since 1956).[55] Hardin greatly admired Malthus and considered the *Essay on Population* to be a 'much misunderstood work, yearly buried by critics and yearly resurrected by its own vigor', and he respected the 'sons of Cambridge'.[56] Hardin at times appeared misanthropic, questioning the desirability of the survival of the human race because 'this can certainly not be proved from any point of view that is demonstrably "objective"'.[57] In his discussion of regulating competition between countries, Hardin gave a hypothetical example of pacifist countries where the peace is broken by a country which increases its fertility: 'the competitive use of human gonads in a pacifistic world is every bit as vicious and productive as is the militaristic use of atomic bombs'.[58]

The key issue for Hardin was the question raised since the publication of *The Origin of Species*: was humanity a part of nature or did it stand above it? If humanity were a part of nature, then it would be subject to nature's laws (including evolution). For example, Hardin saw clear, Malthusian, limits to population growth: 'man, the slender reed that thinks, can alter the force and direction of natural forces somewhat, but only within limits'.[59] But if humanity stood above nature, then Hardin believed that 'utopia must include positive eugenics as well' and advocated for policies to control population. So, while the explicit language of eugenics may have been stripped out of Hardin's later works advocating population control.[60] It can be clearly seen that it is this thinking that implicitly underpins this perspective.

In Hardin's famous article on the tragedy of the commons, he draws explicitly on Malthus again and asks that, 'we explicitly exorcize the spirit of Adam Smith in the field of practical demography' with specific criticism reserved for 'the invisible hand'.[61] The invisible hand here could be interpreted to be 'natural selection', whereas Hardin had stronger preferences for a much more 'visible hand', i.e., eugenic selection. Because Hardin argued that it was:

> a mistake to think that we can control the breeding of mankind in the long run by an appeal to conscience . . . People vary. Confronted with appeals to limited breeding, some people will undoubtedly respond to the plea more than others. Those who have more children will produce a larger fraction of the next generation than those with more susceptible consciences. The difference will be accentuated, generation by generation.[62]

Given Hardin's eugenicist bent, the 'Hardinian taboo', which infers population controls for certain segments of society, implicitly advocates for eugenicist policies.[63]

The other famous advocates for population control were Paul and Anne Ehrlich. While their work has explicitly eschewed eugenics, they do occasionally use turns of phrase that could be misconstrued. For example, 'the people of the UDCs [underdeveloped countries] will be unable to escape from poverty and misery unless their populations are controlled. Today, these countries have larger populations than they can properly support, given their physical and biological resources'.[64] For neo-Malthusians, the cause of poverty was overpopulation and thus the key to development was a reduction in population.

The question of whether population growth would outstrip the means of production was a persistent worry since the end of the nineteenth century. An early prediction of the carrying capacity of the planet was made by the geographer Ernst Georg Ravenstein (1834–1913) in 1890. He saw food availability (explicitly not natural resources, such as coal and iron) as the main constraint on population growth and predicted a maximum carrying capacity of 5.9 billion by the year 2072, but he also anticipated voluntary checks to population growth.[65] A later estimate by Raymond Pearl in 1925 was more pessimistic. Applying a logistic curve (an 'S' shaped curve) to global population, Pearl estimated a maximum carrying capacity of 2 billion.[66] This estimate reinforced views that food supplies would be unable to match the increases in population.[67] In *The Shadow of the World's*

Future, the Australian statistician George Knibb (1858–1929) aimed to define the 'limited population carrying capacity, under various conditions, of our earth'. This was most explicit in a chapter 'New Malthusianism and Man's Future', where Knibb argued that the world was overpopulated and that the population growth experienced since 1800 'cannot continue under any circumstance whatsoever: it must diminish'.[68]

Population growth was a fear that drove the early environmental movement as the increase in population meant greater pressure on the Earth. This was a continuation of interwar concerns over optimum population. One of the earliest writers of this ilk was William Vogt, who highlighted the links between population growth and environmental degradation. For example, he associated settlement and agricultural development of land in the US Great Plains with the creation of conditions for the 'dust bowl', thus highlighting the limited carrying capacity of the Earth. In the context of China's rapid population growth, Vogt declared that there was 'little likelihood that we have seen the end of famine'.[69] Vogt also predicted that Japan 'will probably have to face famine unless she takes quick and effective action to check her population increase'.[70]

This intellectual lineage followed on to Paul Ehrlich, who was an entomologist by training, and he provocatively declared in *The Population Bomb* (published in 1968) that:

> the battle to feed all of humanity is over. In the 1970s the world will undergo famines – hundreds of millions of people will starve to death in spite of any crash programs embarked upon now . . . each year food production in these countries falls a bit further behind burgeoning population growth, and people go to bed a little bit hungrier. While there are temporary or local reversals of this trend, it now seems inevitable that it will continue to its logical conclusion: mass starvation.[71]

At the time that Paul Ehrlich's *Population Bomb* was written, global population had approximately doubled in the first sixty years of the twentieth century (see Figure 3.4). Ehrlich's message clearly resonated with the wider American public as he appeared on the *Tonight Show* and the 1973 movie *Soylent Green* depicted an overpopulated hellscape where people had unwittingly resorted to cannibalism as oceans were depleted. These fears about humanity's ability to feed itself were not confined to the United States. Writing in 1971 the Anglo-French philosopher Edward Goldsmith (1928–2009) concluded that, 'a serious world food shortage appears inevitable' and that 'it would be extremely naïve to suppose that we in Britain will not be affected by these developments'.[72] Fears of famine still persist. The science writer Julian Cribb warned of a famine crisis that was 'arriving even faster than climate change' in his 2010 book *The Coming Famine*.[73]

Neo-Malthusian views influenced the environmental movement in the immediate post-Second World War period and warned of possible renewed wars if population pressures were unresolved.[74] The views of the neo-Malthusians culminated in the misanthropic view that 'people are pollution' or rather, in the more extreme, that people were seen as a cancer on the planet.[75] This led to increased interest in family planning and sterilization in developing countries.[76] As Ehrlich sensationally wrote in *The Population Bomb,* 'we must have population control at home . . . by compulsion if voluntary methods fail' and 'population control must be established and supported in underdeveloped countries'.[77] Essentially, this put the interests of developing countries against the interests of some in developed countries. This led to further studies on animal populations, the most infamous being John Calhoun's (1917–95) concept of the 'behavioural sink', which showed population collapse in rodent populations living under utopian conditions, reinforcing the view that population growth would lead to crisis.[78]

The only problem with these predictions is that famines of such enormous scale have not (yet) materialized, primarily because of the productivity of the agricultural sector.[79] One of the most famous predictions was by the chemist William Crookes (1832–1919) who, in 1898, had warned that the world would run out of wheat by 1931.[80] Crookes was hopeful though that chemistry would provide a solution 'and postpone the day of famine', but he feared that available sources of nitrogen were not enough to meet the 'unlimited nitrogen required to substantially increase the world's wheat crop'. The world did not run out of wheat and it was helped by the discovery of artificial fertilizers via the Haber-Bosch process, the most important innovation of the twentieth century; the significance of the achievement led to a Nobel Prize for Fritz Haber (1868–1934)[81] in 1918.[82] The application of scientific methods to agriculture had increased food production, something that did not go unnoticed by an editorial in *Nature* thirty years after the publication of the *Wheat Problem*.[83]

The prognosticators of doom in the immediate post-Second World War era did not foresee the impact of the green revolution (IR8 was released in 1966 – see below) in improving agricultural yields, just as the benefits of the Haber-Bosch process were not anticipated. The Nobel Peace Prize was awarded to Norman Borlaug (1914–2009) in 1970 for his role in the Green Revolution. Borlaug explicitly addressed the Malthusian arguments in his Nobel lecture:

> Some critics have said that the green revolution has created more problems than it has solved. This I cannot accept, for I believe it is far better for mankind to be struggling with new problems caused by abundance rather than with the old problem of famine.[84]

Borlaug, a PhD scientist with an expertise in plant pathology and genetics, was inspired by the poverty he witnessed during the Great Depression. For Borlaug, it was poverty, not overpopulation, that was the cause of hunger.

Since the Green Revolution, agricultural productivity has continued apace with population growth.[85]

With the improvements in agricultural performance famines effectively 'became history', as the economic historian Cormac Ó Gráda painstakingly documents.[86] The impact of famines had declined, thanks in large part to improvements in public health knowledge as well as medical technology. The largest famines in relative terms (famine deaths as a percentage of population) were in the nineteenth century; these were the classic Malthusian famines. Although paradoxically, the largest famine in history, the Chinese Great Leap Forward Famine, took place in the mid-twentieth century.[87] In a sense, Vogt was right that China would not avoid a famine, but the cause was not overpopulation. Rather, the Chinese famine, like other major twentieth-century famines (e.g., Ukraine, Bengal, and the Netherlands), was man-made owing to wars or totalitarian regimes.[88] This distinction is best typified in the work of Amartya Sen, who argued that the Great Bengal Famine during the Second World War was caused by an entitlement failure, the ability to acquire food through market-based institutions, and not the availability of food *per se*.[89] This assessment led to research on whether the famine was due to a decline in food availability or if it was in fact man-made. The available evidence suggests that there was some element of food availability decline (the 1942 Aman harvest was damaged by a fungus) but there is greater support to the view that the Bengal famine was a man-made catastrophe. Thus, there would have been no Bengal Famine had there been no World War.[90]

Development in the Shadow of the Cold War

Both the United States and the USSR emerged victorious from the Second World War. Even though the UN was meant to act as an independent body with equal representation for all nations, the United States and the USSR were first among equals. They sat as permanent members on the UN Security Council, alongside fellow victors of the Second World War (Britain and France), as well as China (as the largest country in Asia). The Security Council had a veto over any non-procedural motion in the UN, thus limiting the effectiveness of the UN General Assembly. Geopolitical rivalry between the US and the USSR led to the Cold War (1947–89), marking a distinction with the interwar period, and signalled a change in the global balance of power. The USSR offered an ideological alternative to free market capitalism and the perceived threat of communism influenced government policy in Western countries. For example, placing a restraint on income inequality; this was especially pertinent in the case of Western European countries that were in close proximity to the USSR and led to variations in free market capitalism.[91]

In the immediate aftermath of the Second World War, the prevailing view was that the United States held a strategic advantage as it was the sole nation to possess nuclear weapons. This calculus changed when the Soviets successfully developed their own nuclear capabilities in 1949, much sooner than had been expected by the US intelligence community. The discussion on the optimum US response to the communist threat boiled down to three (not mutually exclusive) options: build up the American military, provide military assistance, or provide economic assistance. Following rapid demobilization post-Second World War, neither the Republican-controlled Congress nor the American people had an immediate desire to spend tax dollars on any of these actions.[92] However, events in Europe, where Greece looked like it would fall into communist hands, changed US perceptions. This laid the ground for the so-called 'domino theory', as there was a fear that if Greece fell then next would be Turkey, and so on. This also had applicability outside of Europe, particularly in Asia.

On 6 March 1947, President Harry S. Truman (1884–1972) began making the case for his policy of containment and it is often reported that he said that, 'the whole world should adopt [the] American system [and] the American system could survive in America only if it became a world system'.[93] While this quote is often repeated, it appears to be a paraphrase and it is doubtful whether the President actually wrote the speech.[94] The surviving record of the speech given at Baylor University does not include the quote but it does outline the view that the US leadership would determine the direction of the global economy as 'we [the US] are the giant of the economic world. Whether we like it or not, the future pattern of economic relations depends on us . . . The choice is ours. We can lead the nations to economic peace or we can plunge them into economic war.'[95] A few days after the Baylor Speech, President Truman addressed a joint session of Congress and outlined what became known as the Truman Doctrine:

> At the present moment in world history nearly every nation must choose between alternative ways of life. The choice is too often not a free one. One way of life is based upon the will of the majority, and is distinguished by free institutions, representative government, free elections, guarantees of individual liberty, freedom of speech and religion, and freedom from political oppression. The second way of life is based upon the will of a minority forcibly imposed upon the majority. It relies upon terror and oppression, a controlled press and radio; fixed elections, and the suppression of personal freedoms. I believe that it must be the policy of the United States to support free peoples who are resisting attempted subjugation by armed minorities or by outside pressures. I believe that we must assist free peoples to work out their own destinies in their own way. I believe that our help should be primarily through economic and financial aid which is essential to economic stability and orderly political processes.[96]

Militarily, the Truman Doctrine led to the formation of the North Atlantic Treaty Alliance (NATO) in 1949 and set the groundwork for future US military interventions in Korea (1950–53) and Vietnam (1965–73) as attempts to contain the spread of communism.

The Truman Doctrine also established US policy towards non-communist developing countries for the next twenty years and created a 'massive American aid program'; however, this aid was conditional and required US oversight. The aid for European reconstruction was known as the Marshall Plan and though Asia and Africa did not receive Marshall Aid, additional assistance was provided to non-communist countries to ensure that 'economic advancement was to be promoted'.[97] Point 4 of the Truman Doctrine also provided for the 'benefits of our scientific advances and industrial progress available for the improvement and growth of underdeveloped areas' and for the provision of aid and technical assistance.

The Cold War also held sway within the USSR and influenced geostrategic decision-making, notably in Stalinist policies to support communist orientated nationalists outside the USSR. In turn, this influenced whether the United States chose to intervene and whether it sought to influence European colonial powers, but this was sometimes complicated by other geostrategic considerations. For instance, the United States acted against the Dutch in Indonesia partly because a non-communist nationalist leader was poised to take power. This approach contrasted with how the United States engaged with the French in Vietnam where the nationalist force was communist aligned; another consideration at play was that the United States needed French support in Europe with the reconstruction of Germany.

Decolonization in Asia advanced rapidly, a crucial factor was Japan's role during the inter-war period, which exposed the vulnerabilities of the European imperial powers. The Philippines gained independence in 1946, followed soon after by India. The region drew increased international focus following the Communist victory in China in 1949. The strategy of containing communism became a significant driver of decolonization, as China's shift was quickly followed by the outbreak of the Korean War (1950–53), and a prolonged conflict in French Indochina. There were some exceptions. For example, in the case of India the strategic decision was to be non-aligned with neither the United States nor the USSR, but this ambiguity enabled it to play both sides off each other when it was in its (i.e. India's) interest.[98] African decolonization was more protracted compared to Asian experiences. Africa had not been a major theatre of the Second World War (albeit with campaigns in North Africa) and had less leverage on European colonial powers. The main turning point in Africa was the Suez Crisis in 1956, when Egypt nationalised the Suez Canal. France and Britain launched a failed military offensive to regain control of the canal. This event both kick-started decolonization in earnest and also changed the dynamics between former European colonial powers and the United States.

The spheres of influence and political alignment of the world during the Cold War gave a new terminology to describe the international order: 'First World', to denote the capitalist liberal democracies, the 'Second World', those in the Soviet-Comecon sphere of influence, and the 'Third World', those non-aligned with either group. Although the Third World was unaligned, it came to be associated with poorer developing countries. It was in the Third World where the threat of the spread of communism gave Western countries, particularly the United States, greater impetus to engage in international development. This was done via intergovernmental institutions in which the United States had greater control and oversight. The main vehicle for this was via the International Bank for Reconstruction and Development (IBRC), founded at the 1944 Bretton-Woods Conference. The original goal of the IBRC, now more widely known as the World Bank, was to provide loans to aid with the reconstruction of Europe, but this soon proved superfluous as it was dwarfed by US Marshall Aid.[99] The World Bank switched to its second mission and effectively became a development institution with a focus on 'Third World' countries.[100] Similarly, the foundation of USAID in 1961 had its origins in Cold War geostrategic considerations. This was demonstrated most clearly by the role of USAID in Vietnam, where it acted as a counterpoint to US military operations. Between 1962 and 1975, Vietnam received the lion's share of USAID economic assistance. USAID's presence in Vietnam peaked in 1968 with 5,100 personnel employed 'developing Vietnamese institutions and economic and social services' but this collapsed when the US military withdrew from Vietnam in 1975.[101] Tellingly, overseas aid fell as a share of GDP after the end of the Cold War as it no longer held the same geostrategic significance.[102]

Another dimension of the Cold War was US support for the Green Revolution by offering the promise of a better future, rooted in the belief that Communism appealed to the poor and hungry. The United States backed initiatives to boost agricultural productivity and promote an alternative vision of prosperity. One of the most notable efforts was the establishment of the International Rice Research Institute in the Philippines in 1960, funded by the Ford and Rockefeller Foundations. The institute aimed to develop rice varieties that were 'fertilizer-responsive, photoperiod-insensitive, disease-resistant, and short-strawed'. Its breakthrough came in 1966 with the release of IR8, a high-yield strain of rice that exceeded expectations; early trials showed it could increase yields by a factor of ten. This surge in food production offset the famine warnings of the neo-Malthusians (IR8 was released two years before Ehrlich's *The Population Bomb* was published), but it also contributed to rapid population growth.[103]

The Cold War impetus for development is probably most clearly expressed in Walt Rostow's 1960 book *The Stages of Economic Growth: A Non-Communist Manifesto*.[104] Rostow saw the Soviet Union as being an aggressor nation intent on world domination and imposing communism on the world. This scenario could only be avoided if the non-Communist world demonstrated three things: military deterrence, the possibility that underdeveloped countries could enter sustained take-off under democracy, and that there was an alternative to communism for Russia itself.[105] Thus, in the wider Cold War context, the relative economic performance of the United States vis-à-vis the USSR mattered. A lot of credence was given to the growth of the USSR, which appeared to have caught up with the United States 'in major fields of technology' by the 1950s, especially with the launch of the first Sputnik satellite in 1957. The US economy was growing at a respectable 3.2 per cent in the 1950s, but this paled in comparison with the record growth seen in Japan and Germany (although in the case of the latter they were simply recovering from the wartime destruction).

The competition between economic ideas meant greater pressure to understand the drivers of growth and to ensure that countries succeeded least they be tempted to trial an alternative economic system, giving greater context to the neoclassical growth models that were discussed in Chapter 3. Controversially, the US CIA continuously overestimated the size of the Soviet economy and it is often alleged that some of this overestimation may have been to frighten authorities (and the American people), as well as to secure additional resources for the CIA itself.[106] The United States had also opened up and had greater trade (export and imports) with countries throughout the world, beginning to run a balance of trade deficit from the start of the 1970s. The United States required thriving capitalist countries for international trade and a growing communist world was not in the material or strategic interests of the United States.[107]

The Cold War also provided impetus for a revolution in the US approach to scientific funding. The Manhattan Project and other wartime endeavours had demonstrated the immense benefits of applied science. The framework for the US approach to science was outlined in 1945 by Vannevar Bush (1890–1974), who was the director of the Office of Scientific Research and Development during the Second World War. In *Science – The Endless Frontier*, Bush outlined a vision for US economic growth based on technological progress:

> It is equally clear that public health, higher standards of living, conservation of national resources, new jobs and investment opportunities- in short, the prosperity, well-being and progress of the American Nation - all require the continued flow of new scientific knowledge. Even if a nation's manpower declines in relative numbers, even if its geographical frontiers become fixed, there always remains one inexhaustible national resource - creative scientific research.[108]

Bush saw science policy as essential for public health, national security and economic growth by 'increasing scientific capital'. The proposals from *Science – The Endless Frontier* established the federal funding mechanisms to support academic research. In the early years of the Cold War, US science policy was orientated towards 'defense and defense needs, like the space program'. This focus was intensified by Cold War developments, particularly the USSR's launch of Sputnik I, and scientific research was seen as a way to win the Cold War. US universities became the main focus for scientific research spending and came to be seen as engines of growth with the rise of patents arising from basic scientific research.[109] Scientific research was also implicitly seen as a way to overcome Malthusian constraints on resources and population (e.g., the research on food production).

The Environmental Revolution

Greater environmental awareness emerged in the post-Second World War era, culminating in the first Earth Day on 22 April 1970.[110] The rise of the environmental movement of the 1960s in the United States is often viewed as part of a wider cultural revolution, alongside antiwar protests, the civil rights movement, and the feminist movement. The conventional narrative about the origins of (Western) environmentalism emphasizes the influential role of Rachel Carson's (1907–64) book *Silent Spring*, published in 1962, which highlighted the impact of pesticides entering the food chain.[111] Carson's biographer described her work as one of the rare books that 'changed the course of history', placing *Silent Spring* alongside *The Wealth of Nations*, *Das Kapital* and *On the Origin of Species*.[112]

The fact that environmental awareness did not emerge until the 1960s suprised some historians since environmental problems and pollution associated with economic growth were generally well and long-standing concerns regarding the ecological impact of overpopulation dated from the interwar period.[113] This delayed environmental consciousness can be explained in part by the preoccupation, within the political left, with material issues and the fight for greater social equality, as well as the distractions that the Cold War created in terms of regional conflict and a focus on defence matters.[114]

The early environmental movement, inspired by neo-Malthusian ideas, was largely elite-driven and conservative in orientation. The shift of environmentalism from the political right to the left was catalyzed, in part, by the work of William Vogt.[115] The significance of Vogt to the nascent environmental movement was twofold. First, he changed the interpretation of the role of humans from being a group affected by the environment to having a direct effect on the environment itself. Secondly, Vogt revised the idea of 'carrying capacity' and saw it as a relationship between humanity and the environment. Vogt defined it as the, 'ability to provide food, drink, and shelter to the creatures that live on it'. The carrying capacity was a simple 'bio-equation', which was the ratio between the biological potential of the land ('the ability of the land to produce plants for shelter, for clothing, and especially for food') and the environmental limits of production. As greater pressure was placed on the land by human beings, so too were they placed on the carrying capacity. The idea of carrying capacity became a key part of modern ecology and remains at the core of the Planetary Boundaries framework (discussed in Chapter 1 and 9). Some of Vogt's concerns could arguably have been anticipated at the end of the Second World War, given both the over-intensive use of land and the allocation of chemicals to bomb manufacturing rather than fertiliser production.[116]

Another important precursor to Carson was John Kenneth Galbraith's *The Affluent Society*, which is now seen as an important part of the emergence of environmentalism.[117] Galbraith was critical of economic growth as a policy goal and he argued that the newfound affluence was not being used to its full capacity as many public needs were left unmet.[118] The best-selling book contained an evocative passage relating to the environment (and the passage continued to be included in various revisions of the work):

> The family which takes its mauve and cerise, air-conditioned, power-steered and power-braked automobile out for a tour passes through cities that are badly paved, made hideous by litter, blighted buildings, billboards and posts for wires that should long since have been put underground. They pass on into a countryside that has been rendered largely invisible by commercial art. (The goods which the latter advertise have an absolute priority in our value system. Such aesthetic considerations as a view of the countryside accordingly come second. On such matters we are consistent.) They picnic on exquisitely packaged food from a portable icebox by a polluted stream and go on to spend the night at a park which is a menace to public health and morals. Just before dozing off on an air mattress, beneath a nylon tent, amid the stench of decaying refuse, they may reflect vaguely on the curious unevenness of their blessings. Is this, indeed, the American genius?[119]

On the occasion of the fiftieth anniversary of *The Affluent Society*, Galbraith reflected on this widely quoted passage and wondered whether his work had contributed to the environmental movement. He felt that a 'larger concern for the environment, if still too weak, has become evident since the original edition'.[120]

Modern environmentalism was also the result of greater awareness of the pollution associated with economic activity (as well as concerns over population growth). One of the most infamous pollution episodes in the post-Second World War era was the Great Smog of London in 1952 that killed an estimated 8,000 Londoners (the event is discussed in more detail in Chapter 8). The response in the UK was to introduce environmental protection and a shift away from high-sulphur sources of domestic heating that led to a dramatic improvement in air quality. Elsewhere, industrial activity was linked with other adverse environmental and health effects. One of the most extreme cases was the discovery of a new disease in Minamata Bay, Japan, in 1956 (Minamata Disease), caused by mercury poisoning resulting from effluent from a new industrial plant.

Decolonization and Cold War politics were also important as a backdrop to the emergence of a global environmental movement. International organizations and Nongovernmental Organizations (NGOs) focused on conservation issues in the immediate post-Second World War period. The biologist Julian Huxley (eldest brother of Aldous Huxley, the author of *Brave New World* (1932)) became the founding director of the United Nations Educational, Scientific and Cultural Organization (UNESCO) in 1946. Huxley, who had co-authored the ecology text *The Science of Life*, had lobbied for the inclusion of the 'S' (Science) in the title of UNESCO. Although Huxley was an influential conservationist, his views as a eugenicist (a life fellow of the Eugenics Society from 1925 and its president from 1959 to 1962) were also a key influence.[121] Huxley espoused views on overpopulation as part of his vision for UNESCO, albeit not in explicitly eugenicist terms, and was successful in getting population control seen as a legitimate part of international aid.[122] However, he found it difficult to get UNESCO to fund conservation efforts which led him to look to alternative means to forward these efforts. Huxley was influential in the establishment of NGOs to advance preservationist and conservationist goals. These early environmental NGOs were founded in the wake of decolonization with a view to the preservation and conservation of nature in former colonies. The International Union for Conservation of Nature (IUCN), founded in 1948, and the World Wildlife Fund (WWF), founded in 1961, were both global in outlook but, as the historian Stephen Macekura illustrated, in practice their focus was predominantly on Africa.[123]

In this broader environmental context, Rachel Carson's revelation that the pesticide Dichlorodiphenyltrichloroethane (DDT) had entered the wider food chain sparked widespread public outrage.[124] DDT, first synthesized in 1874, was repurposed as an inorganic pesticide in 1939. The perceived success of DDT as a pesticide, effective against malaria-spreading mosquitos, led to the award of a Nobel Prize in medicine to the Swiss chemist Paul Hermann Müller (1899–1965) in 1948. Thanks to Carson it is is now known that DDT has more harmful effects and can enter the wider food chain and led to an asterisk for this particular Nobel Prize.[125] In the same year that Hermann was awarded the Nobel Prize, William Vogt, anticipating Carson, raised the alarm about the dangers of DDT in *Road to Survival*:

> Many insects, such as those which pollinate fruit trees and parasitize destructive insects, are extremely valuable to man, which is one reason why biologists throughout the world are alarmed by the widespread and unselective use of DDT.[126]

It was Carson's work, however, that led to an almost universal ban on DDT, in spite of attempts by vested interests to debunk her work. Carson's influence stemmed from her identification of a grave environmental problem and her articulation of its connection to the evolving power relationship between humanity and the natural world. She observed that humanity alone had acquired the capacity to alter nature and contended that, since the 1930s, 'the most alarming of all man's assaults upon the environment is the contamination of air, earth, rivers, and sea with dangerous and even lethal materials', which is largely irreversible in both the body and in nature.[127] It was to the pesticide DDT that *Time Magazine* applied the analogy of the domino theory, previously evoked during the Cold War as part of the Truman Doctrine, because the effects of DDT rippled through the entire ecosystem.[128]

Carson was followed by a steady stream of influential intellectual contributions of early environmentalism.[129] A key theme that emerged was limits to economic growth, in effect echoing earlier Malthusian arguments of absolute resource scarcity. One of the most famous contributions was Hardin's study of 'common pool resources' and the suggestion that limits to growth were imposed by difficulties restricting access to these resources.[130] The economist Nicholas Georgescu-Roegen (1906–94) also saw limits to future growth caused by the entropy law of thermodynamics, that governed how economic processes transformed low entropy resources into high entropy goods and wastes.[131] The Ehrlichs also saw physical boundaries to the planet as clear evidence of limits to growth and placed emphasis on the laws of thermodynamics as a scientific basis for the limits.[132] They concluded that 'we are living beyond our means, "spending our capital", depleting what are essentially non-renewable resources'.[133]

With the expansion of environmental writing, ideas of the early ecological movement became mainstream in public discourse, including within economics.[134] Kenneth Boulding[135] used a spaceship metaphor to argue that economic thinking needed to acknowledge the finite nature of natural resources. [136] Boulding suggested that past economic activity had considered resources as though they were unlimited. In Boulding's view, a change in mindset was required, one which would prioritize (natural) stock maintenance and technological change which would place less demands on this stock: 'that is, less production and consumption.'[137] He suggested that the planetary impact of human activity had to be viewed from a systems perspective and that the Earth system was running at a deficit by using up energy that had been stored in the past.[138] Boulding hypothesized that the Earth as a system suffered from an imbalance, created primarily by those societies and industries that actively and aggressively depleted the existing stock of non-renewable fossil fuels. He proposed to focus on renewable energies and a reduction of consumption of non-renewables through recycling and related activities. This was to become a blueprint for a sustainable future in which consumption was measured and assessed in terms of its long-term global impact.

Criticism of unbridled economic growth emerged from the 1960s onwards. The excessive focus on economic growth was described as 'growthmanship' by the economist Colin Clark (1905–89) or 'growthmania' by the economist Herman Daly (1938–2022).[139] Clark described growthmanship as the excessive focus on economic growth as a policy objective, such as the UN development decades, and the obsession with comparing countries based on growth rates alone. He was also critical of simple proposals that equated increases in investment with economic growth.[140] Daly, the founder of the ecological economics school of thought, was somewhat more optimistic in his work than his supervisor, Georgescu-Roegen.[141] Daly's concept of 'steady-state' economics expanded on Boulding's theme of stock control by proposing that modern economies could continue to advance in qualitative terms instead of increasing outputs in quantitative terms.[142] For Daly, the issue related to the obsessive focus on GNP (Gross National Product) growth which was a flow, but this had neglected negative externalities associated with GNP growth and thus overlooked the implications of growth in GNP for capital (i.e., the stock).

Others questioned the desirability of economic growth as a policy objective given the associated environmental costs. The economist Ezra Mishan (1917–2014) questioned whether, after accounting for disamenities such as pollution, economic growth actually meant an improvement in well-being. Mishan was particularly critical of how economic growth was measured and that GNP was 'treated with [an] unabashed reverence', so much so that 'apparently one has but to consult it to comprehend the entire condition of society'.[143] Writing in 1971, Mishan argued that there were limits to economic growth and he referred to GNP as a measure of 'gross national pollution'. He argued that a more appropriate index of economic welfare would subtract the various disamenities from GNP and that 'when GNP is trimmed down to size in this way, it is surprising how unimpressive the progress over the past half century looks'.[144] A counter-argument of economists was that the issue was not economic growth *per se* but the pricing system, that pollution was the result of the lack of a price for externalities and thereby a misallocation of resources.[145] In any case, this led to calls to change how economic activity was measured.

Limits to Growth

One major influence on modern environmentalism was the Club of Rome's *The Limits to Growth (LTG)*, published in March 1972, with a follow-up study responding to various critiques published in 1974.[146] The significance of *LTG* can not be overstated. The report's legacy continues to this day and is a key influence on the Planetary Boundaries approach to measuring existential risk and continues to be cited within academic scholarship.

LTG utilized the system dynamics framework developed by MIT management professor Jay Forrester (1918–2016). The model (*World2*) was outlined in his 1971 book *World Dynamics*. *LTG* was the result of an MIT-based project which updated and applied a version of Forrester's model (*World3*) to the global economy. The intellectual underpinnings of *World Dynamics* were Malthusian, as Forrester outlined:

> Ever since Malthus stated his propositions relating population and food some 150 years ago, the validity of his assumption that food imposes an ultimate limit on population has been debated. The continued growth of population and the rise in the productivity of agriculture are often cited to refute Malthus. But it is undeniable that Malthus stated one ultimate barrier to unending population expansion. His assertion is not erroneous; it is merely incomplete.[147]

The incompletion, as far as Forrester was concerned, was that Malthus had not specified other constraints on population growth.[148] The *World3* model was based on a series of equations that linked population, capital investment, natural resources, pollution, and food production. Effectively it is an attempt to model the interrelation between each component.[149] The starting point was that growth in each of the variables had been exponential up to that point and that exponential growth could not be expected to continue. Forrester sought to determine what would bring the fall in growth and what would be the 'barriers when growth goes too far'.[150] Forrester's model effectively predicted a collapse in world population in the early twenty-first century.

The work of the *LTG* was undertaken by an interdisciplinary research team but with a core expertise in system dynamics. The report was provocative with a central message identifying an 'overshoot and collapse' of the global economy. *LTG* was a non-technical summary of a computer model of the global economy designed at MIT. The report focused on an assumed exponential growth in population, industrialization, and pollution and its impact on food production, and consequential resource depletion more generally. In conclusion, it warned of a collapse of the global economic system within 100 years (see Figure 4.2). *LTG* concluded that:

1. If the present growth trends in world population, industrialization, pollution, food production, and resource depletion continue unchanged, the limits to growth on this planet will be reached sometime within the next one hundred years. The most probable result will be a rather sudden and uncontrollable decline in both population and industrial capacity.
2. It is possible to alter these growth trends and to establish a condition of ecological and economic stability that is sustainable far into the future. The state of global equilibrium could be designed so

that the basic material needs of each person on earth are satisfied and each person has an equal opportunity to realize his individual human potential.

3. If the world's people decide to strive for this second outcome rather than the first, the sooner they begin working to attain it, the greater will be their chances of success.[151]

A central focus of *LTG* was on the depletion of non-renewable resources (such as aluminium, chromium, coal, cobalt, iron, lead, manganese, and mercury), which would precipitate this global collapse. In one scenario, available global resources were assumed to double but even this did not prevent a collapse (see Figure 4.2). The report was so widely read that a contemporary cover of *Newsweek* ran with the headline 'Running out of everything' next to a picture of Uncle Sam looking into an empty cornucopia.[152] The report also coincided with the oil crisis of October 1973 to March 1974, which saw oil prices quadruple (see Figure 4.3). This seemed to support the gloomy prediction that humanity was running out of resources.

In the atomic age, *LTG* was not a niche exercise, but the hugely influential computer model helped to mainstream views of how the world was analyzed and presented to the public. An early example of concern

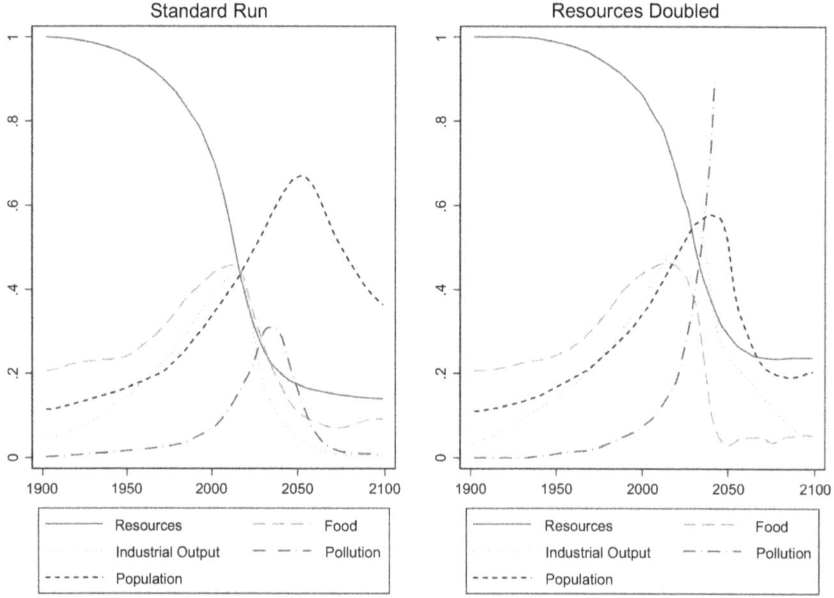

FIGURE 4.2 *World model standard run. Note: Resources doubled was a scenario whereby the modellers assumed 'new discoveries or advances in technology can double the amount of resources economically available'. Meadows et al. (1972), Limits to Growth, p. 126.*

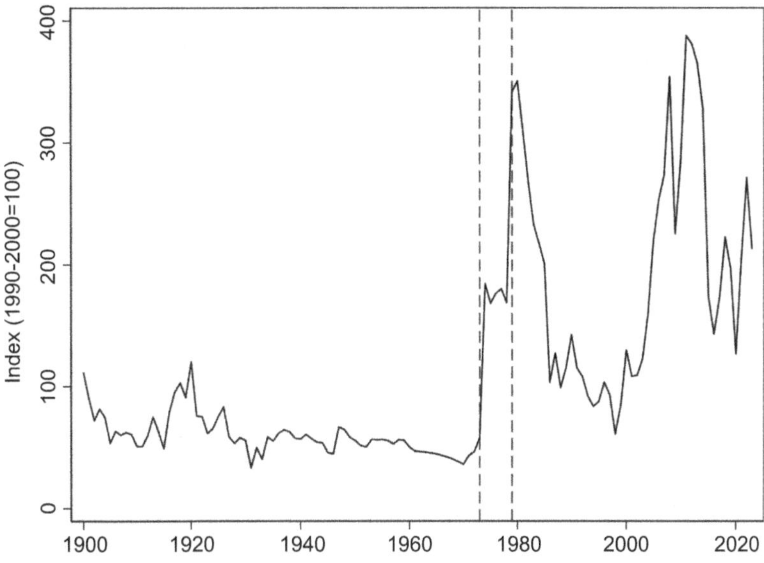

FIGURE 4.3 *Index of crude oil prices in 2000 dollars (1990–2000 = 100). Source: BP Statistical Review of World Energy 2021 & Statistical Review of World Energy 2024.*

over the destructive power of nuclear weapons can be seen in *The Bulletin of the Atomic Scientists*' Doomsday Clock which launched in 1947 (see Figure 4.4). Luminaries of twentieth-century physics helped to establish the *Bulletin*.[153] The *Bulletin* was a periodical intended to be a 'discussion forum for urgent issues at the intersection of science, technology, and society'.[154] The *Bulletin* continued to use an endorsement from the Nobel laureate Albert Einstein (1879–1955) in its masthead, that stated that the *Bulletin* 'has become widely recognized, in America and abroad, both as the best and most complete source of authoritative information on the social aspects of atomic energy, and as a forum for the discussion of the relevant problems, open to all points of view, held in this field by American and foreign, natural and social scientists'.[155]

In the aftermath of the Second World War, the monthly *Bulletin of the Atomic Scientists* became a focal point for those 'concerned about science and public policy'. It was intended to be internationalist and to create a 'social order of knowledge production' initially established as a vehicle to advocate for reducing the risk of nuclear war.[156] In the early 1970s, the *Bulletin* broadened its editorial remit to include 'environment, energy sources, problems of the less developed world, population, and foreign policy'.[157] Climate change became a major theme from the 1990s, although it had first received coverage in 1978.[158] It is evident that the *Bulletin* is an articulation of the concerns of a broad scientific community that recognized a broad

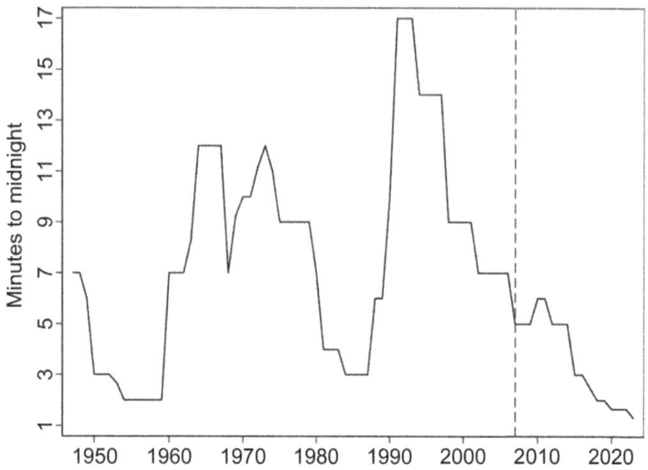

FIGURE 4.4 *Doomsday clock, 1947–2023. Note: Climate change was incorporated in the Doomsday clock in 2007. Source: Bulletin of the Atomic Scientists.*

array of global risks. For example, the climatologist Derek Winstanley, in his 1981 review of the meteorologist Harold W. Bernard's *Greenhouse Effect*, concluded that the 'greenhouse effect poses a high risk for mankind' but that there was too much uncertainty for immediate action to be taken given the swings in scientific opinion.[159]

The broadening of topics covered in the *Bulletin* highlights how the scientific community was perceiving the changing landscape of risk, often employing interdisciplinary considerations. One example was the physicist David Rittenhouse Inglis (1905–95), a contributor to the development of the A-bomb at Las Almos, who argued that Malthusian dynamics (*à la* Hardin and Ehrlich) could only be escaped through the intensive use of nuclear energy.[160] The chemical engineer Noel De Nevers (1932–2019) outlined the case for technological solutions to population growth in response to neo-Malthusian arguments such as Hardin's projections, while others argued that there were no technological solutions to population pressures.[161] The molecular biologist John W. Gofman (1918–2007) drew inspiration from the work of Carson when outlining an 'environmental crisis' resulting from adverse side effects of technological innovation.[162] Similar counter techno-optimistic views were presented by the *Bulletin*, such as the article by the physicist Gerald Feinberg (1933–92), that highlighted the potentially threatening effects of some emerging innovations (such as genetic engineering).[163]

The *LTG* was a bridge between different catastrophic fears because it linked scenarios of gradual resource depletion to catastrophism.[164] If neo-

Malthusians feared that overpopulation was the cause of war, this would have grave implications in the age of atomic weaponry. The *Bulletin* gave wide discussion of *LTG*, in part because of the widespread attention it had received, whereby, 'the business world seem[ed] to give an authority to this work that other dire and oracular statements have failed to capture'.[165] Writing in the *Bulletin*, Garrett Hardin was sympathetic to the message of the *LTG* and its computer-model-derived output. But he was not surprised because it confirmed his worldviews, noting that, 'we do not really need a computer to reach [the conclusion]'.[166] The *Bulletin* also published more critical readings of the *LTG* such as the physical chemist R. Stephen Berry (1931–2020) who highlighted contemporary criticism of Forrester's *World3* model and showed how changing the parameters of the model could upend the findings, foreshadowing later critiques.[167] While Berry was somewhat critical of *LTG* and its methods, this was sympathetic criticism.[168] There was also a noteworthy interview with the economist (and Nobel laureate) Gunnar Myrdal (1898–1987) that sought his opinion on a wide range of issues from the US civil rights movement, the Vietnam War, and *Limits to Growth*. For Myrdal, it was clear that the world needed to 'prepare for the fact that there are limits to growth' and he saw population growth as a central factor in the 'environmental problem'.[169] Only towards the end of this interview were any allusions to nuclear war made. Equally noteworthy is the comment by the soviet geophysicist Yevgeny Fedorov (1910–81) who deviated from the views of *LTG* by arguing, in line with Carson, that it was not scarcity of resources but the limited absorptive capacity of the planet to cope with increased pollution that was the main risk to humanity.[170]

Contemporary Responses to *The Limits to Growth*

While the modern legacy of *LTG* has been an uncritical acceptance of the warnings, contemporaries were less convinced. Writing soon after *LTG* was published, Carl Kaysen (1920–2010), the former director of US National Security and then director of the Institute of Advanced Studies at Princeton, accused *LTG* of 'crying wolf'. Kaysen highlighted the various flaws with the model, the overlooking of technological progress, the treatment of population growth, and a lack of an adjustment mechanism. But he also praised the report for drawing attention to some real problems such as population growth, pollution, and the unintended side effects of technology. For Kaysen, the report did not draw enough attention to more pressing international threats: nuclear war and the inequality in the international distribution of wealth. Therefore, Kaysen concluded that 'a good sentry does not cry up tomorrow's wolves and ignore today's tigers'.[171]

One of the most stinging rebuttals of the entire approach of *LTG* came from the Science Policy Research Unit at the University of Sussex. This was an interdisciplinary research team that looked at various components of the *LTG*. The resulting report, *Thinking about the Future*, was published in the United Kingdom in 1973 and also appeared in the United States with the punchier title *Models of Doom*; the US edition also included a reply from the Meadows *et al.* team.[172] Some of the main criticisms related to the data, or rather the lack of data. Many of the model parameters were inferred based on guesswork. The old aphorism 'garbage in, garbage out' was quite applicable in the case of the *LTG*; given the Malthusian preferences of the team, it is perhaps best described as 'Malthus in, Malthus out'.

The mathematical physicist Sam Cole critically evaluated the structure of the *World2* and *World3* models. The main distinction between the models was that there were three times as many equations in *World3* but that the quality of data underpinning these equations had not improved. In *World2*, Forrester had only used 2 data points; as Cole explained, 'the only real data which appear to have been used in Forrester's model are the world population figures for 1900 and 1970. For the most part the model is based on his vision of how the real world operates'.[173] In *World3* there were numerous assumptions used, such as inferring time series data (data measured over time) from cross-sections (data measured at one point in time across countries).

When it came to sensitivity analysis, Cole and the mathematician Robert Curnow found that the model was highly sensitive to the parameters chosen and that the model specifications were the ones that showed collapse; the assumptions drove the results.[174] There was nothing in the model to prevent collapse, there were no adaptive feedback processes embedded. The model made pessimistic assumptions. If the model was run backwards then 'Forrester's guesswork' led to unrealistic predictions about the past. If the model started in 1850 instead of 1900, then the model would show a collapse in 1970. Clearly, the world had not collapsed in 1970, and this would invalidate the internal consistency of the model and its results. The model also led to inconsistent results if there was a split between developing and developed countries. More importantly, and unsurprisingly, if Adam Smith, rather than Robert Malthus, was the inspiration for the model, it would have led to different conclusions about the limits to growth.

Subsequent analysis by Cole and Curnow, published in *Nature*, reaffirmed that the *World2* and *World3* models were highly sensitive if run backwards and led to some unrealistic conclusions. The main implication was that the parameters of the model were unstable and that this was driven by the assumptions.[175] These criticisms of the model are reflective of wider criticisms, such as other critiques published in the journal *Nature*, that also highlighted the sensitivity of the models to the assumptions and that it was 'too early for policy conclusions' based on the *World2* and *World3* models.[176]

LTG did not go unnoticed within the world of economics, especially among those who had studied economic growth. Jay Forrester, an MIT professor in the Sloan School of Management, saw economists as the biggest critics of both his *World Dynamics* and the *LTG*.[177] Given that the *LTG* was essentially an MIT-affiliated study and also that the leading authorities on economic growth were either based at MIT (Solow) or had studied there (Nordhaus and Weitzman), it effectively became an MIT internal dispute; or more accurately, an internal dispute of MIT's Sloan School of Management. Robert Solow later recalled, 'I thought that its message was mostly hot air. I have not changed my mind about them', although he later felt that the situation may have changed given the resource-intensive economic growth experienced by India and China.[178]

The opening line of Solow's initial views on the *LTG* was that his MIT colleague was 'either the Christopher Columbus or the Dr. Strangelove of this business'.[179] Solow quoted an interview that Forrester had given where he had defined the composition of his 'problem-solving group': they were to be made up of successful professors but should purposefully exclude social scientists because they 'always want to get to the bottom of a particular problem. What we want to look at are the problems caused by interactions'.[180] Given this disdain for social sciences, it is then perhaps unsurprising that *World Dynamics*, effectively a book on economic growth, contains only thirteen references and none of which are to any work by economists, but instead were primarily self-citations of Forrester's own work.[181] It is somewhat curious though, given the renowned expertise in MIT at the time, that Forrester would not consult his colleagues in the economics department or even use his work to chastise their efforts. In fact, the capital-output ratios implicit in the *World2* and *World3* models appear to be more of the Harrod-Domar type of economic growth model rather than the neoclassical model that Solow had inspired (see the discussion in Chapter 3). Perhaps greater cross-campus dialogue could have helped inform the *World2* and *World3* models. The main argument that Solow presented in his 1973 article was that the assumptions Forrester made drove his results; change the assumptions and the conclusions would change too. For example, Solow highlighted the assumption that population growth was positively correlated with income, something that went against the lived experiences of countries undergoing demographic transition. The model was seen as parameterized to show collapse.

Economists continued to engage with the various iterations of the *LTG*. One of the most vocal critics was William Nordhaus, who highlighted how the underlying *LTG* model overlooked existing economic theory, invented concepts *de nouveau* and set model parameters so that it only showed collapse. An initial critique by Nordhaus published in the *Economic Journal* in 1973 argued that changing some key assumptions in Forrester's *World Dynamics* model changed the outcome dramatically;[182] Nordhaus similarly dismissed updates to the *LTG* as 'Lethal Model 2'.[183]

Countering some of the claims was evidently still on Solow's mind when he gave an address to the American Economic Association in December 1973, acknowledging that he, 'like everyone else, [had] been suckered into reading the *Limits to Growth*'.[184] This led to a series of studies that incorporated exhaustible (non-renewable) resources more explicitly in models of economic growth.[185] It also led to the foundations of the economic approach to sustainable development and Inclusive Wealth. These focused on achieving intergenerational equity via the re-investment of rents from exhaustible resources into reproducible capital (such as buildings, machines and tools), discussed in Chapter 6.[186]

In the various critiques of the *LTG*, the focus predominantly was on non-exhaustible resources, the aspect most frequently emphasized in the study. Nordhaus was sanguine about the pollution element of the *LTG* model, stressing that growth need not result in increases in pollution (in terms of toxic gases) and placed emphasis on the global warming/climate change prognosis of the *LTG*, noting how, 'the cost of greenhouse warming in the middle of the next century (or of policies to slow greenhouse warming) would be in the range of 0 to 2 percent of world income'.[187] Similarly, Martin Weitzman focused exclusively on the exhaustible resource constraint set by the standard model of the *LTG*. Using data from the first iteration of the World Bank research programme on Inclusive Wealth (see discussion in Chapter 6 on the origins of this programme), Martin Weitzman assessed the likelihood that the world was running out of resources. He came to the optimistic conclusion that resource scarcity was not binding given that technological change was, 'maybe 40 times larger than the required adjustment for depletion of exhaustible resources'.[188]

This narrative that economists had won the debate with *LTG* also overlooks a contemporary response to Nordhaus from Forrester and colleagues.[189] In their response, they argued it was Nordhaus who was wrong, and it was he who had misinterpreted the model. For Forrester *et al.*, the systems model should be analyzed as a whole and not broken into subcomponents, as was done by Nordhaus, because this was how the system interacts and it is the interactions that drive the results. While Nordhaus had portrayed Forrester as a neo-Malthusian peddling a disproven theory, Forrester embraced this identity and instead accused Nordhaus of misunderstanding Malthus. A view, it appears, that many ecologists of the time would relate to.

What these critiques and responses to the *LTG* overlooked, however, was one key aspect in the second scenario that emphasized pollution as a constraint on growth, primarily CO_2 emissions. The *LTG* predicated that if CO_2 emissions continued to grow at 0.2 per cent per annum and if fossil fuel consumption continued unabated, then atmospheric CO_2 concentration would reach 380 parts per million (ppm) by 2000; remarkably the recorded figure in 2000 was not far off this, reaching 370 ppm (as shown in Figure 4.5).[190] This rise in CO_2 concentrations was

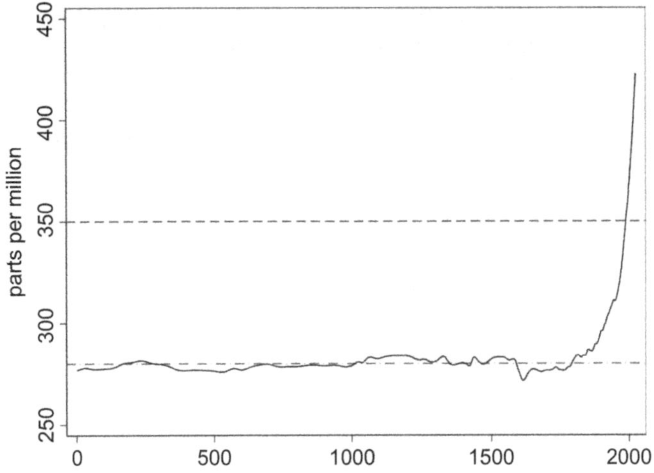

FIGURE 4.5 *Atmospheric Concentrations of CO_2 (parts per million), 0–2023. Note: Horizontal dashed line at 280 ppm indicate the pre-industrial average atmospheric CO_2 concentration. Horizontal dashed line at 350 ppm indicates the safe level of CO_2 in the atmosphere (crossed in 1989). Sources: C. MacFarling Meure et al. (2006). Law Dome CO_2, CH_4 and N_2O ice core records extended to 2000 years BP.* Geophysical Research Letters, *33; Met Office Climate Dashboard https://climate.metoffice.cloud/greenhouse_gases.html#datasets.*

not a foregone conclusion as the *LTG* noted, 'if man's energy needs are someday supplied by nuclear power instead of fossil fuels'. However, the *LTG* warned of global warming 'by the laws of thermodynamics' and that 'thermal pollution may have serious climate effects, worldwide, when it reaches some appreciable fraction of the energy normally absorbed by the Earth from the sun'.[191] Thus, the underlying theory of the economics of sustainable development (presented in Chapter 6) that was directly influenced by the *LTG* is inherently biased towards a focus on exhaustible resource constraints with less emphasis on the climatic change aspects of *LTG*. Boulding, in his 'Spaceship Earth' essay, was more prescient, noting that, 'it seems to be in pollution rather than in exhaustion that the problem is first becoming salient'.[192]

Perhaps the last word should go to Walt Rostow, formerly of the MIT parish although in pariah status at the time that *LTG* was published.[193] Rostow praised the *LTG* for 'the virtue of posing and dramatizing effectively a real set of problems,' and he also welcomed the broad, holistic methodology rather than a narrow, siloed approach. That being said, he outlined five structural problems that ultimately undermined the model: the global nature of the model overlooked regional and interregional dynamics; the model was weakly grounded in facts; its rudimentary treatment of technology and resource constraints; the absence of any price mechanism; and a naïve policy prescription that was unviable.[194]

Ultimately, the provocations of the *LTG* forced economists to think about resource scarcity and environmental preservation. This can be seen in the later work of Solow, where he explicitly addresses the topic of sustainable development.

Conclusion

In the post-Second World War period, the idea of development evolved into a more holistic concept from its original inception as synonymous with economic growth. As the great development economist Arthur Lewis articulated, development meant, 'that it gives man greater control over his environment and thereby increases his freedom'. This freedom was not just about choice, but it also banished the spectre of Malthusian checks (freedom from famine, plague and pestilence).[195] The increasing development of the world coincided with greater environmental awareness in the West and demands for environmental protection. These two opposing concepts converged in June 1972 at the Stockholm Conference on the Human Environment,[196] as articulated in the conference declaration:

> A point has been reached in history when we must shape our actions throughout the world with a more prudent care for their environmental consequences. Through ignorance or indifference we can do massive and irreversible harm to the earthly environment on which our life and well being depend. Conversely, through fuller knowledge and wiser action, we can achieve for ourselves and our posterity a better life in an environment more in keeping with human needs and hopes. There are broad vistas for the enhancement of environmental quality and the creation of a good life. What is needed is an enthusiastic but calm state of mind and intense but orderly work. For the purpose of attaining freedom in the world of nature, man must use knowledge to build, in collaboration with nature, a better environment. To defend and improve the human environment for present and future generations has become an imperative goal for mankind - a goal to be pursued together with, and in harmony with, the established and fundamental goals of peace and of worldwide economic and social development.[197]

The conference led to the establishment of UNEP, the first UN agency to be housed in a developing country (headquartered in Nairobi, Kenya). Ultimately it paved the way for the concept of 'Sustainable Development', which became popularized in the 1980s.[198] The concept was elaborated in the 1980 World Conservation Strategy, which was prepared by IUCN with financial support from UNEP and the WWF.

Although the 1972 Stockholm conference is seen as the fusion of the opposing concepts, some issues relating to development were unresolved. One of the biggest challenges lies with the experiences of decolonization in Africa. By 2000, 45 per cent of countries in Sub-Saharan Africa were poorer than they were at independence.[199] An early study by development economists William Easterly and Ross Levine attributed 'Africa's growth tragedy' to its ethnic fragmentation.[200] This division was due in large part to how borders were derived during the colonization period. Recent research has stressed the persistence of institutional patterns introduced in the colonial period for explaining later developments.[201] Nobel laureates Daron Acemoglu, David Johnson, and James Robinson showed how institutional patterns set up during colonial times persisted and continued to affect economic development to this day, a finding echoed by other studies.[202] The slow development of former colonies due to institutional legacies is one of the arguments put forward by Acemoglu and Robinson in their book *Why Nations Fail*.[203]

An important backdrop to the discussion in this chapter was the influence of Malthusian thought, although here we must acknowledge that the idea of population pressure has a substantially longer lineage than Malthus and concern over population growth is a very old problem. One of the earliest surviving examples comes from the Carthaginian Christian philosopher Tertullian who, writing in the 200s, viewed the issues of overpopulation in what we now consider modern Malthusian terms:

> Surely it is obvious enough, if one looks at the whole world, that it is becoming daily better cultivated and more fully peopled than anciently. All places are now accessible, all are well known, all open to commerce; most pleasant farms have obliterated all traces of what were once dreary and dangerous wastes; cultivated fields have subdued forests; flocks and herds have expelled wild beasts; sandy deserts are sown; rocks are planted; marshes are drained; and where once were hardly solitary cottages, there are now large cities. No longer are (savage) islands dreaded, nor their rocky shores feared; everywhere are houses, and inhabitants, and settled government, and civilized life. What most frequently meets our view (and occasions complaint), is our teeming population: *our numbers are burdensome to the world*, which can hardly supply us from its natural elements; our wants grow more and more keen, and our complaints more bitter in all mouths, while Nature fails in affording us her usual sustenance. In very deed, *pestilence, and famine, and wars, and earthquakes* have to be regarded as a remedy for nations, as the means of pruning the luxuriance of the human race; and yet, when the hatchet has once felled large masses of men, the world has hitherto never once been alarmed

> at the sight of a restitution of its dead coming back to life after their millennial exile. (emphasis added)[204]

Population growth has been a longstanding concern over the past two centuries, traditionally focused on the risks posed by rising populations. In contrast, the more pressing challenge today is the opposite: declining fertility rates. The significant decline in fertility rates threatens the foundations of modern economic systems and the models of economic growth discussed in Chapter 3.[205] Yet such concerns about falling fertility are largely absent in much of the discussion in later chapters. This omission seems to reflect the continued dominance of more traditional, Malthusian fears about overpopulation, that have overshadowed emerging demographic realities.[206]

The *LTG*, with its periodic updates, continues to be a source of inspiration for modern environmentalists. It is acknowledged by the proponents of Planetary Boundaries that their approach, 'builds on and extends approaches based on limits-to-growth'.[207] *LTG* was also influenced by the environmental intellectual tradition that had preceded it and referred to some of the key texts outlined in this chapter, such as the Ehrlichs' work, to support claims that food pressures were already evident.[208] It also attempted to utilize work by Boulding and Daly as philosophical support for the idea of a 'nongrowing state for human society'.[209] This in turn has been influential for modern-day proponents of degrowth (a.k.a nongrowing), discussed in Chapter 9.

A recent assessment of *LTG* viewed system dynamics as discredited and flawed, both as a tool for advanced forecasting and for global risk assessment and management, largely because of the fact that many of the predictions of the *LTG* failed to materialize.[210] This assessment is not shared by the wider scientific community, however, as there continues to be an active system dynamics research network and there are periodic updates to the predictions of the *LTG*.[211] Forrester is still held in high esteem, as evident by a glowing biography that emphasized his contributions to the establishment of the *System Dynamics Review*.[212] Put simply, there is a disconnect between social science and system dynamics scholars. This is unsurprising given how Forrester held no truck for how social scientists approached topics, but this intellectual hubris can lead to siloed thinking and the development of groupthink; the same applies to social scientists who did not engage with system dynamics.

Both *LTG* and the oil crisis led to a series of studies by economists that explicitly incorporated natural resource use into their evaluations. The main point that I wish to stress is that the *LTG* research, for all its shortcomings, singles out perhaps the most crucial parameter: CO_2 concentrations in the atmosphere and their connection with the climate system, and critical limitations imposed on modern life (both production and consumption).

Ignoring this linkage leaves the competitor models, many of them economic, equally flawed, even if their assumptions are more realistic. This is a point I will return to in Chapters 5 and 6 when I discuss how economies are measured (the link between population growth, emissions, and atmospheric CO_2 is shown in Figure 4.6). The distinction between CO_2 emissions and the atmospheric concentration of CO_2 provides an important illustration of the difference between flows and stocks. CO_2 emissions (flows) have risen sharply from 1960 to 2023, however the atmospheric concentration (stock) has increased at a slower pace because of carbon sinks, such as forests and oceans, that have absorbed a large share of emissions (around 30 and 25 per cent of emissions respectively).[213] Underappreciating the role of these natural carbon sinks (our natural capital) risks placing much greater pressure on the planet.

A final point is that the Doomsday Clock, in the opinion of its scientific supporters, was intended to show how close humanity was to a man-made extinction event. It has teetered on the brink of midnight many times in its seventy-five-year history but has tended downward since the mid-2010s (ssee figure 4.4). At the turn of the millennium nuclear risk was still highest on the agenda of the *Bulletin*, but since 2007 climate

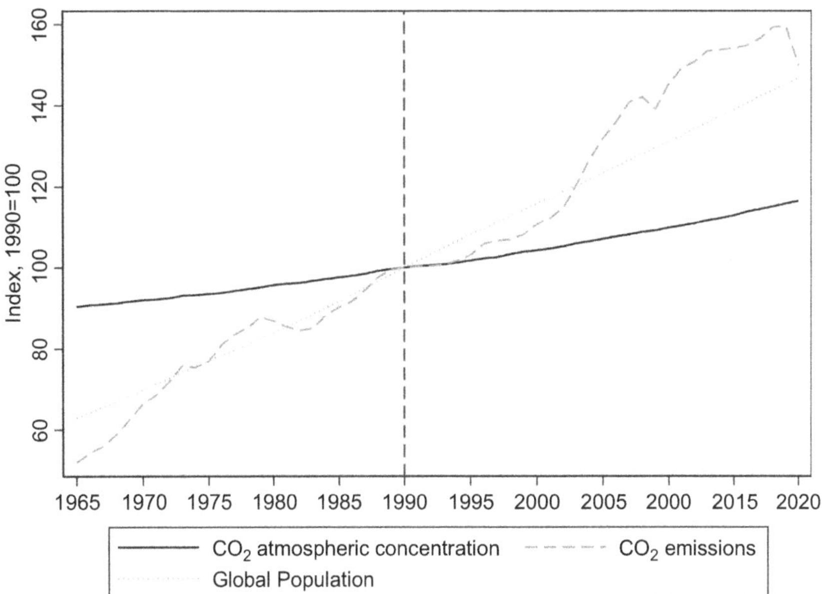

FIGURE 4.6 *Global CO_2 atmospheric concentration, CO_2 emissions and population, 1965–2020 (index 1990=100). Sources: See Figure 4.5, Figure 4.3, Figure 3.4.*

change was incorporated in the analysis, reflecting the wider concerns of society and calls for the elevation of 'Earth's natural science within the family of sciences'.[214] The Doomsday Clock is no longer dominated by any single risk; rather, a multitude of catastrophic risks are now under observation.

Part III

History of Measurement

CHAPTER FIVE

Measuring the Wealth of Nations

A History of National Income Accounting

To count is a modern practice, the ancient method was to guess; and when numbers are guessed, they are always magnified.

SAMUEL JOHNSON (1709–84), *A JOURNEY TO THE WESTERN ISLANDS OF SCOTLAND.*[1]

Macroeconomic statistics attempt to *quantify* the *qualitative* concepts developed by Adam Smith and his successors. They come under the broad umbrella of national accounts and measure various aspects of income and wealth (capital). Writing in the seventh edition of his *Economics* textbook, Paul Samuelson described national income as, 'one of the most important topics in all economics' and a 'yardstick of an economy's performance'.[2] Today Gross Domestic Product (GDP) is the most widely used measure of economic activity.[3]

A modern textbook definition of GDP is that it measures the market value of all final goods and services produced within a given period of time within a country.[4] People are most familiar with aggregate demand as the sum of consumption (C), investment (I), government purchases (G), and net exports (exports–imports). The usual caveats are that it measures output at market prices, it excludes intermediate goods so that value is only counted once, and it includes tangible goods and intangible services. The time parameter means it only includes goods and services currently produced, not past production, and it measures this within the confines of a nation state (although it is possible to scale up or down). Lastly, only legal activities are included within official figures, although there are various estimates to account for illicit and informal activity, which can be substantial.[5] National statistics offices estimate GDP using an agreed international template (the UN System of National Accounts), making for a consistent and comparable measure across time and space.

What is seldom mentioned in modern textbooks is that GDP is a twentieth-century construct and that its creation goes hand-in-hand with the emergence of macroeconomics as a distinct branch of economics. There were two major events that led to its creation: the Great Depression (1929-1939) and the Second World War (1939-1945).[6] Understanding what was happening to the economy during the Great Depression was an important driver in the development of national statistics. While wartime demands required government planners to know the state of munition and armament production, and this provided a key spur to the development of GDP (or rather GNP). The first official estimates of the national income of the United States, United Kingdom, and Germany all date to this period. The measurement is built on a foundation of Keynesian interpretations of the economy which, as we have seen in Chapter 3, were focused on short-run fluctuations.[7]

The Second World War, in particular, ushered in a 'revolution' in the generation and use of economic statistics in policymaking.[8] The creation and collation of economic statistics, particularly relating to official estimates of aggregate economic statistics, changed both how economics was practiced and how it was taught. Writing in 1986, Alec Cairncross (1911–98), a distinguished twentieth-century British economist and one of the first PhD students in economics at the University of Cambridge, recalled how economics had changed over his lifetime. The economics he was taught at the University of Glasgow in the 1920s was based on Alfred Marshall's *Principles of Economics*, which was primarily theoretical. But at Cambridge he witnessed the changes first hand, both theoretical in terms of new Keynesian-based theories, and also empirical with the greater use of econometrics (statistical analysis applied to economic data).[9]

National accounting as currently practiced may be a twentieth-century construct, but its roots are in the empiricism of seventeenth- and eighteenth-century political arithmetic. The economist and statistician Colin Clark was one of the innovators in comparative national accounts. Clark, whose estimates were used in the work of John Maynard Keynes, was very explicit in his admiration for William Petty (1623–87), one of the pioneers of 'political arithmetic' and who Clark thought had 'started [economics] on the right lines'. In Clark's view, Adam Smith (and other classical economists) had 'twisted [economics] out of shape' compared to the empirical focus taken by the political arithmeticians. This perspective comes in part from Smith's theoretical focus but perhaps also from a throwaway sentence in *The Wealth of Nations* that he had 'no great faith in political arithmetic'.

Clark sought to redress this balance and twentieth- and twenty-first-century macroeconomic views are more of the mould of political arithmeticians than of the wider Smithian views of the nature and causes of the wealth of nations.[10]

Despite his lack of faith in political arithmetic, Smith played no small part in the statistical revolution of the nineteenth century and in what the philosopher Ian Hacking describes as the 'avalanche of numbers' that formed the basis of twentieth-century national accounts.[11] Smith was a 'long standing' friend and correspondent of John Sinclair (1754–1835), who was the first person to use the term 'statistics' and 'statistical' in the English language.[12] Sinclair had come across the term 'statistic' in his travels in Germany where it meant, 'species of political inquiry . . . for the purpose of ascertaining the political strength of a country or questions respecting the matters of State'. Sinclair, however, applied a different meaning to the word statistic: 'an inquiry for the purpose of ascertaining the quantum of happiness enjoyed by its inhabitants, and the means of its future improvement'.[13] The German meaning of the word was closer in spirit to the political arithmetic that Smith reviled, while Sinclair's adaptation of the word appears to be closer to what the work of Smith, and also Clark, implied. Although it must be acknowledged, as Sinclair recounted, that Smith witnessed first-hand the value of statistical information from his role as a Customs official, and without this experience, 'he would not have otherwise known or believed how essential practical knowledge was, to the thorough understanding of political subjects'.[14]

Not only was Scotland at the forefront in conceptualizing the economy but it was also at the forefront of the *measurement* of the economy. John Sinclair's *Statistical Account of Scotland* was published in twenty-two volumes between 1791 and 1799. The work, published shortly after the death of Adam Smith, was a colossal undertaking which surveyed parishes throughout Scotland to gain insight into the social and economic conditions of the country. Sinclair's work can be seen as a culmination of Scottish Enlightenment principles.[15] Coincidentally, not only was the Scottish Enlightenment the home of statistics but also the home of the visual representation of data. One of the famous contributions to statistical visualization was the innovative use of graphs by the Scottish engineer and political economist William Playfair (1759–1823) in his *Commercial and Political Atlas*.[16] Playfair's innovative use of graphs arose from a lack of information on annual trade for Scotland, so instead he used bar charts to illustrate statistics at a single point in time.[17]

This chapter will outline the history of attempts to measure the economy. First the role of political arithmetic and the evolution of statistics in the nineteenth century will be highlighted followed by a discussion of the twentieth-century origins of national income accounting and attempts to measure the wealth of nations. Various challenges to national income accounting emerged in the twentieth century and the negative aspects of economic growth, such as poverty, inequality, and environmental degradation, are ignored in the calculation of GDP.[18] An alternative Inclusive Wealth-based metric will be discussed in Chapter 6 and challenges to the hegemony of GDP will be discussed in Chapter 9.

The Statistics Revolution

The twentieth-century development of macroeconomic statistics built on foundations dating from the late eighteenth and early nineteenth centuries. While there is a long lineage of the term 'statistic', with the etymology of the word relating to the 'knowledge of the state' traced back to German and Italian usage.[19] Within Germany there was a distinction between statists and 'table statistician', the former theorized about states while the latter accumulated information about states. The statists, known as cameralists, were an influential school of thought in Germany and in other European countries, such as Denmark; this was an alternative to the mercantilist approach predominant in Britain.[20] 'Table statisticians' were looked down upon and a German polemic, written in 1806, described it as 'brainless busy work . . . these stupid fellows disseminate the insane idea that one can understand the power of a state if one just knows its size, its population, its national income, and the number of dumb beasts grazing around'.[21]

The collection of statistics is a choice about what information is needed and for what purpose. Historically states collected information primarily for bureaucratic administration. States were involved in warfare and needed to raise armies, for this they needed to secure funds through taxation, and, in the era of mercantilism, they needed to track trade flows. These are the key features of early statistics and as states expanded the need for information grew.[22] Here can be seen how the statistics generated by the state were effectively a new technology for bureaucratic administration.[23] As a technology, Kranzberg's first law of technology applies, 'it is neither good nor bad; nor is it neutral'.[24] By this the historian Melvin Kranzberg (1917–95) meant that any technology interacts with its environment and these impacts can go beyond the original purpose, or rather the intention, of the technology. What mattered (and continues to matter) is how these data are subsequently used in statecraft.

The creation and collection of information led to the development of statistics as a distinct branch of mathematics in the nineteenth century with pivotal inputs from figures such as the Belgian polymath Adolphe Quetelet (1796–1874) who applied mathematical methods from astronomy to social statistics. Quetelet developed the concept of the normal man and is probably familiar to most people today from his index, more widely known as the Body Mass Index. This led to new ways of interpreting the information that was being collected. The eugenics movement also strongly influenced the early development of statistics. Francis Galton, studying heredity, introduced concepts like correlation and regression, which Karl Pearson later formalized through tools such as the Pearson correlation coefficient and the chi-squared test.[25]

The origins of social measurement in Britain are traced back to the 1660s with William Petty's work on national income and the work of John Graunt on bills of mortality, although there has been a long-standing debate over Petty's contribution to Graunt's work.[26] John Graunt (1620–74), a draper by trade, is seen as one of the first demographers and epidemiologists. In his work he estimated the population of London and England using the Bills of Mortality.[27] William Petty,[28] a physician by training, worked on estimating the population, income and wealth of both England and Ireland.[29] His original motivation was to provide a quantitative framework to mobilize resources in preparation for war. Petty's approach was novel in that it involved quantification; however, some of his numbers were speculative and 'invested his calculations with a spurious authority'.[30] Other work in this lineage includes Gregory King (1648–1712) who provided detailed estimates of national accounts, social tables, and income distribution for England.[31] Further work on political arithmetic in the eighteenth century tended to focus on demographic aspects of society, overlooking wealth and income as emphasized by Petty. Part of this divergence can be explained by the tendency to equate population size with national wealth, as seen in the writings of David Hume.[32] Within the Germanic tradition, one of the pioneers was J. P. Suessmilch (1707–67) who, like Petty, was a physician by training but became interested in political arithmetic from the perspective of demography.[33]

A continuation of this approach to statistics is seen in the collection of data using periodic censuses. The Swedish and the US censuses were uniquely eighteenth-century inventions, but most countries in Western Europe had implemented censuses in the nineteenth century and the practice spread to other parts of the world. Censuses were used to analyse state capacity along the lines of political arithmetic, the original Germanic statist interpretation of statistics. In the context of nineteenth-century industrialization, censuses were a way for countries to monitor the effect of industrialization through its impact on population.

The first official British census took place in 1801. Given this occurred just three years after the publication of Malthus' *Principles of Population* many, including the current administrators of the UK's census,[34] have assumed that Malthus played a pivotal role in its establishment. The extent of his influence is likely overstated. The census was more likely to have been influenced by an essay written by John Rickman (1771–1840) on the benefits of a national population count for army recruitment, especially during the Revolutionary/Napoleonic Wars.[35] Rickman's influence is evident in his role in supervising the first census.

Angus Maddison (1926–2010), the famous compiler of historical GDP (whose obituary was published in the *Economist* magazine), saw political arithmetic as the antecedent to modern national income accounts.[36] However, using a broader understanding of political arithmetic as an antecedent of statistics, the origins of national accounting can be seen in the development of statistics as a way to understand society, breaking away from individual narratives. Statistics supplanted political arithmetic in the early nineteenth century with a focus on collecting information about a variety of societal issues. While 'statistical thinking' was common across Europe and North America, it was the British who were the most enthusiastic adherents and welcoming of the new ways of quantifying society.[37] The focus of early statisticians in Britain was on the ills associated with industrialization, which were primarily equated with urbanization. The Victorian approach to statistics is perhaps best typified by Charles Babbage (1791–1871), one of the founders of the London Statistical Society, who quipped that, 'the errors that arise from the absence of facts are far more numerous and more durable than those which result from unsound reasoning respecting true data'.[38] This view of statistical thinking was echoed by Florence Nightengale (1820–1910), another famous statistician, who wished to fund a chair in applied statistics 'for some teaching how to use these statistics in order to legislate for and to administer our national life with more precision and experience'.[39] Statistics were presented in quantitative form because numbers were equated to facts.[40]

Although Britain is often seen as being a leader in statistical thinking, it was somewhat of a laggard in terms of statistical measurement. By European standards, Britain was late to introduce civil registration of births, deaths, and marriages, trailing behind other European countries, such as Holland, Belgium, Italy, Austria and France.[41] Here though the influence of the wider statistical movement can be seen. For example, Adolphe Quetelet was an important influence on the development of statistical thinking in Britain. Quetelet, who was 'charged by the [Belgian] Government to furnish the result of the different censuses which have been taken', was the 'star witness' at a UK parliamentary inquiry into the benefits of civil registration. When giving evidence, Quetelet appealed to English national sentiment as he lamented that:

> It is indeed a subject of wonder to every intelligent stranger, that in a country so intelligent as England, with so many illustrious persons occupied in statistical inquiries, and where the state of the population is the constant subject of public interest, the very basis on which all good legislation must be grounded has been never prepared; foreigners can hardly believe that such a state of things could exist in a country so wealthy, wise and great.[42]

The 1830s are seen as a period of a 'great burst in official, as in private, statistical activity' in Victorian Britain and the emergence of 'statistical thinking'. This was marked in series of landmark events that formalized the advent of the statistical age: the creation of a statistical office at the Board of Trade in 1832, the foundation of the Statistical Society of London in 1834, the introduction of vital registration in July 1837, the first publication of the *Journal of the Statistical Society of London* in May 1838, and the 1841 census.[43] The goal of the *Journal* was that it 'will become an important instrument for developing and diffusing the knowledge of truth, and for detecting and removing error and prejudice' and 'aims, like other sciences, at truth, and advances, *pari passu*, with its development'. Although founders of the London society included luminaries of political economy (Robert Malthus and Charles Babbage), the *Journal* was clear that, 'the Science of Statistics differs from Political Economy, because although it has the same end in view, it does not discuss causes, nor reason upon probable effects; it seeks only to collect, arrange, and compare, that class of facts which alone can form the basis of correct conclusions with respect to social and political government'.[44]

The increased interest in statistics led to a wider array of statistical information being produced, although these efforts were often disjointed. While the state collected various information, there were no official attempts to aggregate statistical series until the 1930s and 1940s onwards. Among the relevant economic series produced by early statisticians was Augustus Sauerbeck's price index from 1846 to 1886. Sauerbeck, a wool merchant who became interested in tracking prices for commercial purposes, was motivated by a desire to contextualize the sharp fall in commodity prices in the 1880s, in an era formerly known as the 'great depression'. He noted that the severity of the price decline was not widely appreciated without 'very extensive statistics and of[*sic*] a comparison of various periods'.[45]

The evolution of 'statistical thinking' in Britain can be seen in the work of the eminent statistician William Farr (1807–83). Farr had been appointed to the newly formed General Registry Office (GRO) in 1839 with the title of 'examiner and compiler of abstracts', relating to vital registration. His title was later elevated to that of superintendent of the statistical department of the GRO in 1842. The historian Edward Higgs shows that civil registration of vital statistics in Britain began as a way to track and protect property rights, but Farr created 'unforeseen uses for the registration data'.[46] Farr remained at the General Registrar's office in the statistical department until he retired in 1880. He worked on forty-one annual reports of the Registrar General and also worked on the development of life tables based on vital registration.

In his 1864 presidential address to the London Statistical Society, Farr outlined two branches of statistics: population and property. The former was typified by the periodic censuses as well as the annual registration of vital statistics. Farr saw the latter as a study of wealth, by which he meant, 'riches in land, in horses, sheep, and the cattle on a thousand hills, in grains and crops, in precious metals, in minerals, and in merchandise'. Farr envisaged this as being a threefold division into agricultural, industrial, and commercial statistics, with an additional branch of financial statistics to focus on public and private finance. Statistics were thus seen as an essential part of science that 'reveal laws, and arm man with power over man and over nature'.[47]

Farr saw the state (or rather the office of the Registrar General) as key to furnishing the various statistical returns necessary to 'sustain the statistical reputation of England in the face of Europe'. Yet, writing sixty years later, Alfred Marshall lamented the lack of statistics on wealth and that the 'history of the growth of wealth is singularly poor and misleading'. Marshall attributed this to the fact that there had not been any systematic attempt to collect the necessary information by government agencies. The exception here, of course, was the United States which had collected information on income and wealth through its decadal census.[48]

There were, however, various private efforts by individuals to estimate the 'property statistics' along the lines that Farr described. One such example comes from the work of the Irish statistician Michael Mulhall (1836–1900) who published a series of cross-country estimates of wealth in various statistical books published between 1880 and 1896.[49] Mulhall's motives were simply that it is 'important for us to know every ten years the progress made by nations in the various branches of industry and finances, as to take census of their population', and that 'it is unquestionably of the highest importance to ascertain approximately the earnings and wealth' of nations.[50]

Mulhall's approach was to find statistics, or estimates, from various countries and make comparisons. In his works he provided estimates of both the income of nations where he kept a distinction between income and capital ('or wealth of nations').[51] While earlier editions of the *Dictionary of Statistics* provided little in the way of commentary, the 1892 edition of the *Dictionary* included both income and wealth collated from a range of authors and based on his tabulations of land, livestock, houses, furniture, as well as infrastructure. From his compilation of data, Mulhall estimated that the United States occupied first place followed by Australia and the United Kingdom. In *Industry and Wealth,* Mulhall's underlying methodology was formally introduced: it was a crude approximation of national income and wealth which appeared to arbitrarily assign income to different classes, but it was purported to have been applied across countries which made estimates consistent and comparable.[52]

Mulhall's work was not universally well received, although, as the economist Arthur Bowley (1869–1957) later reflected, the work 'had its utility but (as Professor Alfred Marshall warned me) it was marred by the inclusion of extravagant guesses with ascertained facts'.[53] Although Mulhall had been a long-standing fellow of the Royal Statistical Society (elected in 1880), his work was not favourably reviewed in the *Journal of the Royal Statistical Society*, one review came under the heading 'the abuse of statistics'.[54] His work received scathing reviews elsewhere primarily because of the lack of source attribution with one reviewer writing that 'the statistical specialist has long regarded with justifiable suspicion any statement which emanates from this writer' and another remarking that it represented an 'uncritical use of data'.[55] Nor were historians kind; Mulhall was 'accused of guesswork, exaggeration, and gross inaccuracy' and his casual approach of using pictures to represent various statistics was also lambasted as they contained 'such inaccuracies as to leave the method in doubt'.[56] A later edition of the *Dictionary of Statistics* compiled by the statistician Augustus D. Webb (1880–1953) was much better received by critics particularly because it was more thorough with its inclusion of the sources of the various statistical tables,[57] including estimates of national income and wealth for the UK based on work of the statistician and economist Robert Giffen (1837–1910) as well as a reference to previous estimates of UK national income.[58]

While Mulhall's work may not have been held in high esteem by his contemporaries, he was later lauded by Paul Studenski (1887–1961)[59] and Angus Maddison as being a pioneer in cross-country comparisons of national income and wealth. Part of the criticism of Mulhall can be seen as a misunderstanding of his purpose. From the perspective of a statistically focused reviewer, Mulhall had missed the point of statistics by extrapolating aggregates from averages because 'the purpose of statistics is to ascertain typical conditions, not totals which are meaningless'.[60] Yet, it is the aggregate that modern macroeconomic measurement is concerned with rather than the average and so, while flawed, Mulhall's exercises were precursors to aggregation (i.e., macro-measurement). Here then we see the contrast between statistics as a collection of information and 'facts', and statistics as a distinct methodological and analytical approach.

The main difficulty with the work of Mulhall was that it was a private compendium of statistical data and many of the estimates would have been conjectured. A contemporary statistical textbook saw Mulhall's work in this light as being a private collation of information suitable for 'general use', but it made a distinction between this and 'official statistics' that were collected by government agencies.[61] So while Mulhall made various estimates, he was collating the work of others (often unattributed), but he was hampered by the fact that some information was simply unknown. For example, it was not until 1907 that the first Census of Industrial Production was undertaken in the UK and any estimates prior to this would have been crude. The United Kingdom lagged the United States in this area as the United States had undertaken a census of industrial production 100 years earlier; so comparisons between the United Kingdom and the United States would not have been based on comparable information. It was also no coincidence that the motivation for the introduction of a UK census of production was to ascertain how British domestic production was faring against foreign imports and to support the calls for greater tariff protection (e.g., see discussion of Britain's relative decline in Chapter 7).[62] There was simply a knowledge gap that was being filled by amateur statisticians.

In fact, it was Australia, a British colony, that was a pioneer in the production of official national income estimates. Starting in 1887 these estimates, the work of the engineer and statistician Timothy Coghlan (1856–1926), were published in the annual statistical abstracts (published as *The Wealth and Progress of New South Wales and The Seven Colonies of Australia*).[63] Coghlan's work, which made use of official statistical information, was strikingly modern and has been deemed comparable to the work of Clark and Kuznets described below as he focused on production by sector, distribution and use, and made distinction between national and domestic income. Coghlan's work has been seen as being in the tradition of political arithmetic but given his role as government statistician, it is more of a bridge between political arithmetic, statistics, and national accounts.

Standardization of National Accounts

National (income) accounting came of age in the early decades of the twentieth century. Key to this was agreement on standard definitions and terminology so that national accounts could be estimated and compared over time and space. One of the biggest contributions to the standardization of national income and wealth accounting was an annual conference on *Research in Income and Wealth* hosted by the US-based National Bureau of Economic Research (NBER). The NBER is a private nonprofit organization founded in 1920 for the quantitative study of the US economy. Its main objectives are to focus on quantitative analysis and provide impartial assessments of the economy.[64] Key to the role of the NBER in national accounting was Nobel laureate Simon Kuznets (1901–85), a Belarusian-born economist, who had completed a PhD at Columbia University under the mentorship of the economist Wesley Clair Mitchell (1874–1948), the first director of the NBER. At the behest of Mitchell, Kuznets worked on US national income in 1931 and led the team that developed the first estimates of US national income. Kuznets estimated US national income from 1929 to 1932, the key years of the Great Depression. His report was presented to Congress in 1934 and became a best-seller as it revealed the full extent of the crisis.[65] The report showed that national income had decreased by 50 per cent from 1929 to 1932.[66]

Kuznets was also instrumental in establishing the *Research in Income and Wealth* conference, which brought together academics and government officials to discuss key issues in relation to national accounting. Another notable figure involved in the early years of the conference was Nobel laureate Milton Friedman (1912–2006) who was Kuznets' research assistant at the time of the conference and also edited the early editions of the conference volumes.[67] The first *Research in Income and Wealth* conference in 1936 outlined a general conceptualization of national income accounting, discussing key issues such as what to include in national income measures, and how they should be deflated.[68] Other foundational topics discussed were establishing definitions, outlining how key accounting methodologies could be implemented, and how balance sheet terminology could be incorporated in a consistent manner;[69] notably defining a key distinction between national product and national income.[70] Kuznets also played a key role in standardizing US national accounts during the Second World War and used GDP to plan the US military and civilian economies during the War.

Kuznets is rightly lauded as a pioneering figure in the empirical measurement of what had previously been an elusive conceptualization of the economy. Another important figure was the British economist and statistician Colin Clark who was active in the early development of national income estimates for the UK in the 1930s and, more importantly, contributed to the study of cross-country comparative studies.[71] Clark's 'brilliant private efforts' to estimate national income were used by Keynes in his 1940 pamphlet *How to Pay for the War*, although with a proviso that: 'the following note accepts Mr. Colin Clark's statistics, but not his concept of gross national income'.[72] Both the works of Clark and Kuznets are referenced in *The General Theory* and helped Keynes to quantify his theories.[73]

Keynes' other criticism of Clark's work was that because they were private endeavours they did not have access to various statistics that 'only a government can collect', thus rendering Clark's work closer to a guesstimate. This places Clark as a descendant of the old political arithmetic tradition, something that Clark embraced as he saw Petty as an idol.[74] Similar to Kuznets, Clark operated within the radius of economic policy and worked briefly from 1930 to 1931 as a statistical assistant to the National Economic Advisory Council, the first body established to provide economic advice to the UK government. It was while working at the Council that Clark interacted with Keynes, who was instrumental in bringing him to Cambridge as a lecturer in statistics. Working as a lone academic, Clark published estimates of UK national income in 1932 and 1937.[75] In *National Income* he outlined his definition of national income as:

> the money value of the goods and services becoming available for consumption during that period, reckoned at their current selling value, plus additions to capital reckoned at the prices actually paid for the new capital goods, minus depreciation and obsolescence of existing capital goods, and adding the net accretion of stocks, also reckoned at current prices.

Clark also came at the question from the other side seeing the market value of goods and services as being equal to income. He was also aware of some conceptual challenges, for example, how to account for household labour and estimate the value of housework. Some of Clark's definitions were not without criticism, but overall his approach was welcomed and, given the level of detail provided, it was a considerable improvement on existing estimates.[76] *National Income and Outlay* involved estimates of national income from producer, expenditure, and income approaches.[77] Key sources used in Clark's work were the *Occupation and Industry* reports of the British Census as well as the *Census of Production*.

Efforts to establish agreed international standards to measure national income date from the Second World War. The economist Edward F. Denison (1915–92) presented a report to the 1944 *Research in Income and Wealth* conference on efforts to standardize definitions for national income statistics between representatives of the United States, United Kingdom and Canada. It is notable that the definitions agreed are very similar to how we define national income today:

> **Net national product** measures the value of goods and services produced in the private sector of the economy valued at market prices, after deduction of depreciation charges, plus government services valued at cost. In other words, it is the total value of currently produced goods and services flowing to government, to business for net capital formation, and to consumers.
>
> **Gross national product** or gross national expenditure measures the value of goods and services produced in the private sector of the economy valued at market prices, before the deduction of any allowance for the consumption of durable capital goods during the period, plus government services valued at cost. [emphasis added][78]

Britain had developed extensive national accounts during the Second World War, thanks primarily to the efforts of Nobel laureates James Meade (1907–95) and Richard Stone (1913–91). Although the influence of the NBER conferences was acknowledged by Stone in his UN memorandum on national accounting.[79] Thus, the efforts at standardization were a collective endeavour.

After the Second World War these efforts resumed and there was a greater push towards agreed international standards, with consistent definitions, for calculating national income statistics. These developments must also be viewed in light of other post-Second World War efforts at reconstructing the international economy, particularly the Bretton-Woods currency system as the national income statistics placed particular emphasis on monitoring balance of payments.[80] Part of the motivation for standardization was that 'a broad basis will be available for international comparisons far more satisfactory than anything which could be obtained in the past'.[81] The threefold system of national income based on income, production, and expenditure made it possible to cross-check and give more reliable estimates.[82] The agreed standards became known as the UN System of National Accounts (SNA). Table 5.1 presents the three different approaches outlined in the 1947 UN System of National Accounts, which continue to serve as the foundation for the classification of national income.

The UN SNA remain the basis for international comparison, although as economies became more sophisticated so too did the revisions to the System of National Accounts. The first SNA guidebook was relatively concise at fifty pages, whereas the revisions in 1993 and 2008 were substantially bulkier

TABLE 5.1 National Income, Net Product, Net Expenditure.

National Income	Net National Product at factor cost	Net National Expenditure at factor cost
Income shares a) Wages, salaries, etc b) Interest c) Operating surpluses, and net dividends received from the rest of the world	Net products a) Productive enterprises i. Agriculture ii. Mining iii. Manufacturing iv. Net rentals b) Banks and other financial intermediaries c) insurance companies and social security funds Payments to factors of production by final consumers a) Persons b) Public collective providers Net income received from the rest of the world	Current domestic expenditure on goods a) Persons b) Social security funds and public collective providers Domestic net capital formation a) Persons b) Public collective providers c) Business enterprises d) Construction, works, and durable equipment e) Inventories f) Gold and silver bullion and coin Net expenditure by the rest of the world on goods and services
		Less insurance claims paid to enterprises and transfers to insurance reserves in respect of the increase in accruing liability to business policy-holders *Less* allowances by enterprises for bad debts*Less* indirect taxes net of subsidies *Less* social security contributions of employers

Source: UN (1947). Measurement of National Income and the Construction of Social Accounts, Table 3.

affairs.[83] The 2025 revision to the SNA now contains thirty-nine chapters with additional supplementary material.[84] While the SNA have expanded in complexity they have not evolved to address well-known flaws with the metric such as the production boundary, environmental degradation, and the distribution of income.[85]

One of the main reasons for the mass adoption of the standardized SNA system was its practical benefits. Administrators saw the advantages first-hand during the Second World War where it was 'an important tool for resource mobilisation'.[86] Post-Second World War it became a useful tool for assessing policy and for comparing country performance against peers. Key figures in the development and dispersion of standardized methodology were Simon Kuznets, Milton Gilbert (1909–79), and Richard Stone. Of the three, it was Gilbert, an economic statistician, who played an influential role as head of statistics and national accounts at the Organisation for European Economic Cooperation (OEEC) (established in 1948, and precursor to the OECD) from 1951 until 1960.[87] Gilbert had been head of the national income division of the US Department of Commerce and was responsible for the production of US national income estimates in the 1940s. As head of statistics at the OEEC, Gilbert encouraged national statistical agencies to adopt the UN SNA. Other important factors in ensuring countries adopted the standard were the use of national income for both Marshall Aid allocation and NATO commitments. At the same time, Stone facilitated adoption by providing a training programme in implementing the new system at the University of Cambridge.[88] While Kuznets was instrumental in establishing the International Association for Research in Income and Wealth (IARIW), an international equivalent to the *Research in Income and Wealth* conference and advising governments that were establishing national accounts.[89]

The UN SNA was not the only agreed international standard. In the post-Second World War era, the Soviet bloc had adopted a different standard known as 'Material Product System' (MPS) which had a different approach to measuring economic activity.[90] While the USSR was in the UN, it was under no obligation to adopt the UN SNA, neither was it a member of the OEEC or NATO, and hence there was no imperative for it to conform.[91] Under MPS economic activity was divided into 'material production' and 'non-material services', the former was considered national income while the latter was treated as consumption of the former. MPS also used official prices rather than market prices to value economic activity and MPS focused on physical output rather than financial flows.[92] This makes a clear distinction between MPS and UN SNA approaches. This can help explain why some economists infamously believed that the USSR was growing faster than the US during the Cold War.[93] China, the largest global economy today (using purchasing power parity, see Table 5.2), was a late convert to UN SNA as a measure of economic activity. China had operated under a MPS framework

TABLE 5.2 Largest economies and fastest growing, 2023.

	GDP PPP (constant 2021 international $)			GDP per capita PPP (constant 2021 international $)		
	Level in 2023	Growth (2022–23)	Growth (1995–2019)	Level in 2023	Growth (2022–23)	Growth (1995–2019)
1	China	Macao SAR, China	Equatorial Guinea	Luxembourg	Macao SAR, China	Equatorial Guinea
2	United States	Guyana	Liberia	Singapore	Guyana	China
3	India	Armenia	Qatar	Ireland	Armenia	Myanmar
4	Russian Federation	Congo, Dem. Rep.	Myanmar	Macao SAR, China	Ukraine	Bosnia and Herzegovina
5	Japan	Tajikistan	Rwanda	Norway	Fiji	Armenia
6	Germany	Rwanda	China	Switzerland	Mauritius	Georgia
7	Brazil	Fiji	Ethiopia	Brunei Darussalam	India	Rwanda
8	Indonesia	Samoa	Bosnia and Herzegovina	United Arab Emirates	Samoa	Azerbaijan
9	France	India	Iraq	United States	St. Vincent and the Grenadines	Cambodia
10	United Kingdom	Georgia	Cambodia	Denmark	Tajikistan	Liberia

Source: World Development Indicators

from 1952 to 1984, then used both MPS and UN SNA from 1985 to 1992, and from 1993 to present China adheres solely to the UN SNA.[94]

Measurement Challenges and Limitations

When Samuelson, cited in the introduction, was referring to national income in the 1970s he meant Gross *National* Product (GNP); similar focus on GNP was found in other macroeconomics textbooks of the time. Since the 1990s there has been a shift in emphasis towards Gross *Domestic* Product (GDP), which is now the most widely used measure of economic activity and it was reflected in later editions of Samuelson's textbook.[95] While the decision to analyse GDP or GNP may appear moot, the choice to focus on the domestic or the national matters. For, as highlighted by the economist Edward Denison (1915–92), national income represents the income of the citizens of a country while domestic income represents the income of a country some of which may not accrue to residents.[96]

In addition to GDP there are other measures of income included in the national accounts. Gross National Product (GNP) is the value of goods and services produced by the residents of a country and thus subtracts net overseas income. Net Domestic Product (and Net National Product) allow for depreciation of fixed capital. Regardless of the measure used, the standard transformation of GDP (GNP) is per capita, which simply divides GDP (GNP) by a country's population. This provides an indication of the mean income level but does not reveal anything about its distribution.[97] Another commonly used transformation is the calculation of growth rates over time; this is simply a way of representing the change in GDP (GNP). Within mainstream media representation, economic growth is usually presented as the percentage growth of GDP (GNP) over a short period of time (quarterly or annually). Before taking changes into consideration an estimate of real GDP (GNP) is needed to isolate changes in prices from changes in quantity. For this a GDP (GNP) deflator is needed which is usually based on the prices of goods and services that comprise GDP (GNP).

There are various conceptual issues that make the measurement of national income challenging. First is the issue of *qualitative* change in goods. Many of the products have changed over time and some might completely disappear, while others change with new features added to them. Take the example of a modern refrigerator with smart features compared with a refrigerator of the 1970s or 1980s. The product performs the same task, but the new models are more energy efficient and have additional features such as telling you when you are out of milk. Such qualitative changes can be very rapid, especially when it comes to ICT goods. Take the example of laptops; prices fell significantly over time but there was a huge increase in processing power. Also new devices (smart phones) were created that performed the functions of several traditional personal electronic devices.

In terms of services, it is difficult to make comparisons across countries as many services are not traded, for example haircuts, funerals and restaurants. This makes it difficult to evaluate cross-country differences using market prices. There has also been an increasing variety of new goods and services, and these are not tracked on a regular basis by statistical agencies.[98] One solution to these problems has been to use hedonic pricing (estimating value using prices and attributes of products) to ascertain the value of the new attributes. While this may solve issues related to measurement in one country, if all countries do not adopt the same approach, it can distort the comparative growth picture. For example, Maddison highlighted how the United States had adopted hedonic pricing to a greater extent than Western European countries and Japan, which resulted in an elevated US growth performance relative to its peers.[99]

Another issue relates to the production boundary and how to account for goods and services that are acquired without exchange. The solution to this problem is to use imputed prices to determine the value of resources that are not exchanged. The imputed method uses values for similar market-based goods or uses input prices to infer value. The distinction between imputed and market-based prices may distort comparisons across countries where there are differences in public and private provisions of goods and services, such as the value of public healthcare (in the United Kingdom and Canada) which would differ to that of a market-based economy such as the United States.[100]

Two distinctly modern issues relate to the treatment of 'free' goods and global supply chains. In the case of 'free' goods, such as YouTube or Wikipedia, the service is free at the point of use but their funding models differ: YouTube generates revenue from advertisers, while Wikipedia relies on donations to its parent organization. There has been an argument that perhaps the value that users get from these 'free' services is not being fully reflected in current accounting practices and that imputation of willingness-to-pay for these services should be inferred. The other modern issue relates to global supply chains and determining where exactly production accrues, leading to distortions to GDP.[101] Ireland is one of the most infamous examples of this as many multinationals have shifted profits there due to its low corporate tax policy. Irish officials have responded by generating a modified gross national income (GNI) to show a deglobalized estimate of Irish national income. The results of this exercise show a sizeable wedge between GDP and the modified GNI (which was roughly 25–30 per cent lower).[102]

While national accounting gave countries a quantitative measure of how they compared relative to other countries (how rich or poor they were), such international comparison is easier said than done because of challenges related to exchange rates (do we use market exchange rates which can be volatile or use a fixed exchange rate?), the fact that some goods and services are not traded, and differences in preferences and needs across countries. To overcome this, several attempts have been made to estimate standardized international currencies.

Colin Clark's work on comparative economic growth pre-empted these concerns and is considered to be his biggest contribution as it set out a methodology for comparing countries across time and space.[103] Clark's approach was empirical as he 'dismay[ed] the continued preference for the theoretical' among academic economists. In *Conditions of Economic Progress*, Clark introduced an 'international unit' (I.U.) as a way to make comparisons across countries with different price levels and differences in preferences. The I.U. was set relative to the US dollar and is defined as 'the amount of goods and services which could be purchased for $1 in the US'. Clark's estimates, while crude, showed a sizeable gap had emerged between industrial and non-industrial countries and that the world was 'a wretchedly poor place'. Clark found that the United States had the highest level of income per worker, with the United States, Canada and New Zealand each exceeding $1,000 I.U., while China and India had much lower figures of $120 and $200 I.U., respectively.[104] Reviewing the book in the *Economic Journal*, the economist and statistician (and Clark's replacement as Keynes' Research Assistant) Erwin Rothbarth (1914–44) was both complimentary of the breadth of the exercise but also bewildered by the lack of a theoretical framework guiding the study.[105] Although Clark provided various estimates, he presented them uncritically, in a sense echoing the approach of Mulhall, but unsatisfactory to a modern economist. It was the lack of consistency and quality of estimates across countries that ultimately marred the work.

Further progress in international comparability came from the Irish statistician Roy Geary (1896–1983), whose work was later refined by the Palestinian economist Salem Khamis (1919–2005). Geary, while working as a consultant for the FAO in the 1950s, devised an international unit of comparison that was subsequently formalized. The aim was to compare national incomes using a common numeraire, thereby avoiding distortions from exchange rates. This approach became known as the Geary–Khamis international dollar.[106] Today the most common way that cross-country comparison is done is through purchasing power parity (PPP) which adjusts exchange rates by the price level of countries. PPP exchange rates have been collected in large-scale international surveys. As the Nobel laureate Angus Deaton dryly observed, the international comparison project was 'like the Olympics' because they occurred infrequently and there were very few participants in initial rounds of these exercises; this has increased over time from 60 countries in 1985 to 199 in 2011.[107] Table 5.2 presents information on the richest countries in absolute and relative terms. In absolute terms, the Chinese economy is now the largest in the world based on PPP.[108] But on a per-person basis, the richest economy is Luxembourg. In fact, the top five countries in the per capita ranking are all relatively small countries.

Table 5.2 also presents information on growth rates of economies. Macao is top in terms of absolute and per capita growth from 2022 to 2023, this is a rebound from the Covid-19 pandemic when tourism and gambling re-opened. However, over the period 1995–2019 (so excluding the Covid-19 shock), Equatorial Guinea had the highest growth rates. This is surprising because of the continued macroeconomic travails of the country but the high growth rates can be explained by an oil boom and bust.[109]

The economist Phyllis Deane (1918–2012) was another pioneer in national income accounting. The significance of Deane's work was that she had applied the concepts developed in the most advanced countries (United Kingdom and United States) to a context in what was to become the developing world (or what Deane referred to as 'backward countries'): Rhodesia (Zimbabwe), Nyasaland (Malawi) and Jamaica. The project began in 1941 and preliminary findings were presented at the conference on *Research in Income and Wealth* in 1944.[110] Deane applied the framework developed by Meade and Stone but encountered conceptual difficulties measuring non-market income in the case of Rhodesia where a lot of agricultural produce was for self-subsistence.[111] Following guidelines, most of the 'income' of the farmers would be excluded, while the main market-based activity, copper mining, was produced by capital owned by overseas investors.[112] Furthermore, most of the subsistence farming was undertaken by women whose domestic labour was excluded in industrial countries too. Following standardized practices would thereby lead to biased findings regarding the living conditions of residents and Deane instead argued for idiosyncratic accounting based on local conditions. In a follow-up study, Deane argued that the measurement issues were not insurmountable but that an accurate estimate of national income required the development of a reliable statistical apparatus to record the relevant information needed.[113]

This point relates to the intended purpose of national income accounting. From the outset, Kuznets was explicit about the limitations of national income accounting: 'the welfare of a nation can, therefore, scarcely be inferred from a measurement of national income as defined above'. These definitional issues related to the production boundary of houses, the omission of odd jobs, the exclusion of services rendered from durable consumption goods, capital gains/losses, and also that it did not take the distribution of income into account.[114] Many economists agree that GDP is not a measure of welfare; for example, the economist John R. Meyer (1927–2009) disagreed with critiques of GDP as a well-being indicator because GDP 'does not do what it was never intended to do, i.e., measure social welfare'.[115] However, it is correlated with various welfare indicators therefore allowing textbooks to argue that GDP was a measure of 'economic well-being'.[116]

One of the most salient oversights in how GDP can mismeasure economic well-being is that environmental degradation is overlooked. This is most clearly seen in the case of pollution associated with economic activity which should be associated with a negative value as it reduces societal welfare. Instead it is omitted and thus leads to a distortion of how we view economic growth, as was highlighted by the economist Nicholas Muller in the case of the United States from 1950 to 2016.[117]

Measuring the Economy in the Long-run

Much of the work of economic historians since the 1960s has been the estimation of historical GDP.[118] Historical data is able to contextualize both modern and historic development experiences.[119] One of the main influences in extending estimates of national income into the past was Simon Kuznets through his own work but also through that of his students, culminating in a much lauded volume published in the early 1970s.[120] Even Walt Rostow grudgingly praised Kuznets achievements despite the fact that Kuznets had used his historical estimates to criticize Rostow's 'take-off' hypothesis (see discussion in Chapters 3 and 7).[121]

In the UK, leading figures in the estimation of long-run national income were Phyllis Deane and Charles Feinstein[122] (1932–2004), who were both affiliated with the Department of Applied Economics at the University of Cambridge, the home institution of both Meade and Stone.[123] Deane's experience estimating national income in colonial settings was an asset when estimating historical accounts.[124] Her work coincided with the publication of a volume of British historical statistics which set a template for scholars in other countries to replicate historical estimates of GDP.[125] Feinstein's work was an impressive annual series of UK national accounts from 1855 to 1965 which estimated historical accounts and merged these with the official estimates from the modern era.

Angus Maddison[126] was another pioneer in the estimation of historical national accounts.[127] Maddison's original motivation for his historical work was to understand why growth differed among countries; especially during the so-called 'Golden Age' of high economic growth after the Second World War to 1972. Maddison was then further motivated by the growth slowdown after 1973 in Western European countries.[128] In later work, Maddison saw his efforts as a quantification of Adam Smith's view of the world with a comparative perspective on why some countries were rich and others poor.[129] For Maddison, an understanding of the contemporary economy was not possible without an understanding of the past. His initial work was well respected, for example, he was commended by Kenneth Boulding in a review in the journal *Science*.[130] In subsequent research, Maddison attempted to estimate GDP figures as far back as the year 1, but these were only for a small number of countries and the bulk of data was from the 1950s onwards (based on the post-Second World War adoption of national accounts).[131] But some of these historical estimates should be treated more as informed conjectures rather than as firm quantitative evidence. Or rather, as Vaclav Smil refers to them, as 'qualitative impressions'.[132] Others have been less kind and have highlighted the limitations in terms of the population numbers that Maddison relied on extensively, while others have claimed that Maddison became bolder in the 'mysteries of his craft'.[133] In his final book, Maddison stressed that his work was an attempt to show how the world had gradually evolved during the mercantilist era and that there was no pre-1800 Malthusian trap.[134]

When Angus Maddison died, his work was continued by colleagues at the University of Groningen. This work on historical GDP has been continued to the present day by the Maddison Project which collects and collates data on GDP over time and space. These data have been widely used by growth economists to study the dynamics of long-run growth.[135] The most recent update of the Maddison Project has streamlined estimates of GDP across a more geographically diverse array of countries.[136] One of the major contributions of this exercise has been identifying the timing of the 'Great Divergence' between Europe and Asia. These updates place emphasis on the 'spectacular increase in GDP' and, according to these estimates, global average income per capita increased 13-fold in the 200 years between 1820 and 2020.

Taking account of Smil's criticism of long-run GDP, these are shown as an index in Figure 5.1 to give a qualitative impression of growth over time. Economic growth accelerated slowly over time; it took 100 years for the first doubling of income per capita, and the next doubling only took 60 years, before doubling again in 40 years. There are significant differences across countries. The region that experienced the largest absolute increase in GDP per capita was the 'Western offshoots' (United States, Canada, Australia, New Zealand), followed by Western Europe. East Asia experienced the highest relative increase (a 24-fold increase in GDP per capita), although the 2022 level was under half of that of the Western offshoots. While the poorest countries were located in Sub-Saharan Africa, where GDP per capita grew but only at a very modest rate.

Returning to the original Maddison motivation for undertaking historical estimates of GDP growth rates, Table 5.3 uses the latest Maddison database to update one of the tables from Maddison's 1982 book *Phases of Capitalist Development*. The same country selection is presented, with the addition of China to highlight the rapid increase in economic growth seen there in recent times. There are some subtle differences between Maddison's original estimates and the ones presented in Table 5.3. For example, UK growth is revised down for the earlier phases but revised up for the 1973–79 phase. The period 1950–72 stands out as a 'Golden Age' and European countries and Japan never experienced such high levels of economic growth again. European economic growth has been very low since the 2008 financial crisis. Notably, the only country to experience 'Golden Age' levels of economic growth since the 1970s is China.

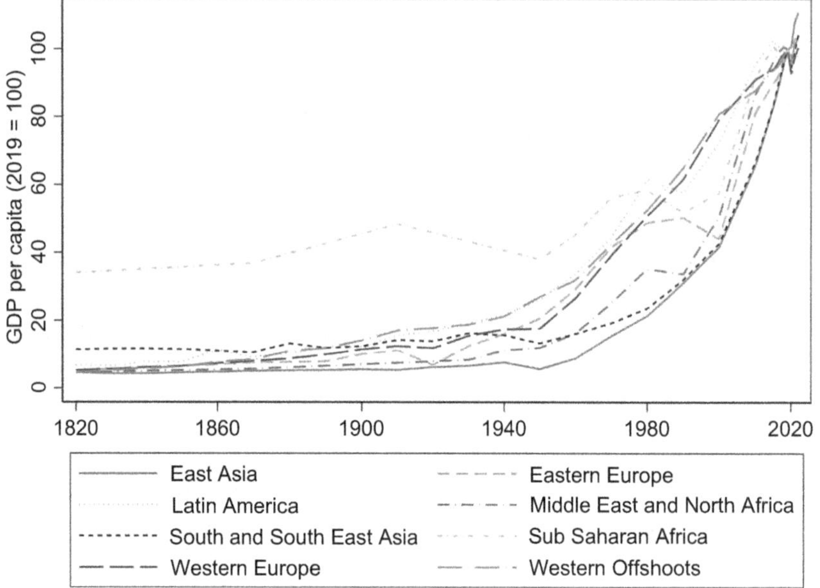

FIGURE 5.1 *Index of real GDP per capita, 1820–2020. Source: MPD version 2023: J. Bolt and J. L. van Zanden (2024). Maddison-style estimates of the evolution of the world economy: A new 2023 update. Journal of Economic Surveys, 1–41.*

Simply comparing growth rates is misleading as growth can be simply a reflection of a country's starting point. Countries that already have a higher income tend to grow at a slower rate. This is a concept known as convergence in the theory of economic growth and it is a prediction of the Solow growth model (see Chapter 3). Figure 5.2 illustrates the growth rates of countries from the Maddison database compared with the initial level of GDP per capita at two different starting points (1820 and 1950). Although there are clearly some countries that experience catch-up growth (those above the lines) as suggested by theory, there are still a lot of divergent experiences which do not fit into this narrative.

Historical GDP estimates can be used to infer the level of inequality *between* countries. This is shown in Table 5.4. The gap between the countries with the largest and smallest GDP per capita grew substantially over time. In 1820, the GDP per capita of the poorest country (Nepal) was 20 per cent of the GDP per capita of the richest (UK); by 1913 the poorest country (Malawi) was only 4.8 per cent of the richest (United States). In 2022, the GDP per capita of the poorest country (Central African Republic) was only 0.40 per cent of the GDP per capita of the richest (Qatar). Through the use of historical GDP, researchers have also estimated the implied levels of

TABLE 5.3 Growth of output (GDP at constant prices) per head of population, 1700–2022.

	1700–1819	1820–69	1870–1913	1915–49	1950–72	1973–79	1973–1989	1990–2007	2008–2022	1820–79	1820–2022
Australia		4.20	1.32	1.05	2.39	2.08	1.96	2.68	1.13	2.34	2.25
Austria		0.95	1.46	1.08	5.33	3.25	2.51	2.45	0.59	2.21	2.07
Belgium	(0.06)	1.86	1.06	0.84	3.54	2.73	2.25	2.00	0.66	1.66	1.62
Canada		1.19	2.37	1.60	2.74	3.10	2.28	1.79	0.60	2.20	1.97
Denmark		0.90	1.62	1.61	3.28	1.80	1.80	2.39	0.90	1.65	1.66
Finland	(0.09)	1.43	1.54	2.13	4.14	2.43	2.91	2.26	0.16	2.25	2.12
France	0.26	1.42	1.36	1.69	4.03	2.57	2.05	1.63	0.44	1.89	1.75
Germany	0.28	0.87	1.57	0.74	5.66	2.88	2.19	2.32	1.10	1.81	1.80
Italy	(0.02)	0.14	0.96	1.07	5.05	3.45	2.78	2.00	0.05	1.42	1.42
Japan	(0.06)	0.11	1.29	0.78	8.11	2.99	3.09	1.28	0.46	2.76	2.36
Netherlands	0.08	0.90	0.97	1.88	3.40	2.19	1.68	2.84	0.84	1.55	1.60
Norway		1.00	1.76	1.97	3.27	4.04	3.05	5.43	1.12	1.95	2.23
Sweden	0.12	0.67	2.08	2.32	3.18	1.81	1.78	2.37	0.74	1.84	1.80
Switzerland		1.33	2.34	1.08	3.73	0.74	1.64	2.79	1.02	2.01	2.02
UK	0.37	1.25	0.88	0.95	2.14	2.24	2.25	1.92	0.37	1.25	1.30
United States	(0.29)	1.27	1.74	1.21	2.60	2.40	2.22	1.83	0.96	1.63	1.62
China	(0.36)	(0.12)	0.32	0.52	2.81	3.91	4.56	5.52	6.14	1.97	3.66

Source: MPD version 2023: J. Bolt and J. L. van Zanden (2024). Maddison-style estimates of the evolution of the world economy: A new 2023 update. Journal of Economic Surveys, 1–41.

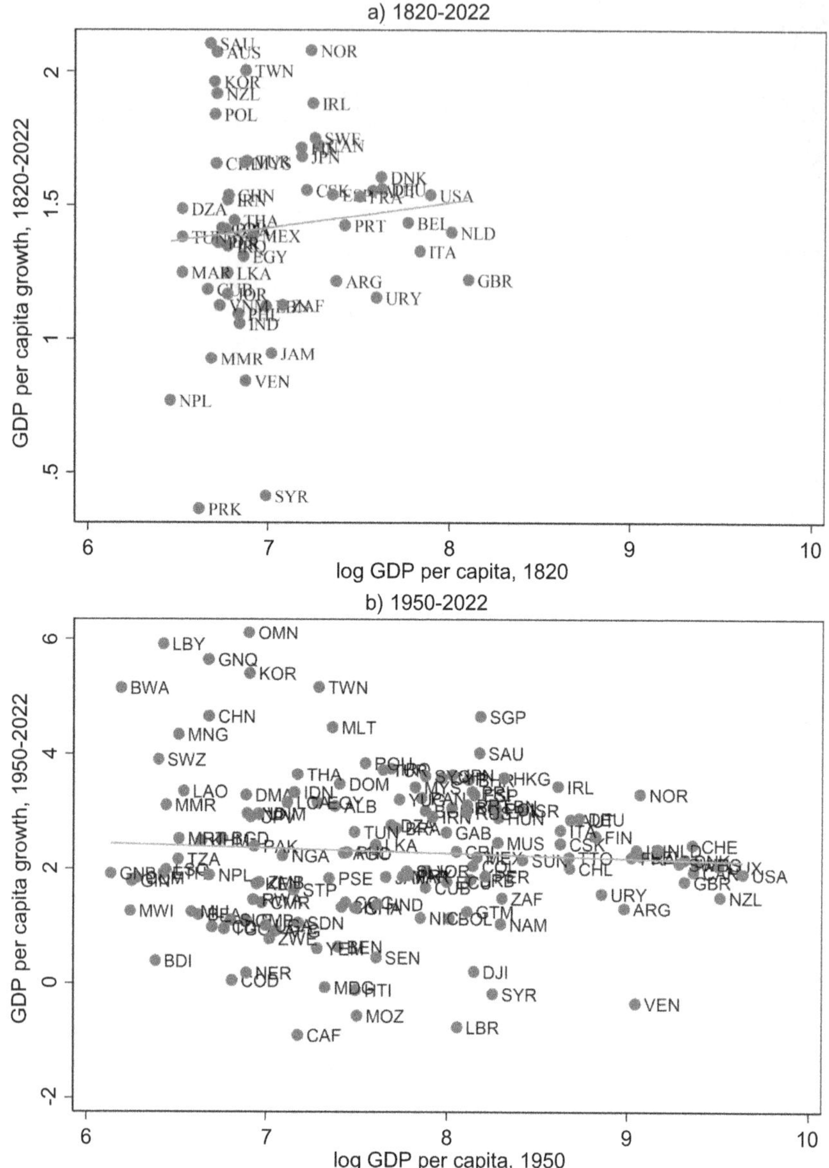

FIGURE 5.2 *Measuring Global GDP growth, 1820–2022. Source: MPD version 2023: J. Bolt and J. L. van Zanden (2024). Maddison-style estimates of the evolution of the world economy: A new 2023 update. Journal of Economic Surveys, 1–41.*

TABLE 5.4 Distribution of GDP per capita across countries

	1820	1913	1950	1973	2022
	GDP per capita, 2011 prices				
Median	968	1862	2175	5255	13072
Mean	1257	2851	3930	7755	19754
Standard Deviation	615	2265	6241	8607	20789
Coefficient of variation	49	79	159	111	105
Minimum	641	487	462	746	596
Maximum	3306	10108	48436	68407	149171
Range (max – min)	2665	9621	47974	67661	148575
Gini coefficient	0.24	0.40	0.55	0.51	0.51
Number of countries	55	75	167	168	169

inequality between countries which rose from a Gini coefficient (where 0 means perfect equality and 1 means perfect inequality) of 0.49 in 1820 to a high point of 0.67 by the 1980s. Subsequent estimates have shown a gradual fall in between-country inequality since the 2000s, and this fall has been driven by the rise of China. [137]

There are various issues with long-run estimates of GDP; for example, the issues highlighted by Phyllis Deane in her work on colonial economies. Firstly, any issue with the concept of GDP in the modern era only gets amplified the further back the concept is pushed. Take the question of production boundaries. Most modern production takes place in the market but the further back in time we go the more likely a greater share of production took place in households, which simply gets overlooked in these estimates of GDP. What may appear to be an increase in GDP may actually be structural changes in the economy. Similarly, production often used enforced labour (serfdom or slavery), but this is glossed over when economic activity is aggregated. Environmental impacts are completely overlooked, even though pollution and carbon emissions co-evolved with GDP.[138] The recent developments in economic history, with some extension of GDP estimates as far back as the thirteenth century,[139] have not acknowledged the negative externalities associated with economic growth.

Measuring the Wealth of Nations

Modern national accounting has tended to focus predominantly on measuring income, or rather the attention of users of these statistics is towards national income (GDP).[140] The reason for this, as John Hicks explained in a lecture to the International Statistical Institute in 1969, was that 'measuring capital is the nastiest job that economists have set to statisticians'.[141] Hicks made the analogy to a limited liability company; it has both running accounts which state the operations over a given year as well as a balance sheet which accounts for all assets and liabilities. The same principle, he argued, should apply to national accounts. Measuring capital in practice, he saw, was plagued with difficulties and 'it cannot be expected that he [the statistician] will be very successful'. Given the various issues with capital theory (discussed in Chapter 3), it is no wonder that the economist Charles Hulten thought that 'national income accounting would be a relatively simple matter were it not for "capital"'.[142]

While great progress was made estimating national income in the interwar period, estimates of national wealth were in a more rudimentary shape. This was despite the *Research in Income and Wealth* conferences being explicitly focused on both national income *and* wealth from the outset. For example, at the second conference Simon Kuznets presented definitions and methodological approaches to measuring wealth.[143] The economist Raymond W. Goldsmith (1904–88) later explained that:

> the complete neglect of the balance sheet aspect of social accounting may seem strange when the balance sheet is so obviously an integral part of the accounts of any business enterprise or even of any other economic unit such as a household, and when the integration of balance sheet and income account is an essential feature of the system of modern double entry bookkeeping that underlies, or should underlie, social accounting.[144]

In the immediate post-Second World War period, Goldsmith outlined some methodological considerations from a national balance sheet perspective, including the distinction between national wealth and national income. He was disheartened by the challenges of estimating wealth and failed to provide any estimates.[145] It was only one year later though that Goldsmith made a marked advancement by estimating national wealth using what is now known as the perpetual inventory method (PIM), an approach that is still used as the standard way to estimate capital.[146] PIM used annual information on capital expenditures (i.e., investment) to infer a benchmark estimate of wealth and this was the basis for Goldsmith's later work on US wealth in the immediate post-Second World War period.[147] Goldsmith also attempted to make international comparisons but this was not possible because similar historical estimates had not been made for other countries.

This continued to be a challenge for cross-country studies of economic growth.[148]

Capital estimates were of course important in the growth theory of the twentieth century. The Harrod-Domar models (discussed in Chapter 3) had emphasized capital as the main source of growth, and this spurred greater effort to measure investment and capital. Although incremental capital-output ratios (that is, the change in capital (i.e., investment) required to generate an increase in output) were easier to measure than capital stocks.[149] However, the use of aggregate production functions in the work of Solow and others required estimates of capital as well as detailed information on labour, and later human capital.

One of the ground-breaking studies of long-run growth was the economist John Kendrick's (1917–2009) work on US productivity. Using a GNP series from Kuznets and capital data from Goldsmith, Kendrick showed that 75 per cent of US GDP per capita growth from 1889 to 1953 was driven by productivity growth, TFP (Total Factor Productivity, also known as the Solow residual).[150] Later work by Dale Jorgenson (1933–2022) showed that factor inputs (capital and labour), not productivity, were the biggest drivers of growth and that only in one sub-period (1960–66) was productivity more important than input growth. Jorgenson's conflicting findings were driven by how capital and labour were weighted in the production function. While Jorgenson's approach emphasized heterogeneity in capital productivity, both Kendrick and Solow operated under the assumption that capital was homogeneous.[151]

A further spurt of measurement of capital was driven by 'the growing influence of economists on economic history'.[152] This was inspired by the work of Walt Rostow who had framed his theories of 'take-off' around increases in net investment rates (see Chapter 3). This led to research endeavours to estimate historical capital stocks, such as the work of Charles Feinstein for the UK, which explicitly sought to test Rostow's claims.[153] Other notable developments in the long-run estimation of capital came from the work of Robert Gallman (1926–98) who estimated US capital stock for the nineteenth century.[154] As well as Maddison's standardized estimates of capital stock for France, Germany, Netherlands, Japan, the United States, and the United Kingdom.[155] Economic historians have also attempted to explain the underlying drivers of growth,[156] availing of modern growth theory and growth accounting. The results from this research agenda showed how technical change was the main driver of economic growth over time in Western countries, although experiences in Asian countries have highlighted the importance of capital accumulation.[157]

Standardized estimates of capital were compiled as part of a cross-country project initiated by the economists Robert Summers (1922–2012), Irving Kravis (1917–92), and Alan Heston (1934–2024) in the 1970s. The three economists were associated with the University of Pennsylvania, and their project became known as The Penn World Tables (*PWT*). The motivation for the study was the 'unsatisfactory procedures generally followed in the past' whereby cross-country comparisons were being based on nominal (current) prices and not constant prices. The data was in real terms building on international price comparisons undertaken by Summers, Kravis and Heston working with the World Bank.[158] The original database (*PWT1*) contained real GDP, real consumption, and real fixed capital formation for 119 countries in 1950 and from 1960 to 1977.[159] Subsequent updates of the *PWT* included more variables and more time periods. For example, *PWT4* contained data on 17 variables (and 2 variables for centrally planned economies) for 130 countries; it was *PWT4* that was used in one of the early empirical studies on economic growth.[160] *PWT5* contained data on 27 variables from 1950 to 1985 for 138 countries, including the necessary data to compare productivity across countries.[161] Version 8 of the *PWT* moved to the University of California, Davis and the University of Groningen but retained the Penn trademark. The updated *PWT* includes estimates of total factor productivity and capital stocks across countries.[162]

Human capital has been a prominent feature of endogenous growth theory (see chapter 3). A 2001 OECD definition of human capital included, 'the knowledge, skills, competencies and attributes embodied in individuals that facilitate the creation of personal, social and economic well-being'.[163] Within cross-country studies of economic growth, human capital is seen as one of the biggest drivers of economic growth.[164] The early empirical growth models used indicators such as literacy rates or enrolment rates in school, and, following the work of economists Robert Baro and Jong-Wha Lee, consistent cross-country estimates of the number of years of schooling are now available.[165]

While the importance of human capital is widely acknowledged, assigning a precise value to the stock of human capital has proven more challenging. Writing in 1961, the Nobel laureate Theodore Shultz (1902–98) bemoaned the absence of human capital from national accounts.[166] The Nobel laureate Gary Becker's (1930–2014) work on human capital was motivated by contemporary growth theory and the finding that produced capital 'at least as conventionally measured, explains a relatively small part of the growth of income in most countries'. Human capital then became another way to explore the drivers of economic growth.[167]

Human capital is now firmly embedded as a key part of the capital stock. As shown in Chapter 3, Irving Fisher had thought of human capital as part of wealth (see Figure 3.7). The lineage of thinking of humans as a form of capital can be traced back to William Petty and Adam Smith. In the 1890s the economist Joseph Shield Nicholson (1850–1927) estimated that the 'living capital' in the UK was at least equal to the value of produced capital. Another early study by the radical economist John Raymond Walsh from the 1930s estimated the discounted lifetime earnings of people at different levels of education as a way to value human capital. Walsh argued that higher education, especially professional training, functioned like a capital investment that yielded returns and that these returns usually exceed costs; but because access to education depends on family resources and motives beyond profit, the education 'market' is imperfect and socially inefficient. This approach was continued in work from the 1960s onwards. John Kendrick attempted to quantify 'total capital' which included both produced and human capital, where the stock of human capital was estimated as the accumulated 'rearing cost' up to age fourteen. Kendrick found that the rates of return were higher to human capital than to nonhuman capital and that 'it is hard to escape the conclusion that society has been underinvesting in human beings relative to nonhuman capital'.[168] Despite these conclusions, the prevailing approach to valuing human capital has tended to focus on the discounted lifetime earnings, as demonstrated by Dale Jorgenson and Barbara Fraumeni.[169]

For non-economists, wealth is not thought of in the same way and other indicators of wealth would be the performance of stock markets, the value of real estate, or holdings of precious metals (gold and silver). Academic research that considers wealth from this perspective tends to focus on the distribution, or rather the concentration, of wealth. For example, the economist Edward Wolff uses survey data to show the change in household net worth over time. The main finding from this line of research is that there is a greater concentration of wealth but that the change in wealth inequality varies enormously depending on movements in asset prices.[170] This is similar to the approach taken by Thomas Piketty who used capital to illustrate the distribution of wealth over time (i.e., inequality).[171] Nuance to this narrative of rising inequality comes from the fact that although wealth is more concentrated, the accumulation of wealth varies over the lifetime, with older groups more likely to have accumulated wealth.[172] Also, Piketty's approach has been challenged and his earlier findings have been revised downwards based on reinterpretation of the original data.[173]

The Wealth of Nations and the Growth in Productivity

Given that growth theory indicates that technological progress is the main driver of economic growth (e.g., see Chapter 3), it would be amiss not to discuss the empirical application of growth theory. This can be ascertained through the application of what is known as growth accounting which involves accounting for changes in inputs (capital and labour) and output (GDP) over time and applying the standard Cobb-Douglas formula (see discussion in Chapter 3).[174] The residual from this accounting exercise is referred to as TFP and, in applications across countries, TFP is seen as the biggest driver of economic growth. As was highlighted in Chapter 3, one of the most famous contributions to this theory is Robert Solow's model of long-run economic growth. Although, Solow had been more cautious highlighting that since his work was published the prevailing notion had been to downplay the role of capital and 'while this had been a move in the right direction, it should not be allowed to go too far' and he even questioned whether there was likely to be a residual during different time periods and even during the industrial revolution itself.[175]

Unperturbed by this warning, many have bravely applied growth accounting across time and space. The findings from these applications show greater convergence in TFP across high-income countries since the 1870s and a decline in the variance in productivity growth among the G16.[176] Trend TFP growth from the *PWT11* is shown in Figure 5.3 for the G7. The trend growth reflects the slowdown in productivity growth that has been pronounced since the mid-twentieth century. The 'Golden Age' is clearly visible in terms of the high productivity growth of the G7 as they converged with the United States, but these high rates of productivity growth were not sustained.

The United States, long the leader of the technological frontier, has also experienced a slowdown in TFP growth. The economist Robert J. Gordon argues that the century of American economic growth from 1870 to 1970 was an exceptional anomaly.[177] He highlights the decline in TFP, what he describes as 'the best measure of the pace of innovation and technical

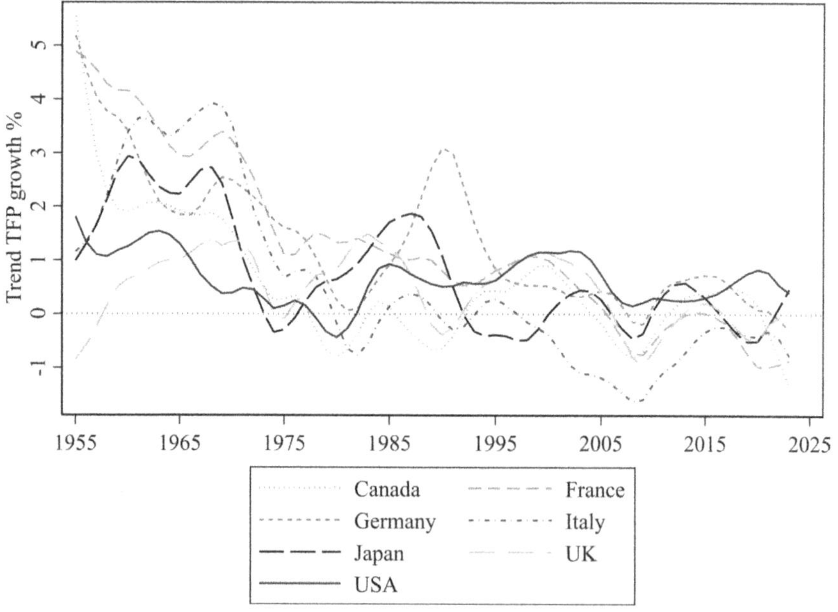

FIGURE 5.3 *Trend TFP growth in the G7 1955–2023. Source: Data from PWT11.*

progress', as key evidence for this claim. Since 1970, TFP growth has slowed significantly, growing at only 'a third of the rate achieved between 1920 and 1970'. According to Gordon, this reflects a slowdown in innovation as 'many of the innovations made possible by computers and information technology have already occurred'. This interpretation is contested, however. For example, the economist Dietrich Vollrath argues that the slowdown in economic growth is actually a marker of success and that some of the slowdown could be attributed to an ageing (and retiring) population leaving the workforce, which reduces labour force participation and thus overall growth.[178] Others argue that we are mismeasuring the economy, and that the production function may be misspecified, especially as new technologies such as artificial intelligence (AI) are developed, or that there is a lag in reaping the gains of new technologies.[179] A recent review points to multiple factors, from mismeasurement and weaker capital deepening to reduced spillovers, slower trade, and declining allocative efficiency.[180]

As China has apparently overtaken the United States (that is according to the World Bank's estimated PPP measure of GDP, shown in Table 5.2), an obvious question arises: how does China compare with the United States in terms of TFP growth (see Figure 5.4)? The answer depends very much on the data source. Earlier iterations of the Penn World Table (*PWT 10*) suggested that China's growth record since the 1950s has been driven

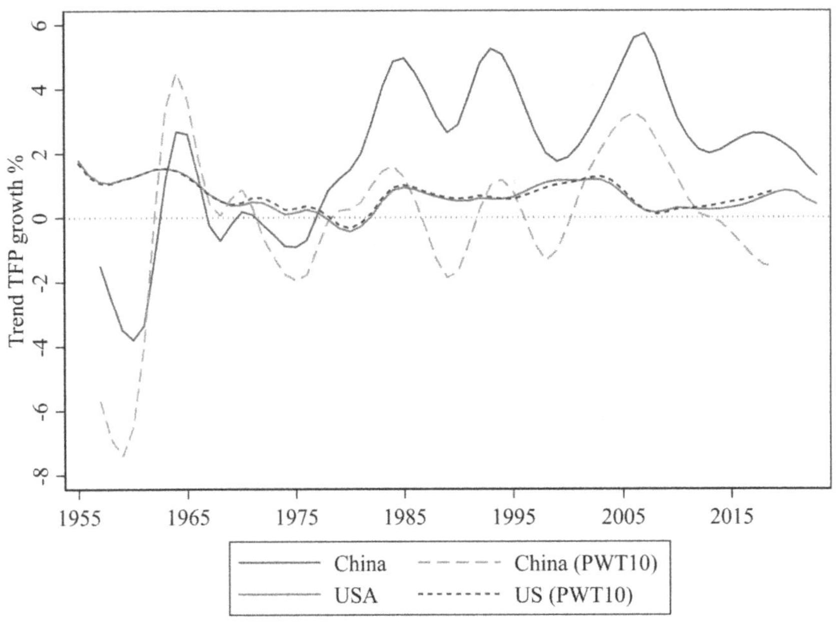

FIGURE 5.4 *Trend TFP growth in China and the United States, 1955–2019. Source: Data from PWT11* and *PWT10.*

primarily by capital accumulation rather than improvements in productivity. According to this view, TFP growth was negative or very weak in the Maoist decades (especially during the Great Leap Forward famine (1958–62)), became positive after the market reforms of 1978, and slowed again in the 2010s.[181] Negative TFP growth in the early years reflects severe structural and institutional disruptions rather than declines in innovation per se. Following the post-1978 reforms, Chinese TFP growth turned positive and contributed increasingly to economic expansion; more recently, however, trend TFP growth has again weakened,[182] reflecting a broader slowdown compounded by demographic ageing and the misallocation of persistently high investment into lower-return sectors.[183]

However, this entire narrative changes under *PWT* 11. A major revision to the *PWT* methodology replaced the earlier adjusted GDP estimates for China with China's official national accounts and incorporated new PPP estimates and updated human-capital and labour-share measures. These changes substantially raise China's measured real GDP growth and, as a consequence, its implied TFP growth. In *PWT* 11, China's TFP growth since the 1980s appears dramatically stronger and China's TFP performance at times approaches or even surpasses that of the United States. This does not mean China has actually overtaken the United States in technological efficiency. Rather, it highlights how sensitive TFP measurement can be. The longstanding caveat about the reliability of official Chinese statistics therefore remains relevant: the shift in *PWT* methodology eliminates earlier downward adjustments, but it does not resolve the underlying measurement challenges.[184]

If (and it is a big *if*) TFP is a reliable indicator of innovation, then the future of economic growth does not look bright given the slowdown in TFP growth across the world's two largest economies. While the extent of China's slowdown depends on the dataset used, *PWT* 11 in particular paints a more favourable picture, the broader trend of weakening productivity growth remains. The only light at the end on the horizon is of course the revolution in artificial intelligence (AI), though this too carries significant existential risks.[185] Whether AI will have an effect on aggregate productivity only time will tell. There are conflicting perspectives on the likely outcome. Daron Acemoglu is notably cautious, arguing that current AI technologies are excessively capital-intensive and orientated towards automation rather than innovation, and therefore are likely to have only a modest effect on TFP growth.[186] By contrast, Philippe Aghion and Simon Bunel view Acemoglu's estimates as excessively conservative and offer a more optimistic assessment, suggesting that AI, particularly when it complements rather than substitutes for human labour, could generate substantially impact on TFP growth.[187] Others, such as the management scholar Ethan Mollick, are overly optimistic and see AI as a revolutionary technology.[188] My view is that AI, at present, is a highly resource-intensive technology, requiring significant amounts of energy, processing power, water, and network infrastructure. These costs must be fully accounted for before we can responsibly conclude that it is a revolutionary or a sustainable solution. Yet, as the preceding pages have shown, predictions are hard, and the dismal science does not have the best track record when it comes to predicting the impact of technology. None other than Robert Solow once quipped:

> what everyone feels to have been a technological revolution, a drastic change in our productive lives, has been accompanied everywhere, including Japan, by a slowing- down of productivity growth, not by a step up. *You can see the computer age everywhere but in the productivity statistics* (emphasis sic).[189]

Conclusion

The development of macroeconomic statistics can be seen as the culmination of 'statistical thinking'. Quantifying abstract concepts created 'facts' that governments and dissenters could point to as signs of progress or regress. Yet, what statistics were collected and communicated represented decisions made about what society deemed to be important information to collect at a particular point in time.

The methodology underpinning national accounts was developed in the 1930s and 1940s to understand the Great Depression and to support economic planning during the Second World War. Many of the contributors to the development of national accounts were luminaries of twentieth-century macroeconomics. While national income measurement has evolved, modern challenges stem from the growth of services. The SNA system was originally designed when production was paramount, but today many economies are service-based, making accurate measurement more difficult.

While recognized, various disamenities associated with economic activity, such as inequality, pollution and climate change, were not included in national accounts when they were first formulated. They continue to be excluded from the measure of progress that most governments track. This has led to increasing criticism directed explicitly at GDP as well as the unwavering focus on GDP growth as a policy goal.

Kenneth Boulding described national income accounting (GNP) as:

> one of the great inventions of the twentieth century, probably almost as significant as the automobile and not quite so significant as TV. The effect of physical inventions is obvious, but social inventions like the GNP change the world almost as much.[190]

Given Boulding's infamous criticism of economic growth, one may be tempted to assume that Boulding was being facetious; however, his argument was that macroeconomic measurement helped avert policy disasters. Boulding believed that without GNP the 1960s would not have been as successful in the United States; GNP was very useful for monitoring short-term fluctuations, but he was critical of GNP as a measure of long-term welfare. Boulding saw GNP as 'too gross', and by this he meant that it included pollution and that this needed to be 'netted out'.

Measuring economic growth has enabled economists to summarize 'facts' before generating new theories (or sometimes after theories were formulated). 'Stylized facts' of economic growth were first summarized according to Nicholas Kaldor in 1961 and then later updated by the economists Charles Jones and Paul Romer in 2010. For Kaldor, the facts were based on a narrow range of advanced countries with extant estimates of national accounts, whereas Jones and Romer had access to both the *PWT* and the Maddison GDP series.

Kaldor outlined six stylized facts:

1. Continued growth of aggregate volume of production and in the productivity of labour; with 'no recorded tendency for a falling rate of growth of productivity'.
2. A continued increase in the amount of capital per worker; 'whatever measure of "capital" is chosen in this connection'.
3. A steady rate of profit on capital.
4. Steady capital-output ratios; 'at least there are no clear long-term trends, either rising or falling'.
5. A high correlation between the share of profits in income and the share of investment in output.
6. Appreciable differences in the rate of growth of labour productivity and of total output in different societies.[191]

Kaldor's facts were really about physical capital and related to the mid-twentieth-century discussions on economic growth (Chapter 3). Jones and Romer updated the 'facts' but with more of a focus on the contributions of new growth theory:

1. Increases in the extent of the market (Driven by globalization).
2. Accelerating growth over time, 'For thousands of years, growth in both population and per capita GDP has accelerated, rising from virtually zero to the relatively rapid rates observed in the last century.'
3. Variation in modern growth rates.
4. Large income and TFP differences.
5. Rising human capital.
6. Long-run stability of relative wages.[192]

From the evidence presented so far in the chapter, it is clear that the facts have generally held up quite well, although the slowdown in TFP growth is worrying.[193] As economies continue to evolve, so too must the tools we use to measure them. Meeting the demands of the twenty-first century will require renewed efforts to define key concepts and standardize methodologies, enabling the development of macroeconomic statistics that are better suited to future needs. Today there are various criticisms of the macroeconomic measurement of the economy both from within the economics profession and without. For example, the Nobel laureate Robert Fogel (1926–2013) argued that GDP is an inadequate measure of the long-run performance of an economy as it understates the value of improvements in human health as indicated by techno-physio evolution.[194]

The measurement of the economy has evolved, from the early foundations of political arithmetic to national statistics, and ultimately to the development of national accounts in the mid-twentieth century. This evolution occurred simultaneously with transformations in the economy itself. Yet, what remains underemphasized thus far is a sustained focus on the *wealth* of nations. While Adam Smith deliberately framed his analysis around wealth, modern macroeconomic statistics largely reflect a twentieth-century Keynesian emphasis on income. The measure of the economy that is predominantly tracked is national income, but this is not the wealth of nations. While related concepts, they are distinct. This has led to renewed calls for a greater focus on wealth and how it is distributed but also on how we think about our wealth more broadly. The issue is best summarised by two figures of standing within the history of economics: Paul Samuelson noted that wealth was needed to make comparisons of well-being across countries, but as Alfred Marshall highlighted how 'estimates of the wealth of other countries have to be based almost exclusively on estimates of income'.[195] The question of wealth is the topic of the next chapter.

CHAPTER SIX

Measuring the Inclusive Wealth of Nations

A History of Wealth Accounting

While there were early initiatives to change how economies were measured, a major shift in emphasis occurred in the 1980s following the publication of the *UN Commission on Environment and Development* (more widely known as the Brundtland Commission). The Brundtland report, published in October 1987, explicitly called on the World Bank to support 'environmentally sound projects and policies'. Acknowledging some of the environmental work of the World Bank, the Brundtland report recommended that 'this should be accompanied by a fundamental commitment to sustainable development by the Bank'.[1] This call did not go unheeded and the World Bank established a dedicated central environmental unit, as well as environmental units in its four regional offices.[2] Key to the changes within the World Bank was lobbying by environmental organizations. This resulted in an amendment to the 1989 *International Development and Finance Act* by California Democratic Representative Nancy Pelosi, which required greater environmental consideration by the Bank.[3] The Act would only authorize the US Treasury Secretary to pay the World Bank subscription provided it had 'established an environmental unit with responsibility for the development, evaluation, and integration of Bank policies, projects, and programs designed to promote environmentally sustainable development in borrower countries' and 'provide[d]s for an increase in the number of environmentally beneficial projects and programs financed by the Bank'.[4]

The efforts to implement the proposals of the Brundtland Commission led to a focus on the so-called 'constant capital' approach to measuring sustainable development. This approach was based on the work of Robert Solow who was awarded the Alfred Nobel Memorial Prize in Economic

Sciences in October 1987 (coinciding with the publication of the Brundtland report). Solow, famous for his work on growth, had expanded his work on intergenerational welfare and in the year prior to receiving his Nobel Prize had published a study on how countries could improve intergenerational welfare by maintaining the level of capital through the re-investment of the proceeds from natural resources rents.[5] This, and subsequent work by Solow and others, became the foundation of how the World Bank approached the measurement of sustainable development.[6] Thinking in terms of all forms of Inclusive Wealth (produced, human, and natural) is now foundational to how international organizations have viewed economic sustainability.[7]

Solow's 1986 article was based on two pivotal works from the 1970s that were inspired by *The Limits to Growth* (LTG) (see discussion in Chapter 4). The first was Solow's own 1974 article on intergenerational justice and exhaustible resources (discussed in Chapter 1) and a follow-up study by the economist John Hartwick who expanded and generalized Solow's original study. In fact, Hartwick's study was also inspired by a seminar by the economist Anthony Scott (1923–2015), a pioneer in the economics of natural resources, who had speculated on what Canada's wealth might have been if it had reinvested all of its natural resource rents.[8] The *LTG* was also an influence on early work on the economics of sustainable development undertaken at the World Bank. This can be most clearly seen in the 1993 World Bank report *World Without End* which emphasized that the only limits to growth were 'if economies are not managed in an environmentally sensitive way'. The report highlighted the importance of measuring sustainable development through changes in capital (produced, natural and human), while also keen to highlight how the *LTG* had underestimated existing reserves of various natural resources.[9] The World Bank was a leader in the measurement of Inclusive Wealth from the 1990s onwards.

Theoretical advances accompanied empirical measurement. The economist Partha Dasgupta, working with colleagues including Ken Arrow, has been among the most influential in developing alternative theoretical measures of wealth.[10] Dasgupta's main criticism of conventional measures of the economy, such as GDP, is that they only capture flows: they tell us what happened in a given period but 'nothing about what lies ahead'. Also that GDP measures 'gross' economic activity, without accounting for the depreciation of capital (in all its forms) used in the process of production and consumption. To address these shortcomings, Dasgupta proposed Inclusive Wealth as an alternative and complementary framework. He defined it as the 'social worth of an economy's entire capital base' and that this was comprised of manufactured capital, human capital, natural capital and knowledge.[11] Dasgupta outlined a theory whereby the change in Inclusive Wealth was a predictor of future changes in well-being, therefore increasing Inclusive Wealth signified improvements in social well-being and sustainable development.[12] This was also thought of explicitly in Smithian terms as a 'measure of the nation's opulence' where sustainable development could be defined as the 'creation of wealth (or, at worst, the non-destruction of wealth)'. Dasgupta sought to return economics to a focus on wealth instead of income (GDP) or *ad hoc* measures of well-being (such as HDI) and he also saw Inclusive Wealth as the most appropriate metric for cross-country comparisons of well-being.[13]

Thus, a key component of the Inclusive Wealth approach was natural capital, defined in the UN system of Environmental-Economic Accounting as, 'environmental assets that are naturally occurring living and non-living components of the Earth, together constituting the biophysical environment, which may provide benefits to humans'.[14] This effectively was a rediscovery of an older tradition and a re-appreciation of the idea of 'natural capital'.[15] Economists had long thought of natural capital in some way but there have mainly been differences in what is included (i.e., counted) and how it is valued. An early attempt to value natural capital published in *Nature* estimated that it was worth almost double the value of global GNP; although it is unclear if the valuation included elements of both the stock and the services provided (flows) making it an inappropriate comparison with GNP (i.e., a flow).[16]

The maintenance of the capital stock (broadly defined) maps onto the views of Adam Smith. Although Smith did not think explicitly in terms of Inclusive Wealth, he did see natural capital being converted into produced capital and discussed the inter-relationship between skilled labour and capital. Human capital derives its value from the specialization of labour (differences in labour Smith saw as an outcome of the division of labour) and the importance of education. Smith also saw the importance of raw materials, and he provided an important insight into some of the valuation challenges inherent in natural capital. This is most infamous in the water-diamond paradox (as discussed in Chapter 2); this paradox is still of paramount importance when it comes to the valuation of natural capital and Inclusive Wealth more generally. In effect, what economists had done was rediscover Adam Smith's approach to economics. Or, as Anthony Scott explained, 'there is no need for a new and grandiose theory of resources; what is needed is for society to actually apply its understanding of the theory of production and of the behaviour of the firm to a different situation'.[17]

While Inclusive Wealth has sometimes been seen in terms of the 'Beyond GDP' debate, this is a red herring. Inclusive Wealth and GDP should be seen as complementary measures of the economy. GDP is an excellent tool for monitoring short-term fluctuations in the business cycle: that was its original purpose. Inclusive Wealth, on the other hand, has the potential to be a better measure of well-being over longer time horizons.[18] It has also been argued that GDP can be adjusted to provide a sustainability signal, this is true but this only adjusts current GDP and does not inform us about what is happening to the capital used to generate future income.

The main point that I wish to emphasize is that Inclusive Wealth is difficult to measure and that inconsistencies are leading to confusing signals when the theory of Inclusive Wealth is applied by different research teams working in silos. I wish to convey that Inclusive Wealth is a better measure of environmental concerns and that public policy in the twenty-first century requires high-quality measures of Inclusive Wealth, but more than that, an understanding of whether different types of wealth are substitutable. How much substitution exists in reality is an important and unanswered question which I return to in Chapter 10.

In this chapter, I will outline where the idea of Inclusive Wealth fits with how economists have thought about the environment and outline the theory of Inclusive Wealth. While there has been greater interest in the idea of 'natural capital' in the past three decades, this has built on a longer tradition within economics; it is this longer tradition that I seek to explore.[19] I will also discuss the various efforts to measure the Inclusive Wealth of nations. I will demonstrate the role of the World Bank in estimating Inclusive Wealth. I will also highlight some divergent findings from the estimates of Inclusive Wealth in the work of the World Bank and the UNEP.

The Treatment of the Environment in Economic Thinking

Environmental economics is a modern field of economics that explicitly sees the economy as operating within the confines of the environment, and thus is more in line with environmental thinking. It explores issues relating to interactions between the economy and the environment, such as pollution control, natural resource management, and the 'amenity value' of nature (characteristics such as pleasantness or aesthetics that influence and enhance people's appreciation of an area).[20] It focuses on a broad array of environmental issues, including design of environmental policy, valuation of non-market goods and services (for example, ecosystem services), and benefit-cost analyses that take account of the value of nature.

Figure 6.1 is a visualization of the environment-economic system as widely understood within environmental economics.[21] The economy exists *within* an environmental system, and the environment provides essential global life-support, without which there would be no life on the planet. The environmental system also provides vital raw materials that are used directly in the production of goods and services (GDP), which in turn is associated with well-being. Further, the amenity value of nature can also improve the well-being of society. A by-product of the economic system is waste, via pollution at local and national levels, and the environment is used as a waste sink. The accumulation of waste then has an impact on all aspects of Inclusive Wealth, which in turn would affect well-being. For example, acid rain can damage buildings and infrastructure, and it can also cause damage to natural capital. Similarly, air pollution can have adverse

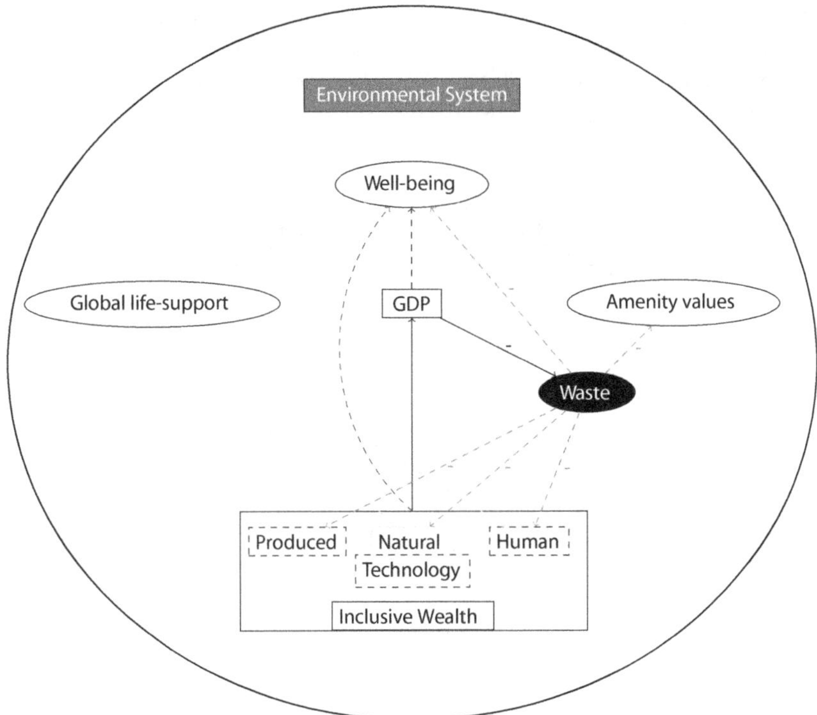

FIGURE 6.1 *Stylistic representation of the Environmental-Economic system. Note: This combines Figure 1.3 with an adaptation of Figure 1.1 from N. Hanley, J. F. Shogren and B. White (2019),* Introduction to Environmental Economics. *Oxford: Oxford University Press.*

effects on health (of people and natural capital) and ultimately on well-being. Or, at the most extreme, future climate change could damage all forms of Inclusive Wealth and lead to lower output and reduced well-being. Therefore, there is a trade-off between the benefits that are received from the increased consumption of goods and services and the negative externalities[22] that are associated with this increased consumption. Within environmental economics, this is represented as a trade-off between the costs and benefits associated with pollution-generating activity. As waste is a by-product of economic activity, the optimum level of pollution is likely not zero (unless it is hazardous toxic waste), nor is unrestricted pollution an optimal outcome. The social optimum is somewhere in between.

Environmental economics as a distinct field of study emerged in the 1970s. The main academic journal in the field was launched in 1974 (the *Journal of Environmental Economics and Management*) and the first undergraduate textbook on environmental economics, written by the pioneering environmental economist David Pearce (1941–2005), was published two years later. This new field built on intellectual foundations over the preceding 200 years.[23] Some of the core principles of environmental economics (resource scarcity and pollution) can be found in earlier writing. Economists in Britain, writing in the late eighteenth and early nineteenth century, saw resource scarcity as a constraint on economic growth and well-being (as discussed in Chapter 3). Land was seen as the major constraint since population growth was checked by diminishing returns to agriculture. Effectively, there was seen to be a race between technology (in the agricultural setting implying new seeds, farming tools, etc.) and population (see Figure 3.6). This foreshadowed the future debates on resource scarcity (resources available per person) from *LTG* (discussed in Chapter 4). While the earlier pessimism of Malthus and others need not be founded, the issue today is distinguished by a race between technology and climate.[24]

Another notable contribution comes from Stanley Jevons's *Coal Question*, published in 1865, which focused on the 'exhaustion of coal' (a case of absolute scarcity) and, given the contemporary importance of coal, the implications this had for long-run British economic growth. Jevon's made a foray into a contentious debate about the abundance of British coal reserves. The mineral surveyor John Williams (1732–95), writing in 1789, believed that UK coal reserves were only sufficient for a few more years, whereas forty years later the geologist Robert Bakewell (1768–1843) believed that coal reserves would last another thousand years.[25] Jevons made the distinction between physical depletion (absolute quantity of the reserves available) and economic availability (coal that was extractable at relatively low cost).[26] Economic availability was more of a concern than physical availability as it would lead to increasing prices across the economy.[27] The work was so influential that Jevons received a letter from William Gladstone (1809–98), then Chancellor of the British Exchequer, stating 'it makes a deep impression upon me, and strengthens the convictions I have long entertained, but with an ever growing force, as to our duty with regard to the National Debt'.[28] Jevons's work encouraged a state inquiry (the *Royal Commission on the Coal Question*, appointed in 1866 and published in 1872) into the coal resources of the UK. The Commission showed that coal reserves were even greater than Jevons himself had estimated.[29]

Running out of natural resources appears to be perennial concern. In the nascent stage of the US oil industry there was a fear that new oil fields would be impossible to find. In 1908 the US President Theodore Roosevelt (1858–1919) was so concerned about declining oil reserves that all US state governors were invited to the White House to discuss. The following year, the US Geological Service released new estimates of reserves and calm was restored.[30]

A further landmark was Harold Hotelling's (1895–1973) classic study on the economics of exhaustible resources. In the opening paragraph, Hotelling foreshadows the concerns of *The LTG*:

> Contemplation of the world's disappearing supplies of minerals, forests, and other exhaustible assets has led to demands for regulation of their exploitation. The feeling that these products are now too cheap for the good of future generations, that they are being selfishly exploited at too rapid a rate, and that in consequence of their excessive cheapness they are being produced and consumed wastefully has given rise to the conservation movement.[31]

Speaking to the issue of economic scarcity, Hotelling sought to answer what the optimum rate of extraction was in the present and the future given the finite availability of resources. He made the point that price (rather the difference between the price of the commodity and the cost of extraction) of a non-renewable resource would have to rise at the same rate as the rate of interest over time. This became an important contribution, especially in the world of resource scarcity.[32] Expansions of Hotelling's approach led to the formation of a branch of economics focused on non-renewable resources.[33]

The work of Arthur Pigou (1977–59) on externalities is often seen as foundational in environmental economics.[34] This is particularly with regard to proposals to address externalities. Taxes on emissions are seen as a way to reduce negative externalities by putting a price on the activity that has an impact on third parties (for example, a tax on a pollution-generating activity or directly on emissions). Likewise, subsidies would encourage activities that have positive externalities (for example, subsidies to beekeepers). But here Pigou was drawing on the formal conceptualization of the ideas of externalities developed by Alfred Marshall, his predecessor at Cambridge, who explicitly linked externalities from fisheries with market failure.[35] Where the issue at the heart of the problem is that there are no property rights to open access ocean fisheries and that an individual firm could achieve constant returns to scale (two boats could catch twice as much fish as one boat).[36] But if many firms increase their fleet of boats, the stock of fish declines, meaning they have to travel further to catch as many fish as before.[37] There are earlier examples too. Writing in the eighteenth century, the Marquis de Condorcet (1743–94) used external effects of agriculture as an argument for government intervention when the exercise of private property rights by one individual violated those of another.[38] Similarly, Adam Smith thought in terms of external effects and unintended effects when discussing justice in *The Theory of Moral Sentiments* (see Chapter 1).

There has been greater engagement with the problem of pollution from economists in the twentieth century, especially in terms of discussing ways of controlling pollution from industrial activity, where pollution is typically seen as a by-product of goods produced. Pigou himself used factory smoke as an example of an external effect.[39] Yet his analysis was too simplistic, since pollution in industrial England was not merely a matter of factories pitted against the interests of society. In reality, all coal-consuming households contributed to pollution: domestic hearths could not reach the high temperatures necessary for complete combustion of coal. Locals were aware of this problem, and the solutions they proposed were not taxes but ways to improve fuel efficiency and thereby reduce harmful emissions.[40]

Research on externalities proliferated in the immediate post-Second World War period.[41] Since the 1960s, the focus of economists has been on ways to reduce pollution at the least cost to society, especially through the use of market-based instruments, such as taxes or permits.[42] While they are commonly referred to as Pigouvian taxes, this has distorted the origins as much of the initial work on pollution pricing was not particularly associated with Pigou.[43] Later approaches drew on the work of the economist Howard Scott Gordon (1924–2019) and the biologist Garrett Hardin, and emphasized common property as a driver of many environmental problems.[44] As there are no private property rights, individuals pursue their private interests without taking wider social interests into consideration.[45] One solution here, drawing on the work of Nobel laureate Ronald Coase (1910–2013), argues for the allocation of property rights as an alternative solution to externalities, paving the way for market-based environmental regulation. Another approach, drawing on the work of Nobel laureate Elinor Ostrom (1933-2012), argues that individuals prioritizing personal gain and neglecting the well-being of society (known as the tragedy of the commons) is not inevitable and highlights how it can be avoided through collective action, as people work together to provide a common objective.[46]

The Idea of Natural Capital

The environment and natural resources have played a pivotal role in shaping conceptions of sustainable development, and economists drew on existing approaches that treated them as components of the broader capital stock. Increased interest in economy-environment interactions date from the 1970s.[47] This is evident in the work of Martin Weitzman who argued that, 'strictly speaking, pools of exhaustible natural resources ought to qualify as capital, and so should states of knowledge resulting from learning or research activities'.[48] Efforts to conceptualize wealth more broadly can be traced further back. For example, William Vogt highlighted that economists did not include the 'vulnerable biotic potential' in their definitions of capital and that we had been 'living on our resource capital'.[49] Another example is Boulding's views on societal welfare as being derived from 'its total capital structure including its human capital'.[50] However, there were other contributions that bear a strong resemblance to current thinking.

Economists have long seen natural resources as capital.[51] For example, Irving Fisher saw natural resources as part of the capital stock and grouped these together in land (see Figure 3.7). Another example is the agricultural economist Lewis Cecil Gray (1881–1952) who argued that the capital value of an exhaustible resource (like a coal mine) was equivalent to the present value of all future net surpluses it can yield.[52] Anthony Scott gave extensive treatment to natural resources as part of the broader capital stock in his 1955 book *Natural Resources*. He highlighted that natural resources should be seen as part ('and only a part') of the stock of 'social capital', alongside man-made capital, in the production of goods and services.[53] Scott made a distinction between 'specific' resources, those that were privately owned (such as mines), and 'non-specific' resources that were commonly owned (such as fisheries).[54] Following on from Scott's approach led to the explicit inclusion of natural resources, both 'exhaustible' and 'replenishable', in economic models.[55] This was done explicitly to account for the externalities associated with extraction but also to account for conservation as an additional motive in decision-making. Natural resources were conceptualized in terms of conventional economic theory and as such natural resources were conceived 'in parallel in theory to the use of capital', with terms such as capital and investment used to conceptualize the use of natural resources.[56]

This approach was a reversal of the omission of land in economics whereby land had been incorporated into capital.[57] This omission, in part, appears to have been a reactionary response by American economists, such as John Bates Clark (1847–1938),[58] to the radicalism of the radical (and popular) economist Henry George (1839–97)[59] who had called for a universal tax on land rents.[60] These issues played out in how the capital was defined, including in the first use of the term 'natural capital' in 1909.[61] Only recently has the significance of natural capital been (re)discovered.[62]

One of the closest examples to the current understanding of Inclusive Wealth comes from Arthur Pigou.[63] The fourth edition of Pigou's *The Economics of Welfare*, published in 1932, had a chapter that explicitly referred to 'what is meant by maintaining capital intact' which described coal as a form of capital:

> Coal, for example, if left alone, will last without change of form for an indefinite number of years; but, none the less, the 'life' enjoyed by coal in the lake of capital, i.e. the period covered between its entrance and its exit, is almost always very short . . . We have now reached the conclusion that the *maintenance of capital intact* for our purpose requires that all ordinary physical deteriorations in the capital stock should be made good. But what exactly do we mean by making good? When a capital stock deteriorates, e.g. through wear and tear, its material components do not disappear from the world, but merely become rearranged in a way that renders them less useful to mankind. Thus what has really disappeared is a physical arrangement embodying a certain sum of values, which we

> may for convenience measure in money, To make this good there must be added to the capital stock new arrangements of matter embodying a sum of values equal to this sum . . . if the failure to provide replacements is carried to the point that henceforward none whatever are forthcoming, the stock of capital must, of course, eventually disappear altogether . . . In this event, however, humanity will take no interest, for the demise of the last capital item will certainly have been preceded by that of the 'last man'.[64]

Pigou distinguished between changes in capital stock caused by price fluctuations and those caused by changes in quantity. He argued that only the latter represented a real decline in capital. This view was forward-thinking and aligns in some ways with the modern concept of Inclusive Wealth, discussed below.

What is perhaps most notable about Pigou's idea of 'maintaining capital intact' is how it was received by his contemporaries, particularly by the Nobel laureate Friedrich Hayek (1899–1992). Pigou's approach was strongly criticized by Hayek who focused on two related issues. First, Hayek questioned whether economic focus should be on preserving capital or ensuring a stable income stream, arguing that the latter was more important, especially since income could come from sources beyond capital. Second, he challenged what he saw as Pigou's 'materialist' view of capital as a measurable substance, particularly when accounting for capital obsolescence. Hayek's analysis was mostly limited to produced capital, and he treated capital as a homogeneous entity requiring measurement in monetary terms; something Pigou disputed. Hayek approached the issue from a microeconomic perspective, focusing on the firm, whereas Pigou took a macroeconomic view centred on 'the national dividend'. John Hicks recognized these differing perspectives and sought a middle ground between them.[65] Later, the economist Maurice Scott (1924–2009) further developed the idea of maintaining capital intact by extending it to include natural capital, anticipating many aspects of today's Inclusive Wealth discussions. Yet, the debates of the 1930s and 1940s, like broader disputes about the nature of capital (explored in Chapter 3), remained unresolved.[66]

Thinking in terms of stocks is also a part of the related, but separate, ecological economics tradition. Ecological economics emerged as a distinct branch of economics in the 1980s and its approach to environmental issues differs subtly from that of environmental economics.[67] This difference is perhaps most apparent in the treatment of natural capital. In particular, the two fields conceptualize natural capital in disparate ways, a contrast made especially clear in the work of Herman Daly, who described a no-growth steady state as one with 'constant stock of physical wealth (capital) and a constant stock of people (population)'.[68]

Table 6.1 compares the approaches to Inclusive Wealth in both the environmental and the ecological schools of thought. For environmental

TABLE 6.1 Distinction between Physical and Monetary Units of different forms of capital.

	Physical	Monetary
Units	Physical units	Currency ($/£/€, etc)
Total Wealth	N (Aggregation problem)	Y
Produced Capital	N (Aggregation problem)	Y
Natural Capital	N (Aggregation problem)	Y
Critical Natural Capital	Y	Not needed
Human Capital	N (Aggregation problem)	Y
Substitution	N (Aggregation problem)	Y

Note: Table is based on Table 4.1 from Pearce and Warford, *World Without End*.

economists, all forms of capital are aggregated using a common denominator (a monetary valuation in $, £, € or ¥) whereas ecological economists focus more on physical units of measurement. The focus on physical units can create a problem when it comes to aggregation; how do we compare a change in the number of polar bears with a change in the number of wild salmon or the change in Amazonian ecosystems and changes in copper mines in the Amazon? A similar aggregation problem would be seen in other measures of capital (see Chapter 3). When measured in monetary units, all forms of capital can be aggregated, and this allows for the assumption of substitution which is a controversial aspect of the exercise. The other notable differences between the approaches of environmental and ecological economics are an abhorrence of discounting and a downplaying of the role of prices within the ecological school.[69] An excessive focus on valuation can also mislead as prices (and values based on these) increase with scarcity, so increasing natural capital in monetary terms could actually signal scarcity (although they *should* be valued in constant prices).[70] Essentially the differences boil down to the distinction between weak and strong sustainability and the preference for weak or strong has implications for how sustainable development is approached.[71]

Since the 1990s, the UN's system of Environmental-Economic Accounting (SEEA) has offered a middle ground in debates over weak and strong sustainability. First adopted in 2012, the UN SEEA tracks both the physical quantities of resources and their monetary values. The SEEA now underpins the valuation of natural capital in the Inclusive Wealth framework.[72]

Sustainable Development and the Theory of Inclusive Wealth

Early contributions to the idea of sustainable economic growth came in the 1970s in response to environmental critiques of economic growth. In a 1973 article, Nobel laureates William Nordhaus and James Tobin (1918–2002) proposed a rule for sustainable per capita consumption whereby: 'per capita consumption cannot be sustained with zero net investment; the capital stock must be growing at the same rate as population and the labor force'. This implied a need for capital deepening (or 'capital widening'). They also distinguished between 'growthmen' who would emphasize investment in produced capital and human capital, and conservationists who stressed the importance of natural capital.[73] Around the same time, Martin Weitzman argued that net national product should be defined as the maximum level of consumption that could be attained 'without running down capital stocks', understood broadly to include produced, natural, and knowledge (and ideas) capital.[74]

Part of the increased drive for inclusion of natural capital as a part of wealth relates to the idea of Sustainable Development (SD) which became a prominent theme in international policy dialogue from the late 1970s onwards. A clear definition of SD remains elusive as there were (and are) several, sometimes contradictory, interpretations of the concept.[75] The Brundtland Report, one of the most widely cited interpretations of SD as a concept, defined SD with inter- and intra-generational equity considerations (see Chapter 1).[76] The Brundtland definition has been the jumping off point of economists engaging with the concept of SD.[77] Such as the best-selling 1988 *Blueprint for a Green Economy (Blueprint 1)*[78] which formulated a comprehensive policy response only two years after the publication of the Brundtland Commission. Valuing the environment and incorporating it in conventional economic models was central to *Blueprint 1* and the focus was on maintaining the aggregate capital by 'substituting man-made for natural environmental capital'; although the report also emphasized a 'constant natural capital approach'.[79]

The theoretical underpinning of *Blueprint 1* was an article by Robert Solow published in 1986 which focused on the intergenerational allocation of natural resources. The approach was built around economic theory from the 1970s, drawing on Weitzman, and resting on the so-called Hartwick Rule, as this described how consumption can be constant over time by re-investing rents from natural resource extraction into other forms of capital.[80]

In the original Hartwick and Solow implementations, natural capital could be reinvested in produced capital but it was later interpreted to be capital 'in the broadest sense to include everything, tangible and intangible, in which the economy can invest or disinvest, including knowledge'.[81] Although the key issue, as perceptively outlined by the economist Karl-Göran Mäler (1939–2020), was the assumption of substitutability between physical and natural capital.[82]

John Hartwick's theoretical approach was devised in an era when the concern was over the implications of the depletion of exhaustible resources (i.e. the *LTG*), but it was later shown that the 'Hartwick-rule' could also be applicable to the issue of global warming.[83] The environmental economists Kirk Hamilton (1951–2024) and Giles Atkinson explored the issue of including air pollution in national accounts. For the case of local pollutants, the issue is relatively straightforward as the pollution damage can be deducted from GDP. The much thornier matter relates to who actually pays for transboundary pollution: should it be the polluter ('polluter pays') or the victim? Hamilton and Atkinson's view was that in the case of savings rules 'some portion of a given country's total savings should, at least notionally, be set aside in order to compensate the recipients of the pollution emitted and transferred across international boundaries'. Given this principle, the issue then became how to value the cost of emissions and for this the 'marginal social cost of a tonne of a pollutant' was used. The adjustments for air pollution led to sizeable deductions and led to negative Genuine Savings[84] (a measure of the *change* of Inclusive Wealth) in the case of the UK.[85] Although this approach has not been embraced in many of the empirical applications discussed below.

The tilt towards natural capital and constant capital approaches in the 1980s coincided with the emergence of endogenous growth theory (see Chapter 3). This helps account for why less attention was given to human capital explicitly in early work on Inclusive Wealth (and also why human capital was subsequently incorporated within the framework). The initial approaches to the economics of SD were explicitly focused on integrating the SD approach within the dominant neoclassical paradigm. This is best illustrated by a chapter in the 1995 *Handbook of Environmental Economics* that explicitly focused on neoclassical growth models and their compatibility with sustainability; only one paragraph was allocated to a brief discussion of endogenous growth.[86]

The constant capital approach has within it two distinct implementations: one requires non-declining *total* wealth (weak sustainability) and another requires non-declining *natural* capital (strong sustainability).[87] The weak sustainability approach, effectively an extension of Solow's neoclassical growth model to incorporate exhaustible resources, assumes perfect substitutability between different types of capital and the monetization of natural capital (this relates to the issues outlined in Table 6.1).[88] For example, a $1 decrease in the value of natural capital (such as oil) can be compensated by a $1 increase in produced capital. Whereas the strong sustainability approach deems that a decrease in a physical unit of natural capital (such as a hectare of forest) cannot be replaced by an increase in the quantity of other forms of capital.[89] The issue of substitutability is contentious but research has shown that technological advances can enhance the array of substitution possibilities, however the extent of substitutability is difficult to determine empirically.[90] Thus, much as Pearce explained in *Blueprint 3*, how one chooses to approach SD, from a weak or strong perspective, is a matter of belief. But, if a country fails a weak sustainability test, such as negative change in Inclusive Wealth, it will in all likelihood not pass a strong test either.[91] Also, the demarcations are not rigid and weak sustainability frameworks can be adjusted to incorporate strong sustainability constraints.[92]

Another important issue relates to the treatment of technological progress. The idea behind technological change is that more consumption could be generated with fewer inputs or that it can facilitate the substitution of natural capital. From this perspective technological progress can help maintain a constant capital. Taking this approach, Martin Weitzman argued that technological progress, approximated by Total Factor Productivity (TFP) growth, could be worth approximately 40 per cent of GDP. This was an enormous estimate of the value of technological progress (or rather TFP growth), one that would easily offset environmental depreciation that was valued at 1 per cent of GDP. This led Weitzman to conclude that omitting technological progress would 'understate an economy's sustainability'.[93] The case for including exogenous technological progress within a measure of Inclusive Wealth was strong in light of the widespread evidence that residual productivity plays a central role in the consumption growth of OECD countries.[94]

Partha Dasgupta also considered the stock of knowledge as a crucial part of wealth and saw that any attempt to measure wealth without discussion of TFP as incomplete.[95] Although Dasgupta was more critical of simply using the growth in TFP to infer technological change as TFP growth may have been due to measurement error; for example, some factors of production (notably natural capital) are excluded in the measurement of TFP.[96] In a later co-authored study, Dasgupta and colleagues argued that technological change 'could be regarded as an increment to knowledge capital, beyond what is captured in human capital'. This was conceptualized as seeing the value of time passing as a capital asset.[97] In empirical applications, Dasgupta highlighted that TFP comprised 90 per cent of the change in wealth per capita in the case of India.[98] Although Solow, when commenting on the methodology, could not be persuaded that 'it makes sense to treat calendar time as a kind of capital stock'.[99]

Population growth has also been a concern, since rising numbers, whether from longer life expectancy, immigration, or high birth rates, require a corresponding increase in wealth to avoid its dilution across more people.

By contrast, when population is falling, wealth need only be maintained for per capita wealth to rise (capital deepening). Early studies in this vein highlighted the need to account for population growth, noting that simple measures of saving could be misleading because they failed to allow for the future needs of a larger population.[100] This led to a key criterion for sustainability: the focus on changes in wealth *per capita*. Recent applications similarly highlight the importance of maintaining adequate savings rates in the face of population growth.[101]

Considering the change in Inclusive Wealth per capita rather than GDP per capita growth entails a focus on aspects of both the environment and development, this then also makes a distinction between Inclusive Wealth and the Human Development Index (HDI) (discussed in Chapter 4). In this context theoretical models framed Inclusive Wealth as an indicator of well- being. The constant capital approaches were interpreted as being a welfare-orientated measure, particularly that it was a capabilities-based but also outcome-based definition of SD (i.e., means of achieving as well as the ends of obtaining SD).[102] The capabilities-based approach draws on the work of Amartya Sen who saw capabilities (that is, what a person can do) as being a better way to compare well-being rather than judging outcomes (that is, what a person has).[103] In the capability framework, the focus is on the ability to achieve a standard of living and therefore well-being.[104] The means-based approach viewed sustainability as a path where the (per capita) real values of changes in capital stocks are non-negative (i.e., constant or increasing). Whereas an outcome-orientated approach saw an SD path as one where well-being (or utility) is non-declining. The constant capital approach linked both sides of the equation as it represented well-being while indicating if a country had the means to achieve well-being, as shown in the work of Dasgupta.[105] Although, as was highlighted by Charles Hulten, the gross and net measures of income are complementary. The gross measure is needed to inform us about economic growth while the net measure is more appropriate as a welfare indicator. As a result, these are not rival concepts but should be seen as complementary.[106]

In his 2001 book *Human Well-Being and the Natural Environment*, Dasgupta illustrated the relationship between both approaches and showed how Inclusive Wealth, in particular the change in wealth, equates to future well-being.[107] Inclusive Wealth is seen as the foundation of future income and hence welfare, as changes in wealth (saving/investment) provide an indication of the feasibility of future ((un)sustainable) development paths.[108] Therefore, unlike GDP, the innovators in terms of 'constant capital' and Inclusive Wealth saw these concepts as being welfare orientated. As a result, the wealth approach has resonated with the broader movement of sustainability sciences and is now seen as integral to the measurement of SD.[109] One of the attractions of Inclusive Wealth is that, under certain assumptions, it can be used to assess both the capabilities-based and the outcome-based approaches to SD.[110] Another attraction is that it is firmly grounded in UN SNA framework (and compatible with System of

Environmental-Economic Accounting) and can be used to measure and compare countries in a consistent manner.[111]

An alternative endogenous sustainable growth framework was developed independently (also inspired by the *LTG*) by Philippe Aghion and Peter Howitt. This approach emphasized the so-called 'AK' and Schumpeterian endogenous growth models (discussed in Chapter 3) and they placed emphasis on technology as key to sustainable development because innovations were seen as the way to save the environment. The endogenous approach highlighted the role of 'resource saving innovations' and 'environmentally friendly technologies' as solutions to environmental problems ensuring SD.[112] This approach is in line with Weitzman, discussed above, although for Weitzman TFP is exogenously determined. Green innovation is also seen as central in a recent update by Aghion and colleagues, who regard innovation as crucial to improving living standards 'despite the constraints of limited natural resources and the necessity of combating global warming'. In the most recent iteration Aghion and co-authors make a distinction between 'polluting technologies' and 'environmentally friendly' technologies, arguing that polluting technologies can be path dependent and thus there is a need for the state to intervene to encourage the latter over the former.[113] However, there has been limited discussion of the alternative endogenous approach within the Inclusive Wealth framework and there is no explicit integration of endogenous growth in the empirical applications discussed below. Nevertheless, the ideas of endogenous growth clearly influenced the evolution of the Inclusive Wealth concept.

Inclusive Wealth Accounting

As with the early history of national income discussed in Chapter 5, the earliest efforts to measure Inclusive Wealth were undertaken by lone scholars. The focus on SD from the 1980s led to the creation of indicators that focused on changes in capital broadly defined which includes produced, natural and later human capital. At the outset the traditional concept of capital was extended only to include natural capital, reflecting the fact that the concepts originally emerged from environmental considerations (the S, and not the D, in SD) and that it was contemporaneous to the emergence of endogenous growth.[114]

An early attempt to rethink how economic progress should be measured came from William Nordhaus and James Tobin, who developed a 'Measure of Economic Welfare' (MEW). This reclassified categories from GNP into consumption, investment, and disamenities. Nordhaus and Tobin's MEW offered a different view of US economic growth from the 1920s to the 1960s: MEW grew much more slowly than Net National Product (NNP). Although GDP was not part of their original study, it is shown in Figure

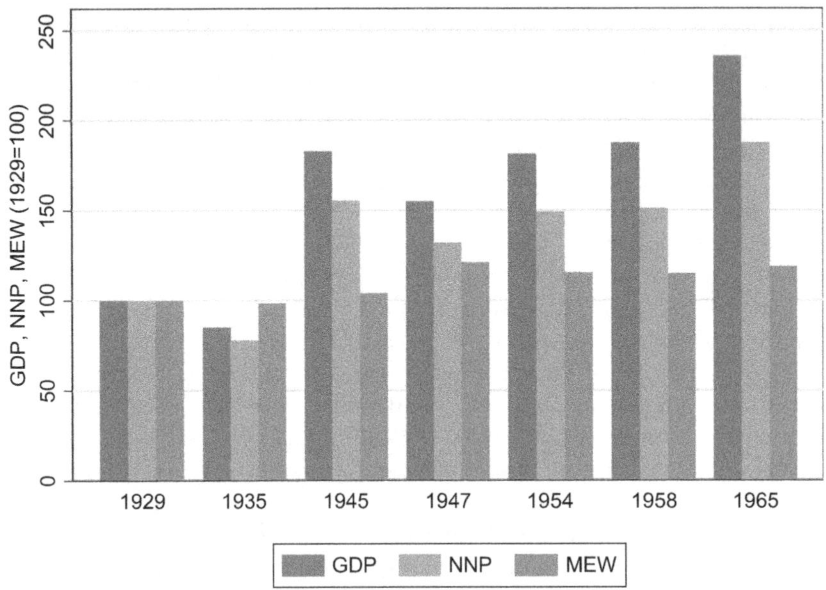

FIGURE 6.2 *Gross Domestic Product, Net National Product, and Measures of Economic Welfare for the United States, 1929–1965. Source: Nordhaus and Tobin (1973) for NNP & MEW; see Figure 3.3 for GDP.*

6.2 alongside the MEW and NNP to underscore the contrasts; GDP growth was more than twice that of MEW. Although MEW yielded striking results subsequent research shifted attention to other dimensions of wealth.

Preliminary work published by the World Bank in 1988 highlighted the inconsistent treatment of the environment within conventional SNA approaches along two lines: 'the costs of environmental protection (defence spending) and the depletion and degradation of natural resources'. For the former, the issue was that the cost of environmental protection, for example treatment of pollution, was considered a source of income despite the fact it was addressing an environmental problem. For natural resources the issue was that they were not being treated like produced capital and were being undermined. The report deemed that the issue of environmental defence spending was greater in industrialized countries while the treatment of natural resources was a greater issue in lower-income countries. The solution for both was the recommendation for greater environmental and natural resource accounting.[115]

A pioneering empirical study by Resources for the Future, a US-based environmental think-tank founded in 1952, emphasized national income adjustments. The 1989 report focused on estimates of an income-based measure, *Net* Domestic Product, using Indonesia as a case study. The *Net* referred to a deduction of resource rents (for oil, timber, and subsoil assets) from GDP. The report showed that from 1971 to 1984 the adjusted growth rate, as measured by NDP, was half the rate of GDP.[116] Despite these stark conclusions, the income-based approach was not widely adopted and subsequent work has tended to focus more on wealth-based indicators because adjustments to capital were more consistent with economic theory (or rather capital theory) and also because adjustments to GDP are more complicated in practice.[117]

The first estimates of the change in Inclusive Wealth were produced by David Pearce and Giles Atkinson in 1993. The estimate was a savings indicator based on two forms of capital, 'natural' and 'man-made', with a simple defining rule for sustainability that savings must be greater than depreciation. This was a 'weak sustainability' indicator because it made an explicit assumption of perfect substitutability between the two forms of capital (i.e., if natural capital was depreciated, it could be offset by an increase in man-made capital, and vice versa). The idea behind this indicator was that savings rates had to be positive in order for a country to be on a sustainable path and the underlying argument was that 'even on a weak sustainability rule many countries are unlikely to pass a sustainability test'. Of a sample of 18 countries, 8 were deemed to be sustainable, 2 were marginally sustainable, and 8 were unsustainable. In an update published in 1995, Pearce and Atkinson increased their sample to 22 countries, 11 of which were deemed sustainable, 3 were marginal, and 8 were unsustainable.[118] This approach also featured in *Blueprint 3* where Pearce showed that the depreciation of natural capital in the 1980s implied that the UK was on an unsustainable path (discussed in more detail in Chapter 8).[119]

Perhaps the biggest practical contribution in this domain was the work of Kirk Hamilton (1951–2024), a former researcher on national accounting at Statistics Canada. Hamilton studied at University College London (UCL), the so-called 'London School', in the early 1990s under David Pearce. Hamilton drew on his professional experience to develop a methodological approach to greening national accounts. In a 1994 article he showed how a sustainability indicator could be developed by expanding the definition of assets from the UN SNA. In 1997 he co-authored a book with five fellow environmental economists that detailed how environmental considerations could be included in macroeconomic concepts where emphasis was put on 'Genuine Savings' (defined as a measure of net savings that took account of depreciation of all assets).[120] Hamilton subsequently had a long career leading the environmental economics unit at the World Bank. Under the leadership of Kirk Hamilton, the World Bank was at the vanguard of measuring the Inclusive Wealth of nations, with initial estimates starting in 1995.[121]

Hamilton benefitted from the changing political landscape of the World Bank where an Environment Department had already been established in 1987 and issues of environment and development, including information on natural resources, were included in its flagship *World Development Reports* from 1992.[122] In Pearce and Warford's *World Without End* report there was discussion of the theory of 'nondeclining capital stocks' comprised of produced, human, and natural capital. The empirical the focus of *World Without End* had been on sustainable income. This was defined as GDP minus depreciation of produced capital and depreciation of natural capital because 'no logic can support including one form of depreciation and not the other'.[123] The first discussions of 'expanding the capital' came in a 1994 report *Making Development Sustainable*. A wealth-based indicator was proposed, based on Robert Solow's work, which included physical, natural, human, and social capital.[124]

The first estimates of both 'Genuine Savings' and Inclusive Wealth appeared a year later in the report *Monitoring Environmental Progress*.[125] The Genuine Savings indicator, based on the work of Pearce and Atkinson and earlier work by Kirk Hamilton, focused on net savings adjusted for environmental depletion and that 'where Genuine Savings is negative, it is a clear indicator of unsustainability'. These estimates were described as 'optimally inaccurate indicators' because they contained information to signal that there may be a problem but because they did not include information on investment in human or health capital[126] they were misleading on the real signal of sustainability. It was proposed that future directions would 'incorporate estimates of saving through education and health investments'.[127] A subsequent article published by Kirk Hamilton and Michael Clemens provided estimates of Genuine Savings from 1970 to 1993. The notable distinction was the inclusion of education spending in the Genuine Savings metric because 'investing in human capital is a type of endogenous technical progress'.[128]

Despite the active research within the World Bank's Environment Department, it is striking that the 1995 *World Development Report*, the World Bank's flagship report, gave limited attention to this work. The Report, which included a table on forestry and freshwater use, commented that:

> no conceptual framework that integrates natural resource and traditional economic data has yet been agreed on. Nor are the measures shown in this table intended to be final indicators of natural resource wealth, environmental health, or resource depletion. They have been chosen because they are available for most countries, are testable, and reflect some general conditions of the environment.[129]

The lack of awareness of the work in the environmental unit of the World Bank suggests that, even in the World Bank, research continued to operate in silos.

Subsequent estimates of Genuine Savings included produced, natural, and human capital; the inclusion of human capital was more aligned with the broad concept of capital. To illustrate the concept, measures for 'world' Genuine Savings taken from the World Development Indicators database are shown in Figure 6.3. The top line represents gross saving as a share of Gross National Income (GNI), subtracting depreciation of fixed capital gives a lower level of saving. Subsequent deductions for natural resource use lower the rate even further. Then incorporating education spending increases the savings rate. The main message conveyed in Figure 6.3 is that gross savings overstates the level of savings relative to the depreciation of produced and natural capital. Investment in human capital (i.e., education) can offset this but this is a partial measure of human capital as it does not account for the loss in human capital through emigration, exits from the labour force and death. Nor does it account for the gains to human capital through immigration or experience gained in the workforce.

Figure 6.4 presents a visualization of the two largest economies in the world from the perspective of Genuine Savings. Panel a illustrates the widely known fact that Chinese levels of gross investment were higher than the United States. Panel b indicates the level of net savings (after deducting for the consumption of produced capital). Over the period 2011 to 2021, the rate of depreciation has been eight percentage points higher in China than in the United States. Panel c highlights green savings, net savings deducting for natural resource use. Again, over the last ten years that these estimates

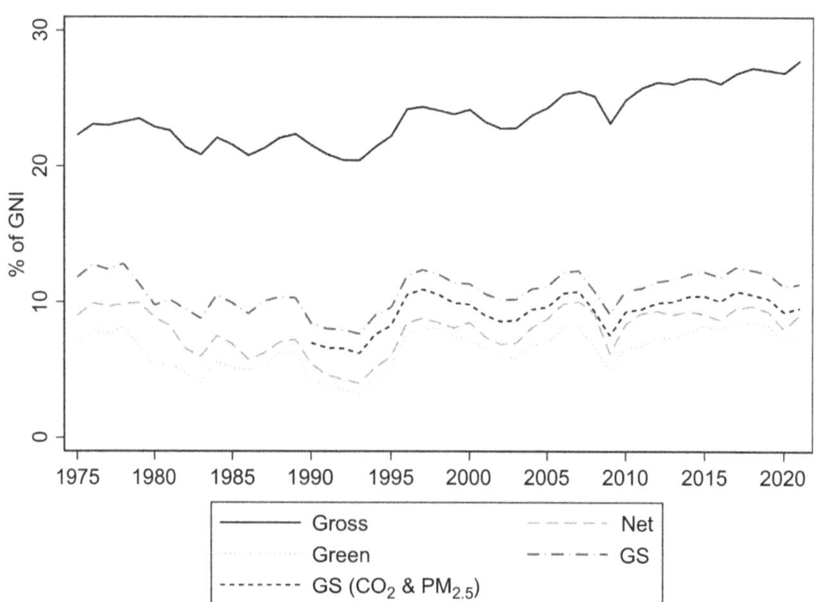

FIGURE 6.3 *Measures of Savings for the World, 1975–2021. Source: World Bank World Development Indicators.*

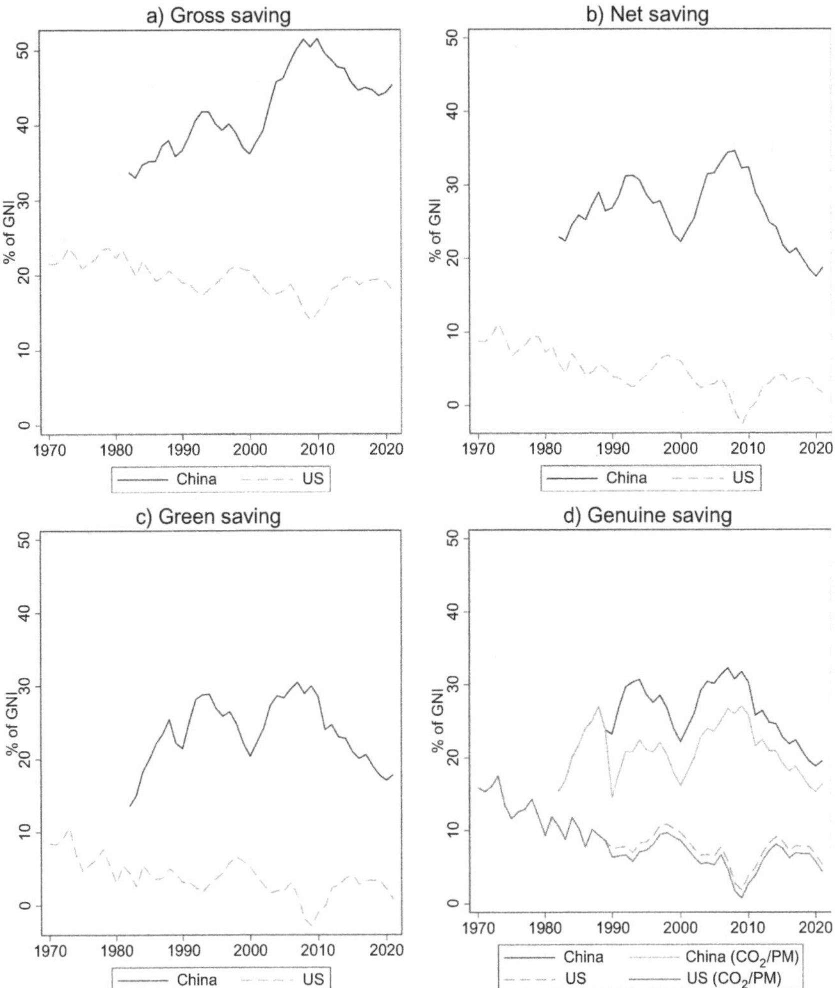

FIGURE 6.4 *Savings metrics for the United States and China, 1970 to 2021. Note: The data for China was only available from 1990 onwards whereas data for the United States was returned from 1970. This highlights the disparities within the series as there is uneven coverage across countries within the existing database. Source: World Bank World Development Indicators.*

are available, Chinese resource depletion was four times the rate of the United States. Panel d illustrates trends in Genuine Savings, presented with and without damages from CO_2 emissions and $PM_{2.5}$. The adjustments for pollution show much higher damage costs for China (3 times) than for the United States, reflecting the higher emissions in China in recent years. The World Bank does not incorporate TFP as suggested by the theoretical research but given the importance of TFP (as shown in Figure 5.4) this seems likely to be a serious omission.

This approach to measuring SD through changes in capital stock also appeared in UN reports in the early 2000s. For example, the 2003 *Handbook of National Accounting* explicitly refers to the 'capital approach' and states that 'long-term sustainability of development is seen to depend upon the maintenance of natural capital (in addition to other forms of capital)'.[130] A 2009 UN report deemed that wealth was comprised of five capitals: financial capital (stocks, bonds and currency deposits); produced capital; natural capital; human capital; health capital; and social capital.[131] In later applications (discussed below) the focus has been on produced, natural, and human capital. There is also reference to the Genuine Savings approach in a 2004 OECD report on measuring sustainable development, however the chapter is written by Kirk Hamilton who placed emphasis on the work being done by himself and others at the World Bank.[132]

Building on its work in the 1990s, the World Bank continued its leadership in wealth accounting with the publication of its reports on the *Wealth of Nations*. The first report was published in 2006 and there have been periodic updates since.[133] The latest in this line of reports, *Changing Wealth of Nations Report* (CWON), was released in 2024. The World Bank estimates produced, natural, and human capital, as well as financial flows to measure 'Comprehensive Wealth' (an equivalent to the concept of 'Inclusive Wealth'). In the latest report there are wealth estimates from 1995 to 2020 for 152 countries. An important question is whether these measures of Inclusive Wealth provide what Hamilton and Clemens describe as 'useful new information' compared to existing metrics such as GDP (as in Chapter 5).[134]

Table 6.2 shows the top ten countries in terms of their Comprehensive Wealth and growth in wealth. This can be cross-referenced with Table 5.2 which ranked the ten largest and fasted economies based on GDP. The top two largest economies ranked by wealth are still the United States and China, but now Japan ranks third and Germany fourth as India is pushed down the list and Russia does not feature in the top 10. In terms of the fastest-growing economy in the recent past, only Qatar features in both Tables 6.2 and Table 5.2. Half of the list of the countries with the highest wealth per capita also appear in Table 5.2, but only Bosnia and Herzegovina and Azerbaijan features as a fast-growing economy in both Table 6.2 and 5.2. The distinct difference in the rank order demonstrates that there is some new useful information gleaned from the estimates of Inclusive Wealth.

Using the latest CWON data it is also possible to compare the growth of Inclusive Wealth with the growth in GDP (as in Table 5.3). The growth rates of various forms of capital are shown in Table 6.3. Given the available data, it is not possible to make a full comparison with Table 5.3; instead two sub-periods, 1995 to 2007 and 2008 to 2020, are highlighted. For 1995 to 2007, the rates of growth for the various components of wealth are on the

TABLE 6.2 Largest economies and fastest growing economies (according to Inclusive Wealth).

	Domestic Comprehensive Wealth (real chained 2019 US$)			Domestic Comprehensive Wealth per capita (real chained 2019 US$)		
	Level in 2020	Growth (2019–20)	Growth (1995–2020)	Level in 2020	Growth (2019–20)	Growth (1995–2020)
1	United States	Maldives	Azerbaijan	Switzerland	Maldives	Azerbaijan
2	China	Bangladesh	Maldives	Iceland	Bosnia and Herzegovina	Maldives
3	Japan	The Gambia	Qatar	Norway	Oman	St. Lucia
4	Germany	Ethiopia	Jordan	Australia	Bangladesh	Vietnam
5	France	Uganda	St. Lucia	Luxembourg	Bulgaria	Bosnia and Herzegovina
6	United Kingdom	Honduras	Djibouti	United States	Costa Rica	Korea, Rep.
7	India	Costa Rica	Vietnam	Qatar	North Macedonia	Dominican Republic
8	Australia	Türkiye	Angola	Denmark	Romania	Kazakhstan
9	Canada	Ghana	Dominican Republic	Sweden	Qatar	Peru
10	Brazil	Slovenia	Honduras	New Zealand	Serbia	Montenegro

Source: CWON 2024

TABLE 6.3 Growth in Inclusive Wealth per capita (%).

	1995–2007				2008–2020			
	Physical	Natural	Human	IW	Physical	Natural	Human	IW
Australia	2.46	–0.65	0.70	1.09	1.93	2.04	0.29	1.01
Austria	2.41	–0.73	0.68	1.21	1.43	–0.46	0.68	0.65
Belgium	1.98	–1.04	1.28	1.08	1.60	–0.63	0.72	0.44
Canada	2.91	0.49	1.42	1.87	2.31	–0.88	0.28	0.59
Denmark	2.08	0.23	0.81	1.18	1.08	–2.27	0.09	0.20
Finland	2.59	–0.17	2.00	1.90	1.91	–0.29	0.38	0.65
France	1.78	–0.64	1.00	1.09	1.35	–0.26	0.50	0.57
Germany	1.81	–1.15	0.46	0.90	1.25	0.31	1.05	0.92
Italy	2.18	–0.99	1.68	1.62	0.58	–0.04	0.73	0.55
Japan	1.65	–1.02	0.14	0.72	–0.09	–0.10	0.54	0.19
Netherlands	2.38	–2.35	1.32	1.26	0.98	–5.78	0.70	0.10
Norway	2.53	–0.53	1.34	1.56	2.40	–1.95	–0.06	0.23
Sweden	0.62	–0.32	0.97	0.62	0.71	–0.94	0.43	0.25
Switzerland	1.59	–0.46	0.38	0.60	1.11	–0.63	0.29	0.08
UK	2.05	–1.62	1.29	1.06	1.05	–3.49	0.47	0.13
United States	2.87	–0.82	0.54	1.08	1.26	1.09	0.33	0.55
China	13.80	–0.32	1.19	2.03	13.15	–0.07	0.43	2.00

Source: CWON 2024

whole much lower than the rates of growth of GDP, while for 2008 to 2020 a similar slowdown in growth rates is also evident. The case of China is revealing. The growth in produced capital was more than double the growth in GDP per capita but there was a marked slowdown in the growth of human capital and a decrease in natural capital, making the overall growth of comprehensive wealth lower than that of GDP per capita.

Effectively Table 6.3 is showing the growth of *inputs* that generate GDP (Table 5.3), revealing what is driving productivity growth and ultimately economic growth. As productivity and human capital are key drivers of economic growth, we can get a sense of where the possible causes of the growth slowdown lie. It is notable that there has been a marked reduction in natural capital, something that does not feature prominently in economic growth research. Figure 6.5 shows the distribution of global wealth, highlighting that human capital has constituted the dominant share since 1995. It also indicates a declining share of natural capital over the same period which corresponds with the slow growth of the total stock of natural capital. The reduced share of natural capital is even more apparent when considered on a per capita basis, as illustrated in Figure 6.6, which shows a marked decline in global natural capital per person.

Although Figure 6.6 indicates a steady increase in Inclusive Wealth, driven largely by growth in produced and human capital, the trajectory of

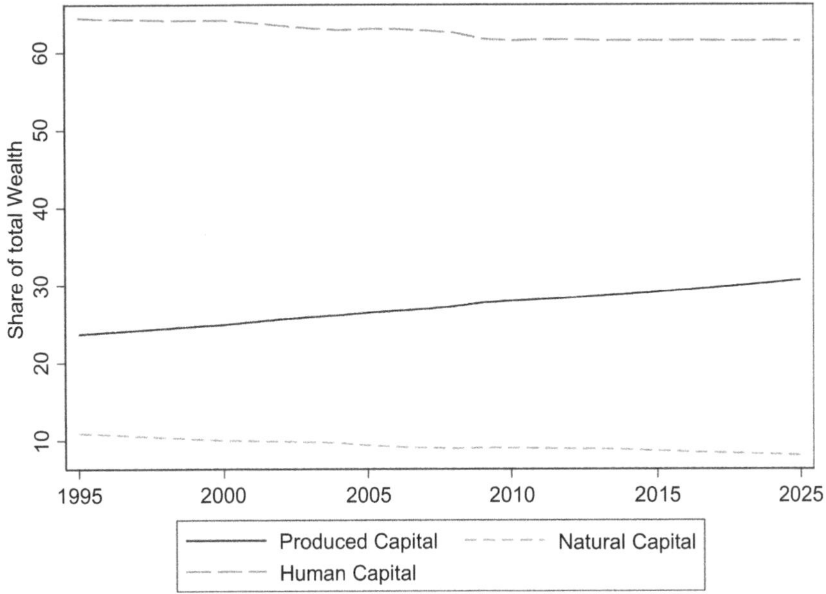

FIGURE 6.5 *Distribution of global Inclusive Wealth by type of assets. Source: CWON 2024.*

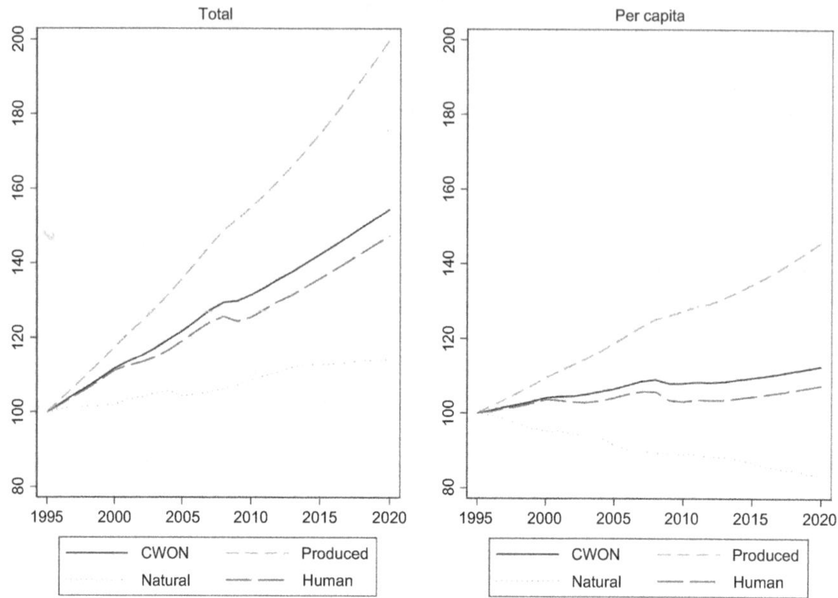

FIGURE 6.6 *Index of components of Inclusive Wealth, 1995–2020 (1995 = 100). Source: CWON 2024.*

natural capital presents a more complex picture. Although the total stock of natural capital has remained stable or even grown modestly since 1995, its per capita value has declined significantly. This decline reflects the pressure exerted by population growth. However, with global fertility rates falling, population is projected to peak much earlier within this century, which may moderate future declines in per capita natural capital. Still, the figures raise important questions about sustainability.

Given that China and the United States are the world's largest economies, Figure 6.7 compares growth in GDP per capita and Comprehensive Wealth per capita over the period 1995–2020. In the United States, the two series exhibit strong co-movement, suggesting that output growth has been broadly supported by wealth accumulation. In China, by contrast, the two measures diverge, with comprehensive wealth rising more slowly than GDP, highlighting the imbalance between the pace of economic expansion and underlying wealth accumulation.

Using the information on Inclusive Wealth, it is also possible to compare the distribution of wealth between countries using Gini coefficients. Table 6.4 shows that wealth inequality between countries is higher than income inequality (Table 5.4) but that wealth inequality between countries fell over the period 1995 to 2020. The largest inequality was initially in terms of produced capital, but this slightly declined from 0.80 to 0.76 between 1995

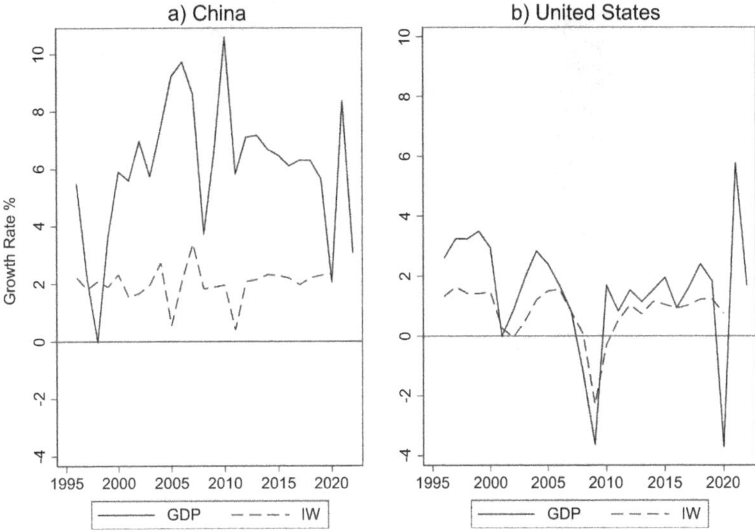

FIGURE 6.7 *Growth of Comprehensive Wealth per capita and GDP per capita, United States and China 1995 to 2020. Source: CWON 2024.*

and 2020. The lowest inequality was in terms of natural capital which fell from 0.65 to 0.61. These Gini coefficients for the various capitals were higher than those reported for GDP per capita (0.51 in 2022 (see Table 5.4)). The trends in between country inequality of wealth per capita and GDP per capita are presented in Figure 6.8. The figure indicates considerably higher levels of between-country inequality for Inclusive Wealth per capita.

Inclusive Wealth Estimates of International Organizations

The UN Environment Programme began producing several reports on Inclusive Wealth in the 2010s and has followed the lead of the World Bank by providing estimates of Inclusive Wealth.[135] UNEP follows an approach developed by Ken Arrow, Partha Dasgupta and co-authors.[136] In the original study by Arrow and colleagues so-called 'health capital' featured as the largest source of wealth, it was based on the value of increased life expectancy. This element of Inclusive Wealth was a key part of early UNEP reports but was quietly abandoned. It seems to have been dropped given the various inconsistencies in the approach, or, as Robert Solow put it, the 'tail was wagging the dog'.[137]

TABLE 6.4 Distribution of Comprehensive Wealth per capita across countries.

	1995				2008				2020			
	Prod.	Natural	Human	Wealth	Prod.	Natural	Human	Wealth	Prod.	Natural	Human	Wealth
Median	3669	9538	16606	37060	5594	8285	8643	41555	8643	7020	25230	47344
Mean	26539	23393	69992	132347	35714	18998	43512	144142	43512	15121	91511	149106
Standard Deviation	56431	68345	116624	224051	74093	51979	84677	234048	84677	37254	143370	232565
Coefficient of variation	213	292	167	169	207	274	195	162	195	246	157	156
Minimum	71	496	628	4324	105	256	263	4343	263	200	700	4821
Maximum	292598	709805	677007	1252130	408720	561540	408068	1137727	408068	387232	735422	1144246
Range (max-min)	292527	709309	676379	1247806	408615	561284	407805	1133383	407805	387032	734721	1139425
Gini coefficient	0.80	0.65	0.70	0.69	0.79	0.63	0.69	0.68	0.76	0.61	0.69	0.67

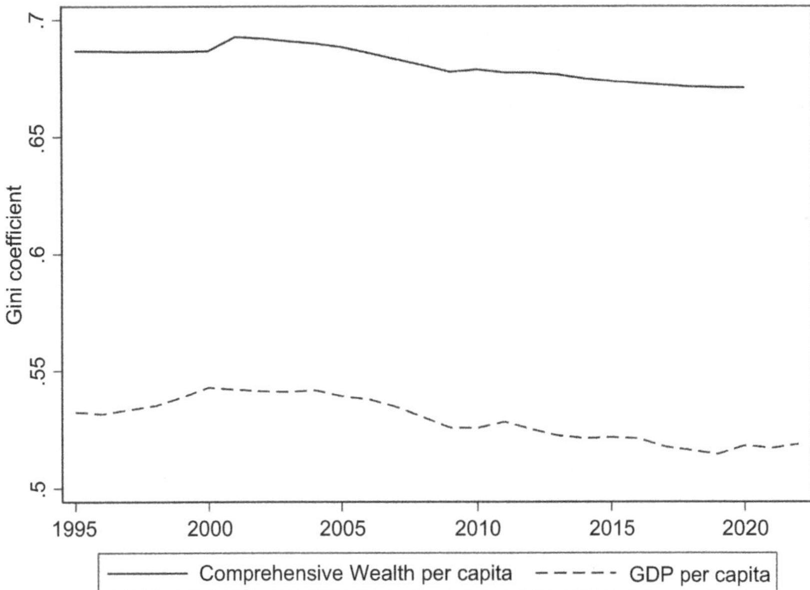

FIGURE 6.8 *Inequality in the Comprehensive Wealth and GDP between countries. Source: Author calculations, data from CWON 2024 and WDI.*

UNEP has also published an Inclusive Wealth report in 2023, but the UNEP team has been far less forthcoming with their data (none of which is publicly available). In a companion article published by the lead authors of the 2023 UNEP report it was stated that 'the datasets generated and/or analyzed in the current study are not publicly available. However, these data are available from the authors upon reasonable request and subject to certain conditions'.[138] I have not been given access to this data despite several requests, so comparisons between the approaches of UNEP and the World Bank are limited.

The World Bank and UNEP tend not to compare their respective definitions and methods. The discrepancies in terms of measurement of both international organizations were highlighted in a 2024 study by myself and co-authors.[139] The main differences related to the measurement of natural and human capital which resulted in divergent wealth indices. This is shown in Figure 6.9 which compares the growth rates in Inclusive Wealth as estimated by both the World Bank and UNEP. The implicit assumption is that there should be a close correlation between these estimates (i.e., that both should tell us that the wealth is increasing or decreasing) but the resulting picture shows that there are conflicting signals. Two of the biggest outliers, Qatar and Iraq, were highlighted as they are purported to be the most unsustainable according to UNEP but sustainable according to the World Bank.

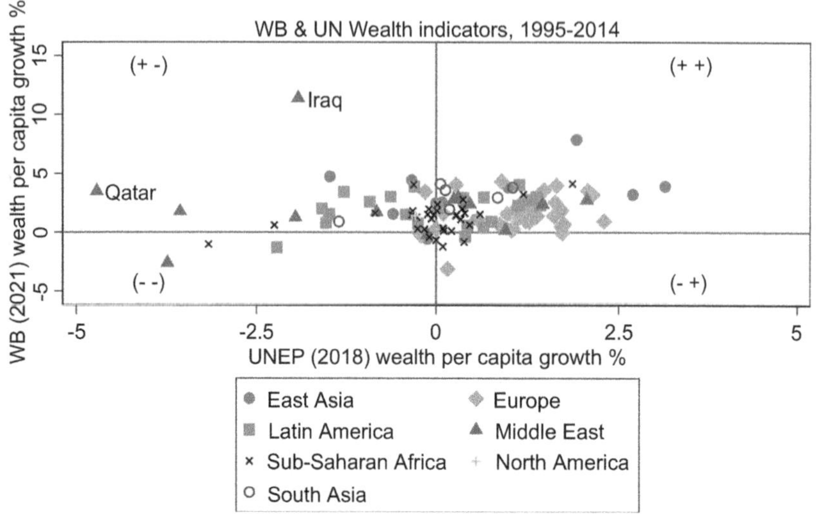

FIGURE 6.9 *Growth in Wealth per capita (CWON 2021 v UNEP 2018).*

On the surface the underlying methodologies of the World Bank and UNEP appear similar, where the treatment of natural capital on the whole follows the UN SNA and the Environmental Economic Accounts, although there are distinctions in how they are aggregated.[140] Table 6.5 outlines the components included in both the World Bank and UNEP measurements of Inclusive Wealth. The produced capital series is almost identical because both use the standard Perpetual Inventory Method approach (discussed in Chapter 5). For natural capital, there are differences in terms of how non-renewable natural capital is measured but a similar approach is used for renewables. There are subtle differences when it comes to valuing human capital in both approaches.

Table 6.6 highlights that in terms of the coverage of assets included in natural capital, these were almost identical. Particularly in the case of non-renewable natural capital. But as shown in Table 6.5 this was one of the divergences in methodology. The World Bank used conventional Hotelling approaches to value the non-renewable resources by providing an estimate of the present value of future earnings from the resources. UNEP instead choose to value the physical reserves by an estimate of a 'shadow price' (an estimated price where no market price exists). This is more in line with Fisherian approaches to measuring capital (Chapter 3). While for renewable natural capital it is difficult to assess, the categories suggest a strong overlap in coverage. Thus it appears that the main difference is in how fossil fuels were valued by the respective groups. As the World Bank and UNEP are international organizations, they are both reliant on data that is publicly available through national statistical agencies and thus there are similar

TABLE 6.5 DISTINCTION BETWEEN COMPONENTS OF WEALTH.

	Comprehensive Wealth (World Bank)	Inclusive Wealth (UNEP)
Produced Capital	Perpetual Inventory Method (machinery, buildings, equipment, intangible wealth and mineral exploration) urban land)	Perpetual Inventory Method (machinery, buildings, equipment, intangible wealth and mineral exploration)
Natural Capital	Non-renewables	
	Discounted Earnings (fossil fuels and minerals)	Stock * Shadow Price (fossil fuels and minerals)
	Renewables	
	Stock * shadow price (timber, agricultural land, protected areas, mangroves and marine fisheries)	Stock * shadow price (timber, agricultural land)
Human Capital	Discounted value of life time earnings of the working population	Based on returns to education, using population educational attainment
Net Foreign Assets	Sum of external assets & liabilities	-
Pollution Damages	Direct (excluded) Indirect (depreciation of produced and natural capital)	Direct (Carbon damages) Indirect (depreciation of produced and natural capital)
Adjustments		Total Factor Productivity Carbon Damages Oil Capital Gains

Source: E. McLaughlin, C. Ducoing, and N. Hanley (2024). Challenges of Wealth-based Sustainability Metrics: A Critical Appraisal.

data sources underpinning both estimates. The main difference between the estimates appears to be methodological choices that are shown in Table 6.5.

A comparison of the World Bank's 2024 update with UNEP's 2018 estimates (shown in Figure 6.10) indicates some convergence, although notable discrepancies remain. How much these differences matter will depend on how we interpret these metrics. For example, if the discrepancies

TABLE 6.6 ASSETS INCLUDED IN NATURAL CAPITAL.

	UNEP	World Bank
	Non-renewable Natural Capital	
Fossil Fuels	Oil	
	Natural Gas	
	Coal	
Minerals	Bauxite	
	Copper	
	Gold	
	Iron Ore	
	Lead	
	Nickel	
	Phosphate	
	Silver	
	Tin	
	Zinc	
	Renewable Natural Capital	
Agricultural Land	Cropland	
	Pasture land	
Fisheries	Marine fisheries	
	-	Mangroves
Forest Resources	Timber	-
	Non-timber forest products	-
	-	Ecosystem services
Protected Areas	-	Protected areas

Source: E. McLaughlin, C. Ducoing, and N. Hanley (2024). Challenges of Wealth-based Sustainability Metrics.

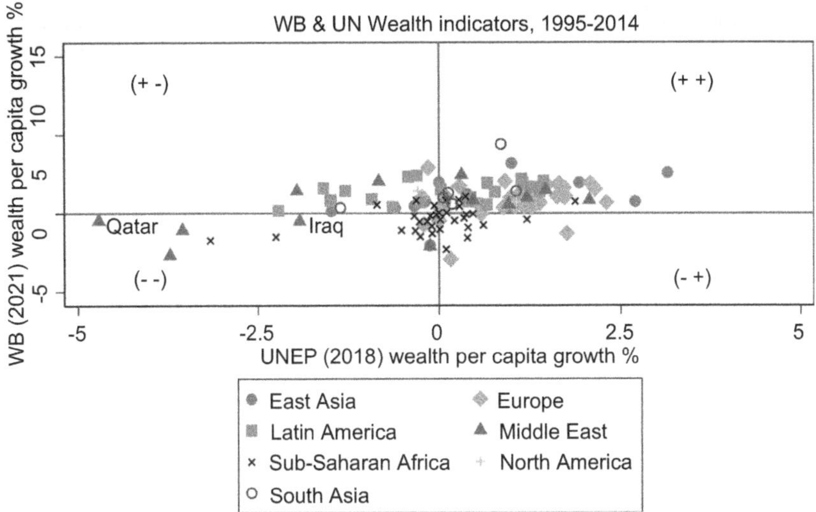

FIGURE 6.10 *Growth in Wealth per Capita (CWON 2024 v UNEP 2018). Note: World Bank (2024) reports wealth data for 150 countries from 1995–2020. UNEP (2018) reports wealth data for 140 countries from 1990–2014. Only 130 countries are reported in both WB and UNEP data – these are the data presented here for the period 1995–2014. Source: World Bank (2024) & UNEP (2018).*

are only in 'smaller' countries and are not evident in larger countries then maybe these are inconsequential for a global sustainability signal. Figure 6.11 attempts to reconcile this by comparing population-weighted and GDP-weighted comparisons of both the World Bank and UNEP measures. Clearly the weighting improves the comparability of the metrics, but the question becomes what the appropriate weight is to use when making comparisons.

Direct comparison between the latest UNEP and World Bank reports is not possible without access to the underlying UNEP data. An indirect comparison can, however, be made by examining the estimates of Gini coefficients shown in Table 6.4 alongside the 2023 UNEP report. The UNEP data suggests that between-country inequality in human capital has remained fairly constant, that the Gini coefficient of produced capital has fallen, and that natural capital has risen. The World Bank data presents a somewhat different picture: produced capital inequality has fallen, human capital was constant, but natural capital inequality declined. Nevertheless, both UNEP and World Bank data indicate that overall inequality in Inclusive Wealth is similar, around 0.68, and on a modest downwards trend. In short, the total indices align but their subcomponents do not.

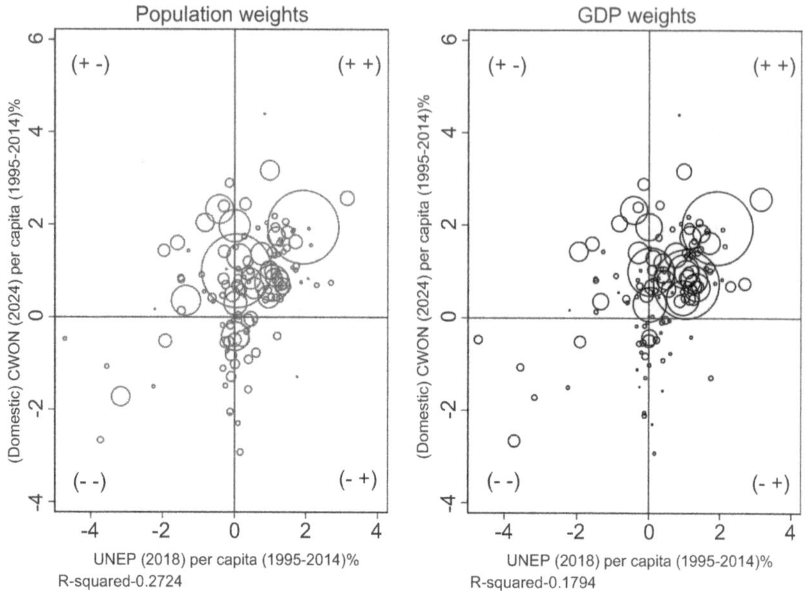

FIGURE 6.11 *Weighted Comparison of World Bank and UNEP measures of Inclusive Wealth.*

The differences between the World Bank and UNEP arise from a lack of standardization of definitions and methods. There has been no equivalent of the 1930s and 1940s conferences on *Research Income and Wealth* to bring both sets of statisticians together to reconcile their methodological differences. Or perhaps a better analogy is the distinction between national income as measured by SNA and by the alternative Material Product System (MPS) approach used in the Union of Soviet Socialist Republics (USSR) (see Chapter 5). Ultimately this is a difference in how capital is measured which places it within the scope of capital controversies (as discussed in Chapter 3).

The World Bank stated that each of its CWON reports 'has introduced incremental improvements to the accuracy of wealth estimates by gathering better-quality and more extensive data on resource production and reserves, and improving the valuation approach'.[141] The 2024 CWON report introduced revisions to the underlying methodology and inclusion of new non-renewable resources (cobalt, lithium, and molybdenum) as well as an adjustment to how the capital series are deflated. The 2023 UNEP report did not increase its coverage of non-renewable resources, and it excludes these important natural resources. Yet, neither the World Bank nor UNEP accounts for other important materials that have been highlighted as being critical to modern economies, such as sand or salt used in the manufacture of semiconductors and fertilizers.[142]

National Estimates of Inclusive Wealth

Ultimately the issue is that international organizations are estimating national wealth using only data that is readily available across countries. While this is more sophisticated than the work of early compilers of estimates of National Income statistics (such as Mulhall and Clark discussed in Chapter 5), it is similar in that researchers are relying on information that is publicly available without direct access to official data. As the fine print from the 2021 CWON report states, 'the World Bank does not guarantee the accuracy of the data included in this work'.

So, what about country-level estimates of wealth? While there have been various efforts to introduce standards, these have faced resistance from various interest groups who might stand to lose out if new regulations based thereon are adopted.[143] Yet, similar to national income estimates in the 1930s, both the United States and the United Kingdom have been leading the way with other countries independently experimenting with wealth accounts.

The US experiment with greening national accounting is perhaps the most telling. The first estimates of green GDP were published by the Bureau of Economic Analysis (BEA) of the US Department of Commerce in 1994; the same government institution that published the early national income estimates in the 1930s.[144] Inspired by the Brundtland Commission, the Bureau published satellite accounts. There was immediate political backlash against the release of the estimates from interest groups (coal mining) most at threat from alternative accounting perspectives. This led to an inquiry into greening national accounts, chaired by William D. Nordhaus and including evidence from Kirk Hamilton. The subsequent report, *Nature's Numbers*,[145] recommended that the BEA's estimates of green national accounts be resumed. The report concluded that:

> extending the U.S. national income and product accounts (NIPA) to include assets and production activities associated with natural resources and the environment is an important goal. Environmental and natural-resource accounts would provide useful data on resource trends and help governments, businesses, and individuals better plan their economic activities and investments. The rationale for augmented accounts is solidly grounded in mainstream economic analysis.

Political developments are key to understanding why there was limited uptake of these measures. The first-term Clinton administration lost midterm elections in 1994. The political will to implement recommendations from *Nature's Numbers* dissipated and caused the proposals to be shelved. On the whole Democrats had been in favour of greening the national accounts, the only exception being a Democratic representative from the coal mining state of West Virginia.[146] The initiative was revived by the Biden Administration when a national strategy for environmental national accounts was announced in 2022, almost thirty years after the original BEA estimates were published. Since this announcement the political sands have once again shifted. A new administration has committed to 'drill, baby, drill', placing natural capital at risk and pitting different interest groups against one another.

The UK's experience of releasing Inclusive Wealth accounts is less dramatic but also revealing of challenges. The UK Office of National Statistics (ONS) released its own version of Inclusive Wealth in November 2024 based on the UNEP approach.[147] The underlying ONS series, shown in Figure 6.12, highlights the decline in natural capital from 2005 to 2022 and the stagnation in human capital. Both are key components of the UK's productivity stagnation (see Chapters 7 and 8). However, media coverage was ambivalent. The *Financial Times* reported that the resulting estimates

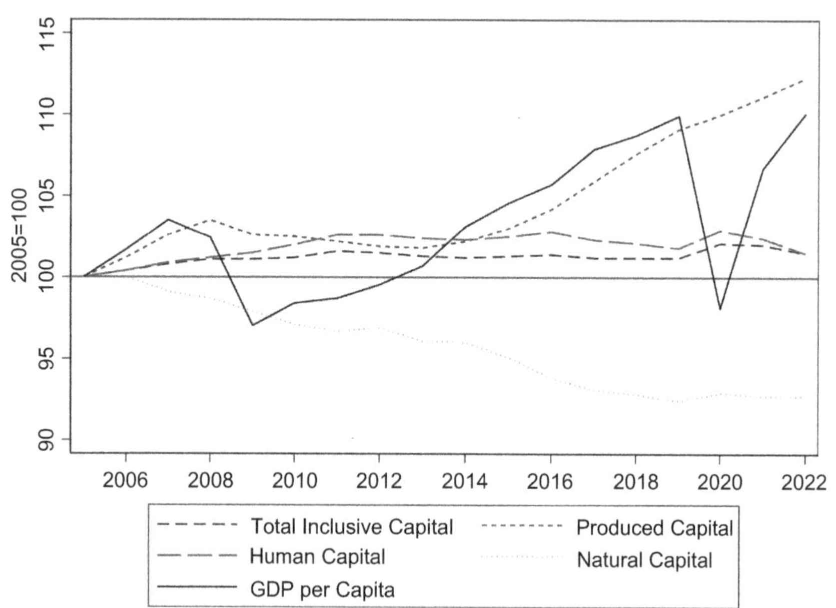

FIGURE 6.12 *ONS Index of Inclusive Wealth per capita and GDP per capita, 2005–2022. Source: ONS (2024). UK inclusive wealth and income accounts: 2005 to 2022.*

were 'a bit of a mess', particularly as the series showed very little change in Inclusive Wealth from 2005 to present.[148] Although, the ONS data shows a similar trend to that shown by the World Bank estimates (Figure 6.6). An optimistic interpretation is that the UK (like the World) is weakly sustainable but the decline in natural capital would worry someone with strong sustainability preferences.

The Change in Inclusive Wealth Over Time

Surveying the research on the economics of sustainable development in the early 1990s, David Pearce and colleagues reflected on why Sustainable Development as a research area emerged. They argued that:

> it is more likely that the literature is simply emphasising sustainability because it has been neglected in the past. In turn, that neglect arises from the widely shared belief that sustainability was not in doubt in the past. Only now that apparent global risks exist that could reduce the well-being of future generations has the need for thinking about sustainability emerged.[149]

The concern about sustainability in the present in turn influenced how historians have revised their interpretations of the past. An early study was by Kirk Hamilton and Michael Clemens who estimated Genuine Savings for developing countries from 1970 to 1993. The publication of the historical time series helped contextualize and establish trends of sustainable development. The main finding was a persistently negative Genuine Savings in Sub-Saharan Africa.[150]

A historical emphasis on wealth might bring the SD research into the orbit of what the economic historian Nicholas Crafts (1949–2023) referred to as the 'capital-fundamentalist' interpretation of economic development associated with Rostow (see discussion in Chapter 7).[151] But Crafts himself was more circumspect when it came to environmental economics. In his 1993 pamphlet *Can Deindustrialisation Seriously Damage Your Wealth*, Crafts had experimented with estimates of MEW and showed that the growth in UK MEW was similar to GDP growth from 1979 to 1989.[152] Crafts' openness to the ideas of environmental economics is further reflected in an historical study of Genuine Savings by the economist Mar Rubio, Crafts' former PhD student. Rubio's study applied the concepts of Genuine Savings to Venezuela and Mexico and showed that both countries had experienced prolonged periods of negative Genuine Savings, but they had not experienced a decline in well-being. Rubio argued that a measure of the terms of trade, or rather the capital gains for the countries' stock of natural resources, was missing from the measurement of Genuine Savings.[153]

Once this was accounted for there was no discrepancy, thus highlighting the importance of completeness of accounting.

Further applications of Genuine Savings came in the 2010s. A study of Genuine Savings in Sweden highlighted the role of pollution in early industrialization. While estimates of British Genuine Savings from the industrial revolution to the present were used to test the theory of whether Genuine Savings was a good indicator of changes in well-being. The study found that Genuine Savings worked as a predictor of well-being over the long run but that it did not work as well without the inclusion of a measure of technological progress.[154] There were similar findings in the cases of the US, Germany, Australia, and Ireland, but not for Sweden.[155] Other studies have used Genuine Savings as a way to nuance the economic history of Ireland, showing a slow rate of Genuine Savings in the 1950s when Ireland experienced a severe recession.[156] The most recent work in this area is an attempt to create a Maddison-style database of Genuine Savings by Cristian Ducoing, Les Oxley and McLaughlin. Similar to Maddison, the goal is to ascertain the trends in the indicators over time to ascertain the likely path of SD.[157] This study highlighted the importance of the inclusion of measures of carbon emissions and how the carbon price can change the signal one gets from the historical record.

Given the more recent shift towards wealth accounting by the World Bank and UNEP, there have been fewer historical estimates of Inclusive Wealth. One exception was a study that compared the methodologies of the World Bank and UNEP using the case of Britain from 1760 to 2000. The study found marked differences in how the Inclusive Wealth of Britain was measured depending on the methodology that was invoked (further discussed in Chapter 8).[158] Consequently, the uncertainty about which methodology to apply has led to lower engagement with the economics of the SD framework among the economic history community.

Conclusion

Inclusive Wealth accounting emerged from the nascent field of environmental (and ecological) economics. This approach saw the economy as embedded within the environmental system. It sees Inclusive Wealth as a means-based indicator of SD. Alternative foci have led to two different ways to think about sustainable development: weak and strong. The former advocates non-declining total capital whereas the latter emphasizes non-declining natural capital.

The theoretical lineage of wealth accounting is peppered with contributions from numerous Nobel laureates (Solow, Arrow, Sen, Tobin and Nordhaus). The application of this theory paralleled early attempts to measure national income. The first estimates were done by lone scholars but in the 1990s the mantle was taken up by the World Bank. UNEP also began to report Inclusive Wealth estimates in the 2010s but these have conflicted with the metrics produced by the World Bank. Overall, there is useful information provided by the measurement of Inclusive Wealth and it is not simply a repetition of narratives based on GDP growth. However, greater coherence is needed between the measures of Inclusive Wealth generated by both the World Bank and UNEP before they can be adopted *en masse*. An arbitrary preference for one over the other will not facilitate comparison across countries.[159]

The theoretical literature has evolved alongside empirical estimates, yet there remains scope for improvement and a need for greater alignment. Academic research has largely continued to frame sustainability in terms of Genuine Savings (the change in Inclusive Wealth), while acknowledging the limitations of existing measures and proposing ways to refine and expand them.[160] By contrast, international organizations have increasingly emphasized wealth-based indicators, though typically without providing empirical justification for preferring one metric over another.

Producing Inclusive Wealth estimates takes time. Even though the World Bank and UNEP have published reports more often in recent years, they still lag behind major events. The 2021 and 2024 World Bank reports, for instance, did not cover the aftermath of Covid-19; the 2024 *Changing Wealth of Nations* only went up to 2020. Similarly, UNEP's 2023 report stopped at 2019. By contrast, the Genuine Savings metric, widely used in academic research, can be updated more easily (although it appears it is no longer being updated by the World Bank), though international organizations may worry about its reliability. A comparison with population statistics helps illuminate the situation. Inclusive Wealth reports are like national censuses: detailed, important, but infrequent. In between, governments rely on annual birth and death registrations to track population changes, even though those figures never quite match the full census. Inclusive Wealth accounting works in much the same way. Comprehensive reports remain essential, but while waiting for them, tracking changes through Genuine Savings is a practical way to stay up to date.[161]

A further issue that warrants deeper discussion is the treatment of technological progress. Earlier contributions, notably Martin Weitzman's work, tended to assume a steady continuation of TFP growth (at c. 1% per annum growth).[162] However, the slowdown in productivity growth, as measured by TFP and documented in Chapter 5, has implications that extend beyond output growth. Despite this, it has received little attention in the debates around Inclusive Wealth. Indeed, the latest UNEP report appears to conflict with the current understanding of productivity trends, asserting that 'all countries experienced different but significant increases in total factor productivity'.[163] Contrary to these claims, the 2024 IMF country report documents a 'broad-based slowdown' in TFP growth across advanced and emerging economies.[164]

Effectively, political economy will determine if nation-states choose to adopt and adhere to these metrics. Where politics can sideline such efforts if they draw attention to inconvenient truths, then international organizations might be free from such domestic political pressures. However, International organizations do not have complete access to information, and these estimates are clearly second-best, but it is better than the alternative of no estimates. Yet, the future is uncertain. Support for the UN and the World Bank fluctuates depending on the whims of governmental forces in power. The World Bank took its environmental turn in the late 1980s and early 1990s under pressure from US Democrats, but the 2024 US election brought in a Republican party that had no qualms about offering only conditional financing to the World Bank with the aim of 're-focusing' it on its 'core mission'.[165] The UN is also under severe financial pressure due to budgetary shortfalls and may be forced to cut expenditure.[166] The situation has been exacerbated by the Republican administration who have reviewed all financial contributions to international organizations, with particular focus on certain UN agencies.[167] Although the future of wealth accounting in the World Bank and UNEP is uncertain, wealth-based metrics remain an essential investment. It seems imperative for a clear consensus if progress is to be made on measuring the Inclusive Wealth of nations and it seems that this progress can only come from nations and that we cannot fully rely on international organizations.

In summary, there has been ongoing debate in the scholarship advocating for alternatives to GDP as a measure of economic performance, with some proposing Inclusive Wealth as a potential substitute. The two should be viewed as complementary: GDP reflects an economy's productive capacity, while Inclusive Wealth captures the welfare outcomes of the growth process. In the following chapters, I will use the history of the United Kingdom as a case study to explore whether applying concepts from Inclusive Wealth can provide meaningful insights, or 'useful new information', to better understand the history of economic growth in the UK.

Part IV

History of Economic Growth

CHAPTER SEVEN

A Brief History of Britain's Economic Growth, 1750–2020

In early 2025 the UK Office of National Statistics released GDP figures showing that the UK had experienced back-to-back quarterly declines in GDP per capita at the end of 2024. These figures by themselves were very low (−0.23% and −0.14%), probably not too far from 0, and were revised away in further revisions, similar to how an earlier contraction had been revised away.[1] Much more alarming, though, were the consecutive quarters of declining GDP per person.[2] The figures available at the end of 2024 showed that GDP per person in the UK remained below its pre-Covid-19 levels. In the summer of 2025, however, the ONS revised its GDP figures, lifting the overall level of output and altering the underlying narrative to some extent. Even after these revisions, GDP per capita in 2024 stood just 0.12 percent above its pre-pandemic level.[3] This compares very poorly with the experience of the United States, where GDP per person was around 6 per cent higher than before Covid-19 levels, highlighting the stark scale of the UK's underperformance. It has been customary of late to blame all the ills of the British economy on the 2016 Brexit referendum,[4] but many of these issues predate Brexit and there is a deeper story to be told.

Taking a longer perspective, Britain[5] today has a higher standard of living than at the time of Adam Smith and it also has higher living standards than at the peak of the British Empire. The difference is relative. Britain, or rather England, in Adam Smith's time was the wealthiest country in the world and today it is not. Britain was the first industrial nation and the most powerful country in the world (*Pax Britannica*), then it experienced a long period of relative decline;[6] this decline is relative to the performance of its peers, as shown in Table 7.1. Britain was overtaken by the United States in the early twentieth century. The United States quickly took a commanding lead and, besides the blip of the Great Depression, showed no indication of relinquishing its lead throughout the twentieth century.

TABLE 7.1 UK Relative GDP per person (UK = 100 in every period).

	Canada	Germany	France	Italy	Japan	United States	China
1770s		60	62			84	
1780s–1790s		59	59				32
1800s–1850s	45	56	55	71	38	84	25
1850s–1890s	52	54	57	48	28	93	16
1900s–1910s	78	63	61	47	31	120	12
1920s–1930s	80	71	78	53	43	124	11
1940s–1960s	103	75	75	59	44	135	8
1970s–1990s	118	104	109	98	106	142	11
2000s–2020s	117	115	102	96	100	143	31

Source: MPD version 2023: J. Bolt and J. L. van Zanden (2024). Maddison-style estimates of the evolution of the world economy: A new 2023 update. Journal of Economic Surveys, 1–41.

Perhaps the United States could alternatively be considered the outlier in that it persistently outperformed its peers. Removing the United States from the picture, Britain was still one of the wealthiest countries in the world up until the 1970s; Britain remained ahead of its European peers and the largest-growing economies in Asia. Britain was still ahead of France and Germany in the mid-twentieth century but then lost its preeminent place due to slower growth. Japan converged and overtook Britain in the 1980s, and by the 1990s Britain fell behind almost all of the G7 countries and despite a flurry in the 1990s and early 2000s, it continued to lag behind (see Figure 7.5). The UK's relative decline is demonstrably a modern phenomenon brought about solely in the past half century rather than an historic legacy. One of the main issues driving the relative decline has been the productivity slowdown, a global phenomenon but one that has been particularly pronounced in Britain.

In this chapter I will give a brief overview of the UK's history of economic growth, outlining the current narratives that are effectively based on comparative GDP performance over time. I will show how Britain's economic history has been interpreted, and revised, through the lens of economic growth theory that was discussed in Chapter 3. As new theories of economic growth came into fashion, they influenced the interpretation (or reinterpretation) of Britain's past. This, however, should be a two-way process; knowledge of history should also inform theory, and economic historians have contributed to this by emphasizing the importance of path dependence, the idea that past decisions can have persistent effects and constrain the present.[7] Different theories of economic growth help to contextualize different facets of Britain's history.

Ultimately, it is within the work of Adam Smith that we see the genesis of the different hypotheses, for example, productivity growth in the division of labour, capital accumulation and also the importance of institutions. Smith was clear: 'it is this effort, protected by law, and allowed by liberty to exert itself in the manner that is most advantageous, which has maintained the progress of England towards opulence and improvement in almost all former times, and which, it is to be hoped, will do so in all future times'.[8] Yet, Smith also emphasized England's geographical advantages (the fertility of its soil, extensive coastline and many navigable rivers) that were important for manufacturing and trade.[9] The subsequent applications of theory have stressed part of the picture but not enough emphasis has been placed on the interlinkages between all explanations; they need not be, and should not be, mutually exclusive.

The Industrial Revolution

The Industrial Revolution was marked by a sustained increase in economic growth rather than a one-off increase in living standards. It was associated with a shift from agriculture to industry, the growth of cities, and an increase in agricultural output to feed the increasingly urban population. There were also improvements to transport and a reduction in sailing times that facilitated the growth of international trade. Most notably there was an increase in technological change, innovation, and productivity growth.[10]

Dating the start of the Industrial Revolution has been subject to much debate. The economic historian Arnold Toynbee (1852–83) was the first English writer to use the phrase 'industrial revolution', dating the start to 1760. Subsequent revisions saw it moved forward to the 1780s, but also back to the 1600s. It is now seen as a reflection of gradual improvements, an industrial evolution rather than a revolution *per se*.[11] The dating of the Industrial Revolution to the 1760s has a lot to do with a series of inventions in the cotton industry (spinning jenny, water frame and spinning mule which increased productivity in spinning and weaving) which was an emblematic industry of the revolution. Other key inventions in the iron industry were the use of coal as the main source of fuel which paved the way for future developments. Another crucial innovation related to the invention and improvements of steam engines, first by Thomas Newcomen (1663–1729) and later by James Watts (1736–1819), with subsequent improvements and applications to transport in the 1830s, although the full impact of the steam engine was not felt until the 1870s, almost 100 years after the original Watt patent.[12] The Industrial Revolution also saw increases in coal mining which was facilitated by the improvements in steam engines and the transport revolutions (fuelled by coal) also helped transport coal (this is discussed in greater detail in Chapter 8).

The historical record offers a crucial arena in which to test competing theories of economic growth, with the Industrial Revolution being interpreted through a wide range of theoretical lenses. The twentieth century saw different theoretical perspectives used to analyse the Industrial Revolution, such as Harrod-Domar models, neoclassical-inspired analyses, and endogenous growth models (see discussion in Chapter 3).[13] The view that the Industrial Revolution marked a dramatic discontinuity, a 'take-off' using Rostow's aeronautical metaphor, was challenged from the 1980s onwards. The current consensus view is one of a gradual increase in economic growth, inspired by the application of growth accounting derived from neoclassical growth models. Although there continued to be voices expressing their disquiet with such views, an early analysis of revised output and manufacturing indices indicated that there was indeed a structural break that made 1780 to 1851 'a distinctive macroeconomic epoch'.[14]

New growth theory was applied to the Industrial Revolution from the 1980s onwards. To the fore in these applications was Nick Crafts who, in a long and influential research career, looked to see if the new growth theory could help provide a better understanding of the industrial revolution.[15] In an early study, Crafts sought to distinguish between the Romer approach which emphasized increasing returns to capital, and subsequent models, such as by Lucas, that placed emphasis on human capital.[16] Crafts showed how new growth theory could only partially explain the Industrial Revolution but that there was still scope for 'exogenous' macro inventions, these were technological innovations that were invented overseas.[17] Crafts drew on the work of the Nobel laureate Joel Mokyr who noted that 'if England led the rest of the world in the Industrial Revolution, it was despite, not because of her formal education system.' Mokyr placed particular emphasis on the Scientific Enlightenment and the development of a culture of science throughout western Europe, however it was England where the applied science came of age. The view of Mokyr was that English workers were skilled at tinkering, micro-innovations, and applying concepts developed elsewhere.[18]

Crafts' early assessment that new growth theory did not fully explain the Industrial Revolution was challenged by economic historians David Greasley (1951–2021) and Les Oxley who illustrated the limitations of Crafts application of new growth theory. They showed that human capital, broadly defined, was compatible with the record of British economic growth.[19] In later work Crafts was more sympathetic towards endogenous growth applications to British economic history. For example, he was critical of neoclassical paradigms because they assumed convergence with the leader but not that the leader would be surpassed.[20] In his last book, a survey of British economic growth from the Industrial Revolution until the 2008 financial crisis, Crafts framed his analysis around endogenous growth and saw it as a way to understand both the Industrial Revolution and also the drivers of innovation in the British economy.[21]

Why Britain?

One of the big questions in economic history is why the Industrial Revolution started in Britain,[22] and it has become, as Crafts put it, 'a search for the Holy Grail'.[23] There are effectively two complementary approaches to the question: one explaining the supply of innovation and the other explaining the demand for innovation.[24] Joel Mokyr focused on the emergence of technological change and, across a series of books, argued that a distinctive culture of science and useful knowledge was central to the Industrial Revolution. While the Enlightenment was a pan-European movement, Mokyr distinguished between macroinventions and microinventions; the macroinvention were major breakthroughs associated with scientific advances, while microinventions were the incremental improvements made by skilled mechanics and entrepreneurs, helping to explain why Britain, in particular, surged ahead. Mokyr further argued that the growing stock of useful knowledge interacted with favourable institutions in Britain to produce sustained technological progress. As European and North American institutions changed through wars and revolutions, other countries began to catch up, and by 1914 Britain was 'first among equals'.[25]

The economic historian Robert Allen offered a different meta-narrative for why the Industrial Revolution occurred first in England. Allen's 'high wage' hypothesis argues that relative factor prices, the costs of inputs used in production, created strong incentives for technological changes.[26] England had high wages and the cost of capital (or rather the cost of energy) was low. The high wage scenario also created conditions for greater savings and thus higher capital accumulation. This generated strong incentives to substitute capital for labour in England and created the conditions for the Industrial Revolution because, as Allen concluded, it was only profitable to invent in England and not elsewhere.[27] Allen further explained England's high wage economy was partly an outcome of the Black Death which caused a dramatic fall in population, and that these high wages were maintained by colonial expansion and the associated increase in trade, as well as the growth in cities. In this model, urbanization was a key driver of both efficiency and higher wages. The explicit example that Allen used was that of textiles where he outlined hypothetical cost schedules for spinning jennies (new technology) and spinning wheels (older technology) in both a high wage and a low-wage economy. The framework, drawing on the work of Daron Acemoglu, highlighted the importance of relative factor prices in incentivizing innovation, as well as market size.[28] In addition to the cost of the machinery, the unit cost of research and development was also included. In the low-wage setting this additional cost would further deter innovation, but this could also have affected innovation in the high wage economy if the unit R&D costs were high and thus undermining the signal from the relative factor prices. Although here market size is important as it would reduce the size of unit R&D cost by spreading the cost over a bigger market.

While Allen's approach offers a very attractive endogenous growth-inspired interpretation of economic history (and it is now appearing in economic textbooks), it is not without its detractors and it has led to a series of debates that have focused on components of the relative price hypothesis, namely Allen's real-wage estimates. Early critiques centred on the calorific content implied in Allen's cost of living indices as they underestimated the calorific needs of women and children. They also show that perceptions about family size were flawed, and that the labour of women and children had been overlooked.[29] Another methodological critique centred on the construction wage data used by Allen and showed how the 'wages' were actually payments to contractors who in turn withheld a margin from their payments to labourers and craftsmen. This margin was sizeable, up to 30 per cent, and this meant that the wage data was overstated and that the wages may not in fact have been wages.[30] A further critique returned to the issue of spinning wages highlighting that these were lower than originally thought and it was argued that this undermined the 'high wage' hypothesis.[31]

The most recent foray into this debate is a series of contributions from the economic historians Morgan Kelly, Joel Mokyr and Cormac Ó Gráda.[32] In an early study, it was highlighted that most inventions were not labour-saving and that the high wages were a symptom, not a cause, of the Industrial Revolution. Instead, greater emphasis was placed on the contribution of human capital, broadly defined to include both education and health, to the Industrial Revolution. This was illustrated using evidence that showed British workers as being taller, stronger, longer lived and thus more productive than their French counterparts. This environment improved the capabilities of workers in Britain. It was also shown that, contrary to Allen's hypothesis, within Britain it was regions with *low* wages that industrialized; this was because skilled mechanics were found in these regions. This built on an earlier study of watchmakers that showed high productivity growth in the high-tech sector at the time, and that it was spillovers from industries such as these that made the Industrial Revolution British.[33] While this is supportive of an endogenous growth framework, it is ultimately a very Smithian story about economic growth in the eighteenth century.

Institutions are also widely seen as a fundamental cause of the Industrial Revolution. The main focus has tended to be on the role of the changing political institutions in Britain as well as economic institutions, such as the patent system, and how these led to secure property rights. Although how much legal protection patents offered before the 1830s has been questioned.[34]

The 'Glorious Revolution'[35] tends to be the event which garners the most attention in this strand of research because it placed greater constraint on the executive in Britain vis-à-vis France and other European countries.[36] Although this high politics interpretation has been questioned as there is no clear link between the 'Glorious Revolution' and the industrial revolution.[37] In the work of Kelly and colleagues, important institutional features of England are highlighted such as the poor law system which offered a modicum of education to the poorest and helped improve labour quality. Another institutional feature was the guild system in England which differed from its European peers and was self-regulating ensuring that apprentices received adequate training. Again, this institutional interpretation has its roots in *The Wealth of Nations*.

Another important event, although less celebrated, is the religious freedom and subsequent suppression of views that occurred during the political revolutions of the Civil War and Republican era (1642–60).[38] The Marxist historian Christopher Hill (1912–2003) placed the later economic revolutions in the context of the political revolutions in Britain in the 1600s, the pinnacle of which was the 'Glorious Revolution' with the change in the royal line from Stuarts but this was also associated with radical religious changes that had profound influences on society.[39] The religious freedom of the of the 1640s saw the emergence of religious groups (e.g., Quakers) that have played a key role during the later industrial revolution.

Capital Formation and the Industrial Revolution

One of the most contentious debates in economic history relates to the role of capital. The reason for the debate stemmed from the work of Walt Rostow who had argued that a 'necessary but not sufficient condition' for sustained economic growth was a rise in the net investment to national income ratio from around 5 per cent to 10 per cent.[40] Rostow also emphasized that there would be a leading sector and that institutions were required to facilitate economic growth. Originally Rostow tentatively dated the period of 'take-off' for Great Britain as 1783 to 1802, but he subsequently revised this to be 1783 to 1830. Effectively Rostow was drawing on the work of contemporary growth theory, the Harrod-Domar model (see chapter 3), as well as the work of development economists, such as Arthur Lewis.

Rostow's work was widely popular outside of economics and, in the eyes of one reviewer, this was perhaps why many of his peers disliked his work.[41] An entire conference was devoted to debating/criticizing Rostow's work with both Simon Kuznets and Robert Solow being vocal critics of Rostow's approach. Kuznets pointed to the fact that there was no sudden increase in net national capital formation, rather a steady evolution of investment rates, while Solow bemoaned the lack of a coherent theoretical framework in Rostow's work.[42] Writing in response to Rostow's original *Stages*, the economic historians Phyllis Deane and John Habakkuk (1915–2002) wrote that, 'if national income data for the eighteenth century are suspect, capital formation data are virtually non-existent'. After reviewing the evidence Deane and Habakkuk found that the 'quantitative data for the period do not support a shift of this order of magnitude'.[43] Deane and Habakkuk did not dismiss the claim that investment was important, rather they disputed that there was a rapid rise in investment in such a concentrated period of time.

Throughout his work Rostow emphasized an annual investment rate of 10 per cent as an 'essentially tautological' way of defining 'take-off'.[44] In later work, he argued that there was general agreement over the increase in investment in Britain, but that debate was over the magnitude of the rise. Deane and Cole, and later Crafts, were somewhat sympathetic to the idea that the investment ratio rose, but they suggested this happened over a more extended period and that only a 'slow acceleration' was visible from the 1740s.[45] While subsequent work by Charles Feinstein denied a sharp rise in the investment ratio, he instead argued that the gross domestic investment ratio had already reached 12 per cent by the 1780s and changed little over the next 50 years.[46]

The evidence that Rostow later used were estimates of *gross* investment; despite this Rostow still maintained that depreciation was about 'one-fifth to about one-half of gross investment'.[47] The gross investment series used by Rostow was a series constructed by Phyllis Deane that showed a gradual rise in gross investment from 5.5 per cent of GDP in the 1830s to 8.2 per cent by the 1850s. Although Deane herself commented that, 'the most striking feature of these results is the rather low proportion of national expenditure they show as devoted to domestic fixed capital formation'.[48] Rostow continued with his line of argument and later editions of *The Stages of Economic Growth* were unchanged bar appendices that directly addressed the various criticisms he had received. One curiosity of the critiques was their focus on *gross* investment, whereas Rostow posited *net* investment as the relevant measure for sustained growth.[49]

While the sweeping generalizations of *Stages* led to greater engagement and stinging criticism, in the eyes of a reviewer of Rostow's Festschrift his 'more scholarly works have stood the test of time better'.[50] In his earlier work Rostow had seen investment as a broader concept which included both traditional capital as well as 'land and other natural resources, as well as scientific, technical, and organizational knowledge'.[51] The definition of take-off in earlier work was also more modest and was intended to be a shift from agriculture to industry. Thus, Rostow's broader generalization in *Stages* and response to criticism distracted from an innovative intellectual contribution and one that has been overlooked in the various attempts to debunk *Stages*.

Slavery and the Industrial Revolution

Long-distance trade was an important backdrop to the Industrial Revolution, with raw materials imported and finished goods exported; it enabled the specialization that drove industrialization in Britain and allowed the country to feed itself. Slave-based commerce was central to the Atlantic economy from the 1600s to the early 1800s. The 'Triangular trade' was between Europe, America, and Africa; whereby Europe exported manufactures to America and Africa, raw materials were exported from America to Europe, and slaves were traded from Africa to America, via Europe.[52]

Slavery is a part of the Industrial Revolution story that is often overlooked in conventional accounts.[53] The path-breaking study was by the Trinidadian political leader and historian Eric Williams (1911–81) who argued that slavery played a key role in the Industrial Revolution as profits from the slave trade helped to finance the Industrial Revolution.[54] Williams further argued that it was economic forces, not humanitarian concerns that led to the removal of slavery as it was, 'mature industrial capitalism [that] destroyed the slave system'. Slavery, it was argued, was essential to Britain's development in the eighteenth century. Some historians have argued that the slave trade was also key to the development and integration of financial markets within the UK.[55] While Williams argued that his study was equally applicable in other colonial contexts where slavery was used, such as France, only Britain was home to the Industrial Revolution. This lends credence to the view that there were other factors at play and that perhaps it was more than profits from the slave trade that led to the Industrial Revolution.

The question of how much slavery contributed to the Industrial Revolution is, of course, disputed. The economic historian Stanley Engerman (1936–2023) estimated that slave trade profits equated to about 0.5 per cent of British national income by 1770 and that the share of UK investment that was derived from slave trade profits was 'low' at between 2.4 to 10.8 per cent.[56] Similarly, the economic historian Patrick O'Brien estimated that the profits from the trade with the periphery (which included the slave trade) contributed a small fraction to gross investment (about 10 per cent) in the early 1800s and thus were unlikely to be a large component of investment during the Industrial Revolution.[57]

The view that slavery played a small role in the Industrial Revolution was challenged by the economic historian Barbara Solow (1923–2014)[58] who argued that William's thesis was compatible with established understanding of the British Industrial Revolution. Solow argued that while slave trade profits were 7.8 per cent of British investment, they equated to 40 per cent of private investment. Solow also showed how the colonial trade could have had a wider impact on British economic growth; she illustrated how the colonial trade provided a way to prevent diminishing returns to capital in Britain and thereby prevent a fall in British profit rates. The colonies, by importing manufactures from Britain, provided a ready market for British industrial activity and the British West Indies took 37 per cent of British domestic exports in 1772–73 and 57 per cent in 1797–98.[59]

The question about the role of slavery and the Industrial Revolution was revisited in a recent study by economists Stephen Heblich, Stephen Redding and Joachim Voth. Their focus was on the 1833 Abolition of Slavery Act and the 1837 Slavery compensation records where £20 million was paid by the British state to compensate slaveholders (5 per cent of GDP). Heblich and colleagues linked the slavery records with industrial employment in Britain. The findings were that slavery increased local incomes in places with the greatest involvement in the slave trade by 40 per cent. However, a limitation of this approach was that it used records from the end of the slave trading period and employment at the tail-end of the First Industrial Revolution to infer the impact of slave trading eighty years previously. The figure of £20 million was based on the net present value of the slaves and not the annual profit from slave trading; thus, the implied investment rates from 1833 would actually be much lower and it does not tell us what the likely investment rates would have been in the 1700s. Also, the location of slave trading and industrialization does not appear to be a clear match. For example, Bristol was a large slave trading hub, but it was not an epicentre of the Industrial Revolution.[60] Furthermore, other detailed studies of the underlying historical data suggest that the compensation funds were directed towards the city of London rather than the industrial north-east.[61]

Catching Up and Falling Behind

During the Industrial Revolution, in comparison with the experiences of countries today, Britain had low investment rates, low human capital accumulation (in terms of formal education), and low rates of TFP growth. This can be explained by the fact that Britain was the pioneer, there were no other countries to emulate and there was no way to 'catch-up' or 'leap-frog' because Britain set the technological frontier.[62] Towards the end of the nineteenth century, British economic growth slowed somewhat but the acceleration of economic growth in the United States was much more impressive.

The United States was much larger, both geographically and in terms of population, which created incentives to spur further innovation. The population of Britain was double that of the United States in the 1820s but the United States experienced rapid population growth due to immigration and overtook Britain in terms of population for the first time in 1855. By the start of the twentieth century the British population was half that of the United States,[63] falling to a fifth by the start of the twenty-first century (see Figure 7.1). The United States attracted immigrants and was able to benefit

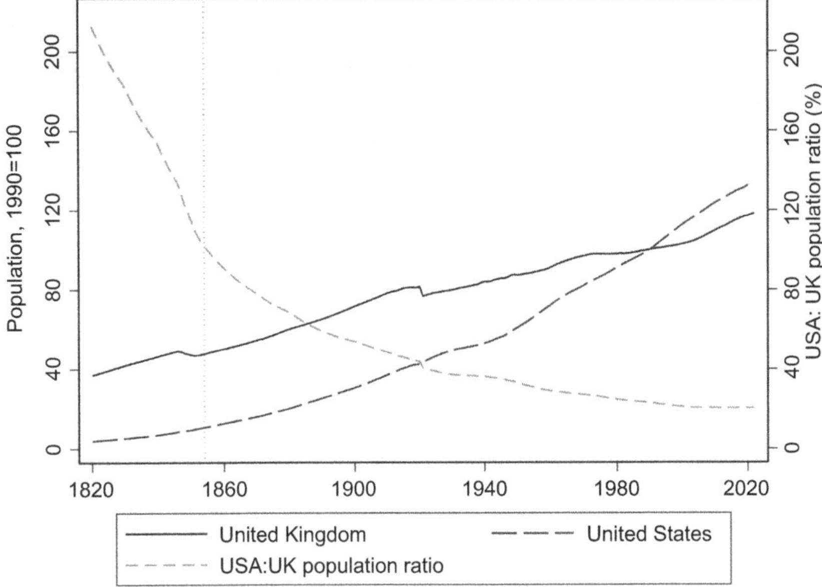

FIGURE 7.1 *UK and US population growth, 1820–2022 Note: Vertical line indicates when the US population overtook the UK's. Source: See Table 4.1.*

from their human capital without incurring the direct cost of education. The United States also had an advantage in terms of natural resources, as it was amply supplied with all sorts of minerals and fossil fuels.[64] The United States simply had a higher growth potential than Britain and it was reflected across many different indicators, and this led to a shift in technological leadership from Britain to the United States. This is shown in Figure 7.2 where the United States was the first country to converge, and overtake, British levels of GDP per capita.

The business historian Alfred DuPont Chandler (1918–2007) argued that the size and rapid growth of the US domestic market in the late nineteenth century made it uniquely profitable to build large, integrated enterprises that coordinated mass production with mass distribution. This scale allowed firms to lower unit costs, exploit high-volume throughput and reinvest in managerial hierarchies, marketing networks and technological innovation, making the United States the 'seed-bed for managerial capitalism'. Crucially, Chandler stressed that 'expanding markets were . . . essential to maintaining mass production and mass distribution, and the United States had the fastest growing market of any industrializing nation', with key indicators ('population, output, and income') all growing faster than in Western Europe and Japan.[65] In a sense, the US experience illustrates Adam Smith's dictum, 'that the division of labour is limited by the extent of the market'.

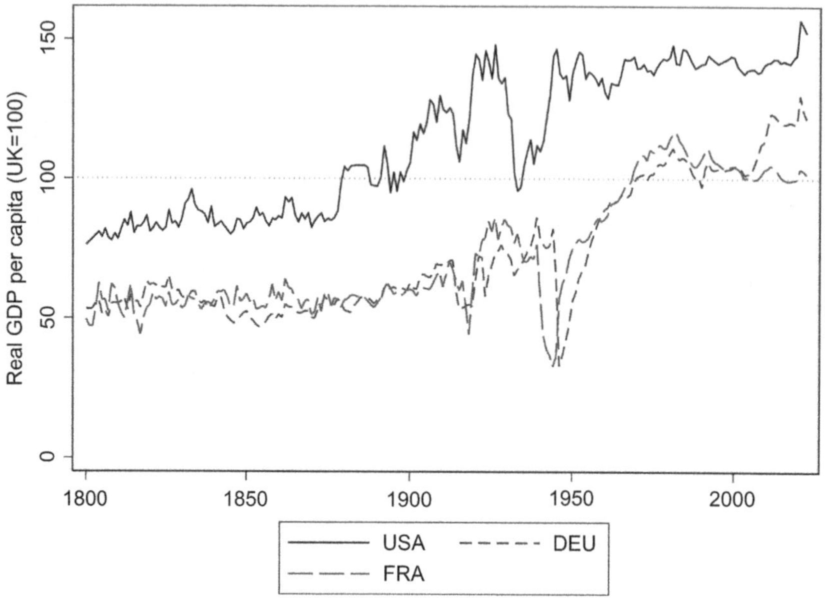

FIGURE 7.2 *UK relative GDP growth (UK = 100 in every year). Source: See Table 7.1.*

One aspect of this higher growth potential comes from the early adoption of machine tabulation for the 1890 US census, which was a precursor of computer processing in the United States. Machine tabulation was required to process the increasing array of data attained by the censuses that was required by American administrators and demanded by US politicians. Although Herman Hollerith, the inventor of machine tabulation (punch cards), read a paper on the benefits of machine tabulation to the Royal Statistical Society in 1894, it was not until the 1911 English census that Britain trialled machine tabulation using machines developed on the US census twenty years earlier.[66] Hollerith's innovations ultimately led to the creation of IBM and the wider application of machine tabulation to business processes, helping to secure US dominance in the field. The conditions driving early adoption of computing were shaped in part by America's large and growing population, and by the 1950s the United States continued to lead Britain in computer applications.[67]

The debate about Britain's relative decline relates to the slowdown in economic growth and the question whether countries were catching-up or if Britain was falling behind. The slowdown in UK growth led to debates about whether (and when) there was a climacteric in the UK's slowdown. Some had dated it to the 1870s and 1880s, associating it with the 'long depression', a period of deflation at the end of the nineteenth century. Although it appears to have been primarily driven by a general shift to a relatively lower growth regime rather than a climacteric.[68]

Productivity growth in US manufacturing is one of the driving forces influencing the convergence of the two countries.[69] Manufacturing indices from the United Kingdom and the United States show the dramatic growth in US manufacturing productivity over the period of the UK's relative decline, shown in Figure 7.3. From 1855 to 1870 UK industrial production grew at 2.97 per cent per annum while US industrial production grew at 3.73 per cent. From 1870 to 1913, UK industrial production growth fell to 2.22 percent per annum while the US rate of industrial production growth increased to 5.28 per cent per annum, more than double the UK rate.

The problems of the UK related to its first mover advantage during the Industrial Revolution; the success of the Industrial Revolution sowed the seeds of later decline.[70] Because of its early start, the geographic location of industries was no longer optimal and difficult to change. While Britain had paved the way during the First Industrial Revolution, there was a reluctance to change within these older industries and the UK lagged behind the development of new industries which were at the forefront of the second Industrial Revolution (such as petrochemicals, aviation, the internal combustion engine, and electricity). The general tendency was for Britian to slip behind and lose the advantages it held in 1870.[71]

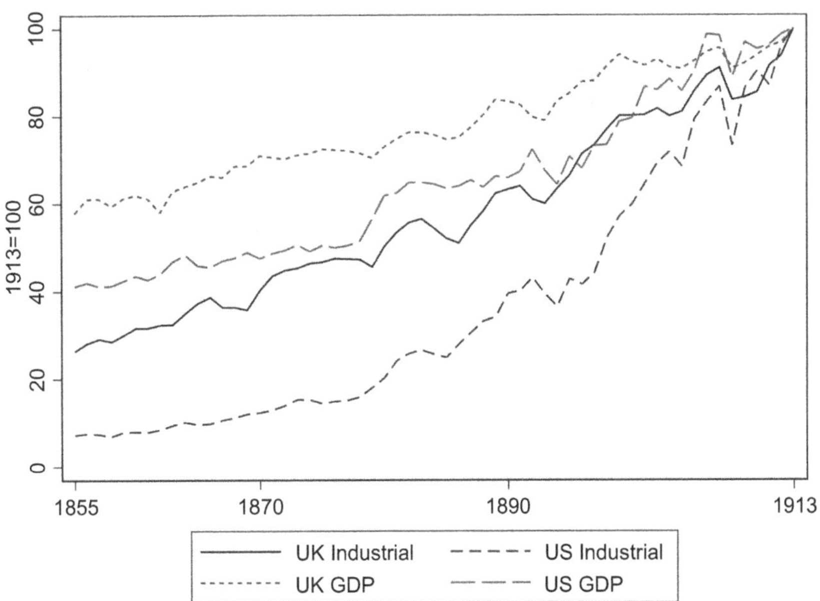

FIGURE 7.3 *UK and US Industrial production indices. Sources: Feinstein (1972). National income, output and expenditure of the United Kingdom 1855–1965; Davis (2004), 'An Annual Index of U. S. Industrial Production, 1790-1915'.*

The UK's relative decline prompted questions about whether Victorian Britain failed by not adopting new technologies.[72] British industry tended to be fragmented, which made it difficult to adopt new technologies and, in a reversal of the Bob Allen argument discussed above,[73] some US inventions did not pay to adopt in Britian.[74] In this context, Britain had low-paid but highly skilled workers whereas the United States faced a shortage of skilled workers alongside an abundance of raw materials. US inventions were therefore ideally suited to US conditions.

Another controversial aspect to the debate over Britain's relative decline is the role of international trade. Britain had adhered to free trade whereas its leading industrial competitors operated under sizeable tariff barriers. US tariff rates were roughly 5 times the level of UK tariffs between 1875 and 1914.[75] British industry was therefore exposed to the full vagaries of international competition, although with sheltered access to its colonial markets. Ironically, Britain was a major source of capital for its competitors and was a net investor in the United States.[76] Overseas investment was high which led to criticism about the lack of investment in the home market. But if the growth of manufacturing in overseas markets was higher, then this implied greater profitability, and British investors were only responding rationally to the investment opportunities.

The shift in technological leadership from the United Kingdom to the United States led to the view that Britain was penalized for its early industrial start.[77] The issue then was if Britain's resources were locked-in to an established pattern of production and whether intervention, via tariff protection, was needed to develop newer industries.[78] Although how effective such protection would have been in practice is likely to have been limited. It is more likely that the protection would have been directed towards older labour-intensive industries rather than the newer more capital-intensive industries of the second industrial revolution.[79]

The two world wars were dramatic shocks to the existing economic structures. The First World War was in part driven by Britain's relative decline and the ascent of Germany which began to supersede Britain as an industrial producer. The First World War caused enormous dislocation, and the post-war recovery was staggered and resulted in various frictions that were unresolved. Part of the issues related to structural problems with the old staple industries which faced increased competition in the inter-war War. New industries emerged in the inter-war period, but these tended to be located in the south of the country leading to a change in the economic geography of the UK.

The global economy was spluttering during the inter-war period and global trade fell as countries around the world began to introduce restrictive trade policies during the Great Depression. While the chronology of the Great Depression is US-centric, Britain's immediate post-First World War experience was worse than the 1929-32 Great Depression period. Britain saw a bigger annual decrease in exports (30 percent fall) in 1921 than in any year during the Great Depression (37.5 percent fall from 1929-32).[80] The 1920s were effectively a lost decade for the British economy. While Britain experienced a relatively mild downturn in the 1930s, this perspective risks obscuring the depth and persistence of economic weakness during the 1920s. The 1919-20 recession was the worst in modern British economic history, and the recovery was slow and protracted. Many factors contributed to the slump of the 1920s, including fiscal retrenchment following the War, the 1918-19 influenza pandemic, monetary tightening, and the loss of southern Ireland.[81] However, a major factor in Britain's post-war malaise was the decision to return to the gold standard (a fixed exchange rate regime) which led to an overvalued pound, and this had immediate implications for competitiveness and employment in regions with traditional export-orientated industry.[82] It was not until September 1931 that Britain decided to abandon the gold standard and sterling was no longer at a competitive disadvantage. Another key facet of the inter-war period was that Britain had amassed an enormous war debt. This was partially relieved with a restructuring of the debt in 1932, but it placed severe restrictions on the fiscal capacity of the state.[83] The United Kingdom did not, however, have a banking crisis similar to the United States because of the branch-banking style of the UK banking system.[84] The effect of the 1920s slump is shown in Figure 7.4 by comparing the trajectories of GDP in the United Kingdom after its 1918 peak with that of the United States following the 1929 peak.

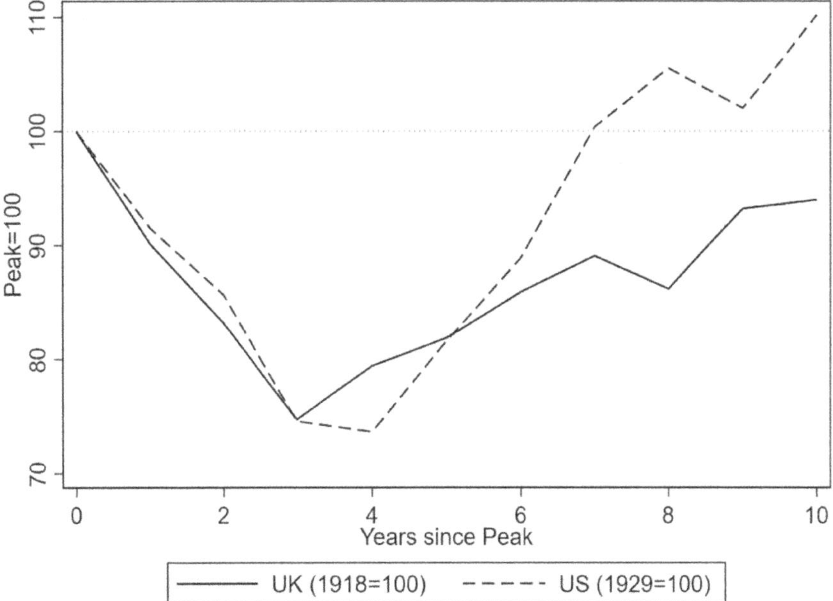

FIGURE 7.4 *Divergent Recovery Paths: UK (Post-1918) and US (Post-1929). Source: Bank of England, A Millennium of Macroeconomic Data; Louis Johnston and Samuel H. Williamson (2025). What Was the US GDP Then? MeasuringWorth.*

Both economies experienced a sharp initial contraction, but the downturn was more prolonged in the UK in the 1920s. While the United States began to recover within five years and surpassed its pre-crisis peak within a decade, the United Kingdom's recovery was much slower and the pre-crisis level was not regained until 1934.[85]

The De-Industrial Revolution and the "British Disease"

On the whole, the economic historian Sidney Pollard (1925–98) was at pains to stress that, while Britain had experienced relative decline in the late Victorian period, the economy was 'fundamentally sound'. This view of soundness, however, was not transferred to his assessment of British economic growth in the post-Second World War era where he concluded that: 'The faults of the decline after 1945 are not to be shuffled off to earlier generations; they remain firmly the responsibility of those who controlled Britain's economic fortunes in those years.'[86]

Sidney Pollard's 1982 book *The Wasting of the British Economy* opened with a bar chart that showed GNP per capita for fifteen countries in 1950 and 1978; this was done to highlight the relative decline of the UK.[87] I continue the Pollard comparison in Figure 7.5 and present GDP per capita using the latest Maddison data for the same fifteen countries as Pollard. The sub-figures in Figure 7.5 are sorted from lowest to highest in each sub-period to highlight the rank order of Britain over time. Similar to Pollard it starts in 1950, but it also records 1972 (the year before the oil crisis), 1980 and 2000. Compared to itself, the UK economy grew over time as GDP per capita increased from $11,061 in 1950 to $31,946 in 2000. However, compared to other countries the UK had the lowest rate of growth and was overtaken. It is clear that Britain goes from being at the top end of the spectrum in 1950 to the tail-end by 2000, but this relative decline happened during the first phase from 1950 to 1972. By the end of the 1970s Britain had ranked last in terms of GDP per capita. What drove this relative decline, and does it really matter?

Britain was a leader in the de-industrial revolution. At the outset this was viewed with concern before being embraced by the political classes as a sign of success. Structural changes in the British economy saw services comprising a larger share of economic activity. Services comprised 49 per cent of gross value added in the 1950s, in the 1970s this had risen to 59 per cent and by the 2000s this had increased to 77 per cent.[88] While other countries followed suit, none had embraced deindustrialization as emphatically as Britain. Nick Crafts, writing in 1996, noted that the 1980s supply-side reforms meant that 'a more optimistic assessment of comparative performance became

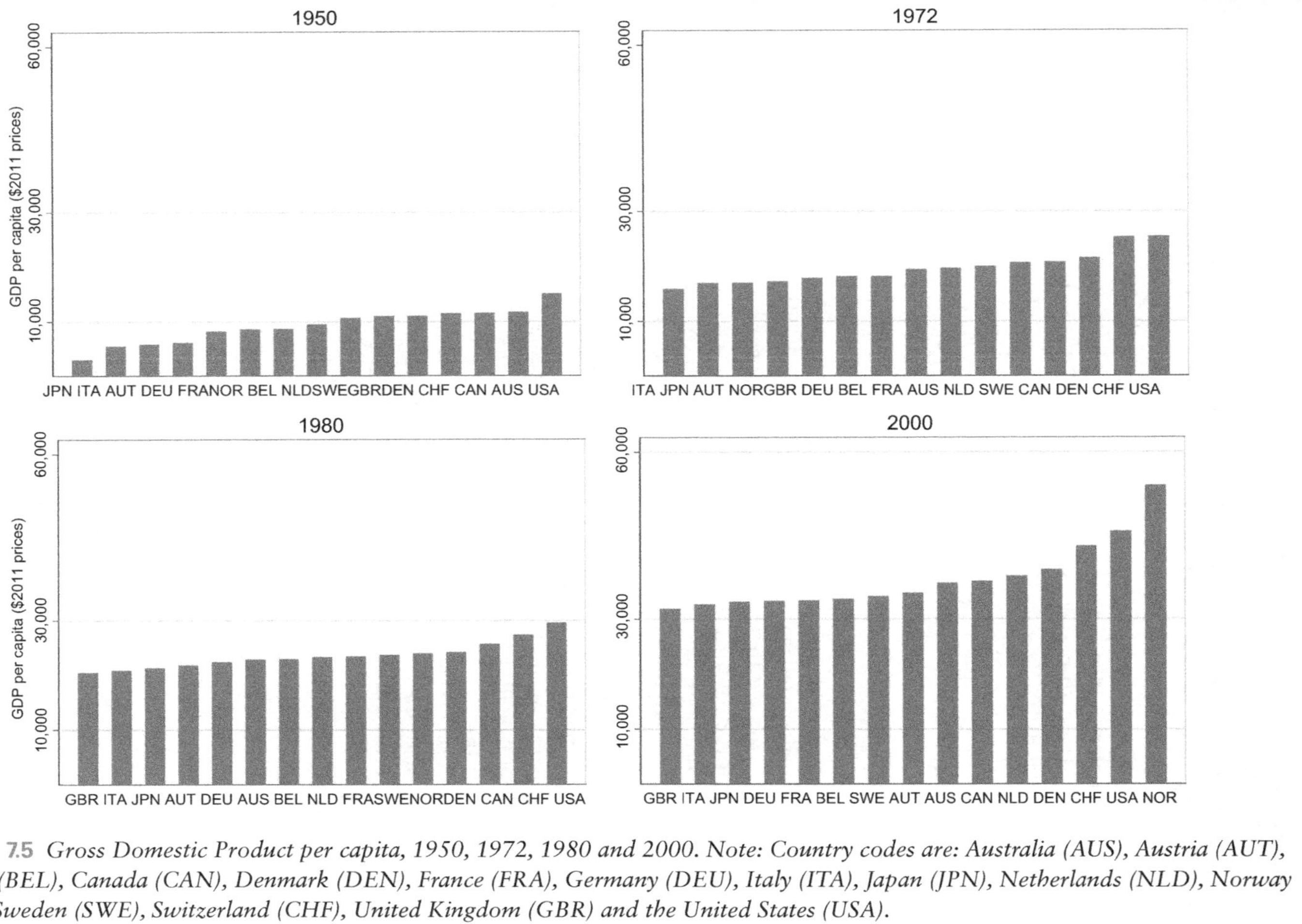

FIGURE 7.5 *Gross Domestic Product per capita, 1950, 1972, 1980 and 2000. Note: Country codes are: Australia (AUS), Austria (AUT), Belgium (BEL), Canada (CAN), Denmark (DEN), France (FRA), Germany (DEU), Italy (ITA), Japan (JPN), Netherlands (NLD), Norway (NOR), Sweden (SWE), Switzerland (CHF), United Kingdom (GBR) and the United States (USA).*

possible'.[89] Others, however, warned that the 'de-industrial revolution' could undermine future British economic growth.[90]

Britain arose victorious from the Second World War, but it also found itself as the leading debtor nation.[91] By 1950 it was still Europe's foremost industrial nation as its competitors had been severely damaged by the war. But in the subsequent twenty-five years, the so-called 'Golden Age', Britain grew slower than other countries in Western Europe and they eventually converged and overtook Britain (see Table 7.1).[92] The UK's performance in the 'Golden Age' was better than anything historically experienced by Britain but in comparison with its peers it was poor and this led to a strand of research emphasizing a 'British Disease'.[93] While most of this growth from the competitors would be expected, it was effectively 'catch-up' growth where countries could adopt the latest productive technology from the 'leader'. In the post-Second World War world it was clear that the United States was the leader of the technological frontier and countries in Western Europe adopted the latest US technologies (via investment and management practices). The economic historian Alexander Gerschenkron (1904–78) argued that countries that are backwards can take advantage of the technology of the leader.[94] This concept was expanded by the economist Moses Abramovitz (1912–2000) who referred to 'social capability' as the ability to absorb the latest technology from the leader, this depended both on human capital as well as institutions (such as trade unions) that facilitated adoption.[95] In this context, it was British 'social capabilities' which may have prevented the adoption of new technology.

One aspect of this is labour relations. Crafts highlights how the high rate of unemployment in the 1920s and 30s was rooted in Britain's early start in the Industrial Revolution because unemployment was concentrated in the regions of the old staple industries. The high unemployment of the interwar period was followed by periods of low unemployment in the 'Golden Age'. The high unemployment of the 1920s and 30s influenced how politicians in the post-Second World War period perceived and responded to the issue. This led to greater government intervention and a policy of full employment to prevent high levels of unemployment recurring, a consensus view that persisted until the 1980s.[96] Here the issue appears to be that in the trade-off between unemployment and inflation (the so-called Phillips curve), British policymakers favoured low unemployment as highlighted in Figure 7.6.

The 1950s to 1970s were characterized by what were known as 'stop-go' economic policies as Britain had to contend with periodic balance of payments crises, caused by an excess of imports (inflows) over exports (outflows). In the go phase, there was a boom with some export growth, but this led to an increase in imports and a sudden stop. The stop-go years were therefore characterized by periods of economic expansion followed by contractions, as restrictive policies were introduced to curb imbalances created by the booms. The key variable was that the British

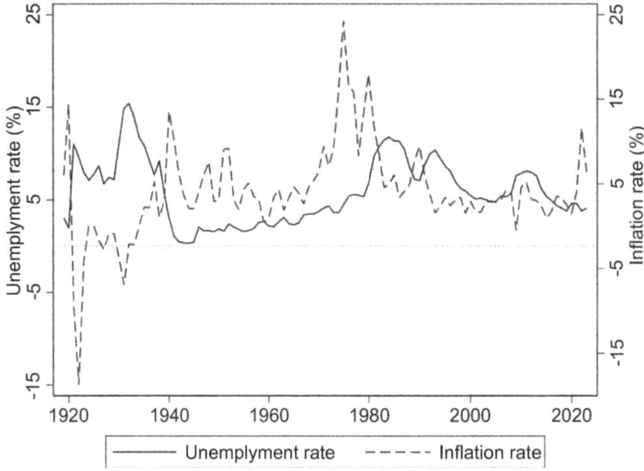

FIGURE 7.6 *British unemployment and inflation, 1920-2024*

government, along with other Western countries, had decided to adopt a fixed exchange regime vis-à-vis the US dollar and the initial exchange rate was chosen at a high level. In such a fixed exchange rate system, as opposed to the flexible exchange rate systems that we are more familiar with today, the exchange rate cannot adjust automatically to a balance of payments crisis. Instead, governments attempted to manage their imports and to increase exports.

The main issues are related to increases in imports and a decrease in exports. This is best illustrated by looking at the current account (that is the difference between exports and imports). For the period up to the First World War, Britain had a current account surplus meaning that its exports were greater than its imports. But after the First World War, as the economy was in a weakened position, Britain struggled to regain a current account surplus, as shown in Figure 7.7. This mattered most in the period of the international currency regimes when Britain adhered to fixed exchange rates. In the interwar period, as previously noted, Britain resumed the Gold Standard at its pre-war level and had an overvalued currency. Britain effectively devalued in 1931 when it left the Gold Standard. In the post-Second World War era Britain was again on a fixed exchange regime, the so-called Bretton-Woods system. Dollar shortages pushed European countries into crisis and the difficulty achieving a current account surplus put pressure on the pound which was forced to devalue twice in September 1949 (30 per cent devaluation) and again in November 1967 (14 per cent devaluation).[97] The fact that Britain devalued led to speculation that it may devalue again, for example there was recurring speculation that there would

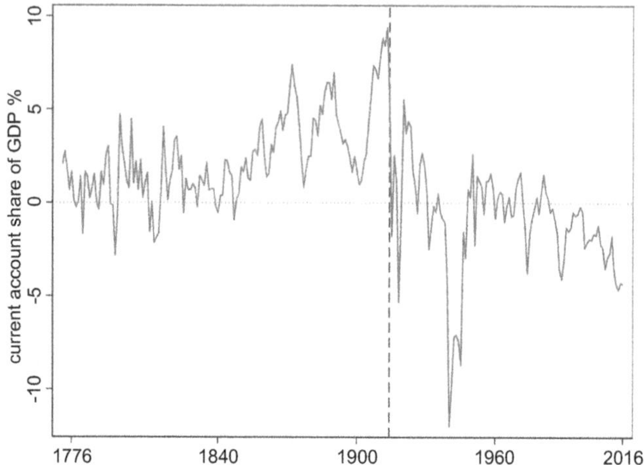

FIGURE 7.7 *Current account as a percent of GDP, 1776–2016. Note: Dashed vertical line indicates the start of the First World War. Positive values indicate that exports are greater than imports and negative values indicate that imports are greater than exports. Source: Bank of England, A Millenium of Macroeconomic Data.*

be a devaluation of sterling in 1955 following a dock strike that affected British exports.[98]

An important part of Britain's relative recovery in the post-1973 period was its entry into the European Economic Community (EEC). The European 'Golden Age' had coincided with the creation of the Common Market for Coal & Steel in 1952 and the European Economic Community (EEC) in 1957; effectively the EEC created a larger market for the economies of Europe. Crafts argued that competition 'cured the British disease'. The interwar period was characterised by a reduction in competition that persisted into the immediate post-war era; competition only improved again from the late 1970s onwards.[99] An important aspect of the increase in competition was EEC membership, Crafts showed how EEC membership was better for the UK than proponents of membership in the 1970s had anticipated and that it slowed Britain's relative decline vis-à-vis France and Germany. The main benefits of EEC entry were a reduction in protection and an increase in competition which boosted UK productivity. Britain was at the forefront of efforts to remove trade barriers and to establish a single market in Europe in the 1980s and 1990s.[100]

The low rate of investment is often seen as one of the principle causes of the decline of manufacturing in UK. The United Kingdom persistently recorded lower rates of investment than the United States, Germany, France and Japan; and lower rates of gross investment compared to Organisation for Economic Co-operation and Development (OECD) countries.[101] Persistent under investment translated into a lower capital stock in UK manufacturing. The UK was also found to be deficient in human capital investment and to exhibit a lower rate of net investment.[102] Crafts, drawing on insights from new economic growth theory, placed emphasis on 'broad capital', which includes human capital, rather than on narrow measures of physical investment,[103] he highlighted how the UK had lower levels of educational attainment than its European peers.

Facets that led to the low investment rate in the UK were high marginal tax rates, lack of competition which meant a misallocation of resources, aggressive mergers which discouraged R&D in firms, and an industrial policy of 'picking winners'. Overall, this meant a neglect of human capital and innovation. As the UK continued to operate as a global power the industrial strategy of 'picking winners' meant attempts to support industries with strategic military connections. The UK governments success of picking winners was very limited. Other avenues which hurt UK manufacturing were misaligned macroeconomic policies; for example, the UK has had an overvalued exchange rate which hurt UK manufacturing. This dates from the Thatcher era (more discussion on this in Chapter 8).

Another key feature of the post-Second World War period was the expansion of the public sector in Britain following nationalization pushes of the Labour government. This brought several struggling sectors of the economy into public ownership. These sectors tended to be capital-intensive and required substantial public investment. The public ownership of industry and the poor performance of these publicly owned companies led to a call for privatization (or 'denationalization') as it was argued that the public sector crowded out private enterprise. Although many of the newly privatized sectors operated in uncompetitive sectors, the introduction of competition would lead to greater uncertainty and likely led to 'sweating assets' (maximizing the use of existing assets) rather than new investment in fixed capital.[104]

Deregulation and privatization of the Thatcher era led to the expansion of a financial services sector in Britain. Effectively, as the economists Michael Kitson and Jonathan Michie argue, this amounted to a UK equivalent of *de facto* industrial policy by giving preferential treatment to financial services and to the City of London.[105] This ultimately came at the expense of manufacturing interests. Also, as Crafts noted, the 2007-8 financial crisis was a very costly crisis that led to a permanent reduction in trend GDP growth.[106] The UK still has not recovered to its pre-2008 trend nor is it likely that it will do so in the immediate future, as shown in Figure 7.8.

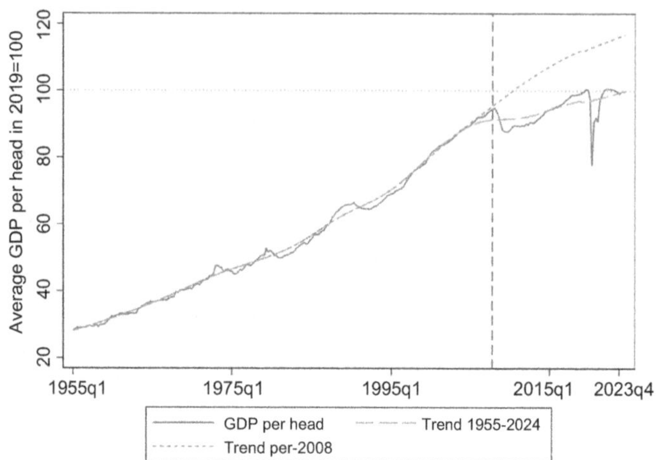

FIGURE 7.8 *Index of GDP per capita and trend (1955–2024 and pre-2008), 1955 to 2023. Note: Index set to the average of GDP per head in 2019q1, 2019q2, 2019q3 and 2019q4. Trends are compared relative to GDP per head in 2019. Source: ONS (2024). 'First Quarterly Estimate, Q3 (July to Sept) 2024', November 2024.*

Summary: A long-run Perspective on UK Productivity

In sum, Britain started the world on the path of modern economic growth. The worries and fears of the classical pessimists (discussed in Chapter 3) were misplaced as British economic growth continued unabated. Yet, Britain has experienced relative decline, and it no longer leads the world. British growth performance in the twentieth century was weak, and the twenty-first century has seen a continuation of this trend. Ultimately the UK's slowdown is driven by the fall in productivity growth. UK productivity peaked in the mid-twentieth century and despite the best efforts of policymakers of all persuasions, it has not been possible to reverse this trend.

The UK's productivity slowdown in the early twenty-first century is unprecedented in recent economic history, growth in output per hour has barely risen since the 2007–8 financial crisis and has not returned to pre-crisis levels (see Figure 7.9).[107] One aspect of this has been the UK's low rate of public investment, something which has been a purposeful political decision. Such cuts in public spending and investment were shown to be related to the rise in support for the UK Independence Party (UKIP) and voting for Brexit.[108]

Figure 7.10 presents the trend of UK TFP growth from 1761 to 2022. UK productivity has waxed and waned over the years. A recent account

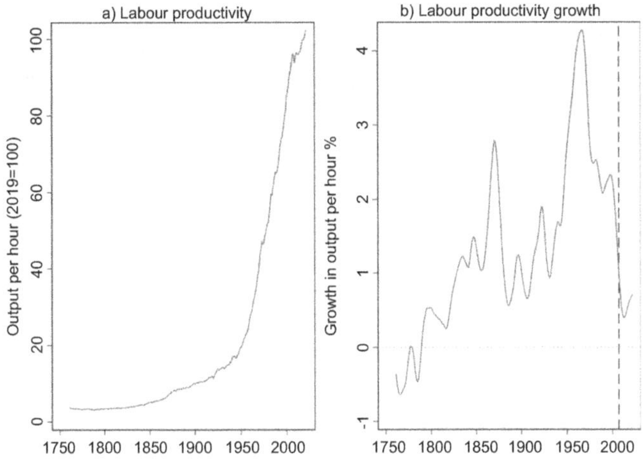

FIGURE 7.9 *Labour productivity: Output per hour and growth in output per hour, 1760–2022. Note: The vertical line represents the year 2007. Source: Bank of England, A Millennium of Macroeconomic Data; and ONS (2024) Output per Hour, UK.*

of British economic history sees low TFP growth in the early Industrial Revolution followed by an increase in the mid-nineteenth century.[109] TFP peaked in the mid-twentieth century and fell thereafter. The view of TFP peaking mid-twentieth century echoes a strand of macro economics, most notably the work of economist Robert Gordon, that sees major technological innovations peaking in the mid-twentieth century.[110]

Nick Crafts referred to the Britain's long-run TFP performance as a 'roller coaster' and, writing in 2021, he had hoped that the 'descent to the nadir' after the 2007–8 financial crisis had been reached.[111] It appears that British TFP decline had not bottomed out and it continued to decline. UK productivity has stagnated since the early 2000s and has been in decline since the 2007–8 financial crisis. This low productivity growth is unprecedented in modern UK economic history. In some sense this is reassuring as the First Industrial Revolution had negative and low TFP growth, but this was trending upwards. From this perspective, the recent decline in GDP per capita could be a reflection of the UK's low investment rate and low rate of productivity growth and also Brexit (although the decline in UK productivity pre-dates this).[112] Recent evidence suggests that the biggest factor explaining the slowdown in UK economic growth has been the fall in TFP growth and this fall is concentrated in knowledge-intensive, technology-intensive, and digital-intensive sectors of the economy.[113] The slowdown in TFP growth has been extrapolated to be 'a slowdown in innovation'.[114]

Over time, there has been convergence in TFP growth rates among high-income countries, and this is seen as having driven convergence with the

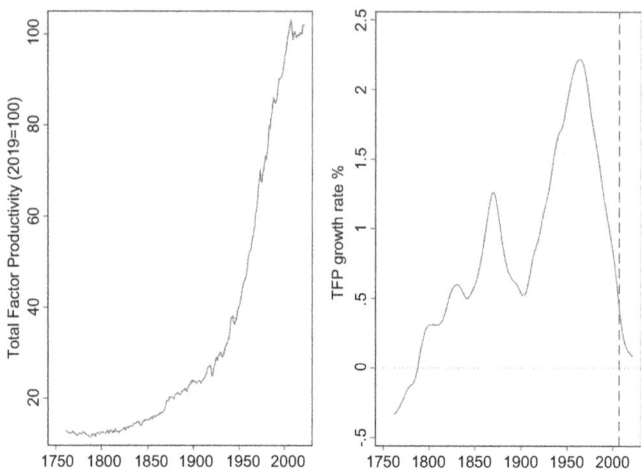

FIGURE 7.10 *Growth in UK Total Factor Productivity. Note: The vertical line represents the year 2007. Source: Bank of England, A Millenium of Macroeconomic data; and ONS (2024) Growth Accounting, Multi-factor productivity Estimates, UK.*

United States.[115] This is highlighted in Table 7.4 as the United States had a low rate of TFP growth compared to historic levels. Crafts, in his 1993 pamphlet *Can Deindustrialisation Seriously Damage Your Wealth*, highlighted the United Kingdom's TFP performance relative to France, Germany, Japan and the United States. He attributed the UK's growth slowdown to the fall in TFP growth, a view that contradicts a more optimistic earlier interpretation which saw UK TFP growth as keeping pace with other countries.[116]

Table 7.2 draws on the latest version of *PWT* to compare TFP growth in the UK relative to the same countries as Crafts, as well as those listed in Figure 7.5.[117] What stands out is the UK's relatively low TFP growth. Over the full period from 1955 to 2023, the UK records the lowest average rate of TFP growth. Across sub-periods there were times when the United Kingdom performed better than other countries, such as the United States in 1974–89 and Japan in the 1990s, but in both instances these relative positions were reversed. More broadly, the table also highlights the universal post-1973 productivity slowdown, the particularly sharp collapse in Japanese TFP growth after 1990, and the exceptional resilience of US productivity after 1990 and even after 2008. Taken together, these patterns suggest that the UK's productivity problem reflects a long-standing tendency towards underperformance rather than the effect of a single episodic shock.

In January 2025 the UK Labour government announced plans to 'turbocharge AI' as an engine of economic growth.[118] It remains to be seen

TABLE 7.2 TFP in comparative perspective, growth per annum (%)

	1955–2023	1954–73	1974–89	1990–2007	2008–23
France	1.31	3.61	1.23	0.60	–0.53
Germany	1.36	2.86	0.97	1.15	0.19
Japan	0.76	2.07	0.82	0.06	–0.04
United Kingdom	0.44	0.89	0.52	0.61	–0.36
United States	0.65	1.10	0.20	0.79	0.43
Weighted	0.77	1.89	0.46	0.51	0.06

if the AI revolution will be able to change the trend of UK productivity growth. Some pessimistic assessments argue that AI would lead to a very modest increase in TFP growth, around 0.5 to 0.7 per cent over the next ten years.[119] In the grand scheme of things this is a very small increase but given the flatlining of UK TFP growth it would signal a modest improvement.

CHAPTER EIGHT

Measuring the Inclusive Wealth of a Nation

Great Britain, 1750–2020

Much has already been written highlighting Britain as the birthplace of the Industrial Revolution. This chapter adds a different perspective to the existing historical scholarship as it will measure the performance of the British economy through the lens of Inclusive Wealth. I will show the evolution of some key aspects of Britain's Inclusive Wealth over time and emphasize the shift in reliance on natural resources towards physical and human capital.

Natural capital is a larger component of wealth in low to middle-income countries today, so we might expect natural capital to play a larger role in the British economy in the past. Similarly, higher-income countries today tend to see a change in their wealth composition with other forms of capital comprising a larger share of wealth.[1] Countries that are relatively rich in natural resources should be expected to show higher rates of economic growth because resource abundance and resource discovery can lead to short-term increases in growth rates and resource windfalls that can be invested into other productive assets (e.g. physical and human capital).[2] The environmental economist Ed Barbier refers to this as a 'frontier expansion hypothesis'. Barbier argues that this can explain why countries with abundant natural resource endowments can be successful and that to sustainably exploit natural resource endowments, the profits from natural resources must be reinvested in productive economic investments. He also argues that the failure of resource-based development to yield sustained economy-wide benefits can be attributed to one of these propositions being violated.[3]

Often countries with large natural resource endowments have exhibited relatively low rates of economic growth. This pattern became known as the 'the resources curse': countries with higher levels of 'resource dependence' tend to experience lower economic growth rates.[4] The idea emerged as an empirical observation that natural resource abundance has a negative relationship with GDP growth, first identified by the economic geographer Richard Auty and, independently, by the economists Jeffrey Sachs and Andrew Warner.[5] It also connects to an older line of research on the 'Dutch Disease' which described the effect of the impact of natural gas extraction on the Dutch currency in the 1970s: the appreciation (rise in the exchange rate) of currency due to resource exports had an impact on the competitiveness of other sectors (e.g., agriculture, manufacturing).[6] Natural resource abundance has been found to affect the quality of institutions, increasing inequalities and leading to corruption and rent-seeking that hamper innovation and growth. Several studies have highlighted the importance of institutions for avoiding the resource curse and maintaining positive Genuine Savings.[7]

The UK's economic history described through the lens of aggregate figures can overlook some important facets of its development, one of which is the importance of natural capital in its economic development. For the Industrial Revolution itself, coal is often seen as playing a crucial role as was implied by Allen in his discussion of the cost of capital inferred through the low cost of coal, as well as in the work of the economic historian Tony Wrigley (1931–2022).[8] Other scholars saw the UK's resource abundance as an explanation for the Industrial Revolution emerging in the British Isles and not in China.[9] Important facets of later development included the discovery of oil, the role of forests, and pollution from economic activity. Britain then makes an ideal case of applying concepts of Inclusive Wealth using its historical experience to shed light on the theory itself and how this framework can help our understanding of economic history.

The Inclusive Wealth framework can help analyse issues relating to Britain's 'productivity puzzle', the decline in productivity growth discussed in Chapter 7. One key argument that the chapter will make is that the root of Britain's recent productivity problems may not be because of the 2007–8 financial crisis, as assumed by many commentators, but may reflect pre-existing trends and the role of oil in the economy. In doing so, I will reopen an old debate about the influence of oil on the British exchange rate and how policy decisions fifty years ago may have had lasting impacts to this day.

In what follows I present some illustrative trends in some important dimensions of the United Kingdom's Inclusive Wealth paying particular attention to developments within natural capital. Aggregating all forms of capital into an index requires a common denominator (for this exercise it is pounds) in order to make comparisons across natural capital measured in different physical units. I have highlighted key aspects relating to the physical stock (e.g., tonnes of coal) as well as the monetary value of the stocks.

'Subterraneous Forests': Coal and the Fossil Fuel Revolution

The UK was one of the earliest coal-producing nations and how coal was mined influenced the subsequent pattern of mining. Coal was first used as a source of fuel in Britain owing to a shortage of wood and restrictions placed on wood use. Towns were surveyed for accessible coal seams; it was these seams that were originally mined using open-cast (i.e., surface) techniques. This search for coal led to the emergence of geological expertise.[10] The mining regions that emerged in the 1700s continued to be the main centres of mining over the nineteenth century, these were: Cumberland, Lancashire, North Wales, South Wales, the South-West, the West Midlands, the East Midlands, Yorkshire, the North-East, and Scotland.[11]

Mining also saw the application of new technologies which helped reduce the cost of mining. For example, steam engines were first used for pumping water from mines and later for winding coal and workers in and out of the shafts. Early Newcomen steam engines, although cumbersome, were used to pump water and helped reduce the cost of deep mining. It is estimated that there were seventy-eight Newcomen steam engines distributed across various coal regions between 1718 and 1733. After the Newcomen patent expired the number of steam engines increased significantly. Before the invention of the Boulton and Watt steam engine, it is estimated that there were 321 steam engines in total distributed across various coal mines in Britain.[12] The Boulton and Watt engine was both cheaper to operate but also more efficient and this meant that steam power became more widely adopted by the 1780s and substituted for horse power (although smaller mines still found it cost-effective to use horse power).[13] By 1800 there were 828 steam engines of all descriptions in use across Britain's coal mining regions.[14]

The increased demand for coal led to the opening of new mines and increased investment in mining, but this type of expansion was limited and instead production was intensified in the existing mines aided by 'improving mining technology.'[15] Mining expansion therefore meant going to greater depths. This was initially hazardous due to drainage and ventilation issues, but technological improvements enabled coal mining to overcome these constraints. The economic historian Michael Flinn (1917–83) highlights that mining was also facilitated by complementary technological developments and investment in other sectors of the economy, such as better infrastructure to transport coal by water, road, and rail.[16] A point also applicable to the later 1800s too.[17] The primary concern for the coal industry was the threat of diminishing returns. This was largely mitigated by technological advancements, both within the industry itself and across the broader economy. As Flinn observed, 'in spite of the need to go ever deeper, and to carry coal even further both underground and on the surface, the real costs of mining coal were unlikely to have risen significantly in the long run and may even have fallen'.[18] The tension between diminishing returns and technological innovation persisted throughout the later nineteenth century and ultimately shaped the industry's profitability.[19] By the early nineteenth century, easily accessible coal seams had been depleted, and the necessity of deeper mining to sustain production remained pressing.[20] This gave rise to fears of resource exhaustion, most famously voiced by William Stanley Jevons in *The Coal Question* (1865). Nevertheless, the 1871 UK *Coal Commission* sought to reassure the public by estimating that the country had sufficient coal reserves to last another 300 years (see Chapter 6).[21]

There is an important distinction between the physically available resources and what is technologically feasible, given costs, to extract. Improvements in technology enable deeper reserves to be extracted and to mine from previously less-accessible seams. What is considered an economically viable reserve, however, depends on the prevailing price levels and the costs of extraction. There was also a conflicting pressure as cumulative production exerts an upward influence on costs, even as technological progress pushes costs down.

Various estimates of UK coal reserves are shown in Table 8.1. There was a lot of variation in the estimates as the opinions of geologists changed, and what was considered economic to extract varied with changes in geological knowledge, technology, and market prices. The estimates published by the 1905 Royal Commission give the most detailed assessments of what total reserves were at a point in time, but this is not equivalent to an economic reserve. While later reports placed greater emphasis on economic reserves. The 2010 estimate was made by the World Energy Council which noted that the decline of the UK coal industry was 'accompanied by a sharp decrease in economically recoverable reserves' but that there were also 185 billion tonnes estimated to be in place and 40 billion of which 'is deemed to be recoverable'.[22] Overall, it is clear from Table 8.1 that Britain did not exhaust its coal mines.

The coal industry went into decline in the early 1900s. This was not driven by the physical depletion of stocks, but by rising costs (labour was still the largest share of costs) and falling prices, as exports weakened in the face of increasing international competition (from Polish and German coal). Another factor in the declining coal price was a fall in domestic demand caused by the rise in the supply of alternative fuels.[23] The decline in coal output is also partly a consequence of the war disruptions. Coal miners were put in reserved occupation status during the First World War, but as the war

TABLE 8.1 Coal reserves and extraction, 1866–2010 (million tonnes).

Year of estimate	Known	Possible	Reserve estimate at time	Total extraction from 1750 to date of reserve estimate	Total extraction at date as % of reserve
c. 1866			85,544	3,381	3.95
c. 1870	97,526	100,917	198,433	3,822	1.93
c. 1905	106,153	40,721	146,874	9,881	6.73
c. 1912			186,494	11,721	6.29
c. 1915			235,000	12,528	5.33
c. 1940	20,500	13,376	33,877	18,265	53.92
c. 1945–6			54,604	19,441	35.60
c. 1947			49,387	19,639	39.76
2010	262	2,527 [40,000]	2,789 [185,000]	27,302	

Source: McLaughlin et al. (2014, 2017). 'Historical wealth accounts for Britain'.

progressed more miners were recruited to the war effort, which ultimately had an effect on labour productivity.[24]

One of the main issues with the British coal mining industry was that it was fragmented; for example, in 1913 there were 1,439 firms operating 2,648 mines.[25] Coal mining was also labour-intensive, there were 1,088,427 miners employed in 1913. Labour costs were 75 per cent of total costs and initially there was resistance to mechanization.[26] Prior to nationalization in 1946, there was a gradual rationalization of the coal mining industry with closures occurring from 1924 through to the 1930s and by 1938 there were 1034 firms operating 1870 mines. There was also a reduction in the number employed, falling to 798,547 in 1938; a 27 per cent reduction from the 1913 level.[27] The post-Second World War era saw the terminal decline of the British coal industry. It could be argued that the coal industry is a case of the British economy in miniature. There was an increase in mechanical cutting but very little else was mechanized in the coal industry and labour productivity was low especially by international comparison.[28] British coal operated in a protected home market until 1970 after which it was exposed to greater competition.[29]

Coal was a significant component of the British economy in the nineteenth century and its contribution, as a share of GDP, peaked in the early twentieth century (shown in Figure 8.1). The significance of the coal industry was outlined by the 1925 Coal inquiry: coal employed one-twelfth of the population, and the value of its annual output was £250 million (c. 5.77 per cent of GDP). Coal made up 10 per cent of UK exports by value and 80 per cent by volume and 'by furnishing outward cargo for a large amount of shipping, it cheapens freights for the imports on which we depend for our vital needs'.[30] The steady expansion of the coal industry from the 1700s onwards led to what the economic historian Tony Wrigley describes as an 'energy revolution', and by the mid-1800s there was a tenfold increase in energy consumption in Britain; with coal providing 92 per cent of this energy.[31] The importance of coal in the Industrial Revolution is indicated by the fact that cities that were further away from coal fields had lower population growth. This is also corroborated in studies that show that high coal prices reduced the likelihood of the development of cotton mills and limited the size of mills in 1838.[32] The effect of coal on the British economy differed from that of oil in the later twentieth century because of the competition for labour among different mining and manufacturing sectors. Miners' wages tended to be volatile and rose and fell with the price of coal, which in turn was influenced by the demand from other sectors of the economy.[33]

Another way to appreciate the significance of coal to the British Industrial Revolution is to look across the Irish Sea. Natural resource abundance (or lack thereof) has been a key feature of Irish economic history

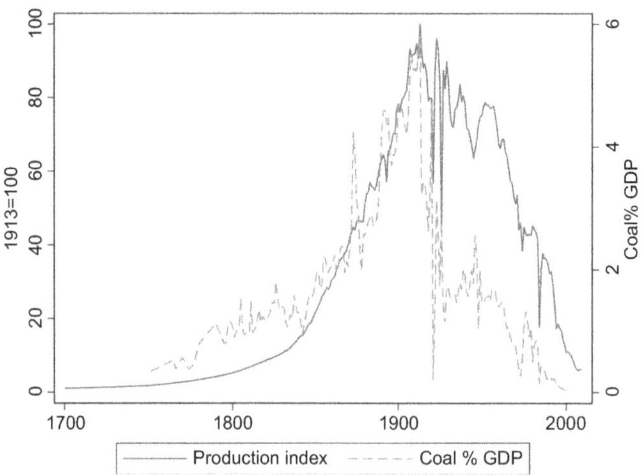

FIGURE 8.1 *UK coal production index (1913=100), 1700–2008. Source: Data from McLaughlin et al. (2014, 2017), 'Historical wealth accounts for Britain'.*

where the traditional view was that Ireland was lacking in the resources (i.e., coal) most commonly associated with early industrialization.[34] This view was challenged by Joel Mokyr, who argued that because Ireland was geographically close to the major coal producer it could import coal from Britain making resource scarcity less of a barrier to development.[35] This argument has been revised in more recent work which suggests that apart from Belfast, located in close proximity to the coal-producing regions of Scotland, high internal transport costs were a barrier to coal access and this ultimately hindered Irish industrial development.[36]

British Disease? North Sea Oil and Gas

The decline of coal was a European-wide phenomenon, precipitated by the availability and consumption of low-cost oil. Unlike with coal, Western Europe (including the UK) was not abundant in oil reserves in the early-twentieth century and the production of oil was concentrated in other parts of the globe (the Middle East, Russia, the Americas, North Africa and the Caribbean). Part of the motivation for European efforts to discover oil was the geopolitical risk associated with the major oil-producing regions of the world. When one of the UK's main oil suppliers, the Anglo-Iranian oil company, was nationalized in 1951 it led to a three-year shutdown of production. Further geopolitical events, such as the Suez Crisis in 1956 and the 1967 Arab-Israeli war (Six-Day War), led to oil shortages. As the UK (and other European countries) was a net importer of oil this had serious ramifications for UK energy security. This led to an active search for oil and gas in the North Sea by Dutch, German, Norwegian, and British interests in the 1950s and 1960s. Initially the emphasis was on natural gas, however discovery of major oil reserves at Ekofisk in 1969 changed this focus.[37] The impact of resource discovery is clear in terms of the reduction of UK oil imports following the rapid increase in production in North Sea oil from 1975, and the UK became a net exporter of oil from 1981 to 2005.

By the early 1970s it was estimated that about 26 per cent of world reserves were found offshore. Technological advances in offshore drilling, particularly from the late 1950s onwards, played a crucial role in enabling the extraction of North Sea oil. Key developments in exploration, drilling, and production techniques significantly improved deep-sea capabilities, making it possible to tap into previously inaccessible reserves. Although the Dutch had found gas off Groningen in the 1950s, drilling was delayed until the jurisdictional claims between the bordering countries were resolved. Once development began, the North Sea provided a stern test of the capabilities of the nascent oil industry as rigs were required to withstand waves as high as thirty metres and drilling at greater water depths. Offshore drilling was expensive but the rise in oil prices helped improve the profitability of the endeavours, helped by the fact that, compared to coal production, oil was not labour-intensive.[38]

When the North Sea came onstream the UK government was bullish. In the UK Department of Energy's 1978 white paper on the *Challenge of North Sea Oil* it was stated that 'the benefits of North Sea oil have already begun to flow'. The white paper saw oil as a chance for the UK to boost material well-being because 'our living standards, which were among the highest in Western Europe a quarter of a century ago, are now among the lowest'. It was expected that North Sea oil and gas would be worth the equivalent of 3 per cent of gross national income (GNP) and there was also an aspiration that it would lead to an increase in government revenue, in the region of an additional £4,000 million a year. The main expected benefits though were in the effects that North Sea oil would have on the balance of payments because of both the reduction in oil imports and the hope for increased exports.[39] One immediate aspect of the oil effect was on the exchange rate, and it was noted that the 'market rate for sterling may be stronger than would otherwise be justified by the underlying competitive position of the United Kingdom'. There was a hope that the North Sea oil revenues would be used in investment for the 'permanent improvement in our economic and industrial efficiency, and consequently in our national standard of living'. [40]

Oil is therefore an integral part of modern UK macroeconomic history and played an important role in the UK economy in the 1970s and 1980s, especially when international oil prices were so volatile.[41] Oil is an international commodity where global market conditions dictate the value of the commodity. As shown in Figure 4.3, oil prices rose dramatically in the 1970s due to geopolitical events. A spike in 1973 followed an embargo by members of the oil cartel, the Organization of Arab Petroleum Exporting Countries (OAPEC), against countries that supported Israel during the Yom Kippur War (1973 Arab–Israeli War). Another shock in 1979 followed the fall in Iranian oil production due to the Iranian Revolution. Despite a brief period of lower prices in the 1990s, oil remained at elevated levels with further peaks in 2008 and 2011. While prices were volatile, the volume of UK oil production (measured in barrels) and reserves (measured in tonnes) was steadily declining (see Figure 8.2 and Figure 8.4).

Vertical lines for the year 1976 are highlighted in Figures 8.3 and Figure 8.4 because, as the economist John Kay noted, '1976 was the last year before oil had any significant effect on the balance of payments or productive structure of the domestic economy'.[42] The 1985 House of Lords *Report on Overseas Trade* also documented the importance of oil: 'after 1979 output of manufacturing industry fell and has not recovered to previous levels. *Much of the growth that has mainly occurred in GDP is attributable to oil*' (emphasis added). The oil bonanza was so spectacular that it contributed a large part to the UK's GDP growth. In 1983 and 1984 respectively, oil accounted for 17 per cent and 20 per cent of UK GDP growth.[43]

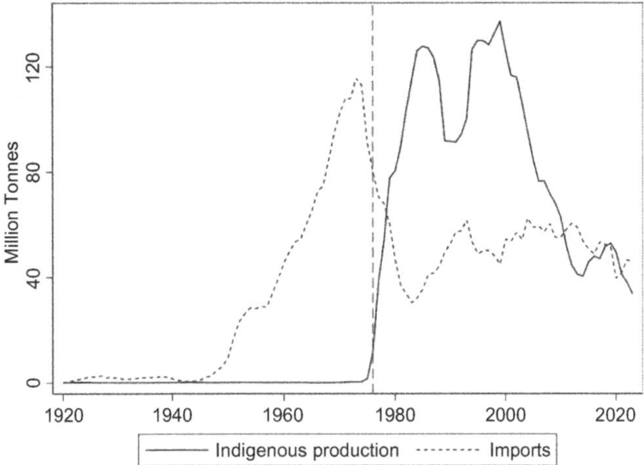

FIGURE 8.2 *UK oil imports and indigenous production, 1920–2023. Source: Data from McLaughlin et al. (2014, 2017), 'Historical wealth accounts for Britain' and update from Digest of UK Energy Statistics (DUKES).*

The oil discovery had an immediate effect on the British economy. North Sea oil accounted for one-eighth of British oil consumption by 1976 and five-ninths by 1978. Sidney Pollard highlights how the oil bonanza impinged on every sector of the British economy. Annual investment in the oil fields exceeded £2 billion and was a quarter of all British capital formation and between one-third and two-fifths of the investment came from British companies.[44] The oil bonanza generated new wealth and jobs, particularly in the Scottish city of Aberdeen where 19,000 new jobs were created. The oil boom ended the periodic balance of payments crises that Britain faced in the post-Second World War era and led to an appreciation of sterling. The revenues from oil found their way to the British Exchequer and went into current government spending. Ultimately Pollard concluded, 'the oil boom thus helped both to explain and to compensate for the decline of manufacturing industry in the later 1970s'.[45]

The verdict of the 1985 UK House of Lords *Committee on Overseas Trade* was that 'oil has become a major factor in Britain's balance of trade and in the growth of the economy as a whole'.[46] The increased oil production had an impact on the UK exchange rate that appreciated by roughly 40 per cent.[47] Although at the time, International Monetary Fund (IMF) economists referred to a 70 per cent appreciation in the real exchange rate and attributed it to sterling becoming a Petrocurrency.[48] The increased production of oil in the North Sea coincided with a shift from manufacturing to services and increased deindustrialization. The conventional narrative equates this with reforms of the Thatcher government and 'neoliberalism'; the oil shock is often overlooked.[49]

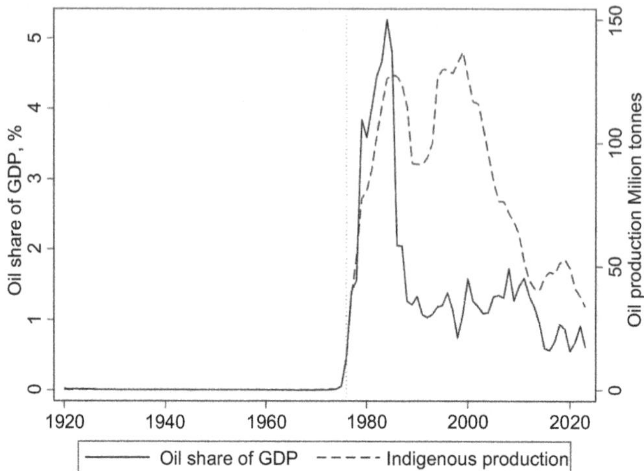

FIGURE 8.3 *Oil as a share of GDP. Source: Data from McLaughlin et al. (2014, 2017). 'Historical wealth accounts for Britain' and update from Digest of UK Energy Statistics (DUKES).*

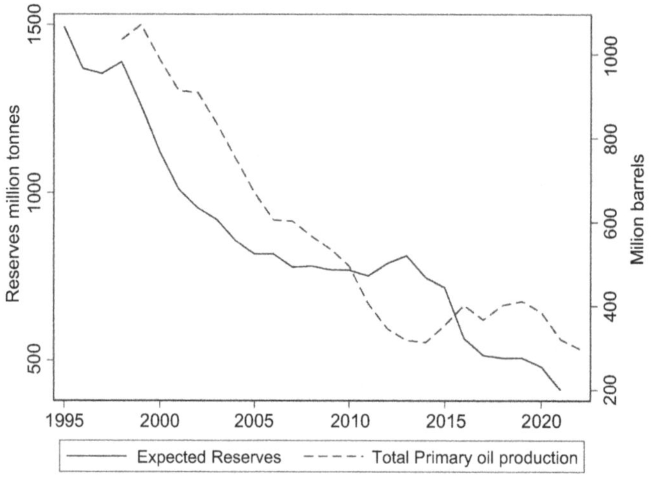

FIGURE 8.4 *Expected Oil Reserves and Physical Production. Source: Data from McLaughlin et al. (2014, 2017), 'Historical wealth accounts for Britain' and update from Digest of UK Energy Statistics (DUKES).*

Contemporaries were aware of a possible 'Dutch Disease' scenario (or rather a new chapter in the 'British Disease', as discussed in Chapter 7) where the resource boom sector would affect the exchange rate and reduce competitiveness of the manufacturing sector. For example, the economists

Peter Forsyth and John Kay argued that 'the contraction of manufacturing output, and an increase in domestic absorption of imported manufacturers, are - whether desirable or not - [are] the only means by which the British economy can benefit from the North Sea oil' and that this was via the appreciation of the exchange rate.[50] Other macroeconomic models of the time, however, had assumed that depreciation, or an implied devaluation, of sterling would drive economic growth. For example, the economist Ajit Singh (1940–2015) argued that Britain should introduce import controls in order to strengthen the UK manufacturing base and negate the impact of North Sea Oil on the exchange rate.[51]

The Forsyth and Kay assessment of the macroeconomic implications was debated, one vocal critic being the economist Patrick Minford who disputed the view that the oil discoveries would lead to a real appreciation of sterling and argued that the appreciation, if it were to occur, would be of a small magnitude (3 per cent).[52] From this perspective, the appreciation of the pound meant a reduction in import prices, lower inflation, and a gradual reduction in interest rates. This would then lead to an increase in modernizing investment. Clearly outlining what exactly the impact that the currency appreciation had on the UK economy is complicated by the fact that manufacturing operated in an era of rising oil prices. The economist Charlie Bean points to the fact that the counterfactual in the absence of North Sea oil would need to account for the fact that the price of oil had increased, and it would require a greater manufacturing and/or service sector to pay for the imports of oil if the UK had not tapped the North Sea.[53]

What is needed is a counterfactual to the UK case, a country that also used sterling but that did not see such a drastic shift to services. A plausible counterfactual could be Ireland which had left its historic peg (fixed exchange rate) with sterling just as the pound effectively became a petrocurrency (see Figure 8.5). Concerns in Ireland prior to breaking the sterling link were that it would lead to an Irish currency appreciating against sterling. In fact the opposite happened; Irish exports became more competitive vis-à-vis their British counterparts simply through exchange rate movements that were driven by the price of oil.[54] The Irish and UK exchange rates relative to the US dollar are shown in Figure 8.5. The Irish punt was consistently trading below the pound sterling after the peg was broken, this initially led to higher inflation in Ireland but eventually led to price stability.[55] The Irish decision to break the sterling link has been seen as a saving grace for Ireland in the early 1980s and, 'no longer tied to sterling, Ireland was sheltered from what would have been a significant loss of competitiveness'.[56]

Further support for the importance of North Sea oil is the events immediately prior to the oil coming on stream. In 1976 the UK government was forced into a bailout from the International Monetary Fund to stabilize the sterling exchange rate. The IMF crisis is seen as a watershed in economic policy formulation from the Keynesian-inspired demand management towards the Thatcher-era neoliberal reforms.[57] The main issue was the

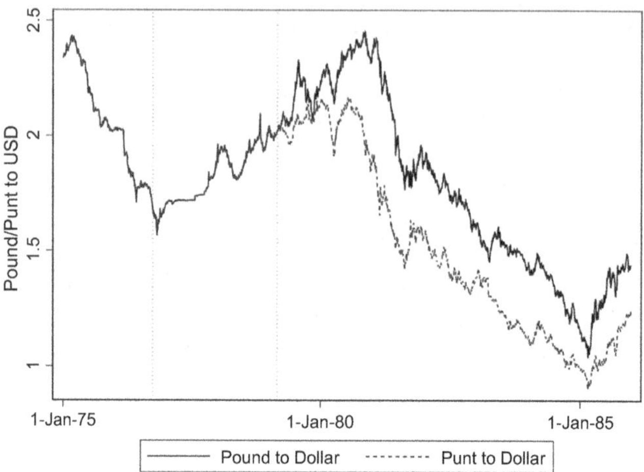

FIGURE 8.5 *Punt to dollar and pound to dollar nominal exchange rate, 1975 to 1985. Note: The blue vertical line represents the period when the UK went to the IMF (September 1976). The red dashed line represents the Irish break of the sterling peg (March 1979). Sources: Exchange rate data from the Bank of England and the Central Bank of Ireland.*

increase in public borrowing and a falling exchange rate (shown in Figure 8.5). In early 1976 there was even a view that the UK Treasury was intending a controlled depreciation of sterling to improve the competitiveness of UK manufacturing. The pound experienced a steady decline vis-à-vis the US dollar in 1976, from $2 in January to under $1.80 by June. It fell to its nadir against the dollar in 1976, trading at under $1.60 by the end of October before it rose again on the back of North Sea oil funds. The falling exchange rate implied increasing inflation. Contemporaries were buoyed by the prospect of a North Sea bailout with the *Financial Times* running the headline 'From the IMF to the North Sea'. By the time North Sea oil was flowing, the UK's fortunes had changed. Alec Cairncross surmised that, 'for the first time since the war and in strong contrast to the 1970s, the 1980s opened with a large and growing surplus and an enviable freedom from the expectation of payments difficulties'.[58]

In the early days of the North Sea, Lord Selsdon (Malcolm McEacharn Mitchell-Thomson (1937–2024)), while sharing the optimism that the North Sea would mark a break in Britain's relative decline, gave a note of caution:

> There are considerable fears that the Government, for one reason or another, will squander and waste in consumption the benefits of the North Sea, that our reserves will run out by 1990 and that we shall be back in a stop-go cycle probably stopping long before then. We should bear in mind that that need not happen.[59]

Similarly, Robert Solow, writing only a decade after the North Sea oil was on stream, felt that 'the British government has been wasting the windfall of North Sea oil'.[60] The reason for this view was that the UK government had given preference to the current generation over future generations and had used oil revenue to fund current expenditure rather than use it for investment in future productive capacity. Most controversially, the UK never implemented a sovereign wealth fund to manage its oil wealth. A study of a simulated UK sovereign wealth fund showed how the establishment of such a fund in 1975 could have led to a substantial fund of £354 billion by 2018.[61] Establishing such a fund in 1975 may not have been realistic given the political issues of the time (e.g., the UK IMF bailout during the 1976 sterling crisis), but establishing a fund in the 1980s and early 1990s is something that could have been undertaken. Take the example of Norway, which discovered its first oil field in 1969 and began production in 1971; however, it was not until 1990 that Norway established its sovereign wealth fund.[62] Today, Norway's sovereign wealth fund is worth 18,218 billion NOK (£1,329 billion) and Norway is held up as an exemplar in the management of natural resources.

In the recent past the *Financial Times* have depicted the UK's hypothetical lost output from falling productivity by comparing Britain's economic performance with a hypothetical scenario if pre-2008 crisis trends

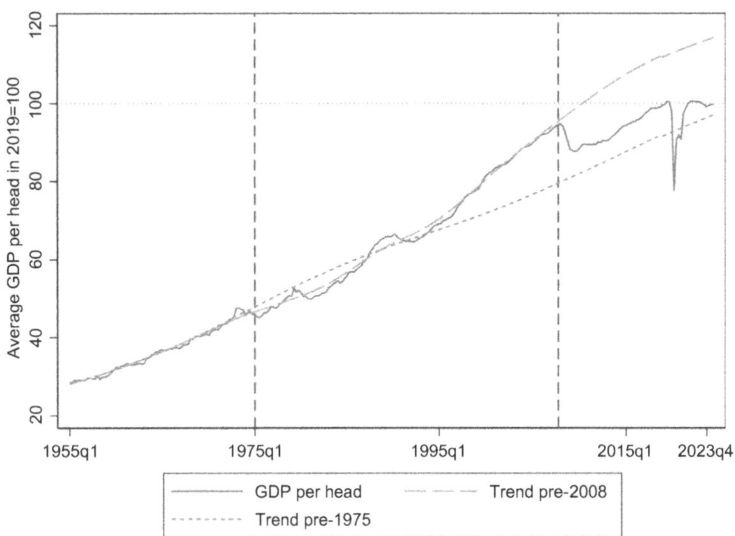

FIGURE 8.6 *Index of GDP per capita and trend (pre-1975, and pre-2008), 1955 to 2023. Note: Index set to the average of GDP per head in 2019q1, 2019q2, 2019q3 and 2019q4. Trends are compared relative to GDP per head in 2019. Source: ONS (2024). 'First Quarterly Estimate, Q3 (July to Sept) 2024', November 2024.*

continued.[63] In Figure 7.8 I compared the trend in UK GDP per capita from 1955 to 2023, with a pre-2008 trend. If a pre-oil trend was included in that figure instead of the pre-2008 trend, as shown in Figure 8.6, then it would appear that the UK is effectively back to where it would have been if no oil had been drilled from the North Sea. Essentially, North Sea oil led to a short-run increase in economic growth, as expected, but as the oil proceeds were not reinvested in the British economy it did not lead to a long-run increase in economic growth.

Forestry Reborn

At the start of the twentieth century, the UK had the lowest rates of area under forest per head in Europe and the second lowest rate of forest area as a share of land. In response to these alarming figures, the German-born forester Wilhelm Schlich (1840–1925) urged that 'an effort must be made to increase the area under timber in this country'.[64] Writing almost a quarter of a century later, the British geographer Laurence Dudley Stamp (1898–1966) noted that 'we in England are apt to get a very wrong impression of the general European timber position' because the UK was still ranked last in terms of forest cover.[65] The figures that Stamp highlighted were 3.9 per cent of forest land coverage in the UK compared to 31 per cent in Europe. This hid some regional distortion as Scotland had double the UK rate of forestry (6 per cent), England was also higher with 5.1 per cent forest area, and it was Ireland that brought down the average with a tiny fraction of land devoted to forestry (1.5 per cent); however, the figures for the three kingdoms were incredibly low relative to the rest of Europe.

The UK and Ireland are believed to have been densely wooded in the medieval period and the low forest coverage dates to the 1700s. Deforestation coincided with increases in agricultural land and is believed to be associated with the enclosure of commons.[66] The total woodland area is estimated to have been relatively static for most of the 1700s and 1800s but experienced a dramatic decrease during, and immediately after, the First World War.[67] Although, earlier writers thought that there was a gradual decrease over time that was driven primarily by unsustainable harvesting practices as replanting did not keep pace with felling.

Timber was mainly used for firewood, construction, and shipping.[68] As shown in Table 8.2, Britain has historically been a net importer of timber, primarily from European countries, and thus less attention was given to the domestic forestry sector.[69] Only 15 per cent of timber consumption came from domestic supplies and domestic cut represented a decreasing fraction of British timber consumption, from 27 per cent in 1846 to 6 per cent by 1911.[70] Large increases in the share of domestic production came during the First World War, around 57 per cent but the total consumption dropped after the war.[71] Therefore, the increased sustainability of British forests was supported by importing forest products.

Interest in arboriculture grew in the late nineteenth century leading to a handful of parliamentary enquiries in the 1800s. It was not until the 1920s that the UK Forestry Commission was established and only in 1924 that the first Forestry Census was undertaken. Even with the annual publication of reports of the Forestry Commission, and publication of the journal *Forestry* in 1927, there was no regular coverage of issues needed to generate estimates of UK forestry stocks.[72] The discussion below brings together the various sources to give a sense of trends in UK forestry.

The first Census of Woodlands gave an authoritative return of woodland coverage in Britain. This came in the immediate years following the end of the First World War and a second Woodland Census, in 1947, followed the Second World War. With the Woodland Censuses a distinction was made between *economic* woodlands, woodlands maintained with the object of producing timber for commercial purposes, and *uneconomic* woodlands, woods maintained for objects other than commercial production.[73] An early Forestry Commission report written in 1927 believed that a large area, 'at a rough estimate 450,000 to 500,000 acres', had been felled during

TABLE 8.2 Imports and exports of timber, 1850–2000.

	Thousand m³		
	Imports	Exports	Net Imports
1850–54	3253	20	3233
1886–1890	10169	71	10098
1909–13	19224	120	19103
1915–19	10949	41	10909
1925–30	27211	56	27155
1934–38	30234	9	30225
1960	36000	800	35200
1970	40300	1200	39100
1980	34700	2300	32400
1990	48400	4700	43700
2000	48595	7660	40935

Source: McLaughlin et al. (2014, 2017). 'Historical wealth accounts for Britain'.

the First World War and in its immediate aftermath.[74] Writing in 1949, the Forestry Commission believed that devastated woodlands 'were the result of exploitation' and that 19 per cent of the total woodland had been felled during the two world wars. Of this, two-thirds had been located in Scotland, and the majority of the felled woodland was in private ownership.[75] Prior to the census of woodlands there were a number of estimates of the area of woodland reported in the agricultural returns and some historic estimates are combined to provide the estimates of forest coverage presented in Figure 8.7.[76]

The Forestry Commission estimated that prior to the outbreak of the First World War annual production was 1.27 million m^3 and it was subsequently estimated that this was slightly higher, in the region of 1.42 million m^3.[77] The geographers Laurence Dudley Stamp and Stanley Henry Beaver (1907–84) stated that, 'during the First World War, the volume of timber obtained from British woodlands was estimated at 1,000,000,000 cubic feet [28.32 million m^3] or roughly one-third of the volume standing in 1914'.[78] Although, these estimates of the First World War production are much higher than more recent estimates.[79] The estimates pre-1960 appear to be underestimates of total woodland produce. For example, Stamp and Beaver took 'no account of hedgerow timber, branchwood, or the trees in amenity woodlands and

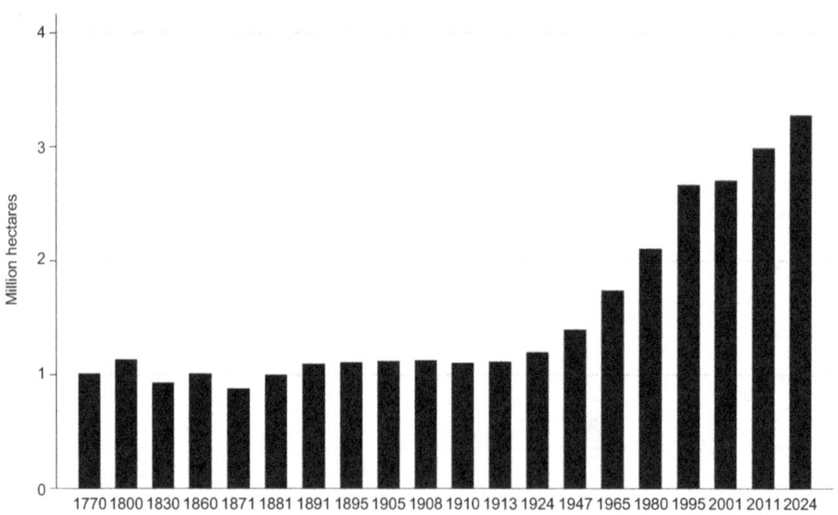

FIGURE 8.7 *Area of British woodland (million hectares) and woodland as a percentage of total land, 1770–2024. Source: McLaughlin et al. (2014, 2017), 'Historical wealth accounts for Britain'; Forest Research (2024), Forestry Facts & Figures 2024.*

parks'.[80] There are few estimates of increment pre-1923 but these estimates have been deemed questionable.[81]

British afforestation was the success story of the twentieth century, helped in no small part by the import of timber to meet consumption needs. In the immediate post-First World War period, there was a consensus that British forestry was on an unsustainable path.[82] Purposeful management has led to an increase in forest coverage and placed forestry on a more sustainable footing. In contrast to the fossil fuels discussed previously, forestry is a renewable resource. Forests, if carefully maintained, can increase in size and provide a constant source of well-being. The increase in UK forest cover raises a number of practical issues from an accounting perspective. Within the Inclusive Wealth approach, there has been a change to how forestry is measured. The early empirical approach taken by the World Bank, as outlined in the *Manual for Calculating Adjusted Net Savings*, gave the following treatment of forestry:

> Since wood stocks can be renewed, extraction of wood is not necessarily a disinvestment in the future and need not be counted against adjusted net savings . . . Net natural growth is not added to savings when it is positive, although this will bias the estimates against sustainability. [83]

As a result of this accounting decision forestry is continuously recorded as zero for the UK from 1970 to present in the World Bank series of Genuine Savings (GS).[84] In the same period of time there was an increase in estimated stocks of standing timber in Britain: increasing from 75 million m^3 in 1947 to 336 million m^3 in 2011.[85] This clearly has added to the Inclusive Wealth of the nation (see Figure 8.8). At the same time Britain's increased forest stock was supported by imports of timber. Whether global forestry also experienced a net gain would depend on the sustainability of forestry practices elsewhere. Thus, the sustainability of one country may (or may not) come at the expense of sustainability elsewhere.

Forests are also useful as proxies for biodiversity. It is biodiversity loss that ecologists are perhaps more concerned with, and economic growth is often seen as a contributory factor in biodiversity loss.[86] The greatest challenge in assessing the relationship between economic growth and biodiversity lies in the difficulty of accurately measuring biodiversity. Because direct measurement is difficult, studies exploring the link between biodiversity and economic growth often rely on proxy indicators, such as forest cover.[87] Other studies use the 'proportion of species' as an approximation of biodiversity and these metrics are based on tropical rainforest (habitat) remaining, i.e., deforestation.[88] Similarly, historical estimates of biodiversity in Britain would also need to rely on forest coverage as a proxy. Based on the suggestive evidence presented here, this would indicate a modest improvement in biodiversity over time.[89]

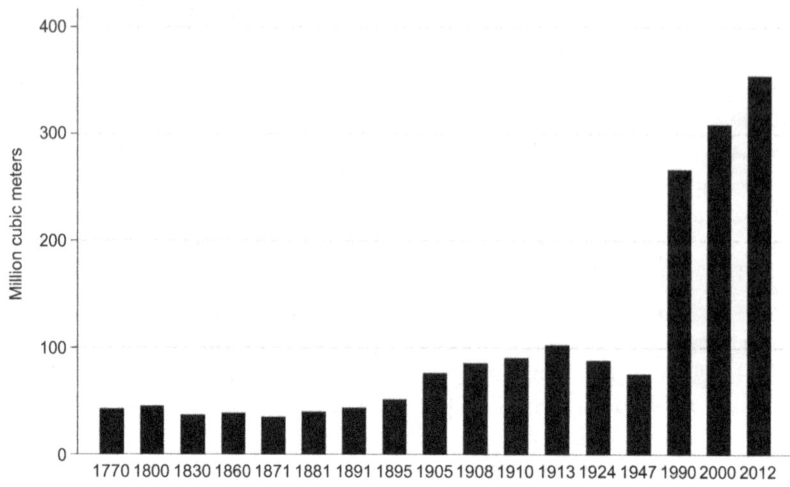

FIGURE 8.8 *Standing volume of timber of timber, 1750–2012. Source: McLaughlin et al. (2014, 2017), 'Historical wealth accounts for Britain'; Forestry Commission (2014), National Forest Inventory.*

Pollution and the Industrial Revolution

One of the most iconic images of the British Industrial Revolution is that of smoke billowing from factory smokestacks.[90] While pollution is depicted in imagery it has been neglected somewhat in historical research because this information was not monitored with any great precision until the gradual introduction of atmospheric and water pollution monitors. Contemporaries were aware of the pollution (atmospheric and water) that came part and parcel with industrialization.[91] Using a variety of source material, such as weather diaries, the atmospheric chemist Pete Brimblecombe recreated the history of atmospheric pollution in London. He showed how pollution was linked to the prevalence of rickets as particulates suspended in London's air-obscured ultraviolet radiation.[92]

Historically, the more visible aspects of pollution, such as smoke and smog, were the target of advocates for cleaner air. Contemporary responses to pollution also explain the residential sorting of UK cities, as the affluent were able to move to the west side of cities and the poorer residents were located in the east in the path of prevailing winds.[93] Damage to property through acid rain was also an issue, particularly in areas that specialized in chemical manufacturing. When pollution caused property damage one early solution was for private landowners to exercise their property rights and litigate for compensation. This was more easily done if it was possible to identify the polluter.[94]

I have highlighted trends in historical emissions of CO_2 and SO_2 for the UK in Figure 8.9. These pollutants are insightful to discuss because they differ in terms of their global and local impact. CO_2 is a global pollutant; regardless of where it is emitted the impact will be felt at a global level, whereas SO_2 is a local pollutant with impacts concentrated in the surrounding region. SO_2 is also interesting because the damages can occur away from the source of emissions, which was most infamous in the case of acid rain where damages were felt in Scandinavia despite emissions originating in the UK. SO_2 is also correlated with other local air pollutants, such as particulate matter, and thus likely to give a good approximation of air quality. One of the main sources of emissions was the burning of coal, especially for domestic heating, and UK coal had a high sulphur content.[95] The 1925 Coal Commission reported that it was recognized that coal burning 'causes serious danger to health and damage to property'. This has been corroborated by recent research suggesting that air pollution was a major contributor to mortality in London in the nineteenth and early twentieth centuries.[96]

Historical estimates of CO_2 and SO_2 are based on energy consumption (effectively coal and then later oil and gas).[97] As fuel consumption increased so too did the emissions of CO_2 and SO_2. The large reduction in SO_2 was driven primarily by improvements in environmental quality following the 1956 Clean Air Act, which led to a reduction of coal consumption for domestic heating in the UK. A strand of economic research emerged in the 1990s that looked at the relationship between economic growth and pollution. These studies found an 'inverse U'-shaped relationship between income and pollution, known as an 'environmental Kuznets curve'. That is pollution started at low levels when income levels were also low, pollution then rises

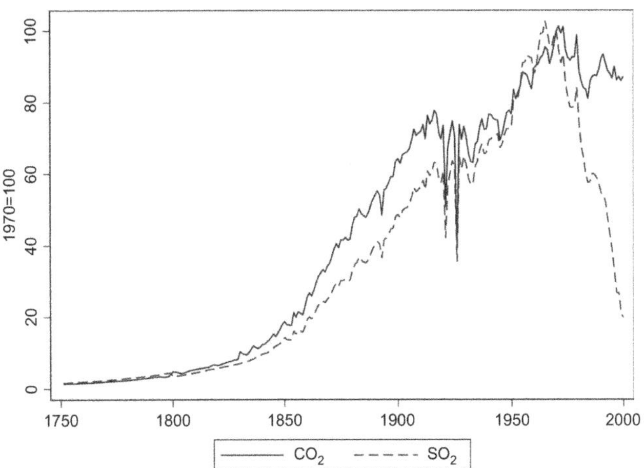

FIGURE 8.9 *UK CO_2 and SO_2 emissions, index 1970=100. Source: McLaughlin et al. (2014, 2017), 'Historical wealth accounts for Britain'.*

as income grows, and eventually declines after reaching a peak, while income continues to increase.[98] Statistical analysis of historical emissions shows how there was an inverted-U shaped relationship between SO_2 and CO_2, and economic growth.[99] The decrease in emissions was primarily driven by more stringent environmental regulations.[100] Coincidently, 100 years before these modern studies, British climatologist Frederick Brodie found a similar inverse U-shaped relationship for foggy days (a consequence of coal smoke) in London in the period 1871–1903. Brodie argued that in the initial years, coal was burned extensively but over time technological and regulatory changes induced decreases in coal burning.[101]

The push for greater environmental regulation in the UK was driven by the Great London Smog of 1952 (mentioned in Chapter 4), one of the worst air pollution events in modern British history. The smog was caused by a period of cold weather on which fog mixed with the soot from the combustion of fossil fuels, primarily coal but also diesel engines. A high-pressure zone had settled over southern England and this caused a temperature inversion that trapped the smog over the city.[102] The Great London Smog caused the death of 4000 people in the immediate aftermath and up to 8000 deaths in the following months.[103] A recent study demonstrated the long-term impact of the London Smog and found that exposure in utero reduced later human capital development in terms of fluid intelligence, poor respiratory health, and lower years of education.[104]

In the traditional research on Inclusive Wealth and Genuine Savings carbon emissions and particulate damages are subtracted from net investment. This is done by placing a value on carbon emissions, known as the Social Cost of Carbon (SCC), and multiplying emissions by the SCC. The SCC is effectively an attempt to value the future damage costs of carbon emissions. For climate change what matters most is the concentration of carbon (cumulative emissions, measured in parts per million) in the atmosphere, so the further back in time, the lower the concentration of carbon (see Figure 4.5). Complicating this is the long life span of carbon once it is in the atmosphere, the 2006 *Stern Review of the Economics of Climate Change* had an estimate of 5–200 years but more recent estimates suggest carbon may have an even longer life-span.[105] The extent of the reduction to net investment then depends on the size of the SCC applied.[106] A similar principle can apply to other pollutants and the reductions to net investment can be substantial no matter what country they are applied to.[107]

In any case, clearly the reduction in pollution has added value to UK national wealth. Air pollution is a major driver of premature deaths across the world today and is linked with cardiovascular disease.[108] The damage associated with air pollution, usually translated into health damages, is not trivial: estimates place it at between 0.7 to 2.8 per cent of GDP in the United States in the early 2000s. Accounting for such externalities can change our understanding of economic growth; for example, the economist Nicholas Muller illustrates how incorporating air pollution changes the growth narrative of the early 2000s in the United States as pollution fell, and how GDP grew faster than an environmentally adjusted measure of GDP in the United States in the mid-twentieth century.[109] Perhaps greater acknowledgement of the contribution of pollution control to the health and well-being of the British people can offset some of the shortfall in 'economic growth' discussed in Chapter 7.

Human Capital

Despite the UK's early lead in the Industrial Revolution, formal education provision was limited.[110] While the work of Morgan Kelly, Joel Mokyr and Cormac Ó Gráda (discussed in Chapter 7) placed emphasis on human capital, the UK lagged behind peer countries when it came to the formal provision of education until the start of the twentieth century. The biggest developments were the introduction of the universal primary education in 1870.[111] Provision for secondary education was scant and higher education was still the preserve of the elite until the twentieth century.[112] Human capital increased in importance over time and in the early twentieth century, what the Nobel laureate Claudia Goldin referred to as the 'human capital century', UK human capital attainment lagged behind the United States particularly in terms of secondary education.[113] There was a significant increase in secondary enrolment rates as part of welfare state reforms following the Second World War and the number of pupils in state-funded secondary education doubled between 1950 and 1970.[114]

As human capital increased in importance in economic discourse, economic historians began to estimate various indicators of educational attainment and human capital formation. One of the earliest studies looking at human capital was by the historical demographer Roger Schofield (1937–2019), who looked at the rise of literacy through various indicators, one of which was the ability to sign one's own name using data from the Registrar General of Births, Deaths, and Marriages. Schofield found that illiteracy rates were around 60 per cent for women and 40 per cent for men in the mid-1700s; 100 years later there was a 10 percentage point decrease in illiteracy for both men and women, and by 1911 illiteracy had fallen to 1 per cent for both.[115] More recently, economic historians have attempted to quantify numeracy using age statements from historical records such as the census. When people report rounded ages, that is ages ending in '0' or '5', this is known as 'age heaping' or 'digit preference'.[116] Efforts to measure numeracy using this approach show that Britain had relatively high levels of numeracy compared to other countries but also that periods of economic turmoil led to decreases in numeracy and future earnings. Estimates of numeracy show an increase from 76 to 93 per cent between 1620 and 1720 and that by the 1830s numeracy was close to 100 per cent.[117]

Nick Crafts incorporated estimates of human capital in his measures of 'broad capital accumulation' that showed a general increase in the number of years schooling, from 2.3 years in the early decades of the nineteenth century to 6.75 years by 1899–1913.[118] Figures 8.10 and 8.11 show a clear rise in human capital as measured by enrolment rates at different levels of formal education and also the average years of education.

Experience is also a key part of human capital and an important development in this regard is the increase in life expectancy, particularly in the first half of the twentieth century. Life expectancy at birth was fairly flat for most of the 1700s and began to rise from the 1850s, increasing slightly from 43 years in 1850 to 46 years by 1900, and by 1939 life expectancy at birth was 64 years. The biggest increases in the twentieth century were driven by improvements in medical knowledge and the development of antibiotics. Historically, infectious diseases were the main causes of death; they were 45 per cent of deaths in 1850 and 36 per cent in 1900. By 1939 deaths caused by infectious diseases had fallen to 15 per cent.[119] A clear factor offsetting these gains was the huge loss to human capital during the world wars. The First World War led to a lost generation, and such a huge loss would be difficult to capture in any monetary measure of human capital. The First World War was also immediately followed by one of the worst global pandemics in modern history. The 1918 influenza pandemic

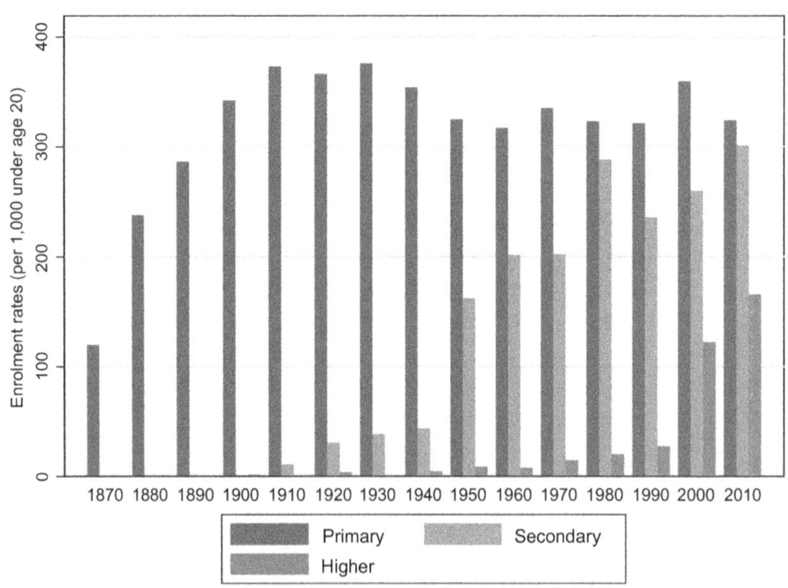

FIGURE 8.10 *Primary, Secondary and Higher Enrolment rates, 1870–2010. Source: V. Carpentier (2020), A historical dataset on UK education 1833–2019.*

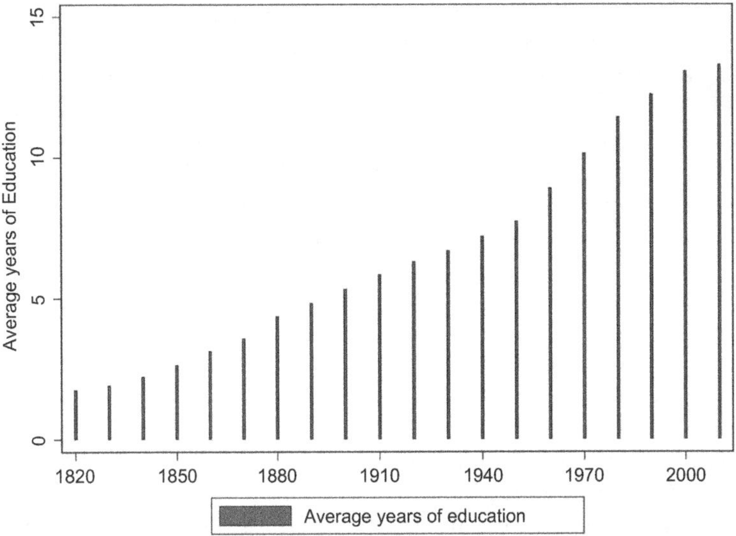

FIGURE 8.11 *Average Years of Education, 1870–2010. Source: B. van Leeuwen and J. van Leeuwen-Li (2015), Average Years of Education. http://hdl.handle.net/10622/KCBMKI, accessed via the Clio Infra website.*

had an unusual mortality profile that affected people of working age, a so-called 'W'-shape distribution.[120]

Another factor that also affects experience is the duration of unemployment. Prolonged periods of unemployment mean a loss of skills and knowledge (a phenomenon known as unemployment hysteresis) and can lead to human capital decay.[121] The idea of unemployment hysteresis dates to the 1980s when Britain was seen as a prime exemplar due to higher unemployment rates than peers from the Organisation for Economic Co-operation and Development (OECD), although the applicability of the concept to the UK is contested.[122] The experience following the 2008 crisis led to a renewed interest in the concept of hysteresis, with recent evidence emphasizing its significance, particularly in the United States after the Great Recession.[123]

Migration is obviously an important part of the accumulation of human capital because some of the investment in human capital is lost to emigration or investment in other countries is received via immigration.[124] In the nineteenth century and up until the 1960s, UK net migration was negative (more people were emigrating than were immigrating). From the 1990s UK net migration has been positive (more people immigrating than were emigrating) with a rapid increase in the level of net migration in the 2020s.[125] The UK was both a recipient of immigrants but was also a source of emigrants that migrated to parts of the British Empire as well as to North

America. In terms of the latter, the majority of British migrants to the United States were reported to have been skilled and thus the human capital that they acquired in Britain was a loss to Britain (brain drain) and a gain to the United States.[126] Similarly, the influx of (skilled) immigrants (brain gain) would have been a boon to the stock of British human capital. Factoring net migration into accounts of British Inclusive Wealth can technically be overcome when assessing the value of human capital as it takes the population as a whole into consideration. However, it can make assessments of the changes in the stock (flows) a challenge and can lead to under (over) estimates of human capital accumulation when net migration is positive (negative).

Incorporating human capital into an Inclusive Wealth framework requires placing a monetary valuation on human capital. As was highlighted in Chapter 5, there are a number of approaches to do this. One of which is to use the current spending on education although this does not necessarily give an indication of educational attainment. Figure 8.12 is drawn from the work of the education historian Vincent Carpentier. It shows public spending on education in the UK as a share of GDP rising over time.[127] Education spending was a large share of public spending, but this also coincided with a rise in the number of private schools which more than doubled between 1951 and 2005 making public spending on education a partial indicator of human capital investment.

Expenditure on education is a measure of the change in human capital and does not provide information on the stock. Measuring the value of the stock of human capital follows the innovative approach pioneered by the economists Dale Jorgenson and Barbara Fraumeni who discounted the

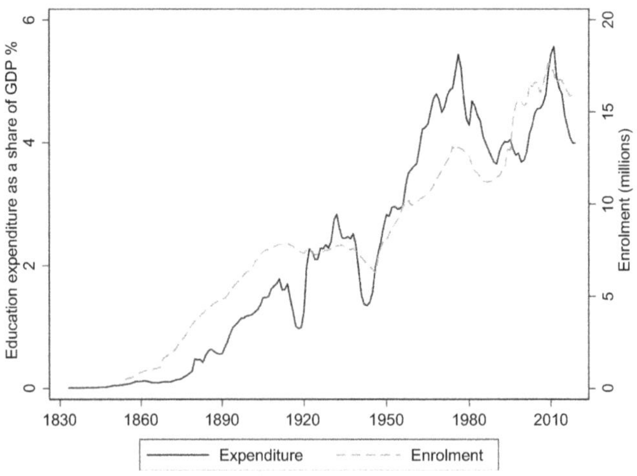

FIGURE 8.12 *Public education spending as a share of GDP, 1833–2019. Source: V. Carpentier (2020), A historical dataset on UK education 1833–2019.*

lifetime earnings of workers to get a present value of the stock of human capital (see Chapter 5).[128] The UK Office of National Statistics (ONS) follows this approach to estimate the stock of human capital and the ONS estimates show that the stock of human capital is approximately sixteen times the level of GDP per capita.[129] A similar approach has been taken to estimate human capital historically and it shows a thirteenth-fold increase in human capital per worker from 1760 to 2009.[130]

Estimating the UK's Inclusive Wealth

Colleagues and I have estimated the UK's Inclusive Wealth from 1760 to 2000. The measure of Inclusive Wealth was made up of net capital (taking account of depreciation of capital), natural capital, and human capital. The natural capital components included the value of agricultural land, fossil fuels (coal, oil and gas), minerals (iron, tin, copper, lead and zinc) and forestry. It excluded the value of biodiversity and pollution damages, so it should be viewed as an approximation of natural capital.[131]

In our original work both the World Bank and the UN Environment Programme (UNEP) approaches to valuing natural capital were used (the approaches discussed in Chapter 6), and there were notable differences between them. Here I have updated the figures to be consistent with the approach of the World Bank post-2018. Figure 8.13 shows the distribution of the capital stocks that comprised the United Kingdom's Inclusive Wealth from 1760 to 2000. Human capital was the major form of capital throughout.

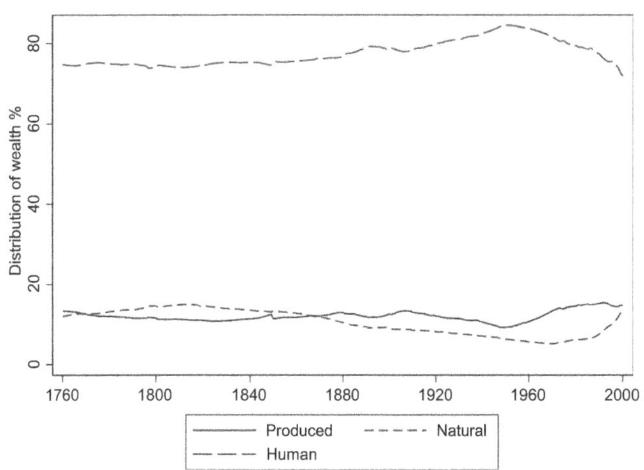

FIGURE 8.13 *The composition of wealth, 1760–2000 (%). Source: McLaughlin et al. (2014, 2017), 'Historical wealth accounts for Britain'.*

In 1760 around 14 per cent of total wealth was natural capital, but only 1 per cent of this was accounted for by minerals. The contribution of natural capital to wealth diminished over the next 200 years but increased after 1970 with the exploitation of North Sea fossil fuel reserves. In the 1970s oil and gas represented more than 70 per cent of all natural capital. The share of produced capital in wealth was relatively stable and increased to over 10 per cent in the twentieth century.

Growth rates of the various components of Inclusive Wealth are shown in Table 8.3 alongside the growth in GDP per capita. On balance, the growth in Inclusive Wealth aligns with the growth in GDP per capita but it also shows some subtle differences. Over the entire period, growth in Inclusive Wealth and GDP per capita are aligned but within sub-periods there are noticeable divergences. There are periods when the growth in Inclusive Wealth is lower than that implied by the growth in GDP per capita (1820–69, 1950–72, 1973–89) and periods when the growth in Inclusive Wealth is higher (1760–1819, 1915–49, 1973–79, 1990–2000).

There is clear alignment between the growth of produced and human capital and GDP per capita growth but disparities in the growth of natural capital are more pronounced depending on the chosen methodology. If the World Bank approach is used there is a trend towards increasing growth in the natural capital stock from below 1 per cent per annum

TABLE 8.3 **Growth in GDP per capita and wealth per capita.**

		Inclusive Wealth components				
	GDP	Produced	Natural (World Bank)	Natural (UNEP)	Human	Wealth
1760-1819	0.16	0.24	0.89	0.71	0.57	0.57
1820-1869	1.25	1.05	0.45	-0.43	0.90	0.85
1870-1913	0.88	0.88	0.01	2.73	0.83	0.75
1915-1949	0.95	0.41	0.55	11.46	1.49	1.30
1950-1972	2.14	3.42	0.80	-2.08	1.45	1.63
1973-1979	2.24	3.08	4.35	28.43	2.22	2.46
1973-1989	2.25	2.40	3.66	6.29	1.64	1.87
1990-2000	1.84	1.84	8.15	-2.54	1.44	2.15
1820-2000	1.05	1.08	1.11	2.47	1.02	1.04

Source: McLaughlin et al. (2014, 2017). 'Historical wealth accounts for Britain'.

until 1972 and then an acceleration, primarily driven by oil, from 1973 onwards. The UNEP approach offers nuance to this as it shows periods of extensive use of natural capital that were followed by a later decline in natural capital.

Genuine Savings of the United Kingdom

An alternative way to look at Inclusive Wealth is to look at the *change* in Inclusive Wealth via the Genuine Savings indicator. The first estimate of the United Kingdom's Genuine Savings was made by David Pearce and appeared in *Blueprint 3* for the years 1980 to 1990 (shown in Figure 8.14). Pearce used gross saving, deducted depreciation of fixed capital (net saving), and depreciation of natural capital (Adjusted Net Saving). The resulting figure shows negative Adjusted Net Saving (ANS) during the early 1980s at the peak of the oil bonanza. Pearce, however, never included human capital in his estimates of ANS, so it is an underestimate of UK sustainable development.[132]

Colleagues and I estimated the change of wealth using net investment, the change in natural capital, and the change in human capital following the approach of the World Bank.[133] These investment-based estimates of Genuine Savings (GS) are of particular interest over the period of the early British Industrial Revolution as they relate to a long-standing debate over the importance of the rise in the savings (or investment) ratio during the Industrial Revolution (see discussion in Chapter 7). With these controversies

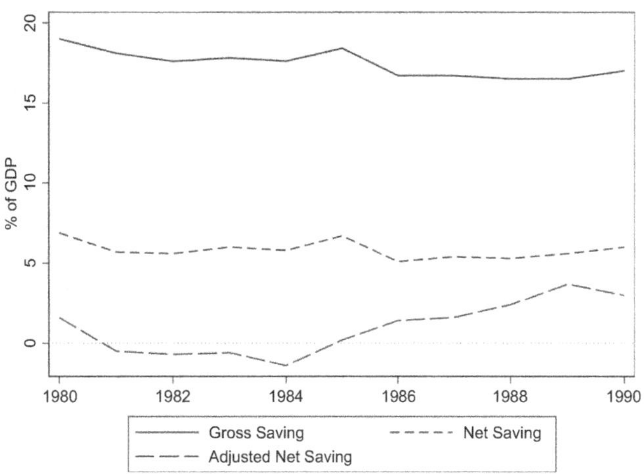

FIGURE 8.14 *UK Adjusted Net Saving, 1980–1990. Source: Pearce (1993). Blueprint 3.*

in mind, estimating GS is effectively re-opening a Pandora's box of economic controversies. Our measure of GS incorporates a wider definition of net investment, similar to those originally envisaged by Rostow and it also aligns with the later work of Solow.

A number of variants of net investment are illustrated in Table 8.4. The first column represents net domestic fixed investment (NFCF), which averaged 0.5 per cent in the 1760s, rose gradually, until the 1830s and peaked during the 'railway mania' of the 1840s. Only using NFCF as the measure of net investment then GS would have been negative in the early periods of the Industrial Revolution. It is difficult to justify limiting net investment to NFCF because it overlooks inventories and works in progress (sometimes defined as circulating capital), both of which were important elements of capital formation during the Industrial Revolution. Countries can also hold wealth in the form of investments in other countries. In the second column of Table 8.4 'Net' refers to NFCF, as well as inventories and overseas investment. Including the latter components of investment offsets the effects of mineral depletion and results in a positive measure of GS in the early years of the Industrial Revolution.

One other aspect of Table 8.4 is the fall in Net (and GS) during the Napoleonic Wars which reflects a drop in overseas investment. Thus, overseas investment played a crucial role in keeping GS positive during periods of falling NFCF and offset natural resource depletion in Britain, a feature that would have persisted until the First World War, and shares similarities with resource-rich countries today that invest overseas. Lastly, Table 8.4 highlights population and GDP per capita growth in the same time periods. The continued positive GS rates meant that the economy was maintaining its wealth intact and keeping pace with population growth.

Figure 8.15 presents the UK GS series for the period 1871 to 2000. It highlights gross investment, net investment (gross minus depreciation), Green investment (which is net investment minus depreciation of natural resources), GS (Green plus education expenditure), and both Green and GS augmented with Total Factor Productivity (TFP). The latter is an idea derived from Weitzman's work that advocated for the inclusion of exogenous technological progress in assessments of (changes in) the capital stocks of a country.[134] The main message from Figure 8.15 is that conventional measurement of investment, gross investment, does not take account of depreciation of fixed capital, so the investment necessary to maintain the physical capital stock. The various adjustments that are made reduce the level of investment from this baseline estimate. The periods of negative investment coincide with the world wars and the massive dislocation of overseas investment and greater use of indigenous natural resources (e.g., timber). The early 1980s appear as a period of negative Green investment, which mirrors the findings of David Pearce shown in Figure 8.14, but this effect is offset by investment in education. In all periods of negative growth

TABLE 8.4 **Mean GS rates (% GDP), 1761–1860 (decade averages).**

	NFCF	NET	Education investment	Forestry	Minerals extraction	GS	Population	GDP per capita
	% of GDP						Growth rate (%)	
1761–70	0.52	1.91			–1.10	0.82	0.60	0.07
1771–80	1.12	3.05		0.05	–1.20	1.90	0.95	0.29
1781–90	1.38	3.44		0.04	–0.80	2.69	0.97	0.05
1791–1800	1.79	4.13		0.03	–0.65	3.50	1.22	0.87
1801–10	2.22	1.97		–0.02	–1.23	0.72	1.26	0.44
1811–20	2.51	5.89		–0.03	–1.35	4.52	1.54	-0.39
1821–30	3.33	7.31		–0.05	–1.69	5.57	1.46	0.77
1831–40	4.27	5.66	0.01	0.01	–1.35	4.32	1.28	1.12
1841–50	5.31	7.62	0.02	0.01	–1.75	5.91	1.20	0.85
1851–60	3.95	7.77	0.08	0.02	–2.47	5.40	1.07	1.58

Source: McLaughlin et al. (2014, 2017). 'Historical wealth accounts for Britain'.

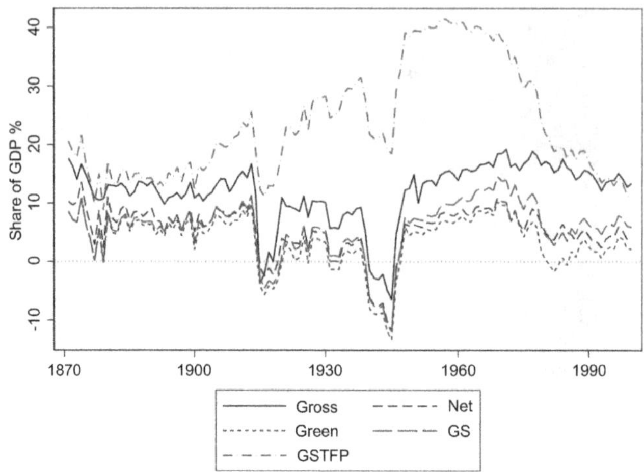

FIGURE 8.15 *Alternative investment measures as % GDP, 1871–2000. Source: McLaughlin et al. (2014, 2017), 'Historical wealth accounts for Britain'; TFP updated using data from Fig 7.9.*

in savings, these are compensated for by the effect of TFP growth. GSTFP indicates a much higher rate of net investment than conventional figures alone but given the slowdown in TFP growth in recent years (see Figure 7.10), this implies a future weakness for the UK economy.

Using the Inclusive Wealth framework can also shed some more light on the United Kingdom's relative decline (see Chapter 7). Figure 8.16 uses World Bank data from the 2011 *Changing Wealth of Nations* report to compare UK savings rates with a weighted and unweighted average of the fourteen other countries that were shown in Figure 7.5.[135] The period of reference is 1970 to 2000 to highlight the years of the 'British Disease' and recovery. What the various figures highlight is that the United Kingdom consistently had a lower savings rate compared to the average of the other countries, this is shown for Gross savings (Quadrant a). When depreciation is included, this translates into a lower net savings rate (Quadrant b) and UK investment was just about covering depreciation of its capital stock. Quadrant c shows Green savings (that is net savings minus resource depletion), and it is clear that the rents from the oil boom were not reinvested into other forms of fixed capital as the rates turned negative in the early 1980s. Quadrant d shows that Genuine Savings, which includes education expenditure to the Green Savings, was still lower than the average of the other countries. While all measures of saving show the United Kingdom had a shortfall compared with other countries, the largest differences were in terms of Green and Genuine Savings during the 1980s.

A more recent update from the World Bank is presented in Figure 8.17. It compares the experiences of the UK with other G7 countries (those listed

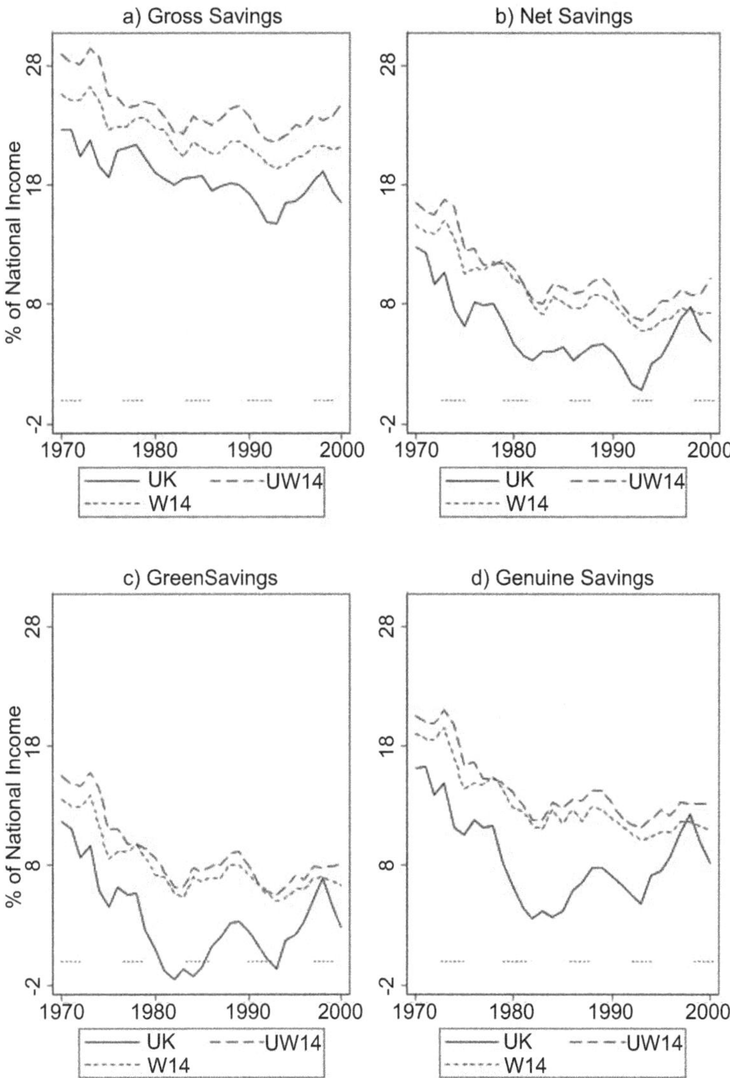

FIGURE 8.16 *UK Gross, Net, Green and Genuine Savings 1970–2000. Note: Countries included in the weighted and unweighted average are those listed in Figure 7.5. Source: World Bank (2011). Changing Wealth of Nations.*

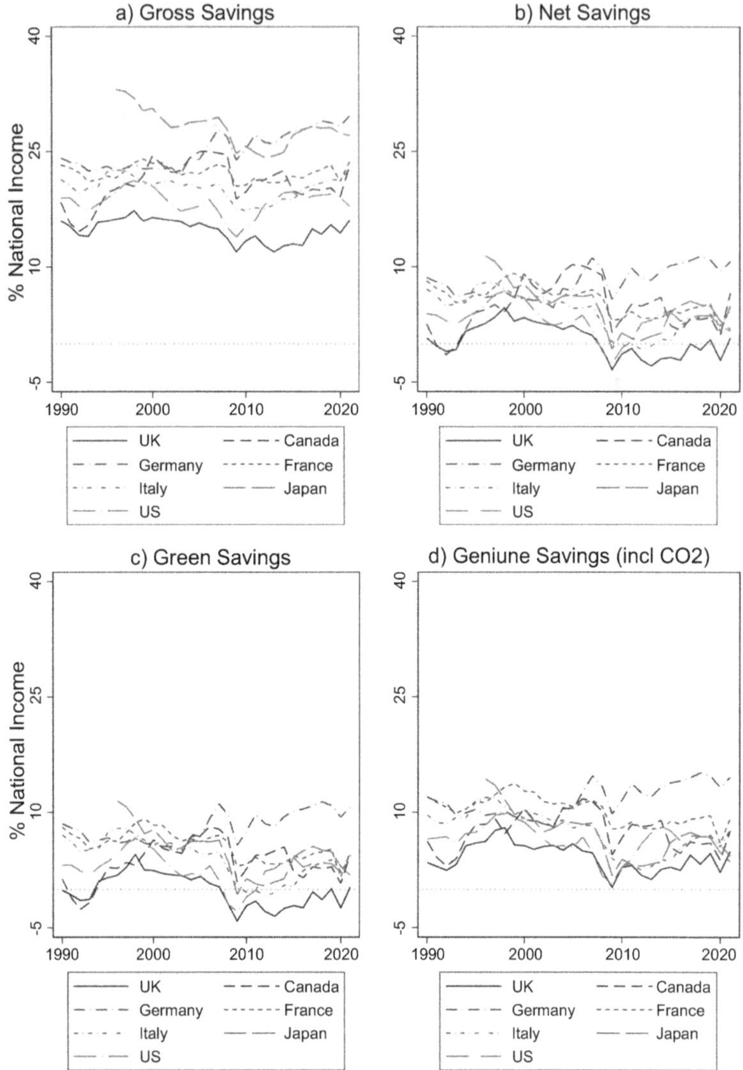

FIGURE 8.17 *Gross, Net, Green and Genuine Savings in the G7, 1970–2021. Note: The World Bank updated its methodology and database. There are some anomalies (for example, series in d) is only available from the 1990s despite estimates from earlier versions of the database starting in the 1970s.The World Bank has only updated these series to the year 2021. See a review by L. McGrath, N. Hanley, and E. McLaughlin (2025), 'Saving or Investing for the Future? Methodology Matters in Inclusive Wealth Accounting'. Heriot-Watt Working Paper, 2025-06. Source: World Development Indicators.*

in Table 7.2). The trends are broadly consistent with Figure 8.16, although some caution is needed because the World Bank databases are not fully comparable; for example, some of the countries from Figure 8.17 have a shorter time series in the updated database.[136] Figure 8.17 shows that the UK had the lowest rate of saving over the period, regardless of how saving was measured. The gap was particularly pronounced for net saving (gross saving minus depreciation) and 'green saving' (net saving minus changes in natural capital), which were negative for much of the late 2000s and early 2010s. Although the UK's GS rate remained positive, it was well below the G7 average, roughly half the rate of the other countries after 2007. The sharp divergence in UK savings rates after 2007 is concerning. Combined with the negative TFP growth reported in Table 7.2, the opposite of what would be predicted by the 'Weitzman Rule', it signals a deeply troubling trend for the UK economy.

Nick Crafts highlighted how a misallocation of resources in the period 1950–70 led to poor growth but Britain in the 1980s had a misallocation of capital and continued to have low investment in physical and human capital. Thus, Crafts concluded that while the Thatcher years may have improved the UK's short-term prospects, but it was an open question whether it halted the UK's long-term relative decline.[137] Similarly, the 1985 House of Lords committee highlighted that Britain had a lower rate of gross investment compared to the United States, Japan, Germany, France, Italy and the OECD.[138] Analysis by Nick Crafts and Mary O'Mahony showed that one of the drivers behind Britain's lag in productivity relative to France and Germany was lower 'broad capital per worker', while relative to the United States it was an innovation gap.[139] Analysis based on GS would corroborate that conclusion as results derived from GS suggest that the UK's decisions made in the 1980s did not halt the relative decline and instead the seeds were sown for a future slowdown. Furthermore, because the focus of industrial policy was on the financial services this may have led to a misallocation of human capital to the financial services sector at the expense of other parts of the economy.

Conclusion

Inclusive Wealth offers a different perspective on long-run economic development in the UK. It stressed the importance of different forms of capital and how they contribute to well-being. The focus on fossil fuels and renewable forestry highlighted contrasting narratives. The UK's coal was never fully depleted but changing market conditions rendered coal production uneconomical. Oil, on the other hand, appears to have run dry.[140] The North Sea was drilled for fifty years, and it has a large, somewhat overlooked, impact on the broader UK economy. Forestry has been a success story of the twentieth century: forest area increased from less than 4 per cent of land coverage to 13 per cent by 2024. The United Kingdom still has one of the lowest areas of forest coverage in Europe and globally,[141] but given the very low base this was a significant improvement and more could be done to increase afforestation. Pollution, the by-product of economic activity, does not get recorded in conventional growth-based accounts of UK economic history but it significantly declined over time. The drop in pollution is undoubtedly a result of the structural changes in the UK economy (i.e., a benefit of the 'de-industrial revolution') but policy has also been key. There have been radical improvements in the United Kingdom's human capital; the population is healthier, lives longer, and is more educated.

Within the wider research on the resource curse, the United States is used as an example of a country that was not resource-cursed by its boon in oil and gas reserves.[142] Yet, the jury is still out on the British case. Perhaps thinking more broadly about wealth can speak to the productivity slowdown. For example, a recent study shows how including natural resources can lead to substantial adjustments to productivity measures.[143] This was also shown in the case of Australia incorporating natural capital into productivity estimates can make a substantial difference to a country's productivity and reinvesting resource rents would have made Australia approximately 30 per cent better off today.[144]

The Inclusive Wealth framework does offer an alternative perspective on the UK economy. Some of the facets discussed here, such as pollution and renewable natural capital, tend to be overlooked in macroeconomic stories about the United Kingdom's economic growth. Yes, the productivity puzzle still exists, but maybe past growth can be revised down along the lines of Muller's analysis for the United States. A more inclusive understanding of our macroeconomic past can help plan for a more sustainable future.

Part V

Alternative

CHAPTER NINE

Can an Inclusive-Wealth-based Approach Safeguard the Future?

Adam Smith greatly admired the French physiocratic approach to political economy, one which saw agriculture as the main source of the wealth of nations. In a complimentary critique, he praised, 'this system . . . with all its imperfections is, perhaps, the nearest approximation to the truth that has yet been published upon the subject of political economy, and is upon that account well worth the consideration of every man who wishes to examine with attention the principles of that very important science'.[1] It is in a similar vein that I consider alternatives to the Inclusive Wealth approach that have emerged in the twenty-first century. This chapter will focus on different economic paradigms to the wealth-based approach,[•] namely 'doughnut economics' and degrowth.[2] One key point is that these critiques focus exclusively on GDP as the measure of the economy yet fail to offer credible alternatives. There are some proposed metrics but the signals they give are driven by arbitrary assumptions.

Both 'doughnut' and 'degrowth' are motivated by the Planetary Boundaries (PBs) approach to defining existential risk; as such the starting point of the chapter is a discussion of PBs. The statistician George Cox (1919–2013) quipped that 'all models are wrong',[3] to this it is often added that some models are better than others. I prefer to think that some models can do more harm than others. The PB model, while highly influential, offers only a partial perspective on global existential risk.[♦] Take, for example, the

---

[•]I have deliberately chosen not to discuss circular economy. I have discussed this elsewhere in the context of its strengths and weaknesses as an indicator of sustainable development: N. Millar, E. McLaughlin and T. Borger (2019). The Circular Economy: Swings and Roundabouts? *Ecological Economics*, 158: 11–19.

[♦]Note that here I purposefully make a distinction between humanity as a whole and social sub-group (geographically isolated societies), such as those identified by the environmental historian Jared Diamond in his book *Collapse* as he focuses on various geographically isolated

discovery of near-earth asteroid 2024 YR4 on 27 December 2024 that was on a trajectory to possibly hit earth on 22 December 2032. The asteroid was initially given a 1 per cent chance of hitting Earth with odds later increasing to 3 per cent, but this was subsequently downgraded when more information about the asteroid's trajectory was analyzed. The fact that the threat was downgraded does not negate the risk that such an event poses given the role of the near-earth objects (NEOs) in the extinction of various species in the geological history of the planet, particularly in the end-Cretaceous dinosaur extinction. Other natural hazards have also been associated with mass extinction events. For example, the end-Permian extinction event has been attributed to volcanic activity (another global catastrophic risk), although other factors such as an extreme El Niño have also played a role.[4] None of these phenomena relate explicitly to the PB framework.

Given the plethora of risks that humanity faces, this highlights the importance of greater awareness and mitigation of such risks. 'Doughnut' and 'degrowth' are effectively proposed solutions to problems relating to PBs and they may work for those risks, but at the expense of greater exposure to other risks. I argue that this is not fully understood or appreciated in the current 'doughnut' or 'degrowth' research.

I do not claim that Inclusive Wealth is a perfect solution, but I do believe that it has saving graces. I will offer a critique of Inclusive Wealth and highlight the limitations of this approach and how these can be overcome. Key issues will be the role of international trade; countries that export natural resources are shown as being unsustainable according to the Inclusive Wealth metrics while countries that import natural resources are sustainable. More effort should be made to account for pollution, both local and transboundary. The completeness of the accounting is also important; are we valuing all our natural resources effectively? This also marks a distinction between Inclusive Wealth and the doughnut approach adopted by the economist Kate Raworth; her adherence to traditional ecological economics is critical of the monetization of natural capital and the division between weak and strong sustainability (see discussion in Chapter 6 and Table 6.1).[5] The crucial issue of substitutability is discussed as well as the implications this raises for the Inclusive Wealth approach. The final point that will be addressed is the treatment of technology: how do we incorporate technological progress effectively into these metrics?

---

societies in the pre-modern period: J. Diamond (2005). *Collapse: How Societies Choose to Fail or Succeed*. Viking: London.

Planetary Boundaries

Planetary Boundaries (PBs) are a way of thinking about existential risks and are a highly influential idea in sustainability science. As previously mentioned, the PB approach sees itself in the same intellectual lineage as *The Limits to Growth* (see Chapter 4).[6] The intellectual underpinnings of the PB approach are system dynamics applied to Earth systems and, as such, the researchers involved tend to be interdisciplinary with specialisms in different areas of Earth systems.[7] The landmark studies have been published in the leading scientific journals (*Nature, Science*, *PNAS*). The pioneering figures involved in the various PB-related works that are cited here have disparate academic specialisms; Johan Rockström's background was in systems ecology and water resource management, Will Steffan (1947–2023) was trained in chemical engineering, and Katherine Richardson specializes in marine science. It is Rockström, Steffan, and Richardson who appear as lead authors on many of the influential studies on PBs. The PB framework is highly regarded, as evidenced by Johan Rockström receiving the Tyler Prize for Environmental Achievement in 2024, one of the most prestigious awards in environmental science.[8] When Will Steffan passed away in January 2023, he was held in such high esteem by the scientific community that he received an obituary in the journal *Nature*.[9]

Works based on the PB framework seek to describe estimated levels of environmental change that minimize risks to the survival of humanity, while humanity's role in driving change in Earth systems is explicitly considered.[10] PB-based research seeks to set boundaries that represent quantifiable markers of 'safe operating spaces' for humanity that, once crossed, could have irreversible consequences for human survival. Although individual boundaries are specified, the inter-linkages and interaction between the various processes effectively make them a composite index of anthropocentric risk to the Earth System. Feedback within the Earth System are therefore continually emphasized as a risk in PB research.[11] Although not explicitly examined in the original studies, anthropocentric climate change is now often given a first-order ranking, with the '2°C guardrail' set as a boundary.[12] In subsequent work, climate change and biosphere integrity are classified as 'core' boundaries that interact with other boundaries.[13] Feedback processes often depend strongly on climate change.[14]

PBs are operationalized at the global level, although in recent iterations there is a focus on local or regional boundaries. PBs measure nine boundaries: Climate change; Rate of biodiversity loss; Stratospheric ozone depletion; Ocean acidification; Biogeochemical flows (Phosphorus and Nitrogen cycles); Change in land use; Global freshwater use; Atmospheric aerosol loading; and Chemical pollution.[15] There are estimates of what would be a 'safe' level for each boundary and also what the current level is. The research team behind PBs have set the boundaries in 2009 and have tracked the global levels ever since with periodic updates appearing in scientific research journals. A recent study showed that Earth is exceeding six of the nine boundaries.[16] The attraction of the PB approach is that they are presented in a visually appealing infographic. It is effectively a diagram of concentric circles with the Earth at the centre. The core circle is divided into nine sectors, with radii used to represent the various boundaries. The graphic represents boundaries that are currently below the Earth's boundaries (in green) or beyond the Earth (with colour coding from yellow to red).[17]

The PB approach distinguishes boundaries which are buffer zones of uncertainty before a critical threshold, while these thresholds are defined as zones that once crossed could push the climate out of the hospitable Holocene conditions in which life has thrived on Earth. This is perhaps best explained in a recent study by Rockström and colleagues that describes the thresholds as 'tipping points that irreversibly destabilize the Earth system' and the safe boundaries are determined by 'assessments of tipping point risks among local and regional tipping elements, evidence on declines in Earth system functions, analyses of historical variability and expert judgement'.[18] They also argue that there is an increased likelihood of tipping points in the Earth system and that there could be a cascade of tipping points.[19] In essence, the PB approach is a modern augmented articulation of William Vogt's idea of the carrying capacity of the planet (see Chapter 4).[20]

Recent iterations of the PBs approach refer to Earth System Boundaries (ESBs). These are distinct from PBs in that they focus on different scales of analysis. At a global level ESBs are identical to PBs, but at sub-global levels ESBs do not equate to PBs. This means that at a local level ESBs are context-specific and do not constitute a global risk. The boundaries are conservative estimates, reflecting uncertainty surrounding the probable impact of a risk while incorporating normative, or rather 'subjective', judgements about risk by adopting the 'precautionary principle'. Rockström and co-authors advocate the use of a so-called '3I justice criteria' which involves a trifecta of justice: inter-species, inter-generational, and intra-generational justice. In practice, this means making normative ESB boundaries that are tighter than they were under the older PB framework, but the thresholds themselves are unchanged. This incorporation of inter-species justice has not led to an approach beyond minimizing human harm.[21] An example of this new focus relates to the climate change boundary, a more stringent '≤1.5°C guardrail' is chosen instead of the previous '2°C guardrail', this boundary is selected to ensure a more just social outcome, but the underlying threshold/tipping point is unchanged. In a 2023 update to the monitoring of PBs, Richardson and co-authors also placed emphasis on 'safe' levels for each boundary based on pre-industrial levels although it did not adhere to the '3I justice criteria'.[22] There is also an upper level derived for each boundary and based on this framework there are now six processes which are currently beyond their boundary; climate change and biodiversity loss are dramatic examples of these.

Many studies rely on PBs as motivating factors,[23] for instance to analyse future threats to public health.[24] Most notable is the Rockefeller-Lancet Commission on planetary health which draws on all PBs to develop measures of human and planetary health.[25] A somewhat different version of 'safe operating spaces' for our health has been developed by the *Dasgupta Review of the Economics of Biodiversity* which specifically focuses on one boundary, biodiversity, arguing that humanity should live within the safe operating space of the biosphere to prevent spillovers of infectious disease from vulnerable wildlife populations.[26]

The PB approach is not without criticism. The political scientists Frank Biermann and Rakhyun Kim are critical of the boundaries as a normative exercise with no input from civil society or government in the selection of the boundaries; the decision over what constitutes boundaries was left to a narrow group of technocrats.[27] In the original PB study, of the twenty-nine authors listed, none were from the global south which hampered the adoption of the framework, effectively re-opening debates surrounding development and environment which have plagued North/South relations since the 1970s (e.g., see Chapter 4).[28] A more radical critique comes from the Breakthrough Institute, an environmental research institute founded in 2007, which argues that the PB framework is 'inherently arbitrary' and that it conflates global and regional issues.[29]

Another critique of the PB research centres on its anthropocentric focus, which restricts analysis to human influence on environments instead of viewing these interactions as a two-way process, where environments can influence human activity.[30] This has led to calls to incorporate socio-environmental interactions within PBs.[31] The interactions of the PBs focus on how human activity impinges on the PBs, rather than stating how PBs affect human activity.[32] Interactions have long been central to other work in this tradition. For example, *The Limits to Growth* thought that there were interactions between environmental and economic activity that could have regional and global consequences. Similarly, the philosopher Toby Ord's assessment of climate change risk saw greater risk through indirect (interaction) effects as compared to direct effects.[33] More recent work in the PB tradition has focused on catastrophic climate change and discusses how climate change could interact with other PB thresholds and other threats such as inequality and fragile states, specifically with projected extreme heat in the future (c. 2070) and what are classified as vulnerable states today.[34]

Thinking beyond Boundaries: Global Catastrophic Risks

There are many types of catastrophes that can befall humanity, and Planetary Boundaries are a partial reflection of these risks. An earlier generation of writers, such as the volcanologist Basil Booth and geologist Frank Fitch in their 1979 book *Earth Shock*, had emphasized a wide array of natural disasters rather than placing emphasis on one aspect of these (i.e., Planetary Boundaries). For Booth and Fitch, '[i]t is obvious that man's selfish and unthinking activities can do serious harm to the environment and make life very much less pleasant for generations to come, but the total destructive power that we can at present generate is still incredibly puny when compared with the awesome forces of the natural world'. Booth and Fitch were not without criticism; they were accused of 'political naivety' due to their superficial treatment of the political dimensions of the various crises.[35]

Analysing PBs in isolation is a mistake and a more coherent approach takes consideration of the wider risks and how they relate to each other.[36] The central focus of the Global Catastrophic Risk (GCR) research is on risks to humanity defined by their scope, intensity, and probability.[37] The scale is global, not local or regional, and the affected group is all of humanity not specific groups. In the GCR framework, a multitude of independent small events do not constitute an existential catastrophe. For an event to be catastrophic requires either a single decisive event, or simultaneous events, or a singular chain of events, with permanent, irreversible outcomes.[38] Outcomes then range from extinction to the failed continuation of the remainder of humanity.[39] The range of possible scenarios is great and ascertaining the likelihood of such events is difficult, given that there is a lack, or absence, of observational data.[40]

If there is a distinguishing characteristic of GCR research, it is that it focuses on specific low probability but high impact events. For example, climate change is clearly related to both GCR and PB concepts, while others may not at first glance appear to be. It could be argued that some natural hazards (e.g., super volcanoes, giant meteors, etc.) would have an effect on specific PBs (e.g., reduced levels of oxygen, light, food, etc.) that could threaten human subsistence. For example, climate variability is naturally driven by volcanic eruptions. This was most spectacularly demonstrated with a series of volcanic eruptions in the 500s which led to global famines (following an eruption in 536 AD) and pandemic (the Justinianic Plague which followed another major eruption in 539/540).[41] The estimated mortality rates from the Justinianic Plague range from 25 to 50 per cent which makes it comparable to the Black Death; although, there has been recent debate downplaying the impact of the pandemic.[42] A similar line of reasoning would relate the risks from hostile acts to impacts on PBs. There is no absolute demarcation line between risks relevant to PB and GCR. Recent research suggested that GCR events can significantly disrupt a critical system, which may or may not be part of a PB, but this does not create a clear distinction.[43]

One of the traditional distinctions between PBs and GCRs is the assumed spread and predictability of the risks concerned: with PBs, as defined above, being gradual and predictable and GCRs being sudden and relatively unpredictable. Or, PBs should be viewed as a system, whereas GCRs can be independent, simultaneous, or chain events. One obvious problem with this distinction is that there are no clear rules for defining events as sudden versus predictable, with much of this depending not only on detailed knowledge of specific events but also specific, often highly politicized, interpretive frames. Clearly much depends on what facts we focus on, as well as how we define a surprise event as compared to a predictable chain of events. Notwithstanding, the strong intellectual foundation of the 'Black Swan' concept in terms of degenerate meta probabilities, fat tails (i.e., rare, but high impact, events), or extreme value events; there too remains a subjective element to the nature of acknowledged surprises, in terms of the fact that the recognition of the fragility of the Earth as system is going to make us more likely to expect risks to materialize and interact with each other.[44]

By framing PBs as existential risks with certainty that belies the uncertainty of the underlying science, it poses the danger of unduly alarming the population. Take the example of the risk associated with NEOs. As the astrophysicist David Morrison and colleagues remind us, the perception of the risks of catastrophic events 'are not directly proportional to actuarial estimates of the causes of human mortality, nor to forecasts of likely economic consequences'.[45] Presenting risks in a simplified manner therefore can confuse people and lead to adverse psychological impacts on the well-being of society. In the case of NEOs a colour-coded Torino scale was designed in the 1990s to communicate the likelihood of a risk ranging from 0 (no hazard) to 10 (certain collision). The scale is based both on the probability of collision and the possible impact.[46] Take the example of asteroid 2024 YR4 mentioned above, it was upgraded to a 3 (meriting attention) on the Torino scale but after further observation, this was downgraded to a 0. Compare this with the latest PB study that reported that several boundaries had been transgressed. What are the implications of this transgression? Does this mean that urgent action is needed or is there some grace? The practical implications are unclear but the visualization as a Planetary Boundary gives the impression of scientific certainty and the message is psychologically alarming. Furthermore, if academics are influenced by the PB approach that may lead to programmes being proposed that both overlook other GCRs and leave us exposed to much greater risks.

The inclusion of GCRs is intended to highlight that, although the PB framework provides a valuable lens for understanding risk, it should not be viewed as the sole framework. An overemphasis on PBs may lead to the neglect of other critical global risks.

Doughnut Economics

The concept of PBs was quickly adopted by the economist Kate Raworth in a 2012 discussion paper written for the British NGO Oxfam.• The discussion paper was circulated in early 2012 and the concept was discussed at the 2012 Rio + 20 conference on sustainable development. Raworth followed up her Oxfam paper with a book in 2017 which was keen to place an emphasis on systems science as a foundation for thinking about the economy.[47] While the 2012 report was placed within the 'beyond GDP' debate, the 2017 book placed greater emphasis on the limitations of GDP and the importance of limits to growth. This places Raworth firmly in line with the tradition established by *The Limits to Growth*; in fact, *LTG* is lauded by Raworth and Donna Meadows (1941–2001), lead author on the *LTG*, is praised as a pioneer in systems thinking.

In her 2017 book, *Doughnut Economics*, Raworth stated that she sought to return economics to the vision of Adam Smith. She characterized Smith's view of economics as a 'goal orientated science', citing a partial quotation from the introduction to Book IV of *The Wealth of Nations*:

> two distinct objects: first, to provide a plentiful revenue or subsistence for the people, or, more properly, to enable them to provide such a revenue or subsistence for themselves; and, secondly, to supply the state or commonwealth with a revenue sufficient for the public services.[48]

However Raworth omitted the beginning of the sentence, 'Political economy, considered as a branch of the science of a statesman or legislator, proposes two distinct objects', which makes clear that Smith was describing the aims of economic policy as they were understood in the 1700s.

In Raworth's adaptation of PBs, her focus was on the striking visualization of the PBs as a circle. Raworth incorporated a concentric circle diagram with an inner ring of social objectives to go alongside the outer ring of the PBs. At the core, Raworth's message emphasized the need to balance the environmental considerations of the PB (the outer ring) with the social implications of actions taken to remedy PB (the inner circle). The annulus (the area between the concentric circles) would imply that there was a balance between the two and this would result in 'a safe and just space for humanity'. Raworth explained that she sought to visualize the environmental

•The case of Oxfam (Oxford Committee for Famine Relief, established by a Quaker-inspired committee) is interesting because the original mission of the charity was to provide famine relief in Greece in 1941–42. Cormac Ó Gráda observed that there is a 'tendency for agencies originally founded as vehicles for famine relief to reinvent themselves as bureaucracies'. Lobbying for sustainable development is arguably quite removed from the original Oxfam mission: C. Ó Gráda (2009). *Famine: A Short History*.

and social systems as setting outer and inner boundaries for an annulus (referred to as a doughnut), within which 'inclusive and sustainable economic development takes place.' In taking this approach Raworth's 'doughnut' brought traditional concerns of development back into twenty-first-century environmental system models. Also, Raworth emphasizes the interactions between the PBs and the social foundations and highlights how ignoring one can be at the expense of the other. In her book, Raworth explained how she sees the 'doughnut' as an alternative framework to GDP growth as it takes a broader array of social indicators into consideration while also staying within PBs. It is never clearly stated how this concept will be operationalized as it requires a balancing of a variety of indicators some of which seem to conflict and overlap with each other.

Although Raworth's 2012 discussion paper frames the doughnut model as a tool for advancing sustainable development and acknowledges the Brundtland Commission's influence, it does not adopt the Brundtland Commission's intergenerational equity definition.[49] Instead, the framework assesses sustainability through the 'current state of human well-being',[50] using social and ecological thresholds as benchmarks. Raworth draws on the 1948 UN Declaration of Human Rights as a starting point for defining the model's 'social foundation'. There were ten social objectives that Raworth emphasized: food, water, income, education, resilience, voice, jobs, social equity, gender equality, and health. These objectives are presented as normative goals, but Raworth does not explain why these particular dimensions were chosen over others. For example, the declaration of human rights contains thirty articles, yet rights such as property (Article 17), personal security and privacy (Article 12), or the right to marry (Article 16) are omitted without discussion. Effectively, the chosen social foundations are based on an arbitrary decision with limited theoretical justification for their inclusion (or exclusion).

The doughnut model has proved very popular and there have been attempts to quantify what would be involved in achieving the balance between the PBs and social foundations. For example, a 2024 study modelled different scenarios at a global level and found that a Raworth-style 'safe and just operating space' was only possible with radical changes to economic activities.[51] Another recent development in this line of research has been the estimation of country-level 'doughnuts', that is national *planetary* boundaries as well as social indicators, by ecological economists Daniel O'Neil, Andrew Fanning, and co-authors.[52] The environmental indicators are CO_2 emissions, Phosphorus, Nitrogen, Land-system change, Ecological footprint, and Material footprint. While the social indicators are: life satisfaction, life expectancy, nutrition, sanitation, income, poverty, access to energy, secondary education, social support, democratic quality, equality, and employment. As estimated, these national-level boundaries do not map on exactly to PBs (global by definition) or to the social foundations from Raworth, but there is a general overlap, and the key CO_2 boundary is included, although in the form of cumulative emissions (a rough proxy for atmospheric concentration).

The study, published in *Nature Sustainability*, reports ratios of recorded values of indicators to their allocated thresholds. If an indicator is greater than the value of the threshold then the intuition is that a country is 'overshooting'. The complication though is setting a country-level boundary for a concept that is, by definition, planetary (i.e., global). How does one define the size of a country, land mass, population, or size of economies?[53] The solution of the Doughnut research teams was to use national population as weights to distribute the global indicator. So the boundary for global cumulative CO_2 emissions, that is national-level estimates of cumulative emissions from 1850 to 1988, are population-weighted shares of cumulative emissions. This approach leads to some interesting, but ultimately arbitrary, results.

I highlight examples based on the United States and China to demonstrate the arbitrariness of these indicators and the ambiguous message that emerges. Firstly, I show the trends for China and the United States as reported in the original study (Figure 9.1). The figures show that China, while overshooting some of its boundaries, is closer to its allocated boundaries than the United States for almost all indicators. This is quite surprising given that China became the workshop of the world in the twenty-first century and in many instances overtook the United States.

A closer inspection of the methodology reveals how these results were achieved. In the original Planetary Boundaries study, the various boundaries are set in absolute levels; that is, they are not with respect to population. This makes intuitive sense because the central issue is the absorbative capacity (or rather Vogt's 'carrying capacity') of the planet which has a tolerance for the total level of the variables, not the amount per person. Yet, in these empirical applications to nation-states, the various thresholds are set as *per capita* thresholds. This is not so intuitive because it means that countries with larger populations get preferential treatment simply because of their size. The CO_2 threshold differs in that it is weighted by population size, but it is a similar idea. The CO_2 threshold per person is the same for China and the United States. Implying that the allocation per person thresholds for China and the United States are identical, but the total thresholds are actually five times greater for China than the United States because China is (was and will be) a more populous country than the United States. In these exercises China is given a higher threshold, but it also has higher levels of the various indicators. So yes, on a per capita basis the United States has 'overshot' but if we think of the absolute levels then China is the nation that is 'overshooting'. Yet in the study in *Nature Sustainability* China is not perceived to be 'overshooting' because it was given very generous, and ultimately arbitrary, 'boundaries' compared to every other country in the world thanks to its large population (see Figure 9.2).

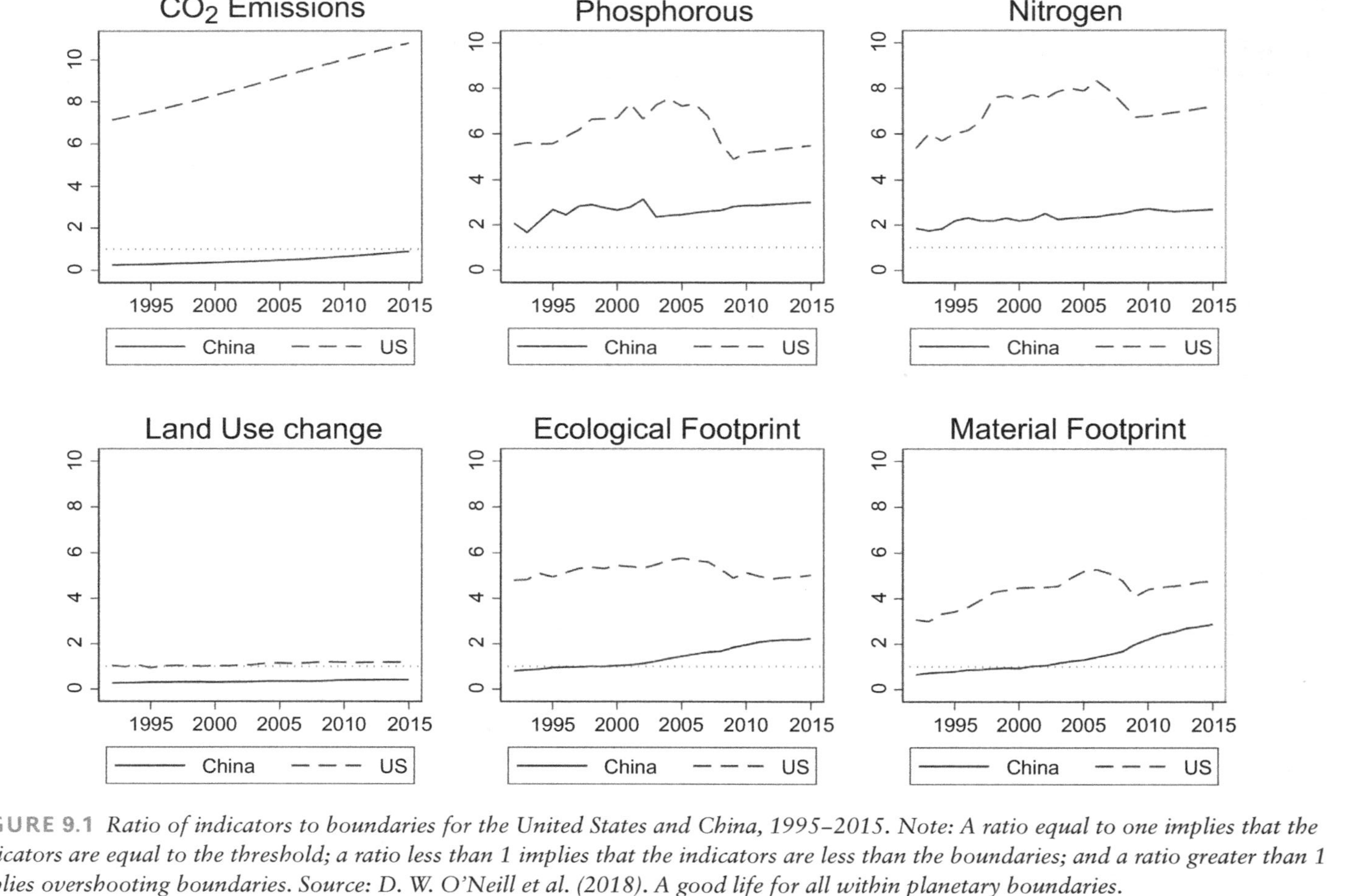

FIGURE 9.1 *Ratio of indicators to boundaries for the United States and China, 1995–2015. Note: A ratio equal to one implies that the indicators are equal to the threshold; a ratio less than 1 implies that the indicators are less than the boundaries; and a ratio greater than 1 implies overshooting boundaries. Source: D. W. O'Neill et al. (2018). A good life for all within planetary boundaries.*

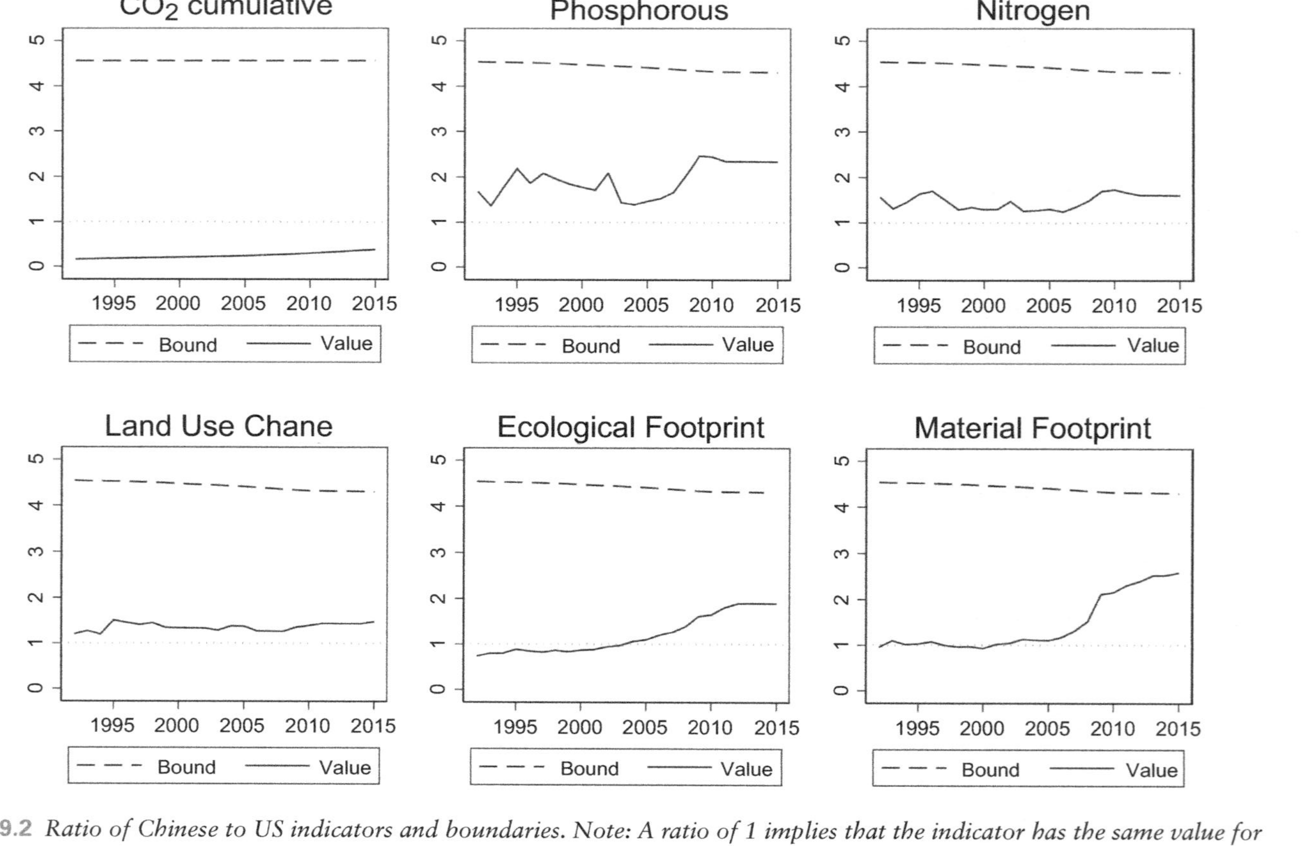

FIGURE 9.2 *Ratio of Chinese to US indicators and boundaries. Note: A ratio of 1 implies that the indicator has the same value for China and the United States; Ratios less that 1 imply that Chinese levels are below the United States; and ratios greater than greater than 1 indicate that China has higher levels. For example, the threshold boundary for Chinese CO_2 is 174,589 cumulative megatonnes, the boundary for US CO_2 is 38,315 cumulative megatonnes, thus the Chinese boundary is 4.5 times greater than the US boundary. Source: D. W. O'Neill et al. (2018). A good life for all within planetary boundaries.*

Also, the CO_2 indicator is equally arbitrary; it is based on cumulative emissions from 1850 to 1988. The endpoint was chosen because this was before the 350 ppm CO_2 boundary was crossed. But given this justification, surely the important point is additional additions to the stock of CO_2 *after* 1988 as the planet has had a limited absorbative capacity to deal with any increase over 350 ppm. If the start date for when the accumulated emissions is changed from 1850 to 1993 (using data from the authors) then the picture looks slightly different. Figure 9.3 illustrates this exercise, in panels a and b, the accumulated indices are set at equals 100. While there was a large increase in accumulated emissions from 1850 to 2015, there was a more rapid increase in the period 1993 to 2015, particularly for China (panel b). Then if we look at the ratio of China to the United States (panel c for cumulative emissions and panel d for annual emissions), the ratio is substantially higher if the accumulated emissions from 1993 are considered rather than 1850. Finally, looking at the ratio of annual emissions, it is clear that Chinese CO_2 emissions have been rising rapidly and have been greater than US emissions since 2009. Therefore, this exercise seems to suffer from an index-number problem, and the arbitrary endpoint of 1988 is what drives the findings.

In any case, there is no theoretical justification for a particular year to benchmark cumulative emissions, so the decisions are made on an *ad hoc* basis. The result of which means that changing these assumptions and decisions yields different conclusions and interpretations. Yet this data was used uncritically in a recent study in *The Lancet Planetary Health* to argue that high-income countries overshoot their ‘fair share of planetary boundaries’. It is unclear then how to interpret these statements given the shaky foundation of the national distribution of planetary boundaries.[54]

Another criticism of the doughnut model is that it does not outline any policy prescriptions to achieve the goals of balancing Planetary Boundaries and social foundations. But this is the point, and Raworth was explicit in this, as she stated that there are ‘no specific policy prescriptions or institutional fixes’ rather her goal was to challenge orthodox, or rather as she sees orthodox, economic approaches to questions such as inequality and the environment.

Yet, the change in mindset that Raworth aims to encourage is somewhat retrogressive as it sees her uncritically accept the discredited arguments of Rostow’s *Stages of Economic Growth*, the Cold Warrior/academic whose arguments were discredited from the 1960s (see discussion in Chapter 7) and *The Limits to Growth* (see discussion in Chapter 4). It has been shown in Chapters 3 and 4 that these ideas were contested and the arguments were shown to be deficient. Also, Raworth effectively dismissed Inclusive Wealth without even explaining the concept, merely noting its existence alongside the Happy Planet Index and the Social Progress Index. Without explaining these concepts, all of which predate Raworth’s ‘doughnut’, it provides no explanation about what is in fact novel about her methodology other than the visualization. Therefore, to be a fully revolutionary (and an evolutionary)

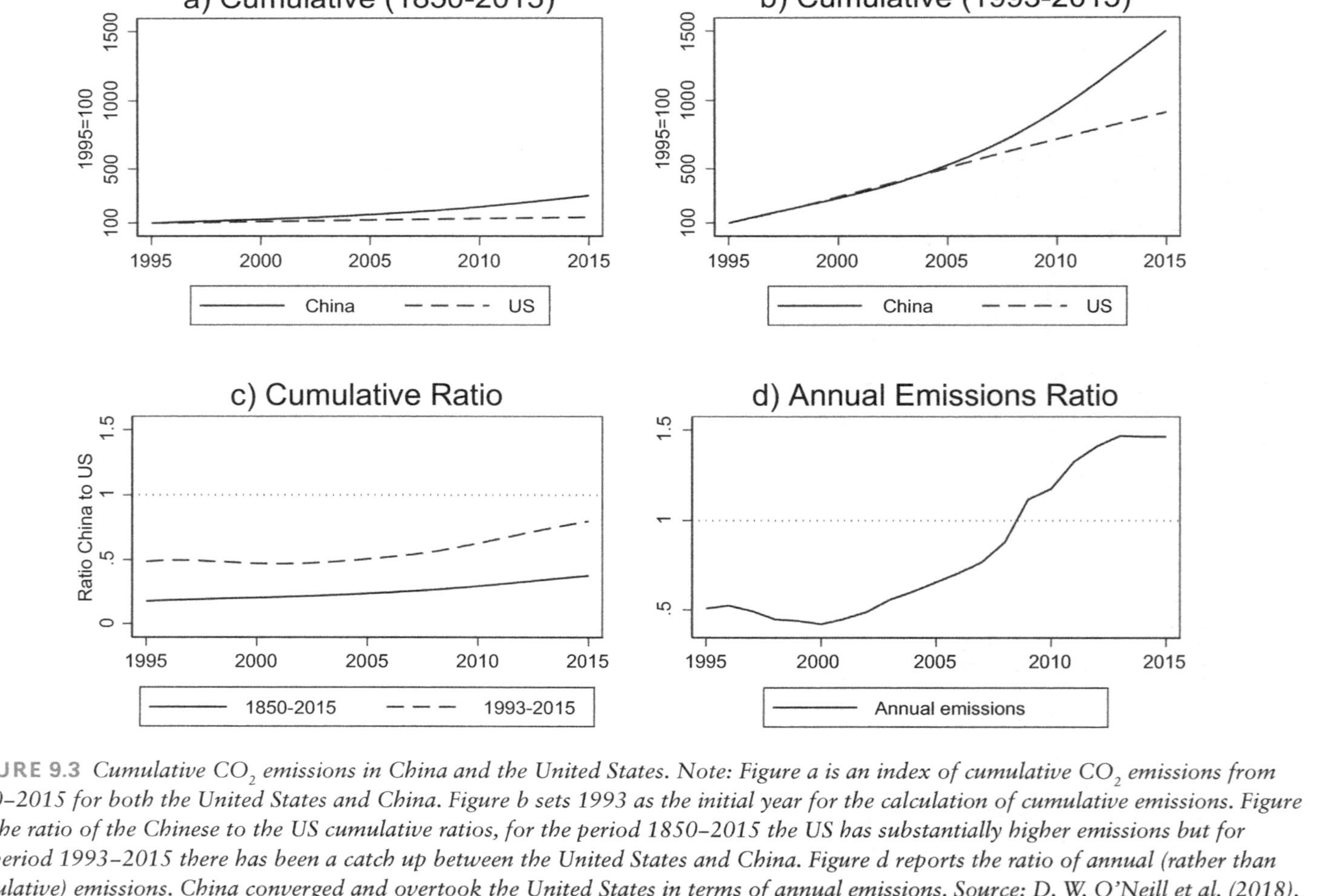

FIGURE 9.3 *Cumulative CO_2 emissions in China and the United States. Note: Figure a is an index of cumulative CO_2 emissions from 1850–2015 for both the United States and China. Figure b sets 1993 as the initial year for the calculation of cumulative emissions. Figure c is the ratio of the Chinese to the US cumulative ratios, for the period 1850–2015 the US has substantially higher emissions but for the period 1993–2015 there has been a catch up between the United States and China. Figure d reports the ratio of annual (rather than cumulative) emissions. China converged and overtook the United States in terms of annual emissions. Source: D. W. O'Neill et al. (2018).*

idea, 'doughnut economics' needs to do more than to reinvent the wheel and completely reimagine economics without re-opening (and not resolving) dormant debates.

Degrowth

As outlined in Chapters 3 and 4, concerns with existential risks related to unbridled economic growth have been expressed since the early phase of the Industrial Revolution. The emphasis of these discourses then shifted in the 1970s towards existential catastrophe related to resource use and environmental pressures. Some believed that this could only be avoided through degrowth. This idea was framed in *Limits to Growth* as 'alter[ing] these growth trends and to establish a condition of ecological and economic stability that is sustainable far into the future'.[55]

Degrowth is the latest element in a long line of critiques of economic growth and uses PBs as a motivating influence.[56] One definition of degrowth is a planned reduction in energy and resource use in an economy.[57] Degrowth has become more popular in recent times. This is clear judging by the frequency of use of the term since the 2000s (judged by frequency of the term on Google Ngrams).[58] An important event popularizing the concept was the first international conference on degrowth hosted in Paris in 2008. The overwhelming majority of scholars active in this area are European, so perhaps they were spurred by greater awareness of the concept or maybe, as the economist Wim Naudé argues, the increase in the popularity of degrowth came because economies in Western Europe had 'degrown'.[59] While degrowth may be a relatively niche research area it still garners attention. A recent review of degrowth studies was widely circulated on social media because it purportedly showed flaws in the methodology of degrowth. The same review article was subsequently reviewed by the *Financial Times*, highlighting the ambiguities of the research.[60]

Defining what advocates mean by degrowth is a challenge as there is such a variety of interpretations. The idea has come to mean everything to everyone. What's more, as ecological economist Giorgos Kallis and colleagues argue, 'degrowth proposals are to a certain extent utopian'.[61] Taking the definition of Kallis and colleagues, the most prominent scholars in the field of degrowth, then:

> Degrowth is defined by ecological economists as an equitable downscaling of throughput, with a concomitant securing of wellbeing. If there is a fundamental coupling of economic activity and resource use, as ecological economics suggests there is, then serious environmental or climate policies will slow down the economy. Vice versa, a slower economy will use fewer resources and emit less carbon. This is not the same as saying that the

> degrowth goal is to reduce GDP; slowing down the economy is not an end but a likely outcome in a transition toward equitable wellbeing and environmental sustainability.[62]

Kallis also defines degrowth in ecological terms, describing it as: 'socially sustainable reduction of society's throughput (or metabolism)' which is 'incompatible with further economic growth, and will entail in all likelihood economic (GDP) degrowth'.[63] Further GDP growth is criticized because of its implied increased use of resources and energy and its waste. This is coupled with the belief that it is unrealistic to think that technological improvement and efficiency gains will allow us to prevent climate change and remove 'pressure on other planetary boundaries'.[64] Others refer to degrowth as 'an umbrella concept that brings together a wide[r] array of ideas and social struggles' with the idea of an 'ecological emergency' arising from the crossing of several planetary boundaries.[65]

The concept has been described as a political agenda to 'plan our way out of ecological catastrophe'.[66] It is also seen as a possible way to mitigate carbon emissions in line with climate targets set out by the Intergovernmental Panel on Climate Change (IPCC). At its most extreme, degrowth is being advocated as a way for local communities to isolate from global climate risk.[67] Climate change is not the sole concern of degrowth, which also emphasizes reducing resource use more generally. Degrowth has been criticized for ambiguity and lack of conceptual coherence. But, as Kallis argued, this is to be expected from a normative social science; in other words, a social science where values are being critically assessed and do not fall neatly into positivist approaches to scientific measurement and testing.[68]

Assuming that capitalism requires continued growth, where 'growth is functional in maintaining economic and social stability', the proposed degrowth solutions imply an anti-capitalist redistribution.[69] Indeed, some authors view the capitalist system as the underlying cause of environmental issues such as climate change.[70] They argue that moving away from a capitalist system and curbing economic growth will help the planet. Although this line of argument overlooks thorny issues such as the fact that environmental disasters occurred under rival communist economic systems, the most infamous example of this being the 1986 Chernobyl nuclear accident, but also the persistent air pollution in Communist China. A degrowth defence here is that, despite ideological differences, communist regimes were also growth-orientated.[71] Therefore, the envisaged alternative to capitalism appears to be a post-capitalist/post-communist eco-utopia.

For Kallis, degrowth implies reduced spending on goods, including some types of public goods, and less investment in new technology:

> we will have to do with less high-speed transport infrastructures, space missions for tourists, new airports, or factories producing unnecessary gadgets, faster cars or better televisions. We may still need more renewable

energy infrastructures, better social (education, and health) services, more public squares or theatres, and localised organic food production and retailing centres.[72]

This line of thinking fails to appreciate that reduced GDP (degrowth) implies lower investment in technologies, such as those necessary for renewable energy.[73] Yet GDP reduction from lower investment is seen as central to degrowth and so is reduced consumption.[74] As degrowth advocates put it, technological advancements must be financed via degrowth, although how this can be achieved is not clearly specified.[75]

One of the main issues is a fundamental misunderstanding of what economic growth is and what drives it. For *The Limits to Growth*, as well as modern degrowthers, it is seen as being *quantity* driven, with a criticism about an insatiable demand for more of the same. This is evident in the writing of degrowthers, such as the anthropologist Jason Hickel, who highlights how growth in GDP requires the continued use of 'energy, resources and waste each year, to the point where it is now dramatically overshooting what scientists have defined as safe planetary boundaries, with devastating consequences for the living world'.[76] But growth in economic theory is much more about quality, not just quantity. This is the role of technological change in economic growth models that were discussed in Chapter 3. It is not about producing more of the same internal combustion engine (ICE) cars from the 1970s but producing more fuel-efficient and better-quality ICE cars as well as developing new electric cars. This in turn creates demand for different resources, such as lithium. One of the best illustrations of this comes from William Nordhaus's study on the price of a unit of light over time as the cost, in terms of hours worked, to produce light changed dramatically (i.e., candles versus fluorescent light bulbs).[77]

The Growing Degrowth Scholarship

Ironically, the one area where degrowth advocates do not complain about growth is in research on degrowth. The continued flurry of research led to not one, but three systematic reviews[♦] of degrowth published in close succession in *Ecological Economics*, the journal of the International Society for Ecological Economics.[78] Oddly, despite apparently following similar search protocols, the reviews come to some different conclusions. Although some of the discrepancies came from how the search protocols were implemented and how the research was categorized.

[♦]Systematic reviews are intended to cover the breadth of scholarship on a given topic, so one is usually sufficient.

The three reviews identified varying numbers of theoretical analyses. For example, in the literature reviewed by the environmental economists Ivan Savin and Jeroen van den Bergh, only 1.9 per cent of the sample (9 studies) used a theoretical model, 1.4 per cent employ an empirical model, 5.5 per cent (31 studies) use quantitative data analysis and 4.1 per cent (23 studies) used qualitative data analysis. This led the authors to conclude that the research is overwhelmingly opinion-based and does not reach a high research standard. Not only this, but they also note: 'both qualitative and quantitative studies tend to not satisfy standards for good research'. Yet the other two reviews identified many more theoretical studies and empirical models (one found that 75 studies used quantitative models to simulate the effect of degrowth policies, and the other found 107 papers that used quantitative modelling).[79] So, are there only a handful of studies that use quantitative methods to assess degrowth? From these systematic reviews, we are none the wiser. But as two of the three reviews conclude that there is a strong strand of quantitative research, presumably this implies that there is.

What the studies actually agreed on was that there is a lack of a coherent definition of what degrowth and/or post-growth is within the research. The multiple definitions have created difficulties for modelling and testing this theory as it is not clearly specified. The lack of a concise theoretical specification makes modelling parameters difficult. One issue became identifying what exactly was classified as 'degrowth research'. A key argument of proponents of degrowth is that it is a *planned* reduction; therefore a recession would not constitute degrowth. But if choices made by, or on behalf of, society (for example, reduced investment due to austerity) led to degrowth, would this be a planned reduction or an unintended consequence?

What the literature reviews show is that there is limited engagement with the concepts within mainstream economics. As the work on degrowth draws inspiration from *LTG*, or rather an 'advanced reincarnation' as Giorgos Kallis and Hugh March see it,[80] perhaps this is the reason why we can see a lack of engagement. As outlined in Chapter 4, *LTG* had predicted an 'overshoot and collapse' of the global economy and was heavily criticized by economists and other scientists. From the perspective of economists, the predictions of the *World3* model were not born out and thus are not worthy of debate.

The main issue appears to be different perspectives on the *LTG* debate. For economists, the debate was won and there is therefore no need for further engagement with proponents of *LTG* (degrowthers). For systems thinkers, they too have been vindicated. Some found that the *LTG* model fitted data thirty years on or even became more relevant over time.[81] There have been studies updating the *LTG* models.[82] The most recent update to the *World3* model shows a similar overshoot and collapse outcome to the original model.[83] Effectively, this is an unsettled scientific controversy where recourse to facts or theory cannot resolve the controversy as both sides see the world in different ways.[84] Although, as the writer and editor Kevin Kelly highlighted, if the *World3* model were run from either 1600 or 1800, it would show collapse a century later. This was a clear test of the model's assumptions and its internal validity, but it was not something done by the original research team (or in the updates). The model would also not predict the Industrial Revolution and, as Dana Meadows explained to Kelly, nor could the model 'take the world from the Industrial Revolution to whatever follows next beyond that'.[85] The *World3* model was designed to show collapse around a century later. Yet, despite these flaws, the *World3* model is still used by proponents of degrowth (and 'doughnut'). It was most recently used in a review article published in *The Lancet Planetary Health* where the simulations of the *World3* model were reproduced but the various issues associated with the model were simply brushed aside.[86]

A Degrowth-based Alternative to GDP

While not exactly an indicator of degrowth, the Index of Sustainable Economic Welfare (ISEW) is an alternative way to measure the economy that was devised by Herman E. Daly and John B. Cobb, pioneers in the field of ecological economics. ISEW is intended to have private consumption as its base and incorporate other aspects overlooked in the measurement of GDP, such as environmental damages.[87] The ISEW is composed of personal consumption adjusted by the income distribution, public non-defense expenditure, investment/capital formation, non-market contribution to welfare services, private defensive expenditure, cost of environmental degradation and deprecation of natural capital. The various components of the ISEW can be tracked over time as well as the index itself. It can show how each component is growing and then this can be compared with conventional measures of the economy, such as GDP growth. [88]

The ecological economists Jonas Van der Slycken and Brent Bleys estimated two variants of ISEW across European countries from 1995 to 2018. The ISEW variants were comprised of the aggregation of unpaid work, consumption, shadow economy and government consumption. From this defence spending, losses from inequality and domestic ecological costs were subtracted. In a second variant, a broader categorization of ecological costs was subtracted as well as a capital adjustment. The central argument was that there is slower growth in ISEW compared with GDP. Yet, re-analysing the data shows that this is actually incorrect and that there is higher growth in ISEW (depending on the variant of ISEW used) than in GDP per capita, among other inconsistencies.[89]

I have produced a visualization based on the UK to highlight the trends in ISEW per capita (variant 1 and variant 2) and GDP per capita growth, shown in Figure 9.4. It is unclear if a focus on ISEW would have resulted in better

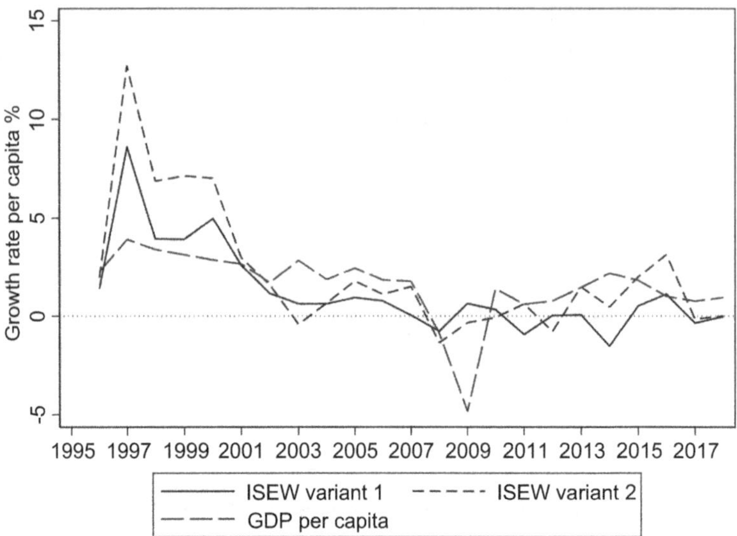

FIGURE 9.4 *Growth rates of ISEW measures and GDP growth for the UK, 1995–2018. Source: J. Van der Slycken, & B. Bleys (2024), 'Is Europe faring well with growth?'.*

outcomes in the UK. While the metric is intended to showcase an alternative economic path than GDP measurement, the metrics (as estimated) would imply less government intervention was required in the 2007–8 financial crisis than actually occurred because according to the ISEW there was only a mild downturn. Policy recommendations based on ISEW would thus vary depending on what aspects of the ISEW were intended to be prioritized. For example, if income distribution is given a higher weight, then policies aimed at predistribution or redistribution would be advocated. Or if reducing environmental degradation was given a higher weighting then policies aimed at this part of the index would be given a greater weighting.

The fundamental issue with the ISEW is that it lacks a coherent theoretical framework. Many of the components are added in an *ad hoc* basis, thus assumptions drive the findings of the index.[90] Any policy decisions made on ISEW grounds could therefore be challenged on the basis of such arbitrariness.

Inclusive Wealth Is the Answer?

There are a lot of similarities between the 'doughnut', degrowth, and the Inclusive Wealth approach. All three see the environment as central to how the economic system functions. The differences are in how each approach tries to incorporate the environment. Doughnut aims to dethrone GDP as a metric and GDP growth as a policy goal, it also aims to supplant economics as an academic discipline with system dynamics. Degrowth is similar although it also has the aim of reducing the economy, via a focus on GDP.

The Inclusive Wealth approach takes a different tack; here the complementary nature of income and wealth is key. The emphasis then is not on replacing GDP but augmenting it and complementing it so as to make it fit for purpose for the twenty-first century. One way of doing so is to integrate Inclusive Wealth more formally into national accounting. By incorporating Inclusive Wealth into national accounts it can provide governments with both a short-term measure useful as a tool for macroeconomic management (GDP), as well as a more forward-looking assessment of future sustainable growth prospects (Inclusive Wealth).[91] By taking the focus away from GDP as an indicator of economic progress we can see if countries are truly growing by augmenting their Inclusive Wealth or if GDP growth is achieved at the expense of other forms of capital. As Dasgupta noted, the 'enormous empirical literature on the sources of economic growth misdirects' because it focuses on GDP growth rather than on the growth of Inclusive Wealth.[92]

That is not to say that I think Inclusive Wealth is a perfect concept, far from it, rather I wish to emphasize that attacking GDP and GDP growth without providing a robust alternative framework seems like a retrogressive step. It is like being a metaphorical ostrich with its head in the sand. If we do not know what is happening to our wealth, then how can it be managed? So, the first step must be to address the shortfalls in our understanding of Inclusive Wealth. I outline a few key issues below and possible solutions. The main issues as I see it relate to international trade, substitution of capital, and the completeness of accounting.

In relation to international trade, the underlying weak sustainability models of Inclusive Wealth are based on the Hartwick Rule which implies reinvesting natural resource rents into other forms of capital. It was shown by the economist Geir Asheim that this rule might not be applicable in open economies because of international trade.[93] For one, the natural resources that are extracted might not be consumed in the countries where they are produced. Or, if prices are set in international markets, then the value of natural capital may experience capital gains (losses) through the vagaries of international commodity markets.

Thankfully there are a number of workable solutions. One of which is to account for terms-of-trade effects, that is the difference between export and import prices. This was the approach taken by the economic historian Mar Rubio when calculating the genuine savings of Mexico and Venezuela, two oil-producing countries in Latin America. Incorporating terms of trade dramatically changed the sustainability signal based on conventional Inclusive Wealth approaches alone.[94] Another approach taken by the environmental economist Giles Atkinson and colleagues is to think in terms of 'virtual sustainability' by monitoring the flow of trade in natural capital and comparing production with consumption.[95]

In terms of substitution, this relates to the original aggregate production function where capital and labour were substitutable (see Chapter 3). Including natural capital within this framework implies a level of substitutability. This is difficult to measure empirically. A well-known example of substitution cited by economists is the replacement of whale oil, once used in candles, with kerosene. William Nordhaus specifically noted that one of the benefits of petroleum's discovery was that it helped preserve the few remaining whales. Or implicitly in the case of Martin Weitzman who used the example in his introductory economics classes and also when discussing substitution in public (as I learned when I met Marty).[96] The idea is simple; before the discovery of petroleum, whales were hunted for their oil and there was a decline in stocks. As the whaling historian Alexander Starbuck (1841–1925) recalled, 'whaling as a business declined; from the scarcity and shyness of whales' but also because of the relative cost of fitting out whaling vessels and rising wage costs.[97] With the discovery of kerosene, this acted as a substitute for whale oil.

This example has a number of caveats. First it was not a substitution of natural capital by other forms of capital, rather it is a substitution within natural capital. The bigger hole in the argument is that whales continued to be hunted, and more whales were hunted *after* the discovery of kerosene (after 1859) than before.[98] The issue was that while the United States had shifted towards greater use of petroleum, other countries did not. Figure 9.5 reflects this by highlighting that after the discovery of petroleum there was no decrease in the price for whale oil. While US catches decreased, globally they did not; the geography of whaling shifted in the twentieth century from the northern to the southern hemisphere. Technology, spurred on by fossil fuels, enabled greater whale catches than had previously been possible. Uses for whale oil evolved; no longer was it simply being used for candles, but it was used to manufacture 'rustproof paint, pharmaceuticals, cosmetics, and a variety of other chemical products'. This included glycerine that was used in explosives during the First World War and there were still uses for whale oil as an engine lubricant until synthetic alternatives were formed. So, whale oil both continued to serve some of its original purposes, while new functions were also developed.[99]

Another example of substitution that is often used is the shift from horses to automobiles in cities (and from horse and plough to tractors in the countryside). Horses were the dominant means of transport in cities in the nineteenth century. The dependence on horses in the nineteenth-century urban economy was most clearly demonstrated during a severe epizootic influenza episode in 1872 when it was estimated that 80–90 per cent of horses in North America had been infected.[100] Although rail and shipping were used for transporting cargo, distribution within cities ran on horsepower; thus, during the epizootic, US cities came to a standstill. In

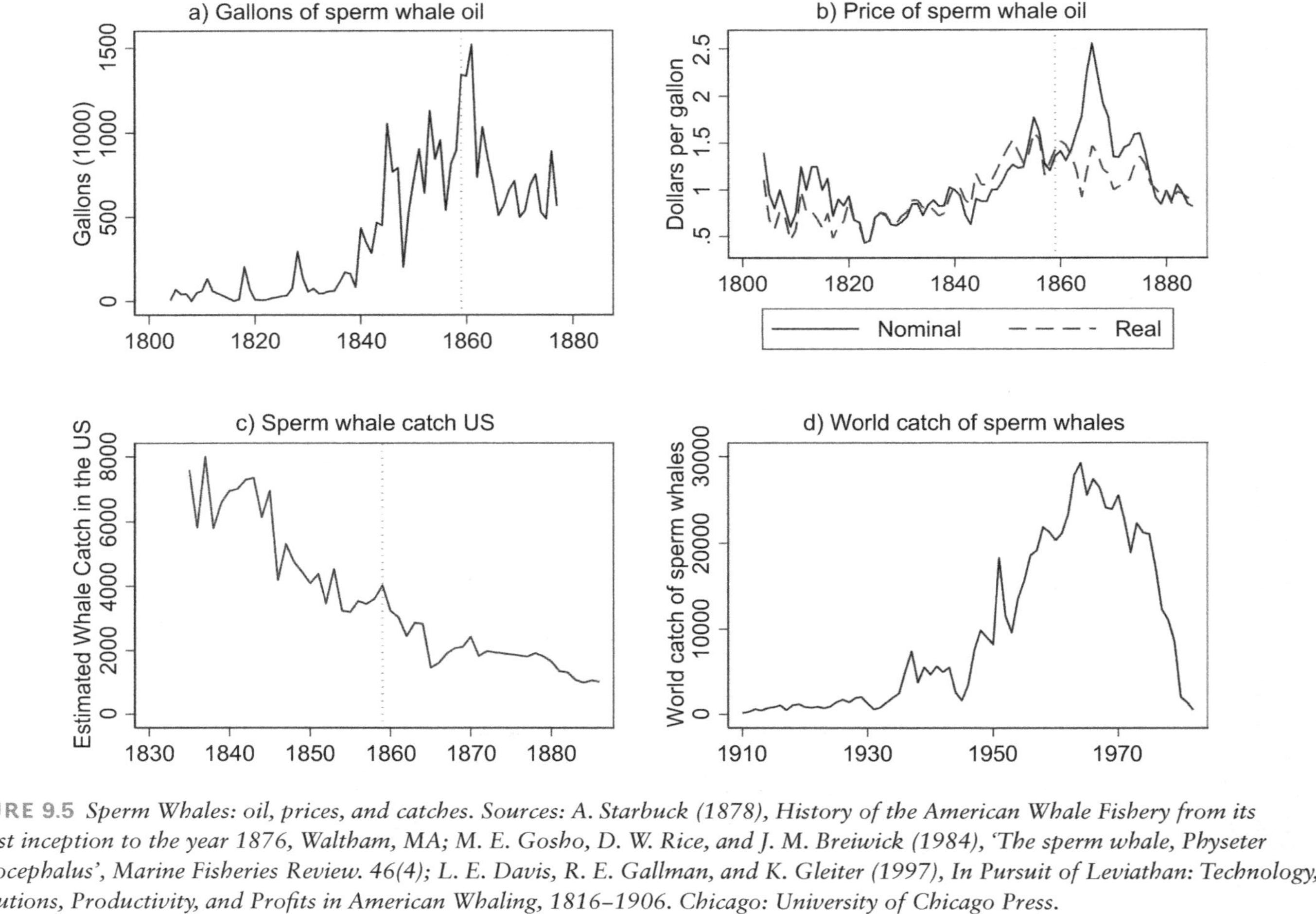

FIGURE 9.5 *Sperm Whales: oil, prices, and catches. Sources: A. Starbuck (1878), History of the American Whale Fishery from its earliest inception to the year 1876, Waltham, MA; M. E. Gosho, D. W. Rice, and J. M. Breiwick (1984), 'The sperm whale, Physeter macrocephalus', Marine Fisheries Review. 46(4); L. E. Davis, R. E. Gallman, and K. Gleiter (1997), In Pursuit of Leviathan: Technology, Institutions, Productivity, and Profits in American Whaling, 1816–1906. Chicago: University of Chicago Press.*

non-epizootic times, the main issue was what to do with the horse manure and urine that were polluting the cities. In the case of horses, there was a fortuitous substitution of produced capital for natural capital. Fossil-fuel-powered automobiles, referred to as horseless carriages, replaced the horse and carriage and changed urban landscapes throughout the world. This solved the problem of horse manure although it created another (and more serious) problem of air pollution associated with the automobiles.[101]

This brings us on to the thorny issue of pollution. Without doubt the modern world generates much value and well-being but a by-product of the goods and services that we consume is pollution. For Inclusive Wealth the issue becomes how to place a price on the social cost of the pollutant to account for externalities. The main considerations here are whether a pollutant is local or global, if it is time-dependent or if it is an immediate flow, and if it has a long-lasting cumulative effect. The scholarship here is led by the focus on climate change and the emphasis on putting a social cost on carbon emissions. Here estimates of future damages to the economy from increases in the atmospheric concentration of CO_2 are estimated; these future damages are then discounted to give a present value.[♦]

Research on the social cost of carbon reveals large variation in estimated prices. Ranging from low values of $20 to $1,455 (and higher) per ton.[102] A recent meta-analysis by the environmental economist Richard Tol shows that the trend is for the social cost of carbon to increase in recent years.[103] Researchers have also included a wider array of pollutants into estimates of the change in Inclusive Wealth and show how this can alter perceptions of growth.[104] The issue of transboundary pollution can be complex, such as CO_2 emissions which have a global impact or the case of acid rain.[105] The implications of these issues may be that some countries might misjudge their sustainability prospects and this could misrepresent how countries contribute to global sustainability. Ultimately, these types of issues could lead to national-level indicators which are misaligned with global problems. One proposed solution has been to develop global metrics which adjust the underlying Social Cost of Carbon (SCC) to take different climate scenarios into consideration.[106] In a recent application, co-authors and I show how the inclusion of CO_2 into measures of the change of Inclusive Wealth can radically alter the picture of global economic growth in the twentieth century.[107]

Inclusive Wealth can also be analyzed in terms of its subcomponents with specific attention given to natural capital. Within natural capital, this is classified as renewable (agricultural land, fisheries, forestry resources, and ecosystem services) and non-renewable natural capital (fossil fuels and minerals). The growth trajectory of natural capital tells a different

[♦]The idea of discounting is that the damages will be greater in the future and by placing a value on these today it is effectively pricing these future damages in the present (see discussion in Chapter 8).

story from that of Inclusive Wealth overall (e.g., see Figure 6.6), and this divergence suggests that natural capital could serve as a distinct indicator in its own right. Tracking natural capital separately allows for a clearer assessment of environmental sustainability, one that is not obscured by increases in produced or human capital.[108] In this view, a rising Inclusive Wealth index may mask the erosion of critical natural assets, underscoring the need for dedicated metrics that reflect the ecological foundations of long-term prosperity. The present system of accounting values all forms of capital and aggregates them in an unweighted index, although in theory, if we knew the 'correct' shadow price, they would be weighted according to their relative value. In principle, weights could also be applied to the indices to focus on the elements of natural capital that are deemed critical. For example, within ecology, keystone species have a disproportionate effect on an ecosystem relative to their abundance, and various keystone species have been identified across different ecosystems.[109] Weighting keystone species within a natural capital framework would thus be in line with existing studies that propose weights to measure keystone communities, although with the caveat regarding the choice of weight.[110] Thus, there is scope for further research into these metrics and to develop more complete measures.[111]

Technology

The last point I wish to raise concerns technology and how it should be incorporated into a measure of Inclusive Wealth. Ultimately, technological progress is a double-edged sword. Technological progress has lifted living standards to incredible heights, but it has also generated serious and often unanticipated side effects. As Joel Mokyr once observed, 'if technological change eventually leads to the physical destruction of our planet, survivors may no longer wish to use the word progress in their descriptions of technological history'.[112]

Technology is difficult to incorporate because what exactly do we mean by this. Do we mean the technology of yesteryear, today, or the future? The historian Neil Ferguson argues that a 'history of the future' can be gleaned from what preoccupied the minds of past science fiction writers.[113] For example, science fiction writers of the past have prognosticated future technological developments, such as Aldous Huxley (1894–1963) who anticipated developments of 4D entertainment but also a eugenically organized society in his 1932 novel *Brave New World*. Science fiction as presented in mass media of television and film depicted visions of both the risks and benefits associated with new technologies.[114] Overall, the science fiction community was very optimistic about what the future would hold.

Taking the techno-optimism of the television show *Star Trek*, which first aired in 1966, as an example, this saw humanity in peaceful coexistence exploring the universe with a plethora of new technologies.

Robert Anson Heinlein (1907–88), one of the leading science fiction writers of the twentieth century, outlined his views of different possible paths of technological growth in his 1952 essay 'Where To?'.[115] Heinlein believed that the 'only way to guess at the future is by examining the *present* in light of the *past*'. His visions for the future saw space travel before the end of the twentieth century and the moon as a retirement home for geriatrics. Heinlein set out his 'rules of prophecy' for predicting future trends in technology and envisaged four scenarios for technological change. The first scenario represented 'stubborn "common sense"' that everything has already been invented and there will not be much improvement in technology. Scenario two represents some improvement but a saturation point where there are diminishing returns. Scenario three represents what he called 'very daring minds,' that 'we will continue along our present rate of progress'. While Scenario four represented 'the proper way to project the curve, because there is no reason mathematically, scientific, or historical, to expect that curve to flatten out, or to reach a point of diminishing returns'. Heinlein believed the future would be more like scenario four because 'the Age of Science has not yet opened'. One only has to look at his predictions about the future to see that the scenario four outcomes were mixed: there is no interplanetary travel and cancer is not conquered, but we have explored the solar system and our phones are small enough to fit in our handbags. Our phones can 'record messages, answer simple queries, and transmit vision' and communism (somewhat) did vanish from the planet. But he was right in one very crucial regard, 'mankind will not destroy itself, nor will civilisation be wiped out'.

The mid-twentieth century exuberance for technological progress was not matched by a comparable realization of material advancement. Most famously, the venture capitalist Peter Thiel captured this sentiment with the remark, 'we were promised flying cars, instead we got 140 characters'.[116] Thiel was bemoaning how the rate of technological progress had slowed; while there was evidence of growth in the Information and Communications Technology (ICT) sector, this was not reflected across the wider economy.[117] The optimistic view of technological progress was also increasingly challenged by environmentalists from the 1960s onwards. The case of DDT serves as a key example: originally introduced to control mosquitos and later widely used as an agricultural insecticide, it ultimately had far-reaching and unforeseen environmental consequences, far beyond what anyone had anticipated. In fact, environmentalists equated technological progress with economic growth, seeing exponential growth in population and pollution which would lead to a collapse of civilization.

An illustration of these contrasting pessimistic and optimistic lenses is the infamous bet between Paul Ehrlich and the economist Julian Simon (1932–

98). The bet originated in the pages of *Social Science Quarterly*, where Julian Simon picked up on an audacious gambit that Ehrlich had proposed: '[i]f I were a gambler, I would take even money that England will not exist in the year 2000'. Simon's proposal was a bet in simple terms ($10,000, $1,000, $100) that 'non-governmental controlled raw materials (including grain and oil) will not rise in the long run'. Ehrlich, who was highly critical of Simon's approach to natural resources and population, agreed to a bet for $10,000 (in 1980 prices) specifying five metals (chromium, copper, nickel, tin and tungsten).♦

The eventual bet was for $1,000 over a ten-year window from October 1980 to October 1990. In the historian Paul Sabin's account of *The Bet*, he portrayed the two protagonists, Paul Ehrlich and Julian Simon, as taking opposing sides of Neo-Malthusian debates surrounding population growth and technology. Ehrlich had warned of a population bomb, while Simon was more sanguine seeing population growth as the 'ultimate resource'.[118] The bet was controversial, perhaps more so because it was Simon who won. Several studies have attempted to see who would win the bet over longer time spans, many showing that Ehrlich would have won. But the popular impression is simply that Simon won and therefore his views were right.[119] As Simon noted in the *Ultimate Resource* 'talk is cheap', he had put money on the line and won.

While Simon's cavalier gamble had paid off, he was effectively representing the optimistic side of the Malthusian debate. Similar optimism can be found elsewhere. For example, writing in 1949, the agricultural economist Merrill Bennett (1897–1969) reflected on the pessimism of neo-Malthusians and whether they were to be proven right or if 'time may prove today's pessimists to have been wrong, as with the pessimists of the past'. For Bennett the future was not written, and it effectively meant a social choice and that, 'to follow the wrong path is to hamper invention, stifle capital accumulation, hinder investment domestically and internationally, and hence to restart the general economic development, one aspect of which is improvement of national diets'.[120]

The optimistic Smithian case is best summarized by Heinlein, who concluded his 'Where to?' essay on technology by highlighting the fact that humanity had not experienced a catastrophic event and that, 'you and I are

♦To describe the exchange as a critical exercise would be generous, given Ehrlich's condescending dismissals of Simon saying at various points that 'Simon is wrong about air pollution . . . Simon is wrong about the economics of mineral resources . . . Simon has been confounded by aggregate statistics he does not understand . . . Nor will I eschew words like "wrong", "incompetent" or even "moronic" in describing works or views of others when the shoe fits': J. Simon (1981). Environmental Disruption or Environmental Improvement? *Social Science Quarterly*, 62(1): 30–43; P. R. Ehrlich (1981). An Economist in Wonderland. *Social Science Quarterly*, 62(1): 44–9.

here because we carry the genes of uncountable ancestors who fought – and won – against death in all its forms. We're tough. We'll survive. *Most of us*'.[121]

Conclusion

The two alternatives to Inclusive Wealth are motivated both by *The Limits to Growth* and the Planetary Boundaries framework; the former was an influential model from the 1970s, the latter an influential paradigm from the 2000s. The doughnut approach aims to place environmental and social bounds on economic activity; the goal of degrowthers is to reduce economic growth as a solution to environmental problems. Both could work as solutions to PBs but would leave humanity exposed to other Global Catastrophic Risks.

Thinking broadly about the world's balance sheet is an intelligent and flexible way to address future catastrophic risks. Action is taken at the level of the nation-state, and this is where the attention needs to be directed. Inclusive Wealth accounting may throw up some inconvenient truths; the question is how to address these challenges in the future in a way that is equitable for both the current and future generations.

The degrowth approach does not see technological solutions as an alternative to degrowth as, in many cases, these are seen as synonymous with economic growth (GDP).[122] As the approaches do not engage with mainstream economics and have evolved along a separate path, this is effectively an unresolved scientific controversy and one that may be irresolvable.

Perhaps the final word should go to an authoritative scientific figure. John von Neumann (1903–57), a polymath who was regarded as 'the smartest man that ever lived',[123] anticipated many of the issues raised by degrowthers. In a 1955 essay, he noted that 'we begin to feel the effects of the finite, actual size of the earth in a critical way'. Von Neumann highlighted various crises from nuclear risks to global warming from the release of carbon dioxide into the atmosphere. But crucially, Von Neumann dismissed prohibiting technologies (that is, degrowth) as a 'pseudosolution' as it is difficult to isolate specific technologies from scientific progress: instead, he advocated for 'patience, flexibility, and intelligence'.[124]

CHAPTER TEN

Concluding Remarks

Each chapter has offered its own concluding reflections, so to conclude the book my intention is to zoom out and identify some broader themes that have struck me as I have worked my way through the material. It is also a moment to reflect on aspects that may not have fully surfaced in the preceding chapters but nonetheless deserve greater attention.

In drawing on Adam Smith's *The Wealth of Nations*, I have shown how prescient his ideas were and how much broader an influence he had than the popular image of him as the father of the 'invisible hand' or as a staunch advocate of free trade and capitalism. Smith cared greatly about the welfare of society, as becomes clear when we see him not as a 'one-book wonder' but as a 'two-book man'.[1] One of my favourite passages from *The Wealth of Nations* reads almost like an echo of the impartial spectator from *The Theory of Moral Sentiments*:

> No society can surely be flourishing and happy, of which the far greater part of the members are poor and miserable. It is but equity, besides, that they who feed, clothe, and lodge the whole body of the people, should have such a share of the produce of their own labour as to be themselves tolerably well fed, clothed, and lodged.[2]

Equity, I would argue, lies at the heart of *The Wealth of Nations*, and it is the same principle that underpins the concept of Inclusive Wealth. The key difference is that Inclusive Wealth extends the idea of fairness beyond the present, incorporating concern for intergenerational equity as well as equity today. Cross-country estimates of Inclusive Wealth reveal significantly higher levels of inequality between nations than conventional income-based measures suggest. This has important implications for future trends in global inequality. Furthermore, elevated levels of wealth inequality within countries point to a deeply uneven distribution of the Inclusive Wealth of nations. It is not enough to consider only the intergenerational distribution of wealth; we must also account for its distribution within generations, and by this measure, we appear to be falling short.

This brings me to an important point: Adam Smith assessed development over long horizons. He looked back to antiquity in order to understand the drivers of opulence, rather than focusing on year-to-year fluctuations. That long-term perspective has largely been lost. Today, we are told we live in an era of 'polycrisis', and governments (and administrations of all kinds) lurch from one emergency to the next. The focus is relentlessly short-term, so much so that those in charge often cannot see the forest from the trees. The shift in focus is understandable. It emerged from the crisis of global capitalism in the interwar years and was driven in large part by the Keynesian revolution. John Maynard Keynes rightly challenged the economic orthodoxy of his day and shifted attention to the short-run stabilization, but I would argue that the pendulum has now swung too far. We need to balance between the short and the long-term. As Keynes himself wrote at the close of *The General Theory*:

> Practical men, who believe themselves to be quite exempt from any intellectual influences, are usually the slaves of some defunct economist. Madmen in authority, who hear voices in the air, are distilling their frenzy from some academic scribbler of a few years back. I am sure that the power of vested interests is vastly exaggerated compared with the gradual encroachment of ideas. Not, indeed, immediately, but after a certain interval; for in the field of economic and political philosophy there are not many who are influenced by new theories after they are twenty-five or thirty years of age, so that the ideas which civil servants and politicians and even agitators apply to current events are not likely to be the newest. But, soon or late, it is ideas, not vested interests, which are dangerous for good or evil.

Ironically, Keynes himself has become one of those very 'defunct economists' whose ideas later generations have clung to, often uncritically, and without sufficient attention to the context in which those ideas originally emerged. The dominant focus on short-run considerations, central to Keynesian policy, has often come at the expense of attention to long-run outcomes. Adam Smith, by contrast, maintained a much deeper concern for long-range dynamics, a perspective that is especially vital when it comes to the challenges of future sustainability. For society to truly prosper across generations, we must learn to balance short-term responsiveness with long-term vision.

I have argued for a more inclusive definition of *The Wealth of Nations*, one that places greater emphasis on natural capital as a fundamental component of a society's total wealth. I have made this case candidly, acknowledging both unresolved issues and the re-emergence of older (often dormant) debates that remain highly relevant in the context of natural capital. In doing so, I have drawn on Paul Samuelson who, after conceding the theoretical significance of the reswitching problem, reminded us that, 'if all this causes headaches for those nostalgic for the old time parables of neoclassical writing, we must remind ourselves that scholars are not born to live an easy existence. We must respect, and appraise, the facts of life'.[3]

Productivity growth was at the heart of *The Wealth of Nations*, and it remains central to both economic growth and sustainable development today. The so-called 'Weitzman rule' implicitly assumed that TFP growth would continue at a steady rate of 1 per cent per annum. While the average trend TFP growth in the United States from 1955 to 2019 was indeed around 1 per cent, this figure conceals a marked slowdown in recent decades; during the 2010s, average annual TFP growth fell to just 0.52 per cent. If this trend persists, the foundations for long-term sustainability are far shakier than Weitzman optimistically envisioned at the close of the twentieth century. Productivity growth is also central to the broader story of modern economic development. The post-2010 slowdown has reignited concerns that we may be approaching the end of sustained economic growth. Some have suggested that the rollout of artificial intelligence across the economy could reverse this trend, but it remains to be seen whether AI can fulfil its promises and restore the vision of a cornucopia of infinite growth. Crucially, one dimension of AI with direct implications for productivity and sustainability is its enormous demand for natural resources. Data centres consume vast amounts of energy, and the hardware underpinning AI (particularly microchips) relies on rare earth elements. These environmental and resource demands must be considered within the framework of Inclusive Wealth as we reassess what sustainable productivity growth truly entails. There is also the thorny issue of existential risk, which makes me deeply uneasy about fully committing to AI without clearer safeguards in place.[4]

This brings us to the case of the UK, who led the world during the First Industrial Revolution but was ultimately unable to sustain that lead. The country's relative decline is evident in its TFP performance, and in recent years it has been characterized by what many have termed a 'productivity puzzle'. A deeper understanding of Inclusive Wealth, rather than a narrow focus on GDP growth alone, may offer new insights into resolving this puzzle. One critical, and often overlooked, piece of the jigsaw appears to be the role of natural resource abundance and the ways in which these resources were managed (or mismanaged) by policymakers over time.

When Smith was writing, he compared the 'opulence' of England with the 'stagnation' of China. Today, the roles have reversed. In the first quarter of the twenty-first century, China has been the growing economy while the UK has experienced stagnation. Property rights and security are important parts of Smith's theory of economic development, and he saw England's economic growth in the eighteenth century as being 'in spite of government extraction'. Here, an analogy could possibly be made with China's rapid growth. Daron Acemoglu and James Robinson have famously distinguished between inclusive and extractive economic and political institutions. According to their theory, sustainable growth tends to emerge in societies where inclusive economic institutions coexist with pluralistic political systems. In China's case, the political institutions are widely viewed as extractive, serving the interests of a narrow elite. Yet the economic institutions are considered to have been broadly inclusive. This combination has underpinned China's remarkable growth, much as England's did in the eighteenth century; it experienced growth in spite of the political constraints. Chinese productivity growth, however, has also been slowing in recent years, mirroring broader global trends. As the country confronts demographic shifts and increasing political centralization, more careful attention will be needed to sustain long-term development.

Reflecting on the key thinkers of both economics and environmental sustainability, it is striking how deeply the Great Depression shaped their worldviews. For John Maynard Keynes, it was the spectacle of mass unemployment. For Robert Solow, it was witnessing joblessness during his formative years. For William Vogt, it was the personal experience of being unemployed. Shocks to the status quo, such as the Great Depression, can alter the course of economic thinking, and by extension, the direction of development itself. In our own time, we have lived through two major global events in the past twenty years. The first was the 2007–2008 global financial crisis, which ushered in a prolonged period of high unemployment. The policy response, sharply lowering interest rates, unleashed a wave of investment in new technologies (as well as asset price inflation), the effects of which are now becoming visible in the ongoing AI revolution. What impact this will have on future generations remains uncertain. The second major event was the Covid-19 pandemic of 2020. Though shorter in duration, it left a deep imprint on societies around the world, not only in terms of lives lost, but also in the uneven and halting return to 'normalcy'. Covid-19 fundamentally shifted how society operates, and in combination with the technological upheavals of AI, it will likely reshape the economic and social order in ways we are only beginning to grasp.

Another point relates to focusing on the wrong crisis. Neo-Malthusians once feared a world overwhelmed by overpopulation and launched a crusade against population growth. These fears were implicit in many of the economic theories discussed earlier in the book. Today, we face the opposite problem: fertility rates are falling below replacement across the world. In 2015, the UN predicted that human population would reach 11.2 billion by 2100. Barely a decade later, in the 2024 UN population predictions, this figure was revised down to 10.2 billion by 2100, and it is predicted that population will peak much earlier than anticipated a decade ago.[5] Rapidly aging societies bring a new set of challenges. Slower population growth translates into lower economic growth, but more than that, it places growing pressure on younger generations to sustain an increasingly elderly and economically inactive population. While demographic decline is not normally framed as an existential risk, it deserves a more prominent place in our discussions of long-term societal stability and resilience.

Another question that I have not dwelled on is what we might call the modern 'commencement of the present disturbances': the unravelling of the post-Second World War international consensus. The global order that emerged in the aftermath of 1945, shaped by Cold War geopolitics and multilateral cooperation, is currently under mounting strain. The elephant in the room is, of course, the two Trump presidencies, which have brought about a cooling of relations between the United States and China over the past decade, what some commentators refer to as 'Cold War II'. Today, we may be witnessing a similarly disruptive shift in international affairs, with Washington DC again at the centre. The second Trump Administration has already targeted institutions such as USAID, universities as centres of scientific research, international trade bodies, and broader frameworks for global cooperation. Many of the institutions central to international development, including those that have helped advance the concept of Inclusive Wealth, now face existential threats. The first Cold War delayed the emergence of environmental thinking, as the attention of both the political left and right was focused on the Cold War. There are signs that 'Cold War II' is leading to the environment again playing second fiddle to national security; for example, in September 2025, the US Environmental Protection Agency, an institution founded in 1970 under the presidency of Richard Nixon (1913–94), announced it would stop collecting emissions data from polluters.[6] In light of this, I would urge global political administrators to consider Inclusive Wealth alongside GDP growth as a measure of national prosperity. It is worth recalling that Adam Smith delayed publication of *The Wealth of Nations* so that he could follow events in the American Colonies more closely; I am not afforded such a luxury here, as Trump's threats of constitutional upheaval in the pursuit of a third term (however likely or unlikely) make a tangible end point of 'Cold War II' seem temporarily out of reach.

A final point concerns the cyclical nature of many of the issues explored in this book. These debates are not new, and they will not be the last of their kind. That is precisely why it is essential to draw the right lessons from history. It is a recurring arrogance of each generation to assume that sustainability crises are unprecedented, that they are the first to grapple with such challenges. The circumstances may differ, but the underlying patterns often rhyme. And while it is easy to destroy, the work of creating, and of sustaining, is far more difficult.[7]

NOTES

Chapter One

1 W. J. Barber (1967). *A History of Economic Thought*. Middlesex: Penguin, p. 23.
2 E. McLaughlin. Where Is the Wealth of Nations in the 21st Century? *Economics Observatory*, 12 July 2023: https://www.economicsobservatory.com/where-is-the-wealth-of-nations-in-the-21st-century
3 D. H. Meadows, D. L. Meadows, J. Randers and W. W. Behrens (1972). *The Limits to Growth: A Report for the Club of Rome's Project on the Predicament of Mankind*. New York: Universe Books; J. Rockström, W. Steffen, et al. (2009). A Safe Operating Space for Humanity. *Nature*, 461(7263): 472–5.
4 W. C. Clark and A. G. Harley (2020). Sustainability Science: Toward a Synthesis. *Annual Review of Environment and Resources*, 45: 331–86.
5 P. Dasgupta (2021). *The Economics of Biodiversity: The Dasgupta Review*. London: HM Treasury.
6 N. Hanley, L. Dupuy and E. McLaughlin (2015). Genuine Savings and Sustainability. *Journal of Economic Surveys*, 29(4): 779–806.
7 P. Dasgupta (2021). *The Economics of Biodiversity*.
8 P. Dasgupta (2025). *On Natural Capital: The Value of the World Around Us*. London: Witness Books.
9 D. Coyle (2025). *The Measure of Progress: Counting What Really Matters*. Princeton: Princeton University Press.
10 Stephen Levitt interview with Robert Solow. Ninety-Eight Years of Economic Wisdom, People I Mostly Admire, 23 June 2023: https://freakonomics.com/podcast/ninety-eight-years-of-economic-wisdom/
11 H. S. Cole, C. Freeman, M. Jahoda and K. L. R. Pavitt (1973). *Models of Doom: A Critique of the Limits to Growth*. New York: Universe Books.
12 This includes the original report and a 2012 update.
13 U. Bardi (2011). *The Limits of Growth Revisited*. Berlin: Springer.
14 V. Smil (2019). *Growth: From Microorganisms to Megacities*. Cambridge, MA: MIT Press, p. 494.
15 The Limits to Growth + 50: Global Equity for a Healthy Planet – Anniversary Webinar Series Episode 1. 2 March 2022: https://www.youtube.com/watch?v=ItLNPn4rXxU
16 A. D. Barnosky, et al. (2011). Has the Earth's Sixth Mass Extinction Already Arrived? *Nature*, 471(7336): 51–7; M. S. Taylor and R. Weder (2024). On the Economics of Extinction and Possible Mass Extinctions. *Journal of Economic Perspectives*, 38(3): 237–59.

17 D. M. Raup and J. J. Sepkoski, Jr. (1984). Periodicity of Extinctions in the Geologic Past. *Proceedings of the National Academy of Sciences*, 81(3): 801–5.
18 W. Hu, Z. Hao, et al. (2023). Genomic Inference of a Severe Human Bottleneck During the Early to Middle Pleistocene Transition. *Science*, 381(6661): 979–84.
19 A. Jha (2011). *The Doomsday Handbook: 50 Ways the World Could End*. New York: Quercus.
20 For example, see: The Next Catastrophe. Politicians Ignore Far-out Risks: They Need to Up Their Game. *The Economist*, 25 June 2020; J. Achenbach (2022). Asteroids! Solar Storms! Nukes! Climate Calamity! Killer Robots! A Guide to Contemporary Doomsday Scenarios – from the Threats You Know About to the Ones You Never Think of. *Washington Post*, 7 November 2022.
21 M. Boyd and N. Wilson (2020). Existential Risks to Humanity Should Concern International Policymakers and More Could be Done in Considering Them at the International Governance Level. *Risk Analysis*, 40(11): 2303–12; M. Boyd and N. Wilson (2023). Assumptions, Uncertainty, and Catastrophic/existential Risk: National Risk Assessments Need Improved Methods and Stakeholder Engagement. *Risk Analysis*, 43(12): 2486–502.
22 W. Steffen, et al. (2015). Sustainability. Planetary Boundaries: Guiding Human Development on a Changing Planet. *Science*, 347(6223): 1259855; J. Rockström, et al. (2023). Safe and Just Earth System Boundaries. *Nature*, 619: 102–11; K. Richardson, W. Steffen, et al. (2023). Earth Beyond Six of Nine Planetary Boundaries. *Science Advances*, 9: eadh2458
23 N. Bostrom and M. M. Ćirković (2008). *Global Catastrophic Risk*. Oxford: Oxford University Press; T. Ord (2020). *The Precipice: Existential Risk and the Future of Humanity*. London: Bloomsbury.
24 Risks from nature can include super volcanoes, meteors, asteroids, comets, supernovae and solar flares, agricultural failure such as a plant virus or super-weed, extreme ice age, a rogue black hole and an anoxic event from oxygen depletion. Risks from the unintended consequences of human activity could include climate change, pandemics, unaligned artificial intelligence, social collapse, accidents in high-energy physics, ecosystem collapse, infertility due to chemicals or biology and inability to procreate due to genetic engineering. Lastly, risk from hostile acts could include nuclear war, bioterrorism and nanotechnology.
25 Risk classification derived from: N. Bostrom and M. M. Ćirković (2008). *Global Catastrophic Risk*; B. Tonn and D. Stiefel (2013). Evaluating Methods for Estimating Existential Risks. *Risk Analysis*, 33(10): 1772–87.
26 V. Smil (2012). *Global Catastrophes and Trends: The Next 50 Years*. Cambridge, MA: MIT Press.
27 F. U. Jehn, J-.O. Engler, C. W. Arnscheidt, M. Wache, E. Ilin, L. Cook, L. S. Sundaram, F. Hanusch and L. Kemp (2025). The State of Global Catastrophic Risk Research: A Bibliometric Review. *Earth System Dynamics*, 16: 1053–84.
28 U. Beck (1992). *Risk Society: Towards a New Modernity*. Translated by Mark Ritter. London: SAGE Publications; U. Beck (2009). *World at Risk*. Translated by Ciaran Cronin. Cambridge, MA: Polity Press.
29 N. Bostrom and M. M. Ćirković (2008). *Global Catastrophic Risk*.
30 J. Rockström, et al. (2023). Safe and Just Earth System Boundaries.
31 J. Vidal (2020). Destroyed Habitat Creates the Perfect Conditions for Coronavirus to Emerge. *Scientific American*, 18 March; WWF (2020).

Covid-19: Urgent Call to Protect People and Nature. https://cdn2.hubspot.net/hubfs/4783129/WWF%20COVID19%20URGENT%20CALL%20TO%20PROTECT%20PEOPLE%20AND%20NATURE.pdf

32 B. Talukder, G. W. van Loon and K. W. Hipel (2022). Planetary Health & COVID-19: A Multi-perspective Investigation. *One Health*, 15: 100416; Global Challenges Foundation (2022). Global Catastrophic Risks 2022: A Year of Colliding Consequences. https://globalchallenges.org/wp-content/uploads/2023/01/GCF_Annual_Report_2022-FINAL.pdf.

33 H. Wang, et al. (2022). Estimating Excess Mortality due to the COVID-19 Pandemic: A Systematic Analysis of COVID-19-related Mortality, 2020–21. *The Lancet*, 399(10334): 1513–36.

34 D. M. Cutler and L. Summers (2020). The COVID-19 Pandemic and the $16 Trillion Virus. *JAMA*, 324(15): 1495–6.

35 T. Ord (2020). *The Precipice*.

36 M. Weitzman (2009). On Modeling and Interpreting the Economics of Catastrophic Climate Change. *Review of Economics and Statistics*, 91: 1–19.

37 J. Rawls (1971). *A Theory of Justice*. Cambridge, MA: Harvard University Press; It is still one of the most widely prescribed readings on philosophy syllabi worldwide: A. Salinas (2021). Readings of Smith by Contemporary Political Philosophers: John Rawls. Adam Smith Works, 22 September 2021. https://www.adamsmithworks.org/documents/alejandra-salinas-reading-adam-smith-john-rawls

38 J. Rawls (1999). *A Theory of Justice*, revised edition. Cambridge, MA: Harvard University Press, p. 252.

39 This is a line of argument that bears a similarity to that used as a rationale for economic actions in the case of climate change; for example, see: W. D. Nordhaus (1991). To Slow or Not to Slow: The Economics of the Greenhouse Effect. *Economic Journal*, 101: 920–37.

40 J. Rawls (1999). *A Theory of Justice*., 256.

41 K. J. Arrow (1973). Rawls's Principle of Just Saving. *The Swedish Journal of Economics*, 75(4), 323–35; R. M. Solow (1974). Intergenerational Equity and Exhaustible Resources. *The Review of Economic Studies*, 41: 29–45.

42 J. Hartwick (1977). Intergenerational Equity and the Investing of Rents from Exhaustible Resources. *The American Economic Review*, 67(5): 972–4.

43 R. M. Solow (1986). On the Intergenerational Allocation of Natural Resources. *The Scandinavian Journal of Economics*, 88(1): 141–9.

44 The World Commission on Environment and Development (1987). [Brundtland Commission]. *Our Common Future: The World Commission on Environment and Development*. Oxford: Oxford University Press.

45 The issue of intergenerational justice is given cursory treatment here but for further reading, see: A. Gosseries (2008). On Future Generations' Future Rights. *Journal of Political Philosophy*, 16(4): 446–74; A. Gosseries (2008). Theories of International Justice: A Synopsis. S.A. P. I. EN. S (Surveys and Perspectives Integrating Environment and Society), 1(1); A. Gosseries and L. H. Meyer (eds) (2009). *Intergenerational Justice*. Oxford: Oxford University Press; J. Taylor (2013). Intergenerational Justice: A Useful Perspective for Heritage Conservation. *Conservation: Cultures and Connections*. https://doi.org/10.4000/ceroart.3510

46 E. R. Gill (1976). Justice in Adam Smith: The Right and the Good. *Review of Social Economy*, 34(3): 275–94; D. McCloskey (2007). Adam Smith, the Last of the Former Virtue Ethicists. *History of Political Economy*, 40(1).
47 N. Cowen (2021). Basic Economic Liberties: John Rawls and Adam Smith Reconciled. *The Independent Review*, 26(2): 263–85.
48 R. E. Backhouse (2002). *The Penguin History of Economics*. London: Penguin.
49 A. Smith. *The Theory of Moral Sentiments (TMS)*, Part II, Section II, Chapter iii.
50 *Wealth of Nations*, Book IV, Chapter. IX.
51 *TMS*, Part II, Section II, Chapter i.
52 *TMS*, Part II, Section II, Chapter ii.
53 *TMS*, Part II, Section I, Chapter i.
54 *TMS*, Part II, Section II, Chapter iii.
55 *TMS*, Part II, Section III, Chapter iii.
56 *TMS*, Part II, Section III, Chapter iii, Chapter ii, 9.
57 J. R. Otteson (2017). Adam Smith on Justice, Social Justice, and Ultimate Justice. *Social Philosophy and Policy*, 34(1): 123–3.
58 A. Sen (2009). *The Idea of Justice*. Cambridge, MA: Harvard University Press; *TMS*, Part IV, Section II, Chapter i.
59 A. Sen (2009). *The Idea of Justice*, pp. 251–2.
60 E. Neumayer (2025). *Weak versus Strong Sustainability: Exploring the Limits of Two Opposing Paradigms*. Cheltenham: Edward Elgar.
61 Ibid.
62 The chapter aimed 'to promote the increasing use of some of those indicators in satellite accounts, and eventually in national accounts, the development of indicators needs to be pursued by the Statistical Office of the United Nations Secretariat, as it draws upon evolving experience in this regard'.
63 UN (2001). Indicators of Sustainable Development: Framework and Methodologies. Background paper no. 3. Department of Economic and Social Affairs; B. Purvis, Y. Mao and D. Robinson (2019). Three Pillars of Sustainability: In Search of Conceptual Origins. *Sustainability Science*, 14: 681–5.
64 B. Purvis, Y. Mao and D. Robinson (2019). Three Pillars of Sustainability: In Search of Conceptual Origins.
65 J. Gupta, et al. (2023). Earth System Justice Needed to Identify and Live within Earth System Boundaries. *Nature Sustainability* 6(6): 630–38; J. Rockström, et al. (2023). Safe and Just Earth System Boundaries.
66 The reconciliation of Smithian and Rawlsian interpretations of justice is a continuing line of inquiry: N. Ben-Moshe (2021). Comprehensive or Political Liberalism? The Impartial Spectator and the Justification of Political Principles. *Utilitas*, 33(3): 253–69.
67 F. Biermann and E. K. Rakhyun (2020). The Boundaries of the Planetary Boundary Framework: A Critical Appraisal of Approaches to Define a "Safe Operating Space" for Humanity. *Annual Review of Environment and Resources*, 45(2020): 497–521.
68 J. E. Stiglitz, A. Sen and J.-P. Fitoussi (2009). *Report by the Commission on the Measurement of Economic Performance and Social Progress*.

69 P. Dasgupta (2021). *The Economics of Biodiversity*; P. Dasgupta and S. Levin (2023). Economic Factors Underlying Biodiversity Loss. *Philosophical Transactions B*, 378: 20220197.

70 Nature (2023). GDP at 70: Why Genuinely Sustainable Development Means Settling a Debate at the Heart of Economics. *Nature*, 620: 246; see the extensive treatment by Dasgupta and Weitzman: P. Dasgupta (2001). *Human Well-Being and the Natural Environment*. Oxford: Oxford University Press; M. L. Weitzman (2003). *Income, Wealth, and the Maximum Principle*. Cambridge, MA: Harvard University Press.

71 Beck and Grande call for a cosmopolitan turn which many international organizations now seem to pursue. *Inclusive Wealth* measures are driven by international organizations rather than nation-states: U. Beck and E. Grande (2010). Varieties of Second Modernity: The Cosmopolitan Turn in Social and Political Theory and Research. *British Journal of Sociology*, 61(3): 409–43; UNEP (2018). *Inclusive Wealth Report 2018*. Cambridge: Cambridge University Press; World Bank (2024). *The Changing Wealth of Nations 2024: Revisiting the Measurement of Comprehensive Wealth*. Washington, DC: World Bank.

72 R. Yamaguchi, M. Islam, and S. Managi (2019). Inclusive Wealth in the Twenty-first Century: A Summary and Further Discussion of Inclusive Wealth Report 2018. *Letters in Spatial and Resource Economics*. 12: 101–11; UNEP (2018). *Inclusive Wealth Report 2018*. World Bank (2024). *The Changing Wealth of Nations 2024*.

73 P. Dasgupta and S. Levin (2023). Economic Factors Underlying Biodiversity Loss.

74 I. W. R. Martin and R. S. Pindyck (2015). Averting Catastrophes: The Strange Economics of Scylla and Charybdis. *American Economic Review*, 105(10): 2947–85.

75 P. Dasgupta (2021). *The Economics of Biodiversity*.

76 D. Coyle (2017). The Political Economy of National Statistics. In C. Hepburn and K. Hamilton (eds), *National Wealth: What Is Missing, Why It Matters*. Oxford: Oxford University Press.

77 Jones adopts a similar to approach weighing up economic growth and AI risk (a GCR) and uses a utility/well-being approach: C. I. Jones (2023). The AI Dilemma: Growth versus Existential Risk. *NBER*, 31837. https://ssrn.com/abstract=4624239

78 K. J. Arrow, P. Dasgupta, L. H. Goulder, K. J. Mumford and K. Olsen (2012). Sustainability and the Measurement of Wealth. *Environment and Development Economics*, 17(3): 317–3; S. Polasky, C. L. Kling, S. A. Levin, S. R. Carpenter, et al. (2019). Role of Economics in Analysing the Environment and Sustainable Development. *PNAS*, 116(12): 5233–8; P. Dasgupta and S. Levin (2023). Economic Factors Underlying Biodiversity Loss.

79 N. Hanley, L. Dupuy and E. McLaughlin (2015). Genuine Savings and Sustainability.

80 E. McLaughlin and M. Beck (2025). Managing and Mitigating Future Public Health Risks: Planetary Boundaries, Global Catastrophic Risk, and Inclusive Wealth. *Risk Analysis*, 45(7): 1607–31; The framework is based on an Inclusive Wealth Schema from Barbier: E. Barbier (2015). *Nature and Wealth: Overcoming Environmental Scarcity and Inequality*. London: Palgrave.

81 F. A. Jonsson and C. Wennerland (2023). *Scarcity: A History from the Origins of Capitalism to the Climate Crisis*. Cambridge, MA: Harvard University Press.

82 M. Diesendorf, G. Davies, T. Wiedmann, J. H. Spangenberg and S. Hail (2024). Sustainability Scientists' Critique of Neoclassical Economics. *Global Sustainability*, 7: e33; there is a similar approach taken by Lina Brand-Correa, et al. (2022). Economics for People and Planet – Moving beyond the Neoclassical Paradigm. *The Lancet Planetary Health*, 6(4): e371–9.
83 Lina Brand-Correa, et al. (2022). Economics for People and Planet.
84 G. Guenther (2024). *The Language of Climate Politics: Fossil-fuel Propaganda and How to Fight It*. Oxford: Oxford University Press.
85 P. R. Erlich and A. H. Erlich (1970). *Population, Resources, Environment: Issues in Human Ecology*. San Francisco: W. H. Freeman and Company.
86 In Chapter 26 of the first edition ('Social Movements and Economic Welfare'): P. Samuelson (1948). *Economics*. New York: McGraw-Hill.
87 P. Samuelson (1970). *Economics*, 8th edition. New York: McGraw-Hill.
88 W. Robert Brazelton (1977). Samuelson's Principles of Economics in 1948 and 1973. *The Journal of Economic Education*, 8(2): 115–7.
89 J. Norman (2018). *Adam Smith: What He Thought, Why It Matters*. London: Allen Lane.

Chapter Two

1 K. Steward (2020). The Bard and the Professor: Adam Smith's Influence on Robert Burns. https://www.adamsmithworks.org/speakings/the-bard-and-the-professor-adam-smith-s-influence-on-robert-burns
2 A. Smith (1776). *An Inquiry into the Nature and Causes of the Wealth of Nations*, A select edition. Edited by Kathryn Sutherland (1998). Oxford: Oxford University Press.
3 A. Smith (1896). *Lectures on Justice, Police, Revenue and Arms Delivered in the University of Glasgow by Adam Smith Reported by a Student and Edited with an Introduction and Notes by Edwin Cannan*. Oxford: Clarendon Press.
4 A. S. Skinner (2006). Francis Hutcheson, 1694–1746. In A. Dow and S. Dow (eds), *A History of Scottish Economic Thought*. London: Routledge.
5 See introduction to the E. Cannan (1904) edited: *An Inquiry into the Nature and Causes of the Wealth of Nations*, by Adam Smith fifth edition. London: Methuen and Co.
6 M. Kelly and C. Ó Gráda (2016). Adam Smith, Watchmaking, and the Industrial Revolution. *Quarterly Journal of Economics*, 131(4): 1727–52.
7 M. Lynch (1992). *Scotland: A New History*. London: Pimlico; N. Phillipson (2016). Smith and the Scottish Enlightenment. In Patrick Hanley (ed.), *Adam Smith: His Life, Thought, and Legacy*. Princeton: Princeton University Press; M. Blum and E. McLaughlin (2019). Living Standards and Inequality in the Industrial Revolution: Evidence from the Height of University of Edinburgh Students in the 1830s. *Economics & Human Biology*, 35: 185–92.
8 T. C. Smout (1969). *A History of the Scottish People, 1560–1830*. Suffolk: Collins.
9 M. Lynch (1992). *Scotland*.

10 See Bank of England. A Millennium of Macroeconomic Data: https://www.bankofengland.co.uk/statistics/research-datasets
11 J. M. Keynes (1933). *Essays in Biography*. London: Macmillan and Co., p. 212.
12 K. Boulding (1971). After Samuelson, Who Needs Adam Smith? *History of Political Economy*, 3(2): 225–37.
13 A. Sen (2016). Adam Smith and Economic Development. In P. Hanley, *Adam Smith: His Life, Thought, and Legacy*. Princeton: Princeton University Press.
14 Throughout I will refer mostly to an edited volume by Kathryn Sutherland as this was the version of *The Wealth of Nations* that I have on my bookcase: *An Inquiry into the Nature and Causes of the Wealth of Nations*. Edited with an introduction and notes by Kathryn Sutherland (1993), Oxford World's Classics. Oxford: Oxford University Press.
15 *WON*, I, ii.
16 *WON*, I, viii.
17 *WON*, I, viii.
18 *WON*, II, i.
19 *WON*, II, v.
20 *WON*, II, iii.
21 *WON*, II, iv; A. Sen (2016). Adam Smith and Economic Development.
22 *WON*, III, iii.
23 *WON*, III, iv.
24 *WON*, III, iv.
25 *WON*, III, i.
26 *WON*, IV, i.
27 *WON*, IV, ix.
28 W. J. Barber (1967). *A History of Economic Thought*, p. 48; M. Schabas and C. Wennerlind (2011). Retrospectives: Hume on Money, Commerce, and the Science of Economics. *Journal of Economic Perspectives*, 25(3): 217–30.
29 *WON*, IV, ii.
30 *WON*, IV, ii.
31 WON, IV, vi.
32 P. Duguid (2003). The Making of Methuen: The Commercial Treaty in the English Imagination. *Revista da Faculdade de Letras. Historia*, 4(1): 9–36; M. Watson (2016). Historicising Ricardo's Comparative Advantage Theory, Challenging the Normative Foundations of Liberal International Political Economy. *New Political Economy*, 22(3): 257–72. N. Dyer (2024). *Ricardo's Dream: How Economists Forgot the Real World and Led Us Astray*. Bristol: Bristol University Press.
33 *WON*, IV, iii.
34 *WON*, IV, v.
35 D. Acemoglu, S. Johnson and J. Robinson (2001). The Colonial Origins of Comparative Development: An Empirical Investigation. *American Economic Review*, 91(5): 1369–401.
36 *WON*, V, iii.
37 A. Sen (2016). Adam Smith and Economic Development.
38 *WON*, V, i.
39 *WON*, V, i.
40 *WON*, V, i, Part i.

41 *WON*, V, i, Part ii.
42 *WON*, V, i, Part ii.
43 *TMS*, Part iv, Chapter 3, Section iv, 37.
44 *TMS*, first edition, Part IV, Section iv, 436.
45 *WON*, V, iii.
46 A. Sen (2016). Adam Smith and Economic Development.

Chapter Three

1 J. K. Galbraith (1984). *The Affluent Society*, 4th edition. London: Penguin.
2 M. Boianovsky (2019). The Development Economist as Historian of Economics: The Case of William J. Barber. *Journal of the History of Economic Thought*, 41(3): 325–33.
3 K. Boulding (1971). After Samuelson, Who Needs Adam Smith?
4 H. W. Arndt (1978). *The Rise and Fall of Economic Growth: A Study in Contemporary Thought*. Melbourne: Longman Cheshire.
5 C. Gide and C. Rist (1915). *A History of Economic Doctrines: From the Time of the Physiocrats to the Present Day*, 2nd edition. Translated by R. Richards. London: George G. Harrap & Co.
6 L. L. Price (1909). Reviewed Works: Cours d'Economie Politique by Charles Gide; Histoire des Doctrines Economiques Depuis les Physiocrates Jusqu'à Nos Jours by Charles Gide, Charles Rist. *The Economic Journal*, 19(75): 416–22.
7 W. J. Barber (1998). Not So Dismal a Science: Reflections. *Journal of the History of Economic Thought*, 20(2): 177–89.
8 Barber's initial research interests were in development economics, influenced by Nobel laureate William Arthur Lewis (1915–91), and he later became interested in the history of economic thought. His reading of history was through the lens of a development economist; this was an era when economists thought that lessons from historical economics could inform the developing world: R. D. C. Black (1960). *Economic Thought and the Irish Question, 1817–1870*. Cambridge: Cambridge University Press.
9 R. Backhouse (2002, 2023). *The Ordinary Business of Life*. Princeton: Princeton University Press; R. Mochrie (2024). *How to Think Like an Economist: Great Economists Who Shaped the World and What They Can Teach Us*. London: Bloomsbury.
10 C. O. Fisher (1922). Reviewed Work: The Ricardian Rent Theory in Early American Economics by John Roscoe Turner. *The American Economic Review*, 12(2): 275–8.
11 R. E. Backhouse (2002). *The Penguin History of Economics*; R. Mochrie (2023). *How to Think Like an Economist.*
12 W. J. Barber (2003). American Economics to 1900. In W. J. Samuels, J. E. Biddle and J. B. Davis (eds), *A Companion to the History of Economic Thought*. Cornwall: Blackwell.
13 W. J. Barber (1998). Not So Dismal a Science.
14 W. J. Barber (1967). *A History of Economic Thought*, p. 107.
15 Ibid., p. 107.

16 C. J. Bliss (1975). *Capital Theory and the Distribution of Income*. Amsterdam: North-Holland Publishing Company.
17 J. Hicks (1974). Capital Controversies: Ancient and Modern. *The American Economic Review*, 64(2): 307–16.
18 W. W. Rostow (1978). *The World Economy: History & Prospect*. London: Macmillan Press; N. D. Kondratieff (1935). The Long Waves in Economic Life. *The Review of Economics and Statistics*, 17(6): 105–15.
19 W. W. Rostow (1975). The Developing World in the Fifth Kondratieff Upswing. *The Annals of the American Academy of Political and Social Science*, 420: 111–24.
20 Dating of the Great Depression follows US chronology, starting with the Wall Street Crash of 1929 until the United States entered the Second World War II: G. Richardson (2013). The Great Depression, 1929–1941. *Federal Reserve History*: https://www.federalreservehistory.org/essays/great-depression
21 R. Mochrie (2023). *How to Think Like an Economist*.
22 E. R. Weintraub (2005). Roy F. Harrod and the Interwar Years. *History of Political Economy*, 37(1): 133–55.
23 It has been argued that we might be underestimating global population, particularly in rural areas: J. Láng-Ritter, M. Keskinen and H. Tenkanen (2025). Global Gridded Population Datasets Systematically Underrepresent Rural Population. *Nature Communications*, 6: 2170.
24 R. E. Backhouse (2023). *The Ordinary Business of Life*.
25 W. J. Barber (1967). *A History of Economic Thought*, p. 17.
26 R. Mochrie (2023). *How to Think Like an Economist*.
27 *The Wealth of Nations* was also not the first systematic treatise on economics in the English language; that honour is reserved for Sir James Steuart's *An Inquiry into the Principles of Political Economy* which was published in 1767. Steuart introduced the term political economy into the English language. Steuart was unusual in that he was part of the Scottish Enlightenment but also a Jacobite and had supported the rebellion in 1745. He was sent to France as an ambassador for the young pretender and did not return to Scotland until 1763. Steuart was also a statist and perhaps why he is not seen in the same tradition as the liberal segment of the Enlightenment. In the time-honoured academic practice, Adam Smith conveniently omits any reference to Steuart's work in *The Wealth of Nations*, although in Steuart we can see the genesis of some of Smith's iconic lines (although not necessarily a focus on capital accumulation). For example, Steuart saw self-interest as the main driving force coordinating the economy: 'The same wind blows upon all; and this wind is the principle of self-interest which engages every consumer to seek the cheapest and the best market.' Smith's writing and prose are clearer and caught the public imagination, without any associated Jacobite baggage, Smith was ultimately a skilled synthesizer of information, skilled at communicating complex ideas to the general public: J. Steuart (1767). *An Inquiry into the Principles of Political Economy: Being an Essay on the Science of Domestic Policy in Free Nations*, Chapter xii, p. 233.
28 W. J. Barber (1967). *A History of Economic Thought*, p. 51.
29 Ibid., p. 25.
30 R. S. Franklin (1976). Smithian Economics and Its Pernicious Legacy. *Review of Social Economy*, 34(3): 379–89.

31 Smith first used the term in an essay written in 1755, 'The Principles which lead and direct Philosophical Inquiries; illustrated by the History of Astronomy', that was later published posthumously. The work, believed to have been written in 1755, refers to 'the invisible hand of Jupiter' when discussing the origins of polytheism. Smith's meaning of 'invisible hand' has been debated and is interpreted as 'ironic' in all three uses by Emma Rothschild, but the usage is seen as distinct by William Grampp: D. Stewart (1799). *Essays on Philosophical Subjects by the Late Adam Smith, LL.D., Fellow of the Royal Societies of London and Edinburgh, to Which Is Prefixed an Account of the Life and Writings of the Author by Dugald Stewart.* London: T. Caddell Jnr.; E. Rothschild (1994). Adam Smith and the Invisible Hand. *American Economic Review* 84(2): 319–22; W. D. Grampp (2000). What Did Smith Mean by the Invisible Hand? *Journal of Political Economy* 108(3), 441–65.

32 *TMS*, Part iv, Chapter i.

33 The adoption of a definite instead of an indefinite article to represent the concept of 'an invisible hand' changes the connotation of the idea. With the definitive article, 'the invisible hand' as the canonical phrase symbolizes the self-regulating nature of markets or systems, whereas the indefinite article, 'an invisible hand', suggests less certainty in the self-regulating nature of markets and that the outcome is not realized in all cases. The use of 'an' continued in Edwin Cannan's 1904 compilation of the fifth edition of *The Wealth of Nations*, where Cannan highlighted the various changes that occurred in the editions 1 to 5 (most edits had been minor such as 'is' for 'it,' 'that' for 'than,' 'becase' for 'because'). Thus, the choice of 'an' and not 'the' in both works written close to two decades apart was a purposeful decision by Smith.

34 C. Gide and C. Rist (1915). *A History of Economic Doctrines*, p. 73.

35 Ibid., p. 65.

36 J. Mokyr (2021). The Holy Land of Industrialisation: Rethinking the Industrial Revolution. *Journal of the British Academy*, 9: 223–47.

37 *WON*, II, iii.

38 *WON*, I, viii.

39 *WON*, II, iii.

40 M. Olson (1982). *The Rise and Decline of Nations: Economic Growth, Stagflation, and Social Rigidities*. New Haven: Yale University Press; D. C. North (1990). *Institutions, Institutional Change, and Economic Performance.* Cambridge: Cambridge University Press; D. Acemoglu and J. A. Robinson (2012). *Why Nations Fail: The Origins of Power, Prosperity and Poverty.* London: Profile Books.

41 S. Ogilvie and A. W. Carus (2014). Institutions and Economic Growth in Historical Perspective. In P. Aghion and S. N. Durlauf (eds), *Handbook on Economic Growth*. Vol 2. Elsevier: Amsterdam, 403–513.

42 M. Smith (2023). Adam Smith on Growth and Economic Development. *History of Economics Review*, 86(1): 2–15.

43 A. A. Young (1928). Increasing Returns and Economic Progress. *The Economic Journal*, 38(152): 527–42.

44 A. Marshall (1920). *Principles of Economics*, 8th edition. London: Macmillan, Book iv, Chapter x.

45 M. Kelly (1997). The Dynamics of Smithian Growth. *The Quarterly Journal of Economics*, 112(3): 939–64.
46 H. Barkai (1969). A Formal Outline of a Smithian Growth Model. *The Quarterly Journal of Economics*, 83(3): 396–414.
47 Thomas Carlyle (1795–1881) decreed that economics was 'not a gay science' but a 'dreary, desolate, and indeed quite abject and distressing one'; his ire was directed towards the opposition of liberal economists towards slavery. Carlyle was a renowned racist and he had declared support for slavery and hence his disproval of the views of economists to the contrary. Carlyle had also displayed hostility to economics in earlier writings; his 1843 *Past and Present* was a subtle nod to the work of Malthus, and he continued to use his 'dismal science' description of economics in later works: P. J. Welch (2006). Thomas Carlye on Utilitarianism. *History of Political Economy*, 38(2): 377–89; F. Machlup (1976). The Dismal Science and the Illth of Nations. *Eastern Economic Journal*, 3(2): 59–63; For some of Carlyle's work, see: https://collections.americanantiquarian.org/freedmen/Manuscripts/carlyle.html
48 C. Gide and C. Rist (1915). *A History of Economic Doctrines*, p. 119.
49 J. M. Keynes (1933). *Essays in Biography*, p. 120.
50 W. J. Barber (1967). *A History of Economic Thought.*
51 R. Malthus (1798 [2007]). *An Essay on the Principle of Population*, 1st edition. New York: Dover Press.
52 R. Malthus (1836). *Principles of Economics Considered with a View to Their Practical Application*, 2nd edition. London: William Pickering, Chapter iv, Section ii, p. 226.
53 W. J. Barber (1967). *A History of Economic Thought*, p. 64.
54 R. Malthus (1836). *Principles of Economics Considered with a View to Their Practical Application*, Book I, Chapter v, Section iii, p. 281.
55 Ibid., Book II, Chapter i, Section ii, p. 312.
56 Ibid., p. 195.
57 A. Bashford and J. E. Chaplin (2016). *The New Worlds of Thomas Robert Malthus Rereading the Principle of Population*. Princeton: Princeton University Press.
58 R. Malthus (1798). *An Essay on the Principle of Population.*
59 A. Bashford (2014). *Global Population: History, Geopolitics, and Lies on Earth*. New York: Columbia University Press.
60 P. R. Erlich and A. H. Erlich (1970). *Population, Resources, Environment*; G. Blanc and R. Wacziarg (2025). Malthusian Migrations. *NBER Working Paper*, 33542.
61 K. Marx (1887). *Capital: A Critical Analysis of Capialist Production*. Vol. 1. Moscow: Progress Publishers, Chapter 25, Section 5, p. 663.
62 J. S. Donnelly (2001). *The Great Irish Potato Famine*. Sutton: Phoenix Mill.
63 A. Fernihough and C. Ó Gráda (2022). Population and Poverty in Ireland on the Eve of the Great Famine. *Demography*, 59(5): 1607–30.
64 L. Clarkson and M. Crawford (2001). *Feast and Famine: Food and Nutrition in Ireland, 1500–1920*. Oxford: Oxford University Press; M. Blum and E. McLaughlin (2019). Living Standards and Inequality in the Industrial Revolution.

65 R. Malthus (1798). *An Essay on the Principle of Population*; M. Blum, C. Colvin and E. McLaughlin (2026). Scarring and Selection in the Great Irish Famine. *Economic History Review*, 79 (1), pp 189-220.
66 The Census of England and Wales showed a population of 8.8 million people in 1801, 12 million in 1821, and 13.8 million in 1831. The Census of Scotland showed a population of 1.6 million in 1801, 2 million in 1821, and 2.3 million in 1831: B. R. Mitchell (1988). *British Historical Statistics*. Cambridge: Cambridge University Press.
67 N. Crafts (2021). Understanding Productivity Growth in the Industrial Revolution. *Economic History Review*, 74(2): 309–38.
68 D. Ricardo (1817). *Principles of Political Economy and Taxation*, Chapter 32.
69 Ibid., Chapter 32.
70 Ibid., Chapter 2.
71 Ibid., Chapter, 7.
72 P. W. Magness and M. Makovi (2023). The Mainstreaming of Marx: Measuring the Effect of the Russian Revolution on Karl Marx's Influence. *Journal of Political Economy*, 131(6).
73 C. Gide and C. Rist (1915). *A History of Economic Doctrines*, p. 449.
74 K. Marx and F. Engels (1888). *The Communist Manifesto*. Translated by Samuel Moore, Penguin Classics edition 2015. London: Penguin.
75 Chapter 10, Section 2, p. 226.
76 K. Marx (1887) *Capital: A Critical Analysis of Capitalist Production*, Chapter 24, Section 3.
77 Ibid., Chapter 25, Section 1.
78 Ibid., Chapter 25. Marx accuses Malthus of plagiarism at numerous occasions: 'Malthus often copies whole pages.'
79 Ibid., Chapter 25, Section 3.
80 C. Gide and C. Rist (1915). *A History of Economic Doctrines*, p. 349.
81 Although there was some progress in the immediate aftermath of Ricardo that foreshadowed later insights: E. R. A. Seligman (1903). On Some Neglected British Economists. *The Economic Journal*, 13(51): 335–6.
82 C. Gide and C. Rist (1915). *A History of Economic Doctrines*, p. 358.
83 J. R. Hicks (1966). Growth and Anti-Growth. *Oxford Economic Papers*, 18(3): 257–69.
84 C. Gide and C. Rist (1915). *A History of Economic Doctrines*, p. 162.
85 J. S. Mill (1909). *Principles of Political Economy with Some of Their Applications to Social Philosophy*. Edited by William James Ashley, 7th edition. London: Longmans, Green and Co., Book IV, Chapter vi.
86 J. F. Schumpeter (1954). *History of Economic Analysis*. Edited from Manuscript by Elizabeth Boody Schumpeter. Oxford: Oxford University Press.
87 J. R. Hicks (1966). Growth and Anti-Growth.
88 A. Marshall (1920). *Principles of Economics*, 8th edition. London: Macmillan, Book IV, Chapter x, Chapter xii.
89 J. R. Hicks (1966). Growth and Anti-Growth.
90 J. M. Keynes (1923). *A Tract on Monetary Reform*. London: Macmillan & Co.
91 J. M. Keynes (1936). *The General Theory of Employment, Interest Rate and Money*. London: Palgrave MacMillan, Chapter 7, p. 75.

92 Ibid., Chapter 8.
93 J. F. Schumpeter (1954). *History of Economic Analysis.*
94 R. F. Harrod (1939). An Essay in Dynamic Theory. *Economic Journal*, 49(193): 14–33; E. D. Domar (1946). Capital Expansion, Rate of Growth, and Employment. *Econometrica*, 14(2): 137–47; R. M. Solow (1956). A Contribution to the Theory of Economic Growth. *Quarterly Journal of Economics*, 70(1): 65–94; T. Swan (1956). Economic Growth and Capital Accumulation. *Economic Record*, 32: 334–61.
95 J. M. Keynes (1936). *The General Theory*, Chapter 9, Part i.
96 H. Hagemann (2009). Solow's 1956 Contribution in the Context of the Harrod-Domar Model. *History of Political Economy*, 41(annual suppl.): 67–86.
97 J. M. Keynes (1936). *The General Theory,* Chapter 7.
98 Trade cycle theory was the focus of his earlier work: R. F. Harrod (1936). *The Trade Cycle.* Oxford: Oxford University Press. Later work focused on growth: R. F. Harrod (1948). *Towards a Dynamic Economics: Some Recent Developments of Economic Theory and their Application to Policy.* London: Macmillan.
99 H. Hagemann (2009). Solow's 1956 Contribution in the Context of the Harrod-Domar Model.
100 M. Frankel (1962). The Production Function in Allocation and Growth: A Synthesis. *The American Economic Review*, 52(5): 996–1022.
101 R. F. Harrod (1939). An Essay in Dynamic Theory. p. 18.
102 S. Yusuf, et al. (2009). *Development Economics through the Decade: A Critical Look at 30 Years of the World Development.* Washington: World Bank.
103 W. Easterly (1997). *The Ghost of Financing Gap: How the Harrod-Domar Growth Model Still Haunts Development Economics.* World Bank Policy Research Working Paper WPS1807.
104 Rostow's influences were Roy Harrod, W. Arthur Lewis (1915–91) and Adam Smith's *Wealth of Nations.*
105 W. W. Rostow (1952). *The Process of Economic Growth.* New York: W. W. Norton.
106 W. W. Rostow (1990). *The Stages of Economic Growth: A Non-Communist Manifesto*, 3rd edition. Cambridge: Cambridge University Press.
107 W. W. Rostow (1956). The Take-off into Self-sustained Growth. *The Economic Journal*, 66(261): 25–48.
108 L. G. Reynolds (1986). *Economic Growth in the Third World.* New Haven: Yale University Press.
109 R. M. Solow (1956). A Contribution to the Theory of Economic Growth; T. Swan (1956). Economic Growth and Capital Accumulation.
110 C. W. Cobb and P. H. Douglas (1928). A Theory of Production. *The American Economic Review*, 18(1): 139–65.
111 P. H. Douglas (1948). Are There Laws of Production? *American Economic Review*, 38(1): 1–41; B. Sandelin (1976). On the Origin of the Cobb-Douglas Production Function. *Economy and History*, 19(2): 117–23.
112 R. M. Solow (1994). Perspectives on Growth Theory. *Journal of Economic Perspectives*, 8(1): 48.

113 M. Abramovitz (1956). Resource and Output Trends in the United States Since 1870. *NBER Occasional Paper* 52.
114 R. M. Solow (1957). Technical Change and the Aggregate Production Function. *The Review of Economics and Statistics*, 39(3): 314.
115 R. M. Solow (1956). A Contribution to the Theory of Economic Growth. p. 81.
116 H. Hagemann (2009). Solow's 1956 Contribution in the Context of the Harrod-Domar Model, p. 83.
117 H. Van den Berg (2013). Growth Theory after Keynes, Part I: The Unfortunate Suppression of the Harrod-Domar Model. *The Journal of Philosophical Economics*, 7(1); A. K. Dutt (2006). Aggregate Demand, Aggregate Supply, and Economic Growth. *International Review of Applied Economics*, 20(3): 319–36.
118 H. Hagemann (2009). Solow's 1956 Contribution in the Context of the Harrod-Domar Model, p. 83.
119 R. M. Solow (1988). Growth Theory and After. *The American Economic Review*, 78(3): 310.
120 R. M. Solow (1959). Investment and Technical Progress. In K. J. Arrow, S. Karlin and P. Suppes (eds), *Mathematical Methods in the Social Sciences, 1959: Proceedings of the First Stanford Symposium*. Stanford: Stanford University Press.
121 F. H. Hahn and R. C. O. Matthews (1964). The Theory of Economic Growth: A Survey. *The Economic Journal*, 74: 779–902.
122 H. W. Arndt (1978). *The Rise and Fall of Economic Growth*.
123 R. J. Barro and X. Sala-I-Martin (1995). *Economic Growth*. New York: McGraw-Hill.
124 N. G. Mankiw, D. Romer and D. N. Weil (1992). A Contribution to the Empirics of Economic Growth. *The Quarterly Journal of Economics*, 107(2): 407–37; R. J. Barro (1997). *Determinants of Economic Growth: A Cross-Country Empirical Study*. Cambridge, MA: MIT Press.
125 J. B. deLong and L. H. Summers (1991). Equipment Investment and Economic Growth. *Quarterly Journal of Economics*, 106(2): 445–502.
126 P. M. Romer (1986). Increasing Returns and Long-run Growth. *Journal of Political Economy*, 94(5): 1002–37; P. M. Romer (1987). Growth Based on Increasing Returns Due to Specialization. *The American Economic Review*, 77(2): 56–62; P. M. Romer (1990). Endogenous Technological Change. *Journal of Political Economy*, 98(5): S71–S102
127 R. E. Lucas (1988). On the Mechanics of Economic Development. *Journal of Monetary Economics*, 22: 3–42.
128 S. Rebelo (1991). Long-Run Policy Analysis and Long-Run Growth. *Journal of Political Economy*, 99(3): 500–21; M. Frankel (1962). The Production Function in Allocation and Growth: A Synthesis.
129 P. Aghion and P. Howitt (1992). Model of Growth Through Creative Destruction. *Econometrica*, 60(2): 323–51; P. Aghion and P. Howitt (1998). *Endogenous Growth Theory*. Cambridge MA: MIT Press; P. Aghion and P. Howitt (2006). Appropriate Growth Policy: A Unifying Framework. *Journal of the European Economic Association*, 4(2–3): 269–314.
130 P. Aghion and P. Howitt (1998). *Endogenous Growth Theory*.

131 M. Frankel (1962). The Production Function in Allocation and Growth.
132 K. Hussein and A. P. Thirlwall (2000). The AK Model of "New" Growth Theory Is the Harrod-Domar Growth Equation: Investment and Growth Revisited. *Journal of Post Keynesian Economics*, 22(3): 427–35.
133 P. Aghion and P. Howitt (2008). *The Economics of Growth*. Cambridge, MA: MIT Press, p. 48.
134 C. Kennedy and A. P. Thirlwall (1972). Surveys in Applied Economics: Technical Progress. *The Economic Journal*, 82(325): 11–72.
135 N. J. Wulwick (1992). Kaldor's Growth Theory. *Journal of the History of Economic Thought*, 14(1): 36–54.
136 N. Kaldor (1961). Capital Accumulation and Economic Growth. In D. C. Hague (ed.), *The Theory of Capital*. London: Macmillan; K. J. Arrow (1962). The Economic Implications of Learning by Doing. *Review of Economic Studies*, 29(3): 155–73; H. Uzawa (1965). Optimum Technical Change in an Aggregative Model of Economic Growth. *International Economic Review*, 6(1): 18–31.
137 F. H. Knight (1944). Diminishing Returns from Investment. *Journal of Political Economy*, 52(1): 26–47.
138 A. Brewer (1983). Reviewed Work: Economics in the Long View. Essays in Honour of W. W. Rostow. 3 Volumes. Models and Methodology: Applications and Cases, Parts I & II by Charles P. Kindleberger, Guida di Tella. *Economic Journal*, 93(271): 650–2.
139 M. M. Postan (1982). Walt Rostow: A Personal Appreciation; D. C. North (1982). The Theoretical Tools of the Economic Historian. In Charles P. Kindleberger and Guido di Tella (eds), *Economics in the Long View: Essays in Honour of W. W. Rostow*. Vol. 1. London: Macmillan.
140 W. W. Rostow (1952). *The Process of Economic Growth*.
141 Ibid.
142 R. M. Solow (1963). *Capital Theory and the Rate of Return*. Amsterdam: North-Holland Publishing Company; G. M. Hodgson (2014). What Is Capital? Economists and Sociologists Have Changed Its Meaning: Should It be Changed Back? *Cambridge Journal of Economics*, 38: 1063–86.
143 C. Bliss, A. J. Cohen and G. C. Harcourt (2005). *Capital Theory Volume* 1. Cheltenham: Edward Elgar.
144 L. Von Mises (1934). *The Theory of Money and Credit*. Translated by H. E. Batson. London: Jonathan Cape.
145 F. H. Hahn and R. C. O. Matthews (1964). The Theory of Economic Growth.
146 See review in: L. Dupuy (2014). *Sustainability and International Trade. Economics and Finance*. Université de Bordeaux L. Dupuy and E. McLaughlin (2019). *Back to the Future: Sustainable Development and Capital Theory*. Mimeo.
147 M. L. Weitzman (2017). Tight Connection Among Wealth, Income, Sustainability, and Accounting in an Ultra-Simplified Setting. In K. Hamilton and C. Hepburn (eds), *National Wealth*.
148 I. Fisher (1896). What is Capital? *The Economic Journal*, 6(24): 509–34.
149 I. Fisher (1906). *The Nature of Capital and Income*. London: Macmillan and Company, p. 19.
150 Ibid., p. 66.

151 C. A. Tuttle (1903). The Real Capital Concept. *Quarterly Journal of Economics*, 18(1): 54–96; I. Fisher (1903). Precedents for Defining Capital. *Quarterly Journal of Economics*, 18(3): 386–408; C. A. Tuttle (1904). The Fundamental Notion of Capital Once More. *Quarterly Journal of Economics*, 19(1): 81–110. I. Fisher (1905). Professor Tuttle's Capital Concept. *Quarterly Journal of Economics*, 19(2): 309–13.

152 J. Hicks (1946). *Value and Capital: An Inquiry into Some Fundamental Principles of Economic Theory*, 2nd edition. Oxford: Clarendon Press, p. 171; Although in a review of Hicks's book the economist Oskar Morgenstern (1902–77) was critical that there was not more attention devoted to capital theory within the work: O. Morgenstern (1941). Professor Hicks on Value and Capital. *Journal of Political Economy*, 49(3): 361–93.

153 J. Hicks (1946). *Value and Capital*, p. 172.

154 E. Osborn (1958). The Wicksell Effect. *Review of Economic Studies*, 25(3): 163–71.

155 A. J. Cohen and G. C. Harcourt (2003). Retrospectives: Whatever Happened to the Cambridge-Capital Theory Controversies? *Journal of Economic Perspectives*, 17(1): 199–214.

156 Robinson asked whether capital should 'be valued according to its future earning power or its past costs'?: "Capital" is not what capital is called, it is what its name is called. The capital goods in existence at a moment of time are all the goods in existence at that moment. It is not all the things in existence.': J. Robinson (1953–4). The Production Function and the Theory of Capital. *Review of Economic Studies*, 21(2): 83.

157 J. Robinson (1953–4). The Production Function and the Theory of Capital. p. 84.

158 Y. S. Chung and Y. C. Chiou (2024). Economic Characteristics of City Bus Operation with a Mixed Fleet: The Influence of Electric Buses. *Transportmetrica A: Transport Science*, 20(3): 2192308.

159 T. Swan (1956). Economic Growth and Capital Accumulation.

160 R. M. Solow (1963). *Capital Theory and the Rate of Return.*

161 Ibid.

162 R. M. Solow (1972). Substitution and Fixed Proportions in Capital Theory. *Review of Economic Studies,* 29(3): 207–18.

163 Arrow's study of learning by doing with an emphasis on increasing returns and Kaldor and the Nobel laureate James Mirrlees (1936–2018) response to Solow's neoclassical model which does away with an aggregate production function: K. J. Arrow (1962). The Economic Implications of Learning by Doing; N. Kaldor and J. A. Mirrlees (1962). A New Model of Economic Growth. *Review of Economic Studies*, 29(3): 174–92.

164 P. A. Samuelson (1966). A Summing Up. *The Quarterly Journal of Economics*, 80(4): 568–83.

165 R. X. Chase (1978). The "Ruth Cohen" Anomaly and Production Theory. *Challenge*, 21(5): 32–9.

166 G. C. Harcourt (1969). Some Cambridge Controversies in the Theory of Capital. *Journal of Economic Literature*, 7(2): 369–405.

167 A. J. Cohen and G. C. Harcourt (2003). Whatever Happened to the Cambridge-Capital Theory Controversies? p. 212.

168 For a modern treatment of the debate see: D. R. Baqaee and E. Farhi (2019). 'The Microeconomic Foundations of Aggregate Production Functions'. *Journal of the European Economic Association*, 17(5): 1337–92.
169 Ibid., p. 210.
170 R. M. Solow (1988). Growth Theory and After.
171 R. E. Lucas (1988). On the Mechanics of Economic Development.
172 J. Hicks (1974). Capital Controversies.
173 A. J. Cohen (2010). Capital Controversy From Böhm-Bawerk To Bliss: Badly Posed Or Very Deep Questions? Or What "We" Can Learn From Capital Controversy Even If You Don't Care Who Won. *Journal of the History of Economic Thought*, 32(1): 1–21.
174 G. C. Harcourt (2022). *Some Cambridge Controversies in the Theory of Capital: Fiftieth Anniversary Edition*. Cambridge: Cambridge University Press.
175 J. K. Galbraith (1958). *The Affluent Society*. London: Penguin.
176 E. R. Weintraub (2005). Roy F. Harrod and the Interwar Years.
177 C. I. Jones and P. M. Romer (2010). The New Kaldor Facts: Ideas, Institutions, Population, and Human Capital. *American Economic Journal: Macroeconomics*, 2(1): 224–45.
178 U. Akcigit (2017). Economic Growth: Past, the Present, and the Future. *Journal of Political Economy*, 125(6): 1736–47.
179 O. Galor (2011). *Unified Growth Theory*. Princeton: Princeton University Press.
180 N. G. Mankiew, D. Romer and D. N. Weill (1992). A Contribution to the Empirics of Economic Growth; C. Jones and D. Romer (2010). The New Kaldor Facts.
181 R. Solow (2009). Does Growth Have a Future? Does Growth Theory Have a Future?
182 O. J. Blanchard (2008). The State of Macro. *NBER Working Paper* 14259; O. J. Blanchard (2025). Convergence? Thoughts About the Evolution of Mainstream Macroeconomics Over the Last 40 Years. *NBER Working Paper* 33802.
183 T. Piketty (2014). *Capital in the Twenty-First Century*. Cambridge, MA: Harvard University Press, p. 58.
184 G. M. Hodgson (2014). What Is Capital? Economists and Sociologists Have Changed Its Meaning: Should It Be Changed Back?
185 R. Solow (2009). Does Growth Have a Future?.

Chapter Four

1 C. Ó Gráda (2024). *The Hidden Victims: Civilian Casualties of the Two World Wars*. Princeton: Princeton University Press.
2 A. Alesina and E. Spolaore (2003). *The Size of Nations*. Cambridge, MA: MIT Press.
3 R. Monastersky. (2015). Anthropocene: The Human Age. *Nature*, 519(7542): 144–7.

4 W. W. Rostow (1978). *The World Economy*, p. 619.
5 W. A. Arthur (1954). Economic Development with Unlimited Supplies of Labor. *Manchester School*, 22: 139–91.
6 Fighting to Save the Earth from Man. *Time Magazine*, 2 February 1970.
7 W. B. Barbier (2011). *Scarcity and Frontiers: How Economies Have Developed through Natural Resource Exploitation*. Cambridge: Cambridge University Press; G. Huff (2007). Globalisation, Natural Resources, and Foreign Investment: A View from the Resource-rich Tropics. *Oxford Economic Papers*, 59: i127–i155; E. Frankema (2010). Raising Revenue in the British Empire, 1870–1940: How Extractive Were Colonial Taxes? *Journal of Global History*, 5(3): 447–7.
8 E. Hobsbawm (1987). *The Age of Empire, 1875–1914*. London: Weidenfeld and Nicolson; A. Hochschild (1998). *King Leopold's Ghost: A Story of Greed, Terror, and Heroism in Colonial Africa*. New York: Mariner Books.
9 See Butcher and Griffiths for discussion of classification of countries: C. R. Butcher and R. D. Griffiths (2020). States and Their International Relations since 1816: Introducing Version 2 of the International System(s) Dataset (ISD). *International Interactions*, 46(2): 291–308.
10 The Covenant of the League of Nations: https://www.ungeneva.org/en/about/league-of-nations/covenant
11 King George V's Speech on Global Affairs. *Belfast NewsLetter*, 24 December 1920 https://creativecentenaries.org/on-this-day/king-george-v-s-speech-on-global-affairs
12 F. D. Lugard (1922). *The Dual Mandate in British Colonial Africa*. Edinburgh: William Blackwood and Son.
13 C. C. Mann (2018). *The Wizard and the Prophet: Two Groundbreaking Scientists and Their Conflicting Visions of the Future of Our Planet*. London: Picador.
14 H. W. Arndt (1981). Economic Development: A Semantic History. *Economic Development and Cultural Change*, 29(3): 457–66.
15 P. N. Rosenstein-Rodan (1944). The International Development of Economically Backward Areas. *International Affairs*, 20(2): 157–65.
16 H. W. Arndt (1987). *Economic Development: The History of an Idea*. Chicago: Chicago University Press.
17 Charter of the United Nations and Statute of the International Court of Justice. UN 1945. https://treaties.un.org/doc/publication/ctc/uncharter.pdf
18 R. Jolly (2005). The UN and Development Thinking and Practice. *Forum for Development Studies*, 32(1): 49–73.
19 UN (1948). *Supplement to Economic Report: Salient Features of the World Economic Situation 1945–47*. Discussion of Report in Economic and Social Council Sixth Session; February and March 1948.
20 H. W. Arndt (1987). *Economic Development*.
21 UN (1951). *Measures for the Economic Development of Under-developed Countries: Report by a Group of Experts Appointed by the Secretary-General of the United Nations*, paragraph 245.
22 UN (1962). *The United Nations Development Decade: Proposals for Action: Report of the Secretary-General*.

23 H. W. Arndt (1987). *Economic Development*; A. Sen (1987). The Standard of Living: Lecture II, Lives and Capabilities. In G. Hawthorn (ed.), *The Standard of Living: The Tanner Lectures*. Cambridge: Cambridge University Press.
24 P. Steeten, S. J. Burki, M. ul Haq, N. Hicks, and F. Stewart (1981). *First Things First: Meeting Basic Human Needs in the Developing Countries*, Oxford: Oxford University Press; M. ul Huq (1995). *Reflections on Human Development*. Oxford: Oxford University Press.
25 H. W. Arndt (1987). *Economic Development*, p. 80.
26 A. Sen (1983). Development: Which Way Now? *The Economic Journal*, 93(372): 745–62.
27 H. W. Arndt (1987). *Economic Development*.
28 Singer worked at the UN from 1947 to 1969: R. Jolly (2008). Hans Singer: The Gentle Giant of UN Economists. *UN Chronicle*.
29 H. W. Singer (1966). The Notion of Human Investment. *Review of Social Economy*, 24: 1–14.
30 S. J. Macekura (2020). *The Mismeasure of Progress: Economic Growth and Its Critics*. Chicago: University of Chicago Press; T. Roy (2011). Morris David Morris (1921–2011). *Economic and Political Weekly*, 46(13): 27–30.
31 A. Sen (2020). Human Development and Mahbub ul Haq. In *Human Development Report 2020: The Next Frontier Human Development and the Anthropocene*. New York: UNDP.
32 M. ul Huq (1995). *Reflections on Human Development*, Oxford: Oxford University Press.
33 *Human Development Report 1990*. New York: UNDP.
34 L. Prados de la Escosura (2022). *Human Development and the Path to Freedom: 1870 to the Present*. Cambridge: Cambridge University Press; recent updates to the HDI include 'planetary pressures-adjusted' this adjustment is done 'to reflect a concern for intergenerational inequality'. However, the adjustment is narrow and only includes carbon dioxide emissions per person and material footprint per person. UNDP (2025). *Human Development Report 2025*. New York: United Nations.
35 Maddison reported global population at 1.56 billion in 1900, 2.53 billion in 1950, and 6.08 billion in 2000: A. Maddison (2009). *Historical Statistics of the World Economy: 1-2008 AD*. There have been debates about the accuracy of population estimates. Recent work by Giovanni Federico and Antonio Tena Junguito argues that global population is not known with much accuracy until about 1950. These new estimates show a slightly larger population in 1900 than estimated by Maddison. The Federico and Tena Junguito population estimate for 1900 is 2.9 per cent higher, at 1.6 million, and the implied population increase between 1900 and 1950 was 57 percent: G. Federico and A. Tena Junguito (2023). How Many People on Earth? World Population 1800–1938. *Working Papers in Economic History 23-01*, Figuerola Institute, Carlos III University of Madrid. http://hdl.handle.net/10016/36431
36 A. Bashford (2014). *Global Population*.
37 R. Malthus (1926). *First Essay on Population, 1798 with Notes by James Bonar*; reprinted for the Royal Economic Society. London: Macmillan.
38 E. Cannan (1916). Review: Population: A Study in Malthusianism by Warren S. Thompson. *The Economic Journal*, 26(102): 218–22.

39 J. M. Keynes (1920). *The Economic Consequences of the Peace*. New York: Harcourt, Brace, & Howe.
40 H. Cox (1922). *The Problem of Population*. London: Jonathan Cape; R. Pearl (1925). *The Biology of Population Growth*. New York: Alfred A. Knopf.
41 C. C. Mann (2018). *The Wizard and the Prophet*.
42 F. Osborn (1948). *Our Plundered Planet*. Boston: Little, Brown, and Company.
43 C. Darwin (1859). *On the Origin of Species by Means of Natural Selection*, 1st edition. London: John Murray; C. Darwin (1872). *On the Origin of Species by Means of Natural Selection*, 6th edition. London: John Murray.
44 N. Barlow (1958). *The Autobiography of Charles Darwin (1809–1882): From the Life and Letters of Charles Darwin. With Original Emissions Restored. Edited with Appendix and Notes by his Granddaughter Nora Barlow*. London: Collins.
45 A. Bashford (2014). *Global Population*; R. Pearl (1925). *The Biology of Population Growth*.
46 D. Worster (1977). *Nature's Economy: The Roots of Ecology*. San Francisco: Sierra Club Books
47 Ibid., p. 192.
48 H. G. Wells, J. Huxley and G. P. Wells (1931). *The Science of Life*. London: Cassel and Company.
49 Ibid., p. 578.
50 W. Vogt (1948). *Road to Survival*. New York: William Sloane Associates, Inc.
51 F. Osborn (1948). *Our Plundered Planet*.
52 P. Levine and A. Bashford (2010). Introduction: Eugenics and the Modern World. In A. Bashford and P. Levine (eds), *The Oxford Handbook of the History of Eugenics*. Oxford: Oxford University Press.
53 F. Galton (1908). *Memories of My Life*. London: Methuen & Co., p. 323.
54 K. Pearson (1903). On the Inheritance of the Mental and Moral Characters in Man, and Its Comparison with the Inheritance of the Physical Characters. *The Journal of the Anthropological Institute of Great Britain and Ireland*, 33: 179–237.
55 G. Gardner (1998). A Martian View of the Hardinian Taboo. *BMJ*, 316(7141): 1386; F. Locher (2013). Cold War Pastures: Garrett Hardin and the "Tragedy of the Commons". *Revue d'histoire Moderne & Contemporaine*, 60(1): 7–36.
56 'Malthus, Darwin, Galton, Fisher, Keynes, Charles Galton Darwin and J. B. S. Haldane . . . as ideas have a heredity of their own': Garrett Hardin (1960). *Nature and Man's Fate*. London: Jonathan Cape; the latter were founders of eugenics. N. W. Gillham (2009). Cousins: Charles Darwin, Sir Francis Galton and the Birth of Eugenics. *Significance*.
57 G. Hardin (1960). *Nature and Man's Fate*, p. 319.
58 Ibid., p. 322.
59 Ibid., p. 325.
60 G. Hardin (1993). *Living within Limits: Ecology, Economics, and Population Taboos*. Oxford: Oxford University Press.
61 G. Hardin (1968). The Tragedy of the Commons. *Science*, 162(3859): 1243–8.
62 Ibid., p. 1246.

63 M. King and C. Elliott (1997). To the Point of Farce: A Martian View of the Hardinian Taboo – The Silence that Surrounds Population Control. *BMJ*, 315: 1441–3.
64 P. R. Ehrlich and A. H. Ehrlich (1970). *Population, Resources, Environment*, p. 2.
65 E. G. Ravenstein (1891). Lands of the Globe Still Available for European Settlement. *Proceedings of the Royal Geographical Society and Monthly Record of Geography*, 13(1): 27–35.
66 R. Pearl (1925). *The Biology of Population Growth*, Figure 30.
67 O. E. Baker (1925). The Potential Supply of Wheat. *Economic Geography*, 1(1): 15–52.
68 G. H. Knibbs (1928). *The Shadow of the World's Future: Or the Earth's Population Possibilities & the Consequences of the Present Rate of Increase of the Earth's Inhabitants*. London: Ernest Benn, p. 103.
69 W. Vogt (1948). *Road to Survival*, p. 219.
70 Ibid., p. 238.
71 P. R. Ehrlich (1968). *The Population Bomb*. New York: Ballantine Books.
72 E. Goldsmith (1971). Conclusion: What of the Future? In E. Goldsmith (ed). *Can Britain Survive?* London: Tom Stacey, p. 244.
73 J. Cribb (2010). *The Coming Famine: The Global Food Crisis and What We Can Do to Avoid It*. California: University of California Press.
74 T. Robertson (2014). *The Malthusian Moment: Global Population Growth and the Birth of American Environmentalism*. New Brunswick: Rutgers University Press.
75 J. Passmore (1974). *Man's Responsibility for Nature*. London: Duckworth; P. R. Ehrlich (1969). *The Population Bomb*.
76 J. Schoen (2005). *Choice & Coercion: Birth Control, Sterilization, and Abortion in Public Health and Welfare*. Chapel Hill: The University of North Carolina Press; I. R. Dowbiggin (2008). *The Sterilization Movement and Global Fertility in the Twentieth Century*. Oxford: Oxford University Press.
77 P. R. Ehrlich (1969). *The Population Bomb*.
78 J. B. Calhoun (1973). Death Squared: The Explosive Growth and Demise of a Mouse Population. *Proceeding Royal Society Medicine*, 66: 80–8.
79 G. Federico (2005). *Feeding the World. Princeton: An Economic History of Agriculture, 1800–2000*. Princeton University Press.
80 W. Crookes (1900). *The Wheat Problem*, 1st edition, reprint 1976. New York: Arno Press.
81 Fritz Haber was controversially awarded a Nobel, not because of his work on synthetic fertilizers but because of his involvement in the development of chemical weapons during the First World War.
82 https://www.nobelprize.org/prizes/chemistry/1918/summary/; V. Smil (2000). Detonator of the Population Explosion. *Nature*, 400: 415.
83 Science and Food Supply (1930). *Nature*, 126: 193–4.
84 Norman Borlaug, Nobel Lecture, 11 December 1970: https://www.nobelprize.org/prizes/peace/1970/borlaug/lecture/
85 G. Federico (2005). *Feeding the World*.
86 C. Ó Gráda (2007). *Famine: A Short History*. Princeton: Princeton University Press.

87 C. Ó Gráda (2008). The Ripple That Drowns? Twentieth-Century Famines in China and India as Economic History. *Economic History Review*, 61(51): 5–37.

88 C. Ó Gráda (2007). Making Famine History. *Journal of Economic Literature*, 45(1): 5–38.

89 A. Sen. (1983). *Poverty and Famines: An Essay on Entitlement and Deprivation*. Oxford: Oxford University Press.

90 C. Ó Gráda (2007). *Famine*; M. M. Islam. (2007). The Great Bengal Famine and the Question of FAD Yet Again. *Modern Asian Studies*, 41(2): 421–40; T. Roy (2016). Were Indian Famines "Natural" or "Manmade"? *LSE Economic History Working Papers*, 243/2016.

91 A. Sant'Anna and L. Weller (2020). The Threat of Communism During the Cold War: A Constraint on Income Inequality? *Comparative Politics*, 52(3): 359–81; P. A. Hall and D. Soskice (eds) (2001). *Varieties of Capitalism: The Institutional Foundations of Comparative Advantage*. Oxford: Oxford University Press.

92 S. Ambrose (1971). *Rise to Globalism: American Foreign Policy since 1938*. London: Allen Lane, p. 141.

93 Ibid., pp. 141, 148.

94 Quoted in: N. Chomsky (1967). *American Power and the New Mandarins*. New York: Pantheon Books; A. Pagden (2005). Imperialism, Liberalism, & the Quest for Perpetual Peace. *Dædalus: Journal of the American Academy of Arts & Science*, 134(2): 46–57; but the reported speech was paraphrased see: D. F. Fleming (1961). *The Cold War and Its Origins*, 1917–1950: Vol. I. New York: Doubleday & Co, p. 436.

95 H. S. Truman (1947). Address on Foreign Economic Policy, Delivered at Baylor University, 6 March. https://www.trumanlibrary.gov/library/public-papers/52/address-foreign-economic-policy-delivered-baylor-university

96 Truman Doctrine, 12 March 1947: https://www.archives.gov/milestone-documents/truman-doctrine

97 H. B. Price (1955). *The Marshall Plan and Its Meaning*. Ithaca, NY: Cornell University Press.

98 R. Crockatt (1995). *The Fifty Years War: The United States and the Soviet Union in World Politics, 1941–1991*. London: Routledge.

99 M. Alacevich (2009). The World Bank's Early Reflections on Development: A Development Institution or a Bank? *Review of Political Economy*, 21(2): 227–44.

100 M. Alacevich (2009). *The Political Economy of the World Bank: The Early Years*. Stanford: Stanford University Press.

101 M. Leepson (2000). The Heart and Mind of USAID's Vietnam Mission. *Foreign Service Journal*, 77(4): 20–7; J. Essex (2013). *Development, Security, and Aid: Geopolitics and Geoeconomics at the US Agency for International Development*. Georgia: University of Georgia Press, p. 48.

102 S. Yusuf, et al. (2009). *Development Economics through the Decades: A Critical Look at 30 Years of the World Development Report*. Washington D.C.: World Bank, p. 83.

103 C. C. Mann (2018). *The Wizard and the Prophet*.

104 Rostow himself is an interesting character (already referred to in Chapter 3) as he had an intertwined career as an academic and public servant. The significance

of Rostow's analysis lies not merely in its academic credentials but also his policy influence. As an academic he studied at Yale and Oxford and taught at various Ivy League universities. He resigned a position at Harvard to take up a role, at the behest of the Nobel laureate Gunnar Myrdal (1898–1987), at the Economic Commission for Europe. Rostow then returned to the United States to take up a role at MIT in 1950, via a visiting professorship at the University of Cambridge. It was at MIT that Rostow penned the *Stages of Economic Growth*. As a public servant, he received an OBE for his service in the Enemy Objectives Unit which identified strategic bombing targets in Germany during the Second World War. He spent time at the US state department and assisted with the Marshall Plan and was later an adviser to President Dwight D. Eisenhower (1890–1969). In the 1960s he was a national security advisor to President John F. Kennedy (1917–63) and President Lyndon B. Johnson (1908–73). Rostow was the only one of Johnson's senior advisors who advocated for nuclear non-proliferation. But Rostow was alienated from American academia after his service in the Johnson administration, particularly as he took a pro-war stance during Vietnam. After his public service ended he was told he was unwelcome at MIT and finished his academic career teaching at the University of Texas at Austin: R. Crockatt (1995). *The Fifty Years War: The United States and the Soviet Union in World Politics, 1941–1991*, p. 187; P. C. Bobbitt (2007). Walt Rostow, 7 October 1916–13 February 2003. *Proceedings of the American Philosophical Society*, 151(4): 479–86.

105 W. W. Rostow (1960/1990). *The Stages of Economic Growth*, 3rd edition, p. 134; M. M. Postan (1982). Walt Rostow: A Personal Appreciation; R. Crockatt (1995). *The Fifty Years War*, p. 187; P. C. Bobbitt (2007). Walt Rostow, 7 October 1916–13 February 2003.

106 US General Accounting Office (1991). *Report to the Honorable Daniel Patrick Moynihan, U.S. Senate September. Soviet Union: Assessment of How Well the CIA Has Estimated the Size of the Economy*. GAO/NSIAD-91-274 NSIAD-91-274 Soviet Economy: Assessment of How Well the CIA Has Estimated the Size of the Economy.

107 R. Crockatt (1995). *The Fifty Years War*, pp. 114–15.

108 V. Bush (1945). *Science the Endless Frontier*, 75th anniversary edition. Reprinted in celebration of the National science Foundation's 70th anniversary.

109 E. P. Berman (2012). *Creating the Market University: How Academic Science Became an Economic Engine*. Princeton: Princeton University Press.

110 A. Rome (2003). 'Give Earth a Chance': The Environmental Movement and the Sixties. *Journal of American History*, 90(2): 525–54.

111 R. Carson (1962). *Silent Spring*. London: Penguin Books; P. Sabin (2013). *The Bet: Paul Ehrlich, Julian Simon, and Our Gamble over Earth's Future*. New Haven: Yale University Press; S. Macekura (2015). *Of Limits and Growth: The Rise of Global Sustainable Development in the Twentieth Century*. New York: Cambridge University Press.

112 R. Carson (1962/2000). *Silent Spring. Introduction by Lord Shackleton. Preface by Julian Huxley, with a New Afterword by Linda Lear*. London: Penguin Books; L. Lear (1998). *Rachel Carson: Witness for Nature*. Boston: Mariner Books.

113 R. E. Lutz (1985). Chemical Fallout: Rachel Carson's Silent Spring, Radioactive Fallout and the Environmental Movement. *Environmental Review*, 9(3): 210–25; A. Bashford (2014). *Global Population.*

114 M. Beck and B. Kewell (2014). *Risk: A Study of Its Origins, History and Politics.* London: World Scientific.

115 Vogt came from a modest rural background in Long Island, New York. In his early teens, Vogt moved to Brooklyn, a transition that appears to have left a lasting impression. He was the first in his family to attend college, choosing to study French literature and deliberately avoiding science and mathematics subjects. Much like how the Great Depression profoundly influenced economic thought (as discussed in Chapter 3), it also inadvertently shaped the development of modern ecology. During the Depression, Vogt, then working as a drama critic and amateur birdwatcher, lost much of his income. He was helped through this lean period by his birdwatching network. His first peer-reviewed science work on dovekie deaths appeared in the journal of the Ornithologist Union, *The Auk*, and he later became editor of the journal *Bird-Lore*. This path eventually led him to a role as a scientific advisor for the Compañía Administradora del Guano in Peru, where he studied the declining guanay population, the seabirds essential to the guano industry. These experiences deeply shaped Vogt's ecological worldview and his conviction in the interdependence of ecosystems. Note there is some discrepancy as Warde and colleagues believe that Vogt was 'trained in ecology at St. Stephen's (now Bard) College'. The entry into the *American National Biography* makes no reference to the study of ecology, rather that he left Bard 'with a BA, having won the poetry prize and edited the college literary magazine': P. Warde, L. Robin and S. Sörlin (2018). *The Environment: A History of the Idea.* Baltimore: John Hopkins University Press; R. Harmond (1999). Vogt, William (15 May 1902–11 July 1968). *American National Biography.* Oxford: Oxford University Press; C. C. Mann (2018). *The Wizard and the Prophet.*

116 P. Warde, L. Robin and S. Sörlin (2018). *The Environment: A History of the Idea*; E. P. Odum (1971). *Fundamentals of Ecology*, 3rd edition. Philadelphia: W. P. Saunders Co; H. T. Odum (1971). *Environment, Power, and Society.* New York: Wiley; C. C. Mann (2018). *The Wizard and the Prophet.*

117 A. Rome (2003). Give Earth a Chance.

118 H. W. Arndt (1978). *The Rise and Fall of Economic Growth.*

119 J. K. Galbraith (1958). *The Affluent Society.* London: Penguin.

120 J. K. Galbraith (1998). *The Affluent Society.*

121 P. Weindling (2012). Julian Huxley and the Continuity of Eugenics in Twentieth-Century Britain. *Journal Modern European History*, 10(4): 480–99.

122 J. Huxley (1946). *UNESCO Its Purpose and Its Philosophy.* Washington, DC: Public Affairs Press; P. Weindling (2012). Julian Huxley and the Continuity of Eugenics in Twentieth-Century Britain.

123 S. J. Macekura (2015). *Of Limits and Growth.*

124 T. N. Takeuchi, N. Morikawa, H. Matsumoto and Y. Shiraishi (1962). A Pathological Study of Minamata Disease in Japan. *Aeta Neuropathologica*, 2: 40–57; R. Carson (1962). *Silent Spring.* Boston, MA: Houghton Mifflin; P. Sabin (2013). *The Bet*; S. Macekura (2015). *Of Limits and Growth.*

125 Paul Müller – Facts. NobelPrize.org. Nobel Prize Outreach 2025. https://www.nobelprize.org/prizes/medicine/1948/muller/facts/
126 W. Vogt (1948). *Road to Survival.*
127 R. Carson (1962). *Silent Spring;* Beck and Kewell (2014). *Risk.*
128 T. Robertson (2014). *The Malthusian Moment.*
129 K. Boulding (1966). The Economics of the Coming Spaceship Earth. In H. Jarrett (ed.), *Environmental Quality in a Growing Economy.* Baltimore: Johns Hopkins University Press; G. Hardin (1968). The Tragedy of the Commons; N. Georgescu-Roegen (1971). *The Entropy Law and the Economic Process.* Cambridge, MA: MIT Press.
130 Critics of Hardin found evidence that users of common pool resources usually developed formal or informal measures to prevent overgrazing: E. Ostrom (1990). *Governing the Commons: The Evolution of Institutions for Collective Action.* Cambridge: Cambridge University Press.
131 N. Georgescu-Roegen (1971). *The Entropy Law and the Economic Process.*
132 P. R. Ehrlich and A. H. Ehrlich (1970). *Population, Resources, Environment,* p. 2.
133 Ibid., p. 56.
134 See Beck and Kewell for further discussion: M. Beck and B. Kewell (2014). *Risk.*
135 Boulding is fascinating in multiple regards, not least because he was a key figure in the shift towards thinking about sustainable development. He had earlier cut his teeth in the capital debates of the 1930s (discussed in Chapters 3 and 6). But he was also the second awardee of the prestigious John Bates Clark medal, that before the introduction of the Nobel Memorial Prize in Economic Sciences in 1968, was considered the highest honour in economics. Boulding never received a Nobel in economics, largely because his research interests diverged from those of mainstream economics. In this respect, he was not unlike his intellectual role model, Adam Smith: K. E. Boulding (1933). The Theory of a Single Investment. *The Quarterly Journal of Economics,* 49(3): 475–94; F. H. Knight (1935). The Theory of Investment Once More: Mr. Boulding and the Austrians. *The Quarterly Journal of Economics,* 50(1): 36–67; T. Mott (2000). Kenneth Boulding, 1910–1993. *The Economic Journal,* 110(464): F430–44.
136 The idea is widely attributed to Kenneth Boulding (1966), although Arndt (1978, p. 139) notes that Ward (1966, p. 17) attributed the term to the architect Buckminster Fuller but provided no reference for doing so: K. Boulding (1966). The Economics of the Coming Spaceship Earth; B. Ward (1966). *Space Ship Earth.* London: Hamish Hamilton; H. W. Arndt (1978). *The Rise and Fall of Economic Growth.*
137 K. Boulding (1966). The Economics of the Coming Spaceship Earth, p. 8.
138 Ibid., pp. 5–6.
139 H. E. Daly (1973). Introduction. In H. E. Daly (ed.), *Toward a Steady-State Economy.* San Francisco: W. H. Freeman and Co.
140 C. Clark (1962). On Growthmanship. *Business Horizons,* 5(1): 35–42.
141 S. Belardinelli and T. Distefano (2022). Back to the Future. Herman Daly: The Economy as a Common Good: https://ilbolive.unipd.it/it/news/back-future-herman-daly-economy-common-good

142 Daly co-founded the International Society of Ecological Economics. H. E. Daly (1977). *Steady-State Economics*. San Francisco, CA: Freeman.
143 E. J. Mishan (1967). *The Costs of Economic Growth*. London: Staples Press.
144 E. J. Mishan (1971). Limits of Economic Growth. In E. Goldsmith (ed.), *Can Britain Survive*. London: Tom Stacey.
145 W. D. Nordhaus and J. Tobin (1973). Is Growth Obsolete? In Milton Moss (ed.), *The Measurement of Economic and Social Performance*. New York: NBER; W. Beckerman (1974). *In Defence of Economic Growth*. London: Jonathan Cape.
146 D. H. Meadows, et al. (1972). *The Limits to Growth*; D. L. Meadows, et al. (1974). *Dynamics of Growth in a Finite World*. Cambridge, MA: Wright-Allen Press.
147 J. W. Forrester (1973). *World Dynamics*, 2nd edition. Cambridge, MA: Wright-Allen Press, p. 2.
148 Ibid., p. 2.
149 U. Bardi (2011). *The Limits of Growth Revisited*.
150 Coincidentally, Forrester was following the approach of Raymond Pearl discussed previously (applying a logistic curve) but Pearl is not cited by Forrester.
151 D. H. Meadows, et al. (1972). *The Limits to Growth*.
152 P. Sabin (2013). *The Bet*.
153 J. Robert Oppenheimer (1904–67), Leo Szilard (18981964), James Franck (1882–1964), and Albert Einstein (1879–1955).
154 D. Kaiser and B. Wilson (2015). American Scientists as Public Citizens: 70 years of the Bulletin of the Atomic Scientists. *Bulletin of the Atomic Scientists*, 71(1): 13–25.
155 B. Nelson (1975). Bulletin of the Atomic Scientists: Thirty Years of Clockwatching. *Science*, 190: 1070–3.
156 P. D. Slaney (2012). Eugene Rabinowitch, the Bulletin of the Atomic Scientists, and the Nature of Scientific Internationalism in the Early Cold War. *Historical Studies in the Natural Sciences*, 42(2): 114–42.
157 B. Nelson (1975). Bulletin of the Atomic Scientists: Thirty years of Clockwatching.
158 D. Kaiser and B. Wilson (2015). American Scientists as Public Citizens: 70 Years of the Bulletin of the Atomic Scientists.
159 D. Winstanley (1981). The Greenhouse Effect. *Bulletin of the Atomic Scientists*, 37(8): 38–9.
160 D. R. Inglis (1971). Nuclear Energy and the Malthusian Dilemma. *Bulletin of the Atomic Scientists*, 27(2): 14–18.
161 N. deNevers (1971). Another Approach to Population Control? *Bulletin of the Atomic Scientists*, 27(3): 34.
162 J. W. Gofman (1971). Nuclear Power and Ecocide: An Adversary View of New Technology. *Bulletin of the Atomic Scientists*, 27(7): 28–32.
163 G. Feinberg (1971). Survival? Yes. But in What Form? *Bulletin of the Atomic Scientists*, 27(5): 27–30.
164 M. Schoijet (1999). Limits to Growth and the Rise of Catastrophism. *Environmental History*, 4(4): 515–30.
165 R. S. Berry (1972). Reflections on "The Limits to Growth". *Bulletin of the Atomic Scientists*, 28(9): 25–7.

166 G. Hardin (1972). We Live on a Spaceship. *Bulletin of the Atomic Scientists*, 28(9): 22–5.
167 R. S. Berry (1972). Reflections on "The Limits to Growth"; W. D. Nordhaus (1992). Lethal Model 2: The Limits to Growth Revisited. *Brookings Pap Econ Act*, 2: 1–59.
168 R. S. Berry (1972). Reflections on "The Limits to Growth"; P. H. Abelson (1972). Limits to Growth. *Science*, 175: 4027.
169 S. Jacobsen (1972). Gunnar Myrdal Comments on: America's Image, Black Rebellion, Limits to Growth and Population Control. *Bulletin of the Atomic Scientists*, 28(9): 5–7.
170 E. K. Fedorov (1972). The Interaction of Man and the Environment. *Bulletin of the Atomic Scientists*, 28(2): 5–10.
171 C. Kaysen (1972). The Computer That Printed out W*O*L*F*. *Foreign Affairs*, 50(4): 660–8.
172 H. S. D. Cole, C. Freeman, M. Jahoda and K. L. R. Pavitt (1973). *Thinking About the Future: A Critique of the Limits to Growth*. Sussex: Sussex University Press; H. S. Cole, C. Freeman, M. Jahoda and K. L. R. Pavitt (1973). *Models of Doom: A Critique of the Limits to Growth.*
173 H. S. D. Cole (1973). The Structure of World Models. In H. S. D. Cole, C. Freeman, M. Jahoda and K. L. R. Pavitt (eds), *Thinking About the Future: A Critique of the Limits to Growth*. Sussex: Sussex University Press, p. 31.
174 Ibid.
175 H. S. D. Cole and R. C. Curnow (1973). "Backcasting" with the World Dynamics Models. *Nature*, 243: 63–5.
176 T. W. Oerlemans, M. M. J. Tellings and H. DeVries (1973). World Dynamics: Social Feedback May Give Hope for the Future. *Nature*, 238(4): 251–5; J. Salerno (1973). Sensitivity in the World Dynamics Model. *Nature*, 244: 488–92.
177 J. Forrester (1973). *World Dynamics*, 2nd edition.
178 R. M. Solow (2009). Does Growth Have a Future? Does Growth Theory Have a Future?
179 R. M. Solow (1973). Is the End of the World at Hand? *Challenge*, 16(1): 39–50; Robert Solow was infamous for using his dry humour rather than engaging in debates, although such an approach may come across as hubristic to those unaccustomed to Solow's personality: R. Mochrie (2024). *How to Think Like an Economist*.
180 R. M. Solow (1973). Is the End of the World at Hand? p. 39.
181 J. Forrester (1973). *World Dynamics*, p. 142.
182 W. D. Nordhaus (1973). World Dynamics: Measurement without Data. *Economic Journal*, 83(332): 1156–83.
183 W. D. Nordhaus (1992). Lethal Model 2.
184 R. M. Solow (1974). The Economics of Resources or the Resources of Economics. *American Economic Review*, 64(2): 1–14.
185 See the symposium on the Economics of Exhaustible Resources published in 1974: *Review of Economic Studies*, 41.
186 R. M. Solow (1974). Intergenerational Equity and Exhaustible Resources; J. M. Hartwick (1977). Intergenerational Equity and the Investing of Rents from Exhaustible Resources.
187 W. D. Nordhaus (1992). Lethal Model 2.

188 M. Weitzman (1999). Pricing the Limits to Growth. *Quarterly Journal of Economics*, 114(2): 691–706.
189 It is alleged that Forrester was not given a right of reply to the Nordhaus critique by the *Economic Journal*: M. Myrtveit (2005). The World Model Controversy. Working Papers in System Dynamics. *Bergen Open Research Archive.*
190 Trends in Atmospheric Carbon Dioxide (CO2), National Oceanic and Atmospheric Administration. https://gml.noaa.gov/ccgg/trends/
191 D. H. Meadows, et al. (1972). *Limits to Growth*, pp. 73–4.
192 K. Boulding (1966). The Economics of the Coming Spaceship Earth.
193 P. C. Bobbitt (2007). Walt Rostow, 7 October 1916 – 13 February 2003. p. 481.
194 W. W. Rostow (1978). *World Economy*, p. 574–5.
195 A. W. Lewis (1955). *The Theory of Economic Growth. Appendix: Is Economic Growth Desirable?*. London: George Allen & Unwin.
196 M. Chick (2019). *Changing Times: Economics, Policies, and Resource Allocation in Britain since 1951*. Oxford: Oxford University Press.
197 Declaration of the United Nations Conference on the Human Environment. 16 June 1972. http://undocs.org/en/A/CONF.48/14/Rev.1
198 J. A. Du Pisani (2006). Sustainable Development – Historical Roots of the Concept. *Environmental Sciences*, 3(2): 83–96.
199 N. Nunn (2007). Historical Legacies: A Model Linking Africa's Past to Its Current Underdevelopment. *Journal of Development Economics*, 83: 171.
200 W. Easterly and R. Levine (1997). Africa's Growth Tragedy: Policies and Ethnic Divisions. *The Quarterly Journal of Economics*, 112(4): 1203–50.
201 E. Akyeampong, R. H. Bates, N. Nunn and J. Robinson (eds) (2014). *Africa's Development in Historical Perspective*. Cambridge: Cambridge University Press.
202 D. Acemoglu, S. Johnson and J. A. Robinson (2001). The Colonial Origins of Comparative Development: An Empirical Investigation; W. Easterly and R. Levine (2003). Tropics, Germs, and Crops: How Endowments Influence Economic Development. *Journal of Monetary Economics*, 50: 3–39.
203 D. Acemoglu and J. A. Robinson (2012). *Why Nations Fail.*
204 Tertullian (c. 203). *A Treatise on the Soul*. Translated by Peter Holmes. Chapter xxx. From The Tertullian Project: A Collection of Material Ancient and Modern About the Ancient Christian Latin Writer Tertullian and His Writings. https://www.tertullian.org/anf/anf03/anf03-22.htm #P2560_840932
205 C. I. Jones (2022). The End of Economic Growth? Unintended Consequence of a Declining Population. *American Economic Review*, 112(11): 3489–527.
206 J. Fernández-Villaverde (2024). Economic Growth and the Demographic Future of Humanity. https://cehd.uchicago.edu/wp-content/uploads/2024/10/Slides_Austin.pdf
207 J. Rockström, W. Steffen, et al. (2009). Planetary Boundaries: Exploring the Safe Operating Space for Humanity. *Ecology and Society*, 14(2): 32.
208 D. H. Meadows, et al. (1972). *The Limits to Growth*, Endnote 10, p. 52.
209 Ibid., p. 171.
210 M. Beck and B. Kewell (2014). *Risk.*

211 U. Bardi (2011). *The Limits of Growth Revisited.*
212 D. C. Lane (2007). The Power of the Bond between Cause and Effect: Jay Wright Forrester and the Field of System Dynamics. *System Dynamics Review*, 23: 95–118.
213 C. L. Sabine, et al. (2004). The Oceanic Sink for Anthropogenic CO2. *Science*, 305(5682): 367–71; J. G. Canadell and M. R. Raupach (2008). Managing Forests for Climate Change Mitigation. *Science*, 320(5882): 1456–7; P. Friedlingstein, et al. (2025). Global Carbon Budget 2024. *Earth System Science Data*, 17(3): 96–1039.
214 While a range of scenarios were discussed by Rothstein et al. (2004a), such as risks from nanotechnology and interstellar risk, Rothstein et al.'s (2004b) summary of the 'rethinking doomsday' articles in the 2004 volume primarily related to nuclear risks: L. Rothstein, C. Auer and J. Siegel (2004). Doomsday for the 21st Century. *Bulletin of the Atomic Scientists*, 60(1): 38–9; L. Rothstein, C. Auer and J. Siegel (2004). Rethinking Doomsday. *Bulletin of the Atomic Scientists*, 60(6): 36–73; When the remit of the clock was changed in 2007 the *Bulletin* covered a range of views, including leading figures in the GCR community: R. H. Socolow (2007). Facing New Unknowns. *Bulletin of the Atomic Scientists*, 63(1): 45–6.

Chapter Five

1 S. Johnson (1791). *A Journey to the Western Islands of Scotland: A New Edition*. London: A. Strahan and T. Cadell.
2 P. Samuelson (1970). *Economics*, 8th edition. New York: McGraw-Hill.
3 P. Samuelson (1970). *Economics*; L. M. Smith (2000). A Study of Paul A. Samuelson's Economics: Making Economics Accessible to Students. PhD thesis, Massey University, New Zealand.
4 N. G. Mankiew (2010) *Macroeconomics*, 9th edition and 10th edition (2019). New York: Macmillan.
5 F. Calderoni (2014). Mythical Numbers and the Proceeds of Organised Crime: Estimating Mafia Proceeds in Italy. *Global Crime*, 15(1): 138–63; P. Restrepo-Echavarria (2014). Macroeconomic Volatility: The Role of the Informal Economy. *European Economic Review*, 70: 454–69; G György and P. Van de Ven (2014). The Non-observed Economy in the System of National Accounts. *Statistics Brief*, 18(1): 1–12.
6 D. Coyle (2014). *GDP: A Brief but Affectionate History*. Princeton: Princeton University Press.
7 D. Coyle (2025). *The Measure of Progress: Counting What Really Matters.*
8 A. Cairncross (1988). The Development of Economic Statistics as an Influence on Theory and Policy. In D. Ironmonger, J. O. N. Perkins and T. Van Hoa (eds), *National Income and Economic Progress: Essays in Honour of Colin Clark*. New York: St Martin's Press.
9 A. Cairncross (1998). *Living with the Century*. Bath: Redwood books.
10 C. Clark (1940). *The Conditions of Economic Progress*. London: Macmillan & Co., p. ix.

11 I. Hacking (1990). *The Taming of Chance*. Cambridge: Cambridge University Press.
12 T. M. Potter (1986). *The Rise of Statistical Thinking*. Princeton: Princeton University Press.
13 J. Sinclair (1798). *The Statistical Account of Scotland*. Vol. 20. Edinburgh: William Creech, p. xiii.
14 J. Sinclair (1831). *Correspondence of the Right Honourable Sir John Sinclar, Bart. With Reminiscences of the Most Distinguished Characters Who Have Appeared in Great Britain, and in Foreign Countries, During the Last Fifty Years*. Vol. 1. London: Henry Colburn and Richard Bentley, pp. 389–90.
15 R. L. Plackett (1986). The Old Statistical Account. *Journal of the Royal Statistical Society*, 149(3): 247–51.
16 W. Playfair (1801). *The Commercial and Political Atlas, Representing by Means of Stained Copper-plate Charts, the Progress of the Commerce, Revenues, Expenditure, and Debts of England*. London: T. Burton.
17 James R. Beniger and Dorothy L. Robyn (1978). Quantitative Graphics in Statistics: A Brief History. *The American Statistician*, 32(1): 1–11.
18 H. W. Arndt (1978). *The Rise and Fall of Economic Growth*; S. J. Macekura (2020). *The Mismeasure of Progress*.
19 V. John (1883). The Term "Statistics": An Etymologically Historical Sketch. *Journal of the London Statistical Society*, 46(4): 656–79.
20 A. Wakefield (2013). Cameralism: A German Alternative to Mercantilism. In P. J. Stern and C. Wennerlind (eds), *Mercantilism Reimagined: Political Economy in Early Modern Britain and Its Empire*. Oxford: Oxford University Press.
21 P. F. Lazarsfeld (1961). Notes on the History of Quantification in Sociology – Trends, Sources, and Problems. *Isis*, 52(2): 277–333; Translation of anecdote from V. John (1884). *Geschichte der Statistic*. Stuttgart: Verlag von Ferdinand Enke.
22 C. Wiggins and M. L. Jones (2023). *How Data Happened: A History from the Age of Reason to the Age of Algorithms*. New York: W. W. Norton & Co.
23 Ibid.
24 M. Kranzberg (1986). Technology and History: 'Kranzberg's Laws'. *Technology and Culture*, 27(3): 544–60.
25 E. Higgs (2004). *Life, Death and Statistics: Civil Registration, Censuses and the Work of the General Register Office, 1836–1952*. Hertfordshire: Local Population Studies.
26 M. J. Cullen (1975). *The Statistical Movement in Early Victorian Britain: The Foundations of Empirical Social Research*. Bristol: Harvester Press; C. H. Hull (1896). Graunt or Petty? *Political Science Quarterly*, 11(1): 105–32.
27 A. Morabia (2013). Epidemiology's 350th Anniversary: 1662–2012. *Epidemiology*, 24(2): 179–83; A. Morabia (2013). Observations Made Upon the Bills of Mortality. *BMJ*, 346: e8640.
28 William Petty was trained as a physician, served as a professor of anatomy at Oxford and a fellow of Brasenose College, and later held administrative roles in Ireland.
29 Although published anonymously, the work was later attributed to Petty posthumously: W. Petty. *The Political Anatomy of Ireland*. London, 1691, reprinted Shannon, 1970.

30 T. Barnard (2013). Petty, Sir William (1623–1687), Natural Philosopher and Administrator in Ireland. In *Oxford Dictionary of National Biography*. Oxford: Oxford University Press.
31 A. Maddison (2004). Quantifying and Interpreting World Development: Macromeasurment before and after Colin Clark. *Australian Economic History Review*, 44(1): 1–34.
32 T. M. Potter (1986). *The Rise of Statistical Thinking*, p. 20.
33 P. F. Lazarsfeld (1961). Notes on the History of Quantification in Sociology – Trends, Sources, and Problems.
34 ONS (2016). The Modern Census. https://www.ons.gov.uk/census/2011census/howourcensusworks/aboutcensuses/censushistory/themoderncensus
35 A. B. Wolfe (1932). Population Censuses before 1790. *Journal of the American Statistical Society*, 27(180): 357–70.
36 A. Maddison (2007). *Contours of the World Economy, 1-2030: Essays in Macro-economic History*. Oxford: Oxford University Press.
37 Theodore M. Potter (1986). *The Rise of Statistical Thinking*, pp. 23, 37.
38 C. Babbage (1832/2009). *On the Economy of Machinery and Manufactures*. Reprint. Cambridge: Cambridge University Press.
39 Letter dated 7 February 1891: K. Pearson (1924). *The Life, Letters, and labours of Francis Galton. Volume II: Researches of Middle Life*. Cambridge: Cambridge University Press, pp. 416–18.
40 M. J. Cullen (1975). *The Statistical Movement in Early Victorian Britain*.
41 Civil registration was first introduced in England in 1837, followed by Scotland in 1854, and Ireland in 1864: E. Higgs (2004). *Life, Death and Statistics*; A. Cameron (2007). The Establishment of Civil Registration in Scotland. *History Journal*, 50(2): 377–95; E. McLaughlin and N. Whelehan (2024). Rethinking the Geography of Distress in Nineteenth-century Ireland: Excess Mortality and the Land War. *Heriot-Watt Accountancy, Economics and Finance Working Papers*, 2024-04.
42 E. Higgs (2004). *Life, Death and Statistics*; British Parliamentary Papers (1833). *Report from the Select Committee on Parochial Registration*. (669), question 960, 998.
43 T. M. Potter (1986). *The Rise of Statistical Thinking*.
44 Statistical Society of London (1838). Introduction. *Journal of the Statistical Society of London*, 1(1): 1–5.
45 A. Sauerbeck (1886). Prices of Commodities and the Precious Metals. *Journal of the Statistical Society of London*, 49(3): 581–648; A. Sauerbeck (1929). Obituary. *Journal of the Royal Statistical Society*, 92(2): 300.
46 E. Higgs (2003). *The Information State in England: The Central Collection of Information on Citizens since 1500*. London: Bloomsbury; E. Higgs (2004). *Life, Death and Statistics*; J. M. Eyler (2021). William Farr (1807–1883). *Dictionary of National Biography*.
47 W. Farr (1864). Opening Address of the President of Section F (Economic Science and Statistics), of the British Association for the Advancement of Science, at the Thirty-Fourth Meeting, at Bath, in September 1864. *Journal of the Statistical Society of London*, 27(4): 459–78.
48 A. Marshall (1920). *Principles of Economics*.
49 M. G. Mulhall (1880). *The Progress of the World in Arts, Agriculture, Commerce, Manufactures, Instruction, Railways, and Public Wealth*. London:

Edward Stanford; M. G. Mulhall (1881). *Balance-Sheet of the World for Ten Years 1870–1889*. London: Edward Standard; M. G. Mulhall (1896). *Industries and Wealth of Nations*. London: Longmans, Green and Co.

50 M. G. Mulhall (1880). *The Progress of the World in Arts, Agriculture, Commerce, Manufactures, Instruction, Railways, and Public Wealth*; M. G. Mulhall (1896). *Industries and Wealth of Nations*.

51 M. G. Mulhall (1881). *Balance-Sheet of the World for Ten Years 1870–1889*. Tables 18, 20 and 21; M. G. Mulhall (1884). *Dictionary of Statistics*. London: Routledge, pp. 469–74; M. M. Mulhall (1892). *The Dictionary of Statistics*. London: Routledge.

52 M. G. Mulhall (1896). *Industries and Wealth of Nations*, pp. 11–12.

53 A. L. Bowley (1953). August D. Webb 1880–1953. *Journal of the Royal Statistical Society. Series A*, 116(1): 104.

54 List of Fellows (1895). *Journal of the Royal Statistical Society*, 58: 10–51; M. de Foville (1887). The Abuse of Statistics. *Journal of the Royal Statistical Society*, 50(4): 703–8.

55 R. P. F. (1897). Review of Industries and Wealth of Nations by Michael G. Mulhall. *Publications of the American Statistical Association*, 5(30): 316–18; R. Mayo-Smith (1897). Review of Industries and Wealth of Nations by Michael G. Mulhall. *Political Science Quarterly*, 12(2): 351.

56 H. Gray Funkhouser (1937). Historical Development of the Graphical Representation of Statistical Data. *Osiris*, 3: 269–404.

57 Review (1912). The New Dictionary of Statistics by Augustus D. Webb. *Journal of Political Economy*, 20(1): 98–9.

58 R. Giffen (1903). The Wealth of the Empire, and How it Should Be Used. *Journal of the Royal Statistical Society*, 66(3): 582–98.

59 Studenski was an 'early bird'. He was one of the very first pilots before he retrained as an academic economist. https://www.earlyaviators.com/estudens.htm

60 R. P. F. (1897). Review of Industries and Wealth of Nations by Michael G. Mulhall.

61 A. Meitzen and R. P. Falkner (1891). History, Theory, and Technique of Statistics. Part Second: Theory and Technique of Statistics. *The Annals of the American Academy of Political and Social Science*, 1(2): Part 2.

62 P. Smith and S. Penneck (2007). 100 Years of the Census of Production in the UK. *Economic & Labour Market Review*, 1: 18–24.

63 P. Studenski (1958). *The Income of Nations: Theory, Measurement, and Analysis: Past and Present; a Study in Applied Economics and Statistics*. New York: New York University Press; B. Haig (2006). Sir Timothy Coghlan and the Development of National Accounts. *History of Political Economy*, 38(2): 339–75.

64 S. Fabricant (1984). Toward a Firmer Basis of Economic Policy: The Founding of the National Bureau of Economic Research. https://www.nber.org/sites/default/files/2021-10/sfabricantrev.pdf

65 D. Coyle (2014). *GDP*.

66 S. Kuznets (1934). National Income, 1929–1932. *National Bureau of Economic Research*, Bulletin 49.

67 M. Friedman (1990). Lunch in Honor of Individuals and Institutions Participating in the First Income and Wealth Conference (December 1936–

January 1937). In Ernst R. Berndt and J. E. Triplett (eds), *Fifty Years of Economic Measurement: The Jubilee of the Conference on Research in Income and Wealth*. Chicago: University of Chicago Press.

68 M. A. Copeland (1937). Concepts of National Income. In *Studies in Income and Wealth*. Vol. 1. New York: National Bureau of Economic Research.

69 C. S. Carson (1990). The Conference on Research in Income and Wealth: The Early Years. In Ernst R. Berndt and J. E. Triplett (eds), *Fifty Years of Economic Measurement*. Chicago: University of Chicago Press.

70 C. Warburton (1937). Accounting Methodology in the Measurement of National Income. In *Studies in Income and Wealth*, Vol. 1. New York: National Bureau of Economic Research.

71 H. W. Arndt (1988). Colin Clark. In D. Ironmonger, J. O. N. Perkins and T. Van Hoa (eds), *National Income and Economic Progress*. New York: St Martin's Press.

72 J. M. Keynes (1940). *How to Pay for the War*. London: Macmillan and Co.

73 J. M. Keynes (1936). *General Theory*.

74 Clark shared many similarities with Petty in that he had studied chemistry at Brasenose College, Oxford, and he was self-taught in economics, and he also spent time as a government administrator. Although Petty was a direct influence, Clark had some indirect Smithian influences as well. The economist Lionel Robbins (1898–1984) recalled that, as a disillusioned chemistry student at Oxford, Clark had attended meetings of the Adam Smith discussion society and 'brought sheaves of statistical matter' that returned the theoretical discussions 'down to earth'. Early in his career Clark had a short stint as research assistant to Allyn Young at the London School of Economics, whose research had focused on the increasing returns arguments from Adam Smith (discussed in Chapter 3). Clark maintained a Smithian influence on his approach to economic growth by focusing on output per worker: L. Robbins (1971). *Autobiography of an Economist*. London: Macmillan & Co., p. 119; A. Maddison (2004). Quantifying and Interpreting World Development.

75 C. Clark (1932). *The National Income, 1924–1931*. London: Macmillan & Co.

76 A. L. Bowley (1937). Review of National Income and Outlay. *Economica*, 4(15): 350–3.

77 C. Clark (1937). *National Income and Outlay*. London: Macmillan & Co.

78 E. F. Denison (1947). Report on Tripartite Discussions of National Income Measurement. In *Studies in Income and Wealth*. Vol. 10. New York: NBER.

79 R. Stone (1947). Definition and Measurement of the National Income and Related Totals. In *UN Measurement of National Income and the Construction of Social Accounts*. Geneva: United Nations.

80 This would become a sticking point in the Bretton-Woods era when countries operated under fixed exchange rates and were forced to play close attention to trade imbalances.

81 UN (1947). *Measurement of National Income and the Construction of Social Accounts*: Report of the sub-committee on National Income Statistics of the League of Nations Committee of Statistical Experts, p. 18.

82 Ibid., Table 3.

83 D. Coyle (2014). *GDP*; See the UN historic versions of SNAs https://unstats.un.org/unsd/nationalaccount/hsna.asp

84 See https://unstats.un.org/unsd/nationalaccount/SNAUpdate/2025/chapters.asp
85 H. Henderson (1996). What's Next in the Great Debate About Measuring Wealth and Progress? *Challenge*, 39(6): 50–6.
86 A. Maddison (2005). Measuring Performance in the World Economic Performance, 1500–2001. *Review of Income and Wealth*, 51(1): 1–35.
87 I. B. Kravis (2018). Gilbert, Milton (1909–1979). In *The New Palgrave Dictionary of Economics*. London: Palgrave Macmillan, p. 5309.
88 A. Maddison (2005). Measuring Performance in the World Economic Performance, 1500–2001.
89 R. F. Fogel (2001). Simon S. Kuznets. *Biological Memoirs*. Vol. 79. Washington, DC: National Academies Press; C. S. Carson (1999). 50-Year Retrospective of the IARIW: The Early Years. *Review of Income and Wealth*, 45(3): 379–96.
90 H. Boss (1986). Origins of the Soviet Material Product System. *Canadian Slavonic Papers*, 28(3): 243–65.
91 A. Maddison (2005). Measuring Performance in the World Economic Performance, 1500–2001.
92 J. van Heijster and D. DeRock (2022). How GDP Spread to China: The Experimental Diffusion of Macroeconomic Measurement. *Review of International Political Economy*, 29(1): 65–87.
93 M. Skousen (1997). The Perseverance of Paul Samuelson's Economics. *Journal of Economic Perspectives*, 11(2): 137–52; D. M. Levy and S. J. Peart (2011). Soviet Growth and American Textbooks: An Endogenous Past. *Journal of Economic Behavior & Organization*, 78: 110–25; D. M Levy and S. Peart (2016). *Escape from Democracy: The Role of Experts and the Public in Economic Policy*. Cambridge: Cambridge University Press.
94 Statistical Bureau of the People's Republic of China and The Institute of Economic Research of Hitosubashi University (1997). The Historical National Accounts of the People's Republic of China, 1952–1995. https://www.ier.hit-u.ac.jp/COE/Japanese/online_data/china/china.htm
95 P. Samuelson (1970). *Economics*, 8th edition; R. J. Gordon (1984). *Macroeconomics*, 3rd edition. Boston: Little, Brown, and Co.
96 E. Dennison (1967). *Why Growth Rates Differ: Postwar Experience in Nine Western Countries*. Washington, DC: Brookings Institution.
97 Recent work has attempted to derive distributional national accounts, for example see: T. Piketty, E. Saez and G. Zucman (2018). Distributional National Accounts: Methods and Estimates for the United States. The *Quarterly Journal of Economics*, 133(2): 553–609.
98 J. E. Stiglitz, A. Sen and J. P. Fitoussi (2009). *Report by the Commission on the Measurement of Economic Performance and Social Progress*.
99 A. Maddison (2005). Measuring Performance in the World Economic Performance, 1500–2001.
100 P. McCarthy (2013). National Accounts Framework for International Comparisons: GDP Compilation and Breakdown Process. In *Measuring the Real Size of the World Economy: Framework, Methodology, and Results of the International Comparison Program – ICP*. Washington, DC: World Bank.
101 K. Dynan and L. Sheiner (2024). GDP as a Measure of Economic Well-Being. In M. R. Reinsdorf and L. Sheiner (eds), *The Measure of Economies:*

Measuring Productivity in an Age of Technological Change. Chicago: University of Chicago Press.

102 Economic Division (2018). GDP and 'Modified GNI' – Explanatory Note. https://assets.gov.ie/4910/181218123252-71a2c297f26b419fa3696d7349e3e788.pdf

103 A. Maddison (2004). Quantifying and Interpreting World Development.

104 C. Clark (1940). *The Conditions of Economic Progress*.

105 E. Rothbarth (1941). Review: The Conditions of Economic Progress by Colin Clark. *The Economic Journal*, 51(201): 120–4.

106 R. C. Geary (1958). A Note on the Comparison of Exchange Rates and Purchasing Power Between Countries. *Journal of the Royal Statistical Society. Series A*, 121(1): 97–9; S. H. Khamis (1984). On Aggregation Methods for International Comparisons. *Review of Income and Wealth*, 30(2): 185–205.

107 I. B. Kravis (1984). Comparative Studies of National Income and Prices. *Journal of Economic Literature*, 22(1): 1–39; A. Deaton (2010). Measuring Development: Different Data, Different Conclusions? In Measure for Measure – How Well Do We Measure Development? *Proceedings of the 8th AFD-EUDN Conference, 2010*: https://www.afd.fr/en/ressources/measure-measure-how-well-do-we-measure-development-proceedings-8th-afd-eudn-conference-2010

108 This is sometimes debated, but most major international institutions rank China as the largest economy by purchasing power parity (PPP). For example, the US CIA Factbook estimates China's 2024 PPP-adjusted GDP at approximately $33.6 trillion, compared to roughly $25.7 trillion for the United States: https://www.cia.gov/the-world-factbook/field/real-gdp-purchasing-power-parity/country-comparison/

109 IMF (2024). IMF Executive Board Concludes 2023 Article IV Consultation with Equatorial Guinea. *Press Release no 24/10*. https://www.imf.org/en/News/Articles/2024/01/16/pr2410-gnq-imf-exec-board-concludes-2023-article-iv-consultation-with-equatorial-guinea

110 P. Deane (1946). Measuring National Income in Colonial Territories. In *Studies in Income and Wealth*. Vol. 8. New York: NBER.

111 S. J. Macekura (2020). *The Mismeasure of Progress*.

112 P. Deane (1948). *The Measurement of Colonial National Incomes: An Experiment*. Cambridge: Cambridge University Press.

113 S. J. Macekura (2020). *The Mismeasure of Progress*.

114 US Senate (1934). *National Income, 1929–32*. Senate document no. 124, p. 7.

115 J. R. Meyer (1974). Comment on Nordhaus and Tobin. Is Growth Obsolete?

116 N. Oulton (2004). Productivity versus Welfare: Or GDP versus Weitzman's NDP. *Review of Income and Wealth*, 50(3): 329–55; N. Oulton (2012). Hooray for GDP! *Centre for Economic Performance*. Occasional Paper 30; e.g., N. G. Mankiew and M. P. Taylor (2014). *Economics*, 3rd edition. Hampshire: Cengage Learning.

117 N. Z. Muller (2019). Long-run Environmental Accounting in the U.S. *Economy NBER, Working Paper*, 25910.

118 N. Crafts (2009). Solow and Growth Accounting: A Perspective from Quantitative Economic History. *History of Political Economy*, 41 (annual supplement): 200–20.

119 H. W. Arndt (1987). *Development.*
120 S. Kuznets (1966). *Modern Economic Growth: Rate, Structure, and Spread.* New Haven: Yale University Press; S. Kuznets (1971). *Economic Growth of Nations. Total Output and Production Structure.* Cambridge, MA: Harvard University Press.
121 W. W. Rostow (1971). Review of Economic Growth of Nations. Total Output and Production Structure. *Political Science Quarterly*, 86(4): 654–7.
122 Feinstein had qualified as a chartered accountant before undertaking academic studies which helped equip him with the tools for national accounting: A. Offer (2008). Charles Hilliard Feinstein 1932–2004. *Proceedings of the British Academy*, 153: 189–212.
123 Charles H. Feinstein (1972). *National Income, Expenditure and Output of the United Kingdom, 1855–1965.* Cambridge: Cambridge University Press.
124 P. Deane and W. A. Cole (1962). *British Economic Growth, 1688–1959: Trends and Structure.* Cambridge: Cambridge University Press.
125 B. R. Mitchell and P. Deane (1962). *Abstract of Historical Statistics.* Cambridge: Cambridge University Press.
126 Maddison had studied at the University of Cambridge at the end of the War and later worked in the economics division at the OEEC/OECD and planning agencies in various countries: A. Maddison (1994). Confessions of a Chiffrephile. *BNL Quarterly Review*, 47(189): 123–65.
127 A. Maddison (1972). Explaining Economic Growth. *PSL Quarterly Review*, 25(102): 211–62. A. Maddison (1983). A Comparison of Levels of GDP Per Capita in Developed and Developing Countries, 1700–1980. *The Journal of Economic History*, 43(1): 27–41.
128 A. Maddison (1964). *Economic Growth in the West. Comparative Experience in Europe and North America.* New York: Twentieth Century Fund; A. Maddison (1982). *Phases of Capitalist Development.* Oxford: Oxford University Press.
129 A. Maddison (2001). *The World Economy: A Millennial Perspective.* Paris: OECD.
130 K. E. Boulding (1964). Review of Angus Maddison's Economic Growth in the West: Comparative experience in Europe and North America *Science*, 146(3648): 1151–2.
131 A. Maddison (2004). Quantifying and Interpreting World Development.
132 V Smil (2019). *Growth.*
133 G. Clark (2009). Review of Angus Maddison's Contours of the World Economy. *Journal of Economic History*, 69(4): 1156–61; T. W. Guinnane (2023). We Do Not Know the Population of Every Country in the World for the Past Two Thousand Years. *Journal of Economic History*, 83(3): 912–38.
134 A. Maddison (2007). *Contours of the World Economy, 1-2030: Essays in Macro-economic History.*
135 A. Maddison (2001). *The World Economy: A Millennial Perspective*; J. Bolt and J. L. Van Zanden (2014). The Maddison Project: Collaborative Research on Historical National Accounts. *Economic History Review*, 67(3): 627–51; A. Deaton and A. Heston (2010). Understanding PPPs and PPP-based National Accounts. *American Economic Journal: Macroeconomics*, 2(4): 1–35.

136 Maddison Project Database, version 2020. J. Bolt and J. Luiten van Zanden (2020). Maddison Style Estimates of the Evolution of the World Economy. A New 2020 Update; MPD version 2023: J. Bolt and J. Luiten van Zanden (2024). Maddison Style Estimates of the Evolution of the World Economy: A New 2023 Update *Journal of Economic Surveys*, 39(2): 1–41.
137 F. Bourguignon and C. Morrisson (2002). Inequality Among World Citizens: 1820–1992. *American Economic Review*, 92(4): 727–4; B. Milanovic (2024). The Three Eras of Global Inequality, 1820–2020 with the Focus on the Past Thirty Years. *World Development*, 177: 106516.
138 See the extensive critique in: V Smil (2019). *Growth*.
139 S. Broadberry, B. M. S. Campbell, A. Klein, M. Overton and B. van Leeuwen (2015). *British Economic Growth, 1270–1870*. Cambridge: Cambridge University Press.
140 D. Coyle (2015). *GDP*; A. J. Field (2019). *Historical Measures of Economic Output*, Second edition. New York: Springer; Maddison (2004). Quantifying and Interpreting World Development.
141 J. Hicks (1981). Measurement of Capital – In Practice. In *Collected Essays on Economic Theory*. Oxford: Oxford University Press, p. 204.
142 C. R. Hulten (1991). The Measurement of Capital. In E. R. Berndt and H. E. Triplett (eds), *Fifty Years of Economic Measurement*
143 S. Kuznets (1938). On the Measurement of Wealth. In *Studies in Income and Wealth*. Vol. 2. New York: National Bureau of Economic Research.
144 R. W. Goldsmith (1951). A Perpetual Inventory of National Wealth. In *Studies in Income and Wealth*. Vol. 14. New York: National Bureau of Economic Research.
145 R. W. Goldsmith (1950). Measuring National Wealth in a System of Social Accounting. In *Studies in Income and Wealth*. Vol. 12. New York: NBER.
146 R. W. Goldsmith (1951). A Perpetual Inventory of National Wealth.
147 R. W. Goldsmith (1962). *The National Wealth of the United States in the Postwar Period*. Princeton: Princeton University Press.
148 E. Denison (1967). *Why Growth Rates Differ*.
149 A. A. Walters (1966). Incremental Capital-Output Ratios. *The Economic Journal*, 76(304): 818–22.
150 J. W. Kendrick (1961). *Productivity Trends in the United States*. Princeton: Princeton University Press.
151 D. W. Jorgenson (1990). Productivity and Economic Growth. In E. R. Berndt and H. E. Triplett (eds), *Fifty Years of Economic Measurement*.
152 F. Crouzet (ed.) (1972). *Capital Formation in the Industrial Revolution*. London: Methuen & Co.
153 C. Feinstein (1978). Capital Formation in Great Britain. In P. Mathias and M. M. Postan (eds), *Cambridge Economic History of Britain*. Vol. 7. Cambridge: Cambridge University Press.
154 R. E. Gallman (1986). The United States Capital Stock in the Nineteenth Century. In S. L. Engerman and R. E. Gallman (eds), *Long-Term Factors in American Economic Growth*. Chicago: University of Chicago Press; R. E. Gallman and P. W. Rhode (2020). *Capital in the Nineteenth Century*. Chicago: University of Chicago Press.

155 A. Maddison (1995). Standardised Estimates of Fixed Capital Stock: A Six Country Comparison. In *Explaining the Economic Performance of Nations: Essays in Time and Space*. Cheltenham: Edward Elgar.

156 N. Crafts (2009). Solow and Growth Accounting: A Perspective from Quantitative Economic History.

157 N. Crafts and P. Woltjer (2021). Growth Accounting in Economic History: Findings, Lessons, and New Directions. *Journal of Economic Surveys*, 35: 670–96.

158 I. B. Kravis, Z. Kenessey, A. Heston and R. Summers (1975). *A System of International Comparisons of Gross Product and Purchasing Power*. Baltimore: John Hopkins Press.

159 R. Summers, I. B. Kravis and A. Heston (1980). International Comparisons of Real Product and Its Composition: 1950–77. *Review of Income and Wealth*, 26(1): 19–33.

160 R. Summers and A. Heston (1988). A New Set of International Comparisons of Real Product and Price Levels Estimates for 130 Countries, 1950–1985. *Review of Income and Wealth*, 34(1): 1–25; N. G. Mankiew, et al. (1992). A Contribution to the Empirics of Economic Growth.

161 R. Summers and A. Heston (1991). The Penn World Table (Mark 5): An Expanded Set of International Comparisons, 1950–1988. *The Quarterly Journal of Economics*, 106(2): 327–68.

162 R. C. Feenstra, R. Inklaar and M. P. Timmer (2015). The Next Generation of the Penn World Table. *The American Economic Review*, 105(10): 3150–82.

163 OECD (2001). *The Well-Being of Nations: The Role of Human and Social Capital*. Paris: OECD.

164 R. J. Barro and X. Sala-i-Martin (2004). *Economic Growth*, Second edition. Cambridge, MA: MIT Press, Chapter 12.

165 R. Barro and J. W. Lee (1993). International Comparisons of Educational Attainment. *Journal of Monetary Economics*, 32: 363–94; R. Barro and J. W. Lee (2001). International Data on Educational Attainment: Updates and Implications. *Oxford Economic Papers*, 53(3): 541–63; R. Barro and J. W. Lee (2013). A New Data Set of Educational Attainment in the World, 1950–2010. *Journal of Development Economics*, 104: 184–98.

166 T. W. Schulz (1961). Investment in Human Capital. *American Economic Review*, 51(1): 1–17.

167 G. Becker (1964). *Human Capital: A Theoretical and Empirical Analysis with Special Reference to Education*, First edition. New York: NBER.

168 J. S. Nicholson (1891). The Living Capital of the United Kingdom. *The Economic Journal*, 1(1): 95–107; J. R. Walsh (1935). Capital Concept Applied to Man. *The Quarterly Journal of Economics*, 49(2): 255–85; J. W. Kendrick (1976). *The Formation and Stocks of Total Capital*. New York: NBER.

169 D. Jorgenson and B. M. Fraumeni (1989). The Accumulation of Human and Nonhuman Capital, 1948–84. In R. E. Lipsey and H. Stone Tice (eds), *The Measurement of Saving, Investment, and Wealth*. Chicago: University of Chicago Press.

170 E. N. Wolff (2017). US Household Wealth Trends, 1983–2010. In K. Hamilton and C. Hepburn (eds), *National Wealth*.

171 T. Piketty (2014). *Capital in the Twenty-First Century.*

172 F. Cowell, B. Nolan, J. Olivera and P. van Kerm (2017). Wealth, Top Incomes, and Inequality. In K. Hamilton and C. Hepburn (eds), *National Wealth.*

173 V. J. Geloso, P. Magness, J. Moore and P. Schlosser (2022). How Pronounced is the U-Curve? Revisiting Income Inequality in the United States, 1917–60. *Economic Journal*, 132(647): 2366–91.

174 The standard Cobb-Douglas formula is $Y = AK^{\alpha}L^{1-\alpha}$, where Y is output (e.g., GDP), A is total factor productivity, K is capital input, L is the labour input, α is the output elasticity of capital, and $1 - \alpha$ is the output elasticity of labour. The assumption of constant returns implies that $\alpha + (1 - \alpha) = 1$.

175 R. Solow (1963). Discussion of the Paper by Professor Cairncross. In W. W. Rostow (ed.), *The Economics of Take-off into Sustained Growth. Proceedings of a Conference Held by the International Economic Association.* New York: St Martin's Press, p. 437.

176 D. Greasley and J. B. Madsen (2006). Employment and Total Factor Productivity Convergence. *Kyklos*, 59(4): 527–55.

177 R. Gordon (2016). *The Rise and Fall of American Growth: The US Standard of Living since the Civil War.* Princeton: Princeton University Press.

178 D. Vollrath (2020). *Fully Grown: Why a Stagnant Economic is a Sign of Success.* Chicago: University of Chicago Press.

179 C. R. Hulten (2000). Total Factor Productivity: A Short Biography. *NBER* 7471; E. Brynjolfsson, D. Rock and C. Syverson (2017). Artificial Intelligence and the Modern Productivity Paradox: A Clash of Expectations and Statistics. *NBER* 24001; E. Brynjolfsson, D. Rock and C. Syverson (2021). The Productivity J-Curve: How Intangibles Complement General Purpose Technologies. *American Economic Journal: Macroeconomics*, 13(1): 333–72.

180 I. Goldin, P. Koutroumpis, F. Lafond and J. Winkler (2024). Why Is Productivity Slowing Down? *Journal of Economic Literature*, 62: 196–268.

181 Z. F. Hu and M. S. Khan (1997). Why Is China Growing So Fast? *IMF Staff Papers*, 44(1): 103–31.

182 IMF (2015). *Regional Economic Outlook: Asia and Pacific.* Washington, DC: International Monetary Fund; L. Brandt, J. Litwack, E. Mileva, L. Wang, Y. Zhang and L. Zhao (2020). China's Productivity Slowdown and Future Growth Potential. *World Bank Policy Research Working Paper*, 9298.

183 D. Muir, N. Novta and A. Oeking (2024). China's Path to Sustainable and Balance Growth. *IMF Working Paper*, WP/24/239.

184 Chinese productivity is notoriously difficult to estimate. The Conference Board provides two alternative estimates of Chinese TFP growth: one based on official statistics and another using the Wu adjustment (formerly employed in the Penn World Tables). The two approaches lead to sharply different conclusions about the trajectory of Chinese productivity growth: The Conference Board, Total Economy Database 2025, https://www.conference-board.org/topics/total-economy-database#Data; See also: L. C. Lee (2025). China's Total Factor Productivity Is Either Extremely Low or Surging Past the United States. *Asia Policy Institute*, 4 December 2025. https://asiasociety.org/policy-institute/chinas-total-factor-productivity-either-extremely-low-or-surging-past-united-states; and T. Hale (2025). The

growing problem with China's unreliable numbers. *Financial Times,* 18 November 2025.

185 C. I. Jones (2024). The AI Dilemma: Growth versus Existential Risk. *American Economic Review: Insights*, 6(4): 575–90.

186 D. Acemoglu (2024). The Simple Macroeconomics of AI. *NBER Working Paper*, 32487.

187 P. Aghion and S. Bunel (2024). AI and Growth: Where do we Stand? Policy note. https://www.frbsf.org/wp-content/uploads/AI-and-Growth-Aghion-Bunel.pdf

188 E. Mollick (2024). *Co-intelligence: Living and Working with AI.* London: Penguin.

189 R. M. Solow (1987). We'd Better Watch Out. *New York Times Book Review*, 12 July 1987.

190 K. Boulding (1970). Fun and Games with the Gross National Product – The Role of Misleading Indicators in Social Policy. In H. W. Helfrich, Jr (ed.), *The Environmental Crisis: Man's Struggle to Live with Himself.* New Haven: Yale University Press.

191 N. Kaldor (1961). Capital Accumulation and Economic Growth.

192 C. Jones and P. Romer (2010). The New Kaldor Facts.

193 B. Herrendorf, R. Rogerson and Á. Valentinyi (2019). Growth and the Kaldor Facts. *Federal Reserve Bank of St. Louis Review*, Fourth Quarter.

194 R. Floud, R. W. Fogel, B. Harris and S. C. Hong (2011). *The Changing Body: Health, Nutrition, and Human Development in the Western World since 1700.* Cambridge: Cambridge University Press; R. W. Fogel, E. M. Fogel, M. Guglielmo and N. Grotte (2013). *Political Arithmetic: Simon Kuznets and the Empirical Tradition in Economics.* Chicago: University of Chicago Press.

195 P. A. Samuelson (1961). The Evaluation of "Social Income": Capital Formation and Wealth. In F. A. Lutz (ed.), *The Theory of Capital.* New York: Stockton Press; A. Marshall (1920). *Principles of Economics.*

Chapter Six

1 Brundtland Commission (1987). *Our Common Future*, pp. 18, 21.

2 J. J. Warford (1987). *Environment, Growth, and Development.* World Bank Development Committee, number 14. Washington, DC: World Bank; J. J. Warford and R. Ackermann (1988). *Environment and Development: Implementing the World Bank's New Policies.* World Bank Development Committee, number 17. Washington, DC: World Bank.

3 S. J. Macekura (2015). *Of Limits and Growth.*

4 H.R.2494 - International Development and Finance Act of 1989. https://www.congress.gov/bill/101st-congress/house-bill/2494/text/rh

5 R. M. Solow (1986). On the Intergenerational Allocation of Natural Resources.

6 R. M. Solow (1993). An Almost Practical Step toward Sustainability. *Resource Policy*, 19(3): 162–72.

7 World Bank (2018). *The Changing Wealth of Nations 2018: Building a Sustainable Future*. Washington, DC: World Bank; World Bank (2021). *The Changing Wealth of Nations 2021: Managing Assets for the Future*. Washington, DC: World Bank; UNEP (2018). *Inclusive Wealth Report 2018*.

8 J. M. Hartwick (1977). Intergenerational Equity and the Investing of Rents from Exhaustible Resources.

9 D. W. Pearce and J. J. Warford (1993). *World Without End: Economics, Environment, and Sustainable Development*. Washington, DC: World Bank.

10 K. Arrow, P. Dasgupta, L. Goulder, G. Daily, P. Ehrlich, G. Heal, S. Levin, K. G. Maler, S. Schneider, D. Starrett and B. Walker (2004). Are We Consuming too Much? *Journal of Economic Perspectives*, 18(3): 147–72.

11 P. Dasgupta (2025). *On Natural Capital.*

12 P. Dasgupta (2001). *Human Well-Being and the Natural Environment*. Oxford: Oxford University Press; P. Dasgupta (2007). Measuring Sustainable Development: Theory and Application. *Asian Development Review*, 24(1): 1–10.

13 P. Dasgupta (2001). *Human Well-Being and the Natural Environment.*

14 System of Environmental-Economic Accounting 2012 Central Framework. UN, EC, FAO, IMF, OECD, World Bank.

15 E. B. Barbier (2011). *Capitalizing on Nature: Ecosystems as Natural Assets*. Cambridge: Cambridge University Press; E. B. Barbier (2019). The Concept of Natural Capital. *Oxford Review of Economic Policy*, 35(1): 14–36; C. Brandon, K. Brandon, A. Fairbrass and R. Neugarten (2021). Integrating Natural Capital into National Accounts: Three Decades of Promise and Challenge. *Review of Environmental Economics and Policy*, 15(1): 134–53.

16 J. Costanza, et al. (1995). The Value of the World's Ecosystem Services and Natural Capital. *Nature*, 387: 253–60.

17 A. Scott (1955). *Natural Resources: The Economics of Conservation*. Toronto: University of Toronto Press.

18 P. Dasgupta and S. Levin (2023). Economic Factors Underlying Biodiversity Loss.

19 C. Brandon, K. Brandon, A. Fairbrass and R. Neugarten (2021). Integrating Natural Capital into National Accounts.

20 N. Hanley, J. F. Shogren and B. White (2019). *Introduction to Environmental Economics*. Oxford: Oxford University Press.

21 N. Hanley, J. F. Shogren and B. White (2007). *Environmental Economics in Theory and Practice*, 2nd edition. London: Palgrave.

22 The idea that an economic activity that results in a private benefit could have a negative impact on a third party.

23 D. Pearce (2002). An Intellectual History of Environmental Economics. *Annual Review of Energy and the Environment*, 27(1): 57–81; A. Sandmo (2015). The Early History of Environmental Economics. *Review of Environmental Economics and Policy*, 9(1): 43–63.

24 J. Simon (1981). *The Ultimate Resource*. Princeton: Princeton University Press; M. Kremer (1993). Population Growth and Technological Change: One Million BC to 1990. *The Quarterly Journal of Economics*, 108(3): 681–716.

25 C. C. Mann (2018). *The Wizard and the Prophet.*

26 S. Jevons' (1865). *The Coal Question; An Inquiry Concerning the Progress of the Nation, and the Probable Exhaustion of our Coal-Mines*. London: Macmillan & Co.
27 A. Missemer (2012). William Stanley Jevons' the Coal Question (1865), beyond the Rebound Effect. *Ecological Economics*, 82: 97–103.
28 Ibid.
29 E. McLaughlin, N. Hanley, D. Greasley, J. Kunnas, L. Oxley and P. Warde (2014). Historical Wealth Accounts for Britain: Progress and Puzzles in Measuring the Sustainability of Economic Growth. *Oxford Review of Economic Policy*, 30(1): 44–69.
30 C.C. Mann (2018). *The Wizard and the Prophet*.
31 H. Hotelling (1931). The Economics of Exhaustible Resources. *Journal of Political Economy*, 39(2): 137–75.
32 K. Arrow and E. L. Lehmann (2005). Harold Hotelling September 29, 1895–December 26, 1973. *National Academies of Sciences, Engineering, and Medicine. Biographical Memoirs*: Volume 87. Washington, DC: The National Academies Press. https://doi.org/10.17226/11522.
33 R. Ferreira da Cunha and A. Missemer (2020). The Hotelling Rule in Non-renewable Resource Economics: A Reassessment. *Canadian Journal of Economics/Revue canadienne d'économique*, 53(2): 800–20.
34 A. C. Pigou (1912). *Wealth and Welfare*. London: Macmillan and Co; A. C. Pigou (1920). *The Economics of Welfare*. London: Macmillan and Co.
35 Market failure occurs when free markets allocate resources inefficiently and fail to maximize overall welfare, often due to externalities, public goods, information asymmetries, or market power; making it a central concern of environmental economics.
36 A. Marshall (1920). *Principles of Economics*.
37 A. Sandmo (2015). The Early History of Environmental Economics.
38 Ibid.
39 Pigou highlighted the additional cost to society from coal burning in terms of 'washing clothes and cleaning rooms, expenses for the provision of extra artificial light, and in many other ways'. These were estimated to have been £290,000 a year (or a £1 a year per person) in Manchester: A. C. Pigou (1932). *The Economics of Welfare*, 4th edition. London: Macmillan, pp. 184–5.
40 I. Kamekawa (2024). Measuring the Cost of Pollution: Economic Life, Economic Theory, and the Origins of Environmental Economics. *Journal of Modern History*, 96(2): 332–61.
41 E. J. Mishan (1971). The Postwar Literature on Externalities: An Interpretative Essay. *Journal of Economic Literature*, 9(1): 1–28.
42 W. J. Baumol and W. E. Oates (1971). The Use of Standards and Prices for Protection of the Environment. In *The Economics of Environment: Papers from Four Nations*. London: Palgrave Macmillan UK, 53–65.
43 H. S. Banzhaf (2020). A History of Pricing Pollution (or, why Pigouvian Taxes Are not Necessarily Pigouvian) *NBER* w27683.
44 H. Scott Gordon (1954). The Economic Theory of a Common-Property Resource: The Fishery. *The Journal of Political Economy*, 62(2): 124–42; G. Hardin (1968). The Tragedy of the Commons.
45 R. N. Stavins (2011). The Problem of the Commons: Still Unsettled after 100 Years. *American Economic Review*, 101(1): 81–108.

46 V. Ostrom and E. Ostrom (1972). Legal and Political Conditions of Water Resource Development. *Land Economics*, 48(1): 1–14; E. Ostrom (1990). *Governing the Commons: The Evolution of Institutions for Collective Action.*

47 Q. Couix (2019). Natural Resources in the Theory of Production: The Georgescu-Roegen/Daly versus Solow/Stiglitz Controversy. *The European Journal of the History of Economic Thought*, 26(6): 1341–78.

48 M. L. Weitzman (1976). On the Welfare Significance of National Product in a Dynamic Economy. *The Quarterly Journal of Economics*, 90(1): 156–62.

49 W. Vogt (1948). *Road to Survival.*

50 K. E. Boulding (1966). The Economics of the Coming Spaceship Earth; K. E. Boulding (1970). *Economics as a Science*. New York: McGraw-Hill.

51 E. B. Barbier (2019). The Concept of Natural Capital.

52 L. C. Gray (1914). Rent under the Assumption of Exhaustibility. *Quarterly Journal of Economics*, 28(3): 466–89.

53 By 'social capital' Scott meant the total capital stock (closer to what we now call Inclusive Wealth) and distinct from the later concept popularized by the political scientist Robert D. Putnam and others in the 1990s. Putnam defined social capital as consisting of networks, norms, and trust that enable collective action and he argued that it had declined in the US: R. D. Putnam (1995). Bowling Alone: America's Declining Social Capital. *Journal of Democracy*, 6(1): 65–78; R. D. Putnam (2000). *Bowling Alone: The Collapse and Revival of American Community*. New York: Simon Schuster.

54 A. Scott (1955). *Natural Resources: The Economics of Conservation.*

55 C. G. Plourde (1970). A Simple Model of Replenishable Natural Resource Exploitation. *American Economic Review*, 60(3): 518–22; N. Vousden (1973). Basic Theoretical Issues of Resource Depletion. *Journal of Economic Theory*, 6: 126–43.

56 C. G. Plourde (1970). A Simple Model of Replenishable Natural Resource Exploitation.

57 M. Gaffney (2008). Keeping Land In Capital Theory: Ricardo, Faustmann, Wicksell, and George. *American Journal of Economics and Sociology*, 67(1): 119–41.

58 Whom a prestigious award in economics is named after, the John Bates Clark Medal: https://www.aeaweb.org/about-aea/honors-awards/bates-clark

59 George was so influential that his work inspired Elizabeth Magie (1866–1948) to create the 'landlord game', which was the influence of the modern board game Monopoly: J. Dodson (2011). How Henry George's Principles Were Corrupted Into the Game Called Monopoly. *Henry George Institute*: https://www.henrygeorge.org/dodson_on_monopoly.htm

60 J. B. Clark (1899). *The Distribution of Wealth: a Theory of Wages, Interest, and Profits*. New York: Macmillan; H. George (1876). *Progress and Poverty: An Inquiry into the Cause of Industrial Depressions and of Increase of Want with Increase of Wealth*. New York: Modern Library; T. M. Dwyer (1982). Henry George's Thought in Relation to Modern Economics. *American Journal of Economics and Sociology*, 41(4): 363–73.

61 A. Missemer (2018). Natural Capital as an Economic Concept, History and Contemporary Issues. *Ecological Economics*, 143: 90–3.

62 P. J. Bryson (2011). *The Economics of Henry George: History's Rehabilitation of American's Greatest Early Economist*. London: Palgrave MacMillan.

63 The Pigou example is typically not included in overviews of the history of natural capital accounting: E. P. Fenichel, J. K. Abbott and S. D. Yun (2018). The Nature of Natural Capital and Ecosystem Income. In P. Dasgupta, S. K. Pattanayak and V. Kerry Smith (eds), *The Nature of Natural Capital and Ecosystem Income. Handbook of Environmental Economics*. Vol. 4. Amsterdam: Elsevier; E. B. Barbier (2019). The Concept of Natural Capital.

64 A. C. Pigou (1932). *The Economics of Welfare*, 4th edition, Chapter iv.

65 F. A. von Hayek (1935). The Maintenance of Capital *Economica*, 2(7): 241–76; F. A. Hayek (1940). *The Pure Theory of Capital*. Norwich: Jarrold and Sons; A. C. Pigou (1941). Maintaining Capital Intact. *Economica*, 8(31): 271–5; F. A. von Hayek (1941). Maintaining Capital Intact: A Reply. *Economica*, 8(31): 276–80; J. R. Hicks (1942). Maintaining Capital Intact: A Further Suggestion. *Economica*, 9(34): 174–9.

66 M. Scott (1984). Maintaining Capital Intact. *Oxford Economic Papers*, 36: 59–73; E. Rothschild (2011). Maintaining (Environmental) Capital Intact. *Modern Intellectual History*, 8(1): 193–212.

67 D. Pearce (2002). An Intellectual History of Environmental Economics.

68 H. E. Daly (1973). Introduction.

69 B. G. Norton and M. A. Toman (1997). Sustainability: Ecological and Economic Perspectives. *Land Economics*, 73(4): 553–68; G. C. van Kooetne and E. H. Bulte (2000). *The Economics of Nature: Managing Biological Assets*. Oxford: Blackwell.

70 E. P. Fenichel and J. K. Abbott (2014). Natural Capital: From Metaphor to Measurement. *Journal of the Association of Environmental and Resource Economists*, 1(1/2): 1–27; M. A. Drupp, M. C. Hansel, et al. (2024). Accounting for the Increasing Benefits of Scarce Ecosystems. *Science*, 383(6687).

71 E. Neumayer (2025). *Weak versus Strong Sustainability*.

72 SEEA (1993). *Handbook of National Accounting: Integrated Environmental and Economic Accounting*. United Nations; SEEA (2003). *Handbook of National Accounting: Integrated Environmental and Economic Accounting 2003*. United Nations; SEEA (2014). *System of Environmental: Economic Accounting 2012 – Central Framework*. United Nations.

73 W. D. Nordhaus and J. Tobin (1973). Is Growth Obsolete?

74 M. L. Weitzman (1976). On the Welfare Significance of National Product in a Dynamic Economy.

75 J. Pezzey (1992). Sustainable Development Concepts: An Economic Analysis. *World Bank Economic Paper* 2; S. Dietz and E. Neumayer (2007). Weak and Strong Sustainability in the SEEA: Concepts and Measurement. *Ecological Economics*, 61: 617–26; M. Qasim (2017). Sustainability and Wellbeing: A Scientometric and Biliometric Review of the Literature. *Journal of Economic Surveys*, 31(4): 1035–61.

76 Brundtland Report (1987). *Our Common Future*; A. Schubert and I. Láng (2005). The Literature Aftermath of The Brundtland Report 'Our Common Future'. A Scientometric Study Based on Citations in Science and Social Science Journals. *Environment, Development, and Sustainability*, 7(1): 1–8; J. Pezzey (1992). Sustainable Development Concepts: An Economic Analysis.

77 For example, G. B. Asheim (1994). Sustainability: Ethical Foundations and Economic Properties. *World Bank Policy Research Working Paper* 1302.

78 There were multiple versions of the *Blueprint for the Green Economy*. I refer to each variant by the number in which they appeared.
79 D. Pearce, A. Markandya and E. Barbier (1989). *Blueprint for a Green Economy*. London: Earthscan, p. 48.
80 M. Weitzman (1976). On the Welfare Significance of National Product in a Dynamic Economy; J. Hartwick (1977). Intergenerational Equity and the Investing of Rents from Exhaustible Resources.
81 R. Solow (1993). An Almost Practical Step toward Sustainability.
82 R. M. Solow (1986). On the Intergenerational Allocation of Natural Resources; K.-G. Mäler (1986). Comment on R. M. Solow, "'On the Intergenerational Allocation of Natural Resources'. *The Scandinavian Journal of Economics*, 88(1): 151–2.
83 K. R. Stollery (1998). Constant Utility Paths and Irreversible Global Warming. *The Canadian Journal of Economics / Revue canadienne d'Economique*, 31(3): 730–42.
84 The concept of genuine savings referred to here differs from the concept of 'genuine saving' that was outlined by Keynes in Chapter 7 of the *General Theory*. In that context, Keynes was referring to the distinction between investment and saving and if investment was made via the creation of credit from the banking system whether 'genuine saving' had taken place.
85 K. Hamilton and G. Atkinson (1996). Air Pollution and Green Accounts. *Energy Policy*, 24(7): 675–84.
86 M. A. Toman, J. Pezzey and J. Krautkraemer (1995). Neoclassical Growth Theory and Sustainability. Measuring Sustainable Development. In D. W. Bromley (ed.), *Handbook of Environmental Economics*. Oxford: Blackwell.
87 D. W. Pearce, K. Hamilton and G. Atkinson (1996). Measuring Sustainable Development: Progress on Indicators. *Environment and Development Economics*, 1: 85–101.
88 R. M. Solow (1956). A Contribution to the Theory of Economic Growth; R. M. Solow (1974). Intergenerational Equity and Exhaustible Resources; P. Dasgupta and G. Heal (1974). The Optimal Depletion of Exhaustible Resources. *The Review of Economic Studies*, 41: 3–28; J. Stiglitz (1974). Growth with Exhaustible Natural Resources: Efficient and Optimal Growth Paths. *The Review of Economic Studies*, 41: 123–37.
89 R. Costanza and H. E. Daly (1992). Natural Capital and Sustainable Development. *Conservation Biology*, 6 (1): 37–46.
90 E. P. Fenichel and J. Zhao (2015). Sustainability and Substitutability. *Bulletin Mathematical Biology*, 77: 348–67; A. Markandya and S. Pedroso-Galinato (2007). How Substitutable Is Natural Capital? *Environmental & Resource Economics*, 37(1): 297–312; F. Cohen, C. J. Hepburn and A. Teytelbom (2019). Is Natural Capital Really Substitutable? *Annual Review of Environment and Resources*, 44: 425–48.
91 K. Hamilton and M. Clemens (1999). Genuine Savings Rates in Developing Countries. *World Bank Economic Review*, 13(2): 333–56.
92 E. G. Irwin, S. Gopalakrishnan and A. Randall (2016). Welfare, Wealth, and Sustainability. *Annual Review Resource Economics*, 8: 77–98.
93 M. L. Weitzman and K.-G. Löfgren (1997). On the Welfare Significance of Green Accounting as Taught by Parable. *Journal of Environmental Economics and Management*, 32(2): 139–53; M. L. Weitzman (1997). Sustainability and

Technical Progress. *Scandinavian Journal of Economics*, 99(1): 1–13; M. L. Weitzman (1999). Pricing the Limits to Growth from Minerals Depletion.

94 S. Ferreira and J. R. Vincent (2005). Genuine Savings: Leading Indicator of Sustainable Development? *Economic Development and Cultural Change*, 53(3): 737–54; J. C. Pezzey, N. Hanley, K. Turner and D. Tinch (2006). Comparing Augmented Sustainability Measures for Scotland: Is There a Mismatch? *Ecological Economics*, 57: 70–4; S. Ferreira, K. Hamilton, J. R. Vincent (2008). Comprehensive wealth and future consumption: accounting for population growth. World Bank *Economic Review*, 22(2): 233-248.

95 P. Dasgupta (2009). The Welfare Economic Theory of Green National Accounts. *Environmental and Resource Economics*, 42: 3–38.

96 P. Dasgupta (2001). *Human Well-Being and the Natural Environment*; P. Dasgupta (2009). The Welfare Economic Theory of Green National Accounts.

97 K. J. Arrow, P. Dasgupta, L. H. Goulder, K. J. Mumford and K. Olsen (2012). Sustainability and the Measurement of Wealth.

98 P. Dasgupta (2014). Measuring the Wealth of Nations. *Annual Review Resource Economics*, 6: 17–31.

99 R. Solow (2012). A Few Comments on 'Sustainability and the Measurement of Wealth'. *Environment and Development Economics*, 17(3): 354–5.

100 K. Arrow, P. Dasgupta, L. Goulder, G. Daily, P. Ehrlich, G. Heal and B. Walker (2004). Are We Consuming Too Much?

101 P. Dasgupta (2001). *Human Well-Being and the Natural Environment*; G. B. Asheim, J. M. Hartwick and R. Yamaguichi (2023). Sustainable Per Capita Consumption under Population Growth. *Resource and Energy Economics*, 73: 101363.

102 N. Hanley, L. Dupuy and E. McLaughlin (2015). Genuine Savings and Sustainability.

103 A. Sen (1983). Poor, Relatively Speaking. *Oxford Economic Papers*, 35(2): 153–69; A. Sen (1984). *Resources, Values, and Development*. Oxford: Oxford University Press; A. Sen (1999). *Development as Freedom*. New York: Random House.

104 A. Sen (1993). Capability and Well-Being. In M. Nussbaum and A. Sen (eds), *The Quality of Life*. Oxford: Oxford University Press.

105 P. Dasgupta (1993). *An Inquiry into Well-Bing and Destitution*. Oxford: Oxford University Press, p. 303.

106 C. R. Hulten (1992). Accounting for the Wealth of Nations: The Net versus Gross Output Controversy and Its Ramifications. *The Scandinavian Journal of Economics*, 94: S9–S24.

107 P. Dasgupta (2001). *Human Well-Being and the Natural Environment*; A Similar approach was taken by Weitzman in his 2003 book, *Income, Wealth, and the Maximum Principle*. Cambridge, MA: Harvard University Press.

108 M. Weitzman (2003). *Income, Wealth, and the Maximum Principle*; M. Weitzman (2017). A Tight Connection Among Wealth, Income, Sustainability, and Accounting in an Ultra-Simplified Setting; D. W. Pearce and G. D. Atkinson (1993). Capital Theory and the Measurement of Sustainable Development: An Indicator of "Weak" Sustainability. *Ecological Economics*, 8(2): 103–8; D. Pearce (2002). An Intellectual History of Environmental Economics; P. Dasgupta (2001). *Human Well-Being and the Natural Environment*.

109 W. C. Clark and A. G. Harley (2020). Sustainability Science: Toward a Synthesis.

110 N. Hanley, L. Dupuy and E. McLaughlin (2015). Genuine Savings and Sustainability.

111 SEEA (1993). *Handbook of National Accounting: Integrated Environmental and Economic Accounting*; SEEA (2003). *Handbook of National Accounting: Integrated Environmental and Economic Accounting 2003*; SEEA (2014). *System of Environmental: Economic Accounting 2012 – Central Framework*.

112 P. Aghion and P. Howitt (1998). *Endogenous Growth Theory*; P. Aghion and P. Howitt (2008). *The Economics of Growth*.

113 P. Aghion, C. Antonin and S. Bunel (2021). *The Power of Creative Destruction. Economic Upheaval and the Wealth of Nations*. Cambridge, MA: Belkap Press of Harvard University Press.

114 D. W. Pearce and R. K. Turner (1990). *Economics of Natural Resources and the Environment*. New York: Harvester; P. A. Victor (1991). Indicators of Sustainable Development: Some Lessons from Capital Theory. *Ecological Economics*, 4: 191–213.

115 S. El Serafy and E. Lutz (1989). Environmental and Natural Resource Accounting. In G. Schramm and J. J. Warford (eds), *Environmental Management and Economic Development*. Washington, DC: World Bank.

116 R. Repetto, W. Magrath, M. Wells, C. Beer and F. Rossini (1989). *Wasting Assets: Natural Resources in the National Income Accounts*. World Resources Institute.

117 K. Hamilton (1994). Green Adjustments to GDP. *Resources Policy*, 20(3): 155–68.

118 Similarly an extension published in 1998 using early World Bank data, also did not include measures of human capital: D. W. Pearce and G. D. Atkinson (1993). Capital Theory and the Measurement of Sustainable Development: An Indicator of "Weak" Sustainability; D. Pearce and G. Atkinson (1995). Measuring Sustainable Development. In D. W. Bromley (ed.), *Handbook of Environmental Economics*. Oxford: Blackwell; D. Pearce, G. Atkinson and K. Hamilton (1998). The Measurement of Sustainable Development. In J. C. J. M. van den Bergh and M. W. Hofkes (eds), *Theory and Implementation of Economic Models for Sustainable Development*. Berlin: Springer.

119 D. W. Pearce (1993). *Blueprint 3: Measuring Sustainable Development*. London: Earthscan, Table 3.6.

120 G. Atkinson, R. Dubourg, K. Hamilton, M. Munasinghe, D. Pearce and C. Young (1997). *Measuring Sustainable Development: Macroeconomics and the Environment*. Cheltenham: Edward Elgar.

121 World Bank (1995). *Monitoring Environmental Progress: A Report on Work in Progress*. Environmentally Sustainable Development Series. Washington, DC: World Bank; World Bank (1997). *Expanding the Measure of Wealth: Indicators of Environmentally Sustainable Development*. Washington, DC: World Bank.

122 World Bank (1995). *World Development Report 1995. Workers in an Integrating World*. Oxford: Oxford University Press, p. 245.

123 D. W. Pearce and J. W. Warford (1993). *World Without End: Economics, Environment, and Sustainable Development*. Washington, DC: World Bank, pp. 52 and 85.

124 I. Serageldin and A. Steer (eds) (1994). *Making Development Sustainable: From Concepts to Action*. Washington, DC: World Bank.

125 The World Bank refers to Inclusive Wealth as 'Comprehensive Wealth', although in the 2006 report there was reference to the term 'inclusive'. Dasgupta had originally referred to the 'notion of wealth advanced here is a comprehensive one' in his 2001 book but the term Inclusive Wealth has become more widely used.

126 Health capital can be considered distinct from human capital as it refers to the value of good health which affects the time that an individual can spend in the workforce: M. Grossman (1972). On the Concept of Health Capital and the Demand for Health. *Journal of Political Economy*, 80(2): 223–55.

127 World Bank (1995). *Monitoring Environmental Progress: A Report on Work in Progress*. Environmentally Sustainable Development Series.

128 K. Hamilton and M. Clemens (1999). Genuine Savings Rates in Developing Countries.

129 World Bank (1995). *World Development Report 1995. Workers in an Integrating World*. Oxford: Oxford University Press, p. 245.

130 United Nations, European Commission, International Monetary Fund, OECD, and World Bank (2003). *Handbook of National Accounting: Integrated Environmental and Economic Accounting*. 1.24.

131 United Nations Economic Commission for Europe (2009). *Measuring Sustainable Development*. United Nations: New York and Geneva.

132 K. Hamilton (2004). Accounting for Sustainability. In OECD (2004). *Measuring Sustainable Development: Integrated Economic, Environmental, and Social Frameworks*. Paris: OECD.

133 S. Dasgupta, K. Hamilton, S. Pagiola and D. Wheeler (2008). Environmental Economics at the World Bank. *Review of Environmental Economics and Policy*, 2(1): 4–25; World Bank (2006). *Where is the Wealth of Nations?: Measuring Capital for the 21st Century*. Washington, DC: World Bank; World Bank (2011). *The Changing Wealth of Nations: Measuring Sustainable Development in the New Millennium*. Washington, DC: World Bank; World Bank (2018). *The Changing Wealth of Nations 2018: Building a Sustainable Future*; World Bank (2021). *The Changing Wealth of Nations 2021: Managing Assets for the Future*; World Bank (2024). *The Changing Wealth of Nations 2024: Revisiting the Measurement of Comprehensive Wealth*. Washington DC: World Bank.

134 K. Hamilton and M. Clemens (1999). Genuine Savings Rates in Developing Countries.

135 UNU-IHDP and UNEP (2012). *Inclusive Wealth Report 2012: Measuring Progress toward Sustainability*. Cambridge: Cambridge University Press; UNU-IHDP and UNEP (2014). *Inclusive Wealth Report 2014: Measuring Progress toward Sustainability*. Cambridge: Cambridge University Press; UNEP (2018). *Inclusive Wealth Report 2018*. UNEP (2023). *Inclusive Wealth Report 2023: Measuring Sustainability and Equity*. Nairobi: UN Environment Programme.

136 K. J. Arrow, P. Dasgupta, L. H. Goulder, K. J. Mumford and K. Olsen (2010). Sustainability and the Measurement of Wealth. *NBER* 16599; K. J. Arrow, P. Dasgupta, L. H. Goulder, K. J. Mumford and K. Olsen (2012). Sustainability and the Measurement of Wealth; A. K. Duraiappah and P. Muñoz (2012).

Inclusive Wealth: A Tool for the United Nations. *Environment and Development Economics*, 17: 362–7.

137 R. Solow (2012). A Few Comments on "Sustainability and the Measurement of Wealth".

138 S. Managi, S. Chen, P. Kumar and P. Dasgupta (2024). Sustainable Matrix Beyond GDP: Investment for Inclusive Growth. *Humanities and Social Science Communications*, 11: 185.

139 E. McLaughlin, C. Ducoing and N. Hanley (2024). Challenges of Wealth-based Sustainability Metrics.

140 SEEA (1993). *Handbook of National Accounting: Integrated Environmental and Economic Accounting. United Nations*; SEEA (2003). *Handbook of National Accounting: Integrated Environmental and Economic Accounting 2003*; SEEA (2014). *System of Environmental: Economic Accounting 2012 – Central Framework*.

141 World Bank (2024). *Changing Wealth of Nations*, p. 98.

142 E. Conway (2023). *Material World: A Substantial Story of Our Past and Future*. London: Penguin Random House.

143 K. Bandhauer, J. Curti and C. Miller (2005). Challenges to Regulatory Harmonization and Standard-Setting: The Case of Environmental Accounting in the US and Canada. *Journal of Contemporary Policy Analysis*, 7(2): 177–94.

144 Bureau of Economic Analysis (1994). *Survey of Current Business. April, 74(4)*. Washington, DC: Department of Commerce.

145 National Research Council. (1999). *Nature's Numbers: Expanding the National Economic Accounts to Include the Environment*. Washington, DC: The National Academies Press. https://doi.org/10.17226/6374

146 G. Wagner (2001). The Political Economy of Greening the National Income Accounts *Newsletter of the Association of Environmental and Resource Economists,* 21: 14–18.

147 ONS (2024). UK Inclusive Wealth and Income Accounts: 2005 to 2022. 13 November 2024. https://www.ons.gov.uk/economy/economicoutputandproductivity/output/articles/ukinclusiveincome/2005to2022

148 C. Giles (2024). The Perils in the Search for the Perfect GDP Alternative. *Financial Times*, 27 November 2024.

149 D. W. Pearce, G. D. Atkinson and W. R. Dubourg (1994). The Economics of Sustainable Development. *Annual Review Energy Economics*, 19: 457–74.

150 K. Hamilton and M. Clemens (1999). Genuine Savings Rates in Developing Countries.

151 W. W. Rostow (1959). The Stages of Economic Growth. *Economic History Review*, 12(1): 1–16; W. W. Rostow (1990). *The Stages of Economic Growth*, 3rd edition. Cambridge: Cambridge University Press; N. Crafts (2009). Solow and Growth Accounting.

152 N. F. R. Crafts (1993). *Can De-Industrialisation Seriously Damage Your Wealth?* London: IEA.

153 M. del Mar Rubio (2004). The Capital Gains from Trade are not Enough: Evidence from the Environmental Accounts of Venezuela and Mexico. *Journal of Environmental Economics & Management*, 48: 1175–91.

154 D. Greasley, N. Hanley, J. Kunnas, E. McLaughlin, L. Oxley and P. Warde (2014). Testing Genuine Savings as a Forward-looking Indicator of Future

Well-being over the (Very) Long-run. *Journal of Environmental Economics and Management*, 67(2): 171–88.

155 N. Hanley, L. Oxley, D. Greasley, E. McLaughlin and M. Blum (2016). Empirical Testing of Genuine Savings as an Indicator of Weak Sustainability: A Three-country Analysis of Long-run Trends. *Environmental and Resource Economics*, 63: 313–38; D. Greasley, E. McLaughlin, N. Hanley and L. Oxley (2017). Australia: A Land of Missed Opportunities? *Environment and Development Economics*, 22(6): 674–98; M. Lindmark, H. N. Thu and J. Stage (2018). Weak Support for Weak Sustainability: Genuine Savings and Long-term Wellbeing in Sweden, 1850–2000. *Ecological Economics*, 145: 339–45; L. McGrath, S. Hynes and J. McHale (2024). Advancing Testing of the Genuine Savings Hypothesis: The Use of Comprehensive Measures of Technical Change for Ireland. *Journal of Environmental Management*, 352: 120072.

156 L. Mcgrath, S. Hynes and J. McHale (2022). Reassessing Ireland's Economic Development through the Lens of Sustainable Development *European Review of Economic History*, 26(3): 399422.

157 E. McLaughlin, C. Ducoing and L. Oxley (2023). Tracing Sustainability in the Long Run: Genuine Savings Estimates 1850–2018. *NBER Working Paper*, 31155.

158 E. McLaughlin, N. Hanley, D. Greasley, J. Kunnas, L. Oxley and P. Warde (2014). Historical Wealth Accounts for Britain.

159 Dasgupta has omitted the work of the World Bank in his discussion of the history of measuring Inclusive Wealth and stated that the UNEP 'has taken the lead in estimating the wealth of nations': P. Dasgupta (2025). *On Natural Capital*; ONS (2022). Inclusive Capital Stock, UK: 2019 and 2020.

160 J. Pezzey (2024). Adjusted Net Savings Needs further Adjusting: Reassessing Human and Resource Factors in Sustainability Measurement. *Journal of Environmental Economics and Management*, 127: 102984; G. B. Asheim, J. M. Hartwick and R. Yamaguchi (2023). Sustainable Per Capita Consumption under Population Growth.

161 E. McLaughlin, C. Ducoing and N. Hanley (2024). Challenges of Wealth-based Sustainability Metrics.

162 M. L. Weitzman (1997). Sustainability and Technical Progress. *The Scandinavian Journal of Economics*, 99(1): 1-13.

163 UNEP (2023). *Inclusive Wealth Report 2023*, p. 122.

164 IMF (2024). *World Economic Outlook. Steady but Slow. Resilience amid Divergence*. Washington, DC: IMF.

165 Trump's Budget Includes $3.2 Billion for World Bank's Fund for Poorest Countries. *Reuters*, 2 May 2025. https://www.reuters.com/world/trumps-budget-includes-32-bln-world-banks-fund-poorest-countries-2025-05-02/

166 A. Russel and A. Hauslohner (2025). Can the UN Save Itself from Irrelevance? *Financial Times*, 23 September 2025.

167 The UN Could Run Out of Cash within Months: America and China are Pushing it to the Brink of Financial Collapse. *The Economist*, 1 May 2025; Withdrawing the United Sates from and Ending Funding to Certain United Nations Organizations and Reviewing United Sates Support to all International Organizations. *White House*, 4 February 2025. https://www.whitehouse.gov/presidential-actions/2025/02/withdrawing-the-united-states-from-and-ending-funding-to-certain-united-nations-organizations-and-reviewing-united-states-support-to-all-international-organizations/

Chapter Seven

1 ONS (2025). Quarterly National Accounts, Q4 (Oct to Dec) 2024 *Office of National Statistics*, 28 March 2025. https://www.ons.gov.uk/releases/gdpquarterlynationalaccountsukoctobertodecember2024
2 ONS (2024). GDP First Quarterly Estimate, UK: October to December 2023. 15 February 2024. https://www.ons.gov.uk/economy/grossdomesticproductgdp/bulletins/gdpfirstquarterlyestimateuk/octobertodecember2023
3 See, S. Fleming (2025). UK's Post-Pandemic GDP Recovery Is Revised Up by Statistics Office. *Financial Times*, 19 August 2025.
4 A recent study has estimated that Brexit has reduced UK GDP by between 6% to 8%. See N. Bloom, P. Bunn, P. Mizen, P. Smietanka, and G. Thwaites (2025). The Economic Impact of Brexit. *NBER Working Paper*, No. 34459.
5 I refer to Britain and the UK interchangeably but primarily I mean Britain (England and Scotland). Most of the historical research on the Industrial Revolution refers to England alone rather than Britain. I purposefully exclude the island of Ireland from most of this discussion as it joined the United Kingdom in 1801 and the southern part of Ireland seceded from the Union in 1922.
6 N. Crafts (1998). Forging Ahead and Falling Behind: The Rise and Relative Decline of the First Industrial Nation. *Journal of Economic Perspectives*, 12(2): 193–210.
7 N. Crafts (2018). *Forging Ahead, Falling Behind and Fighting Back: British Economic Growth from the Industrial Revolution to the Financial Crisis.* Cambridge: Cambridge University Press.
8 *WON*, Book II, Chapter iii.
9 *WON*, Book III, Chapter iv.
10 M. Kelly and C. Ó. Gráda (2019). Speed Under Sail during the Early Industrial Revolution (1750–1830). *Economic History Review*, 72(2): 459–80; E. A. Wrigley (1985). Urban Growth and Agricultural Change: England and the Continent in the Early Modern Period. *The Journal of Interdisciplinary History*, 15(4): 683–728.
11 P. Deane (1965). *The First Industrial Revolution*. Cambridge: Cambridge University Press.
12 N. Crafts (2018). *Forging Ahead, Falling Behind and Fighting Back.*
13 W. W. Rostow (1960). *The Stages of Economic Growth*. Cambridge: Cambridge University Press; N. Crafts (1985). *British Economic Growth during the Industrial Revolution*. Oxford: Oxford University Press.
14 M. Berg and P. Hudson (1992). Rehabilitating the Industrial Revolution. *Economic History Review*, 45(1): 24–50; D. Greasley and L. Oxley (1994). Rehabilitation Sustained: The Industrial Revolution as a Macroeconomic Epoch. *Economic History Review*, 47(4): 760–8.
15 S. Broadberry and T. Hatton (2024). Nicholas Francis Robert Crafts (9 March 1949–6 October 2023). *Biographical Memoirs of Fellows of the British Academy*, 21: 505–24.
16 N. F. R. Crafts (1993). *Can De-Industrialisation Seriously Damage Your Wealth?*

17 N. F. R. Crafts (1995). Exogenous or Endogenous Growth? The Industrial Revolution Reconsidered. *Journal of Economic History*, 55(4): 745–72.
18 J. Mokyr (1992). *The Levers of Riches: Technological Creativity and Economic Progress*. Oxford: Oxford University Press.
19 D. Greasley and L. Oxley (1997). Endogenous Growth or "Big Bang": Two Views of the First Industrial Revolution. *The Journal of Economic History*, 57(4): 935–49.
20 N. Crafts (1998). Forging Ahead and Falling Behind; N. Crafts (1999). Economic Growth in the Twentieth Century. *Oxford Review of Economic Policy*, 15(4): 18–34.
21 N. Crafts (2018). *Forging Ahead, Falling Behind and Fighting Back.*
22 Although Britain experienced an industrial revolution, the majority of the focus has been on England. British and English have been used interchangeably by scholars (e.g., Kelly et al. 2014, 'Precocious Albion', refer to heights of 'British urban convicts' with a note indicating they are the heights of 'English urban convicts').
23 N. Crafts (2010). Explaining the First Industrial Revolution: Two Views. *European Review of Economic History*, 15: 153–68.
24 C. L. Colvin and S. de Pleit (2018). Industrial Revolution and British Exceptionalisim. In M. Blum and C. L. Colvin (eds). *An Economists Guide to Economic History*. London: Palgrave.
25 J. Mokyr (1990). *The Levers of Riches: Technological Creativity and Economic Progress*. Oxford: Oxford University Press; J. Mokyr (2002). The Gifts of Athena: Historical Origins of the Knowledge Economy. Princeton: Princeton University Press; J. Mokyr (2009). *The Enlightened Economy: An Economic History of Britain 1700–1850*. New Haven: Yale University Press.
26 R. C. Allen (2009). *The British Industrial Revolution in Historical Perspective*. Cambridge: Cambridge University Press; R. C. Allen (2009). The Industrial Revolution in Miniature: The Spinning Jenny in Britain, France, and India. *The Journal of Economic History*, 69(4): 901–27; R. C. Allen (2011). Why the Industrial Revolution was British: Commerce, Induced Invention, and the Scientific Revolution. *Economic History Review*, 64(2): 357–84.
27 R. C. Allen (2009). *The British Industrial Revolution in Historical Perspective*.
28 R. C. Allen (2009). *The British Industrial Revolution in Historical Perspective*; R. C. Allen (2009). The Industrial Revolution in Miniature; D. Acemoglu (2002). Directed Technical Change. *Review of Economic Studies*, 69: 781–809.
29 J. Humphries (2013). The Lure of Aggregates and the Pitfalls of the Patriarchal Perspective: A Critique of the High Wage Economy interpretation of the British Industrial Revolution. *Economic History Review*, 66(3): 693–714; see also: R. C. Allen (2015). The High Wage Economy and the Industrial Revolution: A Restatement. *Economic History Review*, 68(1): 1–22.
30 J. Stephenson (2018). 'Real' Wages? Contractors, Workers, and Pay in London Building Trades, 1650–1800. *Economic History Review*, 71(1):

106–32; R. C. Allen (2019). Real Wages Once More: A Response to Judy Stephenson. *Economic History Review*, 72(2): 738–54; J. Stephenson (2019). Mistaken Wages: The Cost of Labour in the Early Modern English Economy, A Reply to Robert C. Allen. *Economic History Review*, 72(2): 755–69.

31 J. Humphries and B. Schneider (2019). Spinning the Industrial Revolution. *Economic History Review*, 72(1): 126–55; R. C. Allen (2020). Spinning their Wheels: A Reply to Jane Humphries and Benjamin Schneider. *Economic History Review*, 73(4): 1128–36; J. Humphries and B. Schneider (2020). Losing the Thread: A Response to Robert Allen. *Economic History Review*, 73(4): 1137–52.

32 M. Kelly, J. Mokyr and C. Ó Gráda (2014). Precocious Albion: A New Interpretation of the British Industrial Revolution. *Annual Reviews of Economics*, 6(1): 363–89; M. Kelly, J. Mokyr and C. Ó Gráda (2023). The Mechanics of the Industrial Revolution. *Journal of Political Economy*, 131(1): 59–94.

33 M. Kelly and C. Ó Gráda (2016). Adam Smith, Watchmaking, and the Industrial Revolution.

34 N. Crafts (2018). *Forging Ahead, Falling Behind and Fighting Back.*

35 Or rather the 'Dutch Invasion' as a standing army of Dutch soldiers occupied the streets of London.

36 D. C. North and B. R. Weingast (1989). Constitutions and Commitment: The Evolution of Institutions Governing Public Choice in Seventeenth Century England. *Journal of Economic History*, 49(4): 803–32.

37 S. Ogilvie and A. W. Carus (2014). Institutions and Economic Growth in Historical Perspective.

38 C. Hill (1976). *The Pelican Economic History of Britain Vol. 2: 1530–1780, Reformation to Industrial Revolution.* London: Pelican.

39 C. Hill (1975). *The World Turned Upside Down: Radical Ideas During the English Revolution.* London: Penguin Books.

40 W. W. Rostow (1990). *The Stages of Economic Growth: A Non-Communist Manifesto*, 3rd edition, p. 37.

41 H. Rosovsky (1965). The Take-off into Sustained Controversy. *Journal of Economic History*, 25(2): 271–5.

42 S. Kuznets (1963). Notes on the Take-off. In W. W. Rostow (ed.), *The Economics of Take-off into Sustained Growth.*

43 P. Deane and H. J. Habakkuk (1963). The Take-off in Britain. In W. W. Rostow (ed.), *The Economics of Take-off into Sustained Growth.*

44 W. W. Rostow (1959). The Stages of Economic Growth. *Economic History Review*, 12(1): 1–16; W. W. Rostow (1963). Introduction and Epilogue. In W. W. Rostow (ed.), *The Economics of Take-Off into Sustained Growth.*

45 P. Deane and W. Cole (1969). *British Economic Growth 1688–1959*, 2nd edition. Cambridge: Cambridge University Press; N. Crafts (1985). *British Economic Growth during the Industrial Revolution.*

46 C. H. Feinstein (1978). Capital Formation in Great Britain. pp. 28–96.

47 W. W. Rostow (1978). *The World Economy*, pp. 374–5.

48 P. Deane (1968). New Estimates of Gross National Product for the United Kingdom, 1830–1914. *The Review of Income and Wealth*, 14(2): 95–112.

49 W. W. Rostow (1960). *The Stages of Economic Growth.*
50 A. Brewer (1983). Review of Economics in the Long View. Essays in Honour of W. W. Rostow. 3 Volumes. *The Economic Journal*, 93(1): 650–2.
51 W. W. Rostow (1952). *The Process of Economic Growth.*
52 R. Findlay (1990). *The Triangular Trade and the Atlantic Economy of the Eighteenth Century: A Simple Model.* Princeton, NJ: Princeton University.
53 M. Berg and P. Hudson (2023). *Slavery, Capitalism, and the Industrial Revolution.* Cambridge: Polity Press.
54 E. Williams (1944). *Capitalism and Slavery.* Chapel Hill, NC: University of North Carolina Press.
55 G. Wright (2020). Slavery and Anglo-American Capitalism Revisited. *Economic History Review*, 73(2): 353–83.
56 S. L. Engerman (1972). The Slave Trade and British Capital Formation in the Eighteenth Century: A Comment on the Williams Thesis. *Business History Review*, 46(4): 430–43.
57 P. O'Brien (1982). European Economic Development: The Contribution of the Periphery. *Economic History Review*, 35(1): 1–18.
58 Barbara Solow (née Lewis) was an outstanding economic historian who wrote on Irish land reform as well as slavery in the Caribbean, she was also Robert Solow's wife. It was Barbara who Robert credited with introducing him to economics.
59 B. L. Solow (1985). Caribbean Slavery and British Growth: The Eric Williams Hypothesis. *Journal of Development Economics*, 17(1985): 99–115.
60 S. Heblich, S. J. Redding and H. J. Voth (2023). Slavery and the British Industrial Revolution. *NBER Working Paper* 30451.
61 M. Anson and M. D. Bennett (2022). The Collection of Slavery Compensation, 1835–43. *Bank of England Staff Working Paper No. 1006.* https://www.bankofengland.co.uk/working-paper/2022/the-collection-of-slavery-compensation-1835-43
62 N. Crafts (1998). Forging Ahead and Falling Behind.
63 In 1921 the estimated population of the British Empire was *c.* 408 million (89 million excluding India). Therefore, the combined population of the British Empire compared favourably with that of the United States. However, the difference was that the population of the United States was united in one territorial jurisdiction and in one federal government, which enabled it to act as a cohesive market more so than the regionally diverse and economically disparate British Empire: Registrar-General (1923). *The Registrar-General's Statistical Review of England and Wales for the year 1921.* London: His Majesty's Stationery Office.
64 G. Wright (1990). The Origins of American Industrial Success, 1879–1940. *American Economic Review*, 80(4): 651–68.
65 A. D. Chandler (1977). *The Visible Hand: The Managerial Revolution in American Business.* Cambridge MA: Harvard University Press; A. D. Chandler (1992). Organizational Capabilities and the Economic History of the Industrial Enterprise. *The Journal of Economic Perspectives*, 6(3): 79–100.
66 H. Hollerith (1894). The Electrical Tabulating Machine. *Journal of the Royal Statistical Society*, 57(4): 678–89; E. Higgs (2004). *Life, Death and Statistics.*
67 J. W. Cortada (1997). Economic Preconditions That Made Possible Application of Commercial Computing in the United States. *IEEE Annals of the History of*

Computing, 19(3): 27–40; J. W. Cortada (2019). *IBM: The Rise and Fall and Reinvention of a Global Icon*. Cambridge, MA: MIT Press.

68 D. Greasley (1986). British Economic Growth: The Paradox of the 1880s and the Timing of the Climacteric. *Explorations in Economic History*, 23(4): 416–44.

69 C. H. Feinstein (1972). *National Income, Output and Expenditure of the United Kingdom 1855–1965*. Cambridge: Cambridge University Press; J. H. Davis (2004). An Annual Index of U. S. Industrial Production, 1790–1915. *The Quarterly Journal of Economics*, 119(4): 1177–215.

70 K. Harly (2014). The Legacy of the Early Start. In R. Floud, J. Humphries and P. Johnson (eds)-, *The Cambridge Economic History of Modern Britain. Volume II. 1870 to Present*. Cambridge: Cambridge University Press.

71 S. Pollard (1989). *Britain's Prime and Britain's Decline: The British Economy, 1870–1914*. London: Edward Arnold.

72 D. N. McCloskey (1981). Did Victorian Britain Fail? In *Enterprise and Trade in Victorian Britain: Essays in Historical Economics*. London: George Allen & Unwin.

73 Or rather that Allen borrowed from John Habakkuk's earlier observations regarding the influence on factor abundance in the search and adaptation of new technologies in the United Kingdom and United States.

74 H. J. Habakkuk (1967). *American & British Technology in the 19th Century*. Cambridge: Cambridge University Press; N. Crafts (2014). Economic Growth During the Long Twentieth Century. In R. Floud, J. Humphries and P. Johnson (eds), *The Cambridge Economic History of Modern Britain. Volume II. 1870 to Present*. Cambridge: Cambridge University Press.

75 K. H. O'Rourke (2000). Tariffs and Growth in the Late 19th Century. *Economic Journal*, 110: 456–83.

76 I. Stone (1999). *The Global Export of Capital from Great Britain, 1865–1914*. New York: Macmillan Press.

77 E. Ames and N. Rosenberg (1963). Changing Technological Leadership and Industrial Growth. *The Economic Journal*, 73(289): 13–31.

78 H. W. Richardson (1965). Over-commitment in Britain before 1930. *Oxford Economic Papers*, 17(2): 237–62.

79 N. Crafts (2018). *Forging Ahead, Falling Behind and Fighting Back*.

80 D. H. Aldcroft (1986). *The British Economy. The Years of Turmoil 1920–1951*. Guildford: Harvester Press.

81 S. Broadberry, J. S. Chadha, J. Lennard, and R. Thomas (2023). Dating Business Cycles in the United Kingdom, 1700–2010. *Economic History Review*, 76(4): 1141–62.

82 M. E. F. Jones (1985). The Regional Impact of an Overvalued Pound in the 1920s. *Economic History Review*, 38(3): 393–401.

83 N. Foley-Fisher and E. McLaughlin (2016). Sovereign Debt Guarantees and Default: Lessons from the UK and Ireland, 1920–1938. *European Economic Review*, 87: 272–86.

84 J. D. Turner (2014). *Banking in Crisis: The Rise and Fall of British Banking Stability, 1800 to Present*. Cambridge: Cambridge University Press.

85 See S. N. Broadberry (1984). The North European depression of the 1920s. *Scandinavian Economic History Review*, 32(3): 159–67; S. N. Broadberry (1990). The Emergence of Mass Unemployment: Explaining Macroeconomic

Trends in Britain during the Trans-World War I Period. *Economic History Review*, 43(2): 271–82; and S. Broadberry and J. J. Wallis (2025). Growing, Shrinking, and Long-Run Economic Performance: Historical Perspectives on Economic Development. *Journal of Economic History*, 85(2): 505–40.

86 S. Pollard (1989). *Britain's Prime and Britain's Decline*, p. 271.

87 S. Pollard (1982). *The Wasting of the British Economy*. London: Croom Helm.

88 Bank of England, A16 Industry GVA shares by SIC.

89 N. Crafts (1996). Deindustrialisation and Economic Growth. *Economic Journal*, 106(434): 172–83.

90 M. Kitson and J. Michie (1996). Britain's Industrial Performance since 1960: Underinvestment and Relative Decline. *Economic Journal*, 106(434): 196–212; W. Eltis (1996). How Low Profitability and Weak Innovativeness Undermined UK Industrial Growth. *Economic Journal*, 106(434): 184–95.

91 C. C. S. Newton (1984). The Sterling Crisis of 1947 and the British Response to the Marshall Plan. *The Economic History Review*, 37(3): 391–408.

92 N. F. R. Crafts (1995). The Golden Age of Economic Growth in Western Europe, 1950–1973. *Economic History Review*, 48(3): 429–47.

93 G. C. Allen (1979). *The British Disease*, 2nd edition. IEA Hobart Paper 67. London: Institute of Economic Affairs.

94 A. Gerschenkron (1962). *Economic Backwardness in Historical Perspective: A Book of Essays*. Cambridge, MA: Belknap Press of Harvard University Press.

95 M. Abramovitz (1986). Catching Up, Forging Ahead, and Falling Behind. *The Journal of Economic History*, 46(2): 385–406.

96 N. Crafts (2018). *Forging Ahead, Falling Behind and Fighting Back*.

97 C. C. S. Newton (1984). The Sterling Crisis of 1947 and the British Response to the Marshall Plan.

98 J. Dow (1964). *The Management of the British Economy 1945–1960*. Cambridge: Cambridge University Press; D. McLaughlin, E. McLaughlin and S. Kenny (2025). Taking a Punt: Monetary Experimentation and the Irish Macroeconomic Crisis of 1955-56. *QUCEH Working Paper*, 25-02.

99 N. Crafts (2012). British Relative Economic Decline Revisited: The Role of Competition. *Explorations in Economic History*. 49(1): 17–29.

100 N. Crafts (2016). The Growth Effects of EU Membership for the UK: A Review of the Evidence. University of *Warwick Working Paper* series, no. 280; See foreword of Lord Cockfield in P. Cecchini (1988). *The European Challenge, 1992: The Benefits of a Single Market*. Aldershot: Commission of the European Communities.

101 M. Kitson and J. Michie (1996). Britain's Industrial Performance since 1960, Table 1; House of Lords (1984–85). *Report from the Select Committee on Overseas Trade* (238-I). Table 3.2.

102 M. Dintenfass (1992). *The Decline of Industrial Britain: 1870–1980*. London: Routledge.

103 N. Crafts (1996). Deindustrialisation and Economic Growth.

104 M. Chick (2020). *Changing Times*.

105 M. Kitson and J. Michie (2014). The De-industrialisation Revolution: The Rise and Fall of UK Manufacturing. In R. Floud, J. Humphries and P. Johnson

(eds), *The Cambridge Economic History of Modern Britain. Volume II. 1870 to Present*. Cambridge: Cambridge University Press.

106 N. Crafts (2014). Economic Growth during the Long Twentieth Century.

107 N. Crafts and T. C. Mills (2020). Is the UK Productivity Slowdown Unprecedented? *National Institute Economic Review*, 251: R47–R53.

108 S. O. Becker, T. Fetzer and D. Novy (2017). Who Voted for Brexit? A Comprehensive District-level Analysis. *Economic Policy*, *32*(92), 601–50; T. Fetzer (2019). Did Austerity Cause Brexit? *American Economic Review*, 109(11): 3849–86.

109 N. Crafts (2021). Understanding Productivity Growth in the Industrial Revolution.

110 R. J. Gordon (2012). Is US Economic Growth Over? Faltering Innovation Confronts the Six Headwinds (No. w18315). *National Bureau of Economic Research*.

111 N. Crafts (2021). The Sources of British Economic Growth since the Industrial Revolution: Not the Same old Story. *Journal of Economic Surveys*, 35(3): 697–709.

112 J. S. Chadha and I. Samiri (2022). Macroeconomic Perspectives on Productivity. *The Productivity Institute Working Paper* No. 030; N. Crafts (2019). The Fall in Potential Output due to the Financial Crisis: A Much Bigger Estimate for the UK. *Comparative Economic Studies*, 61: 625–35.

113 D. Coyle and J-C. Mei (2023). Diagnosing the UK Productivity Slowdown: Which Sectors Matter and Why? *Economica*, 90(359): 813–50.

114 P. Goodridge and J. Haskel (2023). Accounting for the Slowdown in UK Innovation and Productivity. *Economica*, 90(359): 780–812.

115 D. Greasley and J. B. Madsen (2006). Employment and Total Factor Productivity Convergence.

116 N. Crafts (1993). *Can De-Industrialisation Seriously Damage Your Wealth?*, Table 3; A. Cairncross (1992). *The British Economy since 1945*. Oxford: Blackwell.

117 R. C. Feenstra, R. Inklaar and M. P. Timmer (2015). The Next Generation of the Penn World Table. Available for download at www.ggdc.net/pwt. Series: "rtfpna".

118 Prime Minister Sets Out Blueprint to Turbocharge AI, 12 January 2025: https://www.gov.uk/government/news/prime-minister-sets-out-blueprint-to-turbocharge-ai

119 D. Acemoglu (2024). The Simple Macroeconomics of AI. *NBER* Working Paper, 32487.

Chapter Eight

1 E. B. Barbier (2005). *Natural Resources and Economic Development*. Cambridge: Cambridge University Press; J. Sachs and A. Warner (2001). The Curse of Natural Resources. *European Economic Review*, 45: 827–38; F. Van Der Ploeg (2011). Natural Resources: Curse or Blessing? *Journal of Economic Literature*, 49(2): 366–420.

2 G. Wright (1990). The Origins of American Industrial Success, 1879–1940. *The American Economic Review*, 80(4): 651–68; G. Wright and J. Czelusta (2004). Why Economies Slow: The Myth of the Resource Curse. *Challenge*, 47(2): 6–38.

3 E. B. Barbier (2011). *Scarcity and Frontiers.*

4 Where 'resource dependence' was measured as the ratio of natural resource exports as a share of GDP. However, a key issue is how 'resource dependence' is measured and if resource abundance is used instead (resource rents as a share of GDP), then this can lead to different findings, see: C. Brunnschweiler and E. Bulte (2008). The Resource Curse Revisited and Revised: A Tale of Paradoxes and Red Herrings. *Journal of Environmental Economics and Management*, 55(3): 248–64; F. van der Ploeg (2011). Natural Resources: Curse or Blessing?; G. Daw (2025). Natural Resources and Development: New Insights from Strong Curse to Strong Blessing. *Agricultural and Resource Economics Review*, 54(1): 288–341.

5 R. Auty (1993). *Sustaining Development in Mineral Economies: The Resource-Curse Thesis.* London: Routledge; J. D. Sachs and A. M. Warner (1995). Natural Resource Abundance and Economic Growth. *NBER* Working Paper 5398; J. D. Sachs and A. M. Warner (2001). The Curse of Natural Resources; F. van der Ploeg (2011). Natural Resources: Curse or Blessing?

6 W. Max Corden and J. Peter Neary (1982). Booming Sector and De-Industrialisation in a Small Open Economy. *The Economic Journal*, 92(368): 825–48.

7 D. Acemoglu and J. A. Robinson (2012). *Why Nations Fail*, p. 529; G. Atkinson and K. Hamilton (2003). Savings, Growth and the Resource Curse Hypothesis. *World Development*, 31(11): 1793–807; R. M. Auty (2007). Natural Resources, Capital Accumulation and the Resource Curse. *Ecological Economics*, 61(4): 627–34; F. van der Ploeg (2010). Why Do Many Resource-rich Countries Have Negative Genuine Saving?: Anticipation of Better Times or Rapacious Rent Seeking. *Resource and Energy Economics*, 32(1): 28–44.

8 E. A. Wrigley (2010). *Energy and the English Industrial Revolution.* Cambridge: Cambridge University Press.

9 K. Pomeranz (2001). *The Great Divergence: China, Europe, and the Making of the Modern World Economy.* Princeton: Princeton University Press.

10 J. Hatcher (1993). *The History of the British Coal Industry. Volume 1: Before 1700: Towards the Age of Coal.* Oxford: Oxford University Press, pp. 48, 49, 193.

11 M. W. Flinn (1984). *The History of the British Coal Industry 1700–1830: the Industrial Revolution.* Vol. 2. Oxford: Oxford University Press, pp. 5, 29.

12 Ibid., Tables 4.1, 4.2.

13 B. R. Mitchell (1984). *Economic Development of the British Coal Industry 1800–1914.* Cambridge: Cambridge University Press, p. 79; M. W. Flinn (1984). *The History of the British Coal Industry 1700–1830*, pp. 105, 126.

14 M. W. Flinn (1984). *The History of the British Coal Industry 1700–1830*, Table 4.3.

15 B. R. Mitchell (1984). *Economic Development of the British Coal Industry 1800–1914*, p. 70.

16 M. W. Flinn (1984). *The History of the British Coal Industry 1700–1830*, pp. 2–3.
17 R. Church (1986). *The History of the British Coal Industry Volume 3: 1830–1913: Victorian Pre-Eminence*. Oxford: Oxford University Press.
18 M. W. Flinn (1984). *The History of the British Coal Industry 1700–1830*, p. 311.
19 R. Church (1986). *The History of the British Coal Industry Volume 3: 1830–1913*, p. 511.
20 Ibid.
21 Ibid., p. 10.
22 British Parliamentary Papers (1871). *Report of the Commissioners Appointed to Inquire into the Several Matters Relating to Coal in the United Kingdom*. Vol. I. General Report and Twenty-two Sub-reports. H.C., 1871, [C.435] [C.435-I] [C.435-II], XVIII.1, 199, 815; British Parliamentary Papers (1905). *Royal Commission on Coal Supplies*. H.C. [Cd. 2353]; World Energy Council (2010). *2010 Survey of Energy Resources*. London: World Energy Council.
23 B. Supple (1987). *The History of the British Coal Industry Volume 4: 1914–1946: The Political Economy of Decline*. Oxford: Oxford University Press.
24 Ibid., pp. 61, 95.
25 B. Supple (1989). The British Coal Industry between the Wars. Economic History Society. *Refresh*, 9.
26 B. Supple (1987). *The History of the British Coal Industry Volume 4*, pp. 33, 39.
27 B. Supple (1989). The British Coal Industry between the Wars.
28 W. Ashworth (1986). *The History of the British Coal Industry. Vol. 5: 1946–1982: The Nationalized Industry*. Oxford: Oxford University Press.
29 Ibid., p. 47.
30 *Report of the Royal Commission on the Coal Industry (1925) with minutes of evidence and appendices. Vol 1 Report*. Cmd 2600.
31 E. A. Wrigley (2010). *Energy and the English Industrial Revolution*. Cambridge: Cambridge University Press.
32 A. Fernihough and K. H. O'Rourke (2020). Coal and the European Industrial Revolution. *Economic Journal*, 131(635): 1135–1149; N. Crafts and N. Wolf (2014). The Location of the UK Cotton Textiles Industry in 1838: A Quantitative Analysis. *Journal of Economic History*, 74(4): 1103–39.
33 B. R. Mitchell (1984). *Economic Development of the British Coal Industry 1800–1914*.
34 R. Kane (1844). *The Industrial Resources of Ireland*. Dublin: Hodges and Smith.
35 J. Mokyr (1985). *Why Ireland Starved: a Quantitative and Analytical History of the Irish Economy, 1800–1850*. London: George Allen & Unwin.
36 A. Bielenberg (2009). *Ireland and the Industrial Revolution: The Impact of the Industrial Revolution on Irish Industry, 1801–1922*. London: Routledge.
37 D. Chapman (1976). *North Sea Oil and Gas: A Geographical Perspective*. London: David & Charles.
38 H. L. Berryhill (1974). *The Worldwide Search for Petroleum Offshore – A Status report for the Quarter Century, 1947–1972*. Geological Survey Circular 694. US Department of the Interior.

39 Balance of payments was a continual problem from the 1950s to the 1970s, as indicated by Figure 7.6 (see Chapter 7).
40 Department of Energy (1974). *The Challenge of North Sea Oil*. Cmnd 7143.
41 R. Backhouse (1991). *Applied UK Macroeconomics*. Oxford: Basil Blackwell.
42 J. Kay (1984). North Sea Oil and Manufacturing Output. In B. Griffiths and G. E. Wood (eds), *Monetarism in the United Kingdom*. London: Macmillan Press.
43 House of Lords (1984–85). *Report of the Select Committee on Overseas Trade*, paragraph 64. p. 40.
44 L. P. Tempest (1979). The Financing of North Sea Oil 1975–1980. *Bank of England Quarterly Bulletin*, 1(2): 56–60.
45 S. Pollard (1983). *The Development of the British Economy 1914–1980*, 3rd edition. London: Edward Arnold, p. 288.
46 Ibid.
47 M. Chick (2020). *Changing Times*.
48 M. E. Bond and A. Knöbl (1982). Some Implications of North Sea Oil for the UK Economy. *IMF Staff Papers*, 29(3): 363–97.
49 For example, there is no discussion of oil or the North Sea in a recent discussion of neoliberal growth models: N. O'Donovan (2023). Demand, Dysfunction and Distribution: The UK Growth Model from Neoliberalism to the Knowledge Economy. *The British Journal of Politics and International Relations*, 25(1): 178–96.
50 P. J. Forsyth and J. A. Kay (1980). The Economic Implications of North Sea Oil Revenues. *Fiscal Studies*, 1(3): 1–28.
51 A. Singh (1979). North Sea Oil and the Reconstruction of UK Industry. In F. Blackaby (ed.), *De-industrialisation*. London: National Institute of Economic and Social Research.
52 P. Minford (1984). Comment on John Kay's Paper. In B. Griffiths and G. E. Wood (eds), *Monetarism in the United Kingdom*. London: Macmillan Press.
53 C. Bean (1987). The Impact of North Sea Oil. In R. Dornbusch and R. Layard (eds), *The Performance of the British Economy*. Oxford: Oxford University Press.
54 S. Kenny and E. McLaughlin (2022). Political Economy of Secession: Lessons from the Early Years of the Irish Free State. *National Institute Economic Review*, 261: 48–78.
55 J. Kelly (2003). The Irish Pound: From Origins to EMU. *Central Bank of Ireland Quarterly Bulletin,* Spring, 89–115.
56 Fitzpatrick and Honohan saw the lowering of the Irish exchange rate as being favourable to the Irish economy: J. Fitzpatrick and P. Honohan (2023). *Europe and the Transformation of Ireland*. Cambridge: Cambridge University Press.
57 R. Roberts (2016). *When Britain Went Bust: the 1976 IMF Crisis*. London: OMFIF.
58 A. Cairncross (1989). *British Economy since 1945*.
59 North Sea Resources and The Economy. *Hansard*, 388; House of Lords, 8 February 1978.
60 R. M. Solow (1986). On the Intergenerational Allocation of Natural Resources.

61 G. Atkinson and K. Hamilton (2020). Sustaining Wealth: Simulating a Sovereign Wealth Fund for the UK's Oil and Gas Resources, Past and Future. *Energy Policy*, 139: 111273.
62 A. N. Sy, R. Arezki and T. Gylfason (2012). The Economics of Sovereign Wealth Funds: Lessons from Norway. In R. Arezki, T.Gylfason and A. Sy (eds), *Beyond the Curse Policies to Harness the Power of Natural Resources*. Washington, DC: International Monetary Fund.
63 M. Wolf (2024). Britain Needs more than Fiscal Games. *Financial Times*, 6 March 2024; C. Giles (2025). Britain's Productivity Puzzle Is Turning into a Crisis. *Financial Times*, 19 February 2025.
64 W. Schlich (1904). *Forestry in the United Kingdom*. London: Bradbury, Agnew & Co, pp. 17–18.
65 L. D. Stamp (1928). The Forests of Europe: Present and Future. *Empire Forestry Journal*, 7: 185–202.
66 R. Zon and W. N. Sparhawk (1923). *Forest Resources of the World*. Vol. 1. New York: McGraw-Hill.
67 P. Warde (2007). *Energy Consumption in England and Wales, 1560–2000*. Naples: Consiglio Nazionale della Ricerche.
68 N. D. G. James (1981). *A History of English Forestry*. Oxford: Basil Blackwell.
69 I. Iriarte-Goñi and M. I. Ayuda (2012). Not only Subterranean Forests: Wood Consumption and Economic Development in Britain (1850–1938). *Ecological Economics*, 77: 176–84; H. S. K. Kent (1955). The Anglo-Norwegian Timber Trade in the Eighteenth Century. *The Economic History Review*, 8(1): 62–74; L. D. Stamp (1928). The Forests of Europe: Present and Future. *Empire Forestry Journal*, 7: 185–202.
70 W. Schlich (1904). *Forestry in the United Kingdom*.
71 R. Zon (1910). *The Forest Resources of the World*. Washington DC: US Department of Agriculture-Forest Service; H. Hiley (1930). *The Economics of Forestry*. Oxford: Clarendon Press; J. J. MacGregor (1953). The Sources and Natures of Statistical Information in Special Fields of Statistics: Timber Statistics. *Journal of the Royal Statistical Society. Series A* (General), 116(3): 298–322; R. Meigs (1949). *Home Timber Production*. London: Crosby Lockwood and Son.
72 The trade publication *Forestry Journal* published earlier in the 20th century contains a list of timber merchants and importers.
73 T. W. Birch (1936). The Afforestation of Britain. *Economic Geography*, 12: 1–26.
74 *Seventh Annual Report of the Forestry Commissioners year ending September 30th, 1926*. H.C. 1927, IX, (72).
75 *Thirtieth Annual Report of the Forestry Commissioners for the Year Ending September 30th, 1949*. H.C. XIII, (5), pp. 45–8.
76 C. H. Feinstein and S. Pollard (eds) (1988). *Studies in Capital Formation in the United Kingdom, 1750–1920*. Oxford: Oxford University Press; M. L. Anderson (1967). *A History of Scottish Forestry*. 2 Vols. London: Nelson; T. C. Smout, A. R. MacDonald and F. Watson (2005). *A History of the Native Woodlands of Scotland, 1500–1920*. Edinburgh: Edinburgh University Press; H. Schandl and N. Schulz (2002). Changes in the United Kingdom's Natural Relations in Terms of Society's Metabolism and Land-use from 1850 to the Present Day. *Ecological Economics*, 41: 212–13.

77 W. H. Hiley (1930). *The Economics of Forestry.*
78 L. D. Stamp and S. H. Beaver (1954). *The British Isles: A Geographic and Economic Survey*, 4th edition. London: Longmans, Green and Co, p. 158.
79 I. Iriarte-Goñi and M. I. Ayuda (2012). Not Only Subterranean Forests: Wood Consumption and Economic Development in Britain (1850–1938). *Ecological Economics*, 77: 176–84.
80 L. D. Stamp and S. H. Beaver (1954). *The British Isles: A Geographic and Economic Survey.*
81 W. H. Hiley (1930). *The Economics of Forestry*, pp. 12–13.
82 T. W. Birch (1936). The Afforestation of Britain.
83 K. Bolt, M. Matete and M. Clemens (2002). *Manual for Calculating Adjusted Net Savings*. Washington, DC: Environment Department, World Bank.
84 World Bank (2008). Adjusted Net Savings Database.
85 E. McLaughlin, et al. (2014). Historical Wealth Accounts for Britain; Forestry Commission (2012). *Standing Timber Volume for Coniferous Trees in Britain National Forest Inventory Report.*
86 I. K. Otero, S. Farrell, G. Pueyo, et al. (2020). Biodiversity Policy beyond Economic Growth. *Conservation Letters*, 13(4): e12713; J. B. Brauer, D. L. Czech, J. Trauger, et al. (2005). Establishing Indicators for Biodiversity. *Science,* 308(5723): 791–2.
87 E. O. Wilson (2002). *Future of Life*. New York: Alfred A. Knopf; OECD (2001). *OECD Environmental Outlook*. OECD Publishing; P. Dasgupta (2021). *The Economics of Biodiversity.*
88 M. Cropper and C. Griffiths (1994). The Interaction of Population Growth and Environmental Quality. *American Economic Review*, 84(2): 250–4; G. Koop and L. Tole (1999). Is There an Environmental Kuznets Curve for Deforestation? *Journal of Development Economics*, 58: 231–44; E. B. Barbier and J. C. Burgess (1997). The Economics of Tropical Forest Land Use Options. *Land Economics*, 73(2): 174–95; E. B. Barbier and J. C. Burgess (2001). The Economics of Tropic Deforestation. *Journal of Economic Surveys*, 15(3): 413–33; M. C. P. Hansen, V. Potapov, R. Moore, et al. (2013). High-resolution Global Maps of 21st-century Forest Cover Change. *Science*, 342(6160): 850–3; S. Dietz and W. N. Adger (2003). Economic Growth, Biodiversity Loss and Conservation Effort. *Journal of Environmental Management*, 68(1): 23–35; J. H. Mills and T. A. Waite (2009). Economic Prosperity, Biodiversity Conservation, and the Environmental Kuznets Curve. *Ecological Economics*, 68(7): 2087–95.
89 Any inference of an improvement in biodiversity must be qualified by the type of trees that are replanted. In Ireland, for example, the large-scale planting of spruce pine has been associated with the creation of what have been described as 'ecological dead zones', with serious consequences for bird populations: M. Colwell (2018). A Forestry Boom Is Turning Ireland Into an Ecological Dead Zone. *The Guardian*, 10 October 2018.
90 For example, P. J. de Loutherbourg (1801). *Coalbrookdale by Night*. Science Museum London 1952–452; S. Coleman (1822). A View of Bristol from Ashton Park. Bristol Museum, Object Number: K4350.
91 P. Brimblecombe (1977). London Air Pollution, 1500–1900. *Atmospheric Environment*, 11: 1157–62.

92 P. Brimblecombe (1987). *The Big Smoke: A History of Air Pollution in London since Medieval Times*. London: Routledge.
93 S. Heblich, A. Trew and Y. Zylberberg (2021). East-side Story: Historical Pollution and Persistent Neighborhood Sorting. *Journal of Political Economy*, 129(5): 1508–52.
94 A. E. Dingle (1982). The Monster Nuisance of All': Landowners, Alkali Manufacturers, and Air Pollution, 1828–64. *Economic History Review*, 35(4): 529–48.
95 Department of Trade and Industry (2004). *UK Coal Production Outlook: 2004–2016*.
96 *Report of the Royal Commission on the Coal Industry. With Minutes of Evidence and Appendices*. Vol 1. Report [Cmd 2600] P. 23–4; J. Schwartz and A. Marcus (1990). Mortality and Air Pollution in London: A Time Series Analysis. *American Journal of Epidemiology*, 131(1): 185–94; A. Hansell, et al. (2016). Historical Air Pollution Exposure and Long-term Mortality Risks in England and Wales: Prospective Longitudinal Cohort Study. *Thorax*, 71: 330–8; W. W. Hanlon (2024). London Fog: A Century of Pollution and Mortality, 1866–1965. *Review of Economics and Statistics*, 106(4): 910–23.
97 R. J. Andres, D. J. Fielding, G. Marland, T. A. Boden, N. Kumar and A. T. Kearney (1999). Carbon Dioxide Emissions from Fossil-fuel Use, 1751–1950. *Tellus*, 51B: 759–65; T. A. Boden, G. Marland and R. J. Andres (1995). Estimates of Global, Regional, and National Annual CO2 Emissions from Fossil-fuel Burning, Hydraulic Cement Production, and Gas Flaring: 1950–1992. ORNL/CDIAC-90, NDP-030/R6; A. S. Lefohn, J. D. Husar and R. B. Husar (1999). Estimating Historical Anthropogenic Global Sulfur Emission Patterns for the Period 1850–1990. *Atmospheric Environmentī* 33(21): 3435–44; S. J. Smith, H. Pitcher and T. Wigley (2001). Global and Regional Anthropogenic Sulfur Dioxide Emissions. *Global and Planetary Change*, 29: 99–119; S. J. Smith, J. van Aardenne, Z. Klimont, R. J. Andres, A. Volke and S. D. Arias (2011). Anthropogenic Sulf Diox Emissions: 1850–2005. *Atmospheric Chemistry and Physics*, 11: 1101–16.
98 G. M. Grossman and A. B. Krueger (1991). Environmental Impacts of a North American Free Trade Agreement. *NBER Working Paper* 3914.
99 P. Sephton and J. Mann (2016). Compelling Evidence of an Environmental Kuznets Curve in the United Kingdom. *Environmental and Resource Economics*, 64: 301–15.
100 A. Markandya, A. Golub and S. Pedroso-Galinato (2006). Empirical Analysis of National Income and SO_2 Emissions in Selected European Countries. *Environmental and Resource Economics*, 35, 221–57.
101 F. J. Brodie (1905). Decrease of fog in London during recent years. *Quarterly Journal of the Royal Meteorological Society*, 31(133): 15–28; K. Clay and W. Troesken (2011). Did Frederick Brodie Discover the World's First Environmental Kuznets Curve? Coal Smoke and the Rise and Fall of the London Fog. In Gary D. Libecap and Richard H. Steckel (eds), *The Economics of Climate Change: Adaptations Past and Present*. Chicago: Chicago University Press.

102 C. Klein (2012). When the Great Smog Smothered London. *History*.
103 R. Stone (2002). Counting the Cost of London's Killer Smog. *Science*, 298(5601): 2106–7; G. Wang, et al. (2016). Persistent Sulfate Formation from London Fog to Chinese Haze. *Proceedings of the National Academy of Sciences*, 113(48): 13630–5.
104 S. von Hinke and E. N. Sørensen (2023). The Long-term Effects of Early-life Pollution Exposure: Evidence from the London Smog. *Journal of Health Economics*, 92: 102827.
105 N. Stern, et al. (2006). *Stern Review: The Economics of Climate Change*. United Kingdom: UK Treasury, Table 8.1; D. Archer, et al. (2009). Atmospheric Lifetime of Fossil Fuel Carbon Dioxide. *Annal Review of Earth and Planetary Science*, 37: 117–34; M. Inman (2008). Carbon Is Forever. *Nature Climate Change*, 1: 156–8.
106 J. Kunnas, E. McLaughlin, N. Hanley, D. Greasley, L. Oxley and P. Warde (2014). Counting Carbon: Historic Emissions from Fossil Fuels, Long-run Measures of Sustainable Development and Carbon Debt. *Scandinavian Economic History Review*, 62(3): 243–65.
107 L. McGrath, S. Hynes and J. McHale (2021). The Air We Breathe: Estimates of Air Pollution Extended Genuine Savings for Europe. *The Review of Income and Wealth*, 68(1): 161–88.
108 M.B. Hadley, J. Baumgartner and R. Vedanthan (2018). Developing a Clinical Approach to Air Pollution and Cardiovascular Health. *Circulation*, 137(7): 725–42; J. E. Lelieveld, M Fnais, et al. (2015). The Contribution of Outdoor Air Pollution Sources to Premature Mortality on a Global Scale. *Nature*, 525: 367–71.
109 N. Z. Muller and R. Mendelsohn (2007). Measuring the Damages of Air Pollution in the United States. *Journal of Environmental Economics and Management*, 54(1): 1–14; N. Z. Muller (2014). Boosting GDP Growth by Accounting for the Environment. *Science*, 345(6199): 873–4; N. Z. Muller (2020). Long-run Environmental Accounting in the US Economy. *Environmental and Energy Policy and the Economy*, 1.
110 T. J. Hatton (2014). Population, Migration and Labour Supply. In R. Floud, J. Humphries and P. Johnson (eds), *The Cambridge Economic History of Modern Britain*. Cambridge: Cambridge University Press.
111 Somewhat anomalously within the UK, Ireland had already been a recipient of state-funded primary education since 1833.
112 S. Broadberry (2004). Human Capital and Skills. In R. Floud and P. Johnson (eds), *Cambridge Economic History of Modern Britain: Volume 2: Economic Maturity, 1860–1939*. Cambridge: Cambridge University Press.
113 C. Goldin (2001). The Human-Capital Century and American Leadership: Virtues of the Past. *Journal of Economic History*, 61(2): 263–92.
114 R. Millward (2014). The Growth of the Public Sector In R. Floud, J. Humphries and P. Johnson (eds), *The Cambridge Economic History of Modern Britain*. Cambridge: Cambridge University Press.
115 R. S. Schofield (1976). Dimensions of Illiteracy, 1750–1850. *Explorations in Economic History*, 10(4): 437–54.
116 There is a critique of the literature that equates age misreporting with human capital. Some see it as a reflection of state capacity or reflecting a culture of

veneration of elderly. Colleagues and I argue that it could also be distorted by other demographic factors such as emigration: C. L. Colvin, St. Henderson and E. McLaughlin (2024). Age Structure and Age Heaping: Solving Ireland's Post-famine Digit Preference Puzzle. *European Review of Economic History*, 39: 28–48.

117 B. A'Hearn, J. Baten and D. Crayen (2009). Quantifying Quantitative Literacy: Age Heaping and the History of Human Capital. *The Journal of Economic History*, 69(3): 783–808. J. Baten, D. Crayen and H.-J. Voth (2014). Numeracy and the Impact of High Food Prices in Industrializing Britain, 1780–1850. *Review of Economics and Statistics*, 96(3): 418–30.

118 N. F. R. Crafts (1995). Exogenous or Endogenous Growth?

119 L. Shaw-Taylor (2020). An Introduction to the History of Infectious Diseases, Epidemics and the Early Phases of the Long-run Decline in Mortality. *Economic History Review*, 73(3): e1–e19.

120 C. Langford (2002). The Age Pattern of Mortality in the 1918–19 Influenza Pandemic: An Attempted Explanation Based on Data for England and Wales. *Medical History*, 46: 1–20; A. Doran, C. L. Colvin and E. McLaughlin (2024). What Can We Learn from Historical Pandemics? A Systematic Review of the Literature. *Social Science & Medicine*, 342: 116534.

121 T. O'Shaughnessy (2011). Hysteresis in Unemployment. *Oxford Review of Economic Policy*, 27(2): 312–37.

122 A. Cairncross (1992). *The British Economy since 1945*, p. 230; O. J. Blanchard and L. H. Summers (1987). Hysteresis in Unemployment. *European Economic Review*, 31: 288–95; O. J. Blanchard and L. H. Summers (1988). Beyond the Natural Rate Hypothesis. *American Economic Review*, 78(2): 182–7; K. Røed (1997). Hysteresis in Unemployment. *Journal of Economic Surveys*, 11(4): 353–455; D. Webster (2005). Long-term Unemployment, the Invention of 'Hysteresis' and the Misdiagnosis of Structural Unemployment in the UK. *Cambridge Journal of Economics*, 29: 975–95.

123 D. Yagan (2019). Employment Hysteresis from the Great Recession. *Journal of Political Economy*, 127(5): 1993–2568; T. O'Shaughnessy (2011). Hysteresis in Unemployment.

124 C. Batista, D. Han, J. Haushofer, et al. (2025). Brain Drain or Brain Gain? Effects of High-skilled International Emigration on Origin Countries. *Science*, 388(6749): eadr8861.

125 B. R. Mitchell (1988). *British Historical Statistics*; Migration Statistics. House of Commons Library. 2 December 2024. https://commonslibrary.parliament.uk/research-briefings/sn06077/; Net Migration to the UK, 2 December 2024. The Migration Observatory: https://migrationobservatory.ox.ac.uk/resources/briefings/long-term-international-migration-flows-to-and-from-the-uk/

126 B. Thomas (1973). *Migration and Economic Growth: A Study of Great Britain and the Atlantic Economy*, 2nd edition. Cambridge: Cambridge University Press.

127 V. Carpentier (2003). Public Expenditure on Education and Economic Growth in the UK, 1833–2000. *History of Education*, 32(1): 1–15; V. Carpentier (2020). 0 1833–2019. 21 July 2020. UCL Research Data Repository: A Historical Dataset on UK Education 1833–2019.

128 D. Jorgenson and B. M. Fraumeni (1989). The Accumulation of Human and Nonhuman Capital, 1948–84.

129 ONS (2024). Human Capital Stocks Estimates in the UK: 2004 to 2022, released 19 March 2024, ONS Website, Statistical Bulletin.

130 J. Kunnas (2016). Human Capital in Britain, 1760–2009. *Scandinavian Economic History Review*, 64(3): 219–42.

131 E. McLaughlin, N. Hanley, D. Greasley, J. Kunnas, L. Oxley and P. Warde (2014). Historical Wealth Accounts for Britain; E. McLaughlin, et al. (2017). Historical Wealth Accounts for Britain.

132 D. Pearce (1993). *Blueprint 3: Measuring Sustainable Development.*

133 K. Hamilton and M. Clemens (1999). Genuine Savings in Developing Countries; D. Greasley, N. Hanley, K. Kunnas, E. McLaughlin, L. Oxley and P. Warde (2014). Testing Genuine Savings as a Forward-looking Indicator of Future Well-being Over the (very) Long-run.

134 M. Weitzman (1997). Sustainability and Technical Progress; M. Pemberton and D. Ulph (2011). Measuring Income and Measuring Sustainability. *Scandinavian Journal of Economics*, 103: 25–40.

135 Data are from the 2011 *Changing Wealth of Nations* report. These data were used because they are standardized using the same methodology and thus broadly comparable across countries.

136 E.g., see review by L. McGrath, N. Hanley and E. McLaughlin (2025). Saving or Investing for the Future? Methodology Matters in Inclusive Wealth Accounting. *Heriot-Watt* Working Paper, 2025–06.

137 N. Crafts (1993). *Can De-Industrialisation Seriously Damage Your Wealth?*, Table 3.

138 House of Lords (1984–85). *Report from the Select Committee on Overseas Trade*, Table 3.2.

139 N. Crafts and M. O'Mahony (2001). A Perspective on UK Productivity Performance. *Fiscal Studies*, 22(3): 271–306.

140 Oil reserves were estimated at 4.0 billion barrels of oil equivalent (boe) in 2021 with a prospective 11.2 billion boe reserves. This is compared to total production from the North Sea of 46.4 billion boe up to 2021: North Sea Transition Authority (2022). UK Oil and Gas Reserves and Resources as of End 2021.

141 Forest area globally is 31 percent (13039 million hectares). This reflects variation throughout the world. In the EU forest area is 40 percent (400 million hectares), 50 percent (1648 million hectares) in Russia, 21 percent (2989 million hectares) in Africa, 20 percent (3109 million hectares) in Asia, 35 percent (2133 million hectares) in North & Central America, 22 percent (849 million hectares) in Oceania, and 48 percent (1746 million hectares) in South America: Forest Research (2024). *Forestry Facts & Figures 2024: A Summary of Statistics About Woodland and Forestry in the UK.*

142 H. Allcott and D. Keniston (2018). Dutch Disease or Agglomeration? The Local Economic Effects of Natural Resource Booms in Modern America. *The Review of Economic Studies*, 85(2): 695–731.

143 M. Agarwala, M. Burke and J-C. Mei (2024). An Inclusive Wealth Model of Productivity. https://papers.ssrn.com/sol3/papers.cfm?abstract_id=4857812

144 D. Greasley, E. McLaughlin, N. Hanley and L. Oxley (2017). Australia.

Chapter Nine

1 *WON*, Book IV, Chapter IX.
2 K. Raworth (2022 paperback). *Doughnut Economics: Seven Ways to Think Like a 21st-Century Economist*. London: Penguin.
3 G. E. P. Box (1976). Science and Statistics. *Journal of the American Statistical Association*, 71(356): 791–9.
4 A. A. Chiarenza, et al. (2020). Asteroid Impact, Not Volcanism, Caused the End-Cretaceous Dinosaur Extinction. *Proceedings of the National Academy of Sciences*, 117(29): 17084–93; M. Li, et al. (2021). Nickel Isotopes Link Siberian Traps Aerosol Particles to the End-Permian Mass Extinction. *Nature Communications*, 12(1): 2024; Y. Sun, et al. (2024). Mega El Niño Instigated the End-Permian Mass Extinction. *Science*, 385(671): 1189–95.
5 K. Raworth (2017). *Doughnut Economics*.
6 J. Rockström, W. Steffen, et al. (2009). Planetary Boundaries: Exploring the Safe Operating Space for Humanity.
7 W. Steffen, K. Richardson, J. Rockström, et al. (2020). The Emergence and Evolution of Earth System Science. *Nature Reviews Earth & Environment*, 1(1): 54–63.
8 Tyler Prize for Environmental Achievement: https://www.tylerprize.org/laureates/alllaureates
9 L. Hughes and M. Rice (2023). Will Steffen (1947–2023). *Nature*, 615: 29. https://doi.org/10.1038/d41586-023-00519-x; He also received an obituary in the news outlet *The Conversation*: J. Finnegan, P. Canadell and S. J. Lade (2023). We've Lost a Giant: Vale Professor Will Steffen, Climate Science Pioneer. *The Conversation*, 31 January 2023.
10 J. Rockström, W. Steffen, et al. (2009). A Safe Operating Space for Humanity. pp. 472–5; W. Steffen, J. Rockström, et al. (2018). Trajectories of the Earth System in the Anthropocene. *Proceedings National Academy of Science*, 115(33): 8252–9; K. Richardson, W. Steffen, W. Lucht, J. Bendtsen, et al. (2023). Earth Beyond Six of Nine Planetary Boundaries.
11 W. Steffen, P. J. Crutzen and J. R. McNeill (2007). The Anthropocene: Are Humans Now Overwhelming the Great Forces of Nature. *AMBIO*, 36(8): 614–21.
12 J. Rockström, W. Steffen, et al. (2009). A Safe Operating Space for Humanity; J. Rockström, W. Steffen, et al. (2009). Planetary Boundaries: Exploring the Safe Operating Space for Humanity; The '2°C guardrail' target first proposed by William Nordhaus is a risk-averse boundary not derived from modelling but from considering the variation in long-term climate in the 1970s and concluding that 2 was outside the range of human experience: T. Nordhaus (2018). The Two-degree Delusion: The Dangers of an Unrealistic Climate Change Target. *Foreign Affairs*.
13 W. Steffen, K. Richardson et al. (2015). Sustainability. Planetary Boundaries: Guiding Human Development on a Changing Planet; K. Richardson, W. Steffen, W. Lucht, J. Bendtsen, et al. (2023). Earth Beyond Six of Nine Planetary Boundaries.
14 W. Steffen, J. Rockström, et al. (2018). Trajectories of the Earth System in the Anthropocene.

15 J. Rockström, W. Steffen, et al. (2009). A Safe Operating Space for Humanity.
16 K. Richardson, et al. (2023). Earth Beyond Six of Nine Planetary Boundaries.
17 See the Stockholm Resilience Centre Website for the Latest Visualisation of PBs: https://www.stockholmresilience.org/research/planetary-boundaries.html
18 J. Rockström, et al. (2023). Safe and Just Earth System Boundaries.
19 T. M. Lenton, J. Rockström, et al. (2019). Climate Tipping Points – Too Risky to Bet Against. *Nature*, 575: 592–5. https://doi.org/10.1038/d41586-019-03595-0
20 C. C. Mann (2018). *The Wizard and the Prophet.*
21 J. Rockström, et al. (2023). Safe and Just Earth System Boundaries.
22 K. Richardson, et al. (2023). Earth Beyond Six of Nine Planetary Boundaries.
23 A. S. Downing, et al. (2019). Matching Scope, Purpose and Uses of Planetary Boundaries Science. *Environmental Research Letters*, 14(7): 073005.
24 A. J. McMichael (2013). Globalisation, Climate Change, and Human Health. *New England Journal of Medicine*, 368: 1335–43.
25 S. Whitmee, A. Haines, et al. (2015). Safeguarding Human Health in the Anthropocene Epoch: Report of The Rockefeller Foundation–Lancet Commission on Planetary Health. *The Lancet*, 386(10007): 1973–2028.
26 P. Dasgupta (2020). *Interim Report of the Independent Review on the Economics of Biodiversity Led by Professor Sir Partha Dasgupta*. London: H. M. Treasury; P. Dasgupta (2021). *The Economics of Biodiversity.*
27 F. Biermann and R. E. Kim (2020). The Boundaries of the Planetary Boundary Framework: A Critical Appraisal of Approaches to Define a 'Safe Operating Space' for Humanity.
28 F. P. Saunders (2015). Planetary Boundaries: At the Threshold . . . Again: Sustainable Development Ideas and Politics. *Environment, Development and Sustainability*, 17: 823–35.
29 J. Weinkle (2024). How Planetary Boundaries Captured Science, Health, and Finance: The Technological Façade Hiding a Normative Empire. *Breakthrough Institute Journal*, 20.
30 This also touches on arguments for and against ending the Holocene and declaring an Anthropocene which is still widely debated, e.g., see: R. Monastersky (2015). The Human Age. *Nature*, 519: 144–7; M Subramamian (2019). Anthropocene Now: Influential Panel Votes to Recognize Earth's New Epoch. *Nature*. https://doi.org/10.1038/d41586-019-01641-5; While a proposal for a formal recognition of the Anthropocene as a new epoch in the Earth's geological timeline was formally rejected in 2024 by a subcommission of the International Commission on Stratigraphy, anthropocene still exists as a cultural concept: A. Witz (2024). Geologists Reject the Anthropocene as Earth's New Epoch – After 15 Years of Debate. *Nature*, 627: 249–50. https://doi.org/10.1038/d41586-024-00675-8
31 J. F. Donges, R. Winkelmann, et al. (2017). Closing the Loop: Reconnecting Human Dynamics to Earth System Science. *The Anthropocene Review*, 4(2): 151–7.
32 S. J. Lade, W. Steffen, W. de Vries, et al. (2020). Human Impacts on Planetary Boundaries Amplified by Earth System Interactions. *Nature Sustainability*, 3: 119–28; K. Richardson, et al. (2023). Earth Beyond Six of Nine Planetary Boundaries.

33 T. Ord (2020). *The Precipice.*

34 L. Kemp, C. Xuc, J. Depledged, et al. (2022). Climate Endgame: Exploring Catastrophic Climate Change Scenarios. *PNAS*, 119(34): e2108146119.

35 B. Booth and F. Fitch (1979). *Earth Shock: Can Earth Survive Its Natural Catastrophes?* London: Sphere Books; P. J. Smith (1979). Disaster Strikes from the Blue. *Nature*, 279: 654.

36 I. W. R. Martin and R. S. Pindyck (2015). Averting Catastrophes.

37 N. Bostrom (2002). Existential Risks: Analyzing Human Extinction Scenarios and Related Hazards. *Journal of Evolution and Technology*, 9(1); T. Ord (2020). *The Precipice*; M. Rees (2003). *Our Final Hour: A Scientist's Warning*. New York: Basic Books; M. Rees (2018). *On the Future Prospects for Humanity*. Princeton: Princeton University Press; The Global Challenges Foundation Publishes an Annual Assessment of Catastrophic Risk: Global Catastrophic Risks 2021: Navigating the Complex Intersections. https://globalchallenges.org/wp-content/uploads/2021/09/Global-Catastrophic-Risks-2021-FINAL.pdf

38 S. D. Baum, T. M. Maher and J. Haqq-Misra (2013). Double Catastrophe: Intermittent Stratospheric Geoengineering Induced by Societal Collapse. *Environment, Systems and Decisions*, 33(1): 168–80; B. Tonn and D. Stiefel (2013). Evaluating Methods for Estimating Existential Risks.

39 T. Ord (2020). *The Precipice*; T. M. Maher and S. D. Baum (2013). Adaptation to and Recovery from Global Catastrophe. *Sustainability*, 5(4): 1461–79; S. D. Baum, S. Armstrong, T. Ekenstedt, O. Häggström, R. Hanson, K. Kuhlemann, . . . and R. V. Yampolskiy (2019). Long-term Trajectories of Human Civilization. *Foresight*, 21(1): 53–83.

40 B. Tonn and D. Stiefel (2013). Evaluating Methods for Estimating Existential Risks; D. Helbing (2013). Globally Networked Risks and How to Respond. *Nature*, 497: 51–9; K. Kuhlemann (2019). Complexity, Creeping Normalcy and Conceit: Sexy and Unsexy Risks. *Foresight*, 21(1): 35–52.

41 M. Sigl, M. Winstrup, J. R. McConnell, K. C. Welten, G. Plunkett, F. Ludlow, . . . and T. E. Woodruff (2015). Timing and Climate Forcing of Volcanic Eruptions for the Past 2,500 Years. *Nature*, 523(7562): 543–49; L. Mordechai, M. Eisenberg, T. P. Newfield, A. Izdebski, J. E. Kay and H. Poinar (2019). The Justinianic Plague: An Inconsequential Pandemic? *Proceedings of the National Academy of Sciences*, 116(51): 25546–54; T. P. Newfield (2018). The Climate Downturn of 536–50. In S. White, C. Pfister and F. Mauelshagen (eds), *The Palgrave Handbook of Climate History*. London: Palgrave, 447–93.

42 G. Alfani (2024). Epidemics and Pandemics: From the Justinianic Plague to the Spanish Flu. In C. Diebolt and M. Haupert (eds), *Handbook of Cliometrics*. Berlin: Springer; P. Sarris (2022). Viewpoint New Approaches to the "Plague of Justinian". *Past & Present*, 254(1): 315–46.

43 S. Avin, B. Wintle, J. Weitzdorfer, S. S. ÓhÉigeartaigh, W. J. Sutherland and M. J. Rees (2018). Classifying Global Catastrophic Risks. *Futures*, 102: 20–6.

44 N. N. Taleb (2007). *The Black Swan: The Impact of the Highly Improbable*. London: Random House; S. Hochrainer-Stigler (2020). *Extreme and Systemic Risk Analysis: A Loss Distribution Approach*. Berlin: Springer.

45 D. Morrison, C. R. Chapman, D. Steel and R. P. Binzel (2004). Impacts and the Public: Communicating the Nature of the Impact Hazard. In M. J. S. Belton,

T. H. Morgan, N. H. Samarasinha and D. K. Yeomans (eds), *Mitigation of Hazardous Comets and Asteroids*. Cambridge: Cambridge University Press.

46 R. P. Binzel (2000). The Torino Impact Hazard Scale. *Planetary and Space Science*, 48(4): 297–303.

47 K. Raworth (2011). A Safe and Just Space for Humanity: Can We Live within the Doughnut? *Oxfam Discussion Papers*; K. Raworth (2017). *Doughnut Economics*.

48 *WON*, Book IV.

49 The Brundtland Commission is not mentioned in her 2017 book: K. Raworth (2017). *Doughnut Economics*.

50 K. Raworth (2017). A Doughnut for the Anthropocene: Humanity's Compass in the 21st Century. The *Lancet Planetary Health*, 1(2): e48–9.

51 H. Schlesier, M. Schäfer and H. Desing (2024). Measuring the Doughnut: A Good Life for All Is Possible within Planetary Boundaries. *Journal of Cleaner Production*, 448: 141447.

52 D. W. O'Neill, A. L. Fanning, W. F. Lamb and J. K. Steinberger (2018). A Good Life for All within Planetary Boundaries. *Nature Sustainability*, 1: 88–95. https://doi.org.10.1038/s41893-018-0021-4; A. L. Fanning, D. W. O'Neill, J. Hickel and N. Roux (2022). The Social Shortfall and Ecological Overshoot of Nations. *Nature Sustainability*, 5(1): 26–36. Data from: https://goodlife.leeds.ac.uk/national-trends/country-trends/#WLD

53 This remains a subject of ongoing debate. My 8-year-old son (a budding geographer) and I discussed this in relation to the largest state in the United States. He argued convincingly that size should be measured by land area (Alaska), whereas I maintained that it should be measured by population (California).

54 G. Kallis, J. Hickel, D. W O'Neill, T. Jackson, P. A Victor, K. Raworth, J. B Schor, J. K Steinberger and D. Ürge-Vorsatz (2025). Post-growth: The Science of Wellbeing within Planetary Boundaries. *Lancet Planet Health*, 9: e62–78.

55 D. H. Meadows, et al. (1972). *The Limits to Growth*.

56 H. W. Arndt (1987). *Economic Development*; N. Georgescu-Roegen (1971). *The Entropy Law and the Economic Process*; B. G. Baykan (2007). From Limits to Growth to Degrowth within French Green Politics. *Environmental Politics*, 16(3): 513–17; T. Jackson (2009). *Prosperity without Growth?: The Transition to a Sustainable Economy*. London: Routledge; G. Kallis, V. Kostakis S. Lange, B. Muraca, S. Paulson and M. Schmelzer (2018). Research on Degrowth. *Annual Review of Environment and Resources*, 43(1): 291–316; G. Kallis (2019). *Limits: Why Malthus Was Wrong and Why Environmentalists Should Care*. Stanford, CA: Stanford University Press; M. Schmelzer, A. Vetter and A. Vansintjan (2022). *The Future is Degrowth: A Guide to a World Beyond Capitalism*. London: Verso Books; M. Diesendorf, G. Davies, T. Wiedmann, J. H. Spangenberg and S. Hail (2024). Sustainability Scientists' Critique of Neoclassical Economics; J. Hickel (2020). *Less Is More: How Degrowth Will Save the World*. London: Penguin; J. Hickel (2021). What Does Degrowth Mean? A Few Points of Clarification. *Globalizations*, 18(7): 1105–11.

57 J. Hickel (2020). *Less Is More*.

58 E. McLaughlin (2024). Degrowth: Is There any Consensus on Whether It Might be a Good Idea? *Economics Observatory*, 4 November 2024: https://www.economicsobservatory.com/degrowth-is-there-any-consensus-on-whether-it-might-be-a-good-idea
59 W. Naudé (2023). *Economic Growth and Societal Collapse: Beyond Green Growth and Degrowth Fairy Tales*. London: Palgrave Macmillan.
60 A post by the historian Rutger Bregman on the social media platform X (Twitter) had 1.3 million views as of 24 September 2024: https://x.com/rcbregman/status/1831227421896356126; S. Keynes (2024). What's Wrong with Research About "Degrowth"? *Financial Times*, 20 September 2024.
61 G. Kallis, V. Kostakis, S. Lange, B. Muraca, S. Paulson and M. Schmelzer (2018). Research on Degrowth.
62 Ibid.
63 G. Kallis (2011). In Defence of Degrowth. *Ecological Economics*, 70(5): 873–80; G. Kallis (2017). Radical Dematerialization and Degrowth. *Philosophical Transactions of the Royal Society A*, 375(2095): 20160383.
64 J. Hickel (2020). *Less Is More*; J. Hickel (2021). What Does Degrowth Mean?
65 R. Mastini, G. Kallis and J. Hickel (2021). A Green New Deal without Growth? *Ecological Economics*, 179: 106832.
66 G. Kallis (2011). In Defence of Degrowth.
67 G. Kallis (2017). Radical Dematerialization and Degrowth; L. T. Keyßer and M. Lenzen (2021). 1.5 C Degrowth Scenarios Suggest the Need for New Mitigation Pathways. *Nature Communications*, 12(1): 2676; J. Hickel, G. Kallis, T. Jackson, D. W. O'Neill, J. B. Schor, J. K. Steinberger . . . and D. Ürge-Vorsatz (2022). Degrowth Can Work – Here's How Science Can Help. *Nature*, 612(7940): 400–3; O M. Ajulo, J. von Meding and P. Tang (2020). Relocalisation for Degrowth and Disaster Risk Reduction. *Disaster Prevention and Management: An International Journal*, 29(6): 877–91.
68 J. C. Van den Bergh (2011). Environment versus Growth – A Criticism of "Degrowth" and a Plea for "a-growth". *Ecological Economics*, 70(5): 881–90; G. Kallis (2011). In Defence of Degrowth.
69 D. Harvey (1982). *The Limits to Capital*. Oxford: Basil Blackwell; T. Jackson (2009). *Prosperity without Growth?: The Transition to a Sustainable Economy*; D. Harvey (2014). *Seventeen Contradictions and the End of Capitalism*. Oxford: Oxford University Press.
70 For example: J. Hickel (2020). *Less Is More*; and M. Schmelzer, A. Vetter and A. Vansintjan (2022). *The Future Is Degrowth*.
71 G. Kallis (2011). In Defence of Degrowth.
72 Ibid.
73 J. C. Van den Bergh (2011). Environment versus Growth.
74 G. Kallis, V. Kostakis S. Lange, B. Muraca, S. Paulson and M. Schmelzer (2018). Research on Degrowth.
75 R. Mastini, G. Kallis and J. Hickel (2021). A Green New Deal without Growth?
76 J. Hickel (2020). *Less Is More*.
77 W. D. Nordhaus (1996). Do Real-Output and Real-Wage Measures Capture Reality? The History of Lighting Suggests Not. In Timothy F. Bresnahan and

Robert J. Gordon (eds), *The Economics of New Goods*. Chicago: University of Chicago Press.

78 J. O. Engler, M. F. Kretschmer, J. Rathgens, J. A. Ament, T. Huth and H. von Wehrden (2024). 15 Years of Degrowth Research: A Systematic Review. *Ecological Economics*, 218: 108101; I. Savin and J. van den Bergh (2024). Reviewing Studies of Degrowth: Are Claims Matched by Data, Methods and Policy Analysis? *Ecological Economics*, 226: 108324; A. Lauer, I. Capellán-Pérez and N. Wergles (2025). A Comparative Review of De and post-growth Modeling Studies. *Ecological Economics*, 227: 108383.

79 J. O. Engler, M. F. Kretschmer, J. Rathgens, J. A. Ament, T. Huth and H. von Wehrden (2024). 15 Years of Degrowth Research; A. Lauer, I. Capellán-Pérez and N. Wergles (2025). A Comparative Review of De-and post-growth Modeling Studies.

80 G. Kallis and H. March (2015). Imaginaries of Hope: The Utopianism of Degrowth. *Annals of the Association of American Geographers*, 105(2): 360–8.

81 G. M. Turner (2008). A Comparison of the Limits to Growth with 30 Years of Reality. *Global Environmental Change*, 18(3): 397–411; U. Bardi (2011). *The Limits to Growth Revisited.*

82 G. Herrington (2020). Update to Limits to Growth: Comparing the World3 Model with Empirical Data. *Journal of Industrial Ecology*, 25(3): 614–26.

83 A. Nebel, A. Kling, R. Willamowski and T. Schell (2023). Recalibration of Limits to Growth: An Update of the World3 Model. *Journal of Industrial Ecology*, 28(1): 87–99.

84 See, for example, H. T. Engelhardt, Jr and A. L. Caplan (eds) (1987). *Scientific Controversies: Case Studies in the Resolution and Closure of Disputes in Science and Technology*. Cambridge: Cambridge University Press.

85 K. Kelly (1994). *Out of Control: The New Biology of Machines*. New York: Perseus, Chapter 22.

86 G. Kallis, J. Hickel, D. W O'Neill, T. Jackson, P. A Victor, K. Raworth, J. B Schor, J. K Steinberger and D. Ürge-Vorsatz (2025). Post-growth.

87 J. Cobb and H. Daly (1989). *For the Common Good: Redirecting the Economy Toward Community, the Environment and a Sustainable Future.* Boston: Beacon Press.

88 R. Civitillo (2023). Index of Sustainable Economic Welfare. In S. O. Idowu, R. Schmidpeter, N. Capaldi, L. Zu, M. D. Baldo and R. Abreu (eds), *Encyclopedia of Sustainable Management*. Berlin: Springer.

89 J. Van der Slycken and B. Bleys (2024). Is Europe Faring Well with Growth? Evidence from a Welfare Comparison in the EU-15 (1995–2018). *Ecological Economics*, 217: 108054.

90 E. Neumayer (1999). The ISEW: Not an Index of Sustainable Economic Welfare. *Social Indicators Research*, 48: 77–101; E. Neumayer (2000). On the Methodology of ISEW, GPI and Related Measures: Some Constructive Suggestions and Some Doubt on the "Threshold" Hypothesis. *Ecological Economics*, 34(3): 347–61.

91 P. Dasgupta and S. Levin (2023). Economic Factors Underlying Biodiversity Loss.

92 P. Dasgupta (2009). The Welfare Economic Theory of Green National Accounts.

93 G. B. Asheim (1986). Hartwick's Rule in Open Economies. *Canadian Journal of Economics*, 19(3): 395–402.
94 M. del Mar Rubio (2004). The Capital Gains From Trade Are Not Enough.
95 G. Atkinson, M. Agarwala and P. Muñoz (2012). Are National Economies (Virtually) Sustainable?: An Empirical Analysis of Natural Assets in International Trade. In *Inclusive Wealth Report 2012*, 87–117.
96 W. D. Nordhaus (1996). Do Real-Output and Real-Wage Measures Capture Reality?; G. Wagner (2011). *But Will the Planet Notice? How Smart Economics Can Save the World*. New York: Hill and Wang.
97 A. Starbuck (1878). *History of the American Whale Fishery from Its Earliest Inception to the year 1876*. Waltham, MA: Author; M. E. Gosho, D. W. Rice and J. M. Breiwick (1984). The Sperm Whale, Physeter Macrocephalus. *Marine Fisheries Review*, 46(4): 54–64.
98 R. York (2017). Why Petroleum Did Not Save the Whales. *Socius: Sociological Research for a Dynamic World*, 3: 1–13.
99 Ibid.
100 J. P. McClure (1998). The Epizootic of 1872: Horses and Disease in a Nation in Motion. *New York History*, 79(1): 4–22; A. B. Judson (1873). History and Course of the Epizoötic among Horses upon the North American Continent in 1872–73. *Public Health Papers and Reports*, 1: 88–109.
101 G. Wagner (2011). *But Will the Planet Notice?*
102 See discussion in E. McLaughlin, C. Ducoing and L. Oxley (2023). Tracing Sustainability in the Long Run; also see discussion in A. Bilal and J. H. Stock (2025). A Guide to Macroeconomics and Climate Change. *NBER Working Paper* 33567.
103 R. S. J. Tol (2024). Social Cost of Carbon Estimates Have Increased Over Time. *Nature Climate Change*, 13: 532–6.
104 L. McGrath, S. Hynes and J. McHale (2019). Augmenting the World Bank's Estimates: Ireland's Genuine Savings through Boom and Bust. *Ecological Economics*, 165: 106364; L. McGrath, S. Hynes and J. McHale (2022). The Air We Breathe.
105 R. Walgate (1986). UK Denies Responsibility for Scandinavian Acid Rain. *Nature,* 323: 191; K. G. Maler (1989). The Acid Rain Game. *Studies in Environmental Science*, 36: 231–52.
106 J. Pezzey and P. Bourke (2014). Towards a More Inclusive and Precautionary Indicator of Global Sustainability. *Ecological Economics*, 106: 141–54.
107 See discussion in E. McLaughlin, C. Ducoing and L. Oxley (2023). Tracing Sustainability in the Long Run.
108 D. Helm (2016). *Natural Capital: Valuing the Planet*. New Haven: Yale University Press.
109 M. E. Power, D. Tilman, J. A. Estes, B. A. Menge, W. J. Bond, L. S., Mills . . . and R. T. Paine (1996). Challenges In the Quest for Keystones: Identifying Keystone Species Is Difficult – but Essential to Understanding How Loss of Species Will Affect Ecosystems. *BioScience*, 46(8): 609–20; R. F. Denno and D. Lewis (2009). Predator-Prey Interactions. In Simon A. Levin (ed.), *The Princeton Guide to Ecology*. Princeton, NJ: Princeton University Press; I. Shukla, K. M. Gaynor, B. Worm and C. T. Darimont (2023). The Diversity of Animals Identified as Keystone Species. *Ecology and Evolution*, 13(10): e10561.

110 N. Mouquet, D. Gravel, F. Massol and V. Calcagno (2013). Extending the Concept of Keystone Species to Communities and Ecosystems. *Ecology Letters*, 16: 1–8.

111 E. P. Fenichel (2024). A New Era of Economic Measurement for the Environment and Natural Capital. *Review of Environmental Economics and Policy*, 18(2): 321–30.

112 J. Mokyr (1990). *The Levers of Riches*.

113 N. Ferguson (2021). *Doom: The Politics of Catastrophe*. London: Allen Lane.

114 L. Geraghty (2024). Science Fiction Film and Television: The 1950s to the 1970s. In M. Bould, A. M. Butler and S. Vint (eds), *The New Routledge Companion to Science Fiction*. London: Routledge.

115 R. A. Heinlein (1952). Where to? *Galaxy Magazine*.

116 The quote was a subtitle to his funds manifesto: 'What Happened to the Future?'. Although, ironically, Thiel had made his fortune from an early investment in the social media giant Facebook: Facebook Investor Wants Flying Cars, Not 140 Characters. *Business Insider*, 30 July 2011. https://www.businessinsider.com/founders-fund-the-future-2011-7

117 Uncommon Knowledge with Peter Robinson, Interview with Peter Thiel. 9 November 2022. https://www.hoover.org/research/peter-thiel-leader-rebel-alliance

118 P. Sabin (2013). *The Bet*; P. R. Ehrlich (1968). *The Population Bomb*. New York: Sierra Club; J. L. Simon (1981). *The Ultimate Resource*. J. L. Simon (1996). *The Ultimate Resource II: People, Materials, and Environment* Princeton: Princeton University Press.

119 V. Abernethy (1991). How Julian Simon Could Win the Bet and Still Be Wrong. *Population and Environment*, 13(1): 3–7. K. Kiel, V. Matheson and K. Golembiewski (2010). Luck or Skill? An Examination of the Ehrlich–Simon Bet. *Ecological Economics*, 69(7): 1365–7; G. Pooley and M. Tupy (2020). Luck or Insight? The Simon-Ehrlich Bet Re-examined. *Economic Affairs*, 40(2): 277–80; Still widely discussed e.g., Materials Risk Blog: https://materials-risk.com/

120 M. K. Bennett (1949). Population and Food Supply: The Current Scare. *The Scientific Monthly*, 68(1): 17–26.

121 R. A. Heinlein (1952). Where To?

122 G. Kallis, V. Kostakis S. Lange, B. Muraca, S. Paulson and M. Schmelzer (2018). Research on Degrowth.

123 A. Kirsch (2023). The Smartest Man Who Ever Lived. *The Atlantic*, 3 October 2023.

124 J. von Neumann (1955). Can We Survive Technology? *Fortune Magazine*, 1 June 1955.

Chapter Ten

1 N. Phillipson (2016). Smith and the Scottish Enlightenment.

2 Smith. *WON*, Book I, Chapter viii.

3 P. A. Samuelson (1966). A Summing Up.

4 See: *2001: A Space Odyssey. Terminator* (1 & 2), *Matrix*. The list goes on.

5 United Nations (2015). *World Population Prospects: 2015 Revisions*. New York: United Nations; United Nations (2024). *World Population Prospects 2024: Summary of Results*. UN DESA/POP/2024/TR/NO. 9. New York: United Nations.

6 M. Joselow (2025). EPA to Stop Collecting Emissions Data from Polluters. *New York Times*, 12 September 2025.

7 I thank my wife for pointing out (and my 8-year-old for confirming) that this was also the message of the 2025 *Minecraft* movie, bringing Smithian concepts to the next generation as the cycle continues.

INDEX